11/04
ob. 332 $20
2XYMuk

I0669564

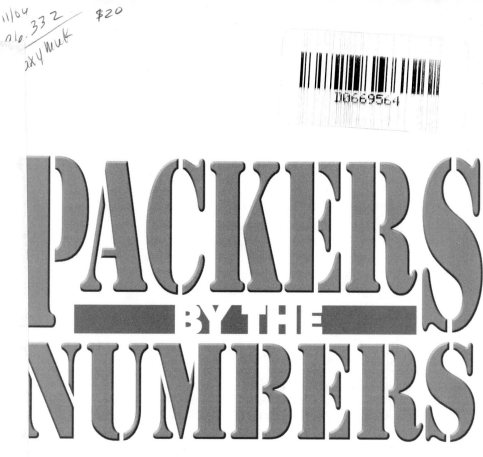

PACKERS BY THE NUMBERS

ersey Numbers and the Players Who Wore Them

DISCARD

John Maxymuk

PRAIRIE OAK PRESS
Black Earth, Wisconsin

REEDSBURG PUBLIC LIBRARY
370 Vine Street
Reedsburg, WI 53959

©2003 John Maxymuk

All rights reserved. No part of this publication may be reproduced or transmitted in any form or by any means, electronic or mechanical, including photocopying and recording, or by any information storage and retrieval system without written permission from the publisher.

Library of Congress Control Number: 2003105896
ISBN: 1-879483-90-4

Project Manager: Anne McKenna
Editor: Jerry Minnich
Designer: Colin Harrington
Cover Photo: Courtesty of the Stiller-LeFebvre Collection

Printed in the United States of America by McNaughton & Gunn.

08 07 06 05 04 03   6 5 4 3 2 1

Prairie Oak Press, a division of Trails Media Group, Inc.
P.O. Box 317 • Black Earth, WI 53515
(800) 236-8088 • e-mail: books@wistrails.com
www.trailsbooks.com

DEDICATION

With love to the stars of my very own home team: Suzanne, Juliane, and Katie.

ACKNOWLEDGMENTS

I would like to thank several people who have helped me with my research. Chad Reese of the Pro Football Hall of Fame, Tom Murphy of the Packers Hall of Fame, Lee Remmel and Zak Gilbert of the Packers Public Relations Department, John Carpentier of Stadium Sports & Antiques, and the staff of the Brown County Library—especially the Local History Department. My colleagues at the Robeson Library of Rutgers University where I work are always supportive and, in particular, InterLibrary Loan maven Mary Anne Nesbit helped me borrow some very obscure materials. Finally, thanks to my editor Jerry Minnich for believing in the project from the start.

REEDSBURG PUBLIC LIBRARY
370 Vine Street
Reedsburg, WI 53959

In 1963 when I was six I started collecting football cards and picked the Packers as my favorite team. Green was my favorite color, and the Packers not only wore green jerseys, but came from an exotic distant place called Green Bay. The name Packers itself was appealing in its oddness—just what was a "Packer" anyway? While the Cowboys' star was alluring to a small boy, the Packers' quarterback had the most apt name a cool signal caller could ever have, Bart Starr. Furthermore, Lombardi's lessons (work hard, do every job the right way every time, never quit, and so on) were the same ones my father taught me. The team also did its part on the field to clinch the deal, winning three straight titles soon after. Beyond their talent, though, the Packers of that time were colorful characters and were written up in newspapers, magazines, and books frequently. As an avid reader, I soaked it all up and then started absorbing the history of the team. I found that Green Bay had a long tradition of quirky characters like Curly Lambeau and Johnny Blood, of exciting performers like Don Hutson and Arnie Herber, and of winning championships. I was hooked and have remained so for 40 years even though I didn't make it to Wisconsin until this past year when researching this book. When my older daughter began to be interested in football, I read her Jerry Kramer's *Instant Replay* as a bedtime story.

The idea of the book came about from the desire to share the knowledge I've accumulated from four decades of reading everything I can find on the Packers. Many books and articles have been written about the team, its coaches, and its players—particularly from the Lombardi era. My basis in this book is uniform numbers. Uniform numbers conjure vivid memories in sports. If you say "3" most sports fans would think of Babe Ruth; Green Bay Packer fans would remember Tony Canadeo. If you say "75" most football fans would think of Mean Joe Greene, but Packer fans would recall Forrest Gregg. However, not all players are that memorable, so where to find the number data? Some NFL teams have compiled comprehensive lists of what number each of their players ever wore and posted that on the team's web site. The Packers' web site is rich in information and very nicely designed but did not include uniform numbers until I had finished two drafts of the manuscript for this book. Much of the data could be found in Eric Goska's wonderful Packer encyclopedia, *Packer Legends in Facts*. More obscure cases were solved through press accounts, team press releases, and actual game programs. Out of the over 1,300 players who have played for Green Bay in its 80+ years in the NFL, I was unable to track down the numbers of only a handful of players. Once the team came out with its authoritative list in the *Packers Media Guide*, I was able to compare notes and ensure the accuracy of the raw data.

Just a list of numbers would make a pretty short and rather dull book, though. The numbers provide the foundation, but I have tried to build an interesting structure on that base. For each number from 1 to 99 I have written a short chapter. Each chapter features one player especially identifiable with that number and often uses him and his career as a launching point into an essay on a broader Packer or football topic. Eight of the chapters are decade chapters that present a snapshot of a particular Packer decade through a range of categories: some are statistical like won-lost records, some are factual like what Hall of Famers played for the team in that period, and many are opinion-based like best and worst trade or best and worst draft of the decade. Each chapter lists all players who have worn the number and provides cross references to other numbers worn by these players. The first player to wear the number and the player to wear it for the longest period are both noted as well. Other notable players are briefly described, as is "one to forget," a player who best would be forgotten for any number of reasons. Finally, a concise bibliography on the player and/or special topic of the chapter is provided for further investigation.

The criteria used to select who represents each number varied from chapter to chapter. I did not always choose the most famous or best player to wear the number. I also have tried to maintain a mix of players from different eras, and that led to quite a bit of shifting around enabled by the fact that players in the leather helmet era especially switched numbers quite a bit. For example, Paul "Tiny" Engebretsen wore number 34 for most of his career but is featured here as 52, which he wore only briefly. I wanted to relate Engebretsen's story, but I also needed to tell about Don Chandler and his role in the 1965 championship. Chandler only wore 34 so he had to stay. Therefore, Engebretsen pushed Frank Winters out from 52, because Tiny's story was more vital to the aims of the book than my fellow New Jerseyan, Frankie Bag of Donuts.

Mike Michalske wore the most numbers as a Packer—nine—but fellow Hall of Famers Arnie Herber and Clarke Hinkle wore eight and seven respectively. In the post-World War II era, Dick Afflis wore a different number in each of his four years in Green Bay from 1951–54, while Steve Collier wore four numbers in his only season as a Packer. Collier tried three different numbers in three replacement games in 1987 and a fourth as a member of the regular roster. However, in time players would become almost interchangeable with their numbers, so much so that the best players even have their numbers retired.

The history of each number represents a different slice of Packer history, and this book attempts to serve as a thematic rather than a chronological approach to Green Bay's rich heritage. Among those themes are accounts of each year the team has played in the post-season, key rivalries, and a host of idiosyncratic topics. Ultimately, the selection criteria was to choose the players who best fit into the stories that I felt most needed to be examined and told.

As a librarian, I am trained to organize information to make it more accessible for users, and I am cognizant of almost everything that has been published on this team. No existing book provides such a team history through its uniform numbers—not to mention a short literature review as well. I have tried to pinpoint the stories we know about the Packers and their players and from what sources we know them. I think my extensive study has permitted me to make a number of interesting connections and observations. My emphasis in this book has been on thoroughness and accuracy, while

I have tried to flavor the narrative with irreverent, intelligent opinions and a sense of humor. I hope that readers find this book fun to read or dip into and a unique resource for research.

HOW TO USE THIS BOOK: The text is designed to be approached by uniform numbers; however, if you want to see all the numbers a Packer wore, Appendix A provides an access point by players' names. If you would like to hopscotch from one chapter to another according to a rough chronological order, Appendix B provides an alternative reading order.

In the text *see* references to chapters are provided when appropriate. For those Packers who are described only in the brief data section at the top of chapters, *see top* references are given. Regarding the number listings both in the chapters and in Appendix A, I used the following conventions:

1) (Henry Burris 2001) Listings within parentheses are players who were eligible to play but never appeared in a game. These players include a handful from the early years who were listed in game programs but are not on the team's official all-time roster because they never got on the field. Of more significance are the team's third quarterbacks. In 1993 the NFL instituted a policy that a team could have a third quarterback suit up and be available for an emergency, but that quarterback would not count as being on the active roster for the game. For example, Henry Burris is not on the team's official roster, but he did suit up in #10 for most of the 2001 season. Danny Wuerffel, the team's third quarterback in 2000, actually appeared in a game and thus does appear on the official roster. Therefore, Burris' listing in this book is in parentheses while Wuerffel's is not.

2) <Curly Lambeau 1925–6> Listings within angle brackets are players who were assigned numbers in a program or dope sheet (the tabloid-sized precursor to game programs) in the years before players wore numbers on their jerseys. Photographic evidence shows that players did not have numbers on their jerseys in 1924 but did in 1927; 1925 and 1926 are questionable. A decade after the Packers started wearing actual uniform numbers, the NFL drafted a rule specifying the size of numbers required as of 1937 on both the front and back of the jersey.

3) Collier 1987r Listings with an "r" after the year are for replacement players who took part in the three non-union league games during the 1987 mid-season players' strike.

Finally, the entries for numbers 1, 2, 6, and 10 are *"cheats."* The subject of those chapters probably never wore that number on the field in a game. For Curly Lambeau (1), Charley Mathys (2) and Cub Buck (10), these were the numbers assigned them in game programs. The case for Vince Lombardi (6) is more complicated and is explained in the entry itself.

PACKER FANS

WHO'S WORN THE NUMBER No Packer has ever worn 00, but the most famous NFL player to wear the number was a Wisconsin native, Jim Otto of the Raiders. Otto was a perennial All Pro center with Oakland and was inducted into the Pro Football Hall of Fame in 1980. Double zero was a double pun for him: first, his name is a palindrome bookended by O's; second, when pronounced, Otto sounds close to "aught oh," i.e., double zero.

ARE PACKER FANS SPECIAL?

•Home games at Lambeau Field have been sold out since 1960. The waiting list for season tickets has grown to over 50,000. It's not unusual for a parent to place his child's name on the waiting list as soon as the baby is delivered.

•Tailgating is a popular activity outside many stadiums around the country. Some claim that it began in Green Bay in the 1950s because of the dearth of quality restaurants in town. In 2002, the Wisconsin Historical Museum in Madison organized the IcOn Wisconsin exhibit of statewide symbols and featured a tailgate party as its central display.

•Fans may not be able to scrounge up tickets to home games at Lambeau Field, but hour and a half tours of the stadium are popular each summer.

•After over 25 years across the street from Lambeau Field, the Packer Hall of Fame moved into the stadium's new atrium with the 2002 renovations. Green Bay was the first sports team to have its own museum, and, fittingly, one of its features is annual recognition of one rooter in the Packer Fan Hall of Fame. The reward for this award includes club box seats for one home game and a road trip to an away game.

•Packers past and present are ever-present in the community. Lambeau Field is on Lombardi Avenue. Other streets in town include Holmgren Way, Lambeau Street, Starr Court, Hutson Street, Isbell Street, Hinkle Street, Favre Pass, Packer Drive and Packerland Drive, in addition to such landmarks as the Ray Nitschke Bridge and Ted Fritsch Park. Formerly there was a Lewellen Road and Canadeo Street, but both disappeared in new development during the 1980s. Dave Robinson and Dave Hampton invested in a subdivision and were rewarded with Robinson and Hampton Avenues. Junior high kids might attend Vince Lombardi Middle School. The East High School football team plays on the same field where the Packers played from 1925–56 as old City Stadium. The site is commemorated with a plaque.

PACKERS BY THE NUMBERS

•When it snows before a game, the stands are shoveled out by fans making no more than $7 an hour.

•When Lambeau Field was resodded after the muddy playoff victory over the 49ers in the 1996 playoffs, 22,000 sections of the old "frozen tundra" were boxed and sold for charity.

•The Packers have had their own "fight song," "Go, You Packers, Go" since 1936.

•Packer fans took the insult of "cheeseheads" and turned it upside down to become a source of pride. They are easily identifiable when wearing foam cheese wedges on their heads.

•Packer players became expert at the Lambeau Leap into the stands after scoring and formed a special connection with the fans in the process.

•Another unique Green Bay tradition has local kids offering their bikes to players at training camp so the players can ride from the practice field to the locker room while the kids carry their helmets.

•Packer fans were chartering train cars to Chicago for the Bears game in the 1920s. Ever since, Packer players are not surprised to find their own cheering section no matter where they play.

•20,000 fans welcomed home the 1929 champion Packers when they returned by train. The players and their wives were whisked onto buses and given an immediate parade through town.

•During the team's train ride home after winning the 1936 championship, fans turned out at each depot in Wisconsin to cheer for the Packers as they rolled through.

•When they won the championship in New York in 1944, over a thousand fans were waiting for them in subzero temperatures at the Green Bay Rail Station.

•When they won Super Bowl XXXI, thousands of fans lined the streets to watch the Packer buses go by and 61,000 filled the stadium, waiting hours in the freezing cold for the Packers to return to Green Bay to celebrate the victory.

Everyone claims to have the greatest fans, especially when they are winning. Every football team has fans who fill their stadium, crazy fans who live and die with the team's fortunes, fans who dress up in strange costumes or remove their shirts in inclement weather, fans who yell and scream and cheer at the excitement on the field, and fans who endure such indignities as personal seat licenses and exorbitant fees for tickets and parking. Only the Packers have fans who actually own the team and don't have to wonder whether some city without a team will try to lure their club away with a better stadium deal and more luxury boxes. The fans own the Packers, and they're not going anywhere.

The Packer ownership is a unique situation in professional sports and dates back to a clever solution to drastic financial problems in the early days of professional football. The industry of professional football arose out of teams put together to represent small Midwestern cities at the beginning of the twentieth century. One such city was

Green Bay, settled in 1634 when French explorer Jean Nicolet crossed Lake Michigan by canoe and landed on the sheltered banks of Green Bay in search of furs and a shorter route to China. Instead he found a scenic and wild setting where he would sign a treaty of friendship with the native Winnebagos. The port of Green Bay would develop over the next 300 years into a major paper mill and cheese processing center by day and a hub for wine, women, and song by night. In the 1920s and 1930s especially, NFL players marveled at the ample supply of taverns and houses of ill repute in the area. The community also displayed a fondness for football. Green Bay featured semi-pro town teams throughout the first couple of decades of the 20th century and even had teams in the late 1890s. When Green Bay was first awarded a franchise in 1921 in the American Professional Football League, as the National Football League was originally called, the Packers were corporately sponsored by the Acme Packing Company. The franchise was revoked at the end of the year for league rule violations, but was reinstated in Curly Lambeau's name the following season. The club was going under financially, when *Green Bay Press Gazette* publisher Andrew Turnbull became involved late in the 1922 season. Under his ingenious and dedicated leadership, the team began a stock sale that would convert the team to a publicly-owned non-profit corporation. In essence, he sold the team to the fans.

During two subsequent times of financial crisis, the fans came to the rescue again. In the midst of the Great Depression in 1931, an allegedly inebriated fan fell through the wooden bleachers in old City Stadium and broke two vertebrae in his back. He sued the team and won a $5,000 judgment that the team could not pay once its insurance company went bankrupt. The team was placed into receivership to protect it from creditors. In order to climb out of that hole, the corporation was reorganized and a limited stock sale was held in 1934. Once again the fans bought shares in the Packers, shares that would never pay a dividend and could only be sold back to the corporation at the original sale price. In the 1940s, the team went into decline on the field and Curly Lambeau began to spend well beyond his means. By Thanksgiving 1949 the team was on the brink of financial ruin. A special intrasquad game was played to raise enough cash to finish the season, and another stock sale was held from 1950 through 1951. Again it was a success and the team was saved. After the Super Bowl triumph in 1997, stock was issued for the fourth time, but this was intended to provide a nest egg for capital improvements and not simply to survive. There are so many shareholders that the corporation's annual meeting is held in Lambeau Field. The annual meeting drew 18,000 in 1998. Green Bay is the last small Midwestern city to survive in today's sports world, and the Packers have done so because their fans, from all over the country, have a stake in this team. There is not another one like it.

FOR FURTHER INFORMATION
Coenen, Craig. "How the Packers Have Lasted 75 Years in Green Bay," *Voyageur*. Vol. 10 No. 2 Winter/Spring 1994. (2-12)

Davis, Russ. "Little Town Leads Them," *Saturday Evening Post*. 11/30/40. (34+)

Doherty, Jim. "In Chilly Green Bay, Curly's Old Team Is Still Packing Them In," *Smithsonian*. 8/9.1 (80+)

PACKERS BY THE NUMBERS

"Football Closeup: Green Bay, Wisconsin," in Barber, Phil. *Football America: Celebrating America's National Passion.* Atlanta, GA: Turner Publishing, 1996.

Furlong, William Barry. "Small Town Smack in the Big Time," *New York Times Magazine.* 10/14/62. (26+)

"How the Packers Do It," *Business Week.* 9/21/63. (52-60)

Morris, David, and Daniel Kraker. "Rooting the Home Team: Why the Packers Won't Leave—and Why the Browns Did," *The American Prospect.* September/October 1998. (38-43)

"Packer Sites," *Voyageur.* Vol. 10 No. 2 Winter/Spring 1994. (14-20)

Reynolds, Quentin. "Football Town," *Colliers.* 11/6/37. (62-5)

Wind, Herbert Warren. "Packerland," *New Yorker.* 12/8/62. (213+)

BEGINNINGS

EARL "CURLY" LAMBEAU
BACK <1925–26> • HEAD COACH 1922–49

WHO'S WORN THE NUMBER <Lambeau 1925–26>

ORIGINATOR Lambeau.

LONGEST TENURE Lambeau.

NUMBER CHANGES Lambeau wore 14 in 1927, 42 in 1928, and 20 in 1929–30.

OTHER NOTABLES None.

ONE TO FORGET None.

EARL "CURLY" LAMBEAU Lambeau Field is one of the most recognizable stadium names in sports, but the man who gave the field its name is largely forgotten today. Moreover, much of what is commonly recalled about Earl "Curly" Lambeau is untrue. The story goes that Lambeau came up with the idea of forming a professional team in Green Bay, got his boss to pay for the uniforms, and installed himself as the team's first coach. In their third year, the Packers joined the fledgling National Football League. In 1922, the Packers were thrown out of the NFL for using illegal college underclassmen, and Curly had to borrow money from a friend to pay the reinstatement fee. The friend raised the money by selling his car in return for the promise to be able to play for the team that year. This account of Curly Lambeau's formation of the Packers is entertaining, but not very accurate.

Larry Names' well-researched four-volume *History of the Green Bay Packers* refutes many of the myths that have grown up around Lambeau and the team's founding. Green Bay football is rooted in the town teams that were annually formed throughout the early years of the twentieth century. Hometown hero Curly Lambeau was the Big Man On Campus at Green Bay's East High School, even coaching the team in 1917 his senior year when regular coach Joe Hoeffel (remember that name) was serving in World War I. Lambeau matriculated at the University of Wisconsin, but soon dropped out to work for his father's construction business. In the fall of 1918, Curly enrolled at Notre Dame on a football scholarship and played in the Fighting Irish backfield alongside the fabled George Gipp of "win one for the Gipper" fame. Meanwhile back in Green Bay, Lambeau's friend Nate Abrams reinstituted a town tradition by forming a town team again. Curly came home in December suffering from tonsillitis and never returned to South Bend. Instead he took a job with the local Indian Packing Company in 1919 and got married to his high school sweetheart

Marguerite. That fall Curly joined up with the men reorganizing the Green Bay football team. Due to Lambeau's prowess and stature, he was elected captain and he arranged with his boss at Indian Packing, Frank Peck, for the company to sponsor the team by paying for uniforms. The team's coach was William Ryan. The Indian Packing Company was taken over by the Acme Packing Company, run by brothers John and Emmett Clair, in 1920 and continued to sponsor the semi-pro Packers.

In 1921 at Lambeau's urging, the Clairs successfully applied for a franchise in the American Professional Football League as the NFL was then called. Joe Hoeffel (remember Lambeau's high school coach?) was named coach and Lambeau was once again captain. At the time, coaches were not permitted to send in plays from the sideline so the captain's job was at least as important as the coach's. The Packers went 3–2–1 in their first season in the league, but then had their franchise revoked because they had used underclassmen for a game late in the season. That was not an unheard of practice at the time, but it was against the rules. At this point the Clairs bowed out of the picture. Lambeau himself was granted a new franchise by the league in July and was now running the team. He enlisted the help of others—especially of *Green Bay Press Gazette* sportswriter George Calhoun who had served as team manager and publicity agent for the team in 1919 to raise money to stake the team. He did not have his friend Don Murphy sell his car to loan Curly the franchise stake in return for a spot on the team. By the middle of the 1922 season, though, the undercapitalized Packers were in financial turmoil again. Calhoun brought in *Press Gazette* publisher Andrew Turnbull who ultimately used a stock sale to raise money and got the team finally on firm financial footing by converting them into a non-profit publicly-owned corporation. Lambeau was in charge of the team on the field.

Eventually, Turnbull, Lambeau and three other community leaders (businessman Leland H. Joannes, Dr. W. Weber Kelly, and attorney Gerald Clifford) became known as "The Hungry Five" and they managed the fortunes of the team for several years to come. Lambeau was the front man. Without him there would have been no Packers, but without the others the team would not have been financially viable enough to continue.

On the field, Curly was a player-coach. As a player, he threw 24 touchdown passes and scored 110 points, both very respectable totals for the 1920s. Three times he was a second team All League selection. As a coach, he was an early proponent of the forward pass as the great equalizer against bigger and stronger opponents. His teams played a fast and exciting brand of football, emphasizing speed and trickery, and they featured colorful stars like Johnny Blood, Red Dunn and Clarke Hinkle. He was one of the first coaches to hold daily practices and an early advocate of the use of game films for preparation and planning. The Packers would be the first team to barnstorm across Hawaii and the first to travel by airplane to a league game.

Above it all, his teams won. He slowly built a championship team in the 1920s. In 1929 he acquired future Hall of Famers Johnny Blood, Cal Hubbard and Mike Michalske as the final pieces, and then won three titles in a row. Only Lombardi's Packers have been able to duplicate that feat throughout league history. When Curly signed Don Hutson in 1935, that led to winning two more titles in the 1930s and one last championship in 1944 during the war. Only the Bears George Halas can match Lambeau's six NFL titles, and that is fitting. The Packers-Bears rivalry was based on the personal rivalry of two great competitors, Lambeau and Halas. Their teams would meet on the football field more than 40 times over three decades, but the two reportedly never once shook hands after any contest. Despite that gridiron enmity, the two did respect one another, and each would come to the aid of the rival's team during times of financial strife.

That competitive fire did not make Curly popular with his players. He was sometimes known as the Belligerent Belgian for his frequent screaming and yelling. One time when he was still playing, Curly was upset with the team's passing attack and inserted himself in the lineup to show the players how to do it. On Cal Hubbard's instigation, the Packers' line stood aside and let the defenders rush in freely and crush Curly. Cal once wondered aloud how they would find six men to serve as pallbearers when Lambeau were to die. Long-time team photographer Vern Biever felt that Lambeau yelled more than Lombardi, and his fines could be extravagant. He once fined the entire team half their weekly paychecks after a subpar performance.

Once the Packers started to fade on the field, Lambeau's self-promoting ways caught up with him. He was a bit of a dandy and was said to spend quite a bit of time in front of the mirror to make sure his hair was just right before going out on the town. Curly had taken annual scouting trips to California in the off season since the 1930s. He was especially attracted to the young starlets and spent an increasing amount of time in California. As the team deteriorated, Curly was said with recrimination to have "gone Hollywood." He abused his expense account. He fired long-time loyalists team doctor W. Weber Kelly and team publicist George Calhoun. Off the field, Green Bay could not compete financially with the rival All America Football Conference. On the field, Curly's offensive and defensive schemes were outdated—the Packers were the next to the last team in the league to move to the T formation. Without a winning team, his domineering, spendthrift ways became intolerable, and he was pushed out. He would resurface almost immediately as the coach of the Chicago Cardinals, but that would last only two losing seasons. That term was followed by two years coaching Washington where he managed a winning record in the second year. However, his two biggest stars (Eddie Lebaron and Gene Brito) left to play in Canada rather than listen to Curly's bellicose blather. When Curly got into a shoving match with owner George Marshall over discipline issues, he was fired during training camp in 1954. When the Packers job opened up again in 1959, Lambeau campaigned for it, but found the team had no interest in a return to the past.

For many years, Curly Lambeau was the Packers, but much to his surprise the team went on without him and eventually rose again. Lambeau may be largely forgotten today, but he was a giant in the early days of pro football. With all his success, Vince Lombardi was never comfortable in Curly's shadow. Vince became extremely upset when shown the cover of the 1965 team yearbook that featured a picture of the recently-deceased Lambeau and was virulently opposed to renaming City Stadium Lambeau Field. But that was the right move to make. Curly was not the sole founder or the first coach, but he led his hometown Packers for 29 years, most of them winning ones, and was elected as a charter member of the Pro Football Hall of Fame in 1963—one of four Packers in that initial class of 17. As he stated in his brief induction speech that day, "I am deeply grateful and very happy to be honored here today. Forty one years ago I came to Canton to get a franchise for Green Bay, Wisconsin. The franchise was issued by Joe Carr at that time, and it cost fifty dollars. And the last time I looked, the Packers were still in the league. Thank you." Curly Lambeau was a flawed man—vain, glorious, hot-tempered, profligate, narrow-minded, and a three-time divorcee—but his team, his life's work, is still flourishing in the league 40 years after those comments. Curly's hometown is still the smallest market with the biggest heart.

Curly Lambeau is second from the left playing defense in a 0-3 loss to the Bears at Bellevue Park on 10/14/23. Although the fierce Packer-Bear rivalry began in 1921, this was the first meeting of the teams since Chicago changed its name from the Staleys to the Bears. *Courtesy of the Stiller-Lefebvre Collection.*

FOR FURTHER INFORMATION

Daley, Arthur. *Pro Football's Hall of Fame.* New York: Grosset and Dunlap, 1968, c1963. (222-33)

The Greatest Packers of Them All. New York: Putnam, 1968. (25-31)

Johnson, Chuck. *The Green Bay Packers: Pro Football's Pioneer Team.* New York: Thomas Nelson and Sons, 1963.

"Lambeau, Curly," in *American National Biography: Volume 13.* New York: Oxford University Press, 1999. (79-80)

"Lambeau, Earl Louis ("Curly")," in *Dictionary of American Biography: Supplement Seven 1961–65.* New York: Scribners, 1981. (451-3)

Names, Larry. *The History of the Green Bay Packers: Book I: The Lambeau Years Part One.* Wautoma, WI: Angel Press of WI, 1987.

———. *The History of the Green Bay Packers: Book II: The Lambeau Years Part Two.* Wautoma, WI: Angel Press of WI, 1989.

————. *The History of the Green Bay Packers: Book III: The Lambeau Years Part Three.* Wautoma, WI: Angel Press of WI, 1990.

————. *The History of the Green Bay Packers: Book IV: The Shameful Years.* Wautoma, WI: Angel Press of WI, 1995.

Packers of the Past: A Series of Articles Reprinted from the Milwaukee Journal Sept. 28 – Dec. 9, 1965. Milwaukee, WI: Milwaukee Journal, 1965. (45-8)

Porter, David L., ed. *Biographical Dictionary of American Sports: Football.* New York: Greenwood Press, 1987. (328-9)

Torinus, John. *The Packer Legend: An Inside Look.* Revised ed. Neshkoro, WI: Laranmark Press, 1982.

Ward, Arch. *The Green Bay Packers.* New York, Putnam, 1946.

1920s IN A BOX
CHARLES MATHYS • QUARTERBACK <1925–26>

WHO'S WORN THE NUMBER <Charles Mathys 1925–26>, (Aaron Brooks 1999).

ORIGINATOR <Charles Mathys 1925–26>.

LONGEST TENURE <Charles Mathys 1925–26>.

NUMBER CHANGES None.

OTHER NOTABLES Aaron Brooks is one of a long line of drafted backups to Brett Favre who had to get his opportunity to start elsewhere. Just like Mark Brunell, Ty Detmer, and Matt Hasselbeck, Brooks had to wait to be traded to become a starter or even to play. In Brooks' first two years in New Orleans he has displayed a lot of talent that is in need of polishing. Like Favre, he has a propensity to take risks, but has not produced as many rewards as Brett just yet.

ONE TO FORGET None.

CHARLES MATHYS Charles Mathys was emblematic of his team and his time. The Packers evolved from a local town team to join the American Professional Football Association (AFPA) in 1921. Green Bay was expelled from the league at the end of the year for using college players, and when they rejoined the league under new ownership in 1922 the AFPA had become the NFL. In that same year, Mathys signed on with Green Bay. He was a local boy like so many of the early Packers and had attended Green Bay's West High School before starting his college career at nearby Ripon. He transferred to the University of Indiana where he was a star quarterback for the Hoosiers. After graduation in 1921, he joined the Hammond Pros of the AFPA and played against the Packers in a 14-7 loss in November.

Mathys, who only weighed between 150-165 pounds, quarterbacked the Packers for five years through 1926, before retiring and being replaced by Red Dunn (see 11). The Packers at the time ran a variation of the Notre Dame Box offense where the quarterback stood about a yard behind the center and then shifted behind the right guard. Mathys would call signals; he often would receive the ball from a center snap and distribute it. In his Packer career, he ran for one touchdown, caught four touchdown passes, and threw 11, including a team-high seven in 1925. After his retirement, he remained in his home town for the rest of his life and served on the Packers Board of Directors for many years. He was elected to the Packer Hall of Fame in 1977 and died in 1983.

FOR FURTHER INFORMATION
"Packer Pioneer Trio," *Pro.* 11/28/76. (64)

HERE IS A SNAPSHOT OF CHARLES MATHYS' ERA:
DECADE HEADLINE: Lambeau Leaps In
WHERE THEY PLAYED: Hagemeister Park (an enclosed field) 1921–22; Athletic Park (a minor league baseball park in Milwaukee) 1922 (one game); Bellevue Field (a minor league baseball stadium) 1923–24; City Stadium (still used as a high school field) 1925–56.
HOW THE GAME WAS PLAYED: Three yards (or less) and a cloud of dust. In the 1920s over 60% of all games ended in shutouts. 0-0 ties were not terribly uncommon. Field position and turnovers decided most games, and a good punter was a highly valued asset. Green Bay was one of only a few teams to see passing as a viable approach to offense.
DECADE WON-LOST RECORD: 61-25-13 .692.
RECORD AGAINST THE BEARS: 6-7-3 (includes 0-1 against Chicago Staleys).
RECORD AGAINST THE GIANTS: 2-1 .
CHAMPIONSHIPS: 1929.
UNSUNG HERO: Andrew Turnbull, Business Manager of the *Green Bay Press Gazette*, became involved with the Packers in 1922. The famous story is that the Lambeau and Calhoun were wondering what to do when heavy rains fell in November of that year. If they played the scheduled game, how could they meet the other team's guaranteed cut when attendance would be minimal? If they cancelled, how viable a franchise would they appear to be to the league? They consulted Andrew Turnbull and his recommendation was to play and he would help them out of their financial difficulties. Although the team was insured against severe weather, the rainfall was three one hundredths of an inch short of meeting the amount needed for a payout. Turnbull's efforts over the following months in the initial Packer stock sale were successful and led to him being named the first Chairman of the Board of Directors of the Green Bay Football Corporation.
HEAD COACHES: Earl "Curly" Lambeau, 1921–49, 61-25-13 for the decade. Technically, Joe Hoeffel coached the team in 1921, but Lambeau was the captain on the field so he ran the game.
BEST PLAYER: Verne Lewellen (see 46).
HALL OF FAMERS: Curly Lambeau, Johnny Blood McNally, Cal Hubbard, Mike Michalske.
PACKER HALL OF FAMERS: Curly Lambeau, Johnny Blood McNally, Cal Hubbard, Mike Michalske, Cub Buck, Boob Darling, Lavie Dilweg, Red Dunn, Jug Earp, Verne Lewellen, Charles Mathys, and Whitey Woodin.
ALL PROS: Tillie Voss, 1924; Verne Lewellen, 1926, 27, 28, 29; Lavvie Dilweg, 1927, 28, 29; Cal Hubbard, 1929; Mike Michalske, 1929.
BEST OFFENSIVE BACKFIELD: 1929—Red Dunn, QB; Verne Lewellen, HB; Johnny Blood, HB; Bo Molenda, FB.
BEST DEAL: Acquiring Cal Hubbard from the Giants. Most accounts indicate that Cal

requested to be released from the Giants so that he could sign with the Packers, closer to his home. Evidently, no compensation was given for this Hall of Famer.

WORST DEAL: Losing Hunk Anderson to the Bears (see *Worst Failure* below).

BIGGEST OFF-FIELD EVENT: The Packers unique nonprofit corporate structure was set in place with the first stock sale in 1923.

BIGGEST ON-FIELD DEVELOPMENT: Lambeau saw that the best way to compete was to embrace the pass. Throughout the decade, the Packers were first in passing yards four times, second twice, third twice, and fourth once.

STRANGEST ON-FIELD EVENT: Dutch Hendrian joined the team in 1924, make that Dutch and his dog. His dog accompanied him everywhere. His dog is in the team picture, was on the sidelines for games, and traveled with the team. Dutch later worked as a character actor in Hollywood.

WORST FAILURE: Having the franchise revoked in 1921 for using college players with remaining eligibility. According to Larry Names in the Chicago game, Lambeau used three college players who came up from nearby Notre Dame. One of these was Hunk Anderson whom George Halas wanted for the Bears. Since there was a league rule, roundly ignored, to only to employ players whose college class had graduated, Halas quietly let it be known what the Packers had done, and Commissioner Joe Carr had the franchise revoked. Lambeau was permitted to apply for a new franchise, but his application was delayed until league meetings in the summer of 1922 by which time Anderson had signed with the Bears. Most reports say the Irish trio played in the December 4 game against Racine.

HOME ATTENDANCE: Incomplete data for only 1924, 1925, 1927–29, 30 games, 151, 439, an average attendance of 5,049.

FIRST GAME: November 23, 1921 a 7-6 victory over the Minneapolis Marines. In the last five minutes, Art Schmael scored the first Packer touchdown and Curly Lambeau kicked the winning extra point.

LAST GAME: December 8, 1929 the Packers pounded the Bears 25-0, the fourth of five straight shutouts they would toss Chicago. The Packers conclude the decade as champions.

BEST GAME: November 24, 1929 the undefeated Packers thoroughly beat the undefeated Giants 20-6, not only knocking off their chief rival for the championship, but also striking a blow for all little towns against the big city boys.

LARGEST MARGIN OF VICTORY: November 6, 1921 43-6 over the Evansville Crimson Giants.

LARGEST MARGIN OF DEFEAT: November 26, 1925 31-0 to the Pottsville Maroons.

BEST OFFENSE: 1929 the Packers scored 198 points.

BEST DEFENSE: 1929 The Packers only gave up 22 points all year in 13 games.

MOST GAMES PLAYED: Jug Earp, 85 games.

MOST POINTS: Verne Lewellen, 211 points.

MOST FIELD GOALS: Cub Buck, 10.

MOST TOUCHDOWNS: Verne Lewellen, 35.

MOST TOUCHDOWN PASSES: Red Dunn, 29. Lambeau had 24.

MOST PASSING YARDS: Curly Lambeau, 4,478. Red Dunn had 3,417.

MOST RECEIVING YARDS: Charles Mathys, 1,506.

MOST RECEPTIONS: Charles Mathys, 90.

MOST INTERCEPTIONS: Curly Lambeau, 21 from incomplete data.

BEST BOOK (ABOUT): Larry Names' *The History of the Green Bay Packers: Book I: The Lambeau Years Part One*, Angel Press of WI, 1987.

NOTED SPORTSWRITER: George Calhoun served as sort of a combination *Green Bay Press Gazette* sportswriter and Packers Public Relations man.

BEST QUOTATION: After the first championship in 1929, each man on the team was presented with a commemorative watch and a wallet with $220 in it. On receiving his, Johnny Blood replied, "I am especially grateful for the check."

UNUSUAL NAMES: Myrt Basing, Adolph Bieberstein, LaVern Dilweg, Rex Enright, Fee Klaus, Adolph Kliebhan, Romanus Nadolney, and Dave Zuidmulder.

NICKNAMES: The Bay City Blues, Bert Ashmore, Bullet Baker, Goofy Jim Bowdoin Cub Buck, Walt "Big Boy" Buland, Tiny Cahoon, Tom "Paddy" Cronin, Sleepy Jim Crowley, Boob Darling, Dukes Duford, Red Dunn, Jug Earp, Gus "Siki" Gardella, Moose Gardner, Buck Gavin, Duke Hanny, Dutch Hendrian, Tubby Howard, Eddie "the Lawrence Flash" Kotal, Curly Lambeau, Ojay Larson, Cully Lidberg, Slick Lollar, Molly Malone, Johnny Blood McNally—"The Vagabond Halfback," Toody McLean, Bo Molenda, Jab Murray, Peaches Nadolney, Pid Purdy, Doc Regnier, Rosey Rosatti, Red Smith, Tillie Voss, Buff Wagner, Dutch Webber, Cowboy Wheeler, and Whitey Woodin.

FASTEST PLAYER: Johnny Blood.

HEAVIEST PLAYER: Cub Buck, listed at times at 280, and appearing every bit of it in photos.

LIGHTEST PLAYER: Nate Abrams, listed sometimes at 5'7" 160 lbs and sometimes at 5'4" 140 lbs which is more likely. Abrams, a veteran of Green Bay town teams, was one of the founders of the Packers.

TOUGHEST INJURY: In 1929, backs Red Dunn and Eddie Kotal were injured against the Bears. Two weeks later in the November 24 20-6 victory over the Giants noted above, Jim Bowdoin was injured in the last minute and had to come out. Until that time, the 11 Packer starters had played the entire game with no substitutes. It was a different game in those days.

LOCAL BOYS: Nate Abrams, Jim Crowley, Curly Lambeau, and Charles Mathys all hailed from Green Bay. Johnny Blood, Cub Buck, Boob Darling, Lavvie Dilweg, Red Dunn, and Whitey Woodin were all from nearby towns.

FIRSTS:

League Game—October 23, 1921, 7-6 over the Minneapolis Marines.

Touchdown—October 23, 1921, a four yard run by Art Schmael; extra point by Curly Lambeau.

Win over the Bears—On September 21, 1924 the Packers beat the Bears 5-0, but it was not considered a league game. The next year on September 27th, the Packers prevailed 14-10 in Green Bay

Championship—1929

Game at City Stadium—The Packers opened their new stadium on September 20, 1925 with a 14-0 win over the Hammond Pros, QB Charles Mathys' original team. It would be their home for 32 years.

PACKERS BY THE NUMBERS

Public Address System—1925, in brand new City Stadium.

Shutout—On October 22, 1922, the Packers and the Milwaukee Badgers played to a 0-0 tie in Milwaukee.

Punt Return for Touchdown—Johnny Blood, 1929, according to David Neft's *The Football Encyclopedia: The Complete History of Professional Football from 1892 to the Present* but I was unable to confirm this in game accounts.

Team Musical Band—1921, the Lumberjack Band, which evolved into the Green Bay City Band in 1923 and the Packer Band in 1939.

LONG TIME SERVICE AND RETIRED NUMBERS

TONY CANADEO • BACK 1941–44, 1946–52

WHO'S WORN THE NUMBER <Cyre 1926>, Monnett 1935, P Miller 1936–38, Feathers 1940, Canedeo 1941–44, 1946–52, R McKay 1944–45, Agajanian 1961. (Number 3 was retired on Tony Canadeo Day at City Stadium on November 23, 1952. Inexplicably, kicker Ben Agajanian wore the number for three games in 1961. Whether Lombardi checked about this with his friend Tony Canadeo is not reported.)

ORIGINATOR Tackle Hector Cyre was one of five Packers from Gonzaga in the 1920s.

LONGEST TENURE Tony Canadeo 1941–44, 1946–52.

NUMBER CHANGES Bob Monnett also wore 18 in 1933, 42 and 66 in 1934, 12 in 1935, 12 and 5 in 1936, 5 in 1937 and 50 in 1938; Roy McKay wore 22 in 1946–47.

OTHER NOTABLES Bob Monnett was an all-purpose back who was elected to the Packer Hall of Fame in 1973. His 2.9 rushing average is the worst in NFL history of backs with at least 500 rushes, but he was an effective tailback who threw for 28 touchdowns against only 26 interceptions.

ONE TO FORGET Beattie Feathers was washed up by the time the former Bear star runner joined the Packers in 1940, and he lasted only one game.

TONY CANADEO Tony Canadeo was born in Chicago in 1919, the same year the Packers began, and was still affiliated with the team at the beginning of the new millennium. He put in more years of service in a variety of capacities than any other Packer. For over 60 years, he was a player, broadcaster, member of the Board of Directors, member of the Executive Committee (including serving three years as treasurer and seven as vice president in the 1980s), and finally Board member emeritus.

As befitting such a mature eminence of the gridiron, his hair went gray at the age of 16 and Tony became known as the "Gray Ghost of Gonzaga" when he attended that Washington university in the late 1930s. The Packers picked him in the seventh round of the 1941 draft, and he became an immediate contributor to the team on both offense and defense. He would play both ways for most of his career. On defense he was a hard-tackling, tough defensive back. On offense, he was the very definition of an all-purpose back, accumulating over 8,000 all-purpose yards in the course of his career. As a runner, he gained 4,197 yards and scored 26 touchdowns; as a receiver he caught 69 passes for 579 yards and five touchdowns; as a punt returner he averaged 11.2 yards on 46 returns for 513 yards; as a kickoff returner he averaged 23.1 yards on 75 returns for 1,736 yards; as a passer he threw for 1,642 yards and 16 touchdowns. He also punted the ball 45 times for a 37.1 yard average and intercepted nine passes. When Cecil Isbell retired after 1942, Tony took on the role of primary passer for the Packer offense in 1943 and led the team to a 7-2-1 record. He made the All League team that year for the first time.

He was a loyal foot soldier both for Green Bay and for his country. He went into the military in 1944 and didn't return to the NFL until 1946. He did manage to play three games in 1944 when he was on furlough to be with his wife for the birth of their first son, Bob. Thus Tony missed out on Curly Lambeau's last title while he was overseas. He didn't even find out the Packers had won the title until three weeks after the victory over the Giants in the championship game.

When he returned from the war, the good times were gone in Green Bay. Don Hutson had just retired, and Lambeau's passing game would never recover. In the postwar years, Curly would increasingly emphasize the run, and Tony became the team's feature back. In 1949, Canadeo became the third man to rush for over 1,000 yards in a season although he finished second in the NFL that year to Steve Van Buren of the Eagles. Of course, Van Buren's Eagles were the champs while Tony's Packers finished 2-10 at the bottom of the league. Gaining 1,052 yards for the last place 1949 Packers was a significant accomplishment, and he made All League for the second time.

When Lambeau was pushed out in 1950, Canadeo was 31 years old. Under new coach Gene Ronzani he would only be a part-time player for the last three years of his career. His last year as a player was 1952 and produced two of his biggest thrills. In his last game against the Bears in his hometown of Chicago, the Packers won 41-28 on November 9. It was the first time the Pack had beaten the Bears in Chicago since Tony's first year of 1941. Two weeks later November 23 was Tony's final home game in Green Bay and was declared Tony Canadeo Day. Once again the Pack won, 42-14 over the Dallas Texans, for their sixth and last victory of the year ensuring a non-losing season for the first time since 1947. Before the game, Tony received gifts and had his number retired, the second Packer to receive that honor. Don Hutson's 14 was retired in 1951; Bart Starr's 15 was retired in 1973; and Ray Nitschke's 66 was retired in 1983. Because the NFL began to discourage the practice, Green Bay made a curious distinction and retired Reggie White's 92 *jersey* in 1999.

Tony was not the fastest or most elusive runner, but he would pound out the yards. Years later, teammates would remember him tearing around the end carrying the ball on a sweep screaming out exhortations to his blockers to clear the way for him. He led the team in rushing five straight seasons interrupted by the War from 1943 through 1949. He was a leader that his teammates admired throughout his career, and in retirement he was called on again by his team. In 1955, Canadeo joined the team's Board of Directors. Other former players who have served on the Packer board include Charles Mathys, Bob Darling, Buckets Goldenberg, Verne Lewellen, Don Hutson, Jim Temp and Willie Davis. Two years later Tony joined play-by-play man Ray Scott to announce televised broadcasts of Packer games during the Lombardi era. As a fellow Jesuit alumnus, he became fast, good friends with Coach Lombardi. Tony was excitable and a "homer" who openly rooted for Green Bay, but also was knowledgeable, good at anticipating plays, and a professional. He was elected to the Executive Committee in 1958 and remained a member of that guiding body through 1993. In 1972, he pushed to hire Joe Paterno as coach, but was outvoted and the job went to Dan Devine.

He came to Green Bay to stay in 1941 and put down roots in town where he was not only a popular former player, but a respected man of the community as well. He raised five children there and worked for decades in the steel business. In 1972 he became ill and nearly died, but was saved by a kidney transplant from his oldest son Bob. As a proper celebration of being alive, he was inducted into the Packer Hall of Fame in 1973. The next year he reached a personal pinnacle by being elected to the Pro Football Hall of Fame in Canton. For six decades on the field and off, Tony Canadeo embodied the competitive spirit and honest dignity of the Packers.

FOR FURTHER INFORMATION

Packers of the Past: A Series of Articles Reprinted from the Milwaukee Journal Sept. 28 – Dec. 9, 1965. Milwaukee, WI: Milwaukee Journal, 1965. (20-3)

Poling, Jerry. *Downfield! Untold Stories of the Green Bay Packers.* Madison, WI: Prairie Oak Press, 1996. (135-9)

Porter, David L., ed. *Biographical Dictionary of American Sports: Football.* New York: Greenwood Press, 1987. (88-9)

Whittingham, Richard. *What a Game They Played.* New York: Harper and Row, 1974. (209-21)

Zimmerman, David. *In Search of a Hero: Life and Times of Tony Canadeo Packers' Grey Ghost.* Hales Corner, WI: Eagle Books, 2001.

HOLMGREN'S CHOICE AND RECENT PLAYOFFS

BRETT FAVRE • QUARTERBACK 1992–

WHO'S WORN THE NUMBER <Lewellen 1925–26>, Schneidman 1935–37, Fusina 1986, D. Dawson 1988, Norseth 1990, Favre 1992–02.

ORIGINATOR Back Verne Lewellen <1925–26> (see 46) or blocking back Herm Schneidman, 1935–37, a teammate of Joe Laws at Iowa. He gained 60 of his 119 career receiving yards on one TD catch against the Giants in 1936.

LONGEST TENURE Brett Favre 1992–02.

NUMBER CHANGES Verne Lewellen wore 21 in 1927, 45 in 1928, 31 in 1929–30, and 46 in 1931–32; Herm Schneidman wore 51 in 1938–39.

OTHER NOTABLES Verne Lewellen (see 46).

ONE TO FORGET Chuck Fusina won the Maxwell award as the best college player in the country in 1978. He spent three years as a backup quarterback in Tampa and then three years as a starter in the USFL before arriving in Green Bay in 1986 to appear in seven games before fading from the scene. He was better than Favre—Irv Favre, Brett's dad.

BRETT FAVRE "Brett who? It's spelled how?" Packer fans had to scratch their heads and wonder what the new GM Ron Wolf was thinking when he traded one of his two number one draft choices for third string Atlanta quarterback Brett Favre on February 10, 1992. Favre had been a high second round pick of the Falcons in 1991, but had spent his rookie year in coach Jerry Glanville's doghouse for being out of shape, not knowing the plays, partying too heartily, and generally being unprofessional in all aspects of his football career. And now the Packers were giving up the 17th pick in the draft for this good old boy whom "Prime Time" Deion Sanders had pegged "Country Time" usually shortened to "Country." Wolf had to be crazy.

Wolf, however, had always liked Favre a lot as a player and would have drafted him number one for the Jets in 1991 if the Jets had a number one choice that year. When the Packers hired Wolf in November 1991, fortuitously their next game was against the Falcons. Atlanta GM Ken Herrock was an old friend of Ron's and indicated that Favre was available. Although Denver and Kansas City reportedly were interested as well, it's doubtful that they were offering a number one pick.

It didn't take long for Packer fans to see what Wolf had seen. New coach Mike Holmgren had planned on bringing Favre along slowly in his complex offensive system, but fate intervened again. The oft-injured starting quarterback Don Majkowski went down with an ankle injury in the first quarter of the third game of the 1992 season against the Bengals, and Favre was forced to grow up fast. For the first three quarters, Favre moved the Packers sporadically, but they trailed 17-3 in the fourth quarter. Brett led the team to two touchdowns, but they still trailed 23-17 with the ball at their own eight with 1:07 to play and no timeouts left. In four plays, he advanced the team to the Cincinnati 35. On the fifth play of the drive with 13 seconds remaining, Favre hit receiver Kitrick Taylor down the sideline for a 35-yard touchdown. Amidst the ensuing celebration, Favre almost forgot that he had to hold the ball for the game winning extra point and he had to be dragged back on the field. The Packers won 24-23 and had found a quarterback and leader. He has started every game since, an NFL record for quarterbacks of 173 straight as of the end of the 2002 season, and the team is 115-58 in that time. In that decade Favre has made so many unbelievable plays that no other quarterback could have accomplished, often turning a broken play into a first down or a score. He has led the Packers to victory 26 times when the team was tied or trailing going into the fourth quarter, perhaps most memorably in 1999 when he tossed game winning touchdowns to beat Oakland, Minnesota and Tampa all in the closing seconds of three of the first four games of the year.

His early success, though, was followed by rough times. The team stood at 3-6 that first year before Favre really got his legs under him and led the team to six straight victories. Then they lost the last game to the Vikings and missed the playoffs. After an inconsistent second season in Green Bay, Favre was close to losing his starting job in his third year in Green Bay when coach Mike Holmgren decided he was fully committed to Brett and told him they would sink or swim together. What then ensued is a familiar story. 11 straight years with over 3,000 yards passing, including three seasons with over 4,000 yards. Five straight seasons and six altogether with over 30 touchdown passes. 314 touchdown passes for his career through 2002. Three straight MVP awards. Two Super Bowl appearances and one championship.

With Brett Favre, the Packers always have a chance to win and are always a contender for the post-season. He overcame a Vicodin addiction in 1996, a bad thumb in 1999, and tendonitis of the elbow in 2000 to still be firing the football harder than anyone else as he enters his early thirties. His record at home has been remarkable, 74-12, while the record of this hearty southerner in home games at 34 degrees or lower is 35-1. His troubles have come in domes and on artificial turf where he has a losing record. That fits his personality. He is naturally enthusiastic, spontaneous and excitable; there is nothing artificial about him. The boyish euphoria he showed running to the wrong sideline in his exhilaration after completing that 54-yard touchdown to Andre Rison to open Super Bowl XXXI was Favre at his most captivating. And he has been enthralling to watch. He clearly loves what he's doing and shows his emotions on the field. His motto always has been, "High risk; high reward," and he keeps the game in perspective by having no regrets when things don't work out.

PACKERS BY THE NUMBERS

What ensured Brett Favre's success was Mike Holmgren's coaching, direction, and faith. Holmgren and Favre had a symbiotic relationship. Holmgren taught Favre how to play quarterback in the NFL; Favre's acceptance of that teaching made the team and the coach successful. In Holmgren's first three years in Seattle, he has not been able to find a suitable quarterback to direct his offense, and the team has been mediocre. Holmgren's skill as a quarterbacks coach is well documented. He converted Steve Young from a high school option quarterback to a drop back passer at Brigham Young and then helped make an NFL quarterback out of Young in San Francisco. He worked well fine-tuning Joe Montana and also made a starting NFL signal caller out of Steve Bono.

Holmgren's track record was well-established when he came to Green Bay, and he became the first winning coach in town since Lombardi. Much was made of some superficial similarities between the two men—both started as high school teachers and coaches, both were primarily offensive coaches, neither held a college or pro head coaching job before coming to the Packers—but they are different men. After all Lisle Blackbourn and Dan Devine started as high school coaches as well, and Gene Ronzani and Lindy Infante were Italian offensive coaches. As for Holmgren, he runs a pass-first offense, while Lombardi ran a run-first offense. Holmgren is more media savvy and has a more obvious sense of humor. Mike has seen several former assistants become successful head coaches in the league, but Vince's former assistants and players were almost uniformly unsuccessful as head men. While Mike runs a tight ship, he is not as strong a disciplinarian as Lombardi—no one could be. The key thing they had in common was winning and that is why both had streets named after them in Green Bay. Ron Wolf has said that hiring Mike Holmgren and trading for Brett Favre were the two most important moves he made in turning around the fortunes of the franchise and those two were intertwined and dependent on each other.

The clearest evidence of that was in the rivalry that sprung up between San Francisco and Green Bay in the late 1990s. The two teams had played one another since 1950, but never with any special feeling. Then Green Bay imported its head coach, two coordinators, and offensive scheme from the Bay Area in 1992. The two teams actually would not meet until the 1995 divisional playoffs when the Packers announced their arrival as a quality team by upsetting the champion 49ers in San Francisco 27-17. The teams have met eight more times since then, five of them with Holmgren coaching the Packers, and Green Bay has lost only once. Five of the nine meetings were playoff games, and four times Green Bay ended San Francisco's season. The Packers had the 49ers number and it drove the West Coasters crazy. They struck back in the late 1990s by importing their new coach, Steve Mariucci, and offensive coordinator, Marty Mornhinweg, from Green Bay in 1997 and signing former Packers like Gabe Wilkins and Travis Jervey as free agents.

In this rivalry, Holmgren and Favre set the tone on offense by beating the 49ers at their own game while Fritz Shurmur's defense pounded on the Niner offense and beat them up. In Holmgren's sixth time coaching against his old team in the 1998 Wild Card Playoff round San Francisco would deliver a surprising counterpunch. It was a great game with Steve Young and Brett Favre exchanging scoring drives and exciting plays. With 4:19 to play, Favre drove the Packers 89 yards in nine plays, firing a 15-yard pass to Antonio Freeman to take a 27-23 lead with two minutes left in the game. Young drove the 49ers right back down the field and threw a 25-yard touchdown to Terrell Owens with three seconds left to win the game 30-27. Owens was covered and the ball should have been knocked down, but first year starter Darren Sharper didn't make the play. In addition, Jerry Rice had fumbled the ball to the Packers several plays before, but the referee ruled him down. The loss ended the Packers' winning streak over their rivals, as well as the Packer careers of Reggie White and Mike Holmgren.

Holmgren left within weeks to become Coach and General Manager in Seattle. Wolf left the Packers just two years later. No one had the foresight to work out an arrangement in 1999 to allow Wolf to move up to a vice presidential role and Holmgren to assume the Packer GM controls. Both teams missed the playoffs in 1999 and 2000, but they did meet twice in the regular season. Green Bay won both contests behind the arm of Brett Favre who had learned Holmgren's lessons well.

In the 2001 season with Holmgren-protege Mike Sherman heading the organization, the reloading Packers made the playoffs for the first time in three years. Their first postseason opponent was once again the revitalized San Francisco 49ers. In the first half, the Pack gained only 76 yards and were behind 7-6. Favre implored Coach Sherman to let him open up the offense in the second half. Green Bay then rolled up 292 yards and 19 points to beat the 49ers for the eighth time in the last nine tries 25-15. They scored on four of their first five possessions after halftime as Favre went 16 of 21 for 226 yards. The next week, though, Green Bay met their doom in a dome. Favre threw six interceptions against the vaunted Rams and three were returned for touchdowns. Favre tried too hard to play at the Rams pace and outscore them, and everything went wrong in the 45-17 loss. The really odd thing was that the defense played pretty well against the Rams, and the Packers offense seemed to be able to move the ball, but eight turnovers were ridiculous. Favre tied a playoff record of six interceptions previously attained by Frank Filchock and Hall of Famers Norm Van Brocklin and Bobby Layne. At least that's good and germane company—in many ways Favre has been like a latter day Bobby Layne. After the game, Favre was quoted as saying, "Whether you lose by one or by 50, whether I throw one [interception] or six, the bottom line is we're going home. It's how we respond. I will be back. My plan is to make everyone forget about today. Life goes on." High risk; high rewards; no regrets. The Packers would return to the playoffs as division champs in 2002, but would exit quickly, losing their first home playoff game ever in a lackluster performance by Favre and the entire team.

When Favre goes into the Pro Football Hall of Fame, perhaps he'll think back to how lucky he was that his gift was not lost. If he had stayed in Atlanta, he could have been buried on the depth chart of a bad team with a questionable offense for several seasons. He could have continued to be blinded by the lights of the big city and never progress. Or maybe he would surface years later on another team as a gritty veteran of some rusty skills who despite some late success never would live up to his full potential like Vinnie Testaverde. However, Favre came to Green Bay to play on the steadily improving Packers with a high-powered offense coached by Mike Holmgren, and his place in football history is secure. His time has been the Favre era in Packer history just as 1935–45 was the Hutson era, and he just may have supplanted Hutson as the greatest Packer of them all. At the very least, his excellence has allowed Packer fans embrace the present with as much vigor as the team's rich past.

FOR FURTHER INFORMATION

Dougherty, Pete. "The Leader of the Pack," in *Heir to the Legacy: The Memorable Story of Mike Holmgren's Green Bay Packers.* Louisville, KY: AdCraft, 1996. (59-65)

"Favre, Brett," *Current Biography Yearbook 1996.* New York: H.W. Wilson, 1997. (130-3)

Favre, Brett, with Chris Havel. *Favre: For the Record.* Garden City, NY: Doubleday, 1997.

Havel, Chris. "Holmgren: The Early Years," in *Heir to the Legacy: The Memorable Story of Mike Holmgren's Green Bay Packers.* Louisville, KY: AdCraft, 1996. (8-15)

"Holmgren, Mike," *Current Biography Yearbook 2000.* New York: H.W. Wilson, 2001. (296-300)

Wolf, Ron, and Paul Attner. *The Packer Way: Nine Stepping Stones to Building a Winning Organization.* New York: St. Martin's Press, 1998. (1-5, 50-7)

1961 CHAMPIONSHIP
PAUL HORNUNG • HALFBACK 1957–66

WHO'S WORN THE NUMBER <O'Donnell 1925–26>, Purdy 1927, R. Baker 1928, (Estes 1928), Monnett 1936–37, Bruder 1938–39, Riddick 1940–42, Hornung 1957–66, Ferragamo 1986, Majkowski 1987, Gilius 1987r, Burrow 1988.

ORIGINATOR End Dick O'Donnell <1925–26> (see top 20) or Pid Purdy, 1927, who was as cocky as one would expect of a 145 pound quarterback. In 1926 he threw one TD pass and 12 interceptions. Nonetheless, he was a skilled kicker and played four years as an outfielder with the White Sox and Reds, batting .293.

LONGEST TENURE Paul Hornung 1957–66.

NUMBER CHANGES Dick O'Donnell wore 20 in 1927–28 and 30 in 1929–30; Pid Purdy had 18 in 1926 and wore 7 in 1927; back Roy "Bullet" Baker also wore 12 and 21 in 1928 and 17 in 1929; Bob Monnett also wore 18 in 1933, 42 and 66 in 1934, 12 and 3 in 1935, 12 in 1936, and 50 in 1938; back Hank Bruder wore 13 in 1931–33, 55 in 1933, 47 in 1934, 27 in 1935–36, and 18 in 1935–38; end Ray Riddick wore 22 in 1942 and 19 in 1946; quarterback Don Majkowski wore 7 from 1988–92.

OTHER NOTABLES Bob Monnett (see top 3); Hank Bruder (see 27); Don Majkowski (see 7).

ONE TO FORGET Kicker Curtis Burrow appeared in his sole NFL game in 1988. He missed his only field goal attempt and two of four extra point tries.

PAUL HORNUNG The only college football player to win the Heisman Trophy on a losing team was Notre Dame quarterback Paul Hornung from the 2-8 Fighting Irish in 1956. He was a remarkably versatile two-way college player; he could pass, run, kick, block, and tackle. In 1956 he finished second in the nation in all-purpose yards, led Notre Dame in eight offensive categories, and even finished second on the team in tackles as a safety. The Packers won a coin flip with the Chicago Cardinals for the 1957 Bonus Pick, the first pick in the draft that year, and picked Hornung. Paul had hoped that he would go to Chicago for the commercial and entertainment options available in the big city. After his first two years in Green Bay, many Packer fans wished that had happened as well.

Hornung looked to be a flop of monumental proportions in those first two years. Much like the long string of option quarterbacks produced by the Universities of Nebraska and Oklahoma over the past few decades, he couldn't throw well enough to play quarterback, couldn't run fast enough to play half-back, and was not big enough to play fullback. Packer coaches Lisle Blackbourn in 1957 and Scooter McLean in 1958 tried him at each backfield position and he excelled at none. He was beginning to look like a more expensive Fred Cone, a part-time fullback and full-time placekicker. Off the field, his swinging lifestyle was resented by fans who wanted better results on the field. Teaming with fellow bachelor Max McGee from the start, the two were spotted frequently in local drinking establishments entertaining a constantly changing series of women. Wild rumors were spread by gossip throughout the small town, and Paul's image suffered. He wanted to be traded and considered retiring.

Enter Lombardi and the resurrection of Hornung's career. Lombardi's assistants did not think much of Hornung in 1959 when they unanimously derided his lack of drive and production and wanted to get rid of him. However, Lombardi's offense was perfectly suited to Paul's multiplicity of talents. His lack of foot-speed was not a great hindrance in Lombardi's dual-back, run-based offense that placed a greater emphasis on the ball carrier picking the right hole to "run to daylight" while the other back ran interference. Hornung and Jim Taylor formed a perfect team. Neither was real big or real fast, but both made great cuts to the hole and each blocked selflessly for the other. Both could catch the swing pass out of the backfield and make something happen. One of the things that jumps out at you when looking at Hornung's statistics are his receiving numbers. In his career, Paul averaged 11.4 yards per catch, which is very high for a back, and scored 12 times out of 130 catches. The other factor that made him perfect for Lombardi's offense was his ability to run the halfback option play. The defense not knowing whether Paul would run or throw made Lombardi's favorite play, the power sweep, that much more effective. It was Paul's favorite play. In his first four years under Lombardi, Hornung completed 18 of 35 option passes for 335 yards and five touchdowns. That's an average of close to 10 yards per pass and kept the chains moving for the Packers.

What Hornung liked to do most, and was best at, was score—in more ways than one. While Lombardi continually fined Hornung and McGee for their off-the-field transgressions, he clearly looked on them as prodigal sons who brought a positive spirit to his club. On the field, Hornung had a nose for pay dirt. In one game against the Colts in 1961 he scored a team record 33 points on four touchdowns, six extra points, and a field goal. Three of the top four scoring games in team history still belong to Paul. As a halfback/kicker, he led the league in points from 1959 through 1961. His 1960 total of 176 points in 12 games has never been surpassed even though teams now play 16 games a season. He dropped off to 146 points in 1961 only because he missed a couple of games after being called up to the Army Reserves during the Berlin Crisis that year. He tried to make up for that in the 1961 title game against the New York Giants.

The 1961 championship game was the first one ever played in Green Bay and would give the town the nickname "Titletown USA." The Packers were favored by 3 1/2 points as the home team, but were forced to punt on their first possession; they would not punt again in the first half. The second time the Packers got the ball, they drove 80 yards in eleven plays highlighted by a 25-yard pass reception by Hornung and Paul's eventual six-yard touchdown run on the first play of the second quarter. After that scoreless first quarter, the Packers were rolling. Ray Nitschke intercepted a Y.A. Tittle pass at the Giants 33 and Bart Starr capitalized with a 13-yard touchdown pass to Boyd Dowler. Hank Gremminger then picked of Tittle at the Giants 36 and Starr capped a six-play drive with a 14-yard touchdown pass to Ron Kramer. Charlie Connerly replaced Tittle and drove the Giants to the Green Bay six, but New York turned the ball over on downs. With time running out in the half, Starr moved the Pack downfield on a 17-yard run by Hornung and a 40-yard pass to Kramer. On the last play of the half, Hornung kicked a 17-yard field goal for a 24-0 lead. In the second half, Hornung would kick two more field goals and Kramer would catch another touchdown pass of 13 yards to complete the scoring at 37-0. For the game Kramer caught four passes for 80 yards and scored 12 points, while Hornung caught three for 47 yards, ran 20 times for 89 yards, and scored 19 points on one touchdown, three field goals, and four extra points. Hornung deservedly was named MVP of this game to go with his league MVP award for the year, and the Packers were champions for the first time since 1944.

Hornung battled injuries in 1962 and played in only nine games and kicked in even fewer. Early in 1963, he and the Lions' Alex Karras were suspended indefinitely by Commissioner Pete Rozelle for gambling—Paul had been betting on his own team to win. Hornung accepted full personal responsibility for his actions and was reinstated the following year. 1964 started well when he kicked three field goals against the Bears on opening day, but quickly deteriorated into a season of injuries and kicking woes. He hit only on 12 of 38 field goal attempts, which helped cost the team a shot at the championship. By 1965, he had lost more than a step, but had two last hurrahs. Late in the year against chief rival Baltimore, he scored five of his eight touchdowns for the year and led Green Bay to a 42-27 victory. In the championship game against the Browns that year, he ran for 105 yards and one score on 18 carries to complement Jim Taylor's 96 yards on the ground as the Packers trampled Cleveland 23-12 for the title. As injuries and age took their toll in 1966, Hornung sat on the bench for the entire first Super Bowl game and watched his friend Max McGee steal the show with seven catches as a reserve. Paul was taken by New Orleans in the expansion draft in 1967, but retired instead. Losing his prodigal surrogate son Hornung brought Lombardi to tears.

Paul Hornung was a man's man and was popular both with women and men. One reason was that he had a good sense of humor about himself. Max McGee would get off a line like, "Paul had a 43-inch chest and a 36-inch head," and Hornung would laugh and answer in kind. The man called "goat" (short for "goat shoulders") by his teammates was a leader the whole team admired and looked up to. Aside from that three-year run of scoring, though, his statistics look a little skimpy. He never rushed for more than 681 yards, never caught more than 28 passes and only had about 3 1/2 years when he was at the top of his game, but he was deservedly elected to the Packer Hall of Fame in 1975. He was not selected for the Pro Football Hall of Fame until his 12th time as a finalist in 1986. He had earned it; he was an all-around football player and a winner, a champion.

FOR FURTHER INFORMATION
Hornung, Paul, as told to Al Silverman. *Football and the Single Man*. Garden City, NY: Doubleday, 1965.

Hornung, Paul, with Tim Cohane. "How Winning Improved My Image," *Look*. 11/20/62. (124-32)

Jenkins, Dan. "The Toe That Lost Its Touch," *Sports Illustrated*. 11/30/64. (30-2)

Johnson, Chuck. *The Greatest Packers of Them All*. New York: Putnam, 1968. (66-75)

Kramer, Jerry, with Dick Schaap. *Distant Replay*. New York: G.P. Putnam, 1985. (61-4)

Maraniss, David. *When Pride Still Mattered: A Life of Vince Lombardi*. New York: Simon and Schuster, 1999. (278-9, 288-90, 336-42, 353-4)

Porter, David L., ed. *Biographical Dictionary of American Sports: Football*. New York: Greenwood Press, 1987. (270-2)

Schaap, Dick. *Paul Hornung: Pro Football Golden Boy*. New York: Macfadden-Bartell, 1962 (No. 13 in the Sport Magazine Library).

———. "Paul Hornung: I'll Make Them Forget," *Sport*. 9/63 (20, 87-9)

———. "The Razzle and Dazzle of Pro Football—and the Game's Golden Boy," *Newsweek*. 10/30/61. (43-6)

———. "The Rough Road Ahead for Paul Hornung," *Sport*. 11/61. (60-87)

Smith, Robert. *Illustrated History of Pro Football*. New York: Grossett and Dunlap, 1977. (245-7)

Wagner, Len. *Launching the Glory Years: The 1959 Packers • What They Didn't Tell Us*. Green Bay, WI: Coach's Books LLC [Jay Bengtson], 2001. (27)

 1961 CHAMPIONSHIP DATA
Green Bay Packers 37
New York Giants 0

December 31, 1961 • City Stadium (Lambeau Field)
Attendance: 39,029 (at $10 per ticket)
Winner's Share: $5,195.44
Loser's Share: $3,339.99
Weather: 21 degrees with a 10 mph wind

KEY STATS	PACKERS	GIANTS
First Downs	19	6
Rush Yards	181	31
Pass Yards	164	99
Total Yards	345	130
Interceptions	4	0
Fumbles Lost	0	1
Penalties	4–16	4–38
Third Down Conversion	7/14	2/12 (0/2 on fourth down)
Halftime score	Packers 24 Giants 0	

LEADERS
Rushing: Paul Hornung 20-89 Alex Webster 7-19

Passing: Bart Starr 10-17-0 164 yds. YA Tittle 6-20-4 65 yds.

Receiving: Ron Kramer 4-80 Rote 3-54

ADDITIONAL FACTS

•On the Tuesday before the game, a confident Lombardi was quoted, "If the field is right, we'll win."

•Defensive end Bill Quinlan and cornerback Jess Whittenton were hospitalized with bad colds three days before the game.

•At the start of the third quarter, Bart Starr scrambled 18 yards from the Packer 37 to the Giant 45 on second and nine and fumbled. The Giants recovered, but the ball was blown dead, plus there was a five-yard illegal procedure penalty on Green Bay. In the confusion, the officials mark off the penalty from the Packer 40 and reset the down to first. Thus, instead of the Giants having the ball or the Packers having a second and 14 from their 32, the Packers had a first and 15 from their 35. Even given the five downs, the Packers had to punt.

•At the end of the blowout, Lombardi pulled his backfield stars one at a time so each got a hometown ovation, Hornung, then Taylor, then Starr.

•Lombardi was carried off the field by Hawg Hanner and Dan Currie.

•One of the congratulatory telegrams received by Lombardi after the game is from President Kennedy: "Congratulations on a great game today. It was a fine victory for a great coach, a great team and a great town."

WINNING
VINCE LOMBARDI • HEAD COACH 1959–67

WHO'S WORN THE NUMBER <Vergara 1925>, <Flaherty 1926>, Bross 1927.

ORIGINATOR End George Vergara <1925> played with the Four Horsemen at Notre Dame. His pro career was cut short by a neck injury. An insurance man, he worked as a college and NFL official and was elected mayor of New Rochelle in 1956. Back Matt Bross, 1927, was another of the five Gonzaga players on the 1920s Packers. All played for Gus Dorais.

LONGEST TENURE All three played for one year.

NUMBER CHANGES None.

OTHER NOTABLES None. Vince Lombardi is number six because he can be counted as the sixth coach of the Packers as an NFL team in two ways. If we count Joe Hoeffel as the first Packer coach, followed by Curly Lambeau, Gene Ronzani, Lisle Blackborn, and Scooter McLean, then Lombardi is the sixth full year coach in Green Bay. Or if we discount Hoeffel and add in the co-coaching pair of Hugh Devore and Scooter McLean who were in charge the last two games of the 1953 season after Ronzani was let go, then Vince is still number 6.

ONE TO FORGET All three, but Bross only lasted two games.

VINCE LOMBARDI Much like Shakespeare's *Hamlet* has been the character most written about in literature, Vince Lombardi who coached in the small hamlet of Green Bay has been the subject of continual analysis by football writers decades after his death. "Horatio, what the hell is going on here?" George Halas and Curly Lambeau were prominent in the establishment of both their teams and the National Football League itself, but they are not recalled much today. Tom Landry and Don Shula were contemporaries of Lombardi who both went on to coach successfully for close to 30 years, but neither is still as commonly lauded as their long-deceased rival Lombardi. Paul Brown, Chuck Noll, Bud Grant... the great coaches come and go, but Lombardi endures above all of them. He is quoted and noted continually and even was portrayed by actor Jerry Stiller in a series of Nike ads in the late 1990s, 25 years after his death. Why?

In a word, winning. "Winning is not a sometime thing; it's an all the time thing. You don't win once in a while; you don't do things right once in a while; you do them right all the time."

(Kramer, *Instant*, 61) Vince Lombardi is the patron saint of winning in America across all fields, not just football. In football, he is so much of an icon that the league championship trophy is named after him. Only Halas and Lambeau won more NFL titles (six) than Lombardi's five, and they did so over a much longer time period. His five titles in seven years was an amazing display of concentrated excellence. As he put it, "One can never achieve perfection, but in chasing perfection, one can achieve excellence." Lombardi's last two championships were won in the first two Super Bowls, and as the first occurrences of that annual American extravaganza they will always be remembered. Moreover, he died relatively young, without the opportunity to sully his coaching mastery of the 1960s in Green Bay with a lower level of success in Washington.

Lombardi was always a teacher at heart and began as a high school teacher and coach in New Jersey. He progressed slowly through the assistant coaching ranks from Fordham to West Point to the New York Giants. In New York he teamed with Tom Landry during the late 1950s to give the Giants probably the best set of offensive and defensive coaches in league history. Head coach Jim Lee Howell stepped back and assumed the role of delegator-in-chief while the Giants achieved success on the field and won the NFL title in 1956. Lombardi was very popular with the Mara family who owned the team and was the heir apparent to take over when Howell retired, but Vince couldn't wait. He took the head job of the 1-10-1 Packers in 1959, and in one year turned the team around.

In Green Bay, he sorted out the talent on hand and put players in the position where they could best contribute to the team. Those he judged could not contribute, he got rid of and replaced with players who could. "I will demand a commitment to excellence and to victory, and that is what life is all about." (Kramer, *Lombardi*, ix) His skills for organization were prodigious, and he had rigorous work habits. The offensive system he installed was, on the surface, as simple as possible, and stood in sharp contrast in the 1960s to Tom Landry's shifting, multi-set passing offense in Dallas. His view was, "Fundamentals win it. Football is two things: it's blocking and tackling." (Lombardi Jr., 7) His was a run-based offense eaturing fewer plays than most teams ran. The complexity was in the multiplicity of options possible off of each basic play. The line took the defenders in the direction they wanted to go, using Lombardi's own devise of "option blocking." The running backs then had to read where the hole opened up and cut back into it. *Run to Daylight* was the title of Lombardi's own football book and "run to win" was a phrase he took from the Bible. On pass plays, receivers were expected to read the defense and break off their routes accordingly. On defense, players had to use their brains to react quickly to the offensive play. "You teach discipline by doing [something] over and over, by repetition and rote, especially in a game like football when you have very little time to decide what you are going to do. So what you do is react almost instinctively, naturally. You have done it so many times over and over and over again." (Lombardi Jr., 97) Lombardi trained his men to be physically fit because "fatigue makes cowards of us all" (Wiebusch, 49) and "the harder you work, the harder it is to surrender." (Wiebusch, 49)

His most familiar line of course is, "Winning isn't everything, it's the only thing." (Wiebusch, 49) What always struck me about that saying was that it was meaningless. It would be like saying, "Football isn't just exciting, it's thrilling." There is not much of a distinction in terms there. Sportswriter Paul Zimmerman insisted that the actual quote from Lombardi after the 1962 championship game was the more coherent "Winning isn't the most important thing, it's the only thing." The original line itself has been attributed by some to various college coaches from the early part of the 20th century. It reliably was traced back to 1940s Vanderbilt coach Red Sanders by Lombardi biographer David Maraniss. Sanders still used the phrase when coaching UCLA in the 1950s and happened to share an agent with screenwriter Melvin Shavelson. When Shavelson was writing the screenplay for a 1953 film called *Trouble Along the Way* starring John Wayne as a football coach, his agent mentioned the phrase. Shavelson put the words in the mouth of Wayne's daughter in the film quoting her father. In Green Bay, it would become one of Lombardi's aphorisms. What it was taken to mean was "win at all costs," but that is not what Lombardi meant. He did not believe that the end justified the means, but rather that proper direction and dedication would lead to the desired end.

Lombardi wanted to win, but he wanted to win the right way. "There are three things that are important to every man in this locker room. His religion, his family, and the Green Bay Packers. In that order." (Kramer, *Instant*, 17) He wanted his team to be fully prepared. He wanted them to block better and tackle harder than the other team. He wanted them to make smart choices on the field. He did not want them to break the rules or to taunt their opponents. He also recognized that he was talking to and about professionals. Professionals are paid to win football games; they are not paid simply to play them. As he flatly stated right from the start to his team, "There are trains, planes, and buses leaving here every day, and if you don't produce for me, you're going to find yourself on one of them." (Lombardi Jr., 231) Professional sports is a harsh business, and there is no substitute for winning. When he saw how his words were being taken in a broader context, he began to amend the saying to variations on "Winning isn't everything, but the desire to win is the only thing," which is certainly more palatable for pee wee football. Even with this, we see how paramount Lombardi placed winning and with good reason.

Lombardi was a master motivator of whom his players still speak reverently today despite the harsh treatment many endured from him. Why did they submit to this torture? They believed in him because they won. Lombardi saw winning as more than something confined to the football field. "Football is the symbol, really, of a lot of things. It is a symbol of courage. It's a symbol of stamina. I think football is a symbol of teamwork, of efficiency...these are the three areas that you would have to say made the United States, made America great. Courage, stamina and teamwork." (Flynn, 23) Lombardi was an extremely popular speaker for business, community, and political groups throughout the turbulent 1960s. Hundreds of times he delivered variations of the same motivational/philosophical speech on Leadership. "I think it is also time in this country to cheer for, to stand up for, to slap on the back the doer, the achiever, a man who recognizes a problem and does something about it, the winner." (Lombardi Jr., 74) Even today, his pithy quotes are everywhere. More than one book has been published that simply compiled and organized quotations from Chairman Vince. If you look on the Web, you'll find several businesses who have appropriated lines from Lombardi to describe their commitment to excellence. His son and namesake Vince Jr. has made a career out of speaking to business groups and writing books on the leadership principles laid out by his father. The influence of this intense and difficult football coach has not faded in 30 years.

Lombardi was no saint. He yelled and screamed and berated his players and staff to get them to improve. He insulted and showed open disdain for members of the press. However, he was a religious and ethical man. Despite his single-minded focus on victory, he could see a larger picture. In his letter of resignation from the Packers, Lombardi wrote that "the championships, the money, the color; all of these things linger only in the memory. It is the spirit, the will to excel; the will to win; these are the things that endure. These are the important things, and they will always remain in Green Bay." (Lombardi Jr., 228) As he once told his quarterback Bart Starr, "The quality of any man's life is in direct proportion to his commitment to excellence." (Flynn, 106) Through Lombardi's commitment, the Packers excelled. Posthumously, he was elected to the Pro Football Hall of Fame in 1971 and the Packer Hall of Fame in 1975.

FOR FURTHER INFORMATION

Briggs, Jennifer, comp. *Strive to Excel: The Wit and Wisdom of Vince Lombardi.* Nashville, TN: Rutledge Hill Press, 1997.

Bynum, Mike, ed. *Vince Lombardi: Memories of a Special Time.* [United States]: October Football Corp., 1988.

Daley, Art. "Lombardi," *Green Bay Packers 2000 Yearbook.* (82-3)

Dowling, Tom. *Coach: A Season with Lombardi.* New York: Norton, 1970.

Flynn, George, ed. *Vince Lombardi on Football.* New York: New York Graphic Society Ltd and Wallyn Inc., 1973.

———. *The Vince Lombardi Scrapbook.* New York: Grossett and Dunlap, 1976

George, Gary R. *Winning Is A Habit: Lombardi on Winning, Success, and the Pursuit of Excellence.* New York: HarperCollins, 1997.

Kramer, Jerry, ed. *Lombardi: Winning Is the Only Thing.* New York: World Publishing, 1970.

Lea, Bud. "Lombardi Left Us 25 Years Ago," *Green Bay Packers 1995 Yearbook.* (71-2)

Lombardi, Jr., Vince. *What It Takes to Be Number One: Vince Lombardi on Leadership.* New York: McGraw-Hill, 2001.

Lombardi, Vince with W.C. Heinz. *Run to Daylight.* Englewood Cliffs, NJ: Prentice-Hall, 1963.

Maraniss, David. *When Pride Still Mattered: A Life of Vince Lombardi.* New York: Simon and Schuster, 1999.

O'Brien, Michael. *Vince: A Personal Biography.* New York: William Morrow, 1987.

Schoor, Gene. *Football's Greatest Coach: Vince Lombardi.* Garden City, NY: Doubleday, 1974.

Wells, Robert W. *Vince Lombardi: His Life and Times.* 2nd ed. Madison, WI: Prairie Oak Press, 1997.

Wiebusch, John, ed. *Lombardi.* Chicago: Follett Publishing, 1971.

MAJIKAL COMEBACKS
DON MAJKOWSKI • QUARTERBACK 1988–92

WHO'S WORN THE NUMBER <Earp 1925–26>, Red Smith 1927, Purdy, 1927, Dunn 1930, E. Svendsen 1937, Jankowski 1938–41, J. Mason 1942–45, Schlinkman 1946–49, Loomis 1951, D. Gordon 1973, Majkowski 1988–92, Landetta 1998, Hanson 1999, Wuerffel 2000.

ORIGINATOR Center Jug Earp,1925–26> (see 39) or guard Red Smith (see top 28)

LONGEST TENURE Don Majkowski 1988–92.

NUMBER CHANGES Jug Earp wore 29 in 1927–28, 9 in 1928, 38 in 1929, and 39 in 1930–32; Red Smith also wore 19 and 28 in 1927 and 15 in 1929; back Pid Purdy had 18 in 1926 and wore 5 in 1927; quarterback Red Dunn wore 11 in 1927–28, 16 and 32 in 1929, 17 in 1930, and 15 in 1931; Earl "Bud" Svendsen wore 53 and 66 in 1939; fullback Eddie Jankowski wore 25 in 1937; defensive back Ace Loomis wore 43 in 1952 and 48 in 1953; Don Majkowski wore 5 in 1987.

OTHER NOTABLES Jug Earp (see 39); Red Smith (see top 28); Red Dunn (see 11); Earl "Bud" Svendsen only played two years in Green Bay but was inducted into the Packer Hall of Fame in 1985 where he joined his brother George; Milwaukee native Eddie Jankowski was Clarke Hinkle's backup but still went into the Packer Hall of Fame in 1984.

ONE TO FORGET Danny Wuerffel won the Heisman Trophy at the University of Florida before spending three dreadful years with New Orleans. He revived his career in NFL Europe and signed with the Packers where he was the third quarterback for the 2000 season. The highlight of his time in Green Bay was getting into a Bears game for the last two snaps, thereby becoming the fifth Heisman Trophy winner to play for the Packers.

DON MAJKOWSKI His name was pronounced Mah-KOW-ski, but he was known as the Majik Man, and for one thrilling season he was just that. Don Majkowski was a quiet, private person off the field, but walked with a cocky swagger on it. He separated his shoulder in his senior year at the University of Virginia and slipped off most teams' draft lists. The Packers picked him in the 10th round of the 1987 draft and he even started five games as a rookie under coach Forrest Gregg. Offensive guru Lindy Infante replaced Gregg in 1988 and continued to cultivate Majkowski's potential.

In 1989 the Majik Man emerged for the one great season of his 10-year NFL career. He led the league in passing yards with 4,318 and led the team to a 10-6 record with 27 touchdown passes. Five of those 10 victories were accomplished by virtue of a furious fourth-quarter comeback led by Majkowski. However, his greatest comeback of the year came in the third game of the year and was unsuccessful. The Packers trailed the Rams 38-7 at halftime before Majkowski led the team to four second-half touchdowns and a field goal only to lose 41-38 when Brent Fullwood fumbled at the Ram one-yard line in the closing minutes. Most of Don's heroics had a happier ending. The Packers would trail the Saints 21-0 before coming back to win 35-34. Majkowski completed 18 straight passes and threw a three-yard scoring strike to Sterling Sharpe with 55 seconds left to win that game by a point. They were trailing the Falcons 21-6 going into the fourth quarter and won 23-21 on Chris Jacke's 22-yard field goal with 1:42 left. They beat the Lions 23-20 in overtime on another Jacke field goal. Majik threw the winning touchdown pass to Sterling Sharpe with nine minutes left in a 20-19 victory over the Vikings that veteran cornerback Dave Brown preserved with two interceptions in the final four minutes. Against Tampa, the Pack were behind 16-14 in the closing minutes when Majik threw an incomplete pass on fourth down. Fortunately, a hands-to-the-face penalty on the Bucs gave Green Bay new life and Majik drove them to the Buc 30 where Jacke kicked a 47-yard winning field goal with no time left. The Packers even handed the eventual Super Bowl champion 49ers a 21-17 loss in San Francisco, one of only two Niner losses all year.

The biggest comeback was against the hated Bears. Majkowski threw a fourth down 14 yard touchdown pass to Sterling Sharpe with 32 second left to pull out a 14-13 win. What made this one special was that it came down to instant replay. Line judge Jim Quirk threw a penalty flag judging that Majkowski was past the line of scrimmage when he unleashed the pass. After a lengthy delay to look at the instant replay, official Bill Parkinson overruled the call and ruled it a touchdown. The Bears were so disgusted that they listed the game with an asterisk in their media book for years. And they were right; he was past the line. The Packers stole the win that day, but could not steal into the playoffs, losing out on tiebreakers in that remarkable season.

Many factors go into an exciting comeback—the importance of the game, the quality of the opponent, how far behind the team was, how late the winning score occurred, and whether the winning score was a touchdown or field goal. The Packers have staged several stirring comebacks throughout their history. The top one most certainly was the Ice Bowl, but setting aside playoff games, here is a top ten countdown in chronological order:

1) 10/27/35 17-14 over the Bears at Wrigley Field. Trailing by 11 with less than three minutes to play, the Packers scored on Arnie Herber's 65-yard touchdown pass to Don Hutson. The Packers kicked off, and Ernie Smith recovered a Bernie Masterson fumble on the next play at the Bear 13. After a few running plays, Herber went to Hutson again, this time for the 3-yard game-winner. For the game, the Bears had six turnovers and the Packers five.

2) 11/30/41 22-17 over the Redskins in Washington. Trailing 17-0 at half in the final game of the season, The Packers came back behind Cecil Isbell's three touchdown passes to Don Hutson to pull out the game and position themselves for a playoff against the Bears for the Western Division crown. Two similar games were a 1965 game against the Lions when the Pack trailed 21-3 at halftime before Bart Starr went six of seven for 221 yards and three touchdowns in the third quarter to lead to a 31-21 win and a 1982 game against the Rams when Green Bay came back from a 23-0 half-time deficit to win 35-23.

3) 9/25/55 20-17 over the Lions in City Stadium. Tobin Rote hit Gary Knafelc with an 18-yard touchdown toss with 20 seconds left to upset the defending Western Division champs on opening day. The following year in Detroit on Thanksgiving, Rote would throw a 13-yard touchdown to Bill Howton with a minute and a half on the clock and safety Bobby Dillon would intercept Bobby Layne with 38 seconds left to beat the Lions 24-20.

4) 9/29/57 21-17 over the Bears at the new City Stadium. Babe Parilli hit Gary Knafelc with a six-yard pass for the winning score with 8:21 left in the first game at what is now known as Lambeau Field.

5) 9/18/66 21-20 over the Browns in Cleveland. The Packers trailed the entire game before beginning their winning drive with 11 minutes left. Over eight minutes later, the Packers had a fourth and eight on the Browns nine-yard line. With all his receivers covered, Starr was forced to throw to Jim Taylor in the flat. Taylor refused to be stopped and broke three tackles to rumble into the end zone. It was Starr's second fourth down touchdown pass to a back in the flat that day as Paul Hornung had caught one earlier.

6) 11/27/86 44-40 over the Lions in the Silverdome. In an exciting back and forth Thanksgiving contest, wide receiver/kick returner Walter Stanley accumulated 287 yards of offense, including an 83-yard punt return for the winning touchdown with 41 seconds left in the game.

7) 11/5/89 14-13 over the Bears at Lambeau Field. The Instant Replay game described above.

8) 9/20/92 24-23 over the Bengals at Lambeau Field. Don Majkowski went down with an ankle injury in the first quarter and first year Packer Brett Favre took over. The Packers trailed the whole game. With 4:11 left, Favre culminated an 88 yard drive with a five yard touchdown pass to Sterling Sharpe to draw within three. The Bengals answered with a field goal to make the score 23-17. After a misplay on the kickoff, the Packers started from their own eight with 1:07 left and no timeouts. In four plays, the Pack-ers got to the Cincinnati 35. On the next play with 13 seconds remaining, Favre hit receiver Kitrick Taylor down the sideline for a 35-yard touchdown.

It was Coach Mike Holmgren's first victory and the beginning of a beautiful friendship between the coach and his new quarterback.

9) 12/18/94 21-17 over the Falcons in Milwaukee. In the last game the Packers would play in the Cream City, their second home, Green Bay kept its playoff hopes alive by pulling out this game with a 67-yard touchdown drive that began with 1:58 left. Brett Favre completed six of nine passes on the drive to get to the Falcon nine. With 14 seconds left, Favre rolled right, found his receivers covered, tucked the ball under his arm, ran for the pylon and just dived in for the winning score. The Packers had no timeouts left so if Favre didn't get in, it is likely that time would have ran out before the field goal team could make it on to the field. Favre's run was reminiscent of a 1970 game against the Bears when Bart Starr surprised everyone by finishing an 80-yard drive in the last two minutes by running in an option play from the five to win the game 20-19.

10) 9/26/99 23-20 over the Vikings at Lambeau. I limited myself to just one of the three brilliant comebacks with which Favre led off the 1999 season. The Packers held their nemesis Randy Moss in check all day until he scored the go-ahead touchdown with 1:56 left. Brett Favre completed five of six passes for 54 yards to bring the Packers to a fourth and one at the Viking 23-yard line. With no time to huddle, Favre didn't bother to call a play. He just read the defense and fired a 23-yard missile to Corey Bradford for the winning touchdown with 14 seconds remaining. Two weeks before Favre had thrown the winning touchdown with 11 seconds left against the Raiders; two weeks later he would hit Antonio Freeman with a 21-yard score with 1:05 left to beat the Bucs.

Favre is the comeback king in Green Bay, but Majkowski had his princely season. He made the Pro Bowl in 1989 and sat out the opening game of the next season in a contract holdout. When he got no free agent offers he joined a lawsuit against the NFL's unfair labor practices that would eventually be successful. While he achieved success off the field, on the field was a disaster. Just as he was beginning to play well, Don was sacked hard on his shoulder in the tenth game of the year and would require rotator cuff surgery. He would never be the same player again. He returned in 1991 with diminished arm strength and injured a hamstring and missed half the season. Majkowski won the starting job under new coach Mike Holmgren in 1992, but as noted above lost his slot to Brett Favre when he went down to an ankle injury in the third game of the year. In 1993 he was a backup in Indianapolis; in 1995 he moved on to Detroit again as a backup. After the 1996 season, he was released and drifted out of football. For one brief, shining season, Majik was among the best quarterbacks in the league. While the team didn't make the playoffs that year, they did provide enough thrills that Don Majkowski will always evoke fond memories from Packer fans.

PACKERS BY THE NUMBERS

FOR FURTHER INFORMATION

Castle, George. "Beers with...Don Majkowski," *Sport.* 9/90. (25-9)

Lieber, Jill. "The Majik Touch," *Sports Illustrated.* 6/11/90. (38-49)

Remmell, Lee. "Greatest Packer Games No. 8," *Pro.* 8/30/75. (38-41)

Rudolph, Jack. "Thrillingest Victories and Toughest Losses," *Green Bay Packers 1960 Yearbook* (48-9)

———. "The Greatest Packer Games in 50 Years," *Green Bay Packers 1968 Yearbook.* (12-19)

Yuenger, Jack. "Knafelc's Key Katches," *Green Bay Packers 1960 Yearbook.* (24-7)

Zimmerman, Paul. "The Majik Show," *Sports Illustrated.* 12/11/89. (34-9)

SPECIALISTS
RYAN LONGWELL • KICKER 1997–

WHO'S WORN THE NUMBER <Lejeune 1925–26>,Uram 1938, Rohrig 1941, B Kahler 1942–44, R. Mosley 1945–46, B Forte 1946–50, 1952–53, Pelfrey 1951, Zendejas 1987–88, A Dilweg 1989–90, Brunell 1993–94, Longwell 1997–02

ORIGINATOR Lineman Walt Lejeune <1925–26> who played for five teams was known as Walt Jean in Green Bay or halfback Andy Uram 1938 (see top 42).

LONGEST TENURE Defensive back Bob Forte 1946–50, 52–53 (see below).

NUMBER CHANGES Andy Uram wore 42 from 1939–43; back Herman Rohrig wore 80 in 1946–47; Bob Forte wore 26 in 1946; end Ray Pelfry wore 26 in 1952.

OTHER NOTABLES Andy Uram (see 42); Bob Forte lost four years to military service, intercepted nine passes in 1947 and 23 overall, and was inducted into the Packer Hall of Fame in 1973; quarterback Mark Brunell was stuck behind Brett Favre, so trading him to Jacksonville allowed him to become a star and the Packers to be able to draft fullback William Henderson and special teams ace Travis Jervey in a trade that made everyone happy.

ONE TO FORGET Quarterback Anthony Dilweg could not live up to his grandfather Lavvie's good name. Lavvie was an All League end several times; grandson Anthony washed out in two years sixty seasons later.

RYAN LONGWELL Ryan Longwell was not supposed to be here. He signed as an undrafted free agent in 1997 with the 49ers who were led by his college coach Steve Mariucci, but was cut early in training camp. Green Bay signed him simply as a second training camp leg. The Packers had released veteran kicker Chris Jacke in the spring and had spent a third-round draft choice on Brett Conway from Penn State to replace him. Conway proceeded to miss three chip shot field goals in his first exhibition game and then worked so hard in practice to correct his mistakes that he injured his leg. Given the opportunity, Longwell seized the job. Conway was put on injured reserve that year and was eventually released. He has bounced around the league ever since due to his unreliability in the clutch.

Longwell, by contrast, has been a model of consistency. His sharp performance saved a very embarrassing situation for the Packers who had wasted a high draft choice and a signing bonus on a kid who could not kick in the big leagues. After his first four seasons, Longwell was the most accurate kicker in league history, converting 111 of 131 field goal attempts for an 84.73% success rate. Remarkably, in the less-than-ideal conditions of wintry Lambeau Field his percentage was even higher. In the 2000 season he led the NFC in scoring with 131 points and kicked the first three game-winning field goals of his career.

On that basis, he signed a large multi-year contract in 2001 and then went out and had the worst year of his career. He missed 11 of 31 field goal attempts which lowered his career percentage to 80.9. His point total of 104 was the lowest of his five-year tenure in Green Bay. He even had an extra point try blocked, the first since 1998. What this really points out, though, is the degree of perfectionism and specialization in the game today.

Don Chandler is remembered fondly as a fine placekicker who solved the kicking woes of the Lombardi threepeat champions. Longwell's field goal percentage of 64.5 in 2001, his worst year, would be within a couple of points of Chandler's best year. If we look at the field goal percentage data throughout team history, we see a steady upward trend both in percentage of field goals made and number of field goals per game. By contrast, the number of touchdowns per game has varied.

1920s			.3 FG/game	1.47 TD/game*
1930s	10 of 32	31%	.34 FG/game	2.32 TD/game
1940s	68 of 167	41%	.54 FG/game	2.66 TD/game
1950s	79 of 169	47%	.66 FG/game	2.61 TD/game
1960s	143 of 280	51%	1.03 FG/game	3.07 TD/game
1970s	166 of 272	61%	1.15 FG/game	1.76 TD/game
1980s	171 of 244	70%	1.13 FG/game	2.38 TD/game
1990s	230 of 289	80%	1.44 FG/game	2.46 TD/game

*42 total FGs; attempt data missing

Special schools sprang up for kickers in the 1980s to help perfect the placekicking art, and two of the most prominent were operated by one-time Packers Ray Pelfry and "Bootin" Ben Agajanian. By the new millennium, the league percentage for field goal was almost 80%. Too much perfection is not good. It takes excitement out of the game which is why the league has made a number of attempts over the last several years to make the job of the placekicker tougher, such as pushing back the kickoff yard line, reducing the tee height for kickoffs, and making them kick new, firmer kicking balls. These sorts of rules changes miss the point, though. Kicking becoming too automatic is symptomatic of the larger problem of excessive specialization brought on by obsessive coaches who want to control everything from the quarterback's play calling to having a specialist to perform even the slightest function on the field—long-snapping for example.

The answer to this specialization problem is simple: reduce the roster size, or at least the active roster size for games. If coaches had fewer slots available, they would have to rely on players being more versatile. They would have to employ more football *players* and fewer "long-snappers," "dime backs," and "pass rushing ends." For a more direct approach, the league could even decree that kickers would have to play a regular position. Pure placekickers first became prevalent in the 1960s. Before that, kicking and punting were handled by regular players—and you better have had a backup on hand in case your placekicker got hurt actually playing football. All of which would make the art of kicking much more uncertain. I love the game today, but if I were king I would make four rule changes: 1) the active roster for any game is 36; 2) Kickers must play a position, although this is probably a moot point after the first change; 3) Again this is probably made moot by the first rule, but substitutions should have a limit. Make teams deal with the strengths and weaknesses of the starting elevens on offense and defense rather than having the coaches mask them with waves of substitutes on each play; 4) As in the pre-World War II days, coaches would not be allowed to call offensive or defensive signals from the bench. Put the game back into the hands of the players. They make enough money to be responsible.

Those suggested rules changes obviously don't have a chance of being instituted, and I may be the only lunatic who would advocate such things anyway. However, they would reintroduce a level of excitement that has been reduced by specialization. Specialization improves performance, but decreases spontaneity.

Ryan Longwell bounced back in 2002 to hit 28 of 34 field goal attempts. He has scored over 100 points each season in the league, and is the fourth leading scorer in team history, trailing only Don Hutson, Chris Jacke, and Paul Hornung. He could pass them all in the 2003 season or, as a kicker, he could lose his touch completely. Kickers are a funny breed. Longwell showed his mental toughness and ability to bounce back from setbacks. He made several All Pro teams in 2000, and there is no reason he couldn't do that again.

FOR FURTHER INFORMATION

Cary, Molly. "Straight as an Arrow," *Milwaukee Journal Sentinel Packer Plus.* Available at www.jsonline.com/packer/news/aug01/longwell30082901.asp.

Wolf, Ron, and Paul Attner. *The Packer Way: Nine Stepping Stones to Building a Winning Organization.* New York: St. Martin's Press, 1998. (138)

DA BEARS
JIM MCMAHON • QUARTERBACK 1995–96

WHO'S WORN THE NUMBER <Woodin 1925–26>, Earp 1928, Borak 1938, D. Dorsey 1988, B. Wagner 1992–93, Borgognone 1995, McMahon 1995–96, Bidwell 2000–02.

ORIGINATOR Guard Whitey Woodin <1925–26> (see top 23) or defensive end Fred Borak from Kenola, WI who played one game in 1938. Earp may have been a typo in the November 18, 1928 game program.

LONGEST TENURE Punter Josh Bidwell 2000–02.

NUMBER CHANGES Whitey Woodin wore 23 from 1927–31 and 25 in 1929.

OTHER NOTABLES Woodin (see top 23).

ONE TO FORGET Dean Dorsey had a three-game tryout as a kicker in 1988 following a three-game tryout in Philadelphia. For Green Bay he kicked one of three field goals and three of four extra points for six total points, tied for about 300th place on the Packers all time list.

JIM MCMAHON Third time's the charm. Twice the Packers came calling on Bear-nemesis Jim McMahon and twice he signed with another team. In 1991 Packers coach Lindy Infante seemed interested, but then signed the tamer Bear Mike Tomczak instead. In 1995, the Packers pursued McMahon only to have him sign with Cleveland because the Browns promised him more playing time and because his family was not interested in moving to an area where Jim was often seen as the devil incarnate. When the Browns released him a few months later, though, McMahon signed at last with Green Bay to serve as Brett Favre's backup.

McMahon was drafted in the first round by the Bears in 1982 and played in Chicago for seven tumultuous but winning years, constantly feuding with his volatile coach Mike Ditka. McMahon was a quarterback who thought and played like a lineman, and he was the respected leader on a loud and boisterous Bear team that won the championship in 1985. His main problem was that he did not have Brett Favre's durable constitution. In his 15-year career, he never played a full season without missing games due to injury. The most notorious injury occurred at the hands of the Packers' Charles Martin (see 94). With Jim as the starter for the Bears, the team's record was 46-15, but they played 101 games in that span and he played in only 66. In his last three years in Chicago, he was able to play in only

22 of 44 non-strike games, so the Bears traded him to San Diego for a third-round pick in 1989. After one season he left as a free agent and signed as a backup in Philadelphia for the Bears' former defensive coach Buddy Ryan. Three seasons later he joined Minnesota and led the Vikings to the playoffs in his one year there. His statistics were never awe-inspiring, but by the time he reached the Vikings he was nothing more than a clever dink-and-dunk specialist whose yards per attempt average dipped to 5.95 down from the 7-8 yard averages he posted in Chicago. Then he signed with Buddy Ryan again, this time in Arizona. Then Cleveland, and finally Green Bay.

McMahon, though, always would be an obnoxious, petulant, cocky Chicago Bear who would never be welcomed by Packer fans. He was the personification of the ancient Bear-Packer rivalry. It's the oldest rivalry in football and nearly the oldest in professional sports. Yankees-Red Sox and Dodgers-Giants in baseball are older and are great rivalries, but they don't have the collegiate intensity that Green Bay-Chicago does. Rivalries usually begin with geography and these two cities are only 200 miles apart, but the Chicago Cardinals never developed as strong a rivalry with either the Bears or the Packers. Packers-Bears has been sustained by other factors: 1) Competitive balance—the Packers and Bears have won more titles than anyone else, 12 and 9 respectively, and have sent the most players to the Hall of Fame, 19 and 24 respectively; 2) Combatants with character—the personal rivalry and competition between George Halas and Curly Lambeau, probably the two most prominent figures in professional football in its early days, fueled the teams' mutual antagonism. It was maintained by such great rivals as Clarke Hinkle/Bronko Nagurski and Ray Nitschke/Dick Butkus; 3) Great Games—so many hard-fought battles going down to the last minute with so many great performers like Don Hutson, Sid Luckman, Walter Payton, and Brett Favre; 4) Irreconcilable Grudges—It's Big City vs. Small City in neighboring states Illinois and Wisconsin. In 1936 a Packer fan ran on the field and ended up slugging one of the Bear players; 5) Tradition—over 80 years and more than 160 games of history and bad blood exist between these two teams.

The first game between the franchises could be said to be on November 27, 1921 when the Packers lost their last game of the year 20-0 to the Chicago Staleys led by end George Halas. It was a game that was highlighted by the first of a long series of cheap shots when the Bears Tarzan Taylor sucker-punched the Packers' Cub Buck and broke his nose. However, Chicago wouldn't become the Bears until 1922 and the Packers would lose their franchise at the end of the season for using three Notre Dame players (Hunk Anderson, Arthur Garvey, and Fred Larson) who played under assumed names either for that Staley game or for the Racine contest a week later. The Packer franchise would be reinstated in Curly Lambeau's name for 1922. There is some evidence that George Halas was behind the revocation of the original Packers franchise in order to push them out of the running for the services of the star guard Anderson, and all three of the Fighting Irish who played for the Packers under aliases would play for the Bears in 1922. At any rate, the Packers and Bears did not play each other in 1922. Thus, many accounts of the rivalry start with the 10/14/23 Bear defeat of the Packers in Green Bay. The first time the Packers beat the Bears was in Green Bay on 9/21/24. Strangely, the game did not count in the standings because the season did not officially begin until the following week. That would be the only year the two teams would not play a league game in

Green Bay until 1974 when the Packer home game against the Bears was held in Milwaukee to the consternation of Green Bay fans. Finally in 1925, the Packers beat the Bears officially for the first time 14-10 behind a Charlie Mathys touchdown pass late in the game. In 1926 and from 1928 through 1933, the rivalry would really heat up as the two teams would meet three times a season, once in Green Bay and twice in Chicago. Between 1928 and 1930, the Packers would win seven games in a row, including five shutouts, and the two teams would end up 6-6-3 against each other in the 1920s.

In the 1930s, the two teams would win six of ten NFL titles between them and six of seven Western Division crowns. Both teams were led by a bruising fullback/linebacker—Clarke Hinkle for the Packers and Bronko Nagurski for the Bears, and their duels were legendary for their ferocity (see 30). 1935 also marked the beginning of Don Hutson's fabulous career which he initiated in emphatic fashion in his first NFL start against the Bears on 9/22/35 when he caught an 83-yard touchdown pass on the game's first play for the only scoring of the day. Later that year he would catch two touchdown passes in the last three minutes of the Packers-Bears rematch to lead Green Bay to a sweep of the Bears that year. Overall, the Packer-Bear split was 10-12-1 in the 1930s. The following decade is when everything fell apart for Curly Lambeau. The Bears were the class of the league while the Packers were steadily slipping. The Packers did manage to tie the Bears for the West in 1941, but lost badly the only playoff game in which the teams ever met. On September 24, 1944, the Packers jumped on top of the Bears 28-0 in the first half, but Chicago staged a furious comeback that tied the game in the fourth quarter. In the last two minutes, Lou Brock scored on a 42-yard run and Ted Fritsch capped the 42-28 Packer victory with a 45-yard interception return for the final tally. Green Bay would win the title that year, but that was Curly's last hurrah. The Bears won 15 and tied one of the 20 encounters in the 1940s. Overall, Lambeau and Halas went against each other 42 times in those 29 years and never once shook hands. However, there was an underlying respect between the two competitors. The Packers loaned Halas $1,500 in order to meet his payroll once during the Depression, and Halas would campaign for the bond needed to build the eventual Lambeau Field in the 1950s. Halas also would serve as one of Curly's pallbearers upon his death.

The post-war period through the mid-1950s was a particularly violent period in the rivalry (see 94), and the 1950s were a nightmare for the Packers. Under coaches Gene Ronzani (a former Bear), Lisle Blackbourn, and Scooter McLean, Green Bay went 5-14-1 for the decade, just one win better than the 1940s. Three times George Blanda would throw late touchdown passes to beat the Pack. The only highlights for Green Bay were the come-from-behind victory over Chicago on September 29, 1957, in the first game in new City Stadium and Lombardi's first game, a 9-6 come-from-behind win over Chicago on September 27, 1959. Lombardi would go 13-5 over Halas and the Bears in his nine years in Green Bay. In 1962 the Packers would beat the Bears 49-0 and 38-7, winning by 81 points en route to a second straight championship. On September 13, 1964 they would win a game with help at the end of the first half from an obscure rule that allows a free kick field goal attempt upon the fair catch of a punt. The Bears would remember this and return the favor by doing the same thing at the end of the game on November 3, 1968 to win 13-10. Some of the greatest performers in the series were active in the 1960s. Mike Ditka,

Dick Butkus, Gale Sayers (754 yards and a 4.7 average in nine games against Green Bay) wore blue jerseys. Ray Nitschke, Bart Starr, and Paul Hornung (121 points in 16 games against Chicago) wore green ones. The green ones won 15 of 20 games during the decade.

The rivalry continued with spirited battles in the 1970s despite both teams being weak, and the Bears won 11 of 20 games in the decade. The 1980s started and ended with a bang for Green Bay. On September 7, 1980 Kicker Chester Marcol's 24-yard field goal attempt in overtime was blocked, but Marcol recovered the ball and ran it in for the touchdown to win 12-6. On November 3, 1989, Don Majkowski's last-second, fourth-down touchdown pass to Sterling Sharpe first was ruled no good because he was past the line of scrimmage when he threw the ball, but the call was overruled by the instant replay official, and the Packers won 14-13. The game became known as the Asterisk Game because the Bears placed an asterisk next to the score in their media guides for the next ten years. In between, Vince Evans would lead the Bears to a 61-7 mauling of Green Bay in the second meeting of 1980 that disturbed coach Bart Starr who felt the Bears were being unsportsmanlike in running up the score. Soon, Mike Ditka would build a powerhouse in Chicago that would defeat Green Bay nine times in a row, and the tenor of the series would again grow very vicious throughout the decade (see 94). The final tally for the 1980s was 11-7 Bears, and the biggest star was Walter Payton, who ran for 2,484 yards in 24 games against the Packers.

Since Mike Holmgren and Brett Favre arrived in 1992, though, times have changed again. Although the Packers lost the first five games of the decade, they won 13 of the next 15, including a series record 10 in a row. Favre's record stands at 18-4 against the Bears, and he has won in all kinds of weather and in all kinds of games. He has been an unsolvable riddle for Chicago and has thrown 38 touchdown passes against the Bears. After 164 games the standings for the series stands at 83-75-6 Bears.

Those who traveled south, not necessarily directly, from Green Bay to Chicago include: Louie Aguiar, Gary Barnes, Edgar Bennett, Connie Berry, Tom Bettis, Brian Cabral, Lee Roy Caffey, Ed Cody, Ron Cox (returned to Chicago after one year in GB), Corey Dowden, Bobby Jack Floyd, Jim Grabowski, Tom Hearden, Bob Hyland (who would eventually return to GB), Bob Jeter, Paul Lipscomb, Keith McKenzie, Ed Neal, David Simmons, Ray Stachowitz, Dick Stahlman, Tillie Voss, Perry Williams, Steve Wright, and Joe Zeller. Henry Burris was the Packers inactive third quarterback in 2001 before seeing action as a Bear the following year. Those who ascended north to a higher clime include: Marty Amsler, Roger Ashmore, Wayland Becker, J.R. Boone, Zeke Bratkowski, Ray Bray, Tony Carter, Greg Clark, Jack Concannon, Ron Cox (see above), Harper Davis, Rob Davis, Bobby Douglass, Wally Dreyer, Chuck Drulis, Ed Ecker, Tiny Engebretsen, Beattie Feathers, Jim Flanigan, Aldo Forte, Dick Gordon, Ken Gorgal, Frank Hanny, Raymont Harris, Perry Hartnett, Tom Heardon, Bob Hyland (see above), Keshon Johnson, Jim Keane, Walt Kiesling, Gene McGuire, Keith McKenzie (returning for a second tour in Wisconsin), Jim McMahon, Steve McMichael, Mark Merrill, Ookie Miller, Rick Mirer, Charley Mitchell, Anthony Morgan, Jim Morrissey, Don Perkins, Washington Serini, Clifton Taylor, John Thierry, Mike Tomczak, Keith Traylor, Pete Van Valkenburg, Bryan Wagner, Ryan Wetnight, Jesse Whittenton, Jerry Wisne, Danny Wuerffel, and Gus Zarnas. Zeke Bratkowski, Walt Kiesling, and John Thierry probably made the most balanced contribution to the two teams. Jim McMahon has one other distinction. He, Tom Bettis, and Tiny Engebretsen are the only three players to play for championship teams in both Chicago and Green Bay.

McMahon would throw only five passes in his year and a half in Green Bay. Coach Mike Holmgren told McMahon at the end of 1996 that he should think about going into coaching. He has the intelligence to do that, but he also has the disposition of a punk. His final act in a Packer uniform was out of a Packer uniform. After the Packers Super Bowl XXXI victory, McMahon was released, but was invited to come with the team to the White House to celebrate the win. McMahon did so in a Bear jersey. Ron Wolf later commented that it didn't bother him since McMahon would never be known as a Packer anyway. That was an understatement.

FOR FURTHER INFORMATION

D'Amato, Gary, and Cliff Christl. *Mudbaths and Bloodbaths: The Inside Story of the Bears-Packers Rivalry.* Madison, WI: Prairie Oak Press, 1997.

Herskowitz, Mickey. *The Quarterbacks: The Uncensored Truth About the Men in the Pocket.* New York: Morrow, 1990. (81-9)

Porter, David L., ed. *Biographical Dictionary of American Sports: Football.* New York: Greenwood Press, 1987. (371-3)

Putnam, Pat. "McMahon with a Golden Arm," *Sports Illustrated.* 11/30/81. (88, 93)

Swain, Glenn. *Packers vs. Bears.* Los Angeles: Charles Publishing, 1996.

OF RUNTS, GRUNTS, AND PUNTS

HOWARD "CUB" BUCK • TACKLE <1925>

WHO'S WORN THE NUMBER
<Buck 1925>, <Cahoon 1926>, Kotal 1927–29, Zuidmulder 1930, Grove 1934, Moss 1948, Parilli 1957–58, Roach 1961–63, Claridge 1965, Stevens 1968–69, Patrick 1970–72, Concannon 1974, Dickey 1976–77, 1979, Troup 1980, Stenerud 1980–83 Del Greco 1984–87, Kiel 1990–91, Aguiar 1999, (Burris 2001).

ORIGINATOR Cub Buck <1925> or back Eddie Kotal 1927–29 (see below).

LONGEST TENURE Kickers Jan Stenerud 1980–83 and Al Del Greco 1984–87.

NUMBER CHANGES Tackle Tiny Cahoon wore 30 in 1927–28 and 40 in 1929; Eddie Kotal had 13 in <1926>; back Dave Zuidmulder wore 12 in 1929 and 41 in 1931; back Roger Grove wore 11 from 1931–35; quarterback Babe Parilli wore 15 from 1952–53 and 16 in 1953; quarterback John Roach also wore 18 in 1961; quarterback Lynn Dickey wore 12 from 1980–85.

OTHER NOTABLES Back Eddie Kotal came out of Lawrence College in Wisconsin and was known as the "Lawrence Flash." He made second team All League when he picked off 10 passes in 1928. He scored 10 touchdowns in his career and was one of the last Packers to play without a helmet. Eddie coached future Packer Ted Fritsch at Stevens Point before returning to Green Bay as one of Lambeau's assistants from 1942–43. Then in the late 1940s, the Rams hired him as the league's first full-time talent scout to run their draft. Perry Moss was not much of a success in his one year in the NFL, but he returned to Green Bay 26 years later as an assistant coach in 1974 and was still coaching arena football 26 years after that.

ONE TO FORGET Of the 10 quarterbacks who wore this number for the Packers, only Parilli and Dickey could play at all. The most inexplicable was Jack Concannon who had already established he could not play over a terrible eight-year career with the Eagles and Bears. After two years in the World Football League, Concannon was signed by Dan Devine as a 31-year-old pretender to the disastrous Packer quarterback depth chart.

CUB BUCK There's a reason the Pro Football Hall of Fame is housed in the small Ohio town of Canton. In the pre-NFL Jurassic Era of professional football, Canton was a giant in the town-team football prevalent at the time. The Canton Athletic Club formed a team in 1905 that would become known as the Bulldogs and would begin a fierce rivalry with the cross-state Massillon Tigers. In 1906 the two teams split a pair of games between them, but the Tigers won the coveted Ohio State title and were known as the best pro team in the nation. Financial instability and a betting scandal caused interest in pro football to dwindle at the time, but things began to improve in the teens. The best football player in the country, Jim Thorpe, signed with Canton in 1915 and the Bulldogs went on to win the Ohio League Championship in 1916, 1917, and 1919. By the next decade, the problems of free-form, freelance professional football led to the organization of the American Professional Football Association in the showroom of a Canton auto dealer in August, 1920. Two years later, the league would change its name to the National Football League. The Canton Bulldogs would win the NFL title in 1922 and 1923, but would be defunct by 1927 as the league outgrew its small-town roots everywhere but Wisconsin.

One of Thorpe's leading blockers in Canton was Howard "Cub" Buck, a mountainous tackle weighing in the range of 280 pounds in a period when 220 pounds was considered very big. Buck had been an All American at the University of Wisconsin before joining Canton in 1916. In that season, he coached the line for the Badgers at his alma mater during the week and on Sundays would meet up with his Bulldog teammates for the professional game. In 1917, he became head football coach at Carleton College in Minnesota and continued with his bifurcated career.

In 1921 the Green Bay Packers joined the new league and Curly Lambeau signed Buck as his first real professional player at $75 a game. The 1919 and 1920, versions of the Packers were essentially professional town teams made up of local players. Although Buck was a native of Eau Claire and had played college ball at UW, he was a five-year veteran of professional football who brought credibility to the franchise and provided an anchor to the line. And for that money, he also worked as the line coach.

Cub was a tremendous competitor with a high voice that could be heard screaming instructions from across the field. He was alternately called "jovial" and "seriousminded" by those who knew him. Stories of his exploits on the field abound. That's Buck giving "donkey ears" to George Vergara in the 1925 team picture. Cub was the victim of the first cheap shot in the history of the Bears-Packers rivalry when Tarzan Taylor broke his nose with a sucker punch in 1921. Slugged by a different Bear on another occasion, he browbeat the opponent for not being a gentleman. When another Bear tried to break his nose with a quick jab, Cub caught the player's arm and broke it with a sharp twist. In an exhibition game against the Lapham Athletic Club of Milwaukee, Buck grabbed two slight scatbacks from Lapham and hoisted them in the air by their belts. While each story is eminently possible, most of these tales are unconfirmed.

What is confirmed is that Cub was a player. He was a force on both the offensive and defensive lines and was a skilled kicker and punter as well. Football was vastly different in those days and kicking and punting abilities were highly valued. From 1922 through 1932, the Packers recorded at least five shutouts each year except 1930 when they only rang up four. And Curly Lambeau was known as an offensive coach! Games were determined by field position, kicking, and mistakes. For example on November 4, 1923, the Packers played the St. Louis All-Stars in a muddy Sportsman's Park. Cub punted 19 times that day, an unofficial league record. (Punting statistics were not kept until 1939.) To show the value of field position, Buck punted five times on first down, once on second, eight times on third, and only five times on fourth down. The only score of the game occurred in the third quarter when Jimmy Simpson of St. Louis fumbled Cub's 50-yard punt and Green Bay recovered at the St. Louis 16. On third down, Cub drop-kicked a 20-yard field goal. The Packers won 3-0 on field position, kicking, and mistakes.

Punting mistakes, though, have haunted the Packers from time to time over the years. On November 29, 1928, the Packers never let the Frankford Yellow Jackets get beyond the Green Bay 30, but lost 2-0 when a bad center snap on a punt went over Verne Lewellen's head and out of the end zone for a safety. The Bears escaped Green Bay with a victory on September 24, 1933, when Bill Hewitt blocked a punt on the last play of the game and recovered the ball for the winning touchdown. In the 1938 title match against the Giants, New York blocked two Green Bay punts in the first quarter leading to nine points in the 23-17 Packer loss. The Pack also suffered blocked punts in the 1939 and 1962 championship games against the Giants, but won both games. When the Rams blocked Donny Anderson's punt to lead to a last minute winning touchdown on December 9, 1967, NFL Films caught the sideline drama of Vince Lombardi summarily rejecting assistant coach Dave Hanner's sound advice to let quicker punter Don Chandler kick. Recently, in the 2003 divisional playoff game against Atlanta, the Falcons blocked a Josh Bidwell punt and recovered the ball for the game's second touchdown in a disappointing Packer loss. Finally, no punter anywhere ever had a worse day than Steve Brousard on opening day 1975, when the Lions blocked three of his nine punts and almost got two others in their 30-16 whipping of the Pack. All three blocks led to touchdowns.

Cub Buck is the only interior lineman/punter in team history as well as the only interior lineman/drop-kicker, although Tiny Engebretsen, Ernie Smith, and Jerry Kramer all were linemen/placement kickers. Cub scored 54 points for Green Bay on 24 of 35 extra points and 10 of 28 field goals. He led the team in scoring in 1923 and even threw a touchdown pass in 1924. In 1923 Buck took on the head coaching job at Lawrence College, and he would stay there for his last three years as a Packer. Cub accepted the head coaching position at the University of Miami in 1926 and retired as a professional football player. After three years in Florida, Cub quit coaching altogether and opened an automobile dealership in Rock Island, Illinois, where he would live the rest of his life until he passed away at 74 in 1966. The Packers' first significant free-agent acquisition, Buck was elected to the Packer Hall of Fame posthumously in 1977.

FOR FURTHER INFORMATION

Daly, Dan, and Bob O'Donnell. *The Pro Football Chronicle: The Complete (Well Almost) Record of the Best Players, the Greatest Photos, the Hardest Hits, the Biggest Scandals, and the Funniest Stories in Pro Football.* New York: Collier Books, 1990. (16)

Packers of the Past: A Series of Articles Reprinted from the Milwaukee Journal Sept. 28 – Dec. 9, 1965. Milwaukee, WI: Milwaukee Journal, 1965. (37-9)

Torinus, John. *The Packer Legend: An Inside Look.* Revised ed. Neshkoro, WI: Laranmark Press, 1982. (15)

Ward, Arch. *The Green Bay Packers.* New York: Putnam, 1946. (51-2)

THREEPEAT I
RED DUNN • QUARTERBACK 1927–8

WHO'S WORN THE NUMBER
<McGaw 1926>, <W. Carlson 1926>, Dunn 1927–28,
Bloodgood 1930, Grove 1931–35, Scherer 1937, Katalinas 1938,
R. Norton 1970, Brousard 1975, Beverly 1975–81, Garcia
1983–84, Prokop 1985, Risher 1987r, Detmer 1993–94,
Hasselbeck 1999–2000.

ORIGINATOR Guard Walt McGaw <1926> who attended
Beloit along with Packer teammate Pid Purdy played in just one
NFL game. Or Red Dunn 1927–28.

LONGEST TENURE Punter David Beverly 1975–81.

NUMBER CHANGES Red Dunn wore 16 and 32 in 1929, 7 and
17 in 1930, and 15 in 1931; back Roger Grove wore 10 in 1934;
end Bernie Scherer wore 40 in 1936, 16 in 1937, and 36 in 1938.

OTHER NOTABLES None.

ONE TO FORGET Punter Steve Brousard was a record setter on
opening day 1975 when he had three punts blocked in one game
as the Lions beat the Packers 30-16. Two were returned for
touchdowns and one was recovered at the Packers six and led to
a third TD. His NFL career lasted three more games in the green
and gold before he was cut with a 31.8 punting average.

RED DUNN Curly Lambeau was the Packers first star passer, but
Joseph "Red" Dunn was their first great quarterback. Red joined
the Packers in 1927 along with former college teammate end Lavvie
Dilweg. Both were born and bred in Milwaukee and both went to
Marquette University. Dunn spent 1924 with the hometown Milwaukee Badgers and then moved on to the Chicago Cardinals for
two years before coming to Green Bay. Each year Red shifted clubs,
the record of the team he left would decline, while the record of
the team he joined would improve. The addition of Dunn to the
Packers signaled their ascension into the elite teams of the league.

Lambeau's offense depended largely on who his passer was.
While he would not install the T formation until the late 1940s,
Lambeau's Packers lined up in a variety of formations over the
years: the Notre Dame Box, the Single Wing, even the Y formation.
The main distinction between them was who would handle the ball
the most. When Red Dunn at quarterback, he lined up close to the
center, but off to the side. While the ball might be passed from the
center to one of the deep backs, usually it was passed to the clos-

est man, Dunn. Dunn never took a direct snap like T formation quarterbacks do, but he was the man distributing the ball. He would hand it off to the deep or wing backs for runs and would drop back to throw on pass plays. After Dunn retired, the quarterback was primarily a blocking back who rarely touched the ball—Buckets Goldenberg, Hank Bruder, and Larry Craig all filled that role. In those years, usually a long snap went to the tailback—Arnie Herber or Cecil Isbell.

Dunn was the team's field general, its signal caller. And who can argue with success? In his five years as a Packer, the team went 47-11-6, a .781 winning percentage. Moreover, they won an unprecedented three consecutive titles. For his part, according to unofficial counts, Dunn caught 50 passes for 618 yards and a touchdown, rushed 80 times for 290 yards and five touchdowns, and completed 275 of 620 passes for 4,641 yards and 48 touchdowns. In addition he kicked two field goals and 48 extra points. Even with the fatter ball used at that time he was an expert at the long pass. On December 9, 1928, he beat the Bears with a 50-yard scoring pass to Dick O'Donnell in the final two minutes of the 6-0 game.

The team's first title came in 1929. Lambeau had signed three future Hall of Famers in the offseason—linemen Cal Hubbard and Mike Michalske and halfback Johnny Blood. The main competition, the New York Giants, were led by ace passer Benny Friedman. When the two undefeated teams met in New York on November 24, it was the fifth game of an eight-game road trip for Green Bay. Dunn and star runner Eddie Kotal were both injured so the Pack played only 12 players in that game, with the only substitution being made in the closing minutes. Hubbard and Michalske led a tough defense that hounded Friedman. Sparked by the passing and punting of Verne Lewellen and the running and receiving of Blood, the Packers scored 14 fourth-quarter points to win 20-6. Frankford would tie the Packers 0-0 the next week, but Green Bay would rebound to win their final two games and cop the title with a 12-0-1 record. The final game was a 25-0 beating of the Bears on December 9, and the Packers returning train was greeted by more than 20,000 fans at the train station. They outscored their opponents 198-22 for the season and recorded eight shutouts, including three over the Bears. At the postseason celebration of the championship, Lambeau paid special tribute to his quarterback. "There is one man on the team I wish to accord a particular tribute. He is a backfield man who has not scored a touchdown this season, but who has few equals in the game. He is Red Dunn. Red always stepped out of the limelight when a touchdown was needed and called plays for other men. At times he would shift a halfback to his position and drop into the vacated post and call a signal that resulted in a touchdown with the halfback going over on a play that he would ordinarily complete himself." (Names, 178)

Again in 1930, Friedman's Giants would prove to be the main rivals. The Packers beat the Giants in Green Bay in October, 14-7. When the teams met again on November 23 at the Polo Grounds, The Packers were 8-1 and the Giants were 10-2. The Giants prevailed 13-6 to move into first place. However, the Giants would lose their next two games before winning their last two to finish 13-4. The Packers would win their next two before being shut out by the Bears 21-0 and just barely escaping with a 6-6 tie in Portsmouth to finish 10-3-1, to win a second consecutive championship.

PACKERS BY THE NUMBERS

Once again in 1931 the Packers were almost undone by some late-season road games. They survived to win a very controversial third consecutive title. The Packers had a 8-0 record before losing to Ernie Nevers' Cardinals 21-13 on November 15 in Chicago. The following week in New York they trailed the Giants in the fourth quarter before Dunn threw a late 19-yard touchdown pass to Hank Bruder to pull out a 14-10 win. Close behind were the newly powerful Portsmouth Spartans. The Packers won their next two, but then lost to the Bears 7-6 on December 6 to finish the year 12-2. Meanwhile the Spartans, who had declined to book a game in Green Bay early in the year, finished 11-3. Portsmouth and Green Bay had "tentatively" scheduled a match for December 13 sometime after the official schedule had been adopted. Now, with nothing to gain and much to lose, Green Bay withdrew from the game. NFL Commissioner Joe Carr declared Green Bay the champs since there was no record of the Packer-Spartan game as part of the official schedule. That ruling was met with delight in Green Bay, but anger in Portsmouth whose fans, ironically, denigrated the Packers as "cheese champs." This flap led to the league tightening its procedures regarding scheduling league games.

Red Dunn retired after the third straight title and the team's record declined from 12-2 to 10-3-1 in 1932. Under current rules with ties counting as 1/2 win and 1/2 loss in a team's winning percentage, they would have won a fourth consecutive title. However, ties did not count in the standings then, so the Bears with one loss and six ties faced off against the Spartans with one loss and four ties to win the NFL championship. Perhaps it was divine retribution for reneging on the Spartans the previous year. Of course the only team to win three consecutive NFL titles since then were Lombardi's Packers from 1965-67.

Red Dunn keeps the ball in 1928 at City Stadium. In his five years with Green Bay, he was the primary ball handler and signal caller on the team, and the Packers won 78% of their games and three straight championships in that time. By comparison, in Brett Favre's best five-year period, the team won 71% of its games. *Courtesy of the Stiller-Lefebvre Collection.*

Red Dunn was an unselfish, versatile player who made his teammates better and regularly led his team to victory. Twice he was named as a second-team All League player. Considering he was competing against the league's first great passer, Benny Friedman, that's not bad. His three league titles are three more than Friedman earned. The unheralded Red was inducted into the Packer Hall of Fame posthumously in 1976.

FOR FURTHER INFORMATION

Cohen, Richard M., Jordan A. Deutsch, Roland T. Johnson, and David S. Neft. *The Scrapbook History of Pro Football.* Indianapolis, IN: Bobbs-Merrill, 1976.

Names, Larry. *The History of the Green Bay Packers: Book I: The Lambeau Years Part One.* Wautoma, WI: Angel Press of WI, 1987. (178-9, 192-3, 204)

Ward, Arch. *The Green Bay Packers.* New York: Putnam, 1946. (86-7)

THE PASSING GAME
LYNN DICKEY • QUARTERBACK 1980–85

WHO'S WORN THE NUMBER
<Abramson 1925>, <Rosatti 1926>, T. Hearden 1927–28,
R. Baker 1928, Zuidmulder 1929, Herber 1930, F. Baker 1931,
Monnett 1935–36, Bratkowski 1963–68, 1971, Del Gaizo, 1973,
Hadl 1974, Milan 1975, Dowling 1977, Dickey 1980–85, Rubley
1995, (Mirer 1998), (Nall 2002).

ORIGINATOR George Abramson <1925> the shortest lineman
in team history at 5'7" made second team All League in 1925 or
Green Bay East High and Notre Dame alumnus Tom Hearden
played in only five games as a back in 1927–8 in Green Bay, but
had a long career in coaching. He was head coach at Green Bay
East High and St. Norbert's for many years before spending
three years as a Packer assistant in the 1950s.

LONGEST TENURE Backup quarterback Zeke Bratkowski was
Bart Starr's ever-reliable relief pitcher form 1963–68 and again
in 1971. He won a number of critical games for the Packers,
most notably the 1965 playoff against the Colts.

NUMBER CHANGES Tackle Rosy Rosatti wore 25 in 1927;
back Roy "Bullet" Baker also wore 5 and 21 in 1928 and 17 in
1929; back Dave Zuidmulder wore 10 in 1930 and 41 in 1931;
Arnie Herber also wore 26 in 1931, 41 in 1932–33, 16 in 1933,
45 and 68 in 1934, 38 from 1935–40, and 19 in 1937; back Bob
Monnett also wore 3 in 1935, 5 in 1936–37 and 50 in 1938 ;
quarterback John Hadl wore 21 in 1975; Lynn Dickey wore
10 in 1976–77 and in 1979.

OTHER NOTABLES Arnie Herber (see 16); Bob Monnett
(see top 3); and Zeke Bratkowski.

ONES TO FORGET Brian Dowling, who was the inspiration
for B.D. in the Doonesbury comic strip from his days at Yale,
threw one incomplete pass as a Packer; T.J. Rubley changed a
Mike Holmgren call with a disastrous audible that cost the
Packers a game against the Vikings in his one appearance in
green and gold; Jim Del Gaizo cost two second-round picks
and completed 43% of his passes for two touchdowns and six
interceptions. Above all, though, once-skilled John Hadl cost the
Packers two number ones, two number twos, and one number
three. In 22 games with Green Bay he threw nine touchdowns,
29 interceptions, and fumbled 11 times.

NUMBER 12

LYNN DICKEY Periodically a glut of highly-rated college quarterbacks come out of college and create a "Year of the Quarterback" draft. The most famous instance was in 1983 when John Elway, Dan Marino, Jim Kelly, Ken O'Brien, Tony Eason, and Todd Blackledge all were selected in the first round. In 1999, Tim Couch, Akili Smith, Donovan McNabb, Cade McNown, and Daunte Culpepper all went in round one, while Shaun King went in round two and Aaron Brooks in round four. The first big quarterback draft, though, was in 1971 when Jim Plunkett, Archie Manning, and Dan Pastorini were picked in the first round, Ken Anderson and Lynn Dickey were picked in the third round, and Joe Theismann went in round four. Dickey, as his luck would dictate, was drafted by the Oilers, who had also picked Pastorini.

Pastorini won the starting job as a rookie, but was being challenged in the preseason of his sophomore year by Dickey when Lynn was driven awkwardly into the artificial turf in an exhibition game and both dislocated and broke his left hip. After a year of rehabilitation, he would challenge Pastorini again in 1973 and 1974, but never quite could beat him out. By 1976, Dickey was rusting on the bench when Packers coach Bart Starr obtained him in a trade. He was given the starting job, but it was a mixed blessing. The Packers offense was awful, with few scoring weapons available. In 1976, with sixth-year-rookie starter Dickey at the helm, the team averaged only 15 1/2 points a game and Lynn went down with a shoulder separation in the 10th game. The next year was even worse on both the offensive and injury fronts. The Packers averaged only 9 1/2 points a game and Lynn had his leg badly broken on the last play of the ninth game of the year. He would not return till late in the 1979 season, missing all of 1978.

By the start of the 1980 season, Dickey had missed 30 of 60 games due to injury in his four years in Green Bay and 53 games altogether in his nine-year career. In that span, he had thrown 25 touchdowns and 60 interceptions. Although the injuries and pain would continue, his career would take off in with the new decade. He had weapons at last: James Lofton as a deep threat, Paul Coffman at tight end, and Eddie Lee Ivery and Gerry Ellis as runners and receivers out of the backfield. John Jefferson would arrive the next year. In the remaining six years of his career, Lynn would throw for 116 touchdowns and 119 interceptions. He would throw for more than 3,000 yards in three seasons, setting a team record of 4,458 passing yards in 1983 when he also led the league with 32 touchdown passes and an average of 9.21 yards per reception.

Dickey ran a wide-open offense for Bart Starr and with the arrival of Jefferson the team would average 23.4 points a game from 1981 through 1985. Unfortunately, they would also give up 22.4 points a game, so their record for those years was just 37-35-1. They made the playoffs only in the strike year of 1982 and went 8-8 every other year, twice for Starr and twice for Forrest Gregg who became coach in 1984.

The most emblematic game of Lynn's years in Green Bay was on Monday night, October 17, 1983, against the champion Washington Redskins. Green Bay would jump on top early when linebacker Mike Douglass recovered Joe Washington's fumble and returned it 22 yards for a touchdown. It was the only big play either defense would make all night. The two teams ran up 1,025 yards of offense, 552 for Washington who had the ball for 39 minutes and 473 for Green Bay who held the ball for only 21 minutes. The teams scored 95 points. Redskin quarterback Joe Theismann threw for 398 yards and two scores, while Dickey completed 22 of 30 for 387 yards and three touchdowns. It was a see-saw battle from the start, and the lead changed hands five times in the last quarter. Green Bay scored on seven of 10 possessions, and Washington scored on nine of 12. Announcer Don Meredith kept saying that the first team to 50 wins, and when reliable Mark Mosely lined up for a 39-yard field goal on the last play of the game with the Skins trailing 48-47, Don's prediction seemed inevitable. Dickey said to his kicker Jan Stenerud, "Can you believe we're going to lose this game?" And then Mosely missed. With a defense that weak, however, endings were often not so happy during Dickey's time.

Dickey's passing skills fit surprisingly well in the historical trend of the Packer offense. Despite playing in a climate that would seem to favor the running game, Green Bay has almost always been known as a passing team. Under Curly Lambeau from 1922 through 1943, the Packers finished first in passing yards eleven times, second eight times, and third three times. They were also regularly ranked first or second in points scored in that time. The team always had one of the best passers in the league, from Lambeau himself to Red Dunn to Arnie Herber to Cecil Isbell, and had two of the greatest receivers in NFL history in Johnny Blood and then Don Hutson. After Isbell and then Hutson retired, Curly could not replace them and his passing game, offense, and team all deteriorated. In the 1950s, about the only thing the Packers could do was pass with Tobin Rote (mostly) throwing to Bill Howton and Max McGee. Under Lombardi, the passing game was downplayed, but still important; it just played off the running game. Dickey brought the pass back to prominence in the 1980s, and subsequent coaches Lindy Infante and Mike Holmgren and his disciples expanded that tendency, lasting to the present day. It may get cold in Lambeau Field, but the passing game can heat things up quickly.

Dickey's last game was the Snow Bowl against Tampa on December 1, 1985, in Lambeau, before only 19,000 fans. Playing in a blizzard that dumped more than a foot of snow in Green Bay that day, Dickey completed 22 of 36 passes for 299 yards in a 21-0 win over the Bucs. Lofton caught six for 106 yards and both running backs, Ellis and Ivery, rushed for over 100 as well. In the following week, Lynn hurt himself on a weight-training machine and he would not play again. He never saw eye-to-eye with Gregg and thus claimed to be relieved when Forrest released him in 1986, ending Dickey's NFL career. He was known as being perhaps the best pure passer in team history and threw the bomb very accurately. Lynn Dickey was the epitome of toughness, coming back time after time from serious injury and playing through chronic pain. He was a notable figure in the team's long tradition of emphasizing the passing game and was inducted into the Packer Hall of Fame in 1992.

FOR FURTHER INFORMATION

Gentile, Domenic, with Gary D'Amato. *The Packer Tapes: My 32 Years with the Green Bay Packers*. Madison, WI: Prairie Oak Press, 1995. (83-5)

Rauen, Karen. "Dickey Led Packers Despite Share of Bad Breaks," *Green Bay Press Gazette Packernews.com*. 12/9/01.
Available online at www.greenbaypressgazette.packernews.com.

Reischel, Rob. "Dickey Remembers Green Bay Fondly,"
Milwaukee Journal Sentinel Packer Plus. 9/19/01.
Available online at www.jsonline.com/packer/news/sep01/dickey20091901.asp.

Riffenburgh, Beau. *Great Ones: NFL Quarterbacks from Baugh to Montana.*
New York: Viking, 1989. (99)

Telander, Rick. "He Takes Great Pains with His Passing," *Sports Illustrated.* 9/26/83.
(24-9)

Wagner, Len. "Lynn Dickey: I Feel I'm as Good as Anybody," *Green Bay Packers 1977 Yearbook.* (4-6)

THE KICKING GAME
CHESTER MARCOL • KICKER 1972–80

WHO'S WORN THE NUMBER
<M. Norton 1925>, <Kotal 1926>, Bruder 1931–33, Horn 1967–70, Marcol 1972–80, Scribner 1983–84, Renner 1986–87, Jacke 1989–96, Bono 1997.

ORIGINATOR Back Marty Norton <1925> tied for the team lead with 36 points and led the NFL with four TD receptions in his one year in Green Bay before jumping to Red Grange's AFL in 1926. Or blocking back Hank Bruder (see 27).

LONGEST TENURE Chester Marcol 1972–80.

NUMBER CHANGES Halfback Eddie Kotal wore 10 from 1927–29; Hank Bruder also wore 55 in 1933, 47 in 1934, 27 in 1935–36, 18 in 1935–38, and 5 in 1938–39.

OTHER NOTABLES Eddie Kotal (see top 10); Hank Bruder (see 27); kicker Chris Jacke came within three points of Don Hutson's all time Packers' scoring mark of 823 points. He was an accurate and reliable kicker for eight years in Green Bay who kicked a team record 17 50+ yard field goals before being replaced by Ryan Longwell in 1997.

ONE TO FORGET Punter Bill Renner had three punts blocked in his three-game 1986 season and still managed to get into three more games in 1987.

CHESTER MARCOL Kicking is a refuge for odd ducks in football who usually stick to themselves on the sidelines. The pressures can be enormous since kickers have no way to make up for a bad kick. They can't go back out there and catch a touchdown pass or make a defensive stop. Everything rides on the few plays they are on the field to kick the ball. Thirteen is a perfect jersey number for the often-ostracized, stressed-out placekicker.

Chester Marcol was as unusual a character as one would expect to find on the gridiron. When he was 16, he emigrated from Poland with his family to Michigan. A star soccer player in Poland, he had never played American football before picking up the game in high school. He played end for Imlay City, but his extremely powerful leg brought him notice from the football coach at Hillsdale College, a small school in Michigan. Marcol had great success at Hillsdale, even setting a field goal distance record by booting a 62-yarder.

Chester was drafted in the second round by the Packers in 1972 and was an immediate sensation on the playoff-bound Pack

NUMBER 13

by leading the league in points with 128 and making both the All Pro and Pro Bowl teams. The Packers thought they had solved their long-standing kicking problem for the foreseeable future. Of course they also thought that they were back as a championship contender. Neither proved true.

Kicking problems periodically plague most teams, and a sorry kicking game can ruin a whole season. It did not help losing Green Bay squads from 1948–50 that Ted Fritsch, their field goal kicker, went 6 of 16, 5 of 20, and 3 of 17 in those three years. Bill Reichardt went 5 of 20 in 1952, followed by Fred Cone's 5 of 16 in 1953. Cone, though, was a generally reliable kicker over the next several years as was his replacement, Paul Hornung. When Hornung was suspended in 1963, though, the kicking game suffered for the Packers, who finished in second place for the next two years. Jerry Kramer made 16 of 34 in 1963 and the returning Hornung was a terrible 12 of 34 in 1964. The poor-quality kicking in 1964 cost the Packers at least a couple of games and a shot at the first-place Colts.

Don Chandler was brought in to rectify that, and he did in 1965 and in 1967, but in 1966 he hit on only 12 of 28 field goal attempts, although the team won the title anyway. After he retired, the next four years were a horror show as a steady parade of inaccurate kickers were brought in and then let go. In 1968 Jerry Kramer, Chuck Mercein, and Mike Mercer went 13 of 29. In 1969 Mercer and Booth Lusteg went 6 of 22. In 1970 Dale Livingston got slightly above water with 15 of 28 field goals, and Tim Webster and Lou Michaels followed that with a 14-of-26 performance in 1971. In all four years a better kicking game could have made a real difference in the won-lost record of the team. Chester Marcol changed those fortunes for a few years, but then he went into decline. Since the 1980s, though, the Packers generally have had consistent kicking from Jan Stenerud, Al Del Greco, Chris Jacke, and Ryan Longwell. The one exception was 1988 when Max Zendejas, Dale Dawson, Dean Dorsey, and Curtis Burrow combined to miss six extra points and 12 of 25 field goal attempts.

As just noted, Chester Marcol continued to be successful for two more seasons, again making All Pro and Pro Bowl teams in 1974 with a league-leading 94 points. Unlike many kickers, Chester was popular and fit in well with his teammates. He fit in perhaps too well as he began to drink heavily. He was injured and sat out most of 1975 and then started using cocaine. He returned as the Packers kicker in 1976, but the last five years of his career was a steady downward spiral. In 1979, due to knee problems, he shared the placekicking with Tom Birney. In 1980 he beat out Birney for the kicking job, but because of his erratic performance and behavior was released after five games and Birney was brought back. Houston brought Marcol in for one game that year, but then his football career was over. His personal life continued to deteriorate as well—drinking, drugs, divorce, and depression all led to an eventual suicide attempt by drinking battery acid in 1986. From that low point, he took a long and slow road to recovery with the help of friends and family.

Chester remains sixth on the all-time list of Packer scorers with 521 points. In his nine years in Green Bay he hit on 61.7% of his field goal attempts, a good figure for his time. He hit some long ones and was known for booming kickoffs. His most famous moment came in his last, sad season. Against the Bears, Marcol attempted a 24-yard field goal in overtime and Alan Page blocked the kick. The ball bounded back into Chester's hands and the slight, bespectacled kicker scooted around the end with it for the winning score. To paraphrase Alex Karras' derisive comment about foreign soccer-style kickers, he had "kicked a touchdown." In 1987, Chester Marcol was inducted into the Packer Hall of Fame, presented by the team's trainer Dom Gentile. Since then he has returned frequently for Packer alumni functions. Remarried with a new family and living on Michigan's Upper Peninsula, he seems to have made peace with his life.

FOR FURTHER INFORMATION

Biever, Vernon J., photography, Peter Strupp ed. *The Glory of Titletown: The Classic Green Bay Packers Photography of Vernon Biever.* Dallas, TX: Taylor Publishing, 1997. (127, 201)

Gentile, Domenic, with Gary D'Amato. *The Packer Tapes: My 32 Years with the Green Bay Packers.* Madison, WI: Prairie Oak Press, 1995. (98-100)

Hintz, Gene W. "We Love Chester," *Green Bay Packers 1973 Yearbook.* (30-3)

————. "Chester Would Like More Work," *Green Bay Packers 1975 Yearbook.* (31-3)

Poling, Jerry. *Downfield! Untold Stories of the Green Bay Packers.* Madison, WI: Prairie Oak Press, 1996. (25-32)

Rubin, Bob. *Green Bay's Packers: Return to Glory.* Englewood Cliffs, NJ: Prentice-Hall, 1974. (107-8)

THE GREATEST PACKER AND THE 1941 PLAYOFF
DON HUTSON • END 1935–45

WHO'S WORN THE NUMBER <Gardner 1925–26>, Lambeau 1927, Lollar 1928, D. Hill 1929, Zuver 1930, Fitzgibbon 1931–32, Blood 1933, Hutson 1935–45.

ORIGINATOR Milt "Moose" Gardner <1925–26> was a large guard from WI who spent five years in Green Bay or Curly Lambeau 1927 (see 1).

LONGEST TENURE Don Hutson 1935–45.

NUMBER CHANGES Curly Lambeau had 1 in <1925–26> and wore 42 in 1928, and 20 in 1929–30; Johnny Blood wore 24 in 1929–30, 20 in 31–32, 26 in 35, and 55 in 1936; back Don Hill also wore 16 in 1929; and back Paul Fitzgibbon wore 18 in 1930 and 49 in 1932.

OTHER NOTABLES The number was officially retired for Don Hutson in a halftime ceremony at the New York Yankee-Packer game on December 2, 1951. Since Packer immortals Curly Lambeau (see 1) and Johnny Blood (see 55) both wore 14 before Don, it deserves retirement for more than one player's exploits.

ONE TO FORGET Slick Lollar, a fullback for three games in 1928.

DON HUTSON Imagine after a Viking punt, Randy Moss gets down in a three-point stance and lines up at defensive end, and you will begin to understand how different professional football was in the 1930s. Don Hutson played end on both offense and defense for the first four years of his career, before muscular blocking back Larry Craig joined the team and allowed Don to move to safety on defense. The Packers were in two championship games in those first four years, so having the undersized Hutson on the defensive line wasn't a fatal flaw in their defense. Players were much smaller then, so Hutson wasn't as manhandled as Moss would be today, but Don was much better suited to safety, where he intercepted 34 passes in his last seven years, altogether grabbing 39 for his career. When he retired, those 39 interceptions were second in league history to Johnny Blood's 40. Although he had never placekicked before coming to Green Bay, Don also booted seven field goals and 172 extra points for 193 points to add to his 105 touchdowns. Skilled as he was on defense and with his feet, however, Hutson is still remembered as one of the best football players ever, primarily because he was the most potent offensive force in the game, leaving records that would not be broken for 40 years or more.

Don grew up in Arkansas as a baseball player and played football only as a senior in high school. At 145 pounds, he drew no interest from college recruiters. When his childhood friend Bob Seawall was offered a scholarship to the University of Alabama, though, he would accept it only if they brought Don along, too. Seawall would drop out after two years, but Hutson became an All American as the end across from Bear Bryant (who would become a lifelong friend). As a senior in the 1935 Rose Bowl, Don caught six passes for 165 yards and two touchdowns as the Crimson Tide upset then-undefeated Stanford, 29-13. In the last year before a pro football draft, free agent Don was pursued by Curly Lambeau and Shipwreck Kelly of the Brooklyn Dodgers. Don used the acumen he gained as a business major and played the two against one another before signing contracts with both of them for what has alternately been described by Don himself as $175 or $300 per game, both very high figures for the time. NFL commissioner Joe Carr awarded Hutson to Green Bay by virtue of the Packers contract being postmarked 17 minutes before the Brooklyn one. Brooklyn was a weak team that would register only two winning seasons during Hutson's years in the league, and they were without a quality passer. Had he gone to Brooklyn, Hutson might be remembered no more than Todd Goodwin, Gaynell Tinsley, and Don Looney—the three receivers other than Don who led the league in receptions from 1935–45.

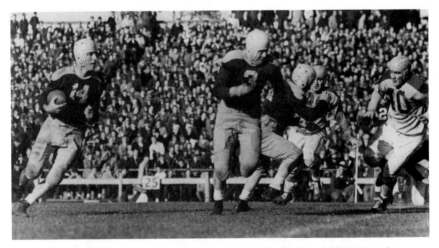

Leading the interference for Don Hutson is Hall of Famer Tony Canadeo who missed the only Packer championship during his long playing career because he was helping overrun the Nazis in 1945. *Courtesy of the Stiller-Lefebvre Collection.*

In Green Bay, Don was blessed with a coach who was devoted to the passing game, a deep team of quality players, and two top passers—first Arnie Herber and then Cecil Isbell. In 11 years he would lead the league in receptions eight times, receiving yards seven times, touchdown receptions nine times, total touchdowns eight times, and scoring five times. In his greatest year, 1942, he led the league with 74 catches for 1,211 yards and 17 touchdowns and a total of 138 points. The nearest receiver caught 27 passes that year. In a game against Detroit in his final year, he caught four touchdown passes and kicked five extra points in the second quarter to set a league record that still stands for points in one quarter.

Hutson was 6'1" and weighed 180 pounds, tall and lanky, and was known as the fastest player of his time. He was quick, a great leaper, and had the best moves and the best hands in the league. He was in the forefront in developing such standard pass patterns as the down-and-in, the stop-and-go and the post pattern. Isbell later said of him, "He was the first one with all the moves. He had good head and shoulder fakes and he had an endless series of changes of pace. It was impossible for one man to cover him and almost impossible for two. He had absolute concentration on the ball; he never heard a footstep in his life, and he'd catch the ball in a crowd almost as easily as he did in the open. And he ran like a halfback after he got it." (Maule, 116)

Beyond all that, he was a very calm and confident player who was impossible to rile. The only thing he lacked was an arresting personality. *New York Times* columnist Arthur Daley wrote a piece on Hutson for *Collier's* in 1944 that stated that Hutson and Isbell were not on speaking terms for their last year together. Since the two roomed together for all five of Isbell's years in the league (as Daley himself would write about years later in the *Times*), one is left with the implication that this questionable tidbit was put in to create some controversy. Ironically in one column, Daley quotes Isbell telling him, "If you ever see that fellow who wrote that we weren't on speaking terms, you can tell him for me that he had it all wrong." (Daley, 16) Hutson was clearly one of Daley's favorites and he would write a column about Don periodically after his retirement from football, generally rehashing the same stories each time: Don catching his first pass for an 83-yard touchdown against the Bears in his first start; speedster defender Dante Magnani covering Don into the end zone when suddenly Don grabs the goal post with his left arm and swings around to catch a touchdown pass with his right; Brooklyn coach Jock Sutherland refusing to believe that Hutson needed to be double-teamed until Don caught eight passes for 126 yards and a touchdown against the Dodgers when they played in 1941; Isbell tossing the shortest touchdown pass then on record, 4 inches, to Hutson in 1942. While Daley would mix up some details like calling it Hutson's first game rather than his first start, the tales are generally true. Hutson was a football player like no other of his time.

Some question how much his numbers were boosted by playing against depleted wartime competition, but his greatest year came in the first year of the war when the competition was still strong. After that, the Packers no longer had a good passer with Tony Canadeo, Irv Comp, and Roy McKay throwing most of the balls. Don was not drafted because he had a wife and three daughters. He kept retiring each year during the war, but Lambeau kept luring him back. For his last year, his salary was a then-astronomical $15,000, but he was worth it. The year after Hutson left, starting tailback Comp completed 28% of his passes for 1 touchdown and 8 interceptions. Don never got to play in a wide-open Split-T formation, but spent his career in Lambeau's variations on the single wing offense that became increasingly outmoded.

To many, Hutson was the Packers. The Bears considered Green Bay a one-man team and keyed on stopping him with double and triple teams. Sometimes that worked and sometimes it didn't, as Hutson caught 83 passes for 14 touchdowns in 22 regular-season games against Chicago. Green Bay was a good team, but the Bears of the early 1940s were the best team in the league. After winning the 1940 championship 73-0 over Washington, they continued their winning ways in 1941 and were undefeated when the Packers met them in Chicago in November with a seven-man line that held the Bears to only 83 yards rushing. The Packers won 16-14. The teams wound up tied for the division title with 10-1 records and met in a playoff before 43,000 fans at Wrigley Field on December 14, 1941, just one week after the attack on Pearl Harbor. (The title game against the Giants one week later would draw only 13,000 fans to Wrigley.) The Bears countered the return of Green Bay's seven-man front and ran for 267 yards en route to a 33-14 victory. The Packers scored first, but the Bears scored the next 30 points, including 24 in the second quarter, despite losing five fumbles. Uncharacteristically, Isbell threw five interceptions and the Packers lost three fumbles as well. The battling Bears clearly intimidated Green Bay, drawing 12 penalties. Hutson had a sore foot and caught only one pass.

After Don's first postseason game in the 1936 championship against the Redskins, he was generally used as a decoy. Against the Skins he caught five passes for 76 yards and a touchdown. In the 1938 title game, he appeared only briefly due to a knee injury. In the other three postseason games he played, the 1941 Bear playoff and title games against the Giants in 1939 and 1944, Don caught five passes for 86 yards and no touchdowns. However, the Giants spent so much time watching Hutson that they lost both games. The period from 1935 through 1945 is rightfully known as the Hutson Era in Packer history. Thanks to his presence, they won three NFL titles in those eleven years.

When he retired for the last time in 1945, his lifetime reception total of 488 was 290 more than closest competitor Jim Benton (who also went to Pine Bluff High School, incidentally). It would not be bested until Billy Howton passed him in 1963, 18 years later. Likewise, his lifetime receiving yardage total of 7,991 was 4,600 yards more than nearest contemporary Benton and was not topped until Howton did it in 1963. His record of 99 touchdown receptions was not exceeded for 44 years until Steve Largent passed Don in 1989. His 105 lifetime touchdowns were surpassed by Jim Brown in 1965. At retirement, Don had accumulated 823 points, more than double Ken Strong's second best total of 410.

Lou Groza would not exceed 823 until 1961. Hutson still is in the record book for having the most seasons and the most consecutive seasons leading the league in touchdowns, points, receptions, receiving yards, and touchdown receptions. He had an unusually healthy attitude about all this, saying that he actually liked when his records were broken because it let him relive a happy part of his life.

Don was a consistent success in business, as well, running bowling alleys

Even on one knee, Don Hutson was the greatest Packer until Brett Favre. During the careers of both these multi-MVP Award winners, Green Bay was often accused of being a one-man team. *Courtesy of the Stiller-Lefebvre Collection.*

and car dealerships, and lived a long and contented life. He would say, "Luck is the thing you need the most to succeed in football, business, or anything. I mean injury luck, business luck, card luck, whatever. And I've always been lucky." (Oates) He also said many times that for every ball he caught in a game he caught a thousand in practice, and both Herber and Isbell attested to long practice sessions with Hutson. Luck is a good thing, but you still have to have the intelligence, diligence, and talent to take advantage of good fortune. Don did, and became a charter member of the Pro Football Hall of Fame in 1963. He was inducted into the Packer Hall of Fame in 1971.

FOR FURTHER INFORMATION

Cope, Myron. *The Game That Was: An Illustrated Account of the Tumultuous Early Days of Pro Football*. New York: Crowell, 1974. (121-30, 160)

Daley, Arthur. *Pro Football's Hall of Fame*. New York: Grosset and Dunlap, 1968, c1963. (151-61)

———. "Wizard of Green Bay," *Collier's*. 11/25/44. (15, 27)

———. "Pass Thrower Extraordinary," *New York Times*. 2/12/45. (16)

Daly, Dan, and Bob O'Donnell. *The Pro Football Chronicle: The Complete (Well Almost) Record of the Best Players, the Greatest Photos, the Hardest Hits, the Biggest Scandals, and the Funniest Stories in Pro Football*. New York: Collier Books, 1990. (296)

Garrity, John. "The Game's Greatest Receiver," *Sports Illustrated*. Fall 1995. (44)

Johnson, Chuck. *The Greatest Packers of Them All*. New York: Putnam, 1968. (87-93)

Maule, Tex. *The Game: The Official Picture History of the NFL and AFL*. New York: Random House, 1967. (118)

Oates, Bob. "Don Hutson," *Los Angeles Times*. 4/30/89. (Sports 3)

Packers of the Past: A Series of Articles Reprinted from the Milwaukee Journal Sept. 28– Dec. 9, 1965. Milwaukee, WI: Milwaukee Journal, 1965. (5-7)

Porter, David L., ed. *Biographical Dictionary of American Sports: Football*. New York: Greenwood Press, 1987. (281-2)

Whittingham, Richard. *What a Game They Played*. New York: Harper and Row, 1974. (119-30, 206)

Williams, Larry. "The Ghost of Green Bay," *Sport*. 12/60. (38-9, 85-8)

Zimmerman, Paul. "The Bronk and the Gazelle," *Sports Illustrated*. 9/11/89. (128-140)

STARR QUARTERBACKS
BART STARR • QUARTERBACK 1956–71

WHO'S WORN THE NUMBER <Basing 1925–26>, Enright 1927, Minick 1928, R. Smith 1929, Dunn 1931, Shelley 1932, P. Young 1933, S. Johnston 1935–38, L. Brock 1940, Lyman 1941, Hinte 1942, Frankowski 1945, Earl Bennett 1946, Tassos 1947–49, Afflis 1951, Parilli 1952–53, Garrett 1954, Brackins 1955, Held 1955, Starr 1956–71.

ORIGINATOR Back Myrt "Biff" Basing <1925–26> (see top 27) or fullback Rex Enright 1927 played for Rockne at Notre Dame and spent two years in Green Bay before launching a college coaching career where he was employed mostly at South Carolina.

LONGEST TENURE Bart Starr 1956–71. The number was retired in 1973.

NUMBER CHANGES Back Myrt Basing wore 27 in 1927; Rex Enright had 20 in <1926>; guard Paul Minick wore 23 and 25 in 1929; lineman Red Smith wore 7, 19, and 28 in 1927; quarterback Red Dunn wore 11 in 1927–28, 16 and 32 in 1929, and 7 and 17 in 1930; Swede Johnston wore 37 in 1934 and 54 in 1936; back Lou Brock wore 16 from 1941–45; guard Earl Bennett also wore 36 in 1946; Dick Afflis wore 62 in 1952, 72 in 1953, and 75 in 1954; quarterback Babe Parilli also wore 16 in 1953 and 10 in 1957–58; Bart Starr also wore 16 in 1956.

OTHER NOTABLES Red Smith (see top 28); Red Dunn (see 11); backup fullback Chester "Swede" Johnston was inducted to the Packer Hall of Fame in 1981; Lou Brock did a little bit of everything for the Packers—running, passing, receiving, punting and playing defensive back—and was inducted in the Packer Hall of Fame in 1982; Dick Afflis (see 72); Babe Parilli was Bart Starr's idol when Babe was at Kentucky and Bart was in high school; Charley "Choo Choo" Brackins was the first black Packer quarterback.

ONE TO FORGET Former Stanford All American quarterback Bobby Garrett sometimes stuttered when he called plays which tends to be a problem in the pros. He threw only 30 passes in his one year in Green Bay. He and Babe Parilli were traded for each other twice.

BART STARR Often in discussions of public affairs people are content to say that history will make the final judgment. But what if history is wrong? After all, history, like journalism, is written by people with a subjective viewpoint. Of course, historical judgments themselves shift as additional information comes to light and as the attitudes of historians change. For a football example we need look no further than Bart Starr, whose luminescence has dimmed a bit over time.

In the 1960s the argument whether Bart Starr or John Unitas was the best quarterback in football was by no means resolved. Many years later, Unitas is still talked about with the likes of Montana, Elway, and Marino as one of the greatest quarterbacks of all time. Starr is mentioned as a deserving Hall of Famer, but not in the upper echelon of quarterbacks. What happened in the interim? Did Unitas win a few more championships after his retirement? Did Starr start throwing interceptions in his backyard? It was a long road to respect for Bart during his career, and somehow much of that has dwindled away in the passage of time and the recording of history's judgment.

Bart Starr was a coveted high school All American who went to Alabama and had immediate success. He led the team to a 61-6 win over Syracuse in the 1952 Orange Bowl, and as a sophomore took the team to the Cotton Bowl where they lost to Rice. In his junior year, he injured his back, and then as a senior sat on the bench because new coach J.B. "Ears" Whitworth decided to go with all sophomores. The Packers drafted Starr in 1956 as a 17th-round draft choice and assigned him number 42 in training camp, obviously not expecting him to beat out Tobin Rote, Paul Held, and Jim Capuzzi. Starr made the team as Rote's backup and took number 15. Over his first three years, Starr showed potential with his accuracy, but his play-calling and leadership were weaknesses, and Rote advised him to build up his arm strength.

Lombardi arrived and Starr was impressed, but the feeling was not mutual. Vince cut the incumbent Parilli and kept Starr around, but gave the starting job first to journeyman Lamar McHan and then to weak-armed tailback Pineapple Joe Francis before finally trying Starr late in 1959. Lombardi's assistant coaches had already written off Bart as a backup at best, but under him the team began to win again. In 1960 Starr and McHan started the season sharing the job until finally Lombardi awarded the job to Bart late in the year, and he led them to their first Western Division crown in 16 years. The Packers would lose the championship game to the Eagles that year, 17-13. Starr's play was not great, but he did not play badly, either. Lombardi was still skeptical and made enquiries of Dallas regarding rookie Don Meredith. In the following year, Lombardi would begin to be convinced. 1960 would be the last time Bart would be on the losing side in a playoff game. The Packers would win every one of the nine postseason games in the 1960s, and Starr would play well in all of them (except the 1965 playoff against the Colts when he was injured on the first play and had to leave the game). He would outplay rival star quarterbacks Y. A. Tittle twice, Don Meredith twice, as well as Frank Ryan, Roman Gabriel, Len Dawson, and Daryle Lamonica all once. Unitas, Montana, Elway, Otto Graham, Bobby Layne would all have bad games in the postseason. Not Bart. His quarterback rating for postseason play is an NFL high of 104.5.

Bart was at his best in a pressure situation. He was a master at calling plays, reading defenses, and switching off to audibles at the line of scrimmage. He often said his goal was to call an entire game of nothing but audibles. His signature play was the surprise pass on third or fourth and short yardage. It was a simple matter of reading the defense. If the defense was bulked at the line against the expected run, Bart would fake to the halfback or fullback and pass to an open receiver. He did it so consistently that it's a wonder that defenses did not adjust better. He threw a 43-yard touchdown to Boyd Dowler in the Ice Bowl on such a calculated risk. Once Starr gained confidence under Lombardi, he had a belief in himself and in his teammates. He generally would take a sack rather than risk an interception, feeling he had a better chance of calling a better play in the huddle to get the first down on the next play even if more yardage was involved.

He did not have as strong an arm as Unitas, but he could and did throw the deep ball. He just made sure his receiver was open. His yards-per-reception figure of 7.85 is virtually identical to Johnny U, and he led the league three times in this category as well as leading three times in passing and three times in completion percentage. Because Lombardi's offense was a ball-control running offense, though, he did not throw enough to accumulate the big passing numbers of Unitas and others. What is often forgotten is that Green Bay's overpowering running attack had dissipated by the second half of the decade. For the three consecutive championships in the latter part of the 1960s the Packers leading rushers were Jim Taylor with 734 yards at 3.5 per carry in 1965, Jim Taylor with 705 yards at 3.5 yards per carry in 1966, and Jim Grabowski with 466 yards at 3.9 yards per carry in 1967. The Packer offense relied on Bart's brains and his arm.

Tight end Marv Fleming once said, "I think Bart Starr was the most honest quarterback there ever was. He had no favorites. If you were open, you were his favorite." (Biever, 63) Center Ken Bowman called him "a great field general. He didn't have the arm of John Elway, but he was a great general. Bart's biggest asset was his brain. He would take things and store them and use them at the most opportune time." (Biever, 69) Bill Curry, who played center for both the Packers and the Colts, added, "Bart Starr's was the strongest personality of a quarterbacks I played with. Unitas had this charismatic way of carrying himself, but he didn't have the presence of Bart in the huddle. Bart was in total command." (Plimpton, 137)

His coach said of him, "Bart Starr is the greatest quarterback who ever played football. Starr is the greatest because he won the most championships. It's as simple as that. Isn't winning the job of the quarterback?" (Flynn, 76) Articles in national magazines and books at the time compared him to Unitas and many sided with Starr. 49er coach Jack Christiansen said, "He is probably the best quarterback in football today and when he retires, which I hope is soon, I expect that he will be recognized as the greatest of all time." (Shecter) If you take away the Packer-Colt matchups in which Green Bay held a 10-7 edge, the records of the two teams for the 1960s were 86-30-5 Packers vs 85-32-4 Colts. The two best teams of the decade were evenly matched— Starr's Packers won five titles; Unitas' Colts won none.

What is most surprising is the opinion of talented *Sports Illustrated* football writer Peter King who wrote a book in 1999 rating quarterbacks through league history. King states clearly that the number one criteria for him is winning and uses it as one of his defenses for choosing Otto Graham as the greatest QB of all time. Starr, however, who won more titles than any other signal caller in history, is ranked number 13. And he doesn't make King's list of top clutch performers either, despite having the highest quarterback rating in NFL history for postseason play. Bart's reputation has sunk back to early 1960s levels when Paul Hornung said of him, "because of myself, and because of Jim Taylor, because of a great offensive team and because of a great defensive team over the years . . . Bart hasn't received as much publicity as he should have." (Hornung, 221) What has been lost in the fog of the past is that the Packers did not always have the most talented team on the field in those championship years, but they always won. Besides Lombardi, the primary reason they won is because Starr consistently excelled and drove his team to victory.

After his playing career ended, Bart was regrettably drawn back to Green Bay as coach. It was a mistake for the team to offer the job to the inexperienced Starr and it was a mistake for him to accept it. It was a mistake that went on for nine years. In addition to the losing, Starr had discipline problems with his players and personality issues with the media covering the team. The whole affair sullied his once pristine image for a time. However, he has risen from that experience and from the personal tragedy of his younger son dying from drugs to once again be a greatly admired figure. He was in the forefront of the effort to pass the bond issue for the Lambeau Field renovations, and his name is consistently in the news linked to the Packers. Once, the Packers' gentlemanly bright star said of his friendly rival from Baltimore, "Unitas was a star when I was still sitting on the bench. I studied film of him for two years before I became a starter, just trying to improve myself. We played them twice a year, and it was always special. I knew I was going against the best quarterback in the game." (Herskowitz, 260) Unitas could say the same of Starr.

FOR FURTHER INFORMATION

Barra, Alan. *That's Not the Way It Was: (Almost) Everything They Told You About Sports Is Wrong.* New York: Hyperion, 1995. (150-72)

Biever, Vernon J., photography; Peter Strupp ed. *The Glory of Titletown: The Classic Green Bay Packers Photography of Vernon Biever.* Dallas, TX: Taylor Publishing, 1997. (63, 67, 69, 71)

Flynn, George, ed. *Vince Lombardi on Football.* New York: New York Graphic Society Ltd and Wallyn Inc., 1973. v. II, (76)

————. *The Vince Lombardi Scrapbook.* New York: Grossett and Dunlap, 1976. (22, 189)

Herskowitz, Mickey. *The Quarterbacks: The Uncensored Truth About the Men in the Pocket.* New York: Morrow, 1990. (254-65)

Hornung, Paul, as told to Al Silverman. *Football and the Single Man.* Garden City, NY: Doubleday, 1965. (221-2)

King, Peter. *Greatest Quarterbacks.* New York: Bishop Books [Time. Inc. Home Entertainment], 1999. (78, 92-7)

Maule, Tex. "A Starr Rises in the Game's Dominant West," *Sports Illustrated.* 10/31/66. (25)

PACKERS BY THE NUMBERS

McCullough, Bob. *My Greatest Day in Football: The Legends of Football Recount Their Greatest Moments.* New York: Thomas Dunne Books, 2001. (211-9)

Plimpton, George. *One More July: A Football Dialogue with Bill Curry.* New York: Harper and Row, 1977. (22-3, 134-7)

Porter, David L., ed. *Biographical Dictionary of American Sports: Football.* New York: Greenwood Press, 1987. (567-8)

Shecter, Leonard. "Bart Starr: Pride of the Packers," *Sport.* 12/67. (60-71)

Starr, Bart, and John Wiebusch. *A Perspective on Victory.* Chicago: Follett Publishing, 1972.

Starr, Bart, with Murray Olderman. *Starr: My Life in Football.* New York: William Morrow, 1987.

Wagner, Len. *Launching the Glory Years: The 1959 Packers—What They Didn't Tell Us.* Green Bay, WI: Coach's Books LLC [Jay Bengtson], 2001. (23)

POSTSCRIPT: I highly recommend iconoclastic sportswriter Allen Barra's take on this topic. Barra is firmly convinced that Starr is the greatest quarterback of all time.

1936 CHAMPS
ARNIE HERBER • TAILBACK 1933

WHO'S WORN THE NUMBER
<J. Harris 1925–26>, Skeate 1927, D. Hill 1929, Dunn 1929,
B. Davenport 1931, Zeller 1932, Herber 1933, Scherer 1937, Biolo 1939,
L. Brock 1941–45, C. Mitchell 1946, Gillette 1947, Cifers 1949, Dreyer
1950, Wimberly 1950–51, Parilli 1953, Starr 1956, McHan 1960, James
1967, Hunter 1971–73, R. Johnson 1976, Sproul 1978, Birney 1980,
Stachowitz 1981–82, Wright 1984–88, McJulien 1991–92, Copeland 1998.

ORIGINATOR Wisconsin's own Jack Harris <1925–26> ran for
three touchdowns in two years as a Packer back or fullback Gil Skeate
1927 was one of five 1920s Packers who were teammates at Gonzaga.

LONGEST TENURE Back Lou Brock 1941–45 (see top 15) and
quarterback Randy Wright 1984–88, the Badger who threw 31 TDs
and 57 interceptions.

NUMBER CHANGES Quarterback Red Dunn wore 11 in 1927–8,
32 in 1929, 7 and 17 in 1930, and 15 in 1931; back Don Hill also
wore 14 in 1929; Arnie Herber also wore 12 in 1930, 26 in 1931,
41 in 1932–33, 45 and 68 in 1934, 38 from 1935–40, and 19 in 1937;
end Bernie Scherer wore 40 in 1936, 11 in 1937, and 36 in 1938;
guard John Biolo also wore 32 in 1939; Lou Brock wore 15 in 1940;
defensive back Wally Dreyer also wore 42 in 1950; Ab Wimberly
wore 43 in 1950 and 85 in 1952; Babe Parilli wore 15 in 1953,
quarterback Bart Starr wore 15 from 1956–71; quarterback Lamar
McHan wore 17 in 1959–60; receiver Claudis James wore 27 in
1967–68; kicker Tom Birney also wore 19 in 1979–80.

OTHER NOTABLES Lou Brock (see top 15); defensive end Ab
Wimberly played in the 1952 Pro Bowl.

ONE TO FORGET Well-traveled quarterback Randy Johnson
bounced into Green Bay to play the last three games of his forgettable
11-year career in which he tossed 51 touchdowns and 90
interceptions. He threw his last pick for the Pack.

ARNIE HERBER It would be hard to find a Hall of Fame football player with a more fairy tale beginning than Arnie Herber. In his teens, he
sold programs at Packer games. A basketball and football star at Green
Bay West High School, he went to the University of Wisconsin and then
transferred to tiny Regis College in Denver, Colorado, after his freshman
year. With the onslaught of the Depression in 1929, he had to drop out
of Regis after only one year. Returning to his home town, Herber found
work as a handyman around the Packer locker room. With nothing to

lose, Curly Lambeau gave the former local hero a tryout and added him to the championship roster in 1930. Veteran Packers treated him with disdain, initially, and called him "Dummy." In his first league game, he threw a touchdown pass. As he slowly began to get playing time and prove himself on the field, they started to call him "Kid." When star full-back Bo Molenda continued to razz Herber, Lambeau sold Bo to the Giants. Within a few years, Herber would be considered the best passer in football and known as "Flash."

Herber was not the first great passer in the NFL—that honor would probably fall to Bennie Friedman who played with the Giants and other teams in the 1920s and early 1930s. However, Arnie was the best of his time and in particular the best deep passer in the game despite not even being a quarterback, but instead a single wing tailback. He was no great shakes as a runner, but was an able punter and defensive back. Herber didn't begin wearing a helmet until 1938 and was probably the last bareheaded Packer. He took a beating, but kept on throwing. His passing numbers do not look very impressive when viewed today, but it should be recalled that the rules of the game, the style of play, and the shape of the ball all were different in those days. He never completed more than 45% of his passes and threw a grand total of 81 touchdown passes, but he led the NFL in passing three times in the 1930s when it was based on passing yardage. In those years, 1932, 1934, and 1936, he also paced the league in touchdown passes.

He had very small hands and compensated by not gripping the football but simply resting it on his palm with his thumb across the laces. With this loose handle he could use his strong right arm to fling rainbow spirals accurately up to 80 yards through the air. Teammate Clarke Hinkle said of Arnie's passing, "He was more accurate at fifty yards then he was at ten." (Cope, 82) Herber confirmed this in the postscript to a famous story told about him. The story goes that a Hollywood film crew was making a short film depicting the amazing skills of pro football players, and the script called for Herber to throw a ball from the fifty yard line and break a pane of glass at the goal line. The director did not even have the cameras rolling for the first take and was shocked when Herber shattered the glass on the first try. Herber then did it again with the cameras rolling. What happened next, Herber recalled years later: "They moved the camera into the end zone for a close up of the football shattering the glass. I wasn't going to be in the picture, so I stood about 10 yards away—and missed." (*Packers*, 23)

It was the deep pass that won the Packers their first championship since the East/West title game playoff format was adopted in 1933. In 1936 they met the Eastern champs, the Boston Redskins, for the championship at the Polo Grounds in New York. The game was played in New York because Redskins owner George Marshall was fed up with the lack of fan support for his team in Boston; indeed, they would become the Washington Redskins in the next season. Green Bay was favored and started off quickly by scoring on a Herber to Hutson touchdown toss in the first three minutes of the game. On third down and five from the Redskin 42, Herber found Hutson all alone on the 20 and Don ran the rest of the way untouched. The Redskins drove down the field and scored a touchdown in the second quarter but missed the extra point so the score stood at 7-6 Packers at halftime.

Green Bay started quickly again in the second half. The key play was a 52-yard pass from Herber to Johnny Blood who was immediately knocked out of bounds at the Redskins eight. Still at the eight on fourth down, Herber found end Milt Gantenbein in the end zone for another touchdown pass and a 14-6 lead. The Packers would clinch matters in the fourth quarter by blocking a Redskin punt at the three. On second down, Bob Monnett ran two yards for the third Green Bay touchdown to complete the scoring in a 21-6 final. Individual statistics from the day are in conflict. The *Milwaukee Sentinel* lists Arnie Herber as completing nine of 23 passes while the *New York Times* says he hit six of 13 passes. It is clear that the Packers outgained the Redskins 153-91 yards through the air and that two of their three scores came through the air and were attributable to the long ball in which Arnie Herber specialized. In freezing temperatures, thousands of exultant Packer fans greeted the team's train when it returned to Green Bay.

Arnie's demise was swift and surprising. He was a friendly, popular player who enjoyed a hearty draught of beer and had a tendency to put on a few extra pounds. During training camp in 1941, Lambeau was concerned about Herber's weight, so Arnie signed a contract with perhaps the first weight clause in NFL history. If he weren't under 200 pounds when weighed each Saturday night, he would be fined $50. Despite the protective clause, he was released before the start of the season, and Curly said it was because of his weight problem. The man who Lambeau would always maintain was the greatest long passer ever was done at 30.

According to research by Larry Names, though, there may have been another reason for the sudden dismissal. It seems that Curly's pregnant second ex-wife came to town to establish residency and to go to court to extract some child support payments from the coach. Lambeau put the word out to hotels throughout town for her to find no rooms available anywhere. Curly was then at the apex of his popularity and power, and local businesses were generally happy to comply with his wishes. With nowhere else to go, Curly's ex turned to her friend Mrs. Arnie Herber and the Herbers put her up in their house. Lambeau gave Arnie an ultimatum to evict his ex. Arnie refused and found himself out of a job. It's interesting that when the Packers' other star tailback Cecil Isbell retired just two years later, he said that he did so because he didn't like the way Lambeau autocratically told respected veterans like Herber they were through.

Herber volunteered for the military during World War II but was rejected for his varicose veins. After being out of football for three years, he would resurface with the New York Giants in 1944 and 1945. Graying, slower of foot and a bit heavy, he would play against the Packers in the 1944 title game. His passing kept the Giants on the move, but four interceptions cinched the game for Green Bay. Arnie would later claim that his biggest thrill in football was when he came off the bench for the Giants in his final year at the age of 35 and threw four second half touchdown passes to defeat the Eagles. He was elected to the Pro Football Hall of Fame in 1966 just three years before his death at the early age of 59. He was elected to the Packer Hall of Fame posthumously in 1972.

FOR FURTHER INFORMATION
Cohen, Richard M., Jordan A. Deutsch, Roland T. Johnson, and David S. Neft. *The Scrapbook History of Pro Football.* Indianapolis, IN: Bobbs-Merrill, 1976. (63)

Cope, Myron. *The Game That Was: An Illustrated Account of the Tumultuous Early Days of Pro Football.* New York: Crowell, 1974. (82)

Daley, Arthur J. "Brilliant Air Atack Gives Packers Victory," *New York Times.* 12/14/36

PACKERS BY THE NUMBERS

Goodman, Murray, and Leonard Lewin. *My Greatest Day in Football.* New York: Barnes, 1948. (113-6)

Johnson, Chuck. *The Greatest Packers of Them All.* New York: Putnam, 1968. (55-6)

Names, Larry. *The History of the Green Bay Packers: Book III: The Lambeau Years Part Three.* Wautoma, WI: Angel Press of WI, 1990. (144-5)

Packers of the Past: A Series of Articles Reprinted from the Milwaukee Journal Sept. 28– Dec. 9, 1965. Milwaukee, WI: Milwaukee Journal, 1965. (23-5)

Porter, David L., ed. *Biographical Dictionary of American Sports: Football.* New York: Greenwood Press, 1987. (260-1)

Swain, Glenn. *Packers vs. Bears.* Los Angeles: Charles Publishing, 1996. (52)

Yuenger, Jack. "He Came to Play," *Green Bay Packers 1962 Yearbook.* (32-3)

1936 CHAMPIONSHIP DATA
Green Bay Packers 21
Boston Redskins 6

December 13, 1936 • Polo Grounds, NY

Attendance: 29,545

Winner's Share: $250

Loser's Share: $180

KEY STATS	PACKERS	REDSKINS
First Downs	7	8
Rush Yards	67	53
Pass Yards	153	91
Total Yards	220	144
Interceptions	1	2
Fumbles Lost	1	2
Penalties	3-15	4-25
Halftime score	Packers 7 Redskins 6	

ADDITIONAL FACTS

•The Packers line outweighed the Skins line 220 to 209 per man.

•The Packers average age was 25 while the Redskins was 24.5.

•The teams and league officials agreed before the game that if the game ended in a tie, the teams would meet again the next week.

•This was the last game for the Boston Redskins; they would move to Washington weeks later.

•Redskins leading runner Cliff Battles left injured after four minutes of the first quarter.

•Riley Smith had two punts blocked and missed an extra point for the first time in 15 tries.

•In the second half the Redskins only gained 3 yards rushing and 14 yards passing.

1939 CHAMPS
CECIL ISBELL • TAILBACK 1938–42

WHO'S WORN THE NUMBER <F. Larson 1925>, <Lidberg 1926>, Darling 1927–28, R. Baker 1929, Dunn 1930, F. Wilson 1931, L. Evans 1933, Bultman 1934, Sauer 1937, Isbell 1938–42, Wheba 1944, Buchianeri 1945, Pregulman 1946, Cody 1947–48, Schuette 1950–51, McHan 1959–60, T. Williams 1967, Tagge 1972–74, Whitehurst 1977–83, Bracken 1985–90, Don King 1987r, Hentrich 1994–97.

ORIGINATOR Center Fred "Ojay" Larson <1925> was one of three Notre Dame seniors to play for the Packers under aliases in 1921 which led to the franchise being revoked or center Bernard "Boob" Darling 1927–28 (see top 29).

LONGEST TENURE Quarterback David Whitehurst 1977–83. Whitehurst was the starter during the two seasons Lynn Dickey missed with a broken leg. He was the first Packer to throw double digit touchdown passes in the 1970s when he tossed 10 in 1978 and 1979. He also threw 17 and 18 interceptions in those years.

NUMBER CHANGES Fullback Cully Lidberg wore 34 in 1929 and 38 in 1930; Boob Darling wore 29 in 1929–31; back Roy "Bullet" Baker also wore 5, 12 and 21 in 1928; quarterback Red Dunn wore 11 in 1927–28, 16 and 32 in 1929, 7 in 1930, and 15 in 1931; guard Lon Evans wore 25 and 65 in 1934, 46 in 1935, 51 in 1936, and 39 in 1937; center Red Bultman wore 45 in 1932–33, 33 and 38 in 1933, and 32 and 52 in 1934; back George Sauer wore 25 in 1935–36; end Ray Wehba also wore 57 in 1944; guard Mike Buchianeri wore 33 in 1941 and 19 in 1944; quarterback Lamar McHan also wore 16 in 1960; returner Travis Williams wore 23 from 1967–70; replacement Don King also wore 32 in 1987.

OTHER NOTABLES Cully Lidberg (see top 34); Boob Darling (see top 29); Red Dunn (see 11); Lon Evans (see top 39).

ONE TO FORGET Green Bay native Jerry Tagge was a wasted number one draft pick. With no competition for the quarterback job, Tagge flopped badly, completing fewer than half of his passes and throwing three touchdowns and 17 interceptions in three years. His failure led to the disastrous Hadl trade.

CECIL ISBELL Single wing tailback Sammy Baugh came into the league in 1937 and left 16 years later as a Hall of Fame quarterback. Sid Luckman joined the Chicago Bears in 1939 to become the first modern T formation quarterback and retired in 1950 as a future Hall of Famer. Cecil Isbell was the Packers number one draft choice in 1938 and may have been the best of the three great contemporary passers, but quit after only five years. A comparison of the passing statistics for each passer over the years that Isbell was active is enlightening:

	G	A	C	%	Yards	YPA	TD	Int	Int %
Baugh (38-42)	51	819	465	56.8%	5,494	6.71	48	60	7.3
Isbell (38-42)	54	818	411	50.2%	5,945	7.27	61	52	2.9
Luckman (39-42)	44	380	196	51.6%	3,782	9.95	28	32	8.4

Or if we make the comparison between the passers' first five years in the league:

	G	A	C	%	Yards	YPA	TD	Int	Int %
Baugh (37-41)	51	765	414	54.1%	5,097	6.66	40	57	7.5
Isbell (38-42)	54	818	411	50.2%	5,945	7.27	61	52	2.9
Luckman (39-43)	54	583	306	52.5%	5,976	10.25	56	44	7.5

This comparison reveals many things. Sammy Baugh threw a lot of short passes and was picked off a fair amount. Sid Luckman was running a passing offense that the rest of the league could not comprehend; his yards-per-attempt figure is eye-popping. The Bears did not throw a lot, but had a lot of long gainers through the air. Overall, Isbell compares very well to both Hall of Famers. His yards per attempt figure is excellent, he threw the most touchdown passes and had the lowest interception percentage by far. Luckman's career yards-per-attempt number would drop to 8.42, still second all-time to Otto Graham; Baugh's number would rise to 7.31 by the end of his career. Baugh was also a league-leading punter and a notable defensive back who intercepted nine passes through 1942. Luckman picked off 10 and was punting for a 40+ average in those years although that average would drop over time. Isbell also had nine interceptions, but was not much of a punter. However, he rushed for 1,522 yards on 422 attempts in his brief career. Baugh rushed for 172 yards in that period, and Luckman's total was negative yardage.

So does Cecil Isbell belong in the Hall of Fame? No, his career was too short. The above numbers indicate, though, that Curly Lambeau was not off base when he said that Isbell was the best passer he ever saw, "Isbell was the master at any range. He could throw soft passes, bullet passes, or feathery lobs. He was the best with Sid Luckman of the Bears a close second and Sammy Baugh of the Redskins a long third. Luckman wasn't as versatile and Baugh couldn't compare on the long ones." (Johnson, *Pioneer*, 78-9) Unlike the other two, however, he never got to play quarterback in the T formation. As a tailback, he would get tackled on every play whether he was involved in it or not. Baugh himself has spoken on how the T extended his career.

Furthermore, Isbell was as fine a passer as there was in the league despite being severely limited by a chronically bad shoulder. Cecil had dislocated his left shoulder several times in college so he started wearing a chain that went from his arm to his torso to keep him from raising his arm too high and damaging the shoulder. "Sure it hampered me some. When I was punting, I couldn't extend my left arm all the way out, so I had to learn to drop the ball one-handed. And I played defense all the time—we didn't have two platoons then—and it wasn't good for tackling. Not that it was so tender, but because it hindered the grasp. My reach didn't have the range it would have had. The other thing was when I was carrying the ball. I couldn't stiff-arm with my left —not effectively any-way." (Johnson, *Greatest*, 53)

Isbell joined the Packers after leading the College All Stars to a 28-16 victory over Sammy Baugh's Redskins in 1938. The Packers already had an All League tailback in Arnie Herber, but Isbell was so talented that the two generally would alternate for Cecil's first three years in the league. Sometimes both would play at the same time and occa-sionally even would throw passes to each other. Slow-footed Herber caught two touch-down passes from Cecil in 1938. Most of the touchdown passes, though, went to Don Hutson. Isbell proved a worthy successor to Herber in getting the ball to Hutson, and the two would enjoy remarkable success together and become good friends.

Isbell's longest touchdown pass was for 92 yards to Hutson in the league All Star game for 1939. His shortest touchdown went to Hutson for four inches in 1942, a sea-son in which Don caught 17 touchdowns and Cecil threw 24. The 24 would stand as a team record until 1983 when Lynn Dickey topped it. From 1940 through 1942, Cecil threw a touchdown pass in 23 straight games, a record that Johnny Unitas would break in 1958 en route to an ultimate total of 47 straight.

The Packers played post-season football in three of Isbell's five years. They lost the title game to the Giants in his rookie year and lost a divisional playoff to the Bears in 1941, but in 1939 they won it all. The 1939 title game was a rematch with the Giants who had won the previous year largely because Hutson missed almost the entire game due to injury. The game was played in Milwaukee to try to cash in on the larger atten-dance possible at the State Fair Grounds. Despite gale force winds, 32,379 fans showed up to cheer on the Packers. The Packers won the toss and chose to put the wind at their backs rather than take the ball. The Giants, just like the previous year, blocked Clarke Hinkle's first punt, but this time missed a field goal try. Later in the first quarter, Green Bay got the ball on the New York 47 and drove the distance in ten plays, including two passes to Hutson. The seven-yard touchdown pass went from Herber to Milt Ganten-bein who was open due to the double coverage on Hutson. Late in the first half the Giants advanced to the Green Bay nine, but the Packers grabbed one of their six inter-ceptions of the game to end the threat. The Giants trailed only 7-0 at the half, but crossed the Packers 30-yard line only once more in the contest.

The second half was all Green Bay. Tiny Engebretsen kicked a 37-yard field goal and Cecil Isbell threw a 31-yard touchdown pass to Joe Laws in the third quarter to make the score 17-0. In the fourth quarter, Ernie Smith kicked a 42-yard field goal and then Bud Svendsen intercepted a pass and ran it back 15 yards to the Giant 15. Full-back Ed Jankowski ultimately punched it in from the Giant one, and the final score was 27-0. It was the worst beating any team had doled out in a title game up to that point, but that record would last only one season until the Bears buried the Redskins 73-0 the next year.

In his five years in the NFL, Cecil Isbell twice was All-League and three times was second-team All-League. He played in four of the five All Star games of the time—once as a member of the 1939 champion Packers and three times as a member of the league All Stars. Isbell said that he had seen Lambeau go up to loyal veterans like Arnie Her-ber and Hank Bruder and tell them they were through, and he determined that would never happen to him. He would quit on his own time. When his alma mater, Purdue, offered him a coaching job at a pay cut in 1943, he took it, so we will never know what he would have accomplished had he stayed a pro longer. He was head coach for three years at Purdue before moving on to coach the Baltimore Colts of the All America Football Conference for a few years. He held a few assistant coaching jobs (including working under Lambeau again on the Chicago Cardinal staff) before leaving football for business in the mid-1950s. He was elected to the College Football Hall of Fame in 1967 and the Packer Hall of Fame in 1972. He died in 1985 and is little remembered, but deserves better.

FOR FURTHER INFORMATION

Gruver, Ed. "Cecil Isbell: A Short Time in the Spotlight," *The Coffin Corner.* Available online at www.footballresearch.com/articles/frpage.cfm?topic'2isbell.

Johnson, Chuck. *The Green Bay Packers: Pro Football's Pioneer Team.* New York: Thomas Nelson and Sons, 1963. (78-82)

———. *The Greatest Packers of Them All.* New York: Putnam, 1968. (52-5)

Packers of the Past: A Series of Articles Reprinted from the Milwaukee Journal Sept. 28–Dec. 9, 1965. Milwaukee, WI: Milwaukee Journal, 1965. (33-5)

Porter, David L., ed. *Biographical Dictionary of American Sports: Football.* New York: Greenwood Press, 1987. (283-4)

 1939 CHAMPIONSHIP DATA
Green Bay Packers 27
New York Giants 0

December 10, 1939 • State Fair Park, Milwaukee

Attendance: 32,279

Winner's Share: $704

Loser's Share: $455

Weather: 25-35 mph north wind

KEY STATS	PACKERS	GIANTS
First Downs	10	7
Rush Yards	131	56
Pass Yards	99	95
Total Yards	230	151
Interceptions	6	3
Fumbles Lost	0	0
Penalties	4-50	5-21
Halftime Score	Packers 7 Giants 0	

ADDITIONAL FACTS

•Curly Lambeau wore green gloves for the game, but his assistant Red Smith wore a green hat, shirt, and tie.

•Giants coach Steve Owen was attending his mother's funeral so New York was coached by assistant Bo Molenda, a former Packer.

•Lambeau's voice was picked up by the sideline announcer's microphone shouting plays to the team on the field, i.e., coaching from the sidelines, which was against the rules at the time.

•The recently erected, makeshift press box swayed precariously in the wind, frightening members of the press.

•Due to a lack of facilities, both teams changed into their uniforms at their hotels.

•The Giants had thrown only 11 interceptions all year before giving up 6 in the title game.

RUNNING QUARTERBACKS
TOBIN ROTE • QUARTERBACK 1952–56

WHO'S WORN THE NUMBER
<Wilkens 1925>, <B. Rose 1926>, <Purdy 1926>, Tuttle 1927,
B. Young 1929, Fitzgibbon 1930, R. Saunders 1931, Monnett 1933,
Bruder 1936–38, L. Mulleneaux 1938, Disend 1940, Shiry 1940,
Vant Hull 1942, Falkenstein 1943, Urban 1944, Kercher 1944,
Keuper 1945–47, Cremer 1948, Ferry 1949, Drulis 1950,
C. Robinson 1951, T. Rote 1952–56, Roach 1961, Duncan 1971,
R. Walker 1974, Danelo 1975, Vataha 1977, Zorn 1985, Shield 1986,
C. Washington 1987r, Tomczak 1991, Pedersen 1996–98, 2001–02.

ORIGINATOR Elmer Wilkens <1925> played six games at end
for Green Bay and lived his whole life in Fort Wayne, Indiana, or
end Golden Gopher George Tuttle who played one game for the
Pack and lived his whole life in Minneapolis.

LONGEST TENURE Tobin Rote 1952–56.

NUMBER CHANGES Quarterback Pid Purdy wore 5 and 7 in
1927; back Paul Fitzgibbon wore 14 in 1931–32 and 49 in 1932;
back Bob Monnett also wore 42 and 66 in 1934, 12 and 3 in
1935, 12 in 1936, 5 in 1936–37, and 50 in 1938; blocking back
Hank Bruder also wore 13 in 1931–33, 55 in 1933, 47 in 1934,
27 in 1935–36, and 5 in 38–39; defensive end Bob Kercher also
wore 23 in 1944; defensive end Alex Urban wore 23 in 1941 and
79 in 1945; Tobin Rote wore 38 in 1950–51; quarterback John
Roach also wore 10 in 1961–63.

OTHER NOTABLES Pid Purdy (see top 5); Bob Monnett (see
top 3); Hank Bruder (see 27).

ONE TO FORGET QB Joe Shield got into only three games in
1986 and never threw a pass, playing behind Randy Wright,
Vince Ferragamo, and Chuck Fusina—all who had passer ratings
in the low 60s.

TOBIN ROTE "The great quarterbacks in future years will have to
run as well as pass to survive pro lines, which seem to get rougher
and faster every season...The pro ends of today are bigger than the
guards and tackles were a decade ago. The defense places greater
emphasis on rushing the passer. The new development in pro football, therefore, will have to be the running quarterback."

That sounds like a description of Michael Vick, Donovan
McNabb, or Daunte Culpepper, today's newest embodiments of the

NUMBER 18

"quarterback of the future" (QOTF), who have both the calibrated arm to hit a receiver at any distance as well the speed, size, and strength to stray far from the safety of the pocket. Among the many current masters of escape are Rich Gannon, Jeff Garcia, and of course Brett Favre. They all follow in the QOTF tradition of Steve Young, John Elway, and Randall "the Ultimate Weapon" Cunningham who also were celebrated for their combination of running and passing abilities. Continuing backward in time, Joe Montana and Joe Theisman were the epitome of mobile quarterbacks who could run if they had to, but were adept at avoiding a pass rush when those lines above were used by Paul Zimmerman to begin the chapter on "Football of the Eighties" in his *The New Thinking Man's Guide to Pro Football* (Simon and Schuster, 1984). Prior to the two Joes, Roger Staubach, Steve Grogan, Greg Landry, and Bobby Douglass carried the QOTF torch and the ball in the seventies (although Douglass threw the ball about as well as one could throw a torch). The origins of the running quarterbacks are often said to date to the sixties when scrambling Fran Tarkenton tried to stay alive behind the porous offensive line of the expansion Minnesota Vikings.

That quotation, however, dates all the way back to 1955 when Paul Brown wrote an article, "I Watch the Quarterback," for the October 28 issue of *Colliers*. And, with apologies to Frankie Albert and Johnny Lujack, the first running quarterback was playing for the Packers at the time, Tobin Rote. In the 1940s the teams in the NFL set aside the single wing offense and moved to the T Formation, and the increase in passing led to an explosion of points. Tobin Rote was a throwback single wing tailback in his talents and a throwback in general for his toughness. In one game, he had his nose broken, left the field for one play, and came back for the next play with blood streaming down his face. In another game, he threw a pass to Ray Pelfry 10 yards downfield. As the defense converged on Pelfry, he lateraled back to Rote who was trailing on the play, and Tobin went for the first down. He could run and throw with equal skill, and he had a long successful career in, remarkably, three professional football leagues.

Rote was a tall, tough Texan born January 18, 1928, in San Antonio. He was a record-setting passer for Rice Institute from 1946 to 1949 and was drafted by the Packers in the second round of the 1950 NFL draft. It was his misfortune to play for some of the poorest teams in Packer history from 1950 through 1956. In those years, the 6'3" 210-pound quarterback led the league twice in attempts, completions, and touchdown passes and once in passing yardage. In addition, he was the first quarterback to lead his team in rushing yards which he did initially in 1951. He repeated that achievement in 1952 and 1956 while finishing second on the team two other times. All this with a yearly rushing average that never fell below 4.5 yards per carry. In 1951, Coach Gene Ronzani installed an early version of the shotgun formation against the Bears to take advantage both of Rote's throwing and running skills. He ran for 150 yards in the second Bears game that year, but also fumbled twice inside the Bears' 15-yard line as the Packers lost. Of course, to fit in on a team that never finished better than 6-6, he led the league in fumbles twice as well.

His second Packer coach, Lisle Blackbourn, referred to Rote as "the greatest competitor I ever saw." However, Blackbourn also noted the signal caller's inconsistency, "When Tobin Rote is hot he is positively the greatest of them all, and when he is cold, well . . ." (Johnson, 49) This is borne out by Rote's statistics. In 1952, he completed 52% of his passes and threw 13 touchdown passes against only eight interceptions for a passer rating of 85.6. The next year he completed only 39% of his passes and threw five touchdowns and 15 interceptions for a rating of 32.4. After his finest year in 1956 when he led the league in passes, completions, yardage, and touchdowns, Blackbourn traded him and Val Joe Walker to Detroit for tackles Ollie Spencer and Norm Masters, guard Jim Salsbury, and halfback Don McIlhenny—no stars but four future starters.

In Detroit, Bobby Layne got hurt in 1957 and Rote led the Lions to a tie for the Western Conference title with the 49ers. After trailing at halftime 27-7 in the playoff, Rote led the Lions back in the second half to win 31-27. In the championship game against the Browns, Rote ran for one score and passed for four others as the Lions trampled Cleveland 59-14. Two years later, though, Rote completed only 38% of his passes and threw 19 interceptions for a passer rating of only 26.8. In 1960 he found himself with the Toronto Argonauts of the Canadian Football League, topping the league in passing with 38 touchdowns and leading his team to a divisional title, although they did not reach the championship game. After three successful years in Canada, Rote had his final hurrah with the San Diego Chargers in the American Football League. In 1963, he led the AFL in passing percentage at 59% and threw for two touchdowns in the Chargers 51-10 drubbing of the Patriots in the championship game. In 1964, he once again quarterbacked the Chargers in the title game, but came up a loser 20-7. He finished his career with a brief appearance for Denver in 1966.

When he died in 2000, he was survived by his wife and three of their four children. Although his career passing percentage is under 46%, he passed for 148 touchdowns and ran for 37 more. His career rushing total of 3,128 yards was a record for quarterbacks later broken by Fran Tarkenton in 1972. His 2,205 rushing yards with Green Bay is still the most of any Packer quarterback. While his greatest triumphs occurred with better teams in larger cities, Tobin Rote's most athletic years were spent in Green Bay where he set the original standard for the running quarterback that continues to evolve today.

FOR FURTHER INFORMATION

Gill, Bob. "Rote and Blanda: Tale of Two Quarterbacks," *The Coffin Corner.* XVI. 1994. Available online: www.footballresearch.com/articles/frpage.cfm?topic'roteblanda.

Johnson, Chuck. *The Greatest Packers of Them All.* New York: Putnam, 1968. (48-50)

Litsky, Frank. "Tobin Rote, 72" [obituary] *New York Times.* 6/30/00. (C19)

Packers of the Past: A Series of Articles Reprinted from the Milwaukee Journal Sept. 28–Dec. 9, 1965. Milwaukee, WI: Milwaukee Journal, 1965. (28-30)

Porter, David L., ed. *Biographical Dictionary of American Sports: 1992-1995 Supplement for Baseball, Football, Basketball, and Other Sports.* New York: Greenwood Press, 1995. (519-20)

GOING HOLLYWOOD
CARLOS BROWN • QUARTERBACK 1975–76

WHO'S WORN THE NUMBER <McAuliffe 1926>, F. Mayer 1927, Red Smith 1927, Bowdoin 1928, (Laabs 1929), Nash 1929, Hanney 1930, McCrary 1931, Michalske 1932, N. Mott 1932, Norgard 1934, Herber 1937, C. Mulleneaux 1938–41, 1945–46, Albrecht 1942, Bucchianeri 1944, Riddick 1946, McDougal 1947, Olsen 1949, Baldwin 1950, Orlich 1951, Carlos Brown 1975–76, B. Douglass 1978, Birney 1979–80, Pisarkewicz 1980, Campbell 1981–84, Schroeder 1994.

ORIGINATOR Jack McAuliffe <1926> was a 155 pound halfback who caught one TD pass in Green Bay and spent his whole life in Butte, Montana or guard Frank Mayer 1927 transferred from Iowa State to Notre Dame where he played under Rockne. He later coached at St. Thomas College in Minnesota.

LONGEST TENURE End Carl Mulleneaux 1938–41 and 1945–46 (see Notables below).

NUMBER CHANGES Lineman Red Smith also wore 7 and 28 in 1927 and 15 in 1929; guard Jim Bowdoin wore 32 in 1929–30 and 34 in 1931; end Tom Nash wore 21 in 1928, 26 in 1929, 37 in 1929–30, and 35 in 1931–32; fullback Herdis McCrary wore 29 in 1929, 28 in 1929–30, 43 in 1932, and 38 and 53 in 1933; guard Mike Michalske wore 36 in 1929–30 and 1937, 28 in 1931, 30 in 1932, 31 in 1933, 24 and 63 in 1934 and 33 and 40 in 1935; end Al Norgard also wore 62 in 1934; tailback Arnie Herber also wore 12 in 1930, 26 in 1931, 41 in 1932–33, 16 in 1933, 45 and 68 in 1934, and 38 from 1935–40; guard Mike Bucchianeri wore 33 in 1941 and 17 in 1945; end Ray Riddick wore 5 from 1940–42 and 22 in 1942; end Dan Orlich also wore 49 from 1949–51; kicker Tom Birney also wore 16 in 1980; receiver Bill Schroeder wore 84 from 1997–01.

OTHER NOTABLES Red Smith (see top 28); Tom Nash made All League in 1931 and 1932 and second team in 1930. He later played for Brooklyn; Arnie Herber (see 16); Mike Michalske (see 33); Carl Mulleneaux was the end opposite of Hutson at the beginning of the 1940s. He caught six TD passes in 1940 and was inducted into the Packer Hall of Fame in 1983.

ONE TO FORGET Drafted number one in 1981 rather than Ronnie Lott who was available, rag-armed quarterback Rich Campbell got into seven games in four years before being cut. He completed fewer than half his passes and threw three touchdowns and nine interceptions in his brief time on the field.

PACKERS BY THE NUMBERS

CARLOS BROWN Carlos Alan Autry was born in Shreveport, Louisiana, in 1952. When he was two his family moved to the San Joaquin Valley in California where they picked cotton to make a living. His parents divorced, and Carlos grew up with his mother's name, Brown. At 6'3" 210 pounds he earned a football scholarship to Fresno State and became the first person in his family to attend college. In 1975, the Packers picked him in the 12th round of the draft, and he made the team as a third string quarterback. He barely played in his rookie year, but when starter Lynn Dickey went down to injury in 1976, Brown started three games late in the season and proved he was overmatched in the NFL. He completed 26 of 74 passes for two touchdowns and six interceptions in those three games. He was cut in 1977 and later played a year in the Canadian Football League.

Through some Hollywood people he had met, he started acting in movies in the late 1970s. He appeared in *North Dallas Forty, Popeye,* and *Southern Comfort* as Carlos Brown. However, in 1981 Carlos met his father for the first time as an adult and went back to Autry, Alan Autry. He continued acting in movies such as *Brewster's Millions* and *Amazing Grace and Chuck* before hitting it big on television. In 1988, he landed the role of Captain Bubba Skinner on the new television series "In the Heat of the Night" and stayed for seven years. From there he starred on another series, "Grace under Fire," for two seasons and then formed his own production company. In 2000, he followed in the footsteps of fellow actor/mayor Clint Eastwood by being elected mayor of Fresno. From growing up as the son of divorced farm workers to the NFL to movies and television to politics—Alan Autry has lived the American dream through hard work and dedication, despite not excelling at anything.

Alan Autry may be the most successful Packer actor, but Green Bay has had its brushes with Hollywood. Curly Lambeau spent increasing amounts of time and money there in the 1930s and 1940s, causing talk that the Green Bay native had "gone Hollywood." A football follies sort of short film called *Pigskin Champions* was released in 1937. It featured the champion Packers in white uniforms cavorting around with a white football while announcer Pete Smith provided a silly voiceover. In 1948, Lambeau announced that a movie called *The Green Bay Story* would be produced that year. Tony Owen, who would produce such 1950s classics as *Traveling Saleswoman, Duel in the Jungle* and *Beyond Mombasa,* even came to Green Bay that summer and was interviewed by the *Green Bay Press Gazette* about the upcoming film. Screenwriter Robert N. Lee was said to be working on the script. Actors being considered supposedly were Dennis O'Keefe, Dennis Morgan, and John Hodiak. Needless to say, most movie proposals are never turned into celluloid and this movie was never produced.

The first successful Packer/actor was Dutch Hendrian who appeared in at least 82 movies although he was uncredited in many of them. He appeared in such films as the *20,000 Years in Sing Sing* (1932) as Prisoner at Rockpile, *Punch Drunks* (1934) as First Plug Ugly, *Navy Blue and Gold* (1937) as Football Official, *Tip-Off Girls* (1938) as wounded thug Dutch, and *Knute Rockne All American* (1940) as Hunk Anderson. Hendrian, who attended four colleges, including Princeton, is remembered as the Packer who brought his dog with him when he joined the team. Dutch's dog was in the team picture for 1925 and on the sideline for games that year. He belonged in Hollywood. Tackle Ernie Smith appeared many times in the 1930s as an extra in movies, as did guard Lon Evans and center Nate Barrager, who forged a career behind the camera as prop man, assistant director,

LITTLE GUYS
ALLEN ROSSUM • KICK RETURNER 2000–01

WHO'S WORN THE NUMBER <Enright 1926>, O'Donnell 1927–28, Lambeau 1929–30, Blood 1931–32, Greeney 1933, Caspar 1934, Sandifer 1952, B. Bailey 1953, D. Miller 1954, Bookout 1955–56, J. Petitbon 1957, Francis 1958–59, Widby 1972–73, Tullis 1978, W. Turner 1979–80, D. Williams 1981, C. Winters 1983, M. Turner 1985, E. Berry 1986, K. Cook 1987, Hargrove 1987r, McGruder 1989, K. Williams 1993, K. Cooks 1998, Rossum 2000–01, M. Anderson 2002.

ORIGINATOR Rex Enright <1926> (see top 15) or end Dick O'Donnell 1927–28 whose greatest moment in his seven years in Green Bay was catching a 35-yard TD pass from Red Dunn with two minutes left to beat the Bears on December 9, 1928.

LONGEST TENURE Dick O'Donnell, Curly Lambeau, Johnny Blood, Billy Bookout, Joe Francis, Ron Widby, Wylie Turner, and Allen Rossum. All spent two years as number 20. Of them, forgettable defensive back Wylie Turner, appeared in the most games in his two years, 28.

NUMBER CHANGES Dick O'Donnell had 5 in <1925–26> and wore 30 in 1929–30; Curly Lambeau had 1 in <1925–26> and wore 14 in 1927 and 42 in 1928; Johnny Blood wore 24 in 1929–30, 14 in 1933, 26 in 35, and 55 in 1936; back Cy Caspar also wore 44 in 1934; defensive back Dan Sandifer wore 23 in 1953; wide receiver Walter Tullis wore 87 in 1979; safety Kerry Cooks also wore 45 in 1998.

OTHER NOTABLES Curly Lambeau (see 1); Johnny Blood (see 55); and Ron Widby who was a decent punter who played a season of professional basketball with New Orleans of the ABA in 1967–68, averaging 2.9 points per game.

ONE TO FORGET Running back Kelly Cook stuck around for 11 games in 1987, rushing two times for three yards and returning 10 kicks for a whopping 14.7-yard average including bobbling one out of bounds at his own one-yard line.

ALLEN ROSSUM Pardon the pun, but in his short time in Green Bay, Allen Rossum had a big impact on the team's fortunes. He is part of an exclusive group of Packers who were small in stature, but persevered to make their mark on team history.

Rossum set an NCAA record with nine returns for touchdowns in his years at Notre Dame. Three were punt returns, three were kick-off returns, and three were from interceptions. The Eagles picked him in the third round in 1998 and he made the team as a return specialist.

In his two years in Philadelphia, Allen fumbled 10 times (although only one was recovered by the other team) and developed a reputation for having poor judgment in returning punts. After the Eagles signed veteran return man Brian Mitchell in 2000, Rossum was expendable and the Packers traded a fifth-round pick for him.

Rossum fit right in and put his past problems behind him. In his first year in Green Bay he was named as an alternate selection to the Pro Bowl after finishing third in the NFC in kickoff returns with a 25.8 yard average and finishing eighth in the conference in punt returns with an 8.6 yard average. His 92-yard kickoff return for a touchdown clinched the win over the Colts and his 90-yard return against the Vikings helped win that game as well. In 2001, he was hampered by injuries for much of the year, but his 55-yard punt return for a touchdown with three minutes left against the Bucs was the game-winning score. He also contributed as a "gunner" or first man down on special teams coverage units and a defensive back in the dime defensive package on passing downs. Like so many players of smaller stature, Rossum was a hustler who was able to compensate for a lack of size with a lot of quickness, speed, and effort. When he moved on to Atlanta as a free agent in 2002, it left a large hole in the Packers' special teams.

Rossum was listed as 5'8", but was probably 5'7 1/2" at best. He was the first Packer to play at under 5'9" since 5'7" Aubrey Matthews. Matthews was a tiny run-and-shoot receiver who passed through Green Bay in 1988 and 1989. In 2002, 5'6" J.J. Moses got a brief two-game shot as kick returner and became the shortest Packer in 75 years. Other 5'8" Packers include returner Vai Sikahema (1991), receiver Clarence Weathers (1990–91), returner Steve Odom (1974–79), guard Earl "Jug" Bennett (1946), guard Pete Tinsley (1938–45), back Paul Fitzgibbon (1930–32), quarterback Charlie Mathys (1922–26), back Eddie Glick (1922), end Herm Martell (1921), and back Art Schmaehl (1921). The only other 5'7" Packers besides Matthews were replacement running back Larry Morris (1987), returner J.R. Boone (1957), back Jack McAuliffe (1926), lineman George Abramson (1925), end Dave Hays (1921–22), and back Ray McLean (1921). Backs Pid Purdy (1926–27) and Marty Norton (1925) were an inch shorter at 5'6". The shortest Packer of all time was co-founder Nate Abrams who was a 5'4" end for one game in the team's first year in the NFL.

Steve Odom had the longest tenure of any of the vertically challenged Packers. He played in Green Bay for six years and was named All Pro in 1975. He ranks with fellow returner Rossum among the best of this group. The other top players here are Charles Mathys who is in the Packer Hall of Fame and guard Pete Tinsley who was a second team All Pro in 1941 and is also in the Packer Hall. Tinsley and Jug Bennett are the very definition of the old term "watch-charm guards," although the shortest lineman in Packer history was George Abramson.

At 178 pounds, Rossum was too muscular to rank among the lightest Packers of all time. The last Packer listed under 170 pounds was 165-pound receiver Jeff Query (1989–91). Other Packers in the 160s include receiver Phil Epps (1982–88), receiver Aubrey Matthews (1988–89), returner J.R. Boone (1957), back Ralph Earhart (1948–49), back Eddie Kotal (1925–29), back Charlie Mathys (1922–26), back Jim Crowley (1925), back Marty Norton (1925–28), back Eddie Glick (1922), end Dave Hays (1921–22), end Herm Martell (1921), back Ray McLean (1921), back Art Schmaehl (1921), and back Buff

Wagner (1921). Steve Odom was only 165 in his rookie year of 1974 but bulked up to 174 for the rest of his career. The only three Packers who weighed under 160 pounds were back Jack McCauliffe at 155 in 1926, Pid Purdy at 145 in 1926–27, and Nate Abrams again at 140 in 1921.

Phil Epps lasted the longest of any of the lightest Packers. The world-class sprinter was able to run away from most danger for seven years in Green Bay and caught 192 passes for 14 touchdowns. He was one of the best players of this group. Again, Steve Odom and Charlie Mathys are included with the top players and back Eddie Kotal, the Lawrence Flash, belongs among the best as well. Kotal was one of the last Packers to play without a helmet. The two lightest linemen both just miss the cutoff here. Center Walter Nieman (1922–24) and tackle Sammy Powers (1921) both may have played at 170 pounds. Some listings have Nieman at 180 and some have Powers at 150. The underpowered Powers lasted only four games. With most linemen around 300 pounds today, football is a different game; however, there is still room for a talented little man, as Allen Rossum has proven.

FOR FURTHER INFORMATION

Cunningham, Michael. "Rossum's Value Difficult to Measure," *Milwaukee Journal Sentinel.* 8/11/01. (1C)

Mertz, Adam. "Rossum's Heroics Are Huge," *Capital Times.* 11/20/00. (1D)

RIVAL LEAGUES
BOB JETER • DEFENSIVE BACK 1963–70

WHO'S WORN THE NUMBER
Lewellen 1927, Nash 1928, R. Baker 1928, J. Evans 1929, Haycraft 1930, Gantenbein 1931–32, Goldenberg 1933, Banet 1937, Tinsley 1938–39 and 1941–45, Sparlis 1946, Cuff 1947, O. Smith 1948–49, DiPierro 1950–51, Jeter 1963–70, Hall 1971–74, Hadl 1975, S. Wagner 1976–79, Jolly 1980, 1982–83, Crouse 1984, Fullwood 1987–90, Fuller 1991, C. Carter 1992, Duckett 1994, C. Newsome 1995–98, G. Berry 2000, Jue 2001–02.

ORIGINATOR Back Verne Lewellen 1927 (see 46).

LONGEST TENURE Bob Jeter 1963–70.

NUMBER CHANGES Verne Lewellen had 4 in <1925–26> and wore 45 in 1928, 31 in 1929–30, and 46 in 1931–32; end Tom Nash wore 19 and 26 in 1929, 37 in 1929–30, and 35 in 1931–32; back Roy "Bullet" Baker also wore 5 and 12 in 1928 and 17 in 1929; end Milt Gantenbein wore 30 and 47 in 1933, 46 in 1933–34, and 22 from 1935–40; blocking back/guard Buckets Goldenberg wore 51 in 1934, 44 in 1935–37, and 43 from 1938–45; quarterback John Hadl wore 12 in 1974; defensive back Charlie Hall wore 44 in 1975–76

OTHER NOTABLES Verne Lewellen (see 46); Tom Nash (see top 19); Milt Gantenbein (see top 22); Buckets Goldenberg (see 43); Pete Tinsley was a 5'8" fireplug who was an anchor on the Packers line for the first half of the 1940s. He was inducted in the Packer Hall of Fame in 1979.

ONE TO FORGET 1987 first-round pick running back Brent Fullwood had enough talent to gain over 800 yards one year and make the Pro Bowl as an alternate, but he never lived up to his potential and ended up rushing for only 1,700 yards in his four years in Green Bay. He once asked his coach Forrest Gregg, "Coach, did you ever play in this league?" He is most remembered for taking himself out of a Bears game in Chicago due to illness and then being seen that night dancing in a Green Bay nightclub. Two days later he was traded to Cleveland for a seventh-round pick and never carried the ball again in the NFL. Fullwood claims that the witnesses lied and he only dropped off his brother-in-law at the club, but he will be a disappointment forever to Packer fans.

BOB JETER In the 1959 Rose Bowl, Iowa rolled over California 38-12. Iowa rushed for 429 yards and was led by junior halfback

Bob Jeter, who set a Rose Bowl record of 194 yards on only 9 carries, including an 81-yard touchdown (another record). After an injury-plagued senior year, Jeter was drafted in the second round of the 1960 draft by Green Bay. Instead, he signed with the British Columbia Lions of the Canadian Football League. It was a decision that would sidetrack his career for several seasons.

After two years in British Columbia, Jeter was traded to the Hamilton Tiger Cats and then was cut in training camp. He came down to Green Bay and was put on the taxi squad for the 1962 season. Vince Lombardi made the same mistake with Jeter that he did earlier with another Big Ten halfback who he didn't think fit the Packer's running style—Herb Adderley. He tried to make wide receivers out of both of them. Fortunately for Adderley, the experiment didn't last too long before he was put at cornerback. Bob Jeter, though, spent two seasons as a reserve receiver before finally being shifted to cornerback in 1965 in his sixth year out of college. He was hurt in the final exhibition game and lost out on the starting job to Doug Hart. By the championship game against the Browns that year, though, he was back in the starting slot, and he made a name for himself in that game by shutting down All Pro wide receiver Paul Warfield. In the next two years he would team with Adderley to shut down the top receivers of many teams.

In the following season of 1966, Jeter picked off five passes and returned two for touchdowns: one for 46 yards against the Colts in the opening game and the other for 75 yards against the Rams in the last game of the year. In that year's title game against the Cowboys, he threw a blanket over Bullet Bob Hayes, and the Packers went on to the first Super Bowl. Cowboys quarterback Don Meredith would say of Jeter that, "In the past, left cornerback Herb Adderley was so good that the opponents picked on Jeter. But now they can't. Jeter has more speed than Adderley and is better at moving up on the end run." The following year, Bob intercepted eight passes, was named All Pro, and went to the Pro Bowl. He was a second-team All Pro in 1968 and went to the Pro Bowl for the 1969 season. He spent one last season in Green Bay before getting into a dispute with new coach Dan Devine in 1971 and being traded to the Bears where he spent the last three years of his career. Although he did not start for the first six years of his career, he was deservedly inducted into the Packer Hall of Fame in 1985.

Jeter was one of a handful of players who rejected Green Bay right from the start. Bob Gain, Randy Duncan, and Bruce Clark were all number-one draft choices of the Packers who went north (or sometimes south) to Canada instead. George Dixon was a 1959 ninth-round Packer pick who became a Hall of Famer in the CFL. Usually it went the other way. Players would wash out in Green Bay and head to Canada. Indian Jack Jacobs, Stan Heath, Al Baldwin, Byron Bailey, Ernie Danjean, Veryl Switzer, Pineapple Joe Francis, Larry Hickman, John McDowell, and Jerry Tagge all failed first in Wisconsin before leaving the country. Jacobs and Bailey would go into the CFL Hall of Fame. Garney Henley was 15th-round choice in 1960 who was cut in training camp and also became a Hall of Famer in the CFL. Urban Henry, Vince Ferragamo, and Henry Burris all came to the Packers from Canada like Jeter, although Henry and Ferragamo had played for the Los Angeles Rams before first heading to the CFL.

All rival leagues to the NFL have had some interaction with the Packers, but usually the effect has been minor. The original American Football League was formed by Red

Grange and his agent C.C. Pyle in 1926 to showcase Grange's talents and make a ton of money. Guard Paul Minick, lineman Dick Stahlman, end Larry Marks, and backs Matt Bross and Marty Norton all played in AFL I for its single year of existence and eventually played for the Packers as they later bounced around the NFL. Grange's own New York Yankee team was admitted to the NFL and lasted two years before folding itself. The Yankee prize for the Packers was Hall of Fame guard Iron Mike Michalske whom they signed as a free agent in 1929. The second and third versions of the AFL each lasted only two years—AFL II in 1936–37 and AFL III in 1940–41. Guard Claude "Cupid" Perry played in AFL II. Center Lee Mulleneaux, brother of Packer Carl Mullenaux, was an All AFL selection for the Cincinnati Bengals in 1937. He played for the Packers in 1938 and then played in AFL III in 1940. Tiny Engebretsen coached the AFL III's Buffalo Tigers in 1941 and his team at times included Johnny Blood. The independent Kenosha Cardinals regularly played against teams in AFL III and also played two exhibition games against Green Bay which they lost by a combined score of 82-2. Their team at times included former Packers Johnny Blood (again) and John Biolo, and future Packers Paul Berezney and Paul Christman.

The All America Football Conference (AAFC) was the next rival league in 1946 and provided a real challenge to the Packers. The post-war Packers could not compete financially against the AAFC teams. They lost their number one pick in 1946, Johnny Strzykalski, and their number one (Ernie Case) and two (Burr Baldwin) picks in 1947 to the AAFC, and then focused on drafting lesser players they thought they could sign in 1948 and 1949. The Packers had little talent worth raiding, but local boy and Packer star Ted Fritsch signed with Cleveland and then changed his mind and jumped right back to Green Bay. In contrast, Glenn Johnson left the AAFC's New York Yankees to join the Packers in 1949. After the AAFC merged with the NFL in 1949, Green Bay picked up some fine players in the dispersal of talent from the folded teams. Kick returner Billy Grimes of the Los Angeles Dons was All Pro in 1950 and both he and defensive end Ab Wimberly, also of the Dons, went to the Pro Bowl. Al Baldwin from the Buffalo Bills had one decent year as a receiver, but former Browns halfback Bill Boedecker had no great impact in his one season in Green Bay.

The most successful rival league was the AFL IV, which operated successfully from 1960 until 1969 when the league fully merged into the NFL. The Packers lost no one of great value from their roster to the AFL. Al Carmichael and Howie Ferguson were former Packers when they signed with the AFL in 1960. Ben Davidson, Howie Williams, and Jan Barrett all ultimately ended up in Oakland, but the best player was Davidson and the Packers had first traded him to Washington. Randy Duncan, the former number one pick who signed instead with the CFL, turned up with the Dallas Texans, but only as a backup. The AFL's biggest effect on Green Bay was in the draft. The Packers could not sign high draft picks Larry Elkins, Jon Morris, Al Dotson, Ode Burrell, and Paul Costa. Of more importance, they lost out on late round sleepers Buck Buchanan, Daryle Lamonica, Jon Gilliam, Gary Cutsinger, Roger Hagberg, Bobby Brezina, Len St. Jean, and Chuck Hurston. Moreover, because of the bidding wars, it cost them a million dollars to sign prize draftees Donny Anderson and Jim Grabowski in 1966. Reacting to the escalating bonuses paid to draft picks and the AFL's initiation of signing raids on NFL quarterbacks, the leagues agreed to merge in 1967.

Rival leagues since 1967 have not been very successful, although the CFL still plods on. The World Football League ran only two years, 1974–45, before going under. Although defensive end Bob Barber came out of the WFL, the main Green Bay connection was in the coaching ranks. Former Packer quarterbacks Perry Moss and Babe Parilli were head coaches in the WFL, as was former Packer assistant Tom Fears. Of most significance, Willie Wood took over the Philadelphia Bell during the 1975 season and thus became the first black head coach of a major league football team.

From 1982 through 1985 the spring football United States Football League tried to go head to head with the NFL. The Packers lost starting defensive end Mike Butler along with kick-blocking tight end Gary Lewis, and lesser lights Allan Clark, Brad Oates, Larry Pfohl, Larry Rubens, and John Thompson to the USFL. Pfohl, the future Lex Luger of the World Wrestling Federation, never actually played for Green Bay, but spent 1982 on Injured Reserve. Those were not devastating losses. Other one-time Packers who went to the USFL included Vickey Ray Anderson, Buddy Aydelette, Bob Barber, Bruce Beekley, Rich Dimler, Kit Lathrop, Mark Miller, Steve Pisarkiewicz, Dave Pureifory, Dave Simmons, Arland Thompson, and Walter Tullis. Aydelette and Lathrop became stars in the new league. When the USFL collapsed, the NFL held a three-round dispersal draft. The Packers had no shot at the biggest prizes—Steve Young, Reggie White, and Gary Zimmerman—but they did pass up receivers Gary Clark and Rickey Sanders, returner Mel Gray, and defensive end William Fuller. Instead they plucked such gems as Buford Jordan, Chuck Clanton, and John Sullivan. Other USFL players who went straight to Green Bay were Mossy Cade, Paul Ott Carruth, Greg Feasel, Nolan Franz, Chuck Fusina, Bobby Leopold, Charles Martin, and Mike Weddington. Chuck Fusina was the All League quarterback of the USFL. Super Bowl tickets will go on sale . . . not quite. Many other former USFL players ultimately passed through Green Bay: Ross Browner, Putt Choate, John Corker, David Greenwood, Joey Hackett, Jim Hargrove, Perry Hartnett, Jerry Holmes, Van Jakes, Ken Johnson, Perry Kemp, Sean Landetta, Van Mansfield, Larry Mason, Aubrey Matthews, Keith Millard, John Miller, Jim Bob Morris, Bob Nelson, Alan Risher, Tommy Robison, Dan Ross, Carl Sullivan, Mickey Sutton, Harry Sydney, and Reggie White. Reggie White? Super Bowl tickets did go on sale after all.

Was the XFL a rival league? That bizarre marriage of wrestling theatrics and professional football was more like an economic and cultural car crash. Former Packers involved included Jahine Arnold, Jonathan Brown, Kerry Cooks, Russell Copeland, Antonio Dingle, Darick Holmes, Leshon Johnson, Charles Jordan, Kivuusama Mays, Basil Mitchell, Roell Preston, Jermaine Smith, Jude Waddy, and James Willis. After its demise, the Packers signed former XFLers Paris Lenon, Kevin Kaesviharn, and Glenn Rountree, but only Lenon made the team. Other football leagues exist today, but not as competitors. The Arena Football League once boasted Packer training camp arm Kurt Warner. So did the NFL's European development league which has been called the World League of American Football, the World League, and now NFL Europe. The Packers send players over almost every year. For example, trackman Bill Schroeder got enough seasoning in Europe to become a starting receiver in Green Bay. The Packers signed journeyman Danny Wuerffel in 2000 after he had led his team to the World League title, which qualified him to be a third-string quarterback in the NFL. With 32 NFL teams, there is only

PACKERS BY THE NUMBERS

so much talent to go around. Still, it wouldn't be surprising for a new rival league to spring up again, although ultimate success is highly unlikely.

FOR FURTHER INFORMATION

Johnson, Chuck. *The Greatest Packers of Them All.* New York: Putnam, 1968. (173-8)

Kramer, Jerry, with Dick Schaap. *Distant Replay.* New York: G.P. Putnam, 1985. (166-8)

Poling, Jerry. *Downfield! Untold Stories of the Green Bay Packers.* Madison, WI: Prairie Oak Press, 1996. (202-4)

FAMILY TIES
LAVVIE DILWEG • END 1927–34

WHO'S WORN THE NUMBER L. Dilweg 1927–34, Gantenbein 1935–40, Pannell 1941–42, 1945, Riddick 1942, D. Evans 1943, Bilda 1944, McKay 1946–47, Rhodemyre 1948–49, Grimes 1950–52, Boone 1953, Papit 1953, B. Roberts 1956, Shanley 1958, Butler 1959, E. Pitts 1961–69, 1971, Staggers 1972–74, M. Lee 1980–90, Billups 1992, McGill 1994–95, B. Brooks 1996–97, D. Holmes 1998, D. Parker 1999–2000, Thibodeaux 2001, Metcalf 2002.

ORIGINATOR Lavvie Dilweg 1929

LONGEST TENURE Cornerback Mark Lee 1980–90 (see Notables below).

NUMBER CHANGES End Lavvie Dilweg also wore 61 in 1934; end Milt Gantenbein wore 21 in 1931–32, 30 and 47 in 1933, and 46 in 1933–34; end Dick Evans wore 53 in 1940; end Ray Riddick wore 5 from 1940–42 and 19 in 1946; halfback Roy McKay wore 3 in 1944–45; center Jay Rhodemyre wore 85 in 1951 and 50 in 1952; returner J.R. Boone also wore 43 in 1953; defensive back Bill Butler also wore 25 in 1959.

OTHER NOTABLES End Milt Gantenbein played the "other" end to Lavvie Dilweg and then Don Hutson so well that he was elected to the Packer Hall of Fame in 1972. He was first team All League once, second team twice, and later coached at Manhattan College; Elijah Pitts was a dependable all-around running back who ran for two touchdowns in the first Super Bowl and was inducted into the Packer Hall of Fame in 1979; Mark Lee was a decent cornerback who played in more games (141) during the nineties than any other Packer.

ONE TO FORGET Lewis Billups played in only five games for the Packers, but earned a whole section to himself in the book *Pros and Cons* by Jeff Benedict and Don Yeager about criminal behavior by NFL players. Billups later did time for a sexual assault and died in an auto accident.

LAVVIE DILWEG LaVern Dilweg was the epitome of the scholar athlete. He graduated from Marquette in his hometown of Milwaukee and then enrolled in the law school there while he took up professional football with the local Milwaukee Badgers in 1926. The team ran into financial difficulties that year and Dilweg's rights were nearly sold to George Halas of the Chicago Bears. Dilweg had no problem with the thought of finishing the season in Chicago, but insisted on being a free agent for the next season so he could return closer to home. Halas would not agree to that, so Dilweg stayed put and signed with Green Bay the next season.

NUMBER 22

In Green Bay, he also began his legal career. He would practice football in the morning and law in the afternoon. He had received some All League consideration in his rookie year in Milwaukee, but in Green Bay he was named All League for his first five years, and then second team for two more years. Only in his final year of 1934 did he not receive any postseason notice. Lavvie had long arms and large hands that he used on defense to ward off blockers. He was a solid wall against the run and was the career league leader in interceptions with 27 when he retired. On offense, even playing for Curly Lambeau who passed more than most, his highest reception total was 25 in the championship year of 1929. Unofficial counts list him with 126 catches for 2,043 yards, a 16.2 yards per catch average, and 12 touchdowns. He also scored twice on interceptions and kicked two extra points for a total of 86 points. Overall, he was consistently excellent, but had no sensational games. Dilweg deserves to be in the Pro Football Hall of Fame as the finest end of his era by far.

He retired after the 1934 season. He would be replaced in the lineup in 1935 by the spectacular offensive force of Don Hutson, who would make it seem as if no one had ever played end before. Since Dilweg worked in the law firm of Gerald Clifford, one of the Hungry Five who managed the team, he took part in one last great event in Packer history. In January 1935 he was the witness as the articles of incorporation for the reorganization of the non-profit Packers were signed by Clifford, Lee Joannes, and Dr. Kelly. Dilweg continued to practice law in Green Bay for several years, but kept busy in other ways as well. He officiated Big Ten football games until 1943. He ran unsuccessful campaigns for state attorney general and U.S. Senator, and then was elected to Congress in 1942. He lost his bid for re-election, but built up a lucrative law practice with his Washington D.C. ties. In 1961 President Kennedy appointed him for a three-year term to the Foreign Claims Settlement Commission and he was reappointed twice by President Johnson. He died just two days after Lombardi's Packers won their third consecutive NFL title in the Ice Bowl, replicating the achievement of the Packers of Dilweg's era. Posthumously, Lavvie Dilweg was a charter inductee into the Packer Hall of Fame in 1970.

Fifty-five years after Lavvie retired and 21 years after he died, another Dilweg wore the green and gold, his grandson Anthony. Anthony Dilweg was a third-round pick in 1989 who made the team as a backup quarterback. His moment of glory came on opening day of 1990 when he got his first NFL start, replacing holdout Don Majkowski, and completed 20 of 32 passes for 248 yards and two touchdowns to upset the Rams 36-24. Later that year he would relieve Majkowski in the fourth quarter against the Cardinals and throw two more touchdown passes to pull out a 24-21 win. By the next year he was out of the league, however. Two father-and-son pairs—the Pitts and the Flanigans—have played for the Packers, and one of the sons played with Lavvie's grandson Anthony. Running back Elijah Pitts would bring his son Ron into the locker room to hang out during the 1960s glory days; in 1988 Ron joined the Packers as a defensive back. He had spent his first two years in Buffalo (where his father was coaching), and would spend the last three years of his career in Green Bay. Jim Flanigan was a rookie linebacker on Lombardi's last title team in 1967. His son, Jim Jr., grew up in the Green Bay area, went to Notre Dame, and then played defensive tackle for seven years for the Chicago Bears. In 2001 he signed with the Packers as a free agent and spent a busy year on the defensive line for his father's team before becoming a salary cap casualty.

These Packers had sons who also played in the NFL:

PACKER	PACKER YRS	HIS SON
Hank Bullough G	1955–58	Chuck Bullough LB
Ted Fritsch FB	1942–50	Ted Fritsch Jr. C
Jim Gillette HB	1947	Walker Gillette WR
Gary Knafelc E	1954–62	Greg Knafelc QB
Bob Kowalkowski G	1977	Scott Kowalkowski LB
Ernie McMillan T	1975	Erik McMillan S
Rich Moore DT	1969–70	Brandon Moore T
George Sauer B	1935–37	George Sauer Jr. WR
Joe Skibinski G	1955–56	John Skibinski FB
Howie Williams DB	1962–63	Gardner Williams DB

These Packers had fathers who also played in the NFL:

PACKER	PACKER YRS	HIS FATHER
Charley Ane C	1981	Charley Ane C
Matt Brock DE	1989–94	Clyde Brock T
Santana Dotson DT	1996–01	Alphonse Dotson DT
Ken Gorgal DB	1956	Alex Gorgal FB
Matt Hasselbeck QB	1999–00	Don Hasselbeck TE
Dave McCloughan DB	1992	Kent McCloughan CB
Rich Moran G	1985–93	Jim Moran DT
Kevin Smith TE	1996	Charley Smith HB
Eric Metcalf PR	2002	Terry Metcalf HB

Five pairs of brothers have played for the Packers. Guards Carl and Marty Zoll played for the team in its first two years in the league although not at the same time. Fifteen years later a third brother, Dick, would play guard for the Rams. Centers George and Bud Svendsen were the first brothers to play together on the Packers, in 1937, but they would not play together in the remainder of their careers. Bud was traded to Brooklyn in 1938, but both were elected to the Packer Hall of Fame. In 1938 both end Carl and center Lee Mulleneaux played in Green Bay, but it would be Lee's only year as a Packer. Carl would stay for several years and go into the Packer Hall of Fame. Back Bob Kahler and his brother Royle, a tackle, were not Hall of Famers or even starters, but they did play together in 1942. Bob would stay for two more years. Linebacker Walt Michaels spent his rookie year, 1951, in Green Bay; 20 years later his brother Lou would spend his last year there as a kicker. In 1966 the Packers drafted Tony Jeter to join his brother Bob, but then traded him to Pittsburgh in training camp before that could happen. Bob Jeter is one of the Packers who had a brother play elsewhere in the NFL:

PACKER	PACKER YRS	HIS BROTHER
Paul Berezney T	1946	Pete Berezney T
Ross Browner DE	1987	Jim DB, Joey DB, and Keith Browner LB
Francis Chesley LB	1978	Al LB and John Chesley TE

PACKERS BY THE NUMBERS

PACKER	PACKER YRS	HIS BROTHER
Bob Cifers HB	1949	Ed Cifers E
Av Daniell T	1937	Jim Daniell T
Harper Davis DB	1951	Art Davis DB
Ty Detmer QB	1992–95	Koy Detmer QB
Greg Feasel T	1986	Grant Feasel C
Bill Forester LB	1953–63	Herschel Forester G
Clyde Goodnight E	1945–48	Owen Goodnight DB
Joey Hackett TE	1987–88	Dino Hackett LB
Jim Hill DB	1972–74	David Hill TE
Tim Huffman T	1981–85	Dave Huffman G
Bob Jeter CB	1963–70	Tony Jeter DE
Carl Jorgensen T	1934	Wayne Jorgensen C
Jim Keane E	1952	Tom Keane DB
Rudy Kuecheberg LB	1970	Bob Kuechenberg G
Gary Lewis TE	1981–84	Darryl Lewis TE
Raleigh McKenzie G	1999	Reggie McKenzie G
Dexter McNabb FB	1992–93	Ed Robinson LB
Rich Moran G	1985–93	Eric Moran T
Dwayne O'Steen DB	1983–84	Bryan Reeves WR
Sterling Sharpe WR	1988–94	Shannon Sharpe TE
Darren Sharper DB	1997–	Jamie Sharper LB
Clifton Taylor FB	1974, 76	Ed Taylor DB
Clarence Weathers WR	1990–91	Robert Weathers FB
Pat West FB	1948	Walt West FB
Doug Widell G	1993	Dave Widell G
Max Zendejas K	1987–88	Luis K and Joaquin Zendejas K
Carl Zoll G	1922	Dick Zoll G
Marty Zoll G	1921	Dick Zoll G

If Tim Hasselbeck ever catches on, then he and his big brother Matt can be added to the above list. The best of all these family pairings was clearly the Sharpe brothers, Sterling and Shannon, who both played at a Hall of Fame level. A little below them, the Sharper brothers, Darren and Jamie, both play at a Pro Bowl level, as did the Browner brothers, Ross and Joey. It's very rare for two members of the same family to experience the same level of success in football. Vince Lombardi's grandson Joe has coached college football and in the XFL; how likely is it that he will surpass the gridiron accomplishments of his grandfather?

FOR FURTHER INFORMATION

Carroll, Bob. "The Best End We Ever Forgot," *The Coffin Corner*. 1986. Available online at www.footballresearch.com/articles/frpage.cfm?topic'lavie.

Johnson, Chuck. *The Greatest Packers of Them All*. New York: Putnam, 1968. (105)

Packers of the Past: A Series of Articles Reprinted from the Milwaukee Journal Sept. 28–Dec. 9, 1965. Milwaukee, WI: Milwaukee Journal, 1965. (8-9)

Porter, David L., ed. *Biographical Dictionary of American Sports: Football.* New York: Greenwood Press, 1987. (142)

Ward, Arch. *The Green Bay Packers.* New York: Putnam, 1946. (59, 86-7)

NO RETURN
TRAVIS WILLIAMS • HALFBACK 1967–70

WHO'S WORN THE NUMBER Woodin 1927–31, Minick 1929, Quatse 1933, Ben Smith 1933, Witte 1934, Mattos 1936, Daniell 1937, Urban 1941, Ohlgren 1942, Kercher 1943, Lankas 1943, D. Perkins 1944, Goodnight 1945–49, Pritko 1949-50, Jansante 1951, Nussbaumer 1951, Sandifer 1953, Capuzzi 1955, Romine 1958, G. Young 1956, Winslow 1960, J. Norton 1963–64, Travis Williams 1967–70, B. Hudson 1972, C. Leigh 1974, T. Randolph 1977, Harvey 1981–83, Clanton 1985, Greene 1986–90, McCloughan 1992, S. Walker 1993, M. Dorsett 1995, Blackmon 1998, B. Jenkins 2001, D. Gordon 2002.

ORIGINATOR Guard Whitey Woodin 1927–31 (see Notables below).

LONGEST TENURE Whitey Woodin 1927–31 and defensive back Tiger Greene 1986–90 who intercepted four passes in five years as a slow backup safety.

NUMBER CHANGES Whitey Woodin wore 9 in <1925–26> and also wore 25 in 1929; guard Paul Minick wore 15 in 1928 and 25 in 1929; tackle Jess Quatse also wore 36 in 1933; defensive end Alex Urban wore 18 in 1944 and 79 in 1945; defensive end Bob Kercher wore 18 in 1944; back Don Perkins wore 53 and 58 in 1943 and 48 in 1945; defensive back Bob Nussbaumer wore 48 in 1946; defensive back Dan Sandifer wore 20 in 1952; defensive back/quarterback Jim Capuzzi wore 26 in 1956; halfback Al Romine wore 85 in 1955; Travis Williams also wore 17 in 1967.

OTHER NOTABLES Whitey Woodin was a consistent, durable, hard-hitting performer on the early Packer lines and was elected to the Packer Hall of Fame in 1973.

ONE TO FORGET Jim Capuzzi showed such promise as a quarterback in 1955 that the Packers moved him to defensive back in 1956 and then moved him out of the NFL in 1957.

TRAVIS WILLIAMS One of the more interesting subplots of Jerry Kramer's diary of the 1967 season, *Instant Replay*, was the pilgrim's progress of rookie speedster Travis Williams from nervous neophyte to the "Roadrunner." Williams was a solidly packed 6'1" 210-pound running back who could run the 100 in 9.3 seconds, but arrived in Green Bay as a raw fourth-round draft choice. The first time he had ever carried a football was as a freshman at Contra Costa Junior College. He transferred to Arizona State and spent two uneventful years there. His first problem in training camp was hanging on to the ball. Vince Lombardi was excited by his talent and speed, calling him the Packers' answer to Cowboy Bob Hayes, but got so frustrated with Williams' fumbling in camp that he had Travis carry a football with him everywhere he went. Something clicked, and he began to get a handle on the ball.

Travis found little to do as a reserve running back in the first half of the year, but it wasn't until the seventh game of the year against the Cardinals on October 30 that he was given a chance as a deep man on the kickoff return team. In that game he gave a glimpse of his spectacular ability by taking a kickoff right up the middle for a 93-yard TD. Two weeks later he returned two first quarter kickoffs by the Browns for touchdowns of 87 and 85 yards. Opposing teams quickly came to the conclusion that it might be smart to kick the ball away from Williams, so he returned only 18 kicks that year. In the next to last game of the year, Travis dropped back four yards deep in his end zone to receive a kick and went 104 yards with it to score his record-setting fourth touchdown of the year. His 41.1-yard average led the league in kickoff returns that year. Even if you took away the 369 yards he gained on his four touchdown jaunts, he still averaged 26.5 yards per try on his other 14 returns. In the first playoff game that year again against the Rams, Travis scored two touchdowns on runs from scrimmage of 46 and two yards to lead the Packers to victory. In the Ice Bowl and Super Bowl II (which occurred on his 23rd birthday) he played sparingly, but he was a major contributor to the championship season. After a rookie year like that, it seemed as if there was no limit to his potential.

Whether it was because of the departure of Lombardi, the overall decline of the team, or personal reasons, Williams never realized the potential he had shown in his first year. In his second season, Travis' kick return average dropped almost in half to 21.4 and his yards per carry from scrimmage went from 5.4 to 1.9. He rebounded a bit in 1969 by leading the team with 536 yards rushing, catching 27 passes, and returning kicks at a 24.6 pace including a fifth TD via a kick return. He even returned a punt for a score that year. He declined again in 1970 and was traded to the Rams. In his only year in Los Angeles he again led the league in kick returns with a 29.7-yard average and scored for a record sixth time. In NFL history, only Ollie Matson, Gale Sayers, and Mel Gray have run as many kickoffs back for touchdowns as Travis. Only the Bears Cecil Turner has ever matched his four-touchdown season. In an exhibition game in 1972, though, he blew out his knee and never played pro football again.

Such is all too often the mercurial career arc of the return specialist. Returners quickly come and go, hoping to leave behind a highlight reel of sensational darts and dashes. According to the Neft and Cohen *Pro Football Encyclopedia*, the first Packer to return a punt for a touchdown was the spectacular Johnny Blood in 1929. However, I found no evidence of this in 1929 game accounts. If not Blood, how about Buckets Goldenberg, who returned a blocked punt 30 yards on October 29, 1933, versus the Eagles? The first full-length punt returned for a TD by a Packer was later that year when Bob Monnett went 88 yards with a Bear punt on December 10, 1933. Long-forgotten back Wuert Engelmann recorded the first kickoff return for touchdown in team history on October 25, 1931, when he went 80 yards against the Providence Steam Roller. Desmond Howard returned the most punts for touchdowns both in a season and as a Packer with three in 1996. Travis Williams obviously holds the team record for most kickoffs returned for touchdown in both a season and as a Packer. He also has the most combined scores on kick and punt returns (six), and was the first Packer to return both a kick and a punt for scores in one season. The first one to score by both punt and kick returns was Andy Uram, who returned a punt 90 yards against Brooklyn in 1941 and a kick 98 yards against the Lions in 1942. Al Carmichael became the first to return a kick 100 yards in 1955, and set a league distance record still unsurpassed by returning a kick 106 yards in 1956 against the Bears. The first Packer to return more than one kick in the same season was again Travis Williams, while Billy Grimes was the first Packer to bring back more than one punt in one year when he scored twice in 1950. Antonio Freeman became the first Packer to score on a punt return in the playoffs when he went 76 yards against Atlanta in 1995. Desmond Howard achieved the only Packer postseason kick return in Super Bowl XXXI and also had a punt return touchdown against the 49ers that year to have the most postseason touchdown returns in team history with two.

These Packers have scored more than once on a return in the regular season:

	PR	KR	Total
Travis Williams	1	5	6
Dave Hampton	0	3	3
Desmond Howard	3	0	3
Steve Odom	1	2	3
Robert Brooks	1	2	3
Roell Preston	1	2	3
Andy Uram	1	1	2
Billy Grimes	2	0	2
Al Carmichael	0	2	2
Willie Wood	2	0	2
Herb Adderley	0	2	2
Jon Staggers	2	0	2
Allen Rossum	1	1	2

By decades, the team has scored on returns:

	PR	KR	Total
1920s	1?	0	1?
1930s	3	1	4
1940s	2	1	3
1950s	6	2	8
1960s	6	8	14
1970s	5	7	12
1980s	4	1	5
1990s	6	7	13
2000s	1	1	2

Travis' numbers make the 1960s the highest scoring decade for Packer special teams. He had the greatest season a kick returner has ever had in his rookie year, but his personal life was haunted by tragedy. Williams had two kids with a third on the way when he first reported to the Packers, and eventually would have seven children with his wife. He and his wife spent his first off-season following Super Bowl II tooling up and down the California coast in a 1951 Jaguar he had purchased. They would stop in a town by the ocean and rent two adjoining rooms, one for them and one for the kids, spend a few days there, and then move on to the next beach town. If ever a player was in need of guidance, it was Travis Williams. He never planned on a life beyond football, so that when his career abruptly ended there was little money saved but a lot of mouths to feed. He worked as a security guard, a truck driver, and a bouncer, but it was never sufficient. The family lost their house, and Travis started to drink heavily. In 1979 he found another man with his wife and assaulted him. Travis ended up in county jail for a year. His wife joined him later that year when she hit and killed a man while driving drunk, and their children went to live with grandparents. In 1985 Travis' wife died from a drug overdose and his mother died from colon cancer. A few months later his sister died from an alcohol-related illness. In the face of this much suffering, Travis ended up homeless on the street, in deteriorating health, drinking heavily. He died of heart failure in 1991 at the age of 45 without a dime in his pocket or a roof over his head in his hometown of Richmond, California. The Packers sent former linebacker Gary Weaver to represent the organization at the funeral, but none of William's old teammates attended. In March 1997 he was inducted into the Packer Hall of Fame in the wake of the first Green Bay Super Bowl triumph since the year of the Roadrunner.

FOR FURTHER INFORMATION

Anderson, Dave. "He Thought Football Was Forever," *New York Times*. 3/5/91. (B9)

Christopulos, Mike. "Travis Williams—The Road Runner," *Green Bay Packers 1968 Yearbook*. (29-31)

Gentile, Domenic, with Gary D'Amato. *The Packer Tapes: My 32 Years with the Green Bay Packers*. Madison, WI: Prairie Oak Press, 1995. (106-8)

Newman, Bruce. "The Last Return," *Sports Illustrated*. 3/11/91. (38-42)

Schaap, Dick, ed. *Instant Replay: The Green Bay Diary of Jerry Kramer*. New York: World Publishing, 1968.

UNDRAFTED FREE AGENTS
WILLIE WOOD • SAFETY 1960–71

WHO'S WORN THE NUMBER B. Jones 1927–28, Blood 1929–30, W. Don Carlos 1931, C. Perry 1932, Sarafiny 1933, Michalske 1934, O'Connor 1935, Laws 1937–45, B. Reid 1952–56, Wood 1960–71, R. McBride 1973, Gray 1975–83, Cade 1985–86, Jakes 1989, Hauck 1991–94, Hayden 1997, Edwards 1999–02.

ORIGINATOR Guard Bruce "Buck" Jones 1927–28 captained the 1925 national champion Alabama team, which won the Rose Bowl, and spent the first two years of his NFL career in Green Bay.

LONGEST TENURE Willie Wood 1960–71.

NUMBER CHANGES Johnny Blood wore 20 in 1931-32, 14 in 1933, 26 in 35, and 55 in 1936; guard Claude Perry wore 26 from 1927–30, 37 in 1929 and 1933, 27 in 1931, 50 in 1934, and 32 in 1935; guard Mike Michalske wore 36 in 1929–30 and 1937, 28 in 1931, 19 and 30 in 1932, 31 in 1933, 63 in 1934 and 33 and 40 in 1935; back Joe Laws wore 38 and 41 in 1934 and 29 from 1935–36; halfback Breezy Reid wore 80 in 1950–51.

OTHER NOTABLES Johnny Blood (see 55); guard Claude Perry (see top 26); guard Mike Michalske (see 33); left-handed Joe Laws was a solid all-around runner, defensive back, and punt returner who was inducted into the Packer Hall of Fame in 1972. He set a league title game record with three interceptions in 1944 and also led the team in rushing that day; safety Johnnie Gray was not as good as Willie Wood, but he was good enough to be elected to the Packer Hall of Fame in 1993.

ONE TO FORGET Cornerback Mossy Cade was obtained for number one and number five draft choices in 1985, but lasted less than two years before getting arrested on sexual assault charges. He served time in prison and never played in the NFL again.

WILLIE WOOD One could argue that the dozen most unlikely Pro Football Hall of Famers are the ones whose careers began after 1935 and who were not drafted by any professional team. Eight of these players arrived in the immediate post-World War II era: tackle Lou Groza, center Frank Gatski, guard Bill Willis, fullback Marion Motley, end Len Ford, fullback Joe Perry, safety Emlen Tunnell, and cornerback Dick "Night Train" Lane. All but Groza and Gatski were black and therefore invisible to the NFL at the time. All but Tunnell and Lane signed with AAFC teams. Tunnell walked into the offices of the New York Giants and talked his way into a tryout. Lane did the same with the Rams. Perry played junior college football, and was spotted playing service ball. The rest all ended up with the Browns. The four later free agents came into the league in the next decade and struggled to find a home. In the sixties, cornerback Willie Brown would sign with Houston and be cut before sticking with Denver and starring with Oakland. Guard Larry Little and center Jim Langer would both fail with the original team that signed them before both succeeded as teammates on the Miami Dolphins. And then there was safety Willie Wood.

Willie Wood grew up in Washington D.C. and went west to college, starting at Coalinga Junior College before ending up at the University of Southern California. At USC Wood was a three-year letterman as a 5'10" running quarterback. His position coach was Al Davis, future owner of the Raiders. Wood broke his collarbone as a senior, and that was the third strike against him. When the NFL draft was held, Willie was ignored as an injured, undersized, black quarterback. He started writing letters to professional teams requesting a tryout, but received no response until Jack Vainisi and Vince Lombardi of the Packers decided to give him a look. Given a chance, he made the Packers in 1960, and it was his good fortune for two reasons. Not only had he gotten in on the ground floor of the Green Bay glory years, but he got to spend two years with one-time free agent Emlen Tunnell, who was winding down his career in Wisconsin. Tunnell, who had been the premier free safety in the league throughout the 1950s and would be the first black inducted into the Hall of Fame, was a generous individual who became both roommate and mentor to Wood. Willie would later say, "Em taught me everything." (Kramer, 162)

Wood made a strong first impression in practice when he laid out Jim Taylor with a solid tackle. Lombardi ordered the play run again, and Willie dropped the larger Taylor again. Lombardi and the whole team were impressed with this little man's toughness. His first appearance on defense came in the sixth game of the 1960 season against Johnny Unitas and the Colts. Starter Jesse Whittenton got hurt and Willie was inserted at left cornerback against All Pro receiver Raymond Berry. Wood repeatedly was beaten and eventually was replaced that day by Dick Pesonen. After the game, Wood was badly shaken and uncertain about his future when Lombardi took him aside and told him to shake it off because he was going to be here as long as the coach was. The coach had good reasons to have confidence in Willie Wood. Although he was not extremely fast, he was very quick and a great leaper—he could dunk a basketball and played pickup hoop games against Elgin Baylor back in D.C. He was said to be able to touch the crossbar of the goal posts with his elbow. Beyond that, he was a smart player and became the surest tackler on the team.

In 1961, Willie won the starting free safety position, replacing the aging Tunnell, and the Packers won their first title in 17 years. Shades of his mentor, he intercepted five passes and led the league in punt returns with a 16.1 average. Two punts he took back for touchdowns. The next year, he led the NFL in interceptions with nine and averaged 11.9 yards per punt return. He also kicked off for the team. Oddly, he was ejected from the 1962 title game when he jumped up quickly to protest a penalty call and accidentally bumped into the official. The most memorable moment of his career came in the first Super Bowl when he intercepted a Len Dawson pass early in the third quarter and returned it 50 yards to the Kansas City five. Elijah Pitts scored on the next play, and the game was essentially over. Wood was later teased about being run down from behind by fellow USC alumnus Mike Garrett, but Willie was never known for his speed and he probably had lost a step by then. Willie is the all-time team leader in most punt returns (187) and most fair catches (102), but after his first five years he wasn't very effective at it. His punt return averages in those first five years were 6.6, 16.1, 11.9, 8.9, and 13.3. After that he never averaged more than 5.3 and his overall average for the last seven years was a pitiful 3.8. As his punt return talents dwindled, though, his safety skills became more highly respected. Wood was named All Pro for the first of six consecutive seasons in 1964. In that same year, he was named to the first of eight straight Pro Bowls. While he never approached Tunnell's 79 lifetime interceptions, Willie is the all-time interception leader for Green Bay with 48 in 12 years, and he returned two of them for touchdowns.

Tunnell started a tradition in Green Bay of high-quality free agent safeties. Wood continued that tradition, and the torch was passed to Johnny Gray in the 1970s, Mark Murphy in the 1980s, and Eugene Robinson in the 1990s. While Wood and Tunnell are the only undrafted Packer players in the Hall of Fame, Green Bay has signed several free agents over the years who have been inducted into the Packer Hall of Fame: tackle Buford "Baby" Ray, fullback Ted Fritsch, fullback Howie Ferguson, safety Johnny Gray, tight end Paul Coffman, fullback Gerry Ellis, and safety Mark Murphy. In the past decade, free agents George Koonce, Bernardo Harris, and Ryan Longwell have all been major contributors to the team. With all the research that goes into the draft each year, it seems less and less likely for an undrafted free agent to achieve stardom. From 1997 through 2001, the Packers signed 46 free agents in the days immediately following the NFL draft. Of those 46, only five made the Packers: Joe Andruzzi, Randy Kinder, Jude Waddy, Basil Mitchell, and Whisper Goodman. They have generally been useful special teams performers, although Andruzzi later started in Super Bowl XXXVI for the Patriots. In 2002, the Packers hit it big with three free agents making the team and contributing to its success—Kevin Barry, Marcus Wilkins, and Tony Fisher. The most likely free agent to make the Hall of Fame next is one who signed but did not stick with Green Bay in 1994—Kurt Warner.

The Packers' greatest free agent, Willie Wood, had the respect of his teammates. Fiery Ray Nitschke said, "I hate to miss a tackle because I know if I do, I'm going to get a dirty look from Willie. He'll kill you with that look." (Kramer, 163) He was a leader on a defense of stars, so it was not surprising that he went into coaching upon retiring as a player after the 1971 season. He served two years as the defensive backs coach in San Diego before becoming the first black head coach of a professional football team with the Philadelphia Bell in the World Football League in 1975. The Bell had a losing record that year before the entire league folded. Willie got a second chance in the Canadian Football League when he took over the Toronto Argonauts from his former teammate Forrest Gregg in 1980. The talent-poor Argos went 6-20 over the next two seasons and Wood was fired. Wood left football for business at that point and moved back to his hometown of D.C. He still returns to Green Bay to watch the Packers and to monitor his area restaurant. He was elected to the Packer Hall of Fame in 1977, and his long-overdue induction to Canton occurred in 1989.

FOR FURTHER INFORMATION

Berghaus, Bob. "Wood Caught Lombardi's Eye," *Milwaukee Journal Sentinel.* 9/6/96. (5)

Gildea, William. "Wood in Hall Will Signal Pack Is Back," *Washington Post.* 8/4/89. (Sports 1)

Johnson, Chuck. *The Greatest Packers of Them All.* New York: Putnam, 1968. (169-71)

Kramer, Jerry, with Dick Schaap. *Distant Replay.* New York: G.P. Putnam, 1985. (160-4)

Maraniss, David. *When Pride Still Mattered: A Life of Vince Lombardi.* New York: Simon and Schuster, 1999. (237-40, 247-8)

Porter, David L., ed. *Biographical Dictionary of American Sports: Football.* New York: Greenwood Press, 1987. (662-3)

Starr, Bart, with Murray Olderman. *Starr: My Life in Football.* New York: William Morrow, 1987. (84-5)

Wood, Willie. "How to Defend Against Passes," *Sport.* 4/65. (114-5)

THE NINETIES AND BEYOND IN A BOX
DORSEY LEVENS • RUNNING BACK 1995–2001

WHO'S WORN THE NUMBER Rosatti 1927, H. Griffin 1928, Woodin 1929, Minick 1929, (Kresky 1930), Englemann 1931–33, L. Evans 1934, Sauer 1935–36, Jankowski 1937, Zupek 1946, P. West 1948, Wizbicki 1950, H. Davis 1951, Losch 1956, Kinard 1957–58, T. Brown 1959, B. Butler 1959, T. Moore 1960–65, Hampton 1969–71, L. Goodman 1973–74, Huckleby 1980–85, Weigel 1987r, P. Collins 1988, V. Clark 1991–92, M. Oliver 1993, Levens 1995–01.

ORIGINATOR Tackle Rosey Rosatti 1927 who attended three colleges and played for three NFL teams.

LONGEST TENURE Dorsey Levens 1995–01.

NUMBER CHANGES Rosey Rosatti had 12 in <1926>; Whitey Woodin had 9 in <1925–26> and also wore 23 from 1927–31; guard Paul Minick wore 15 in 1928 and 23 in 1929; back Wuert Englemann wore 33 in 1930; guard Lon Evans wore 17 in 1933, 65 in 1934, 46 in 1935, 51 in 1936, and 39 in 1937; George Sauer switched to 17 in 1937; Ed Jankowski wore 7 from 1938–41; defensive back Bill Butler also wore 22 in 1959.

OTHER NOTABLES Guard Whitey Woodin (see top 23); guard Lon Evans (see top 39); halfback George Sauer was an All American at Nebraska before spending three years in Green Bay. After his playing career ended, Sauer coached college football and served as a pro football executive. His son George Jr. starred with the Jets in the 1960s. Fullback Ed Jankowski was a first-round draft choice who spent five years with the Packers before World War II. He was elected to the Packer Hall of Fame in 1984. Halfback Tom Moore was also a number one pick and spent most of his career backing up Hornung and Taylor, but was always ready when he got his chances.

ONES TO FORGET Halfback Jack Losch was a first-round flop in 1956, averaging 2.3 yards per carry in his one year in the league and then went into the Air Force. A Williamsport, PA, native, Losch was the star of the Maynard Midgets who won the first Little League World Series in 1947. Cornerback Vinnie Clark was also a first-round flop in 1991, but he lasted two years in Green Bay and six years in the league.

DORSEY LEVENS The essence of Dorsey Levens was displayed at the end of the 2001 season when the eight-year veteran took on the

NUMBER 25

job of kick returner and despite lacking breakaway speed did the best job of any Packer returner for the year. Whatever the team needs, Dorsey will attempt. In high school, he shared the starting running back position. At Notre Dame, he worked his way up the depth chart until briefly reaching the top as a sophomore and immediately suffered a knee injury. After a dispute, he transferred to Georgia Tech and finally got a chance to play in his senior year.

Drafted in the fifth round by Green Bay, he sat on the bench in his rookie year before winning the starting fullback job in 1995. However, his total of 120 rushing yards was the lowest amount for any number two back in team history. Replaced by sturdier blocker William Henderson in 1996, Levens found a niche as a change of pace for starter Edgar Bennett. In 1996, he gained 566 yards on the ground and caught 31 passes. He had his coming out party in the NFC Championship game when he gained 205 yards running and receiving in leading the Pack to an easy triumph. After breaking a 35-yard run on a third and one, Dorsey electrified the crowd on the next play by leaping over the tight coverage of Eric Davis and landing in bounds to make a spectacular 29-yard touchdown grab in the second quarter. In the third quarter he helped close out the win by smartly following his blocks on a 66-yard screen play that led to the Packers' final touchdown of the day. He was also the team's leading rusher in the Super Bowl victory over New England.

When Bennett went down in the 1997 preseason, Levens grabbed the opportunity in his free agent year and showed that he was Bennett's superior, gaining 1,435 yards rushing (second in team history) and catching 53 passes. Much was made at the time of how he seemed to get stronger as the game went on, picking up a large share of his yards in the fourth quarter. However, that's an illusion attributed to many running backs. Usually it's more a case of the defense running out of gas as the game goes on. It's the late running game that allows a team to put the other team away, and that's what the two 1990s Super Bowl teams could do.

His success fell apart too quickly, though. A lengthy holdout in 1998 was followed by a severe ankle injury. Dorsey finally made it back by the end of the year, but the Packers made a quick exit in the playoffs. More injuries have followed in each year since, although Dorsey did gain 1,000 yards on the ground again in 1999. He was supplanted by Ahman Green in 2000 and took a large pay cut to return as a backup in 2001. At one time it seemed a cinch that Dorsey would pass John Brockington's 5,024 rushing yards and trail only Jim Taylor in Packer records. However, he gained less than 400 yards in the millennium and still trailed third-ranking Tony Canadeo's 4,197 yards when he left as a free agent in 2002 and signed with the Eagles.

Dorsey has been a popular player for a number of reasons. He ran hard and bounced off of people, making him hard to tackle. He was a terrific outlet receiver to keep the chains moving when no one else could get open. He was quiet, consistent, and savvy. Besides Brett Favre and Reggie White, what made the Packers winners again in the 1990s were players like Dorsey Levens, well-coached, disciplined guys who would do whatever it took to help their team win. And the Packers won a lot in this last decade:

PACKERS BY THE NUMBERS

 THE PACKERS IN THE 1990s

DECADE HEADLINE: Wolf Pack

WHERE THEY PLAYED: Lambeau Field (known as City Stadium 1957–64), 1957–; County Stadium in Milwaukee, 1953–1994.

HOW THE GAME WAS PLAYED: The West Coast ball control short passing offense is countered by the Zone Blitz and a host of other clever defensive schemes. In the 1990s and beyond the coaches have taken over the game completely, running it as a chess match of situational substitutions and variations on variations of plays and schemes. Wherever he is, Lombardi can probably be heard screaming in front of the television.

DECADE WON LOST RECORD: 93-67 .581 + 9-5 in the playoffs; 33-15 .688 in 2000-02 plus 1-2 in the playoffs.

RECORD AGAINST THE BEARS: 13-7; 5-1 in 2000-02.

RECORD AGAINST THE LIONS: 13-9 (including 2-0 in the playoffs); 5-1 in 2000–02.

RECORD AGAINST THE VIKINGS: 8-12; 4-2 in 2000–02.

RECORD AGAINST THE COWBOYS: 1-9 (including 0-3 in the playoffs).

RECORD AGAINST THE 49ERS: 6-2 (including 3-1 in the playoffs); 3-0 (including 1-0 in the playoffs) in 2000–02.

PLAYOFF APPEARANCES: 1993, 1994, 1995, 1996, 1997, 1998, 2001, 2002.

CHAMPIONSHIPS: 1996 season.

UNSUNG HERO: Bob Harlan joined the Packers organization in the Devine regime and slowly worked his way to the top. In 1991 he hired Ron Wolf and smartly stepped out of the way as Wolf brought the team back to prominence.

HEAD COACHES: Lindy Infante, 1988–91, 10-22 for the decade; Mike Holmgren, 1992–98, 75-37; Ray Rhodes 1999, 8-8; Mike Sherman 2000–02, 33-15.

BEST PLAYER: Brett Favre obviously, but he was ably supported by Reggie White and Sterling Sharpe.

HALL OF FAMERS: None yet, but Favre and White are first-ballot sure things. Sharpe would have had a Hall of Fame career if he hadn't been forced to retire in his prime from a neck injury.

PACKER HALL OF FAMERS: Johnny Holland, Mark Murphy, and Sterling Sharpe, but many will follow.

LEAGUE LEADERS: Robert Brooks—kickoff return avg 1993; Brett Favre—passing yards 1995, 98, 99; passing % 1998; passing TDs 1995, 96, 97; Antonio Freeman—receiving yards 1998; Desmond Howard—punt return avg 1996; punt return yards 1996; punt return TDs 1996; Sterling Sharpe—catches 1992, 93; receiving yards 1992; receiving TDs 1992, 94; Darren Sharper—interceptions 2000; Reggie White—sacks 1998.

AWARD WINNERS: Brett Favre—Most Valuable Player 1995, 96, 97; Offensive Player of the Year 1995, 96; Desmond Howard—Super Bowl MVP 1996; Reggie White—Defensive Player of the Year 1995, 98.

ALL PROS: James Campen, 1990; Sterling Sharpe, 1990, 92, 93; Chuck Cecil, 1992; Jackie Harris, 1992; Leroy Butler, 1993, 96, 97, 98; Chris Jacke, 1993; Reggie White, 1993, 94, 95, 96, 97, 98; Bryce Paup, 1994; Robert Brooks, 1995; Mark Chmura, 1995; Brett Favre, 1995, 96, 97; Desmond Howard, 1996; Eugene Robinson, 1996; Doug Evans, 1997; Craig Hentrich, 1997; Travis Jervey, 1997, 98; Dorsey Levens, 1997; Brian

Williams, 1997; Antonio Freeman, 1998; Roell Preston, 1998; Frank Winters, 1999; Ryan Longwell, 2000; Darren Sharper, 2000.

PRO BOWLERS: Sterling Sharpe, 1990, 92, 93*, 94*; Chuck Cecil, 1992; Leroy Butler, 1993, 96, 97, 98; Reggie White, 1993, 94*, 95, 96, 97*, 98; Bryce Paup, 1994; Mark Chmura, 1995, 97, 98; Brett Favre, 1992, 93, 95, 96, 97*, 2001*, 2002*; Keith Jackson, 1996; Frank Winters, 1996; Travis Jervey, 1997; Dorsey Levens, 1997; Antonio Freeman, 1998; Roell Preston, 1998; Darren Sharper, 2000, 02; Bubba Franks, 2001, 02; Ahman Green, 2001, 02; Marco Rivera, 2002; Donald Driver, 2002. (* selected, but did not play)

BEST OFFENSIVE BACKFIELD: 1996, Brett Favre; QB, Edgar Bennett spelled by Dorsey Levens, RB; William Henderson, FB; Antonio Freeman, FL.

BEST DRAFT CHOICE: Dorsey Levens 1994 5th round or Mark Chmura 1992 6th round. Wolf had a special feel for round #3 picking Robert Brooks in 1992, Earl Dotson in 1993, William Henderson, Brian Williams and Antonio Freeman in 1995, Mike Flanagan and Tyrone Williams in 1996, Brett Conway in 1997, Jonathan Brown in 1998, Mike McKenzie and Cletidus Hunt in 1999, Steve Warren in 2000, and Bhawoh Jue and Torrance Marshall in 2001.

BEST OVERALL DRAFT: 1995, Craig Newsome in the 1st; Darius Holland, William Henderson, Brian Williams and Antonio Freeman in the 3rd; Travis Jervey in the 5th; and Adam Timmerman in the 7th. 1990 also was very good with Tony Bennett and Darrell Thompson in the 1st, Leroy Butler in the 2nd, Jackie Harris in the 4th; and Bryce Paup in the 6th, plus Bobby Houston in the 3rd, Charles Wilson in the 5th, and Lester Archambeau in the 7th. Unfortunately, Bennett, Paup, and Harris all left as soon as they attained free agent status.

WORST DRAFT CHOICES: Cornerback Vinnie Clark was taken #1 in 1991 and never panned out; neither did John Michels taken #1 in 1996.

WORST OVERALL DRAFT: 1991, aside from Vinnie Clark, the only others to make the team were defensive linemen Esera Tualo and Don Davey and fullback Chuck Webb. No studs there.

BEST FREE AGENT: Gilbert Brown was drafted by the Vikings, waived and signed by the Packers; Ryan Longwell was a 49er free agent who was cut and then signed by the Packers.

BEST TRADE: 1992 brought one of the best trades in the history of the league: Brett Favre from the Falcons for a #1 that Atlanta traded to Dallas and was used to pick cornerback Kevin Smith. Ron Wolf of course swung many good deals in his nine years. Keith Jackson and Mark Ingram from the Dolphins for a #2 in 1995. Getting a #5 from the Bucs for Vince Workman in 1992 and turning it into Mark Brunell who was then traded to Jacksonville in 1995 for a #3 (William Henderson) and a #5 (Travis Jervey). Trading Matt Labounty to the Seahawks for Eugene Robinson in 1996. In the new millennium, he sent Fred Vinson and a #6 to the Seahawks for Ahman Green and a #5, got Allen Rossum from the Eagles for a #5 (Tony Stewart) and traded a #4 to the Broncos for Nate Wayne. Wolf knew talent and wasn't afraid to pull the trigger.

WORST TRADE: Nothing earthshaking. The 1999 trade of John Michels to the Eagles for Jon Harris was essentially a deal of number one draft choice flops to save each team the embarrassment of having to cut their own former top pick. Ironically, the Packer coach in 1999 was the Eagle coach who drafted Harris, Ray Rhodes. Neither man made the roster of his new team either.

PACKERS BY THE NUMBERS

BIGGEST OFF-FIELD EVENT: True free agency is achieved by the players. Signing Reggie White makes it a plus for the Packers. Of course, on-field success combined with the salary cap means a constant turnover of good players seeking greener paychecks elsewhere.

BIGGEST ON-FIELD DEVELOPMENT: The Packers become unbeatable at home winning 25 home games in a row from 1995 through 1998.

STRANGEST ON-FIELD EVENTS: On the good side is the Lambeau Leap started by Leroy Butler and perfected by Robert Brooks. On the negative is Sterling Sharpe's threatened walkout over salary issues at the start of the 1994 season.

WORST FAILURE: To hold on to Holmgren, especially in light of Wolf's retirement a mere two years later.

HOME ATTENDANCE: 4, 627,928 in 80 games for an average attendance of 57,849; for the 16 home games in 2000–01 the average attendance was 59,824. From 1990 through 1994, Milwaukee average attendance was 52,850 while Green Bay's was 57,259. The last Packer home game in Milwaukee was on December 18, 1994, ending a 61-year tradition that the Packers had outgrown.

FIRST GAME: September 9, 1990. The Packers beat the Rams 36-24 in a match between two teams that would finish 6-10 and 5-11. The new millennium began with Mike Sherman's first game on September 3, 2000 with a 20-16 comeback loss to the Jets.

LAST GAME: January 2, 2000 marked the last game of the 1999 season and of Ray Rhodes' short tenure—a 49-24 victory over the hapless Cardinals in which the 8-8 Packers tried to roll up the score to win a potential tiebreaker showdown for the playoffs. They didn't deserve it and they didn't make it. The last game actually played in the 1990s was a 29-10 loss to Tampa the week before December 26, 1999.

BEST GAME: On Christmas Eve 1995, the Packers delivered an early Christmas present to their fans by beating the Pittsburgh Steelers 24-19 to win their first Division title in 23 years. The see-saw game went right down to last minute when normally reliable Steeler receiver Yancy Thigpen dropped a fourth down touchdown pass to clinch the Packer victory. A second game of great satisfaction was on November 23, 1997 when the Packers finally got to play the hated Cowboys in Green Bay after losing 7 straight (including 3 playoff games) contests in Dallas. The Packers physically pounded the Cowboys, beating them convincingly 45-17.

LARGEST MARGIN OF VICTORY: 40-3 over the Bears 12/11/94 and 37-0 over the Redskins 9/24/01.

LARGEST MARGIN OF DEFEAT: 31-0 to the Eagles 12/16/90.

BEST OFFENSE: 1996, 456 points, tops in the league.

BEST DEFENSE: 1996, 210 points allowed, tops in the league and also #1 in fewest yards allowed.

MOST GAMES PLAYED: 156, Leroy Butler.

MOST POINTS: 712, Chris Jacke.

MOST FIELD GOALS: 151 out of 196, Chris Jacke.

MOST TOUCHDOWNS: 52, Sterling Sharpe.

MOST TOUCHDOWN PASSES: 235, Brett Favre; + 79 in 2000–02.

MOST PASSING YARDS: 30, 284, Brett Favre; + 11,391 in 2000–02.

MOST RECEIVING YARDS: 5,920, Sterling Sharpe.

MOST RECEPTIONS: 450, Sterling Sharpe.

MOST RUSHING YARDS: 3,548, Dorsey Levens;

MOST INTERCEPTIONS: 36, Leroy Butler.

MOST SACKS: 68.5, Reggie White.

MOST KICKOFF RETURN YARDS: 1,708, Roell Preston.

MOST PUNT RETURN YARDS: 968, Desmond Howard.

BEST BOOKS: What a rich selection: Vernon J. Biever, *The Glory of Titletown: The Classic Green Bay Packers Photography of Vernon Biever*, Taylor Publishing, 1997. Gary D'Amato and Cliff Christl, *Mudbaths and Bloodbaths: The Inside Story of the Bears-Packers Rivalry*, Prairie Oak Press, 1997. Eric Goska, *Packer Legends in Facts: Your Most Accurate Source of Stats, Rosters, Team History and All Team Photos of the Green Bay Packers 1919–1995*, Tech/Data Publications, 1995. Ed Gruver, *The Ice Bowl: The Cold Truth About Football's Most Unforgettable Game*, McBooks Press, 1998. David Maraniss, *When Pride Still Mattered: A Life of Vince Lombardi*, Simon and Schuster, 1999. Dick Schaap, *Green Bay Replay: The Packers Return to Glory*, Avon Books, 1997.

NOTED SPORTSWRITER: Chris Havel of the *Green Bay Press Gazette* seems to have a special pipeline to Favre, having ghostwritten his autobiography. While he can be a bit of an apologist for Brett, the quarterback's perspective often is one we want to hear.

BEST QUOTATION: "When we hired Mike as coach, I could tell he liked the history involved here. He and I knew we had a unique situation. Because the franchise is publicly owned, we didn't have an owner looking over our shoulders. The only two who could mess up this situation were Mike and me."—Ron Wolf "It's an experience that's hard to describe as the coach of that team in that stadium because of the size of the city and the history and tradition of the place. It's one of the best coaching jobs in the world. There's not another team in the NFL like it."—Mike Holmgren

BUBBLEGUM FACTOID: Esera Tualo's 1991 Pinnacle card says, "The tenor has sung the 'Star Spangled Banner' at Oregon State football and basketball games, Portland Trail Blazers basketball games, and, this season, before the Packers game against the Bears...The Tacklin' Tenor is a pretty fair football player, too." Rich Moran's 1992 Bowman card puns, "Moran was born in Moscow, ID—which may explain why he is such a key component of the Packers' 'rushin' game.'" John Jurkovic's 1994 Topps card gives meta info, "Off the field, John's a card collector."

UNUSUAL NAMES: Lester Archambeau, Sanjay Beach, Dirk Borgognone, Shannon Clavelle, Najeh Davenport, Na'il Diggs, Kabeer Gbaja-Biamila, Antonio Dingle, Vonnie Holiday, Darius Holland, Tunch Ilkin, KeShon Johnson, LeShon Johnson, Bhawoh Jue, John Jurkovic, Matt LaBounty, Paris Lenon, Bill Maas, Bryce Paup, Roell Preston, Vai Sikahema, Kittrick Taylor, Esera Tualo, Lance Zeno.

NICKNAMES: Edgar "Emmitt" Bennett, Tony "Alligator" Bennett, Corey "Louisiana Lightning" Bradford, Robert "Shoo-in" Brooks, Gilbert "The Gravedigger" Brown, Terrell "T-Buck" Buckley, Mark "Chewy" Chmura, Chris "Darkside" Darkins, Ty "Chicken Legs" Detmer, Earl "The Big E" Dotson, Santana "Sack-Tana" Dotson, Antuan "The Truth" Edwards, Brett "Country" Favre, Bubba Franks, Herbert "Whisper" Goodman, William "Boogie" Henderson, Darius "Man Child" Holland, Vonnie "Chocolate Thunder" Holliday, Cletidus "Big Block" or "Nuke" Hunt, Keith "K-Jack" Jackson, Travis "Flash" Jervey,

Chucky Jordan, Blair "Popeye" Kiel, Bob "Scooby" Kuberski, Dorsey "The Horse" Levens, Russell "The Conscience" Maryland, Jim "Mad Mac" McMahon, Steve "Mongo" McMichaels, Rick "Oscar" Mirer, Jim "Smells" Morrisey, Andre "Bad Moon" Rison, Tootie Robbins, Eugene "The Prophet" Robinson, Wayne "Big Money" Simmons, William "Mickey" Sutton, Ed "The Tool Box" West, Reggie "The Minister of Defense" White, Gabe "Big Willie" Wilkins, Frankie "Bag of Donuts" Winters.

FASTEST PLAYER: Don Beebe.

HEAVIEST PLAYER: Gilbert Brown, 335 at his best and at his worst 380 or more until he ate himself out of the league.

LIGHTEST PLAYER: Perry Kemp, 5'11" 170 lbs.

TOUGHEST INJURY: Robert Brooks was never the same after tearing his ACL in 1997. Mark Chmura had back problems before he had legal problems. Aaron Taylor tore up both knees before his career even started. Mark D'Onofrio career never did start. Johnny Holland was forced to retire by injury. However, Sterling Sharpe's retirement due to neck injury was the costliest of all.

LOCAL BOYS: Kevin Barry, Dan Davey, Jeff Dellenbach, Bill Schroeder, and Mark Tauscher are all from in-state. Jim Flanagan was born and raised in Green Bay from when his father played for Lombardi's Packers.

FIRSTS:

> **Postseason Punt Return TD**—12/31/95 Antonio Freeman 76 yards against Atlanta
>
> **Postseason Kickoff Return TD**—1/26/97 Desmond Howard 99 yards against New England.
>
> **Trip to the Super Bowl in 29 Years**—1997.
>
> **Victory over the Cowboys in the Decade**—11/23/97 45-17.
>
> **Time in 62 years All Home Games Played in Green Bay**—1995.
>
> **Division Championship in 23 Years**—1995.
>
> **Stock Sale in 47 Years**—1998.
>
> **Shareholders Meeting Held in Lambeau Field**—1998.
>
> **Trip Overseas in 66 Years**—1998 American Bowl preseason game in Japan.
>
> **Black Head Coach with Two Black Coordinators**—1999, Ray Rhodes, Sherman Lewis, and Emmitt Thomas.
>
> **Jersey (Not Number) Retired**—Reggie White.
>
> **Home Playoff Loss**—2003.
>
> **Loss by Brett Favre at Home When the Temperature Was Below 34 Degrees**—2003.

SUPER BOWL II
HERB ADDERLEY • CORNERBACK 1961–69

WHO'S WORN THE NUMBER Perry 1927–30, Nash 1929, Herber 1931, Van Sickle 1933, F. Butler 1934, Blood 1935, Sturgeon 1937, B. Forte 1946, Kelley 1949, Pelfry 1952, Pearson 1952, G. Dawson, 1953, Capuzzi 1956, Gorgal 1956, Adderley 1961–69, W. Walsh 1972, Torkelson 1974–79, 1981, T. Lewis 1983–86, Jay 1987r, Cecil 1988–92, D. Thompson 1994, M. Collins 1997, Swiney 2002.

ORIGINATOR Tackle/Guard Claude "Cupid" Perry 1927–30 was a teammate of Bruce Jones in high school, college and on the Packers. Cupid later played in the AFL II.

LONGEST TENURE Herb Adderley 1961–69.

NUMBER CHANGES Claude Perry wore 37 in 1929 and 1933, 27 in 1931, 24 in 1932, 50 in 1934, and 32 in 1935; end Tom Nash wore 19 in 1928–29, 37 in 1929–30, and 35 in 1931–32; tailback Arnie Herber also wore 12 in 1930, 41 in 1932–33, 16 in 33, 45 and 68 in 1934, 38 from 1935–40, and 19 in 1937; guard Clyde Van Sickle wore 31 and 57 in 1932; center Frank Butler also wore 60 in 1934, 48 in 1935–36, 59 in 1936 and 35 in 1938; halfback Johnny Blood wore 24 from 1929–30 and 55 in 1936; defensive back Bob Forte wore 8 in 1946–50; end Ray Pelfry wore 8 in 1951; defensive back/quarterback Jim Capuzzi wore 23 in 1955; running back Darrell Thompson wore 39 from 1990–93.

OTHER NOTABLES End Tom Nash (see top 19); Arnie Herber (see 16); Johnny Blood (see 55); cornerback Tim Lewis had his promising career abruptly ended by a neck injury; Chuck Cecil was a slow, but hard-hitting safety popular with the fans.

ONE TO FORGET Darrell Thompson was a first-round flop in 1990. He stuck with the team for five years but rushed for only 1,641 yards and an average of just 3.5 yards per carry. He ran for 100 yards in a game only once in his career.

HERB ADDERLEY There's a tendency when talking about great players from the past to extol their virtues to such a great degree that it sounds as if they never made a bad play and were never out of position. Herb Adderley is usually ranked in the top 5-10 cornerbacks of all time, but he was sometimes beaten for touchdowns, too. In the 1965 season, he gave up no touchdown passes in his area all year, and then was beaten to the outside by Gary Collins in the first quarter of the title game against the Browns. Herb had been quoted the week before saying that Collins always went to the post and never to the corner. Of course all Herb's peers gave up scores, too: Night Train Lane, Willie

NUMBER 26

Brown, Lem Barney, Mel Blount, Rod Woodson, and Deion Sanders. "If you never make a mistake, you ought to be a coach," Adderley said. Usually teams would avoid throwing into the area covered by any of these All Pros because the risk of an interception was just too great.

Adderley was drafted first by the Packers in 1961 as a running back from Michigan State. Vince Lombardi didn't think Herb's outside running skills fit in with the style of the Packer running game so he tried to make a flanker out of Adderley. Midway through the season, the transition was not going smoothly, so Lombardi asked veteran Emlen Tunnell to find out if anything was troubling the rookie. Tunnell reported back to Lombardi that Adderley wanted to play defense. When cornerback Hank Gremminger went down with an injury in the Thanksgiving game against Detroit, Adderley replaced him in the lineup and showed an instinctive grasp of the position. By 1962, Herb was starting at cornerback and Gremminger moved to safety.

There is a temptation to compare Adderley to the more contemporary Deion Sanders because the two have a lot of similarities. Both were tall, fast, and shifty runners. Both played in the league for 12 years and intercepted 48 passes. Both returned those picks for an average of over 20 yards, ranking one and two in NFL history of those who intercepted more than 40 passes. Both thrived on man-to-man coverage and were rarely beaten. Both liked to jaw with receivers, telling them that they wouldn't be catching anything today. Both liked to bait quarterbacks by playing off the receiver a bit to try to draw a throw that could be batted away or intercepted. Among the two Hall of Famers though, Adderley was the more complete player. He came up to play the run very well and was known as a hard-hitter who would lay out receivers.

Above all, Herb was a big-play guy. In the first Detroit game of 1962, the Packers were trailing 7-6 in the final minute when Herb picked off a Milt Plum pass at midfield and returned it 30 yards to set up a last-second, game-winning field goal. In 1963 Herb blocked a last-minute potential game-winning field goal against Minnesota and Hank Gremminger ran the block back for a clinching touchdown. In 1965, he returned three interceptions for touchdowns. tying a record achieved earlier in the decade by Dick Harris of the Chargers and Dick Lynch of the Giants and later surpassed by Ken Houston of the Oilers, Jim Kearney of the Chiefs, and Eric Allen of the Eagles. In all, he scored on seven of his 39 interceptions as a Packer, setting the league mark that would be surpassed two years later by Ken Houston's nine (in turn surpassed by Rod Woodson's 10 as of 2001). Herb had a nose for the ball and could turn around a game in a moment. As Bart Starr put it, "After a few years, opponents just quit challenging him." (Starr, 86) He also returned two kickoffs for scores and ended up with a career kick return average of 25.7 yards.

That big-play ability showed up in Super Bowl II against the Raiders following the 1967 season, which had been a rough one for the aging Packers. Starr in particular was injured throughout the year, and many games were a struggle. However, the team was 9-2-1 and had clinched their division before dropping the last two games of the year to the Rams and Steelers. The playoffs were expanded that year so that Green Bay would have to win twice just to get to the Super Bowl. The first playoff game was against Rams in Milwaukee. The Rams were young and had lost only one game all year. After turning the ball over to Los Angeles three times in the first 16 minutes, the Packers settled down and rolled over the confident Rams 28-7, outgaining them by 150 yards. The Packers returned to Lambeau Field the following week to defeat the Cowboys in the Ice Bowl (see 76), and then traveled south to Miami to meet the Raiders.

It was fitting that Lombardi should win his final title against Oakland. The Packers later would be dubbed the "Pride and Poise Boys" because the Packers under Vince were known especially for those two qualities. The game itself had some similarities to the first Super Bowl from the previous year. The Packers felt out the Raiders in the first half, maintaining a slight edge, and then pulled away in the second half. Green Bay drove to a couple of field goals by controlling the ball for 12 1/2 of the game's first 18 minutes. After stopping Oakland on a three-and-out series, Green Bay got the ball back at its 38 with 11 minutes left in the half. Starr sensed a blitz on first down and audibled to weak side pass play to Dowler who got past the secondary and caught an easy 62-yard touchdown pass to push the lead to 13-0. To their credit, the Raiders answered with a 78-yard scoring drive that culminated with a 23-yard pass to Bill Miller to make the score 13-7. After a bad kickoff return and a sack of Starr, Donny Anderson had to punt from his own end zone. The Raiders got the ball on the Packer 40, but couldn't move and George Blanda missed a 47-yard field goal. Willie Wood returned the missed field goal to the eight and the Packers again had to punt three plays later with 23 seconds left. Anderson's punt was muffed by Rodger Bird and Dick Capp recovered for Green Bay at the Oakland 45. Starr completed a nine-yard pass to Dowler, and Chandler kicked a 43-yard field goal to take the Packers into the half with a 16-7 lead.

In the third quarter, the Packers put the game out of reach. A two-yard Anderson touchdown run was set up by Max McGee's final catch as a pro. Dowler was momentarily shaken up, so Max went in and caught one of Bart Starr's patented third-and-one surprise passes for a 35-yard gain. The Packers drove to a fourth Chandler field goal on their next possession and ended the third quarter up 26-7. Adderley applied the final touches to the victory by picking off a pass intended for Fred Biletnikoff and returning it 62 yards for a touchdown. The Raiders, who would gain 180 of their 293 yards in the fourth quarter after the game was already decided, would add a late touchdown on another pass to Miller, but the final score was a convincing 33-14 Packers win. In Vince Lombardi's last game as Packer coach, the offense controlled the ball for 35:38 and won the team's third straight title. Vince would retire less than three weeks later.

Herb Adderley revered Lombardi. Years later he would answer teammate Jerry Kramer's question of whether he still thought of the late coach by saying, "Every day. And I love my father who is also deceased, but I don't think about my father every day." (Kramer, 166) However, problems arose in the next couple of years under new head coach Phil Bengtson. Adderley got angry when he was left off the Pro Bowl roster in favor of teammate Bob Jeter after the 1969 season. Herb blamed Bengtson, although coaches could not vote for or against their own players, and he sparked a 1970 trade to the Dallas Cowboys to play under Lombardi's old rival, Tom Landry.

Reports were that Landry was not happy about any of the former Packers that general manager Tex Schramm was collecting in Dallas—Lee Roy Caffey and Forrest Gregg were brought in the following year. Adderley started two years in Dallas, and the team would go to the Super Bowl both years, winning it in 1971. Cowboy teammate Pat Toomay credits Herb with not only being an outstanding player on the field, but with being a major help in the clubhouse with his positive winning attitude. Toomay even asserts that Herb helped allay racial tensions that were undermining the team. Landry, however, did not like Adderley's playing style; it was too intuitive and did not always stick to the coach's carefully devised scheme. As time went on, Landry berated Adderley more and more for "clueing" or guessing on plays. Herb lost his starting position in 1972 and quietly retired at the end of the year. Although he won a Super Bowl ring in Dallas to go with the two he won in Green Bay, Herb has stated that he never wears the Cowboy ring. He will always be a Packer and was elected to the Packer Hall of Fame in 1981, one year after being inducted into the Pro Football Hall of Fame.

FOR FURTHER INFORMATION

Allen, George, with Ben Olan. *Pro Football's 100 Greatest Players: Rating the Stars of Past and Present.* Indianapolis: Bobbs-Merrill, 1982. (188-9)

Johnson, Chuck. *The Greatest Packers of Them All.* New York: Putnam, 1968. (171-3)

Kramer, Jerry, with Dick Schaap. *Distant Replay.* New York: G.P. Putnam, 1985. (164-6)

Lombardi, Vince, with W.C. Heinz. *Run to Daylight.* Englewood Cliffs, NJ: Prentice-Hall, 1963. (40-1)

Porter, David L., ed. *Biographical Dictionary of American Sports: Football.* New York: Greenwood Press, 1987. (1-2)

Smith, Ron. *The Sporting News Selects Football's 100 Greatest Players: A Celebration of the 20th Century's Best.* St. Louis, MO: Sporting News, 1999. (100)

Starr, Bart, with Murray Olderman. *Starr: My Life in Football.* New York: William Morrow, 1987. (85-6)

Toomay, Pat. "The Specter of Lombardi," Sportsjones web site. Available online at www.sportsjones.com/sj/225.shtml.

1967 SUPER BOWL II DATA
Green Bay Packers 33
Oakland Raiders 14

January 14, 1968 • Orange Bowl, Miami
Attendance: 75,546
Winner's Share: $15,000
Loser's Share: $7,500
Weather: 68 degrees.

KEY STATS	PACKERS	RAIDERS
First Downs	19	16
Rush Yards	160	107
Pass Yards	162	186
Total Yards	322	293
Interceptions	1	0

KEY STATS	PACKERS	RAIDERS
Fumbles Lost	0	2
Penalties	1-12	4-31
Third Down Conversions	5/16	3/11 • 1/1 on 4th down
Time of Possession	35:38	24:22
Halftime Score	Packers 16, Raiders 7	

LEADERS

Rushing: Ben Wilson 17-62 Hewritt Dixon 12-50

Passing: Bart Starr 13-24-0, 202 yds Daryle Lamonica 15-34-1, 208 yds

Receiving: Carroll Dale 4-43 Bill Miller 5-84

ADDITIONAL FACTS

•Game time temperature was 81 degrees warmer than the NFL Championship game against Dallas two weeks before.

•For the three playoff games against the Rams, Cowboys and Raiders, the Packers out-gained their opponents 403 to 274 on the ground and 488 to 428 through the air. Each Packer won an additional $7,950 beating the Cowboys and a normal game salary for beating the Rams.

•Bart Starr's playoff passing line was 44-71-1 for 615 yards and 4 touchdowns.

•Nearly half of Oakland's total yardage, 47 rushing and 90 passing came after the score reached 33-7 in the fourth quarter.

•Jerry Kramer and Forrest Gregg carried Lombardi off the field after his last game as a Packer.

1930s IN A BOX
HANK BRUDER • BACK 1935–36

WHO'S WORN THE NUMBER Basing 1927, Molenda 1928–30, C. Perry 1931, Hinkle 1932, Hubbard 1933, Bruder 1935–36, Midler 1940, Don Miller 1941–42, Ranspot 1942, C. Adams 1943, S. Barnett 1945, Tollefson 1946, J. Jacobs 1947–49, Coutre 1950, 1953, Switzer 1954–55, Symank 1957–62, Mack 1966, James 1967–68, A. Randolph 1971, Austin 1973, C. Taylor 1976, G. Hayes 1984–86, T. Elliot 1987–88, Fontenot 1989–90, T. Buckley 1992–94, C. Jones 1996, M. Blair 1998, T. McBride 1999–02.

ORIGINATOR Back Myrt "Biff" Basing, 1927, led the team in rushing, receiving, and scoring in 1925.

LONGEST TENURE Johnny Symank, 1957–62, undersized, overachieving defensive back who had a long career as an assistant coach in the NFL.

NUMBER CHANGES Biff Basing wore 15 in 1925–26; fullback Bo Molenda wore 30 in 1931–32; guard Claude Perry wore 26 in 1927–30, 37 in 1929 and 1933, 24 in 1932, 50 in 1934, and 32 in 1935; Clarke Hinkle also wore 33 in 1932, 30 in 1933, 1935, and 1937–41, 39 in 1933, 45 and 48 in 1934, and 41 in 1936; Cal Hubbard wore 39 in 1929, 40 in 1930 and 1932, 38 in 1931, and 51 in 1935; back Hank Bruder wore 13 in 1931–33, 55 in 1933, 47 in 1934, 18 in 1935–38, and 5 in 38–39; guard Solon Barnett wore 72 in 1946; guard Charles Tollefson wore 46 from 1944–45 and 77 in 1947; receiver Claudis James also wore 16 in 1967.

OTHER NOTABLES Bo Molenda, star bruising fullback for the triple champs of 1929–31. Molenda had a falling out with Lambeau and was traded to the Giants in 1932 where he later became a coach. He was replaced in Green Bay by Hall of Famer Clarke Hinkle; Indian Jack Jacobs was Lambeau's first T Formation QB after being obtained from the Redskins. He later played in Canada and is in the Canadian Football Hall of Fame.

ONE TO FORGET As the fifth player taken in the 1992 draft, Terrell Buckley was actually a good player, but he never fit in Green Bay. He was too loud before he had done anything to earn the fans' respect. He took too many risks and was beaten too often in coverage. While he never played well enough to justify being taken that high in the draft, he has been a solid performer with several teams over a ten-year professional career.

HANK BRUDER Hank Bruder was known as "Hard Luck Hank" at Northwestern for a series of unfortunate injuries and accidents that befell him on and off the field. He missed half of one year with a broken leg and half of the next with smallpox. At a key moment against Notre Dame in 1930, he fumbled on the goal line, costing the Cats the game. Nonetheless, he also was team Captain and a highly respected, unselfish, versatile performer and a member of the Delta Upsilon fraternity. That versatility was highlighted throughout his nine-year career in Green Bay from 1931–39, almost the entire decade. The 1930s were not a time of flashy statistics, and players still played both offense and defense. Bruder was an all-purpose back. He played defensive back and linebacker on defense as well as quarterback, halfback, and fullback on offense. He was most famous as a blocking back, playing quarterback in Lambeau's Notre Dame Box offense in the 1930s. In that offense the backs started out aligned roughly in a T formation, although the quarterback was not directly under center, and then they shifted right or left before the ball was snapped. For example if they shifted right, the quarterback would slide over behind the right tackle and the right halfback would become a wingback by moving up next to the quarterback but behind the right end. Meanwhile, the fullback would slide to the right behind the quarterback and the left halfback would slide to the right and become the tailback behind the center. The four backs were then set in a box shape or, more accurately, a parallelogram. The center would usually snap the ball to the tailback, or sometimes to the other deep back, who had the option to run, hand off, or pass. The quarterback was a lead blocker similar to the fullback in today's offenses.

In the 1930s Hall of Famers Arnie Herber, Mike Michalske, Coach Curly Lambeau, plus assistant coach Red Smith, end Milt Gantenbein, and versatile back "Hard Luck Hank" Bruder were all keys to the team of the decade—Green Bay. *Courtesy of the Stiller-Lefebvre Collection.*

In his nine years in Green Bay, Bruder threw only 24 passes and caught just 36. He ran the ball 265 times but only 21 times in his last four years when he was increasingly used as a blocker. The Packers played in three title games in those four years, due largely to Herber and Isbell throwing to Hutson, but effective role players like Bruder kept the way clear for the stars to shine. Hank scored 100 points in his Packer years, which was a good total for the time. Twenty-two of those came in one game against Cincinnati in 1934 when he scored three touchdowns and kicked four extra points before taking himself out in the fourth quarter. He was traded to the Steelers in 1940, where he played for one last year. In the off-season, he tried professional wrestling, but broke his shoulder blade in 1932. He then opened a tire shop in Green Bay. During his playing career and beyond he was a strong supporter in the campaign to build a new City Stadium in the mid-1950s. Eventually, he moved back to his native Illinois, where he died in 1970, just two years before being elected to the Packer Hall of Fame.

FOR FURTHER INFORMATION
"Lookin' 'Em Over," *Peoria Journal Star.* 7/1/70. (D2)

 HERE'S A SNAPSHOT OF BRUDER'S TIME:
AIR FORCE ONE—THE 1930s
WHERE THEY PLAYED: City Stadium (still used as a high school field), 1925–56; Athletic Park (a minor league baseball park in Milwaukee), 1933 (1 Game); Wisconsin State Fairgrounds in Milwaukee, 1935–51.
HOW THE GAME WAS PLAYED: Rules changes designed to open up the game to appeal to fans were adapted. Hashmarks were moved in from the sidelines, passers no longer needed to be at least five yards behind the line of scrimmage to throw the ball, and the goal posts were moved back to the goal line. Green Bay, with Arnie Herber and then Cecil Isbell throwing to Johnny Blood and then Don Hutson, was a leading practitioner of the air game.
DECADE WON-LOST RECORD: 86-35-4 .704 + 2-1 in the playoffs.
RECORD AGAINST THE BEARS: 11-12-1.
RECORD AGAINST THE LIONS: (including Portsmouth Spartans): 13-5-1.
RECORD AGAINST THE GIANTS: 8-8 (including 1-1 in playoffs).
PLAYOFF APPEARANCES: 1936, 1938, 1939.
CHAMPIONSHIPS: 1930, 1931, 1936, 1939.
UNSUNG HERO: Joe Carr, NFL Commissioner, who ruled in 1935 that Don Hutson belonged to the Packers. Hutson had signed contracts with both the Packers and the Brooklyn Dodgers. Because the Packers contract was postmarked 17 minutes sooner than the Dodgers contract, Carr awarded Don to Green Bay where he would have a revolutionary effect on pro football. With the less-talented Dodgers who lacked a skilled passer, who knows what kind of career Hutson would have had.
HEAD COACHES: Curly Lambeau, 1921–49, 86-35-4 for the decade.
BEST PLAYER: Don Hutson.
HALL OF FAMERS: Curly Lambeau, Johnny Blood McNally, Cal Hubbard, Mike Michalske, Arnie Herber, Clarke Hinkle, Don Hutson, Walt Kiesling.

PACKER HALL OF FAMERS: Curly Lambeau, Johnny Blood McNally, Cal Hubbard, Mike Michalske, Arnie Herber, Clarke Hinkle, Don Hutson, Nate Barragar, Charley Brock, Hank Bruder, Larry Craig, Boob Darling, Lavvie Dilweg, Red Dunn, Jug Earp, Tiny Engbretsen, Lon Evans, Milt Gantenbein, Buckets Goldenberg, Cecil Isbell, Harry Jacunski, Ed Jankowski, Swede Johnston, Joe Laws, Russ Letlow, Bob Monnett, Baby Ray, Bud Svendsen, George Svendsen, Pete Tinsley, Andy Uram, Whitey Woodin.

LEAGUE LEADERS: Buckets Goldenberg—TDs 1933; Arnie Herber—passing yards 1932, 34, 36; passing TDs 1932, 34, 36; Clarke Hinkle—rushing TDs 1937; TDs 1937; points 1938; Don Hutson—catches 1936, 37, 39; receiving yards 1936, 38, 39; receiving TDs 1936, 38; TDs 1935, 37; Cecil Isbell—rushing avg. 1938.

ALL PROS: Lavvie Dilweg, 1930, 31; Mike Michalske, 1930, 31; Johnny Blood, 1931; Cal Hubbard, 1931, 32, 33; Nate Barragar, 1932; Arnie Herber, 1932, Lon Evans, 1936, 37; Clarke Hinkle, 1936, 37, 38; Don Hutson, 1936, 38, 39; Ernie Smith, 1936; Russ Letlow, 1938.

PRE-PRO BOWLERS: In the 1938 All-Star Game, Clarke Hinkle, Cecil Isbell, and Russ Letlow were all selected to play against the champion Giants.

BEST OFFENSIVE BACKFIELD: 1938—Arnie Herber or Cecil Isbell, TB; Bob Monnett, HB; Joe Laws, HB; Clarke Hinkle, FB.

BEST DRAFT CHOICE: Cecil Isbell, 1938 1st round.

BEST OVERALL DRAFT: 1938. In addition to Isbell, the Packers picked halfback Andy Uram in the 4th round and guard Pete Tinsley in the 9th.

WORST DRAFT CHOICE: Larry Buhler, 1939 first round, a back who played briefly with the Packers.

WORST OVERALL DRAFT: 1936. Aside from #1 pick guard Russ Letlow, only third-rounder end Bernie Scherer made the team as a backup.

BEST FREE AGENT (DRAFT YEARS): Baby Ray, 1938, a giant fixture on Lambeau's line for 11 years.

BEST TRADE: The Packers traded end Tom Nash to Brooklyn in 1932 for a "player to be named later." In 1934 (!) that player turned out to be Tiny Engebretsen, a quality guard and kicker for the next eight years.

WORST TRADE: Selling Bo Molenda, who had personal problems with Lambeau, to the Giants in 1931 when he still had several years left.

BIGGEST OFF-FIELD EVENT: In 1931 part of the bleachers collapsed and a fan was injured and sued the team for $25,000. In 1933, he won a $5,200 judgment. Because the team's bankrupt insurance company refused to pay the claim, the Packers' existence was threatened. The team went into receivership for two years before being reorganized as the Green Bay Packers, Inc. in 1935. To raise cash, 600 shares of stock were sold with the proviso that no dividends would be issued and if the club was sold all profits would go to the local American Legion Post.

BIGGEST ON-FIELD DEVELOPMENT: Larry Craig joins the team in 1939 as a blocking back on offense and covers end on defense, freeing Don Hutson to move to defensive back. This move both preserved Hutson's health and improved the team's defense because Hutson was too slight to play defensive end.

STRANGEST ON-FIELD EVENTS: On September 22, 1935, Packer fanatic Emmet Platten, a local butcher who regularly paid for 15 minutes radio air time before Packer games to speak his mind, spends his time railing against the stupidity of Lambeau for not only signing such a "little guy" as Don Hutson, but for planning to start him against the Bears as well. The following year against the Bears Platten runs onto the field during the game and slugs Bear player Ted Rosequist who is attempting to keep Platten from attacking the referee. On August 25, 1938, the Packers play an exhibition game doubleheader against Johnny Blood's Pittsburgh Pirates, tying the first game 7-7 and winning the "nitecap" 17-0.

WORST FAILURE: The Packers did not win the Championship in 1932 even though they had the best record. At the time, ties did not count in the standings so the Bears with a 6-1-6 record won a playoff against the 6-1-4 Spartans. Had ties been treated as half a win and half a loss like today, the Pack would have claimed a fourth consecutive Championship with a 10-3-1 record. Of course, had they managed to beat the Bears and Spartans in their final two games, they would have won the title anyway.

HOME ATTENDANCE: 553,542 in 50 games (1931 data unavailable) for an average attendance of 11,071. In 1933, the Packers began to play some home games in the bigger city of Milwaukee. In six of the seven years of the decade, the Milwaukee average attendance was higher than the Green Bay average. Overall, Milwaukee averaged 13,281 while Green Bay averaged 12,195.

FIRST GAME: September 21, 1930. The Packers open the decade by shutting out the Cardinals 14-0.

LAST GAME: In the only decade to end with a Green Bay title game, the Packers shutout the Giants 27-0 in Milwaukee on December 10, 1939. (see 17)

BEST GAME: 10/27/35. After Hutson singlehandedly sank the Bears in his first game against them by catching an 83-yard touchdown pass for the game's only score, he did himself one better in the rematch later that season. Trailing 14-3 in the fourth quarter, the Packers rallied with two touchdown passes to Hutson in the final two and a half minutes of the game to win 17-14.

LARGEST MARGIN OF VICTORY: 47-0 over the Pittsburgh Pirates 1938.

LARGEST MARGIN OF DEFEAT: 30-3 to the Bears 1936.

BEST OFFENSE: 1931, the Packer scored 291 points, a total that would not be topped in the league until the 1939 Bears scored 298.

BEST DEFENSE: 1935, Green Bay allowed a league best 96 points, only giving up more than 14 points once.

MOST GAMES PLAYED: 99, Arnie Herber. Hank Bruder and Milt Gantenbein both played in 98.

MOST POINTS: 275, Clarke Hinkle. Hutson had 234 and Johnny Blood had 200.

MOST FIELD GOALS: 13, Clarke Hinkle. Tiny Engebretsen had 12.

MOST TOUCHDOWNS: 38, Don Hutson. Hinkle had 35 and Johnny Blood had 32.

MOST TOUCHDOWN PASSES: 63, Arnie Herber.

MOST PASSING YARDS: 6,199, Arnie Herber.

MOST RECEIVING YARDS: 2,902 Don Hutson.

MOST RECEPTIONS: 159, Don Hutson.

MOST RUSHING YARDS: 3,084, Clarke Hinkle.

MOST INTERCEPTIONS: 28, Clarke Hinkle (data incomplete).

BEST BOOK (About): Larry Names' *The History of the Green Bay Packers: Book II: The Lambeau Years Part Two*, Angel Press of WI, 1989.

NOTED SPORTSWRITER: Oliver Kuechele of the *Milwaukee Journal*. Kuechele coined the term "Hungry Five" to indicate the prime movers of the corporation—Curly Lambeau, Andrew Turnbull, Leland Joannes, Dr. W. Weber Kelly, and Gerald F. Clifford. He also created the nickname "the Vagabond Halfback" for Johnny Blood. He was doing a story on Blood detailing how Johnny had ridden the rails to report to training camp and was going to call the article "The Hobo Halfback." Lambeau requested a classier sobriquet be given to his player. Kuechele also was a leading proponent of the Packers sharing their home games with Milwaukee.

BEST QUOTATION: "In short, this group of Packers reminds one very much of the famed Gas House Gang. 'Anything for a Laugh' appears to be their slogan. Once during yesterday's session four or five of them took time out to chase a squirrel across the field. That the squirrel didn't turn around and chase them was a revelation."—Louis Effrat, "Packers, 30 Strong, Confident of Defeating Football Giants," *New York Times* 11/16/38 (29).

BUBBLEGUM FACTOID: On the back of Swede Johnston's 1935 National Chicle football card, it says that Johnston's father played pro football as well. He is not listed as having played in the NFL, but could very well have played on any number of pro teams that existed in the Midwest prior to the founding of the league in 1921. Green Bay itself had town teams from 1895 until the time of the Packers.

UNUSUAL NAMES: Wayland Becker, Elbert Bloodgood, Averell Daniell, Waldo Don Carlos, Wuert Engelmann, Herdis McCrary, Orrin Pape, Jessie Quatse, Ade Schwammel, Champ Seibold.

NICKNAMES: Megs Apsit, Av "Li'l Abner" Daniell, Tiny Engebretsen, Buckets Goldenberg, Flash Herber, Don "The Alabama Antelope" Hutson, Bruce "Buck" Jones, Tom "Potsey" Jones, Babe Kiesling, Tiger Laws, Buster Maddox, Harry "The Horse" or "The Toe" Mattos, Iron Mike Michalske, Ookie Miller, Buster Mott, Carl "Moose" Mulleneaux, Lee "Brute" Mulleneaux, Nanny Pape, Fat Ken Raddick, Baby Ray, Al "Big Un'" Rose, Russ "Racehorse" Saunders, Zud Schammel, Biff Schneidman, Bunny Schoeman, Ade "Tar" Schwammel, Red Sleight, Tuffy Thompson, and Mule Wilson.

FASTEST PLAYER: Don Hutson.

HEAVIEST PLAYERS: Baby Ray, 6'6" and sometimes up to 260 lbs. Cal Hubbard went at 265 and Walt Kiesling at 260.

LIGHTEST PLAYER: Clarence "Tuffy" Thompson 5'11"170 lbs.

TOUGHEST INJURY: Don Hutson hurt his knee late in 1938 and was ineffective in a brief appearance in the 1938 Championship game loss to the Giants. If he had been healthy, the Packers likely would have won (see 52).

LOCAL BOYS: Arnie Herber and Wayland Becker were from Green Bay; other Wisconsin boys included Milt Gantenbein, Buckets Goldenberg, Ed Jankowski, Swede Johnston, Ken Radick, and Champ Seibold.

FIRSTS:

> **Championship Game**—December 13, 1936, the Packers beat the Boston Redskins in a game Skins owner George Marshall moved to New York due to lack of interest in Beantown. They became the Washington Redskins in 1937 (see 16).

PACKERS BY THE NUMBERS

200 Point Season—234 points in 1930.

Losing Season—1933, 5-7-1.

Kickoff Return TD—Wuert Engelmann 10/25/31 80 yards against Providence.

HB with 10 TD Receptions—Johnny Blood, and it hasn't been done in the NFL since.

Home Game in Milwaukee—On October1, 1933, the Packers lost to the Giants 10-7.

Home Game in December—1939 Championship Game in Milwaukee. Packers would not have another until December 1942. They would not play a December game in Green Bay until December 1951.

Cheerleaders—1931 from the local East and West High Schools.

Post-Season Exhibition Series Outside the US—Packers travel to Hawaii in December 1932 to play three games against local competition and barnstormed in California upon their return stateside.

Packer to Model a Statue—Back Russ Saunders was the model for the head, chest, and shoulders of "Tommy Trojan" on the campus of his alma mater, the University of Southern California.

1970s IN A BOX
WILLIE BUCHANON • CORNERBACK 1972–78

WHO'S WORN THE NUMBER Red Smith 1927, McCrary 1929–30, Michalske 1931, Kurth 1933, G. Maddox 1935, Ed Smith 1937, (Jarrell 1947), Christman 1950, Thomason 1951, Self 1952, 1954–55, Rowser 1967, Harden 1970, Buchanon 1972–78, M. McLeod 1984–85, Watts 1986, R. Pitts 1988–90, Mullen 1995–57, B. Mitchell 1999–2000, Bowen 2001–02.

ORIGINATOR Wisconsin native Richard "Red" Smith, 1927, played guard and back for five teams in five years in the NFL and was a catcher for one game with the New York baseball Giants. Red was better known as Lambeau's assistant coach from 1936 through 1943, when he moved on to the staff of Steve Owen of the Giants. The Red Smith Award is given annually to the person who has made the most significant contribution to Wisconsin sports. Paul Hornung, Ray Nitschke, and Jerry Kramer are all past recipients.

LONGEST TENURE Willie Buchanon 1972–78.

NUMBER CHANGES Red Smith also wore 7 and 19 in 1927 and 15 in 1929; fullback Herdis McCrary wore 29 in 1929, 19 in 1931, 43 in 1932, and 38 and 53 in 1933; guard Mike Michalske wore 36 in 1929–30 and 1937, 19 and 30 in 1932, 31 in 1933, 24 and 63 in 1934 and 33 and 40 in 1935; and tackle Joe Kurth wore 31 and 58 in 1934; defensive back John Rowser wore 45 from 1967–69.

OTHER NOTABLES Red Smith (see above); fullback Herdis McCrary (see top 53); Mike Michalske (see 33); defensive back Ron Pitts was the son of 1960s Packer HB Elijah Pitts.

ONE TO FORGET Paul Christman was an excellent QB with the champion Chicago Cardinal in the late 1940s. However, like the acquisition of John Hadl 24 years later, Christman was finished by the time the Packers got him. At least they didn't give up five high draft picks for him.

WILLIE BUCHANON Willie Buchanon was a shutdown cover cornerback who had great speed and could tackle. Drafted in the first round in 1972, he was named Defensive Rookie of the Year, made the All Pro team once, and was selected for three Pro Bowls. He returned two of his 21 Packer interceptions for touchdowns, and in his rookie year returned a blocked field goal 57 yards for another score. Throughout his years with the Packers, the team was more effective on the defensive side of the ball. By the time he left, the offense was about to take off and the defense was

NUMBER 28

about to collapse. Willie's career was interrupted twice when he broke his left leg in two places in 1973 and when he broke the same leg two years later. In 1978, he led the NFC in interceptions with nine, including four in one game against the Chargers. After that year, his seventh in Green Bay, the Packers traded him home to San Diego for first- and seventh-round draft picks, and he played there for another four years. In retirement, he taught school before going into real estate and becoming active in the San Diego community. He was elected to the Packer Hall of Fame in 1993.

FOR FURTHER INFORMATION

Hintz, Gene W. "Willie Buchanon: A Good Place to Start," *Green Bay Packers 1974 Yearbook.* (45-6)

Poling, Jerry. *Downfield! Untold Stories of the Green Bay Packers.* Madison, WI: Prairie Oak Press, 1996. (196-7)

Porter, David L., ed. *Biographical Dictionary of American Sports: Football.* New York: Greenwood Press, 1987. (76-7)

WILLIE BUCHANON DESERVED BETTER THAN THE DYSFUNCTIONAL DECADE OF THE 1970S: FALLING STARR—PACKERS IN THE 1970S

WHERE THEY PLAYED: Lambeau Field (known as City Stadium 1957–64), 1957–; County Stadium in Milwaukee, 1953–1994.

HOW THE GAME WAS PLAYED: Defenses improved throughout the decade to the point where the NFL loosened up some rules in 1978 to open up the passing game that fans like to see. Green Bay opened the 1970s with a good defense and no offense and reversed that by the end of the decade through diligent incompetence. George Allen started using five (the nickel) and six (the dime) defensive backs on passing downs. More and more coaches called the team's plays; almost all kickers were soccer-style sidewinders.

DECADE WON LOST RECORD: 57-82-5 .413 + 0-1 in the playoffs.

RECORD AGAINST THE BEARS: 9-11.

RECORD AGAINST THE LIONS: 9-9-2.

RECORD AGAINST THE VIKINGS: 4-15-1.

RECORD AGAINST THE COWBOYS: 2-2.

PLAYOFF APPEARANCES: 1 (1972).

CHAMPIONSHIPS: None.

UNSUNG HEROES: Jim Irwin and Max McGee, broadcast partners from 1979–98. Irwin actually started doing Packer play-by-play in 1969. McGee replaced Lionel Aldridge as color analyst ten years later. Irwin and McGee were an enjoyable pair to listen to describe mostly dreadful football in that dry spell of Green Bay history. Irwin's friendly, comfortable style meshed well with the dry wit of McGee, and they helped keep interest alive in some dark days.

HEAD COACHES: Phil Bengtson, 1968–70, 6-8 in 1970; Dan Devine, 1971–74, 25-27-4; Bart Starr, 1975–83, 26-47-1 for the decade.

BEST PLAYER: Fred Carr, much like Dave Robinson, came out of college with the speed and ability to play several positions and became an All Pro linebacker.

HALL OF FAMERS: Bart Starr, Forrest Gregg, Ray Nitschke, Willie Wood, Ted Hendricks, and James Lofton.

PACKER HALL OF FAMERS: Bart Starr, Forrest Gregg, Ray Nitschke, Willie Wood, Lionel Aldridge, Donny Anderson, John Anderson, Phil Bengtson, Ken Bowman, Zeke Bratkowski, John Brockington, Willie Buchanon, Fred Carr, Paul Coffman, Carroll Dale, Lynn Dickey, Gale Gillingham, Johnny Gray, Bob Jeter, Ezra Johnson, James Lofton, Chester Marcol, Larry McCarren, Elijah Pitts, Dave Robinson, Travis Williams, Mike Douglass.

LEAGUE LEADERS: Ken Ellis—punt return avg 1972; Dave Hampton—kickoff return yards 1971; Chester Marcol—FGs 1972, 74; points 1972, 74; Steve Odom—kickoff return avg 1978.

AWARD WINNERS: John Brockington Offensive Rookie of the Year 1971; Willie Buchanon—Defensive Rookie of the Year 1972; Chester Marcol—NFC Rookie of the Year 1972; Dan Devine—Coach of the Year 1972.

ALL PROS: Gale Gillingham, 1970, 71, 74; John Brockington, 1971, 72, 73; Bob Brown, 1972; Ken Ellis, 1972, 73, 74; Chester Marcol, 1972, 74; Jim Carter, 1973; Ted Hendricks, 1974; Fred Carr, 1975; Steve Odom, 1975; Willie Buchanon, 1978; Terdell Middleton, 1978.

PRO BOWLERS: Fred Carr, 1970, 72, 75; Carroll Dale, 1970; Gale Gillingham, 1970, 71, 73*, 74; Willie Wood, 1970; John Brockington, 1971, 72, 73; Willie Buchanon, 1973*, 74, 78; Ken Ellis, 1973, 74; Chester Marcol, 1972, 74; Ezra Johnson, 1978; James Lofton, 1978. (* selected, but did not play)

BEST OFFENSIVE BACKFIELD: 1972—Scott Hunter, QB; John Brockington, RB; Macarthur Lane, RB; Carroll Dale, FL.

BEST DRAFT CHOICE: Cornerback Ken Ellis, 1970 4th round.

BEST OVERALL DRAFT: 1972. Willie Buchanon All Pro cornerback #1 and Chester Marcol #2 league leading kicker were the jewels of this draft, but #6 defensive tackle Dave Pureifory, additional #6 running back Bob Hudson, #8 wide receiver Leland Glass, #10 guard Keith Wortman, and #14 linebacker Larry Hefner all made contributions. Second #1 quarterback Jerry Tagge was a major disappointment.

WORST DRAFT CHOICE: Receiver Barry Smith, a 1973 first-rounder who caught 41 passes for four TDs in three years in Green Bay.

WORST OVERALL DRAFT: 1975, Picks 1, 2, and 3 went to the Rams for John Hadl. A second #2 went to the Dolphins in the Jim Del Gaizo deal. All Bart Starr was able to salvage from his first draft was guard Bill Bain with another #2, running back Will Harrell with another #3, and #4 defensive back Steve Luke.

BEST FREE AGENT: 1978, Paul Coffman.

BEST TRADE: Picking up Ted Hendricks who had signed with the rival World Football League from the Colts in 1974 for an 8th-round pick (Mario Cage). Unfortunately, the Packers let the Mad Stork fly to the Raiders as a free agent in 1975, but the Pack did receive two #1s as compensation (Mark Koncar and Ezra Johnson). Obtaining Lynn Dickey from the Oilers in 1976 for John Hadl, Ken Ellis a #3 (Tim Wilson) and a #4 (Steve Largent) was a good deal, too.

WORST TRADE: Hands down, the John Hadl deal in 1974. Known as the Lawrence Welk trade ("a one and a two and a three"), this trade was one of the worst in NFL history and decimated the franchise. The Packers gave the Rams #1s in 1975 (Mike Fanning) and 1976

PACKERS BY THE NUMBERS

(Dennis Lick), #2s in 1975 (Monte Jackson) and 1976 (Pat Thomas) and a #3 in 1975 (Geoff Reese) for a spent John Hadl. Fanning, Jackson, and Thomas had fine careers for the Rams.

BIGGEST OFF-FIELD EVENT: "Monday Night Football" debuts and accelerates the emphasis on football as entertainment, just another talk show on television.

BIGGEST ON-FIELD DEVELOPMENT: Unhappy players doing angry things on the field. 1974—There is talk of players boycotting the season finale to protest Dan Devine. 1975—Ken Ellis is fined for walking out of training camp twice. 1976—Ken Ellis, Bill Bain, and John Brockington all demand to be traded. 1977—Ken Payne responds with obscenities to an assistant coach. He is fined and then waived. 1979—James Lofton makes an obscene gesture to the fans after being booed for dropping passes and fumbling.

STRANGEST ON-FIELD EVENTS: 1) It was not a good omen that in Dan Devine's coaching debut in Green Bay he was run over by a group of players and broke his leg. 2) Trying linemen on the other side of the ball. In 1972, All Pro guard Gale Gillingham was shifted to defensive tackle and tore up his knee; in 1977, Mike McCoy was moved from defensive tackle to offensive guard for two weeks and was then traded.

WORST FAILURE: The Packers spent the decade looking for a quarterback. They spent five high draft picks on a washed-up John Hadl and two on Jim Del Gaizo (!). They wasted a #1 on Jerry Tagge. When they finally traded for a good one in Lynn Dickey, he broke his leg so severely that he missed two years of action.

HOME ATTENDANCE: 3,879,863 in 72 games for a 53,887 average attendance. Green Bay's average attendance was higher in each year of the decade and for the 10 year period was 55,900. Milwaukee's average was 51,225.

FIRST GAME: September 20, 1970. The Packers are humiliated by the Lions 40-0. Detroit holds Green Bay to five first downs and 114 total yards. The fans reward this ineptitude with a chorus of loud boos and we know the glory years are done. The Lions would cap the season by shutting out the Packers again 20-0.

LAST GAME: December 15, 1979 The 5-11 Packers beat the 2-14 Lions 18-13.

BEST GAME: The playoff-clinching 23-10 victory over the rival Vikings, 12/10/72, was a satisfying game, but my pick is an obscure 10/15/78 shootout with Seattle that the Pack won 45-28. James Lofton starred in the win, which brought the Pack's record to 6-1. Unfortunately, the bubble soon burst and the team ended the season 8-7-1 and out of the playoffs.

LARGEST MARGIN OF VICTORY: 34-0 over the Chargers 11/24/74.

LARGEST MARGIN OF DEFEAT: 40-0 to the Lions, opening day 1970 (see First Game above).

BEST OFFENSE: 1972, they had no passing game, but they rushed their way to the division title.

BEST DEFENSE: 1974, led by All Pro linebacker Ted Hendricks whom they stole for a ninth-round pick, the team allowed only 206 points. Hendricks himself blocked seven kicks that year, but left for Oakland the next year as a free agent.

MOST GAMES PLAYED: 116, Rich McGeorge. Fred Carr played in 112.

MOST POINTS: 502, Chester Marcol.

MOST FIELD GOALS: 118 out of 192, Chester Marcol.

MOST TOUCHDOWNS: 32, John Brockington.

MOST TOUCHDOWN PASSES: 22, David Whitehurst.

MOST PASSING YARDS: 4,974, David Whitehurst.

MOST RECEIVING YARDS: 2,370, Rich McGeorge.

MOST RECEPTIONS: 175, Rich McGeorge.

MOST RUSHING YARDS: 5,024, John Brockington.

MOST INTERCEPTIONS: 21, Willie Buchanon.

MOST SACKS: 30, Ezra Johnson (incomplete and unofficial).

MOST KICKOFF RETURN YARDS: 4,124, Steve Odom.

MOST PUNT RETURN YARDS: 569, Steve Odom.

BEST BOOKS: Steve Wright with William Gildeau and Kenneth Turin, *I'd Rather Be Wright*, Prentice-Hall, 1974. John Wiebusch, ed. *Lombardi*, Follett Publishing, 1971. Bart Starr and John Wiebusch, *A Perspective on Victory*, Follett Publishing, 1972. Ray Nitschke as told to Robert W. Wells, *Mean on Sunday: The Autobiography of Ray Nitschke*, Prairie Oak Press (2d ed.), 1999.

BEST SPORTSWRITER: Cliff Christl of the *Green Bay Press Gazette* who always infuses his writing with a respect for tradition. He later moved to the *Milwaukee Journal-Sentinel*.

BEST QUOTATION: Dan Devine complaining in *Time* of Packer fan abuse of him and his family, "It's been vulgar, malicious and ugly. It makes me sick." Gary Knafelc on Devine's successor Bart Starr, "I'm surprised he accepted the job. He had such a wonderful reputation here that people will expect incredible things of him immediately, and people hate to be disappointed."

BUMPER STICKERS: The Pack Will Be Back and The Pack Is Back.

BUBBLEGUM FACTOID: After three years in the league, Barry Smith's 1976 Topps card stated that, "Barry is a receiver along the style of Raiders' Fred Biletnikoff." Barty Smith's 1979 Topps card says, "Barty is ranked among the top 20 rushers on the Packers all-time list." Scott Hunter's 1973 Topps card puts a positive spin on, "Scott had 43.2 Comp. Pct. In 1972. He threw only 199 times as a result of GB's outstanding ground attack." Willie Buchanon's 1978 Topps card says, "Willie is one of the Packers' more flamboyant dressers." His 1979 card adds, "Willie keeps over 40 plants in his apartment."

UNUSUAL NAMES: Derrell Gofourth, Estus Hood, Ezra Johnson, Chester Marcol, Terdell Middleton, Alden Roche, Dave Roller, Eric Torkelson.

NICKNAMES: Big John Brockington, Jim "Shy" Cheyunski, Mike "Mad Dog" Douglass, Dave "Scooter" Hampton, Ted "The Mad Stork" Hendricks, Mark "Claw" Koncar, Chester "The Polish Prince" Marcol, Larry "the Rock" McCarren, Terdell "TD" Middleton, Dave "Rocky" Osborn, Dave "The Tasmanian Devil" Pureifory, Bucky Scribner, Harry "The Horse" Schuh, Rabbit Vataha, Clarence "Sweeny" Williams, and Wimpy Winther.

FASTEST PLAYER: James Lofton.

HEAVIEST PLAYER: Mike McCoy 285 lbs.

LIGHTEST PLAYER: Charley Wade 5'10" 163 lbs.

TOUGHEST INJURY: Let's see. Willie Buchanon broke the same leg twice. Lynn Dickey injured his shoulder and broke his leg. Gale Gillingham had knee problems. Barty Smith had five knee surgeries. Chester Marcol had problems with alcohol. Eddie Lee Ivery blew out his knee in his first game. In terms of effect on the 1970s, I would probably go with

PACKERS BY THE NUMBERS

Dickey. In terms of long-term effect, who knows how good Ivery could have been?

LOCAL BOYS: Jerry Tagge and Bob Kroll were from Green Bay. Larry Krause was from Wisconsin and attended St. Norberts College.

FIRSTS:

> First Packer Hall of Fame Inductions—1970.
>
> Packer Hall of Fame Building Dedicated by President Ford—April 1976.
>
> "Monday Night Football" Appearance—October 12, 1970, 22-20 over the Chargers
>
> "Monday Night Football" Home Game—November 9, 1970, 13-10 loss to the Colts in Milwaukee.
>
> "Monday Night Football" in Green Bay—October 1, 1979, 27-14 win over New England.
>
> Players Strike—1974, during training camp.
>
> Overtime Game—11/26/78, a 10-10 tie against the Vikings in Green Bay.
>
> Overtime Loss—9/23/79, 27-21 against the Vikings in Minnesota.
>
> Packer QB with Double Digit TD Passes in Decade—1978, David Whitehurst, 10.
>
> 20 Sacks in a Season (Unofficial)—1978, Ezra Johnson.

1940s IN A BOX

CHARLEY BROCK •
CENTER/LINEBACKER 1939–56

WHO'S WORN THE NUMBER Earp 1927–28, McCrary 1929, Darling 1929–31, L. Peterson 1932, Bettencourt 1933, Laws 1935–36, Lester 1937–38, C. Brock 1939–47, B. Wood 1940, H. Williams 1962–63, Dunaway 1968, A. Matthews 1970–75, M.C. McCoy 1976–83, Stills 1985–89, J. Woods 1990, M. Wilson 1992–95, R. Harris 1998; Goodman 2000–01.

ORIGINATOR Center Jug Earp 1927–28 (see 39)

LONGEST TENURE Charley Brock 1939–47

NUMBER CHANGES Center Jug Earp wore 7 in <1925–26> and wore 9 in 1928, 38 in 1929, and 39 in 1930–32; fullback Herdis McCrary wore 28 in 1929–30, 19 in 1931, 43 in 1932, and 38 and 53 in 1933; center Boob Darling wore 17 in 1927–28; end Les Peterson wore 43 in 1934; center Larry Bettencourt also wore 30 and 39 in 1933; Joe Laws wore 38 and 41 in 1934 and 24 from 1937–45.

OTHER NOTABLES Jug Earp (see 39); Herdis McCrary (see top 53); Boob Darling was a top center for five years in Green Bay who was unable to shed his unfortunate childhood nickname. He served for several years on the Packers Board of Directors; Joe Laws (see top 24); Mike C. McCoy was an average cornerback who was a contemporary of defensive tackle Mike P. McCoy.

ONE TO FORGET Dave Dunaway was a second round pick in 1967 who received a large bonus, appeared in only two games for the Packers in 1968, and was out of the league in two years. The team needed a replacement for Boyd Dowler who would retire at the end of 1969, and Dunaway failed to seize the opportunity. Sadly he died young at the age of 56.

CHARLEY BROCK Charley Brock was always a leader. He was captain at Nebraska, captain of the West team in the 1939 East-West Shrine Game, captain of the All-Stars in the 1939 College All-Star game, and he was a pace-setter on the line for the Packers for nine years. Undersized for a center at 180 pounds, he nonetheless was All Pro in 1945 and was a second team selection twice. His job as center in the single wing required him to snap the ball to a tailback several yards behind the line, not simply hand it back to a quarterback under center. He practiced his snaps an hour to an hour and a half a day. Five times he had his nose broken in an interior line scrum.

His primary value was on defense, where he was a terror at linebacker, intercepting 20 passes, recovering more than 11 fumbles (fumbles weren't tabulated till 1945), and scoring four touchdowns on returns. He had a special skill in stripping ball-carriers of the pigskin. In his rookie year, he intercepted a pass, and he chased down a runner close to scoring in the 1939 title game shutout of the Giants.

After his playing career, Brock served as line coach at the University of Omaha in 1948 and then coached the Packers' defense for one year before he was let go in the post-Lambeau transition. Charley had to sue the team for back pay. He became a successful local businessman who formed the Packer Alumni Association, a booster organization, and served as its president for many years. He was elected to the Packer Hall of Fame in 1973 and died in Green Bay in 1987.

FOR FURTHER INFORMATION
Packers of the Past: A Series of Articles Reprinted from the Milwaukee Journal Sept. 28–Dec. 9, 1965. Milwaukee, WI: Milwaukee Journal, 1965. (19-20)

Paustian, John L. "A Tradition at Center," *Green Bay Packers 1974 Yearbook.* (29-31)

 THE WAR YEARS OF CHARLEY BROCK LOOKED LIKE THIS: TWILIGHT OF THE GODS—PACKERS IN THE 1940S
WHERE THEY PLAYED: City Stadium (still used as a high school field), 1925–56; Wisconsin State Fairground in Milwaukee, 1935–51.
HOW THE GAME WAS PLAYED: The Bears perfection of the T formation with a man in motion took hold throughout the league. Green Bay was one of the last teams to move from the Single Wing to the T. The adoption of unlimited substitutions later in the decade led to separate units for offense and defense. In the All America Football Conference, Paul Brown introduced messenger guards to call plays for his quarterback. For many years, calling plays from the sideline had been illegal.
DECADE WON LOST RECORD: 62-44-4 .582 + 1-1 in the playoffs.
RECORD AGAINST THE BEARS: 4-16-1 (including 0-1 in playoffs).
RECORD AGAINST THE LIONS: 16-4.
RECORD AGAINST THE GIANTS: 3-4-2 (including 1-0 in playoffs).
PLAYOFF APPEARANCES: 1941, 1944.
CHAMPIONSHIPS: 1944.
UNSUNG HERO: Vern Biever began snapping pictures at Packer games as an 18-year-old stringer for the *Milwaukee Sentinel* in 1941. In a career that would span over 60 years, his photographs have told the story of the team and its players in an intimate, moving, and exhilarating way, and we remember so many special moments through Biever's photographs.
HEAD COACHES: Curly Lambeau, 1921–49, 62-44-4 for the decade.
BEST PLAYER: Don Hutson. After Hutson's retirement, Tony Canadeo was the team's best.
HALL OF FAMERS: Curly Lambeau, Arnie Herber, Clarke Hinkle, Don Hutson, and Tony Canadeo.
PACKER HALL OF FAMERS: Curly Lambeau, Arnie Herber, Clarke Hinkle, Don Hutson, and Tony Canadeo, Charley Brock, Lou Brock, Irv Comp, Larry Craig, Tiny Engbretsen, Bob Forte, Ted Fritsch, Milt Gantenbein, Buckets Goldenberg, Cecil Isbell, Joe

Laws, Harry Jacunski, Ed Jankowski, Russ Letlow, Baby Ray, Bud Svendsen, George Svendsen, Pete Tinsley, Andy Uram, and Dick Wildung.

LEAGUE LEADERS: Irv Comp—passing yards 1944; Ted Fritsch—TDs 1946; points 1946; Don Hutson—catches 1941, 42, 43, 44, 45; receiving yards 1941, 42, 43, 44; receiving TDs 1940, 41, 42, 43, 44; TDs 1941, 42, 43, 44; points 1940, 41, 42, 44; interceptions 1940; Cecil Isbell—passing yards 1941, 42; passing TDs 1941, 42.

AWARD WINNERS: Don Hutson—MVP, 1941, 42.

ALL PROS: Clarke Hinkle, 1941; Don Hutson, 1940, 41, 42, 43, 44, 45; Cecil Isbell, 1941, 42; Tony Canadeo, 1943, 47; Charley Brock, 1945, Ted Fritsch, 1945, 46; Larry Craig, 1947.

PRE-PRO BOWLERS: Clarke Hinkle, Don Hutson, and Charley Brock all were selected to play in the All-Star Game against the champion Bears in 1940. Hutson, Cecil Isbell and Larry Craig were picked to play the champion Bears in 1941. Brock, Craig, Hutson*, and Isbell* were picked to play the champion Redskins in 1942. (* selected, but did not play)

BEST OFFENSIVE BACKFIELD: 1942—Cecil Isbell, TB; Tony Canadeo, HB; Andy Uram or Lou Brock, HB; Ted Fritsch, FB.

BEST DRAFT CHOICE: Hall of Fame halfback Tony Canadeo, 1941 7th round.

BEST OVERALL DRAFT: 1941. The Packers did not draft well all decade, but in 1941 they picked Canadeo as well as George Paskvan, Ed Frutig, Herman Rohrig, William Kuusisto, and Ernie Pannell—all of whom played for the team although none were stars.

WORST DRAFT CHOICE: Stan Heath, drafted twice, in 1948 as a Future in the 23rd round and in 1949 in the first round. Meant to be the answer at QB, Heath completed 24% of his passes and threw one TD and 14 interceptions in one year before leaving for Canada.

WORST OVERALL DRAFT: 1944. First-rounder Merv Pregulman is the only pick from that draft who ever played for the Packers, and he lasted only a year before being traded.

BEST FREE AGENT: Ted Fritsch, who came out of nearby Stevens Point Teachers College in 1942 to become a team stalwart for nine years.

BEST TRADE: None were especially good, but obtaining Jack Jacobs from the Redskins for Bob Nussbaumer gave the Pack a good quarterback for 1947.

WORST TRADE: Trading Bud Svendsen and Dick Cassiano to Brooklyn for a washed-up Beattie Feathers in 1940.

BIGGEST OFF-FIELD EVENT: The demands of World War II depleted manpower in the first half of the decade, and the league war with the All America Football Conference took its toll on Green Bay in the second half of the decade.

BIGGEST ON-FIELD DEVELOPMENT: After the early retirement of Cecil Isbell, Lambeau would never have another top passer; after the retirement of Don Hutson, he wouldn't have an offense to speak of.

STRANGEST ON-FIELD EVENT: On Thanksgiving 1949, the Packers staged an intrasquad game to raise $50,000 cash to meet ongoing expenses. The Veterans were led by Jug Girard and wore blue uniforms. The Newcomers were led by Stan Heath and wore green. The Veterans won 35-31 before 15,000 fans who braved the snowy weather to support their team. At halftime, Johnny Blood was supposed to land on the 50-yard line in a helicopter, but the weather precluded that. Instead, Verne Lewellen gave a punting demonstration and Arnie Herber threw passes to Blood.

PACKERS BY THE NUMBERS

WORST FAILURE: The refusal of Lambeau to stay current and move to the T formation.

HOME ATTENDANCE: 1,103,683 in 55 games for an average attendance of 20,067. Milwaukee home games drew an average of 18,778, while Green Bay games averaged 21,065. Green Bay's average attendance was higher every year but 1945 through 1947.

FIRST GAME: September 15, 1940. The Packers held the Eagles to minus seven yards rushing, but Philadelphia's quarterback Little Davey O'Brien threw 40 passes and three touchdowns to keep the game close. Green Bay wins 27-20.

LAST GAME: December 11, 1949. The Packers lose to the Lions 21-7, the first of what will be 11 straight losses to Detroit. It was Curly Lambeau's last game with Green Bay.

BEST GAME: Two come to mind. On November 30, 1941, the Packers trailed the Redskins 17-0 at halftime. In the second half, though, Cecil Isbell threw 3 touchdowns to Don Hutson and the Pack won 22-17, enabling them to tie the Bears and force a playoff for the Western Division crown. On October 7, 1945, the Packers scored 41 points in the second quarter against the Lions, including four TD catches and 29 points by Don Hutson. They would go on to win 57-21. The 41 points by a team and 29 by a player are still league records for one quarter.

LARGEST MARGIN OF VICTORY: 54-7 over the Steelers on November 23, 1941.

LARGEST MARGIN OF DEFEAT: 49-3 to the Giants on November 21, 1948.

BEST OFFENSE: 1942. The team scored 300 points for the first time. Isbell threw for over 2,000 yards and 24 touchdowns, while Hutson caught 74 passes for 1,200 yards and 17 scores—all in 11 games.

BEST DEFENSE: 1941. The team gave up 120 points in 11 games with only the Bears managing more than 17 in a game.

MOST GAMES PLAYED: 94, Baby Ray. Ted Fritsch played in 87 and Charley Brock played in 82.

MOST POINTS: 589, Don Hutson.

MOST FIELD GOALS: 33, Ted Fritsch.

MOST TOUCHDOWNS: 67, Don Hutson.

MOST TOUCHDOWN PASSES: 47, Cecil Isbell.

MOST PASSING YARDS: 4,537, Cecil Isbell.

MOST RECEIVING YARDS: 5,089, Don Hutson.

MOST RECEPTIONS: 329, Don Hutson.

MOST RUSHING YARDS: 3,628, Tony Canadeo.

MOST INTERCEPTIONS: 34, Irv Comp.

MOST KICKOFF RETURN YARDS: 1,162, Tony Canadeo.

MOST PUNT RETURN YARDS: 441, Tony Canadeo.

BEST BOOK: Arch Ward, *The Green Bay Packers*. Putnam, 1946. The first history of the team was written by veteran Chicago sportswriter who created both the Baseball All-Star Game and the football College All-Star Game. He was also offered the job of NFL Commissioner in both 1939 and 1940.

NOTED SPORTSWRITER: Art Daley began a lengthy tour of covering the Packers for the *Green Bay Press Gazette* that would culminate with him being elected to the Packer Hall of Fame in 1993. He also originated the *Green Bay Packer Yearbook* in 1960 and edited it for decades.

BEST QUOTATION: Gerry Clifford, the last remaining member of the "Hungry Five," on Lambeau's resignation from the team in 1949, "We've had two good breaks in Green Bay in the last two weeks. We lost Rockwood Lodge and we lost Lambeau. If Lambeau had stayed here for two more years, we would have gone completely busted. We can now go ahead."

UNUSUAL NAMES: Amadeo "Mike" Buchianeri, Beattie Feathers, Clyde Goodnight, William Kuusisto, Nolan Luhn, and Urban Odson.

NICKNAMES: Jug Bennett, Connie "Warhorse" Berry, Charley "Ears" Brock, Red Bultman, Tony "The Grey Ghost of Gonzaga" Canadeo, Tiny Croft, Ralph "Scooter" Earhart, Whitey Evans, Tony "Hawk" Falkenstein, Bob "Chick" Forte, Ted "The Bull" Fritsch, Buddy Gatewood, Jug Girard, Clyde "Nip" Goodnight, Indian Jack Jacobs, Smiley Johnson, Royal "King Kong" Kahler, Red Keuper, Tex McKay, Forrest "Aimee" McPherson, Bomber Nussbaumer, Bulldog Panell, Butch Perkins, Ace Prescott, Stumpy Rohrig, Ken "Rhino" Snelling, Al "Gunga" Sparlis, Damon "Greek" Tassos, and Urban "Jeep" Urban.

FASTEST PLAYER: Don Hutson (still).

HEAVIEST PLAYER: Tiny Croft, 300 lbs in 1942. Ed Neal ranged from 290-300.

LIGHTEST PLAYER: Ross Mosley and Perry Moss, both 5'10" 170 lbs.

TOUGHEST INJURY: Bob Skoglund played one year, 1947, and injured his knee. He was featured on a Bowman football card in 1948, but did not play. Instead, he developed a kidney infection and died in January 1949 at the age of 23.

LOCAL BOYS: Irv Comp, Ted Fritsch, Stan Heath, Ken Keuper, and Evan Vogds all hailed from nearby Wisconsin towns.

FIRSTS:

Team to Travel by Airplane for a League Game—from Chicago to New York for the 11/17/40 game with the Giants.

Packer Team to Score 300 Points in a Season—1942.

Packer Team to Score 50 Points in a Game—11/24/40 50-7 win over the Lions.

Packer Team to Give up 300 Points in a Season—1949.

Packer Team to Lose 10 Games—1949.

Packer Team to Finish Last—1949.

Packer Team to Give up 40 Points in a Game—9/22/40 41-10 loss to the Bears.

Packer to Rush for 1,000 Yards—Tony Canadeo, 1,052, 1949.

Packer to Pass for 2,000 Yards—Cecil Isbell, 2,021, 1942.

Packer to Throw 20 TDs—Cecil Isbell, 24, 1942.

Packer to Convert all PATs in a Season—Don Hutson, 36 of 36, 1943.

Player to Catch Over 70 Passes—Don Hutson, 74, 1942.

Player to Gain 1,000 Yards Receiving—Don Hutson, 1,211, 1942.

HEAD TO HEAD
WITH NAGURSKI
CLARKE HINKLE • BACK 1933, 1935, 1937–41

WHO'S WORN THE NUMBER Cahoon 1927–28, O'Donnell 1929–30, Molenda 1931–32, Michalske 1932, Bettencourt 1933, Gantenbein 1933, Hinkle 1933, 1935, 1937–41, Barragar 1934, Mercein 1967–69, Krause 1970–71, 1973–74, Patton 1979, Whitaker 1981–82, Carruth 1986–88, J.B. Morris 1987r, Webb 1991, C. Harris 1993–94, Henderson 1995–97, A. Green 2000–

ORIGINATOR Tackle Ivan "Tiny" Cahoon 1927–28, of the five 1920s Packers from Gonzaga, the 235-pound Cahoon spent the longest time in Green Bay. He later coached high school football in town.

LONGEST TENURE Clarke Hinkle 1933, 1935, 1937–41.

NUMBER CHANGES Tiny Cahoon wore 10 in 1926 and wore 40 in 1929; end Dick O'Donnell had 5 in <1925–26> and wore 20 in 1927–28; fullback Bo Molenda wore 27 in 1929–30; guard Mike Michalske wore 36 in 1929–30 and 1937, 28 in 1931, 19 in 1932, 31 in 1933, 24 and 63 in 1934 and 33 and 40 in 1935; center Larry Bettencourt also wore 29 and 39 in 1933; end Milt Gantenbein wore 21 in 1931–32, 47 in 1933, 46 in 1933–34, and 22 from 1935–40; Clarke Hinkle also wore 27 and 33 in 1932, 39 in 1933, 45 and 48 in 1934, and 41 in 1936; center Nate Barragar wore 31 in 1931 and 1935, 56 in 1932 and 64 in 1934; replacement Jim Bob Morris also wore 47 in 1987; defensive back Corey Harris wore 81 as a wide receiver in 1992; fullback William Henderson changed to 33 in 1998 when cornerback Doug Evans left.

OTHER NOTABLES Bo Molenda (see top 27); end Milt Gantenbein (see top 22); center Nate Barragar (see top 31); fullback Chuck Mercein was indispensable in the Ice Bowl (see 76); William Henderson has been a solid fullback in recent years; Ahman Green has a chance to set some team rushing records in future years.

ONE TO FORGET Third-round draft choice Chuck Webb was active for only two games and returned two kickoffs for 40 total yards. He reinjured his knee and could not break into a 1991 RB rotation of Darrell Thompson, Keith Woodside, Vince Workman, and Allen Rice—none of whom averaged over 3.9 yards per carry—and then retired.

NUMBER 30

CLARKE HINKLE The drawback to having a long, rich tradition of success like the Packers is that today's players get irritated hearing how great their predecessors were. Teams in the 1970s and 1980s certainly grew weary of hearing about the teams of the 1960s. It wasn't until the 1990s teams had their own success that they could embrace the stars of the '60s themselves. Before the dynasty took off in the 1960s though, those players had to listen to how great the players of the 1930s were. What made that even worse was that they had to hear about heroes of one-platoon football, players who went both ways. Clarke Hinkle wasn't just Jim Taylor, but Ray Nitschke as well. This in itself made for a less explosive game; players got tired. Hinkle said he played pro football for "20 years—10 years on offense and 10 on defense." (Campbell)

Hinkle was an All American fullback and linebacker at Bucknell College in Pennsylvania and was recruited by the New York Giants who invited him to be their guest at a game against Green Bay in 1931. Hinkle was less impressed by the Giants than by the Packers, however, in particular by the size of Cal Hubbard, whom he wanted playing on his side. After starring in the East-West Shrine Game, Hinkle signed with the Packers and spent his entire career with them, missing only six games.

His numbers aren't impressive in today's context, but he was known as a triple-threat star—he could run, pass, and kick with the best. He also was known as a punishing blocker. When he retired, Hinkle held the league record for most yards gained rushing (3,860) even though he had finished among the top five only twice in his career. The Packers passed a lot and spread the rushing carries around. Clarke threw an occasional pass, punted well, and placekicked effectively. He led the league in scoring once, field goals twice, and rushing touchdowns once.

It was his toughness that was celebrated above all. He was known as one of the most difficult men in the league to bring down, inflicting punishment on his tackler just as Jimmy Taylor would 30 years later. On defense, he was as hard a hitter as there was in the league, indeed like Nitschke. His reputation was heightened through his respectful rivalry with legendary Bear fullback/linebacker Bronko Nagurski. Nagurski outweighed Hinkle by roughly 30 pounds, but they were often seen as equals in ferocity. Their battles are still remembered today for their competitiveness. They faced each other for the first time in Hinkle's rookie year, and Nagurski had to be helped off the field after their first collision. Another time on defense, Hinkle made the mistake of waiting for Nagurski to come to him, and the Bronk ran over Clarke and gave him seven stitches in his chin.

Their two most famous encounters are well-documented. On September 24, 1933, in a Packers 14-7 victory, Hinkle went back to punt on third down, which was conventional strategy during the field-position game of the early 1930s. Instead, he took off toward the sideline and Nagurski lit out in pursuit. Seeing that Nagurski had the angle on him, Hinkle decided to go down swinging, literally. As Nagurski approached, Hinkle pivoted and threw his shoulder into Nagurski's face. Both players went down, but only Hinkle got back up. Bronk had to be carried off the field with a broken nose and untold other injuries. Some reports list Nagurski as having cracked his hip as well, and of missing several games. But records show that Nagurski missed no games in 1933, so that part is pure legend.

The second collision happened on November 1, 1936, in a Packers 21-10 win. Hinkle took a handoff from Isbell for his favorite play, a weak-side line plunge in the three hole, and was met thunderously by Nagurski. Hinkle was thrown back into the back-field, but kept his balance and took off around the end for a 59-yard touchdown run. Bear tackle George Musso later remarked that this was the only time he had a back pass him three times on the same play. Strangely, when Hinkle would recall these two inci-dents a decade later for *My Greatest Day in Football*, he would remember them both as coming in losses.

Hinkle was a player who Lambeau knew just how to motivate. Clarke would get so psyched up that he often played the game in a fury, flying around the field hitting peo-ple and making a lasting impact. His teammate Cecil Isbell would say of him years later, "He did not have the pure brute power of Nagurski because he did not have Bronk's size. But he had the knack you see today in a runner like Jim Taylor of exploding at the point of impact. He was a compact runner, and he had the same kind of balance Taylor has—he could take the shock of a tackle, bounce sideways and keep going. And he never quit. He wanted to win more than anyone I ever saw." (Maule, 115-6) Appropriately when he was elected to the Hall of Fame in 1964, he was presented by his long-time friend and rival Bronko Nagurski. Hinkle was inducted into the Packer Hall of Fame in 1972, and his memory was further honored by having one of the Packers' practice fields named after him in 1997.

FOR FURTHER INFORMATION

Campbell, Jim. "Evolution of NFL Players," *Pro!* 1984. Available online at www.footballresearch.com/articles/frpage.cfm?topic'evol-pla.

Cope, Myron. *The Game That Was: An Illustrated Account of the Tumultuous Early Days of Pro Football*. New York: Crowell, 1974. (77-96)

D'Amato, Gary, and Cliff Christl. *Mudbaths and Bloodbaths: The Inside Story of the Bears-Packers Rivalry*. Madison, WI: Prairie Oak Press, 1997. (107-11)

Goodman, Murray, and Leonard Lewin. *My Greatest Day in Football*. New York: Barnes, 1948. (117-21)

Johnson, Chuck. *The Greatest Packers of Them All*. New York: Putnam, 1968. (79-83)

Maule, Tex. *The Game: The Official Picture History of the NFL and AFL*. New York: Random House, 1967. (115-6)

Whittingham, Richard. *What a Game They Played*. New York: Harper and Row, 1974. (91-105)

1962 CHAMPIONSHIP
JIM TAYLOR • FULLBACK 1958–66

WHO'S WORN THE NUMBER Lewellen 1929–30, Jenison 1931, Barrager 1931 and 1935, Van Sickle 1932, Michalske 1933, Kurth 1934, Prescott 1946, Harding 1949, Boedecker 1950, Mann 1950–51, Cone 1952–57, J. Taylor 1958–66, P. Williams 1969–73, Culbreath 1977–79, G. Ellis 1980–86, Hunter 1987r, A. Rice 1991, B. McGee 1992, Teague 1993–5, R. Smith 1998, Vinson 1999, Akins 2000–01.

ORIGINATOR Back Verne Lewellen 1929–30 (see 46).

LONGEST TENURE Jim Taylor 1958–66

NUMBER CHANGES Verne Lewellen had 4 in <1925–26> and wore 21 in 1927, 45 in 1928, and 46 in 1931–32; center Nate Barragar wore 56 in 1932, 30 and 64 in 1934; guard Clyde Van Sickle also wore 57 in 1932 and 26 in 1933; guard Mike Michalske wore 36 in 1929–30 and 1937, 28 in 1931, 19 and 30 in 1932, 24 and 63 in 1934 and 33 and 40 in 1935; tackle Joe Kurth wore 28 in 1933 and 58 in 1934 Bob Mann wore 87 in 1952–54; Fred Cone wore 66 in 1951.

OTHER NOTABLES Verne Lewellen (see 46); Nate Barrager was captain of the USC football team before becoming an All League center in the 1930s. He later worked for 30 years in the film business; Mike Michalske (see 33); receiver Bob Mann was the team's first black player (see 87); Fred Cone was a fullback and placekicker for most of the 1950s; Gerry Ellis led the team in rushing three times and is sixth all-time in team rankings with over 3,800 yards. He also caught 267 passes.

ONE TO FORGET Out-of-control defensive back and special teams player Chris Akins caused a great deal of upheaval with his on-the-field antics before being cut late in the 2001 season. His personal foul penalty in the Atlanta game helped lead to their winning touchdown, and he followed that with a shouting altercation on the sideline with Coach Mike Sherman. Two weeks later he picked up two personal foul penalties against Jacksonville. Finally, he told reporters that the coach had a grudge against him and that he wanted to be waived. He got his wish, as did Packer fans.

JIM TAYLOR Dick Schaap wrote so many articles and books about and with the 1960s Packers that he was practically an honorary teammate. A *Saturday Evening Post* article he wrote about Jim Taylor struck a sour note, though. Sarcastically entitled "Genius at Green Bay," the perspective of the piece was that Taylor was living proof that you didn't have to be very bright to play football. While Schaap may have meant nothing mean-spirited in writing it—Taylor was called "Doody Bird" by his teammates, was known for engaging in doubletalk and malaprops, and was often the butt of their jokes—it seems jarringly cruel when read today. Besides, teammate Henry Jordan probably had a more astute view when he said of Taylor that, "he liked to give the impression he was a rough, tough country boy and mumbled a lot, but if you got him talking finances he came out bright and clear." (Carroll, 168) He may have lacked academic aptitude, but Jim turned out to be a very successful businessman after his career ended.

On the field, he was respected by teammate and opponent alike. Ray Nitschke said of him, "Taylor was in a class by himself. In 15 years with the pros, he's one of the toughest men I ever played against —and we were on the same team. He'd hurt you when you'd tackle him. He was as hard as a piece of granite. He had such strong legs." (Nitschke, 61) Colts guard Jim Parker, Colts tight end John Mackey, and Cowboy tackle Bob Lilly all rated him among the top ten players they ever saw. Sam Huff and Merlin Olsen both ranked him the second toughest player they ever played against. Ever-tactful Norm Van Brocklin put it crudely, but succinctly, "Taylor is tougher than Japanese arithmetic." (Johnson, 58)

When he finished his career with 8,597 yards rushing—all but 390 attained in his nine years in Green Bay—he was third all-time in the NFL behind Jim Brown and Joe Perry (counting Perry's AAFC numbers). He is still number one by a wide margin on the Packers. He ran for over a thousand yards five years in a row and was the only man aside from Jim Brown to win a rushing championship during Brown's career. His league-leading totals of 1,474 rushing yards and 19 TDs in 1962 led to him being awarded the MVP for the year. He rarely fumbled, became a dependable receiver, and was a capable blocker as well. It's no wonder that he was the first of Lombardi's Packers elected to the Hall of Fame in 1976.

Taylor was intensely competitive and felt a special rivalry with Jim Brown. In the handful of times they played against each other, Taylor almost always gained more yards and scored more touchdowns. Of more importance, the Packers won each game. By consensus, Brown was the greatest running back of all time. He had size, strength, great speed, and shifty moves. His special tool was a powerful straight arm that he wielded to push tacklers away. Taylor, in contrast, was smaller, did not have great speed, and did not rely on shifty moves. He was extremely strong (he was one of the first players to seriously lift weights), followed his blocks perfectly, and ran over anyone in his way. Coach George Allen said of his running that, "He ran with his elbows almost as much as his legs. He'd lower his shoulders and swing his forearm out in front of him and flail away with his elbows and hurt people as he ran through them." (Allen, 72) Taylor himself sums up his career simply, "I was just a player. I enjoyed football. I enjoyed contact." (Carroll, 168)

Jimmy felt Lombardi was a master motivator, but the coach thought Taylor disloyal when he played out his option and went home to sign with New Orleans in 1967. He was the heart of Lombardi's offense, though, and Vince always admired him. When Lombardi was coaching the Redskins, Sam Huff remembers his playing and replaying film of Taylor's runs and saying out loud, "Boy, that son of a bitch could run." He had an intense rivalry with Sam Huff. To this day, Taylor will single out Dick Butkus and Joe Schmidt and Bill George as tough opponents, but only says of Huff, "He had a good press agent." (McCullough, 241)

Taylor's greatest moment was the 1962 title game against Huff and the Giants in Yankee Stadium. The Packers were 13-1, first in the league in points scored and fewest points allowed; they beat both the Bears and the Eagles 49-0 that year, but the Lions had displayed some chinks in their armor on Thanksgiving, beating Green Bay handily 26-14. The Giants were no slouches either. They finished 12-2, second in points scored and fourth in points allowed. In addition, the Giants were fired up about being embarrassed 37-0 in previous year's title game by Green Bay.

It was bitterly cold day with the temperature 20 degrees at game time and winds gusting to 40 mph. Some players who also played in the Ice Bowl, including Ray Nitschke, considered the conditions in the 1962 game even tougher. The ground was icy, hard, sharp, and inflicted pain anytime someone was tackled. The wind negated the Giants vaunted passing offense, and this became a game fought in the trenches. Taylor was the workhorse, carrying the ball 31 times for 85 yards, and the Giants, led by Huff, gang-tackled him each time, often getting in some cheap shots after the play was dead. Jimmy needed stitches in his elbow, bit his tongue and was spitting blood the whole game. After the game according to announcer Ray Scott, Taylor's body was black and blue and yellow and purple, a complete mess. In the second quarter, he scored a touchdown from the seven yard line on the only play he wasn't tackled all game. At the half the Packers led 10-0, meaning they had played six championship quarters against the Giants in 1961–62 and had outscored them 47-0. The Giants finally got on the board in the third quarter by blocking a Packer punt and falling on the ball in the end zone, but they never did score on the Green Bay defense. With Jerry Kramer kicking three of five field goals, the final score was 16-7 and the Packers were two-time champs. Sam Huff was forced to concede that the Packers were "36 tough s.o.b.s." Of the 36, Jimmy Taylor was the toughest.

FOR FURTHER INFORMATION

Allen, George, with Ben Olan. *Pro Football's 100 Greatest Players: Rating the Stars of Past and Present.* Indianapolis: Bobbs-Merrill, 1982. (71-2)

Carroll, Bob. *When the Grass Was Real: Unitas, Brown, Lombardi, Sayers, Butkus, Namath and All the Rest: The Ten Best Years of Pro Football.* New York: Simon and Schuster, 1993. (165-9)

Johnson, Chuck. *The Greatest Packers of Them All.* New York: Putnam, 1968. (57-66)

McCullough, Bob. *My Greatest Day in Football: The Legends of Football Recount Their Greatest Moments.* New York: Thomas Dunne Books, 2001. (233-42)

Nitschke, Ray, as told to Robert W. Wells. *Mean on Sunday: The Autobiography of Ray Nitschke.* 2nd ed. Madison, WI: Prairie Oak Press, 1999. (61-2)

Schaap, Dick. "Genius at Green Bay." *Saturday Evening Post.* 11/3/62. (32-38)

"36 Tough Ones." *Newsweek.* 1/14/63. (44)

PACKERS BY THE NUMBERS

 1962 CHAMPIONSHIP DATA
Green Bay Packers 16
New York Giants 7

December 30, 1962 • Yankee Stadium, NY
Attendance: 64,892
Winner's Share: $5,886.57
Loser's Share: $4,166.85
Weather: 20 degrees, dropping to 17 in the second half with a 20-30 mph wind.

KEY STATS	PACKERS	GIANTS
First Downs	18	18
Rush Yards	148	94
Pass Yards	96	197
Total Yards	244	291
Interceptions	1	0
Fumbles Lost	0	2
Penalties	5-44	4-62
Third Down Conversions	5/17	9/17

Halftime Score: Packers 10 Giants 0

LEADERS

Rushing: Jim Taylor 31-85   Alex Webster 15-56
Passing: Bart Starr 9-21-0 85 yds   YA Title 18-41-1 197 yds
Receiving: Boyd Dowler 4-48   Joe Walton 5-75

ADDITIONAL FACTS

•The game was blacked out on television in New York, so Giant fans had to drive 75 miles to view it.

•Willie Wood was ejected from the game for knocking down an official while protesting an interference call.

•Boxing promoter Al Flora offered Sam Huff and Jim Taylor $2,000 for a four-round boxing match.

•Game MVP Ray Nitschke appeared that night as the mystery guest on the "What's My Line" TV show.

• An ironic postscript to the title game coverage by *Newsweek* was a little note they included regarding the NFL employing a team of ex-FBI agents to ferret out gambling rumors involving four teams, with only the Bears named. Of course, Paul Hornung and the Lions Alex Karras would be suspended due to this investigation, and the Bears would win the 1963 title.

ICONOCLAST
TRAVIS JERVEY • RUNNING BACK, 1995–98

WHO'S WORN THE NUMBER Dunn 1929, Bowdoin 1929–30, Comstock 1931–33, Bultman 1934, C. Perry 1935, Becker 1936–38, Biolo 1939, Lusteg 1969, D. Highsmith 1973, Starch 1976, S. Atkins 1979–81, J. Simmons 1986, D Brown 1987–89, Don King 1987r, Avery 1991, J. Stephens 1993, Cobb 1994, Jervey 1995–98, Mealey 2001–02, Westbrook 2002.

ORIGINATOR Quarterback Red Dunn 1929 (see 11).

LONGEST TENURE Running back Travis Jervey 1995–98.

NUMBER CHANGES Red Dunn wore 11 in 1927–28, 16 in 1929, 7 and 17 in 1930, and 15 in 1931; guard Jim Bowdoin wore 19 in 1928 and 34 in 1931; center Red Bultman wore 45 in 1932–33, 33 and 38 in 1933, and 17 and 52 in 1934; guard Claude Perry wore 26 in 1927–30, 37 in 1929 and 1933, 27 in 1931, 24 in 1932, and 50 in 1934; guard John Biolo also wore 16 in 1939; replacement Don King also wore 17 in 1987.

OTHER NOTABLES Red Dunn (see 11).

ONES TO FORGET Former 1,000 yard rushers John Stephens and Reggie Cobb were brought in as free agents to cure the running game in successive years, but Stephens gained only 173 yards in five games and Cobb gained 579 in 16 games, not exactly Emmitt Smith numbers.

TRAVIS JERVEY Colorful characters come in a variety of types on a football team. There are tough guys like Clarke Hinkle, Jim Taylor, Ray Nitschke, and Frankie Winters. There are comic cut-ups like Ted Fritsch, Fuzzy Thurston, and Brett Favre. There are ladies' men like Curly Lambeau, Johnny Blood, Paul Hornung, and Max McGee. And then there are the free spirits who march to the offbeat of their own drum kit. Johnny Blood (again) rode the railroad blinds like a hobo and was dubbed by some the "Magnificent Screwball." His exploits are so legendary that they warrant their own chapter (55).

While all pale in comparison to Blood, some Packers were still goofy. At 6'6" and 250 pounds, tackle Steve Wright was called "Bullwinkle" after the popular cartoon moose on television because of Steve's tendency to run in the wrong direction on some plays. Once in practice, Vince Lombardi was so discouraged by Steve's likeable personality and lackadaisical attitude that the 5'8" coach started flailing away at Wright, trying to get him to hate the coach enough to take it out on the opposing team. In the Ice Bowl, starting tackle Bob Skoronski was injured on one play and the call went out for Wright to replace him. The only trouble was that Steve couldn't find his helmet. Finally he grabbed the closest one he could find and ran onto the field, but he had grabbed Lionel Aldridge's helmet and it was too big for him. He realized this as soon as he went into a three point stance on his first play and Aldridge's helmet slid down over his face so that he couldn't see anything as the ball was snapped. Travis Jervey was of the same cracked mold as Wright.

Top Ten Examples That Travis Jervey Is a Few Yards Shy of the Goal Line

10) Pulled over for speeding in 1997, Jervey was arrested for possession of marijuana. Three days later, the charges were dropped after lab tests revealed that what the police had found was not pot. In the meantime, the Jacksonville Jaguars withdrew a three-year $3.75 million contract offer to the restricted free agent, and he re-signed with Green Bay for $400,000.

9) Pulled over for speeding in his rookie year in Green Bay, he explained to the officer that he had a radar detector, but that the stereo was so loud he couldn't hear it. He was let off with a warning.

8) Again in his rookie year, Travis was having trouble starting a fire in his fireplace. So he doused the wood with gasoline and then threw in a match. After the ensuing explosion, Jervey had to roll around on the floor smothering the fire that was burning the hair off his arms and legs.

7) In the off-season after his rookie year, he slept with a football and carried it around the house to lessen his fumbling problem.

6) When asked what he wanted for Christmas one year, he responded "Night vision goggles and paint ball guns."

5) After scoring the first and only touchdown of his Packer career in a 1998 game against the 49ers, Travis was about to strike his intended end zone surfer pose when he was tackled by his exuberant quarterback Brett Favre.

4) Jervey was such an avid surfer that he invoked the anger of coach Mike Holmgren at Super Bowl XXXII in San Diego by buying a surfboard and hitting the waves while the team was preparing for the Broncos.

3) A few weeks before that Super Bowl, Travis took a pair of needle-nose pliers and removed the braces from his teeth in about 10 minutes because they were driving him crazy. (So that was the problem.)

2) Jervey spent several weeks after Super Bowl XXXI in Costa Rica surfing and bumming around. He liked the people, but was surprised because, "They don't even hardly speak English." He added that, "People don't realize in the United States, people here go straight from high school to college. Everybody goes to college. In Europe, Australia, Brazil, everyone travels for a couple of years. Everybody. Nobody goes straight to school. Because there's no hurry. In the United States, there's this big hurry." Especially on the football field.

1) In his rookie year, Travis apparently thought he was on Animal Planet. He shared a house with LeShon Johnson who reportedly was raising 19 pit

bulls. The two were fined by the state for illegally setting deer traps in their backyard. Jervey wanted his own pet and considered a monkey but heard that they were too difficult to take care of so he settled on ordering a lion cub for $1,000. Accounts differ as to whether the lion was actually delivered before Mike Holmgren told his players they were not allowed to have a lion. They are welcome to tame the ones from Detroit, though.

In the fifth round of the 1995 draft, the Packers' director of college scouting, John Dorsey, advocated selecting Terrell Davis of Georgia. Ron Wolf was apprehensive of Davis' frequent injuries, and instead picked Travis Jervey of the Citadel, who had nearly set a record for accumulating the most demerits at the military school. The Broncos grabbed Davis in the sixth round. Three years later the two would face each other in the Super Bowl. Jervey was a star on special teams, but Davis had become the top running back in the league. Travis was not a bad pick for a fifth rounder, but he was not a Super Bowl MVP. Twice he was chosen as having one of the best physiques in football by *Muscle & Fitness*, and one time he finished fourth in the NFL's Fastest Man competition. Jervey was fast but not elusive, muscular but a fumbler. Therefore, he failed in his bid to replace an injured Dorsey Levens at running back in 1998 before breaking his ankle. However, he was valuable as a Pro Bowl special teams player who was also named to some All Pro teams.

Travis finally made his big score in 1999 when the 49ers signed him to a four-year, $6 million contract despite the broken ankle and promised him a shot at the starting running back slot. In San Francisco, he was slow to recover and claims he took testosterone to help speed the treatment of his ankle, but was detected having used steroids and given a four-game suspension by the league. After two years of more injuries and only seven carries for 49 yards and one TD, the 49ers waived him. He caught on as a special teams guy for the Falcons in 2001, but his football career has begun to slip away.

It was a similar story for Wright. After Lombardi left, Steve was traded from one team to another, traveling first to the Giants then the Redskins, then the Bears, then the Cardinals, and finally to the disastrous World Football League. The road for the maverick is usually a bumpy one. Green Bay was the one place Wright felt at home because it was a brotherhood of individuals intent on the single purpose of winning. Both Wright and Jervey were a bit off center, but were still competitors who strove to win. When Jervey looks back on his career, he will probably recall his years as a special teams player in Titletown as the happiest ones of his career. Winning teams can find a place for a hard-working non-conformist.

FOR FURTHER INFORMATION

King, Peter. "Countdown," *Sports Illustrated*. 10/30/95. (22-9)

Nickel, Lori. "Packers Make Great Escapes," *Milwaukee Journal Sentinel*. 7/31/97. (Sports 1)

Wright, Steve, with William Gildeau and Kenneth Turin. *I'd Rather Be Wright*. Englewood Cliffs, NJ: Prentice-Hall, 1974.

LEAVING THE GAME
MIKE MICHALSKE • G 1935

WHO'S WORN THE NUMBER B. Kern 1929, Englemann 1930, Radick 1931, Hinkle 1932, Bultman 1933, Michalske 1935, C. Clemens 1936, R. Peterson 1937, Weisgerber 1938–40, 1942, Bucchianeri 1941, Sorenson 1943–45, Gatewood 1946–47, Baxter 1948, B. Burris 1949–51, Floyd 1952, B. Clemens 1955, Purnell 1957, Nitschke 1958, Carpenter 1959–63, Grabowski 1966–70, Barty Smith 1974–80, J. Jensen 1981–2, J. Clark 1983–87, Sterling 1987r, Woodside 1988–91, D. Evans 1993–97, Henderson 1998–02.

ORIGINATOR Tackle Bill Kern, 1929, was a second team All Pro in 1929 and 1930 and was later a successful head coach at Carnegie Tech (where he was voted Coach of the Year in 1936) and West Virginia.

LONGEST TENURE Running back Barty Smith 1974–80 (see Forget below).

NUMBER CHANGES Back Wuert Englemann wore 25 from 1931–33; lineman Ken Radick wore 35 in 1930, Clarke Hinkle also wore 27 in 1932, 30 in 1933, 1935, and 1937–41, 39 in 1933, 45 and 48 in 1934, and 41 in 1936; center Red Bultman wore 45 in 1932–33, 38 in 1933, and 17, 32, and 52 in 1934; guard Mike Michalske wore 36 in 1929–30 and 1937, 28 in 1931, 19 and 30 in 1932, 31 in 1933, 24 and 63 in 1934, and 40 in 1935; guard Mike Bucchianeri wore 19 in 1944 and 17 in 1945; center Les Gatewood also wore 77 in 1946; fullback Bob Clemens also wore 35 in 1955; Ray Nitschke wore 66 from 1959–72; fullback William Henderson wore 30 in 1995–97.

OTHER NOTABLES Bill Kern (see above); Clarke Hinkle (see 30); Ray Nitschke (see 66); William Henderson has been a solid fullback in recent years and tied Elijah Pitts' team record for most games played by a Packer running back with 126 in 2002.

ONE TO FORGET Barty Smith was tough with a good work ethic and was a good blocker useful on special teams. However, he was a number one pick as a running back, and as a runner he was terrible. He was slow from the start and then had knee problems. In seven years he gained only 1,942 yards and averaged only 3.6 yards per carry.

MIKE MICHALSKE Iron Mike Michalske was a true 60-minute man. He resisted ever coming out of any game, and with good reason. He was a four-time All Pro and was the first guard elected to the Pro Football Hall of Fame in its second year, 1964. He was inducted in the Packer Hall of Fame in its first year, 1970. On offense he was expert at pulling and leading interference downfield for Packer ball carriers. On defense he was the Lawrence Taylor of his day, blitzing the passer, but was also tough against the run. Benny Friedman, the Giants All League quarterback from the 1920s, picked Michalske for his All Time Team. He claimed Mike was "one of the fastest and most agile of linemen. He was smart, alert, aggressive, and was...never mouse-trapped, never out of position. He was always in the right place at the right time and a deadly tackler." Citing his intelligence, Friedman called Michalske a "quarterback-playing guard. I nominate him for my line coach." (Daley)

Mike was an All American at Penn State in 1925 and played fullback, guard, end, and tackle for the Nittany Lions. He signed with Red Grange's New York Yankees of C.C. Pyle's new American Football League in 1926. The Yankees were the class of that league, but the first AFL folded after only one year. The Yankees joined the NFL but the team itself foundered two years later. In 1929, still owed $400 by the Yankees, Mike became a free agent and signed with the Packers. Along with Cal Hubbard and Johnny Blood, Mike was one of three key Packer acquisitions that year, and Green Bay would take the league title the next three years.

While many things have changed about the game, the basics remain the same. Michalske would once reminisce, "We called it blitzing in those days, too. Our target was the man with the ball, especially the passer. It may not have been exactly ethical, but it was legal in those days to rough the passer, even after he got rid of the ball. We worked him over pretty good. Hubbard and I used to do some stunting in the line to find an opening for a blitz breakthrough. We figured the best time to stop them was before they got started." (*Packers*, 32) For the next four years, the Packers ranked first, fourth, second, and second in points allowed, largely due to Michalske and Hubbard's pressure defense. One of the highlights of his career was in the November 1, 1932, Bears game when Mike's 70-yard interception return for a touchdown was the margin of the 6-2 Packer victory.

After seven years with the Packers and 10 in professional football, Michalske took off 1936 to become head basketball coach and assistant football coach under Ernie Nevers at Lafayette College. He returned to Green Bay in 1937, but would play in only six games before he hurt his back and retired for good. A number of Packers over the years have quit playing for a year only to come back the next, usually with diminishing powers.

In the 1930s, center Nate Barragar sat out 1933 to tend to business concerns after having played three years in the NFL and two with Green Bay only to return in 1934. Barragar was still young and in his prime and would make the All Pro team both of his final years in football, 1934 and 1935. Usually it goes a little differently. Cal Hubbard sat out 1934 to coach college football and did not have a lot left in the tank when he returned in 1935. He finished his career the next year in New York. Tackle Ernie Smith sat out 1938 to play for the Hollywood Stars of the minor league Pacific Coast Pro Football League and returned for only six games in 1939 before quitting for good.

World War II caused all sorts of strange career disruptions. Tackle Ade Schwammel made second team All Pro in 1936 and then quit. Due to the wartime shortage of players, he returned to the Packers six years later to play for two more years. Arnie Herber was cut in 1941, but returned three years later with the Giants and would face the Packers in the 1944 title game. Buckets Goldenberg and Don Hutson probably would have retired earlier than they did if it hadn't have been for the war.

Expanded opportunities caused some players to return in 1960. Al Carmichael and Howie Ferguson had sat out the 1959 season and Fred Cone had missed 1958 and 1959, but all three returned in 1960. Carmichael and Ferguson signed with new AFL teams, the Denver Broncos and Los Angeles Chargers respectively, and Cone turned up on the expansion Dallas Cowboys.

Of course the biggest return of all was Vince Lombardi returning to coaching with the Washington Redskins in 1969 with promising results. But Redskin Bill Anderson sat out 1964 and returned as a Packer who caught only 10 passes in 1965 and 1966. Boyd Dowler retired from the Packers in 1969 only to return as a Redskin in 1971 for his poorest year as a pro. Zeke Bratkowski was brought back from coaching after two years in retirement to resume his backup quarterback duties in 1971. In later years, Reggie White and Robert Brooks were ineffective in their one-year comebacks with the Panthers and Broncos in 2000, but Gilbert Brown surprisingly still was a force on the field after eating himself out of football in 2000.

On the flip side, a handful of Packers left the field too soon. The most obvious is Cecil Isbell, the star tailback who threw for 24 touchdowns and over 2,000 yards to make the All Pro team in his fifth and final year in the league. Tackle Bill Kern retired in 1931 to go into coaching and guard Lon Evans retired in 1938. Both made All Pro in their final years. Ade Schwammel and linebacker Clayton Tonnemaker were second team All Pros in their last years, and Derrel Teteak was still a vital 27-year-old star when he quit in 1957. Red Dunn, Don Hutson, Bill Forester, and Willie Wood all made All Pro in their last year, too, but all were past 30 and could not have had many productive years left, anyway. Packers whose careers were abruptly ended by injury, such as Sterling Sharpe, Johnny Holland, Tim Lewis, and Nelson Toburren, are a whole other category of players who left too soon.

After his playing career ended, Mike Michalske coached football at St. Norbert's and Iowa State until the end of the war. After the war, he served as a line coach for Baylor, Texas A&M, and Texas until he got tired of being fired and left coaching for the business world in 1957. He would live a long life before leaving the field of this earth for good in 1983 at age 80.

FOR FURTHER INFORMATION

Daley, Arthur. "A Dissent from an Expert," *New York Times.* 12/23/49. (24)

Harrington, Denis. *The Pro Football Hall of Fame: Players, Coaches, Team Owners and League Officials, 1963-1991.* Jefferson, NC: McFarland, 1991. (46-7)

Packers of the Past: A Series of Articles Reprinted from the Milwaukee Journal Sept. 28–Dec. 9, 1965. Milwaukee, WI: Milwaukee Journal, 1965. (30-2)

Porter, David L., ed. *Biographical Dictionary of American Sports: Football.* New York: Greenwood Press, 1987. (392-3)

1965 CHAMPS
DON CHANDLER • KICKER AND PUNTER 1965–67

WHO'S WORN THE NUMBER Lidberg 1929, Sleight 1930, Bowdoin 1931, Stahlman 1932, A. Rose 1933, Engebretsen 1935–41, Roskie 1948, J. Spencer 1950–51, Chandler 1965–67, Middleton 1977–81, A. Clark 1982, L. Rash 1987r, L. Mason 1988, Edgar Bennett 1992–96, M. McKenzie 1999–02.

ORIGINATOR Fullback Cully Lidberg 1929 cut his points scored in half each year from 24 as a rookie in 1926 when he was second team All League to 12 in 1929 to 6 in 1930. He was a hard tackler and rugged rusher.

LONGEST TENURE Guard Tiny Engebretsen 1935–41 (see 52).

NUMBER CHANGES Cully Lidberg had 17 in <1926> and wore 38 in 1930; tackle Red Sleight wore 37 in 1931; guard Jim Bowdoin wore 19 in 1928 and 32 in 1929–30; lineman Dick Stahlman wore 36 in 1931; end Al Rose wore 37 and 52 in 1932, 49 in 1934, and 47 in 1935–36; Tiny Engebretsen wore 69 in 1934 and 52 in 1936; back Ken Roskie also wore 50 in 1948; tackle Joe Spencer wore 79 in 1951.

OTHER NOTABLES Tiny Engebretsen (see 52); Terdell Middleton gained over a thousand yards in 1978. No Packer would do that again until Edgar Bennett in 1995; Mike McKenzie is beginning to look like a star at cornerback.

ONE TO FORGET Running back Allan Clark in five games returned four kickoffs for 75 yards and fumbled once in 1982.

DON CHANDLER Don was one of the first punting specialists in the NFL. The first was Pat Brady of the Steelers in 1954, followed by Dick Deschaine of the Packers in 1955. Chandler and Sam Baker joined the league in 1956, the 49ers Tommy Davis came in 1959, and Bobby Joe Green arrived in 1960. This trend toward kicking specialists became the norm in the 1960s. Chandler was originally supposed to be the Giants' place kicker as well, but due to an injury he was replaced by Ben Agajanian. The next year the Giants acquired Pat Summerall, so Chandler did not assume both kicking jobs until his seventh year in the league, 1962.

Chandler was one of the best in the league at both duties. And with his background as a running back, he was very effective at the fake punt which he seemed to try about once a year when the opposition was lax. In his 12–year career, Don rushed the ball 13 times for 146 yards and threw and completed three passes for 67 yards. Since he rarely played in the backfield after the first year, most if not all of these attempts can be assumed to have been fake punts. Only once did he lose yards—11 yards on what was most likely a botched snap in 1962. In Green Bay he ran once for 27 yards in 1965 and once for 33 yards in 1966 before Donny Anderson took over the punting in 1967. In an October 1965 game against the 49ers in Lambeau, Chandler got off a 90–yard punt that traveled 75 yards in the air and over 110 yards out of the end zone with the roll. The Packers had a fourth down at their own ten, and Don booted the ball from his goal line. It landed at the San Francisco 25 and bounded on through their end zone for a touchback.

Chandler had nine good seasons with the Giants, even leading the league in scoring in 1963, but when he had an off year in 1964 coach Allie Sherman was happy to deal him to the Packers for a draft pick. Green Bay was coming off its most disappointing season under Lombardi and much of it was due to the kicking game. When Paul Hornung returned from his 1963 gambling suspension he had completely lost his kicking touch, going 12 of 38 in field goals and missing two extra points. Better kicking could have changed the team's 8-5-1 record to 11-3 and reduced the division winning Colts to 10-4.

Lombardi treated Chandler much differently this time. Chandler was a connection to the old days in New York, so Vince would confide in Don about the team and left him alone about his kicking. Don did straighten out the Packers kicking mess. In 1965, he kicked 17 of 26 field goals and in 1967 he hit on 19 of 29 and made the Pro Bowl for the only time in his career. 1966 was an off year when he hit on only 12 of 28, but Lombardi blamed that primarily on reserve center Bill Curry's high snaps.

1965 was a pivotal year for the reputation of Vince Lombardi. People were starting to suspect the Packers were done with their nice little run. If so, Lombardi would be remembered today as just another good coach from the past, not an icon that the Super Bowl trophy is named after. The Colts had won the West convincingly in 1964 and looked to repeat in 1965. Green Bay and Baltimore had won six of the last seven Western Division crowns, and the Colts reins had been successfully passed from Weeb Ewbank to young Don Shula to perhaps begin a new Baltimore era. The Packers and Colts would meet three times that year, and the Colts would have a different starting quarterback each time. On September 26, the teams met in Milwaukee with Johnny Unitas behind center for Baltimore. Green Bay would win a hard-hitting defensive battle 20-17 behind a fourth quarter 37-yard touchdown pass from Zeke Bratkowski to Max McGee. Zeke had replaced an injured Bart Starr in an uneasy bit of foreshadowing. When the teams met again on December 12 in Baltimore, Gary Cuozzo was starting in place of Johnny Unitas who had been injured the week before. In a thick fog, the game was close for the first half. The Packers led only 14-13 in the last minute when Cuozzo was intercepted by leaping linebacker Dave Robinson at the Packer two-yard line. Robby returned the ball 88 yards to the Colts 10. The Packers scored again to lead at half 21-13 rather than trailing 20-14. In the second half they would rumble on behind Hornung and Taylor who accumulated 127 yards on 32 carries between them. Hornung scored five touchdowns in the 42-27 victory.

In more bad news for Baltimore, Cuozzo separated his shoulder in the second half and halfback Tom Matte had to finish up at quarterback for Baltimore. Equally important, the loss knocked them out of first place. To win the division, Baltimore would have to win its final game against the last place Rams with halfback Matte running the offense and hope that the Packers not beat the 49ers. Amazingly, that's what happened. The 49ers tied the Packers on a last minute John Brodie touchdown pass, and that left Green Bay and Baltimore in a tie for first place. Even though the Packers had beaten the Colts both times in the regular season, a playoff would be held the next week, and Green Bay won the coin flip to determine the location.

With the difference in quarterbacks between Starr and Matte, the Packers were expected to win easily. On the game's first play from scrimmage, though, tight end Bill Anderson fumbled Starr's pass. Linebacker Don Shinnick picked the ball up and headed for the end zone. Starr tried to make the tackle, but got caught up in a crush of bodies and badly bruised his ribs. After one play, the Packers turned the game over to Zeke Bratkowski down 7-0. The game turned into a fierce defensive struggle and after several exchanges of punts, the Colts launched a 67-yard drive to the Packers eight and kicked a 15-yard field goal to go up 10-0 late in the second quarter. The Packers finally began to move the ball and got to the one-yard line on second down. Three straight runs were stuffed by the Colts who took over on downs and ran out the clock still up by 10 at the half.

In the third quarter the Packers got a break when a bad snap on a punt led to the Packers getting the ball on the Colts 35. Green Bay scored in three plays. The next two times the Packers got the ball their drives were stopped by interceptions; they turned the ball over four times in this game. Finally, with nine minutes left, Green Bay got the ball on its 28 and began one final long march that took them to the Colt 20 with two minutes left. On fourth down Chandler lined up to attempt a 27-yard field goal. He booted the ball very high and then turned his head in disgust because he thought he missed it. However, under the goal posts, field judge Jim Tunney ruled the kick good. The Colts could not believe it and never would accept it even decades later. The controversial kick tied the game and caused the goal posts to be raised to 30 feet for the next season. In overtime the defensive battle continued for another 13 minutes. Lou Michaels missed a 47-yard try for Baltimore, but Chandler at last won the game for Green Bay with a 25-yarder right down the middle. The Packers had outgained the Colts 362 yards to 175, but had turned the ball over four times to Baltimore's one. Anderson avenged his early fumble by catching seven more passes the rest of the day.

The next week on a wet, snowy, muddy, Lambeau Field the Packers took on the Cleveland Browns for the title and Chandler was the leading scorer for the Packers with 11 points as they defeated the Browns 23-12. The Browns team bus got stuck in the bad weather traffic and arrived late at Lambeau, where Cleveland was greeted with field conditions not to their liking. Through the rain, sleet and snow, the game was marked by a number of terrific performances. Bart Starr returned with his ribs heavily bandaged and called a brilliant game on offense. At halftime, the Packers led only 13-12 by benefit of a botched extra point by the Browns, but in the second half, the Packer line asserted itself and allowed Paul Hornung to accumulate 105 yards on 18 carries and Jim Taylor to bump forward for 96 yards on 27 carries. Green Bay had one 90-yard drive that culminated with a 13-yard Paul Hornung touchdown run and consumed over seven minutes. Another second half drive lasted 13 plays and resulted in a game clinching field goal. The Packers held the ball for 21 1/2 minutes in the second half. On defense, Ray Nitschke and the Packer line held Jim Brown to only 50 yards rushing and new starting cornerback Bob Jeter shut down ace wide receiver Paul Warfield. The Packers were champs again, and it was "just like the old days," in the words of Paul Hornung.

Chandler's kicking would figure prominently in each of the three championships he was part of in Green Bay. In his bad year of 1966, it was his blocked extra point attempt that allowed the Cowboys to get within range of tying the NFL title game in the last minute. In 1967, he scored 15 of the Packers 33 points on four field goals and three extra points in Super Bowl II over the Raiders. He retired with Lombardi, but reportedly was willing to return in 1968 if he were able to skip weekly practices and just show up on the weekends for games. General Manager Lombardi refused, and it was a big mistake for which new coach Phil Bengtson paid the price. The team would make only 13 of 28 field goal attempts and would miss three extra points as well. More reliable kicking would have won them three or four more games and earned them the divisional title despite the fact that Bart Starr missed half the season with injuries.

At this point, the "what ifs" become really interesting. In the first playoff game they would have faced the 13-1 Colts and probably would have lost badly just as the Vikings actually did. However, the Packers always played the Colts tough and won more than they lost against them so a win was possible. Up next would have been the Cleveland Browns, a good solid team, but one that the Colts smoked. The Packers probably would have run out of gas, but again a win was possible. And who would be waiting in Super Bowl III? Joe Namath's Jets. It was shocking enough when the Jets upset Baltimore, what if they beat the team of the 1960s? Talk about a changing of the guard. Then again, Packer teams normally didn't make the kinds of deadly errors that doomed the Colts in that Super Bowl . . . But Lombardi said no, Chandler stayed home, and the glory days were over.

FOR FURTHER INFORMATION

Johnson, Chuck. *The Greatest Packers of Them All.* New York: Putnam, 1968. (181-8)

Kramer, Jerry, ed. *Lombardi: Winning Is the Only Thing.* New York: World Publishing, 1970. (125-9)

Kramer, Jerry, with Dick Schaap. *Distant Replay.* New York: G.P. Putnam, 1985. (192-6)

Maule, Tex. "Cool Masterpiece," *Sports Illustrated.* 1/10/66. (14-8)

———. "Ghostly Massacre," *Sports Illustrated.* 12/20/65. (22-7)

———. "Packers in a Thriller," *Sports Illustrated.* 10/4/65. (76, 78)

———. "Point of Some Return," *Sports Illustrated.* 1/3/66. (10-3)

Thorn, John. *Pro Football's Ten Greatest Games.* New York: Four Winds Press, 1981. (63-81)

1965 CHAMPIONSHIP DATA
Green Bay Packers 23
Cleveland Browns 12

January 2, 1966 • Lambeau Field

Attendance: 50,777

Winner's Share: $7,819.91

Loser's Share: $5,288.83

Weather: 33 degrees, light snow and rain with a 10 mph wind. Three and a half inches of snow were cleared from the field before game time.

KEY STATS	PACKERS	BROWNS
First Downs	21	8
Rush Yards	204	64
Pass Yards	128	97
Total Yards	332	161
Interceptions	2	1
Fumbles Lost	0	0
Penalties	2-20	3-35
Third Down Conversions	7/15	2/10 1/1 on 4th down

Halftime Score: Packers 13 Browns 12

LEADERS

Rushing: Paul Hornung 18-105   Jim Brown 12-50

Passing: Bart Starr 10-18-1 147 yds   Frank Ryan 8-18-2 115 yds

Receiving: Boyd Dowler 5-59   Jim Brown 3-44

ADDITIONAL FACTS

•Wisconsin Governor Warren Knowles was kept from the game by the snow.

•Hornung said, "The snow reduced their speed down to ours" When asked whether the footing was good, he replied, "Yes, considering that it was muddy and slippery."

•Brown quarterback Frank Ryan completed his first four passes for 77 yards; after that he was 4-14-2 for 38 yards.

•In the second half, the Packers first drive went for almost seven minutes and their second for over eight. The Packers held the ball for 38 of the 56 plays in the second half, and Cleveland gained only 26 yards after intermission.

•Hornung and Taylor carried Lombardi off the field.

PRO BOWL AND ALL PRO HONORS
CLAYTON TONNEMAKER • LINEBACKER 1950

WHO'S WORN THE NUMBER Ashmore 1929, Radick 1930, Nash 1931–32, Vairo 1935, F. Butler 1938, Balazs 1939–41, Flowers 1942–49, (Piotrowski 1947), G. Johnson 1949, Tonnemaker 1950, W. Michaels 1951, B. Clemens 1955, Mestnik 1963, A. Jacobs 1965, D. Conway 1971, D. Rogers 1982, 1984, Wilhite 1987r, M. Haddix 1989–90, R. Wilson 1994, J. Graham 2002.

ORIGINATOR Tackle Marion "Roger" Ashmore 1929 was one of five 1920s Packers from Gonzaga. Roger was the only one to make All League (second team 1928).

LONGEST TENURE Center Bob Flowers 1942–49 a longtime back up who was released after opening day of his eighth year in Green Bay.

NUMBER CHANGES Roger Ashmore wore 46 in 1928; lineman Ken Radick wore 33 in 1931; end Tom Nash wore 21 in 1928, 19 and 26 in 1929, and 37 in 1929–30; center Frank Butler wore 26 and 60 in 1934, 48 in 1935–36, and 59 in 36; Clayton Tonnemaker wore 58 in 1953–54; fullback Bob Clemens also wore 33 in 1955.

OTHER NOTABLES End Tom Nash (see top 19); and linebacker Walt Michaels would have a nice career with the Browns.

ONE TO FORGET A one-time number one pick of the Eagles, running back Michael Haddix spent his last two seasons in Green Bay. His career ended with a bang as he led the team in rushing . . . with the embarrassing total of 311 yards. That's in a 16-game season. That season also represented the second best yards per carry average of his career, 3.2.

CLAYTON TONNEMAKER Native Minnesotan Clayton Tonnemaker had his own Leaf Bubblegum football card in 1948 as a college player. He was co-captain of the Minnesota Gophers football team and an All American in his senior year of 1949. Among his teammates on the powerful Golden Gophers squad was future Vikings Coach Bud Grant. Clayton was drafted number one by the Packers in 1950 and moved right into the starting lineup as a center and linebacker. In his memorable first game as a pro, he made over half the tackles against the Chicago Cardinals. Later that same year in a forgettable game against the Bears, Tonnemaker snapped the ball to the punter and then was stood up by Ray Bray and laid out by a sucker-punch from Fred Davis. Clayton had to be carried off the field. After his rookie year, Tonnemaker would spend the next 32 months in the Army Medical Corps, including a stint in the Korean War. Upon his return to the Packers in 1953, the speedy 240-pound linebacker wreaked havoc on NFL gridirons for only two more seasons before retiring to go into business. His final foray into sports was at the age of 32 in 1960 when he joined the first Minnesota Rugby Football Club in the Midwest Rugby Football Union. He was named to the College Football Hall of Fame in 1980 and died of a stroke in 1996.

Tonnemaker was honored in each of the three years he played in the NFL. In 1950 he was named All Pro in his rookie year. In his first year back from the service he was picked for the Pro Bowl in 1953, and in his last year he was a second team All Pro in 1954. If he had played a few more seasons in Green Bay, he probably would be in the Packer Hall of Fame. The Packers in their long history through 2001 have had 45 players who were named All Pro once and 36 players who were named All Pro for more than one season:

Nine time All Pros—Don Hutson

Eight time All Pros—Forrest Gregg

Seven time All Pros—Jim Ringo

Six time All Pros—Willie Wood, James Lofton, Reggie White

Five time All Pros—Lavvie Dilweg, Henry Jordan, Jerry Kramer, Herb Adderley, Willie Davis

Four time All Pros—Verne Lewellen, Cal Hubbard, Clarke Hinkle, Bobby Dillon, Bill Forester, Gale Gillingham, Sterling Sharpe, Leroy Butler

Three time All Pros—Mike Michalske, Ray Nitschke, Dave Robinson, John Brockington, Ken Ellis, Brett Favre

Two time All Pros—Lon Evans, Cecil Isbell, Tony Canadeo, Ted Fritsch, Bill Howton, Dan Currie, Jim Taylor, Fuzzy Thurston, Chester Marcol, Tim Harris, Travis Jervey

Of these All Pros with multiple selections, all eligible players except Tim Harris have been inducted in the Packer Hall of Fame.

In addition to the 30 Packers who were selected to a single Pro Bowl, 39 players were selected for more than one Pro Bowl:

Nine Pro Bowls—Forrest Gregg

Eight Pro Bowls—Willie Wood

Seven Pro Bowls—Jim Ringo, James Lofton, Brett Favre

Six Pro Bowls—Reggie White

Five Pro Bowls—Jim Taylor, Herb Adderley, Gale Gillingham, Sterling Sharpe

Four Pro Bowls—Bill Howton, Bobby Dillon, Bill Forester, Henry Jordan, Bart Starr, Willie Davis, Leroy Butler

Three Pro Bowls—Roger Zatkoff, Jerry Kramer, Dave Robinson, Carroll Dale, Fred Carr, John Brockington, Willie Buchanon, Paul Coffman, Mark Chmura

Two Pro Bowls—Billy Grimes, Dave Hanner, John Martinkovic, Paul Hornung, Jesse Whittenton, Boyd Dowler, Bob Jeter, Ken Ellis, Chester Marcol, Larry McCarren, Darren Sharper, Bubba Franks, Ahman Green

Of the Pro Bowlers with multiple selections, all eligible players except Roger Zatkoff and Billy Grimes are in the Packer Hall of Fame.

PACKERS BY THE NUMBERS

Finally, in the pre-Pro Bowl All Star Games held from 1938-42, Don Hutson and Cecil Isbell were selected three times, Clarke Hinkle and Charley Brock were picked twice, and Russ Letlow and Larry Craig were chosen once. All of these players are in the Packer Hall of Fame.

If we total all of these post-season honors by position, we can get an idea of what have been the strongest and weakest positions for the Packers through their history. What I did was tabulate each year a Packer was honored with either an All Pro selection, a second team All Pro notice, or a Pro Bowl appointment. For example, in 1956 Bill Howton was named All Pro and selected to the Pro Bowl, so that counts as one honored year for the wide receiver position in the tabulation, just as 1978 does when James Lofton was picked for the Pro Bowl, but not for any All Pro teams. I divided the data into two sections: 1) the 29 years of pre-1950 two-way football and 2) the 52 years of two-platoon football through 2001. I added up all the honored years and divided by the number of starting slots to get a weighted number as a result, i.e., there are two tackle positions so the total number of honored years is divided by two, but there is only one center position so that is not divided. I made an adjustment with defensive tackle and linebacker to take into account the 13-year period when the Packers played a 3-4 defense instead of a 4-3. I also made an adjustment between running backs and wide receivers to reconcile the emergence of the flanker position in the Split T Formation. Dividing the weighted years by the number of years in the time period gives us a final figure to compare relative strength of each position across the two eras. I have ignored special teams performers in the following tables:

TWO-WAY FOOTBALL 1921–49

Position	Honored Years	Weighted Years	Weighted Years/29
End	29	14.5	.5
Tackle	20	10	.34
Guard	18	9	.31
Center	11	11	.38
Backs	42	10.5	.36

TWO PLATOON FOOTBALL 1950–2001

Position	Honored Years	Weighted Years	Weighted Years/52
Wide Receiver	22	11.9	.23
Tight End	7	7	.13
Tackle	9	4.5	.09
Guard	20	10	.19
Center	13	13	.25
Quarterback	11	11	.21
Running Back	15	7	.13
Defensive End	19	9.5	.18
Defensive Tackle	14	8	.15
Linebacker	45	13.8	.27
Cornerback	23	11.5	.22
Safety	25	12.5	.24

These tables indicate a number of things. For the two-way era, end was the strongest position, which is not surprising considering that Don Hutson and Lavvie Dilweg were stationed there for 19 of the 29 years. The honored years were pretty evenly distributed amongst the other positions. Curly Lambeau's Packers were a well-rounded, top-flight team for most of those years, so again this relatively equal distribution of talent is no surprise.

When we look at the table for the two-platoon era, the strongest positions on offense were center and wide receiver (continuing a long tradition of passing offense excellence). On defense, both linebacker and the secondary were positions of strength, while defensive line—particularly defensive tackle—were the weaker positions. Aside from Henry Jordan and Dave Hanner, the Packers defensive middle has often been weak. The weakest position of all is clearly offensive tackle where only Forrest Gregg truly distinguished himself, but tight end and running back have been somewhat weak as well. The last column allows us to compare the two eras to some extent. None of the two-platoon numbers measure up to the numbers generated by the two-way period. Largely, this is a function of there being many more teams and thus greater competition for the same number of spots in the more recent years. However, it is also an indicator of bad to mediocre football often on display in Green Bay in the 1950s, 1970s, and 1980s. Clayton Tonnemaker was an exceptional exception for his time.

FOR FURTHER INFORMATION

Porter, David L., ed. *Biographical Dictionary of American Sports: 1989–1992 Supplement for Baseball, Football, Basketball, and Other Sports.* New York: Greenwood Press, 1992. (491-2)

THE LAMBEAU LEAP
LEROY BUTLER • DEFENSIVE BACK 1990–01

WHO'S WORN THE NUMBER Michalske 1929–30 and 1937, Stahlman 1931, Quatse 1933, Tenner 1935, Scherer 1938 Steen 1939, Van Every 1940–41, Earl Bennett 1946, Girard 1948–51, B. Wilson 1967, M. Carter 1970, Lane 1972–74, Sampson 1978–79, K. Davis 1986–88, L. Butler 1990–2001.

ORIGINATOR Guard Mike Michalske 1929–30 and 1937 (see 33).

LONGEST TENURE Leroy Butler 1990–2001.

NUMBER CHANGES Guard Mike Michalske wore 28 in 1931, 19 and 30 in 1932, 31 in 1933, 24 and 63 in 1934 and 33 and 40 in 1935; lineman Dick Stahlman wore 34 in 1932; tackle Jess Quatse also wore 23 in 1933; end Bernie Scherer wore 40 in 1936 and 11 and 16 in 1937; guard Earl Bennett also wore 15 in 1946.

OTHER NOTABLES Mike Michalske (see 33); Macarthur Lane teamed well with John Brockington at running back for a couple of years.

ONE TO FORGET Local boy Jug Girard was the classic jack-of-all-trades-master-of-none and was ultimately a major disappointment as a first round pick in 1948. He was a disaster at quarterback in 1949, completing only 35% of his passes. In four years he rushed for fewer than 300 total yards, caught under 20 passes, and returned an occasional punt and kickoff. He was a moderately skilled punter who may have been best in the defensive backfield. He spent five years with the Lions and one with the Steelers after leaving his native Wisconsin, so he had some value as a receiver, defensive back, and punter, but not first-round value.

LEROY BUTLER When Leroy Butler was a boy, the bones in his pigeon-toed feet were so weak that he spent most of his time either in a wheelchair or in leg braces. In a fortunate accident, his sister knocked him out of his wheelchair when he was eight years old. Leroy got up, found that he was able to walk without a problem, and then started to run just like the scene in the movie "Forrest Gump." Within no time he was a star athlete in the Jacksonville projects where he grew up.

He befriended another local star athlete in growing up, future Packer teammate Edgar Bennett. Leroy was two years ahead, but he and Bennett played together in high school, at Florida State where Butler helped recruit Bennett, and in Green Bay where Leroy urged his team to draft Edgar in the fourth round in 1992. Leroy himself was a first round pick in 1990 and stepped in immediately as a starting cornerback and a fixture on defense. Were it not for the career-ending broken shoulder blade he suffered in 2001, he would have passed Bart Starr for most games played as a Packer. Nonetheless, with a 12-year career in exclusively in green and gold, he will be remembered as a Packer great. His 38 interceptions trail only Bobby Dillon's 52, Willie Wood's 48, and Herb Adderley's 39 in team annals. His aim was to reach 40 interceptions and 20 sacks, a combination not yet attained and something on which to pin his Hall of Fame chances. He reached the sack goal, but fell two picks short.

Through good seasons and bad, Leroy was an upbeat vocal team leader, always good for a quote and always espousing a winning attitude. He viewed communication with the media as one of his duties as a team leader, taking the pressure off more reticent players. When GM Ron Wolf criticized Butler's conditioning and play during the first half of 1995, Leroy took his anger out on Packer opponents, not on Packer management. He took the criticism to heart and became a greater player. He has been a loyal team player who has restructured his contract on several occasions in order to help the team fit other players under the salary cap. His service to the Packers stands with that of Brett Favre and Reggie White among players of his era, and he was a fan favorite throughout his career. He was tough, durable, and played through injuries. In 1997 he played all season with a badly torn bicep muscle and had an All Pro year.

His versatility was what made so valuable. He was quick enough to cover receivers and hard-hitting enough to come up and make the tackle on running backs. His talent for finding the openings in the line allowed him to be a real threat as a blitzing pass rusher as well. In the Super Bowl season of 1996, Butler finished with 6.5 sacks, only two behind team leader Reggie White, and he had a memorable one-arm sack of Drew Bledsoe in Super Bowl XXXI. The following year the Denver Broncos focused their attack on finding Butler and putting a blocker on him on every play because they had noticed how often he would swoop in and make a big tackle at the line when everyone else was blocked. That strategy paid off for Denver in its first Super Bowl victory.

If for no other reason, Leroy will always be remembered as the originator of the Lambeau Leap that has punctuated Packer touchdowns over the past decade. On the day after Christmas 1993, the Packers pasted the Raiders 28-0 in the final home game of the season, thereby clinching a playoff slot for the first time in 11 years. Green Bay was leading 14-0 in the fourth quarter when Butler forced Raider running back Randy Jordan to fumble. Reggie White recovered the ball and began running for the goal line. As he was being tackled, he saw Butler free and lateraled the ball to Leroy who ran the ball the last 25 yards to the end zone. Some fans were yelling, "jump in the stands," so Leroy kept right on running and made the first Lambeau Leap into the outstretched arms of the fans in the lower end zone seats. He didn't make it all the way into the stands as he was grabbed by the fans, but the interesting thing is that the first Leap was not noted at all in game reports of the time. If not for receiver Robert Brooks taking up the practice two years later in 1995 to gain the fans' confidence and acceptance in replacing Sterling Sharpe as the team's go-to receiver, Leroy's leap of fame would be forgotten.

Brooks' leaps were high and artistic. His proficiency at them led him to record a song called "Jump in the Stands" to commemorate the celebration. The Lambeau Leap has been taken up and tried by many Packer touchdown makers since, and even imitated in other venues (Viking Vault, anyone?) In Lambeau Field, though, it was a spontaneous and special bond between the Packers of the 1995–98 period and their fans. Unlike so many touchdown celebrations that seemed to say no more than, "look at me," the Leap demonstrated a special rapport between the Packers and their fans. The Leap's charm eventually dwindled as it became more ritual than spontaneous celebration, but it was a special symbol of the Packers as the fans' team, and it was owed to the inspiration of Leroy Butler.

In his long tenure in Green Bay, Leroy came up with other bits of joyful choreography, such as the Six Gun Salute he and Brett Favre would exchange after another Favre touchdown pass. Of more importance, Leroy was a four-time All Pro and a four-time Pro Bowler who did everything asked of him by his defensive coaches. At one time, he was probably the best strong safety in the game. In the later years of his career he has served as a coach on the field directing where his teammates should line up and shouting out instructions on what to watch for. Despite being named to the NFL's 1990s All Decade team by the Hall of Fame selection committee, he may well fall short in his ultimate stated goal of reaching the Pro Football Hall of Fame, but his induction in the Packer Hall of Fame is assured and his spot in Packer lore is enduring.

FOR FURTHER INFORMATION

Favre, Brett, with Chris Havel. *Favre: For the Record.* Garden City, NY: Doubleday, 1997. (169, 185-6)

Froberg, Tim. "Butler: Simply the Best," *Green Bay Packers 1998 Yearbook.* (70-2)

Silver, Michael. "Stepping Out," *Sports Illustrated.* 5/19/97. (78-83)

Silverstein, Tom. "Butler Retires, Says He Can't Shoulder the Load Any Longer," *Milwaukee Journal-Sentinel Packer Plus.* Available online at www.jsonline.com/packer/news/jul02/59597.asp.

White, Reggie, with Jim Denney. *In the Trenches: The Autobiography.* Nashville, TN: T. Nelson, 1996. (156-7)

Wilde, Jason. "Butler Shoots for 20-40 Career Marks (Sacks and Picks) to Trigger 'Hall' Chances," *Green Bay Packers 2001 Yearbook.* (48-9)

NEW BROOM
SWEEPS CLEAN
MARK MURPHY • SAFETY 1980–85, 1987–91

WHO'S WORN THE NUMBER C. Perry 1929 and 1933, T. Nash 1929–30, Sleight 1931, A. Rose 1932, S. Johnston 1934, Seibold 1935–36, F. Schammel 1937, T. Jones 1938, Brennan 1939, C. Berry 1940, L. McLaughlin 1941, Reichardt 1952, H. Ferguson 1953–58, L. Hickman 1960, Crutcher 1964, Vandersea 1966, D. Livingston 1970, I. Thomas 1972–73, T. Wells 1975, Moresco 1977, M. Murphy 1980–85, 1987–91, Keshon Johnson 1994, Ty Williams 1996–2002.

ORIGINATOR Guard Claude Perry 1929 (see top 26).

LONGEST TENURE Mark Murphy 1980–85, 1987–91.

NUMBER CHANGES Claude Perry wore 26 in 1927–30, 27 in 1931, 24 in 1932, 50 in 1934, and 32 in 1935; end Tom Nash wore 21 in 1928, 19 and 26 in 1929, and 35 in 1931–32; tackle Red Sleight wore 34 in 1930; end Al Rose also wore 52 in 1932, 34 in 1933, 49 in 1934, and 47 in 1935–36; fullback Swede Johnston wore 15 from 1935–38 and 54 in 1936; tackle Champ Seibold wore 57 in 1934 and 1939–40, 58 in 1936, and 41 in 1937–38; linebacker Tommy Joe Crutcher wore 56 from 1965–67 and 1971–72; linebacker Phil Vandersea wore 83 in 1968–69.

OTHER NOTABLES Claude Perry (see top 26); Tom Nash (see top 19); Swede Johnston (see top 15); tackle Champ Seibold (see top 57); fullback Howie Ferguson (see below); cornerback Tyrone Williams was a steady performer for the Packers.

ONE TO FORGET In 1994 the Packers picked up Keshon Johnson from the Bears. Wrong K. Johnson, though, this defensive back's next stop was back to the Bears.

MARK MURPHY The Packers' pass defense was porous in 1979 so they used four of their 11 1980 draft picks on defensive backs in addition to bringing in free agents like Mark Murphy from West Liberty State College to compete with their existing secondary members in training camp. Murphy broke his wrist in that 1980 training camp, but not before impressing the coaches enough in scrimmages that he was put on the injured reserve list. While recovering from his injury, he studied and learned the safety position thoroughly. When Johnny Gray was injured in 1981, he started seven games at strong safety and nabbed the first three of his 20 lifetime interceptions. In 1982 he returned to special teams duty as the team made the playoffs for the only time in Murphy's career. When Gray was shifted to free safety in 1983, Mark became a regular at strong safety and would remain there the rest of his career.

Whenever he took off his helmet, he was a distinctive smooth-pated figure in green and gold. He had suffered from the mysterious hair loss condition alopecia since he was in third grade and had no hair on his head. On the field, though, he used his head and played more with intensity and intelligence than talent. He was a steady player who hit with power, but lacked speed. His biggest years were those in which he teamed with Chuck Cecil to form the toughest, hardest-hitting, yet probably slowest pair of safeties in the league. Their proclivity for the big hit that could be felt throughout the stadium made them a popular duo with the fans. Murphy led the team in tackles the last four years of his career. Of course, it's not just who makes the tackle that's important, but where the tackle is made. Lindy Infante said that "If I can have 47 Mark Murphys, I wouldn't have to worry about the Super Bowl at all." (Biever, 159) That statement not only sums up Mark Murphy, but tells you all you need to know about Lindy Infante. If he had 47 Mark Murphys, he wouldn't be worrying about the Super Bowl because he still wouldn't be going. It takes a mix of talent and intensity to make a Super Bowl team. Murphy had the intensity to play a valuable role on a winning team, but he never had an abundance of flashy skills.

When Ron Wolf and Mike Holmgren came in, they saw the secondary as a weakness, aside from Leroy Butler. The desire was there, but the speed wasn't. When Murphy came to minicamp and saw himself as third on the strong safety depth chart, he asked to be released and Wolf complied. Murphy did not catch on anywhere else. Cecil lasted one more year in Green Bay before he was let go. They both fell victim to the process of radical change necessary to turn around any long-term losing team. The new regime in this situation needs to examine the personnel closely to see that only those who can play are the ones who stay. Beyond identifying those with simple ability is determining those with a winning attitude. Ron Wolf has said that he was shocked and disappointed by the attitude he found in Green Bay when he arrived. It was not a winning attitude; losing was too easily accepted. He set out to change that as quickly as possible. Firing people is a good way to show that you mean business. After all, professional athletes are paid to win games, not simply to play them. Of the 56 players who played for Green Bay in 1991, 28 or 50% were gone before the 1992 season. From there, Wolf and Holmgren went about restocking the talent pool with successful drafts, and, of most importance, installed the quarterback they wanted in Brett Favre.

Another good player who wore number 37 during tough times in Green Bay ran into this same situation 30 years before. Howie Ferguson was a fun-loving, hard-hitting fullback who never went to college. A scout saw him playing for a service team, and he got a tryout with the Rams in 1952. The Rams were loaded at running back and couldn't use him, but they recommended him to the Packers. Green Bay brought him in as a free agent the next year, and Howie spent the next half-dozen years as the team's starting fullback. In 1955 he finished second in the league with 859 yards rushing in his greatest year. His running style was said to be similar to that of his successor, Jim Taylor, meaning that the shortest distance between two points is straight ahead. Ferguson liked to run over people, not around them. The teams he played for were truly awful, though, winning only 20 of 72 games over those six years.

Lombardi came in and went right about the business of clearing out the dead wood and the dead attitudes in 1959. He had an encounter with Ferguson right away. Howie and Max McGee arrived at training camp a day early, dropped off their stuff, ate lunch with the rookies, and took off for a night of partying. The next day Lombardi lit into them for disappearing because to him once they reported to camp, they were subservient to his rules. McGee saw that discretion was the better part of valor and submitted to the coach. Ferguson chose to argue with Lombardi and was quickly gone. He would play one final year with the Los Angeles Chargers in 1960. Lombardi swept out the players who could not play and those accustomed and comfortable with losing. He was fortunate in that a great deal of unrealized talent was already available to him for molding. Once he settled on Bart Starr as his quarterback, the team was ready to win. The change from 1958 to 1959 was almost as striking as from 1991 to 1992. Of the 38 players from 1958, 16 or 42% were gone by 1959.

Both Howie Ferguson and Mark Murphy were dependable, hard-working players who did their best for weak teams, but who did not have the skills to remain when the talent pool was upgraded. Ferguson went on to make money drilling oil, while Murphy coaches high school football. They both were deservedly elected to the Packer Hall of Fame, Ferguson in 1974 and Murphy in 1998. Of their time in the NFL, Ferguson would probably agree with Murphy that, "I had the ideal job, a job I loved to do, that I'd played for 23 years of my life. I wasn't getting paid for it in junior high or high school or college, but then all of a sudden they're handing me a check? To play a game I love! There were a lot of fun games. That's all that I know, you know, you go out and hit people, and I can honestly say that I enjoyed every game that I played in. It was fun." (Biever, 159)

FOR FURTHER INFORMATION

Biever, Vernon J., photography, Peter Strupp ed. *The Glory of Titletown: the Classic Green Bay Packers Photography of Vernon Biever.* Dallas, TX: Taylor Publishing, 1997. (159)

Burke, Don. "Mark Murphy's Lucky Break," *Green Bay Packers 1989 Yearbook.* (43-5)

Lea, Bud. "Ferguson Was One Wild and Crazy Guy," *Milwaukee Journal Sentinel Packer Plus* 9/15/99. Available online at www.jsonline.com/packer/comm/sep99/leacol16091599.asp.

Poling, Jerry. Downfield! Untold Stories of the Green Bay Packers. Madison, WI: Prairie Oak Press, 1996. (209)

Wolf, Ron, and Paul Attner. *The Packer Way: Nine Stepping Stones to Building a Winning Organization.* New York: St. Martin's Press, 1998. (36)

ALL TIME TEAMS AND HALL OF FAME
CAL HUBBARD • TACKLE 1931

WHO'S WORN THE NUMBER Earp 1929, Lidberg 1930, Hubbard 1931, McCrary 1933, Bultman 1933, Laws 1934, Herber 1935–40. Sample 1942, 1945, Luhn 1945–49, T. Rote 1950–51, Mercer 1968–69, T. Webster 1971, Scales 1975, E. Hood 1978–84, C. Sullivan 1986, N. Jefferson 1987–88, C. Washington 1987r, A. White 1992, B. Pickens 1993, Satterfield 1996, McElmury 1997–98, M. Snider 1999.

ORIGINATOR Center Jug Earp 1929 (see 39).

LONGEST TENURE Defensive back Estus Hood played from 1978–84 mostly as a nickel back whose specialty was getting beaten deep, especially when he began to have knee problems.

NUMBER CHANGES Jug Earp wore 7 in <1925–26>, 29 in 1927–28, 9 in 1928, and 39 in 1930–32; fullback Cully Lidberg had 17 in <1926> and wore 34 in 1929; Cal Hubbard wore 39 in 1929, 40 in 1930 and 1932, 27 in 1933, and 51 in 1935; fullback Herdis McCrary wore 29 in 1929, 28 in 1929–30, 19 in 1931, 43 in 1932, and 53 in 1933; halfback Joe Laws also wore 41 in 1934, 29 in 1935–36 and 24 from 1937–45; Arnie Herber also wore 12 in 1930, 26 in 1931, 41 in 1932–33, 16 in 1933, 45 and 68 in 1934, and 19 in 1937; quarterback Tobin Rote wore 18 from 1952–56; fullback Matt Snider also wore 44 in 2000.

OTHER NOTABLES Jug Earp (see 39); fullback Cully Lidberg (see top 34); fullback Herdis McCrary (see top 53); halfback Joe Laws (see top 24); tailback Arnie Herber (see 16); quarterback Tobin Rote (see 18).

ONE TO FORGET Defensive back Norman Jefferson was "Mr Irrelevant XXII" by virtue of being the last player selected in the 1987 draft. Surprisingly he made the team, and in his two years in Green Bay handled the ball 11 times by returning five punts and six kickoffs. He fumbled five times before he was dropped from the team and headed for Canada.

CAL HUBBARD Robert Cal Hubbard was a big Missouri farm boy who was born at the turn of the last century and who had a celebrated, long, and divergent career in professional sports. After graduating high school, Cal spent a few years working on the farm before enrolling in 1922 at tiny Centenary College in Shreveport, Louisiana, in order to play football for his boyhood hero, Bo McMillan. When

McMillan moved to Geneva College in Beaver Falls, Pennsylvania the next year, Hubbard continued to follow him and sat out of football a year. He then played for McMillan at Geneva from 1924–26 and made All America in his senior year. That final year was highlighted by Geneva's 16-7 upset of mighty Harvard when Hubbard was practically a one-man team. His Geneva roommate, Pip Booth, recalled that "Hubbard moved like a cat and always smashed into the ball carrier with his face or chest. Once I saw him smash down the whole side of a defensive line by himself. He was six to eight years older than most of us, and we looked up to him more as a father than as a teammate." (Jenkins, 82)

He joined the New York Giants in 1927 as they won their first NFL championship; in his second year, he made All Pro for the first of six consecutive years. On offense he played tackle and occasionally end, while on defense he is sometimes credited with being the first linebacker because he would back up off the line to take his stance with the Giants. After those two years, he had had enough of the big city and made known that he wanted to go to Green Bay. He joined the Packers in 1929. History is silent on exactly how this transfer was arranged. Often in accounts of Hubbard's life, his change of teams is referred to as a trade, but the question of compensation is deftly ignored. Hubbard's sister Mary wrote a biography of her brother in his later years, and she stated that the Packers sent Al Bloodgood to the Giants for Cal. However, her text is not very reliable. In this instance, Bloodgood was a Giant teammate of Cal's in 1928 and a Packer teammate of his in 1930.

In any case, Hubbard joined the Packers the same year with fellow stars guard Mike Michalske and halfback Johnny Blood, and Green Bay won the next three championships with their help. That made four in a row for Cal. Hubbard and Michalske shored up the defensive line to the extent that the Packers surrendered only 22 points for the entire 1929 season while Johnny Blood helped them score 198. Curly Lambeau had Cal stay in the line on defense, ending his "linebacker" days. Hubbard was sometimes listed as weighing as much as 270 pounds, but he asserted that he never weighed more than 250 in his playing days, but that was still gigantic stature for those days of two-way football. Opposing quarterback Harry Newman said of Cal, "Green Bay had the most brutal lineman in the game, Cal Hubbard. He played tackle and was about 6'5" and maybe 270 pounds. He played with the same kind of intensity that Dick Butkus did later. We used to say of Cal that even if he missed you, he still hurt you. When he tackled you, you remembered it. I do to this day." (Whittingham, 113)

Hubbard was such an imposing figure that teams tried to provoke him into fights to get him thrown out of the game. The Chicago Cardinals once sent reserve guard Phil Handler out to do just that. Hubbard put up with Handler's harrassment all game until there was a free-for-all at the end of the contest. When all the players were separated, Handler was out cold, with Hubbard standing innocently nearby. Such wisdom would prove useful to Cal as he began to move into a new field, baseball umpire. He started umpiring in the minor leagues in 1928 and worked his way up to the International League by 1931. His football career was winding down. He left the pros in 1934 to be a line coach at Texas A&M for one year, and then returned to Green Bay in 1935. The following year, he saw action with both Pittsburgh and the Giants, but of more importance he was promoted to American League umpire. Over the next 16 seasons as a big league umpire, he worked four World Series and three All Star Games. When a hunting accident marred his vision in 1952, he was promoted to assistant supervisor of umpires and then to American League Supervisor of Umpires in 1954. He held that post until 1969 when he retired.

In that same year, Cal was voted the NFL's greatest tackle for its first fifty years; Don Hutson, Jerry Kramer, and Ray Nitschke also made that same team. In addition, he was selected along with Hutson and Clarke Hinkle to the league's 75th anniversary two-way team; other Packers on the overall 75th anniversary team were Hutson, Nitschke, Ted Hendricks, Jan Stenerud, and Reggie White. Green Bay has selected its own All-Time team on several occasions. On their 25th anniversary in 1946 the team chosen by a Green Bay Press Gazette poll consisted of ends Don Hutson and Lavvie Dilweg, tackles Hubbard and Cub Buck, guards Mike Michalske and Buckets Goldenberg, center Charlie Brock, "quarterback" Arnie Herber, halfbacks Johnny Blood and Verne Lewellen,and fullback Clarke Hinkle. For the 1957 team selected in honor of the opening of the new City Stadium, the only change was Tony Canadeo replacing Lewellen. A 22-man team was selected for the 50th anniversary in 1969, and 15 slots unsurprisingly were filled with Lombardi era players. Along with Hutson, Hinkle, Dilweg, Larry Craig and Bobby Dillon, Cal was one of six old-timers picked—he was chosen at both offensive and defensive tackle. In 1976, teams were selected for both the "Iron Man Era" and the "Modern Era." Cal made the Iron Man team.

Cal is also a member of at least six halls of fame. He is the only man to be a member of both the Baseball and Pro Football Halls, and he is also in the College Football Hall, the Packer Hall, the Missouri Sports Hall of Fame and the Louisiana Sports Hall of Fame. He was inducted into Cooperstown in 1976, and was one of four Packers who were charter members of the Pro Football Hall in 1963 along with Curly Lambeau, Don Hutson, and Johnny Blood. In time they would be joined by 16 other Packers: Herb Adderley, Tony Canadeo, Willie Davis, Forrest Gregg, Arnie Herber, Clarke Hinkle, Paul Hornung, Henry Jordan, James Lofton, Vince Lombardi, Mike Michalske, Ray Nitschke, Jim Ringo, Bart Starr, Jim Taylor, and Willie Wood. Five other Hall of Famers spent brief periods in Green Bay: Len Ford, Ted Hendricks, Walt Kiesling, Jan Stenerud, and Emlen Tunnell. Three were elected in their first year of eligibility—Gregg and Starr in 1977 and Nitschke in 1978. At the other extreme, Willie Wood was elected in his 13th year of eligibility and 10th as a finalist (1985) while Paul Hornung was chosen in his 15th year of eligibility and 12th as a finalist (1980). These 24 men were introduced at their inductions by former teammates, opponents, coaches, and even a Supreme Court Justice:

YEAR	INDUCTEE	PRESENTER
1963	Cal Hubbard	Paul Kerr, President, Baseball Hall of Fame
1963	Don Hutson	Dante Lavelli, Cleveland Browns
1963	Curly Lambeau	Jim Crowley, Notre Dame "Four Horsemen"
1963	Johnny Blood	Byron "Whizzer" White, US Supreme Court Justice
1964	Clarke Hinkle	Bronko Nagurski, Chicago Bears
1964	Mike Michalske	L.C. Timm, Professor, Iowa State University
1966	Arnie Herber	Clarke Hinkle
1966	Walt Kiesling*	Byron "Whizzer" White, US Supreme Court Justice
1967	Emlen Tunnell	Fr. Benedict Dudley, NY Giant Chaplain

YEAR	INDUCTEE	PRESENTER
1971	Vince Lombardi*	Wellington Mara, President, NY Giants
1974	Tony Canadeo	Richard O. Bourguignon, Vice President, Green Bay Packers
1976	Len Ford*	Theodore McIntyre, High School Coach
1976	Jim Taylor	Mrs. Marie Lombardi
1977	Forrest Gregg	Mrs. Marie Lombardi
1977	Bart Starr	Bill Moseley, High School Coach
1978	Ray Nitschke	Phil Bengtson
1980	Herb Adderley	Willie Davis
1981	Willie Davis	Eddie Robinson, Coach, Grambling University
1981	Jim Ringo	Willard "Whiz" Rinehart, High School Coach
1986	Paul Hornung	Max McGee
1989	Willie Wood	Phil Bengtson
1990	Ted Hendricks	Al Davis, President, Oakland/Los Angeles Raiders
1991	Jan Stenerud	Hank Stram, Kansas City Chiefs
1995	Henry Jordan*	Don Kovach, Friend
2003	James Lofton	David Lofton, Son

*Posthumous inductees: Kiesling was represented by Johnny Blood, Lombardi by his son Vince Jr., Ford by his daughter Debbie, and Jordan by his son Henry Jr.

In the NFL, only Green Bay and the New Orleans Saints have their own halls of fame, but other pro football teams have honor rolls of past heroes. Former Packers so honored include Tobin Rote by the Lions, Babe Parilli by the Patriots, Jan Stenerud by the Chiefs, and John Hadl, Bob Laraba, and Jacques MacKinnon by the Chargers. In addition, Indian Jack Jacobs and Byron Bailey are two one-time Packers inducted by the Canadian Football Hall of Fame.

Packers in the College Hall of Fame include: centers Merv Pregulman and Clayton Tonnemaker; tackles Av Daniel, Cal Hubbard, Lou Michaels, Ernie Smith, and Dick Wildung; ends Carroll Dale, Don Hutson, John Jefferson, Ron Kramer, and Keith Jackson; quarterbacks John Hadl, Paul Hornung, Jim McMahon, and Babe Parilli; halfbacks Donny Anderson, Paul Christman, Jim Crowley, Beattie Feathers, Clarke Hinkle, Cecil Isbell, and Bruce Smith; fullbacks Jack Cloud, Jim Grabowski, and George Sauer; defensive ends Ross Browner, Ted Hendricks, and Reggie White; and coach Dan Devine.

As noted above, Hubbard is one of five Packers in the Missouri Sports Hall (along with Paul Chrisman, Dan Devine, Jim Kekeris, and Jan Stenerud) and one of six in the Louisiana Hall (with Willie Davis, Ken Ellis, Max McGee, John Petitbon, and Jim Taylor). He is not in the Wisconsin Hall although Don Hutson, Clarke Hinkle, Cub Buck, Red Dunn, Johnny Blood, Curly Lambeau, Lavvie Dilweg, Arnie Herber, Verne Lewellen, Mike Michalske, Tony Canadeo, Buckets Goldenberg, Vince Lombardi, Lisle Blackbourn, Ray Nitschke, Bart Starr, Willie Davis, Paul Hornung, Jim Taylor, and Jerry Kramer are. A number of other states have prominent sports halls of fame with Packer members. Alabama acknowledged Hutson, Starr and Scott Hunter. Georgia enshrined Zeke Bratkowski and

Tom Nash. Kansas elected Lynn Dickey, John Hadl and Veryl Switzer. New Jersey honored Vince Lombardi and Jim Ringo. Pennsylvania inducted the Michaels brothers, Walt and Lou. Tennessee acclaimed Beattie Feathers, Baby Ray, Harry Schuh and Ron Widby. Texas commemorated Donny Anderson, Bobby Dillon, and Forrest Gregg. This is not an exhaustive list.

Of all that, Cal Hubbard once said, "I am deeply grateful and especially thankful to the fans and the news media for keeping my name alive in the public for so long. It gave me not only a livelihood, but pleasure and satisfaction in my achievements. However, in recent years the halls of fame are forfeiting some of their glamour because they are becoming numerous . . . Sports heroes are glamorized because they are constantly in the limelight, but as I look back over the years that have brought honor to me I realize that I fall short of the dimensions of many of the nation's unsung heroes —the Veterans of Foreign Wars...In their presence I stand in awe." (Hubbard, 102-3) Cal died in 1977.

FOR FURTHER INFORMATION

Gerlach, Larry R. "Hubbard, Cal" in John A. Garraty and Mark C. Carnes, general editors. *American National Biography.* New York: Oxford University Press, 1999. v. 11 (378-9)

Hubbard, Mary Bell. *Strike Three! And You're Out: The Cal Hubbard Story.* MO: Walsworth, 1986.

Jenkins, Dan. "A Lot Packed in a Little," *Sports Illustrated.* 9/20/65. (82-3)

Packers of the Past: A Series of Articles Reprinted from the Milwaukee Journal Sept. 28–Dec. 9, 1965. Milwaukee, WI: Milwaukee Journal, 1965. (15-7)

Porter, David L., ed. *Biographical Dictionary of American Sports: Football.* New York: Greenwood Press, 1987. (277-8)

Reed, William F. "Early Master," *Sports Illustrated.* 9/5/94. (64-5)

Remmel, Lee. "Presenting Packers' All-Time 'Iron Man' Team," *Pro.* 11/21/76. (82-5)

Ronberg, Gary. "Pigskins and Horsehides," *Pro.* 11/28/76. (17c-20c, 85)

Whittingham, Richard. *What a Game They Played.* New York: Harper and Row, 1974. (113)

NUMBER 39

GEAR
JUG EARP • CENTER 1930–32

WHO'S WORN THE NUMBER Hubbard 1929, Earp 1930–32, Hinkle 1933, Bettencourt 1933, Paulekas 1936, L. Evans 1937, Heath 1949, Martinkovic 1951, E. Mann 1968, J. Hill 1972–74, S. Johnson 1979, Meade 1982–83, Burgess 1985, Ken Johnson 1987, Parker 1987r, D. Thompson 1990–93, Prior 1994–98, T. Carter 2002.

ORIGINATOR Tackle Cal Hubbard 1929 (see 38).

LONGEST TENURE Safety Mike Prior 1994–98 a serviceable safety and special teams player.

NUMBER CHANGES Cal Hubbard wore 40 in 1930 and 1932, 38 in 1931, 27 in 1933, and 51 in 1935; Jug Earp had 7 in <1925–26> and wore 29 in 1927–28, 9 in 1928, and 38 in 1929; Clarke Hinkle wore 27 and 33 in 1932, 30 in 1933 and 1935 and 1937–41, 39 in 1933, 45 and 48 in 1934, and 41 in 1936; center Larry Bettencourt also wore 29 and 30 in 1933; Lon Evans wore 17 in 1933, 25 and 65 in 1934, 46 in 1935, and 51 in 1936; defensive end John Martinkovic also wore 47 in 1951 and 83 from 1952–56; defensive back Ken Johnson also wore 41 in 1987; running back Darrell Thompson wore 26 in 1994; Mike Prior wore 45 in 1993.

OTHER NOTABLES Cal Hubbard (see 38); fullback Clarke Hinkle (see 30); two time All Pro Guard Lon Evans was elected to the Packer Hall of Fame in 1978. In his off-seasons, he worked as an actor in Hollywood and later became a long-time official in both pro and college football. Eventually, he was elected Sheriff of Tarnat County (Fort Worth), Texas and served for 24 years; defensive end John Martinkovic (see 83).

ONE TO FORGET Milwaukee's own quarterback Stan Heath was drafted number one in 1949 and completed 24% of his passes for one touchdown and 14 interceptions in his rookie year. He later failed to catch on in Cleveland before fleeing to Canada.

JUG EARP Once he dug in, Francis Louis Earp, was tough to move. He grew up in Monmouth, Illinois, a town of under 10,000 residents at the time. He went to Monmouth High in town. After graduation, he continued his education at Monmouth College, a small Presbyterian school in the community. From there, he branched out to begin his pro football career with the Rock Island Independents, 39 miles away. After two games of his second season in Rock Island, Earp was involved in a salary dispute with management. When Curly Lambeau made him an offer, he couldn't refuse; he jumped to Green Bay and spent the rest of his life there.

PACKERS BY THE NUMBERS

Earp was often spelled "Erpe," and he was known as "Jug" or sometimes "Jugger." Both were short for "Juggernaut" because at 235 pounds he was a large and powerful force in the middle of the line. For 11 years he was the bedrock starting center for the Packers and helped them develop from a good club into three-time champions from 1929 through 1931. He is sometimes credited with originating the one-hand center snap. His one-on-one duels with Bear center George Trafton were such annual battles of scrappy intensity that unfounded stories were repeated that he and Trafton would begin every game by spitting tobacco juice in each other's eye.

Yet, when you look at photographs of the era, the players don't look all that impressive. Jug noted, "We all supplied most of our own equipment in those first years." (Packers, 27) Players generally had only one uniform, and there often wasn't time to wash it out before the next game, especially on lengthy road trips. Sometimes the best a player could do was let his sweaty, muddy uniform dry and then brush off the dried, caked dirt. Not all players wore helmets, and facemasks still hadn't been invented, since it would be difficult to attach anything to the flimsy leather helmets prevalent then. Pads were optional as well. The beginnings of modern, cantilevered shoulder pads did not come until the mid-1930s. Therefore in photographs of the time, players don't look all that formidable with slack shoulders in what appears to be tight long-sleeve t-shirts.

The uniform styles have changed a great deal over time, too. The first team in 1921 had jerseys featuring the words "Acme Packers" on the front, like a sponsored, beer-league softball team might today. In 1923 and 1924, the Pack wore gold jerseys with blue tiger stripes on the sleeves. These stripes were subsequently replaced in 1925 by a darkened blue shoulder area. By 1927, the players began wearing numbers on their backs, and the team tried blue and gold vertical stripes on its jerseys. Then in 1929 and 1930, they went back to solid blue jerseys, but with uniform numbers inside a small circular patch on the chest. From 1931 through 1934, the team again returned to solid navy blue jerseys. The team was still frequently referred to as the "Big Bay Blues" in the newspaper.

In 1935 and 1936, the jerseys were two colors—a solid body with gold shoulders and sleeves. In a 1994 article for the Packer Report, Art Daley recalled the body being navy blue, but an August 30, 1935, article in the *Green Bay Press Gazette* lauded the new gold and *kelly green* uniforms. In 1937, the champion Packers wore myrtle green jerseys with gold numbers, gold helmets, gold pants, and green socks for the College All Star game. These uniforms were made of thick wool and caused the team to wilt during the humid summer night. Clarke Hinkle claimed to have lost 25 pounds in that game. However, in the 1937 regular season, the Packers finally established their first real look: solid blue jerseys with gold numbers and shoulders, gold pants, blue stockings, and gold helmets. Curly's Notre Dame-colored uniform would be the team's standard for the rest of his tenure in Green Bay. He did offer an occasional alternative. In 1939, Curly unveiled white jerseys with green numbers, gold helmets, and white socks. And in 1946, the Packers tried white jerseys with gold shoulders, numbers, pants, and helmets.

With new coach Gene Ronzani came new uniforms in 1950 and 1951: kelly green jerseys and pants, gold numbers, and gold stripes on the sleeve and down the side of the pants. Alternate uniforms featured gold uniforms with green numbers. A third option were plain blue jerseys with gold numbers and gold pants. A fourth option starting in 1952 were white jerseys with green numbers and green pants. When the Packers played the Rams in Los Angeles in 1952, both teams wore gold uniforms and the Rams coach Hampton Pool played the game under protest, although LA prevailed 45-27. Also in 1952, the league made its first attempt to organize the assignment of jersey numbers according to position. This was formally codified in 1973, and updated in 1989.

New coach Lisle Blackbourn brought a return to blue jerseys with gold numbers and added three gold stripes on the sleeves in 1954. As an alternative, jerseys sometimes feature white numbers and stripes, and the pants can be either gold or white. When George Halas refused to have his Bears wear white road uniforms for the 1954 and 1955 Bear-Packer contests in Green Bay, it was hard to tell who was who on the field. Although two teams in dark jerseys had been the norm for the first 30 years of the league, pro football was moving steadily toward popular acceptance and that had to change. TV forced the NFL to insist on teams wearing contrasting colors. In 1956, numbers were added to Packer sleeves. By 1957 and the opening of new City Stadium, the Packers were back to a dark bluish-green jersey with three gold bands on the sleeves, gold numbers, gold pants, and green-and-gold striped socks. Helmets were usually gold, but plain white helmets were worn as well during this time.

Vince Lombardi heralded the last major uniform change in 1959 and simplified the Packers' uniform to its familiar classic design. The green on the jersey was lightened, numbers were white and were also displayed on the sleeve along with a band of five gold and white stripes, gold pants, gold helmets, and green socks with gold and white stripes. In addition, the "G" logo was added to the left side of the helmet. The "G" logo was added to the other side of the helmet in 1961 and names appeared on the back of the jersey in 1970. Since then, the sleeves have grown shorter while numbers moved to the shoulders. A "G" was added to the shoulders in 1984, but was removed in 1990, and in 1997 sleeve and sock stripes were reduced from two white lines within a gold band to just one.

In 1994 the NFL instituted turn-back-the-clock weeks when teams would wear replicas of old-style uniforms as a celebration of league tradition and a chance to market more expensive jerseys to fans. The Packers wore their 1937-50 style blue jersey with gold shoulders. For the 2001 Thanksgiving game against the Lions, both teams wore flashback jerseys—the Packers returning to their 1939 white jerseys described above. The league adopted a policy in 2002 allowing an alternative jersey be worn for one week of the season, and the Packers considered doing something to coincide with the completion of the Lambeau Field renovations in 2003. As a salesman and fan, Jug Earp probably would approve.

The Jugger retired after the 1932 season. At first, he sold cars. Eventually he joined the Office of Price Administration and was head of operations for all of Wisconsin by 1946. In 1950, he came back to the Packers as their publicity director, even though he had never written a press release in his life. He served in that capacity for four years while Gene Ronzani was coach before leaving to go back into sales, employing his natural gift for gab. He once recalled, "People still like to talk about the Packers, and I like to talk about them, too." (*Packers*, 28) Always popular with the fans, he died in 1969, just a year before he was inducted as a charter member of the Packer Hall of Fame.

PACKERS BY THE NUMBERS

FOR FURTHER INFORMATION

Carroll, Bob, Michael Gershman, David Neft, and John Thorn. *Total Packers: The Official Encyclopedia of the Green Bay Packers.* New York: Harper Perennial, 1998. (37)

Daley, Art. "They Weren't Always Green and Gold," *The Packer Report* 10/1/94. (11)

Packers of the Past: A Series of Articles Reprinted from the Milwaukee Journal Sept. 28–Dec. 9, 1965. Milwaukee, WI: Milwaukee Journal, 1965. (27-8)

Ward, Arch. *The Green Bay Packers.* New York: Putnam, 1946. (44-5)

Zimmerman, David. *In Search of a Hero: Life and Times of Tony Canadeo Packers' Grey Ghost.* Hales Corner, WI: Eagle Books, 2001. (51-2)

TROUBLES TROUBLES

EDDIE LEE IVERY • RUNNING BACK 1979–86

WHO'S WORN THE NUMBER Cahoon 1929, Hubbard 1930 and 1932, Michalske 1935, Scherer 1936, B. Lee 1937–42, 1946, Schwammel 1943, A. Forte 1947, Eason 1949, Elliot 1951, B. Aldridge 1953, J. Johnson 1954–58, Hackbart 1960–61, Gros 1962–63, T. Brown 1964–68, Kopay 1972, Van Valkenberg 1974, Harrell 1975–77, Ivery 1979–86, David King 87r, J. Jackson 1992, C. Hayes 1996, Terrell 1998, J. Moore 2000, T. Fisher 2002.

ORIGINATOR Tackle Tiny Cahoon 1929 (see top 30)

LONGEST TENURE Eddie Lee Ivery 1979–86.

NUMBER CHANGES Tiny Cahoon wore 10 in 1926 and wore 30 in 1927–28; tackle Cal Hubbard wore 39 in 1929, 38 in 1931, 27 in 1933, and 51 in 1935; guard Mike Michalske wore 36 in 1929–30 and 1937, 28 in 1931, 19 and 30 in 1932, 31 in 1933, 24 and 63 in 1934, and 33 in 1935; end Bernie Scherer wore 11 and 16 in 1937 and 36 in 1938; tackle Ade Schwammel wore 53 in 1934, 50 in 1935, 50 and 57 in 1936, and 58 in 1944; end Carlton Elliot wore 80 from 1952–54.

OTHER NOTABLES Cal Hubbard (see 38); Ade Schwammel (see top 50); Big Bill Lee was a teammate of Don Hutson at Alabama and an outstanding tackle; safety Tom Brown had the clinching interception in the 1966 championship game against Dallas and played baseball with the Washington Senators.

ONE TO FORGET Pat Terrell, a nine-year veteran safety, was brought in as a free agent in 1998 to help shore up the secondary, but his best days were far in the past.

EDDIE LEE IVERY In television, a story arc follows one particular story from its origins to its dramatic conclusion. The arc of Eddie Lee Ivery's story is one worthy of a soap opera and, unlike fiction, continues on without a closing curtain. The seasons of his career can be seen as a series of stations on an untamed route that fluctuated between the highest peaks and the lowest valleys. He began as a heavily recruited high school athlete and went on to a spectacular tenure at Georgia Tech after breaking his leg in his freshman year. At Tech he gained over 3,500 yards, including 356 in one game against Air Force in his senior year, 1978. As a big, strong, fast running back with great moves and vision, Eddie was a clear first-round pick who went to Green Bay as the 15th player chosen in 1979.

FALLING On his third carry in his very first NFL game against the Bears in Soldier Field on September 6, 1979, Ivery blew out his knee on the new astroturf. Discouraged during his season spent rehabbing the knee, he picks up a new habit, drinking.

NUMBER 40

RISING Eddie comes back in 1980 to lead the team in rushing with 831 yards at 4.1 yards per carry and catches 50 passes for another 431 yards.

FALLING In the first game of the 1981 season against the Bears at Soldier Field, Ivery blows out the same knee again. Another season lost to injury; more frustration ensues with the realization that his speed and moves will decline precipitously.

RISING, BUT NOT AS HIGH Eddie comes back again in strike-shortened 1982 to score 10 touchdowns in nine games. He gains 453 yards and again leads the team, but averages only 3.6 yards per carry.

FALLING Early in the 1983 season, Ivery goes to a party with teammates and gets his first taste of cocaine. Like so many others, he finds cocaine offers relief from his physical and emotional pain, and he becomes addicted. Coach Bart Starr finds out about Ivery's drug use through an anonymous tip and confronts him about it. Ivery spends the second half of Starr's final season as coach in a drug recovery program.

RISING A LITTLE Eddie is still drinking, having problems at home, and experiencing a number of injuries, as well as encountering legal problems that eventually will be resolved. Despite all that, he manages to put together decent part-time seasons in 1984 and 1985. He gains 552 yards in 10 games in the former and 636 yards in 15 games in the latter. His 1985 total again leads the team.

FALLING In 1986, he plays only 12 games, generally as a situational pass receiver out of the backfield, and he spends 1987 on the injured reserve list. In 1988 Coach Forrest Gregg releases him with the comment, "He's had a lot of injuries." Ivery retires and resumes using cocaine.

BUMPY RIDE Ivery and his wife separate in 1990, and he returns to Georgia Tech. In 1992 they divorce, and he gets his degree in management. Briefly, he sobers up and gets a job with an athletic company. He returns to drinking and using cocaine and loses the job. Again he sobers up, and in 1995 is working at a day care center and has custody of his own children. By 1998, he is using coke again, and the children return to their mother in Florida. Finally in that same year, he admits that he has a problem and will always be an addict who must be in an ongoing program to stay clean. Happily, in 2000 Eddie was hired by his alma mater as a strength and conditioning coach and has reunited with his children. His son Eddie Jr. is a heavily recruited high school running back who led his team to the state championship game in 2001.

There are a couple of issues that arise when looking at Eddie Lee Ivery's thrill ride of a career. The first is the prevalence of injuries in the NFL. Football has always been a rough game, and there have always been widespread injuries. Playing with pain is something all players learn about early on. In the last 30 years or so, though, there have been a number of changes. First of all, medical treatment has improved to an astounding degree. With techniques such as magnetic resonance imaging (MRI) and arthroscopic surgery, injuries can be detected with greater accuracy and can be repaired with less invasiveness so that seriously injured players can get back on the field much faster than ever. However, the amount of serious injuries has also increased due largely to bigger, faster players having more violent collisions. A second reason often cited for increased injuries, particularly knee problems, is artificial turf. Players continually rail against artificial turf, but it remains in several stadiums throughout the league. And in the cursed domes, we will never get rid of it.

The second issue regarding Eddie Lee Ivery of course is alcohol and drug abuse. Football players have always abused alcohol. Some of the funniest stories of some of the wildest characters in team history, like Johnny Blood, Max McGee and Paul Hornung, are fueled by heavy drinking. Others like Ivery let alcohol shorten their careers. Linebacker Jim Carter claims that for the meaningless final game against Atlanta in 1974, one player filled his water bottle with vodka and was so drunk he could barely stand by the end of the game. Ultimately, liquor is a legal intoxicant that some people can handle and others can't. As Blood said of one game he played hung over, "I don't know how I did it, but I know I paid for it. Games like that took a few years off my career."

Furthermore, as far back as 1935, Johnny Blood claimed to have experimented with Benzedrine pills that truckers used to stay awake driving, although harder drugs didn't really come into prominence until the last 40 years. These, no one can handle. From pep pills and pain killers since the 1960s, to narcotics since the 1970s, to steroids since the 1980s, drugs have spread throughout the league and among the Packers and have done a lot of damage. The Packers stopped freely distributing amphetamines in the early 1970s and began drug testing in 1977 under Bart Starr and trainer Dom Gentile, a full 13 years before the league began its drug testing program. Over the years, Gentile indicates that a number of players were detected using drugs. The team was able to help some, while others were released. But no system is perfect, and players continue to push the limits. Just in the past few years, we've seen Brett Favre in rehab for pain killers, Jude Waddy punished for steroids, and Cletidus Hunt caught for marijauna. While Eddie Lee Ivery stands as an example of how much damage drugs can do to your life and how hard it is to rise again from all the disaster that may come your way, each player must comprehend this hazard in his own way. Eddie Lee's career was not the last to be lost to injuries; his life was not the last to be battered by drugs.

FOR FURTHER INFORMATION

Berkow, Ira. "When Johnny Blood Rode," *New York Times*. 7/11/82. (sec. V, 5)

Bunn, Curtis. "Light at the End of the Tunnel: Former Tech Rushing Star Sober At Last," *Atlanta Journal and Constitution*. 7/30/00. (1E).

Gentile, Domenic, with Gary D'Amato. *The Packer Tapes: My 32 Years with the Green Bay Packers*. Madison, WI: Prairie Oak Press, 1995. (35-53)

Person, Joseph. "On the Rebound: Ivery Beating Cocaine Habit," *Milwaukee Journal Sentinel*. 8/20/00. (1C)

LOCK UP YOUR DAUGHTERS
EUGENE ROBINSON • SAFETY 1996–97

WHO'S WORN THE NUMBER O'Boyle 1928, Zuidmulder 1931, Herber 1932–33, Laws 1934, Hinkle 1936, Seibold 1937–38, Kell 1939–40, Earhart 1948–49, B. Robinson 1952, M. Johnson 1952–53, Mihaljovich 1954, Nix 1955, B. Freeman 1959, Coffey 1965, Gibson 1972, Osborn 1976, Burrow 1976, Flynn 1984–86, Ken Johnson 1987, Compton 1987r, E. Robinson 1996–97, T. Marshall 2002.

ORIGINATOR Harry O'Boyle 1928 was a 5'9" triple-threat back from Notre Dame of whom Rockne once said, "His chief characteristics were determination and fight, counterbalanced with smartness, intellect and headwork." He worked in management for GM for 30 years.

LONGEST TENURE Safety Tom Flynn, 1984–86, was Defensive Rookie of the Year in 1984 when he intercepted nine passes, but was gone from the team two years later. Fortunately for him, he got to win a Super Bowl with the Giants in 1986.

NUMBER CHANGES Harry O'Boyle wore 42 in 1932; Arnie Herber also wore 12 in 1930, 26 in 1931, 16 in 1933, 45 and 68 in 1934, 38 from 1935–40, and 19 in 1937; Joe Laws wore 38 in 1934 and 29 from 1935–36, and 24 from 1937–45; Clarke Hinkle wore 27 and 33 in 1932, 39 in 1933, 30 in 1933, 1935 and from 1937–41, 45 and 48 in 1934, and 41 in 1936; tackle Champ Seibold wore 57 in 1934 and 1939–40, 37 in 1935–36, and 58 in 1936; defensive back Doyle Nix also wore 45 in 1955; defensive back Ken Johnson also wore 39 in 1987; linebacker/fullback Torrance Marshall also wore 51 in 2001–2002.

OTHER NOTABLES Tailback Arnie Herber (see 16); halfback Joe Laws (see top 24); fullback Clarke Hinkle (see 30); tackle Champ Seibold (see top 57).

ONES TO FORGET Halfback Bill Robinson played two games with the Packers in 1952 and one with the AFL New York Titans in 1960. Defensive end Lou Mihaljovich played nine games with LA in the AAFC in 1948 and then three games with Green Bay in 1954. Wide receiver Paul Gibson spent his entire one game career with Green Bay; defensive back Jim Burrow did the same for his three game career. Altogether, these four players spent nine games in the NFL—all with Green Bay.

NUMBER 41

EUGENE ROBINSON Eugene Robinson was not recruited out of high school to play college football; instead he attended Colgate University on an academic scholarship. He went out for football and played defensive back for the Red Raiders for three years. After earning his degree in Computer Science, Robinson was not drafted by an NFL team. The Seahawks signed him as a free agent, and, like two other undrafted star free safeties who played for Green Bay (Emlen Tunnell who finished up there and Willie Wood), he made the team against long odds. He had a successful but largely anonymous 11-year career in Seattle—named All Pro once in 1993 when he led the league in interceptions with nine and making the Pro Bowl in 1993 and 1994. His 42 lifetime interceptions and experienced leadership attracted Ron Wolf's attention, though. Wolf saw Robinson as one of the final pieces for the Packers Super Bowl run and traded Matt Labounty for him in 1996. In Green Bay, Robinson solidified the secondary, led the team in interceptions, and helped the Packers win Super Bowl XXXI and return to Super Bowl XXXII where they lost to the Broncos. With his contract up, he signed with Atlanta for more money than the Packers were willing to pay and helped lead the surprising Falcons to their first Super Bowl appearance.

Along with his skills on the field, Eugene Robinson was an intelligent, caring, committed Christian with a beautiful and loving family. He published two books, *Diary of a Super Bowl Season* and *It Takes Endurance* in which he expounded further on his beliefs and principles. Known as "The Prophet" and respected throughout the league, he was voted Man of the Year four times in Seattle for his charitable work and continued in this vein in Green Bay and Atlanta. All this work culminated on the day before Super Bowl XXXIII in his being awarded the Bart Starr Award by Athletes in Action, a worldwide Christian athletic group. The Starr Award is given to the NFL player who "exemplifies outstanding character and leadership in the home, on the field, and in the community."

Despite all this, Robinson embarrassed himself on football's biggest stage that very night by being arrested in a sting operation for allegedly offering an undercover cop money for sex. The charges were later dropped in a plea bargain. The effect of this on his team in the Super Bowl was arguable. The Falcons weren't likely to beat the Broncos anyway, but the distraction of their starting free safety keeping himself and several other players awake through the night discussing his arrest was not helpful. Of more importance, of course, is the effect on Robinson's wife and children, who were forced to deal with undeserved national embarrassment. Robinson had spent 36 years building an impressive reputation as a person of the highest integrity, and threw it all away in one minute's time.

Players have been involved in sexual shenanigans from the time Green Bay fielded a football team. In the 1920s and 1930s, Green Bay was a noted hot spot for visiting players because of the large number of bars and brothels there. The irrepressible Johnny Blood was said to have bought up an entire brothel for a night on more than one occasion. Handsome Clarke Hinkle said that players, "had [their] pick of the most beautiful gals in town." (Cope, 85) During the 1950s and 1960s, Paul Hornung and Max McGee were the two most notable ladies men of their era, but reports indicate that there was enough flesh available wherever they went for the whole team to enjoy. Tight end Marv Fleming wrote of players enjoying groupies, group sex, and wife swapping. It makes one wonder whether Blood, Hornung, and McGee still would be looked on simply as lovable rogues if they had lived in today's more publicized and litiguous times. In the 1980s, defensive back Mossy Cade and highly respected James Lofton stood trial in separate sexual incidents. Lofton was acquitted, but Cade was found guilty of sexual assault. Despite his acquittal, Lofton was given the bum's rush out of town. Cade served prison time and lost his career. More recently, politically conservative tight end Mark Chmura was caught playing drinking games in a hot tub with teenagers and was released, even though he was found innocent of the more serious sexual assault charges.

There is nothing new here, of course. Forbidden fruit has driven mankind to irrational disaster since the beginning of recorded time. What is it in the nature of man that inspires us to reach for what we know will only do us harm? Adding the religious angle in the Robinson incident only makes it more provocative as Americans are always on the lookout for any sign of hypocrisy from those who attempt to serve as moral leaders. That's a common motif throughout Western literature dating at least to medieval times when the broad humor of Chaucer and Rabelais lampooned the predilections of a vile, venal, and corrupt clergy. However, Eugene Robinson's unfortunate choice in Miami was not funny at all, just sad and disappointing. He would play another year in Atlanta and one in Carolina, retiring with 57 interceptions in 16 seasons, but he will always be remembered most for one stupid play off the field.

FOR FURTHER INFORMATION
Benedict, Jeff, and Don Yeager. *Pros and Cons: The Criminals Who Play in the NFL.* New York: Warner Books, 1998.

Cope, Myron. *The Game That Was: An Illustrated Account of the Tumultuous Early Days of Pro Football.* New York: Crowell, 1974. (85)

Daly, Dan, and Bob O'Donnell. *The Pro Football Chronicle: The Complete (Well Almost) Record of the Best Players, the Greatest Photos, the Hardest Hits, the Biggest Scandals, and the Funniest Stories in Pro Football.* New York: Collier Books, 1990. (35)

Fleming, Marv, with Bill Burns. "Women Made My Career," *Sport.* May 1977. (70-6)

Madden, Michael, and Will McDonough. "Upstanding Character Is a Beaten Man," *The Boston Globe.* 2/1/99. (D8)

Oates, Tom. "Eugene Robinson," *Green Bay Packers 1997 Yearbook.* (74-5)

Robinson, Eugene, with Kevin Isaacson and Rocky Landsverk. *Diary of a Super Bowl Season.* Iola, WI: Krause Publications, 1998.

1972 PLAYOFF RETURN
JOHN BROCKINGTON • RUNNING BACK 1971–77

WHO'S WORN THE NUMBER Lambeau 1928, O'Boyle 1932, Monnett 1934, McDonald 1935 Schoeman 1938, Uram 1939–43, Duhart 1944, (Kinkade 1945), B. Smith 1945–48, Kranz 1949, Dreyer 1950, Cannava 1950, Carmichael 1953–54, McIlhenny 1957–59, Brockington 1971–77, Landers 1978–79, Ellerson 1985–86, W. Dean 1991, Sydney 1992, L. Johnson 1994–95, C. Dowden 1996, Sharper 1997–02.

ORIGINATOR Curly Lambeau 1928 (see 1).

LONGEST TENURE John Brockington 1971–77.

NUMBER CHANGES Curly Lambeau had 1 in <1925–26> and wore 14 in 1927 and 20 in 1929–30; back Harry O'Boyle wore 41 in 1928; back Bob Monnett wore 18 in 1933, 66 in 1934, 3 and 12 in 1935, 12 and 5 in 1936, 5 in 1937 and 50 in 1938; halfback Andy Uram wore 8 in 1938; defensive back Wally Dreyer also wore 16 in 1950; halfback Al Carmichael wore 48 from 1955–58.

OTHER NOTABLES Curly Lambeau (see 1); Bob Monnett (see top 3); long distance all-purpose back Andy Uram ran 97 yards from scrimmage for a touchdown in 1939, returned a punt 90 yards in 1941, returned a kickoff 98 yards in 1942, and was enshrined in the Packer Hall of Fame in 1973; halfback Bruce Smith won the Heisman Trophy in college, was injured, and never amounted to much in Green Bay; halfback Al Carmichael set a league record returning a kickoff 106 yards despite being under orders from coach Blackbourn not to run back any ball from the end zone. He was elected to the Packer Hall of Fame in 1974; safety Darren Sharper has become an All Pro and a leader on defense.

ONES TO FORGET Guard Dustin McDonald played only one game in the league. So did halfback Al Cannava, but Cannava gained two yards on a run, 28 yards on a pass, 10 yards on a kick return, nine yards on two punt returns, and fumbled in his one-game career.

JOHN BROCKINGTON John Brockington's decline was so swift and severe that Packer fans, almost 30 years later, are still wondering what happened to him. A first-round draft choice out of Ohio State, he was Offensive Rookie of the Year in 1971, setting a record for first-year men by gaining 1,105 yards on the ground. He became the first man to rush for over 1,000 yards in each of his first three years as a pro, was named All Pro once, and went to three Pro Bowls. He was a dominant runner, a brawny blocker, and a more-than-adequate receiver out of the back-field. He led a team that completed fewer than 43% of its passes to the playoffs in his second year. By 1974, he was finished, never to be the same power runner again. Why?

A number of theories have been suggested for the collapse of his career. Most people seem to agree that he got away from his strength of running north/south and began going east/west without hitting the hole. But what caused the change? Trainer Dom Gentile cited an incident in a game against the Bengals in Brockington's rookie year. John's pumping knee hit Bengal safety Ken Dyer in the head, temporarily paralyzing him and ending his career. Gentile felt John was deeply affected by that, but that was only in his third game, and he would reach 1,000 yards three times after that. Others note the trading of Brockington's running mate and lead blocker Macarthur Lane to the Chiefs in 1975, but Brockington's play seriously deteriorated in 1974 with Lane still there. Besides, John's best year was his first one, before Lane arrived, with Donny Anderson as his running mate. In that year, 1971, the team ran for more yards with a higher rushing average than any other season in John's tenure in Green Bay. Brockington himself blames the coaching staff for moving away from his favorite off-tackle slant play and calling more sweeps. Quarterback Scott Hunter remembers yelling at Brockington once for not cutting back on a sweep play and turning upfield where the hole was. At that point, Hunter says he came to the realization that John couldn't turn his shoulders quickly enough to hit the hole and make that play.

Sadly, I think that is the key to understanding what happened to John Brockington. He was a great straight-ahead power runner who couldn't run any other way. Add in the fact that the Packers did not have an effective quarterback throughout his career, and that highlighted his limitations even more. Defenses make adjustments. Brockington's best year was his first, when he averaged over five yards a carry in rushing for more than 1,100 yards. In his second year, his rushing average dropped almost a yard and a half per carry to 3.7—that's an enormous drop, especially for a player in his second year in the league. To his credit, Brockington raised that average back to 4.3 in 1973, but that was the last year he would come close to 4 yards a carry again. Probably what happened is that when defenses began to stop his off-tackle rushes, the coaches put in more wide runs to try to counter the defense, but with Brockington that didn't work. Plan B failed and there was no Plan C because there was no passing attack to loosen up defenses. He finished 1977 with the Chiefs, joining his old pal Mac Lane, and was out of the league the next year.

In his retirement, Brockington sold insurance and turned up in the news in 2001 for a distressing reason—he was undergoing regular dialysis treatments because of kidney problems and was awaiting a kidney transplant. The good news was that scores of his former Ohio State teammates came forward to support their fallen comrade. He still has the second highest total of rushing yards in team history and was inducted in the Packer Hall of Fame in 1984. Above all, he will always be remembered fondly in Green Bay for leading the Packers to their one shining moment in the dark decade of the 1970s, winning the 1972 Central Division Championship.

The 1972 team was the only Packers team to make the playoffs in the 1970s. Its offense was essentially Brockington and Lane running and blocking for each other—together they gained 1,848 yards on the ground. In addition, they finished first and second on the team in receptions with 26 for Lane and 19 for Brockington. The two starting wide receivers, Carroll Dale and Leland Glass, caught 16 and 15 passes respectively. Scott Hunter was a leader at quarterback but had a rag arm from a shoulder separation suffered in college and completed only 43.2% of his passes for a paltry 1,252 yards. The line was a solid drive-blocking unit.

Dan Devine was a failure overall as a coach in Green Bay, but he did put together a team just good enough to win in 1972. His first squad finished last in its division in 1971, but things seemed to be looking up. Brockington and Hunter had arrived in the 1971 draft and cornerback Willie Buchanon and kicker Chester Marcol came in the 1972 draft. Combined with defensive linemen Alden Roche and safety Jim Hill, obtained through trades, these moves pushed the Packers into the playoffs. The defense finished first in the NFC by giving up only 226 points and went from allowing 21 touchdown passes in 1971 to only seven in 1972. Marcol improved the field goal kicking from 14 of 26 to 33 of 48 and led the league in scoring with 128 points. They were not spectacular, but gritty, relentless, and efficient.

Ultimately, they were exposed in the playoffs by George Allen's Redskins who confronted the Packers with a five man defensive line, and Green Bay never countered by opening up the passing offense. Hunter says he wanted to, and offensive coach Bart Starr wanted to, but Devine kept sending in the running plays. Hunter claims that by the second half Devine and Starr were not speaking to each other—Starr did resign his post at the end of the year. The team's limitations were clear, and they would not have another winning season until 1978 when John Brockington was only a memory. For too brief a time, he was among the very best in the league.

FOR FURTHER INFORMATION

D'Amato, Gary. "1972 Packers Surprised NFL," *Milwaukee Journal Sentinel.* 12/24/95. (1D)

Gentile, Domenic, with Gary D'Amato. *The Packer Tapes: My 32 Years with the Green Bay Packers.* Madison, WI: Prairie Oak Press, 1995. (72-73)

Poling, Jerry. *Downfield! Untold Stories of the Green Bay Packers.* Madison, WI: Prairie Oak Press, 1996. (1-6, 94-97)

Youngblood, Kent. "A Team to Remember," *Wisconsin State Journal.* 12/10/95. (1D)

1944 WARTIME CHAMPS
BUCKETS GOLDENBERG • GUARD 1938–45

WHO'S WORN THE NUMBER D. Webber 1928, McCrary 1932, L. Peterson 1934, G. Svendsen 1935–37, Goldenberg 1938–45, D. Wells 1946–49, Kirby 1949, Wimberly 1950, Loomis 1952, Barton 1953, Boone 1953, Hart 1964–71, Mason 1974, A. Thompson 1977–78, H. Monroe 1979, D. Jones 1984–85, L. Morris 1987r, Kinder 1997, McGarrahan 1998–00, M. Smith 2002.

ORIGINATOR Dutch Webber 1928 an end and back who played for seven NFL teams in 42 games (three with Green Bay) over six years.

LONGEST TENURE Buckets Goldenberg 1938–45

NUMBER CHANGES Fullback Herdis McCrary wore 29 in 1929, 28 in 1929–30, 19 in 1931, and 38 and 53 in 1933; end Les Peterson wore 29 in 1932; center George Svendsen wore 66 in 1940–41; Buckets Goldenberg wore 21 in 1933, 51 in 1934, and 44 from 1935–37; end Don Wells also wore 84 in 1946; defensive end Ab Wimberly also wore 16 in 1950–51 and 85 in 1952; back Ace Loomis wore 7 in 1951 and 48 in 1953; returner J.R. Boone also wore 22 in 1953; receiver Aundra Thompson wore 89 from 1979–81.

OTHER NOTABLES Herdis McCrary (see top 53); George Svendsen spent five years as a center/linebacker and was elected to the Packer Hall of Fame in 1972.

ONE TO FORGET Kick returner Jack "Rabbit" Kirby fumbled three times in his brief six-game career in 1949.

BUCKETS GOLDENBERG Charles "Buckets" Goldenberg is not remembered much today, but was considered one of the top lineman in the league during his career and was one of the team's most popular figures for years after his career ended. He was born in Odessa in the Ukraine in 1911, and his family emigrated to the U.S. when he was four. He grew up in Milwaukee and was an All City halfback in high school where he inherited his older brother's posterior-inspired nickname "Buckets." At the University of Wisconsin he starred both in the line and the backfield, and Curly Lambeau signed him to a pro contract in 1933. He spent the next 13 years in a Packer uniform mostly as either number 44 or 43.

Lambeau originally employed Buckets mostly as a single wing quarterback, better described as a blocking back, for his first few years. He led the league in touchdowns with seven as a rookie, but in his backfield years he carried the ball only 108 times and caught 11 passes. Almost half of his carries came in his rookie year, when he backed up Hinkle at fullback, but he was the starting blocking back on the 1936 champions. At 5'10" and 220 pounds, he had the body of a 1930s lineman, and Mike Michalske helped convince Lambeau to convert Buckets to guard, where he spent the last two-thirds of his career. As a guard/linebacker he was first team All Pro once and second team another year. He was known as a flattening lead blocker on offense and a tenacious tackler on defense. Despite his talent and popularity, Lambeau actually traded him and Swede Johnston to Pittsburgh for Pat McCarty and Ray King in 1938 when Johnny Blood became coach of the Steelers. Fortunately for all in Green Bay, the deal fell through when Buckets retired rather than report to Pittsburgh. He returned to Packers for two more championship runs.

In his off-seasons, Goldenberg was a professional wrestler for many years until the travel became too much of a drain on his family life, so he opened a restaurant in Milwaukee in 1941. His restaurant was very successful for decades and featured several large photographs of Packer players in action. Like many former players of his time, he continued as a fan of the team in his retirement and regularly attended all Packer games in Green Bay, Milwaukee, and Chicago. In many ways, he was similar to another guard known more for his nickname than his given name, Fuzzy Thurston. He also served on the Packers Board of Directors from 1953 until the year before he died, 1985. He was inducted into the Packers Hall of Fame in 1971 and was named "Outstanding Jewish Athlete of All Time" by the Green Bay B'nai B'rith lodge in 1969.

Had World War II not occurred, though, it is doubtful his career would have lasted as long. With so many of the young and able in the military, league rosters were filled with the old and damaged. One year, Pittsburgh merged its squad with Philadelphia to form the Steagles, and the next season they merged with the Cardinals to form Card-Pitt. Goldenberg tried to enlist in the army, but he was rejected because his knees were so bad. The Packers continued to field winning teams throughout the War years, and by 1944 enough of the 1940s Bears juggernaut was in the service that Green Bay was able to slip past the Bears and win the Western Division. They would face the New York Giants in the Polo Grounds for the title.

The Packers offense still was centered around getting the ball to Don Hutson, now in his 10th year, but Cecil Isbell and Arnie Herber were both retired, so the lead passer was the erratic Irv Comp. Herber, as it turned out, returned to football with the Giants after three years of retirement and was their leading passer. The paunchy 34-year-old Herber was a year older than Buckets and among the day's participants only the Giants' 38-year-old Ken Strong and 35-year-old Mel Hein were older.

What is most remembered from this low-scoring affair is that the Packers used their main weapon, Hutson, mostly as a decoy, drawing Giant defenders away from the thrust of the Packer attack. The Packers moved the ball well throughout the first half and moved the ball to the Giants one-yard line in the second quarter on a couple of fine runs by Joe Laws and Ted Fritsch. The Giants put on a tough goal-line stand, but on fourth down Fritsch scored by following a hole opened by Buckets. The Packers started another drive late in the same quarter, keyed by a third-and-three 24-yard completion to Hutson at the Giants' 30. After a couple of running plays advanced the ball two more yards, the Giants' defense followed Hutson as he went right. leaving Ted Fritsch all alone at the five to pull in a toss from Comp and walk in with a minute and a half left before halftime.

In the second half, the Packers could do nothing on offense, while Herber filled the air with passes for the Giants. The Giants got one score when Irv Comp fell down on defense and Frank Liebel caught a 41 yard pass to the one. Ward Cuff punched it in from there. However, the Packers picked off Herber four times, including the last one by Paul Duhart inside the Packers' 20-yard line with under five minutes to play to preserve a 14-7 Green Bay victory. Joe Laws had three interceptions and led the Packers with 72 yards rushing. Irv Comp was 3 of 11 passing with three interceptions; Hutson caught two for 46 yards and Fritsch grabbed the 28-yard touchdown. Herber went 8 for 22 for the Giants.

In this game, Buckets was there once more when his team needed him, getting the key fourth-and-goal block that enabled Fritsch to score the first touchdown. He would play one more year and then hang up his cleats along with Don Hutson. Over the next couple of years all of the champion Packers of the two-way era would retire without being replaced adequately. Green Bay would not see another guard of Goldenberg's quality until Kramer and Thurston showed up almost 15 year later.

FOR FURTHER INFORMATION

Grosshandler, Stan. "Buckets," *The Coffin Corner*. 1986. Available online at www.footballresearch.com/articles/frpage.cfm?topic'buckets.

Packers of the Past: A Series of Articles Reprinted from the Milwaukee Journal Sept. 28–Dec. 9, 1965. Milwaukee, WI: Milwaukee Journal, 1965. (13-15)

"Packers Top Giants for Title 14-7," *New York Times*. 12/18/44. (1D)

PFRA Research. "The Least Remembered Championship," *The Coffin Corner*. 1986. Available online at www.footballresearch.com/articles/frpage.cfm?topic'leastrem.

Porter, David L., ed. *Biographical Dictionary of American Sports: 1992-1995 Supplement for Baseball, Football, Basketball, and Other Sports*. New York: Greenwood Press, 1995. (432-433)

 1944 CHAMPIONSHIP DATA
Green Bay Packers 14
New York Giants 7

December 17, 1944 • Polo Grounds, NY
Attendance: 46,016 (including 4,563 servicemen)
Winner's Share: $1,449.71
Loser's Share: $814.36
Weather: 40 degrees and sunny

KEY STATS	PACKERS	GIANTS
First Downs	11	10
Rush Yards	162	70
Pass Yards	73	117

KEY STATS	PACKERS	GIANTS
Total Yards	235	187
Interceptions	4	3
Fumbles Lost	0	0
Penalties	4-48	11-90

Halftime Score: Packers 14 Giants 0

ADDITIONAL FACTS

•The Packers spent the week before the game training in Charlottesville, Virginia.

•The Giants recorded shutouts in six of their ten regular-season games in 1944.

•Vice President John Nance Garner attended the game.

•New York was outgained 141 yards to 24 in the first half.

•Charley Brock, Larry Craig and Don Hutson all went the full 60 minutes.

•The Packers played a sloppy exhibition game in 1944 against the Eagles in Baby Ray's hometown of Nashville, Tennessee. After the game, Lambeau gave Ray a pat on the back and told him that when the Packers won the championship that year, Ray would get the game ball. Lambeau remembered his promise, and Baby got the game ball.

1950s IN A BOX
BOBBY DILLON • DEFENSIVE BACK 1952–59

WHO'S WORN THE NUMBER Marks 1928, Apsit 1932, Caspar 1934, Goldenberg 1935–37, Ray 1938–48, McGeary 1950, D. Stephenson 1951, Dillon 1952–59, D. Anderson 1966–71, Kroll 1972–73, C. Hall 1975–76, V. Anderson 1980, O'Steen 1983–84, Mandeville 1987, Mansfield 1987r, J. Holmes 1990–91, McNabb 1993, Darkins 1996–97, M. Snider 2000, Davenport 2002.

ORIGINATOR End Larry Marks 1928 was the team MVP for the Indiana Hoosiers in 1925 and then played with Mike Michalske on the NY Yankees of the AFL I and the Packers.

LONGEST TENURE Buford "Baby" Ray 1952–56 was a giant-sized lineman for his era, 6'6" and from 250 to 280 pounds. He was the anchor of the Packer line and was elected to the Packer Hall of Fame in 1973. He scouted for Green Bay for many years.

NUMBER CHANGES Back Cy Caspar also wore 20 in 1934; back/guard Buckets Goldenberg wore 21 in 1933, 51 in 1934, and 43 from 1938–45; Baby Ray also wore 58 in 1940; Dave Stephenson wore 69 in 1952 and 53 from 1953–55; defensive back Charley Hall wore 21 from 1971–74; fullback Dexter McNabb also wore 45 in 1992–93; fullback Matt Snider also wore 38 in 1999.

OTHER NOTABLES Buckets Goldenberg (see 43). Baby Ray (see above). Donny Anderson was a late 1960s bonus baby who was picked to replace triple threat Paul Hornung. While no Hall of Famer, Anderson was a good runner, receiver, and punter who fully earned his spurs in the Ice Bowl and Super Bowl II.

ONE TO FORGET Jerry Holmes, veteran cornerback brought in as a free agent from Detroit, was characteristic of the late 1980s plan to breathe new life into the Packers by infusing the team with a wealth of mediocre veterans through Plan B Free Agency. Plan B was role player heaven, allowing everybody but the stars to change teams. Holmes was OK and could have filled a role on a good team, but was of little value on a bad one. Ron Wolf got the Pack on the right path of building primarily through the draft.

BOBBY DILLON Bobby Dillon lost an eye at age 10 in an accident. That hardship did not prevent him from becoming a star defensive back and punt returner at the University of Texas, where he was team captain in his senior year. He continued his success in the pros for the Packers, leading the team in interceptions every year but his final one, becoming a four-time All Pro, and going to

NUMBER 44

four Pro Bowls. Once he picked off a pass he knew what to do with it; he retired with a second-best career 18.8 yard average interception return, and took five in for touchdowns. He stole nine passes in three different seasons, and in one Thanksgiving game against the Lions he nabbed four. Overall, he is still the leading Packer interceptor with a total of 52. Had the Packers been a better team throughout the 1950s, his numbers might have taken him to the Hall of Fame. However, he was elected to the Packer Hall of Fame in 1974 and to the Texas Sports Hall of Fame in 1996. His last season was Lombardi's first, and it was the only year he played for a winner in Green Bay.

FOR FURTHER INFORMATION

Johnson, Chuck. *The Greatest Packers of Them All.* New York: Putnam, 1968. (180)

"Packers Lose a Good Eye: Bobby Dillon Ends Career," *Green Bay Packers 1960 Yearbook.* (10-11)

Poling, Jerry. *Downfield! Untold Stories of the Green Bay Packers.* Madison, WI: Prairie Oak Press, 1996. (172-7)

Porter, David L., ed. *Biographical Dictionary of American Sports: 1992–1995 Supplement for Baseball, Football, Basketball, and Other Sports.* New York: Greenwood Press, 1995. (411)

Swain, Glenn. *Packers vs. Bears.* Los Angeles: Charles Publishing, 1996. (174-6)

BOBBY DILLON'S HELLISH DECADE OF THE HALT AND LAME WENT LIKE THIS:
DARKNESS AT NOON (GAMETIME)—THE PACKERS IN THE 1950s

WHERE THEY PLAYED: City Stadium (still used as a high school field), 1925-56; Lambeau Field (known as City Stadium 1957–64), 1957–; Wisconsin State Fairground in Milwaukee, 1935–51; Marquette Stadium in Milwaukee, 1952; County Stadium in Milwaukee, 1953–94.

HOW THE GAME WAS PLAYED: The T formation became the Split T under the leadership of the Rams, and the game took to the air for a decade of wild scoring. The 1950s also marked the beginning of games being televised nationally. As the game's popularity increased, a string of violent on-field episodes led to rule changes to clean up the game, such as not allowing ball carriers to continue running after they were knocked down, and the outlawing of high tackling and grabbing the face mask (which ironically was introduced as a safety device in the last decade to lessen the incidence of broken noses). Paul Brown moved his Browns to the NFL and continued to use messenger guards to call the plays.

DECADE WON LOST RECORD: 39-79-2 .323.

RECORD AGAINST THE BEARS: 5-14-1.

RECORD AGAINST THE LIONS: 4-15-1.

RECORD AGAINST THE GIANTS: 1-2.

PLAYOFF APPEARANCES: None.

CHAMPIONSHIPS: None.

UNSUNG HERO: Former star player Verne Lewellen served as General Manager from 1954–60 and Business Manager from 1961–67. As Packer executive, Lewellen laid the foundation for Lombardi to take over five years later, got a new stadium built, and got the team on solid financial footing for future success.

HEAD COACHES: Gene Ronzani, 1950–53 14-29-1; Hugh Devore and Scooter McLean fill in for the last two games (losses) of 1953 after Ronzani is fired; Lisle Blackbourn, 1954–57 17-31; Scooter McLean, 1958, 1-10-1; Vince Lombardi, 1959–67, 7-5 for the decade.

BEST PLAYER: Bill Howton (see 86).

HALL OF FAMERS: Tony Canadeo, Jim Ringo, Bart Starr, Forrest Gregg, Paul Hornung, Ray Nitschke, Jim Taylor, Len Ford, Vince Lombardi, Emlen Tunnell, and Henry Jordan.

PACKER HALL OF FAMERS: Tony Canadeo, Jim Ringo, Bart Starr, Forrest Gregg, Paul Hornung, Ray Nitschke, Jim Taylor, Vince Lombardi, Henry Jordan, Phil Bengtson, Al Carmichael, Fred Cone, Dan Currie, Bob Dillon, Boyd Dowler, Howie Ferguson, Bill Forester, Bob Forte, Hank Gremminger, Dave Hanner, Bill Howton, Gary Knafelc, Jerry Kramer, Ron Kramer, John Martinkovic, Max McGee, Tobin Rote, Bob Skoronski, Fuzzy Thurston, Jesse Whittenton.

LEAGUE LEADERS: Al Carmichael—kickoff avg 1955; Billy Grimes—punt return yards 1950; punt return TDs 1950; Paul Hornung—points 1959; Bill Howton—receiving yards 1952, 56; receiving TDs 1956; Tobin Rote—rushing avg 1951; passing yards 1956; passing TDs 1956; Veryl Switzer—punt return yards 1954; punt return avg 1954. Award Winners: Boyd Dowler—Rookie of the Year, 1959; Vince Lombardi.—Coach of the Year, 1959.

ALL PROS: Billy Grimes, 1950; Clayton Tonnemaker, 1950; Bobby Dillon, 1954, 56, 57, 58; Roger Zatkoff, 1954; Bill Howton, 1956, 57; Jim Ringo, 1957, 58, 59.

PRO BOWLERS: Billy Grimes, 1950, 51; Ed Neal, 1950; Dick Wildung, 1951; Bill Howton, 1952, 55, 56, 57; Derrell Teteak, 1952; Ab Wimberly, 1952; Hawg Hanner, 1953, 54; John Martinkovic, 1953, 55; Clayton Tonnemaker, 1953; Roger Zatkoff, 1954, 55, 56; Bobby Dillon, 1955, 56, 57, 58; Howie Ferguson, 1955; Tobin Rote, 1956; Jim Ringo, 1957, 58, 59; Bill Forester, 1959; Forrest Gregg, 1959; Paul Hornung, 1959; Emlen Tunnell, 1959.

BEST OFFENSIVE BACKFIELD: 1959. Bart Starr, QB; Paul Hornung, HB; Jim Taylor, FB; Boyd Dowler, FL.

BEST DRAFT CHOICE: 1956—Hall of Fame quarterback Bart Starr, 17th round — the equivalent of a sixth rounder today.

BEST OVERALL DRAFT: 1958, 1st round—Dan Currie, All Pro linebacker; 2nd round—Jim Taylor, Hall of Fame fullback; 3rd round—Ray Nitschke, Hall of Fame linebacker; 4th round—Jerry Kramer, All Pro guard; 5th round pick Joe Francis spent a couple years as a backup QB before heading to Canada and 6th round pick Ken Gray was cut and became an All Pro guard for the Cardinals.

WORST DRAFT CHOICE: Randy Duncan, 1st round 1959. He never played in the NFL, but played two years in Canada and one as a backup with the Dallas Texans of the AFL.

WORST OVERALL DRAFT: 1954. Max McGee was a great pick in the 5th round, but #1 Art Hunter played one year in Green Bay, went into the service, and then was traded. Their second #1, Veryl Switzer, spent two years in Green Bay before going into the service and then on to Canada, and #2 Bob Fleck was featured on a 1954 Bowman football card, but didn't make the team.

BEST FREE AGENT: Howie Ferguson never played college football. After being in the service, he tried out for the Rams in 1953. When he was cut, the Pack signed him and he became the team's best running back for the decade.

BEST TRADE: Trades sometimes create interesting trails. Defensive end John Martinkovic was obtained from the Redskins in 1951 for end Ted Cook who never played again in the NFL. After several Pro Bowl years in Green Bay, Martinkovic was traded along with tackle Dalton Truax to the Giants in 1957 for a 3rd-round pick in the 1958 draft. Martinkovic's career was over by the time the Packers used the pick on Hall of Fame linebacker Ray Nitshcke. Another example was in 1956; the Packers gave a 5th-round pick to the Browns for journeymen Don King and Gene Donaldson. The Browns used the 1957 pick to grab Henry Jordan. Two years later, the Packers traded a #4 in the 1960 draft (eventually John Brewer) to obtain Henry Jordan, who became a Hall of Fame defensive tackle in Green Bay.

WORST TRADES: The Packers made three dubious trades with the Browns. In 1952, the Packers gave up the rights to Bob Gain who had gone to Canada and a #4 (Zeke Costa) for Dom Moselle, Ace Loomis, Don Schroll, and Dan Orlich. Gain was the only star in the deal, but he was not interested in Green Bay. In the same year, the Packers traded Walt Michaels for Dick Logan, Chubby Griggs, and Zeke Costa. Again, Michaels was the only real player in the deal. Finally, in 1955, the Packers traded Art Hunter who was in the service for Bill Lucky and Joe Skibinski. Once more, Cleveland got the only player in the deal because they were not in desperate need for immediate help.

BIGGEST OFF-FIELD EVENT: Hiring Vince Lombardi in 1959 and giving him total control.

BIGGEST ON-FIELD DEVELOPMENT: Lambeau Field opens as the new City Stadium on September 29, 1957, with Vice President Nixon, "Gunsmoke's" James Arness, and Miss America all in attendance. The Packers beat the Bears 21-17. Having been expanded several times since, Lambeau is still considered the best place to watch a pro football game.

STRANGEST ON-FIELD EVENT: Beating Curly Lambeau's Chicago Cardinals in an exhibition game in August 1950. The Packers would meet Lambeau's Cardinals and Redskins four more times and would go 3-1 in preseason games and 1-0 in regular season contests. Also, Gene Ronzani was fired with two games to go in 1953, but he made the West Coast trip with the team anyway.

WORST FAILURE: The disgraceful 1959 season, 1-10-1.

HOME ATTENDANCE: 1,393,449 in 60 games for an average attendance of 23,224. Twenty-six Milwaukee home games drew an average of 21,347 while 34 games in Green Bay drew an average of 24,660. Green Bay's average attendance was greater than Milwaukee's every year except 1955 and 1956.

FIRST GAME: September 17, 1950. The Packers begin this decade with a new coach, Gene Ronzani, but playing the way they ended the last one by losing to the Lions. The 45-7 score represented the first of five times Green Bay would surrender more than 40 points in the season as they gave up over 400 for the year.

LAST GAME: December 13, 1959. The Packers ensure their only winning season of the decade for coach Lombardi by rolling up 479 yards of total offense and rolling over the 49ers on the Coast, 36-14.

BEST GAME: In the annual Thanksgiving game in 1956, Tobin Rote threw a scoring pass with under two minutes left, and Bobby Dillon intercepted a Bobby Layne pass with 38 seconds left to beat the Lions 24-20. An interesting sidelight was the October 26, 1958 Packer-Eagle game, a turnover-laced battle of cellar-dwellers. The Pack built up a 38-14 fourth-quarter lead only to watch it melt to 38-35. But Ray Nitschke recovered an onside kick with 56 seconds left to clinch the team's only victory of the year.

LARGEST MARGIN OF VICTORY: 42-14 over the Dallas Texans 11/23/52.

LARGEST MARGIN OF DEFEAT: 56-0 to the Baltimore Colts (the former Dallas Texans) 11/2/58. This is the worst loss in the history of the franchise.

BEST OFFENSE: 1952, fifth in the league in both points and yards and with 26 TD passes.

BEST DEFENSE: 1959. Not quite the caliber of Bengtson's championship defenses of the 1960s, but in 1959 he had them headed in the right direction finishing sixth in points allowed but third in yards—a decade-high ranking.

MOST GAMES PLAYED: 96, Dave Hanner. Bobby Dillon played in 94.

MOST POINTS: 455, Fred Cone.

MOST FIELD GOALS: 53, Fred Cone.

MOST TOUCHDOWNS: 43, Bill Howton.

MOST TOUCHDOWN PASSES: 89, Tobin Rote.

MOST PASSING YARDS: 11,535, Tobin Rote.

MOST RECEIVING YARDS: 5,581, Bill Howton.

MOST RECEPTIONS: 303, Bill Howton.

MOST RUSHING YARDS: 2,205, Tobin Rote, QB. Howie Ferguson had the most for a running back, 2,120.

MOST INTERCEPTIONS: 52, Bobby Dillon.

MOST KICKOFF RETURN YARDS: 3,907, Al Carmichael.

MOST PUNT RETURN YARDS: 834, Billy Grimes.

BEST BOOKS (About): Larry Names' *The History of the Green Bay Packers: Book IV: The Shameful Years.* Angel Press of WI, 1995. *Launching the Glory Years: The 1959 Packers—What They Didn't Tell Us,* Coach's Books LLC [Jay Bengtson], 2001. This provides the 1959 assistant coaches' assessment of each player on Lombardi's first team after the eighth game of the season, at which point the club was 3-5 and on a 5-game losing streak. Comments include: Paul Hornung, "I don't see how he can help a good pro club. We need better backs than this." Bart Starr, "A capable fill-in at best." and Ray Nitschke, "Has physical ability, but cannot think. Will never be able to play for us. Trade him."

NOTED SPORTSWRITER: Lee Remmel of the *Green Bay Press Gazette* covered the team from the mid-1940s before becoming the head of public relations for the team in 1974. He was still serving the team into the new century and has personally witnessed over 100 Packer-Bear games. He was elected to the Packer Hall of Fame in 1996.

BEST QUOTATIONS: New York sportswriter and Green Bay native Red Smith wrote of the 1959 1-10-1 Packers, "The Packers overwhelmed one opponent, underwhelmed 10, and whelmed one." Vince Lombardi greeted his new team in 1959 by saying, "Gentlemen, I have never been associated with a losing team, and I have no intention of starting now." He also noted, "There are planes, trains, and buses leaving every day, and if you don't produce for me you're going to find yourself on one." Bart Starr called his wife to excitedly tell her, "Honey we're going to win!"

BUBBLEGUM FACTOID: Ed Neal's 1951 Bowman card tells us that Ed is, "perhaps the strongest man in professional football and one of the biggest . . . Blacksmith in the oil field in the off-season." Bob Zatkoff's 1956 Topps card says, "In the off season he teaches school and you can be sure youngsters in Bob's class have perfect conduct." Bart Starr's rookie 1957 card states, "The flashy freshman proved to be an unusually accurate passer."

UNUSUAL NAMES: Billy Bookout, Ray Bray, Fred Cone, Jerry Helluin, Ace Loomis, Bill Lucky, John Martinkovic, Clarence Self, Washington Serini, Rebel Steiner, Veryl Switzer, John Symank, Len Szafaryn, Jim Temp, Clayton Tonnemaker, Val Joe Walker, Ab Wimberly.

NICKNAMES: Dick "the Bruiser" Afflis, Lefty Aldridge, Jack Rabbit Boone, Charlie "Choo Choo" Brackins, Buddy Brown, Buddy Burris, Al "Hoagy" Carmichael, Pitchin' Paul Christman, Jack "The Flying" Cloud, Rip Collins, Bubba Forester, Pineapple Joe Francis, Bobby "Goose" Freeman, Hawg Hanner, Red Hearden, Pelican Paul Held, Paul "Golden Boy" Hornung, Red Howton, Blackie Jansante, Moose Lauer, Clink McGeary, Babe Parilli, Ray "Crazy Man" or "Tiger" or "Wrong Way" Pelfry, William "The Bull" Reichardt, Breezy Reid, Skiba Joe Skibinski, Trapper Stephenson, Derrel "The Little Thinker" or "The Little Bull" Teteak, Buster Young, and Roger "Zany" Zatkoff—"The Mad Russian".

BEST FOOTBALL NAME EVER: Bart Starr.

FASTEST PLAYER: Probably Bill Howton. Al Carmichael, Veryl Switzer, and Bob Mann were all fast as well.

HEAVIEST PLAYER: Jerry Helluin, 280 lbs.

LIGHTEST PLAYER: J.R. Boone, 5'8" 167 lbs.

TOUGHEST INJURY: Jim Taylor suffered burns from a kitchen grease fire, causing him to miss most of four games in 1959. Taylor's injury coincided with the team's midseason losing streak that cost them any shot of contending for a title.

LOCAL BOYS: Bill Butler, Jug Girard, Ace Loomis, Dom Moselle, Howie Ruetz, and Jim Temp all hailed from Wisconsin.

FIRSTS:

Black Player—Bob Mann, 1950.

Number Retired—Don Hutson's #14, 11/2/51.

Thanksgiving Day Series with Detroit—1951.

Televised Packers Game—10/24/53 31-14 loss to Steelers over the Dumont Network.

Televised Packers Win—10/31/53 35-24 over the Colts.

Regular Season December Home Game in Green Bay—12/2/51 31-28 loss to the Yankees.

106 Yard Kickoff Return—Al Carmichael in a 10/7/56 37-21 loss to the Bears.

Season Spent Entirely in Last Place—1958, 1-10-1.

Winning Season of the Decade—1959, 7-5.

400 Points Given Up—1950.

50 Points Given up in a Game—12/3/50 51-14 loss to the Rams.

WORK ETHIC
ERNIE SMITH • TACKLE 1935–37, 1939

WHO'S WORN THE NUMBER Lewellen 1928, Bultman 1932–33, Herber 1934, Hinkle 1934, Ernie Smith 1935–37, 1939, Kuusisto 1941–45, Wildung 1946–51, Nix 1955, Tunnell 1959–61, Hathcock 1966, Rowser 1967–69, E. Hunt 1970, P. Smith 1973–76, L. Thomas 1987–88, Sikahema 1991, McNabb 1992–93, Prior 1993, K. Crawford 1995, 1999, Cooks 1998.

ORIGINATOR Back Verne Lewellen 1928 (see 46).

LONGEST TENURE Tackle Dick Wildung 1946–51 (see 70).

NUMBER CHANGES Verne Lewellen had 4 in <1925–26> and wore 21 in 1927, 31 in 1929–30, and 46 in 1931–32; center Red Bultman wore 33 and 38 in 1933 and 17, 32 and 52 in 1934; Arnie Herber wore 12 in 1930, 26 in 1931, 41 in 1932–33, 16 in 1933, 68 in 1934, 38 from 1935–40, and 19 in 1937; Clarke Hinkle wore 27 and 33 in 1932, 30 in 1933, 1935, and 1937–41, 39 in 1933, 45 and 48 in 1934, and 41 in 1936; Ernie Smith also wore 61 in 1936; Guard Bill Kuusisto wore 52 in 1946; Dick Wildung wore 70 in 1953; defensive back Doyle Nix also wore 41 in 1955; defensive back John Rowser also wore 28 in 1967; fullback Dexter McNabb also wore 44 in 1993; safety Mike Prior wore 39 from 1994–98; safety Kerry Cooks also wore 20 in 1998.

OTHER NOTABLES Verne Lewellen (see 46); Arnie Herber (see 16); Clarke Hinkle (see 30); Dick Wildung (see 70); New York Giant Hall of Famer Emlen Tunnell came west with Vince Lombardi to finish up his career.

ONE TO FORGET Running back Lavale Thomas played in two games in his two year career from 1987 to 1988, one as a replacement player, and ran for 19 yards and caught two passes for 52 yards.

ERNIE SMITH It is difficult to conceive how different professional sports was 70 years ago. It was not at all major league in the contemporary use of the term. Working conditions were primitive, and pay was paltry. There was no television and no Internet; games were covered on radio or not at all. Newspapers were the media giant, but they relegated all but major league baseball to deep inside the limited sports pages. Football coverage meant college football.

Ernie Smith is an case in point. He was a large All American tackle for Coach Howard Jones' two-time national champion University of Southern California Trojans. He and his linemates averaged

50-55 minutes a game and allowed only two touchdowns all season. Were he playing today with a resume like that, he'd be a high first-round draft choice who would sign an extended contract for millions of dollars a year with several million up front as a signing bonus. His agent would take his cut off the top and help guide the newly rich tackle in ways to invest his new wealth so that he might never have to work again after football. Of course there would be no guarantee on the soundness of those investments or of the person the player selects to manage the money, but the potential is there to be "set for life."

Ernie Smith, 6'2", 220 pounds, graduated in 1933, however, and did not even turn pro immediately. He spent the 1933 and 1934 seasons coaching the USC freshman team and getting started in a career in insurance that would last 53 years. In 1934 he played minor league football near his home with the Southern California Maroons of the Pacific Coast Pro Football League (PCPFL). Finally, in 1935 he signed on with Curly Lambeau and played tackle for three years, twice receiving All Pro consideration and helping the team win the 1936 title. In addition, he handled extra-point kicking and the occasional field goal attempt for the Packers. He dropped out in 1938 to again play close to home for the Hollywood Stars of the PCPFL, but returned for a final NFL season in 1939 as the Pack won another title. He then got on with his real life career, interrupted briefly by a World War II stint in the U.S. Army Air Force. Smith also appeared in movies, roughly 85 according to one source. (Porter, 532) A check of the Internet Movie Database, however, reveals only an Ernie Smith (I) who appeared in one movie in 1936 and one television production in 1966, and Ernie Smith (VIII) who appeared in *That's My Boy* in 1932, playing, in a bit of typecasting, a football player. It's likely that Smith's movie appearances were mostly as an extra. Perhaps he was helped in landing bit parts in films by fellow USC alumni who made a career in movies: actor Ward Bond who played on the 1930 Trojan team, film editor Cotton Warburton who was an All American quarterback from 1932–4, and production staffers Nate Barragar and Russ Saunders who played for the Trojans from 1927–29. Barragar and Saunders also played for Green Bay, and Barragar was a fraternity brother of Smith's. Perhaps even John Wayne, who had played for the Trojans as Marion Morrison in 1925–26, might have put in a word for him.

In sports and, in particular football, the improvement in financial rewards was gradual. Magazine articles on the team in the 1930s noted how Packer players were fully integrated into the town. Former players were part of the scenery. Charlie Mathys ran a ground glass business. Jug Earp was a car salesman. Lavvie Dilweg was an attorney. Verne Lewellen was prosecutor. Current players had regular jobs to support their football sidelight. Dave Zuidmulder was a fireman. Arnie Herber ran a clothing store. Hank Bruder ran a tire company. George Svendsen had a gas station. Milt Gantenbein sold insurance.

Football cards in the 1940s and 1950s regularly listed players' off-season occupations: Jerry Helluin ran a gas station, Howie Ferguson worked in the oil fields, Al Carmichael was a movie stunt man, and so on. In the 1960s the sport's popularity allowed the pay to increase to a living wage—$20,000 on average by 1963. In Green Bay, post-season playoff bonuses became a regular thing to be figured in a player's budget during that decade. Off-season occupations were still listed on cards, but it was more likely the career the player was preparing for after his playing days were over. In the 1970s, as average salaries passed $50,000, occupations began to disappear from trading cards and be replaced by hobbies. By the 1980s, average salaries would stretch to six figures, making football a very well-paying full-time job in which off-season conditioning was seen as part of the job requirements; not many players waited until training camp to get into shape. In the 1990s, true free agency arrived and football's non-guaranteed contracts with salaries reaching seven figures were supplemented by the more important lump sum signing bonus to invite the aforementioned phrase "set for life."

While no one wants to go back to the football or the playing/working conditions of Ernie Smith's time, that era's lack of guaranteed money and the resultant need for players to prove their worth on the field every day produced a competitive work ethic that was good for the game. The need for players to continue proving their worth and earning their keep after a sports career ended was a good example for the nation. Today's model of athletes as entertainers who have hit the lottery is a far less positive image.

FOR FURTHER INFORMATION
Porter, David L., ed. *Biographical Dictionary of American Sports: 1992–1995 Supplement for Baseball, Football, Basketball, and Other Sports.* New York: Greenwood Press, 1995. (531-532)

TRIPLE THREAT
VERNE LEWELLEN • BACK, 1931–32

WHO'S WORN THE NUMBER Ashmore 1928, Lewellen 1931–32, Gantenbein 1933–34, L. Evans 1935, Letlow 1936–42, 1946, Fries 1943, Tollefson 1944–45, R. Clemons 1947, Olsonoski 1948–49, Nichols 1951, Gremminger 1956–65, Glass 1972–73, Luke 1975–80, Harrison 1987r, Richard 1988, Workman 1989–92, M. Robinson 1996, Bolden 1998, Artmore 1999.

ORIGINATOR Tackle Roger Ashmore 1928 (see top 35).

LONGEST TENURE Defensive back Hank Gremminger 1956–65 intercepted 28 passes in a decade in Green Bay. He was better at safety than cornerback and was elected to the Packer Hall of Fame in 1976.

NUMBER CHANGES Roger Ashmore wore 35 in 1929; back Verne Lewellen wore 4 in <1925–26> and 21 in 1927, 45 in 1928, and 31 in 1929–30; end Milt Gantenbein wore 21 in 1931–32, 30 and 47 in 1933, and 22 from 1935–40; guard Lon Evans wore 17 in 1933, 25 and 65 in 1934, 51 in 1936, and 39 in 1937; Russ Letlow also wore 62 in 1936; guard Charles Tollefson wore 27 in 1946 and 77 in 1947; center Larry Olsonoski wore 74 in 1948.

OTHER NOTABLES Milt Gantenbein (see top 22); guard Lon Evans (see top 39); guard Russ Letlow (see 72).

ONE TO FORGET On a team desperate for receivers, Leland Glass caught 26 passes in 26 games in his two years.

VERNE LEWELLEN Were it not for an arm injury, Verne Lewellen might have become a star pitcher for the Pittsburgh Pirates and never have come to Green Bay. How different Packer history would have been had that occurred. Lewellen was one of the most intelligent, talented, and versatile men ever to work for the Pack, and his influence was felt on the team for decades both on and off the field.

At Lincoln High School in Nebraska, Lewellen played on two unbeaten football teams including the 1918 state champions, starred on the 1920 state basketball champions, and led his school to two track championships. Verne graduated with a law degree from the University of Nebraska. While there, he displayed enough pitching talent to interest the Pittsburgh Pirates, and captained the football team that delivered the only two defeats Knute Rockne's "Four Horsemen" would suffer in their three years together. One of the key elements of Nebraska's victories over Notre Dame in 1922 and 1923 was Lewellen's running, passing, punting, and defensive work. One of the Four Horsemen, Jim Crowley, recommended the skilled Lewellen to his old high school coach in Green Bay, Curly Lambeau. Curly signed Verne in 1924, and the Nebraskan would spend nine years as a Packer, pacing the team in scoring five times.

For his part, Lewellen, once said that he found Green Bay attractive because it was the "city with the college spirit." (Names, I, 179) He was not disappointed, and Green Bay was not disappointed with him. Verne could do everything well on the football field. At the halfback position, the 6'1" 180-pound Lewellen was one of the best runners in the league and was also a skilled pass receiver in addition to being adept at throwing the fat football of the day. On defense he was a sure-tackling defensive back. Above all, he was known as the finest punter of his time. In the community, he was so popular that he was elected District Attorney for Brown County as a Republican in 1928 and was reelected in 1930. Teammate Lavvie Dilweg ran in the Democrat primary for the same office in 1928, but was defeated, so the team was spared potential locker room campaigning for a Verne v. LaVern match during the 1928 season.

There are virtually no official statistics for the period that Lewellen played, but unofficial press counts provide a good picture of Lewellen's talents. In over 100 games Verne ran the ball 708 times for 2,410 yards and 37 touchdowns. He caught 84 passes for 1,265 yards and 12 touchdowns. He completed 122 of 335 passes for 2,080 yards and nine touchdowns, and punted the ball 681 times for a 39.5 yard average. It should be noted that in the 1920s, punting was a more vital function than it is today. Teams played a ball-control game and would punt from anywhere and on any down. One reason his punting average stands at 39.5 yards is that teams would often punt from inside the opposing teams 40 yard line and would aim the ball for the sidelines, the coffin corner kick that would bury the opponent near his own goal line. In defense of Lewellen, it should also be noted that his total of 681 punts is hundreds greater than his nearest contemporaries; he was the punting king of the 1920s.

In the single wing offense, versatility was a necessity in the backfield. Each back had to be able to take a snap from center and handle the ball. Backs at that time were ideally supposed to be triple threats—able to run the ball, pass the ball, and kick the ball with equal skill—and Lewellen met that ideal as well as anyone in the league. Kicking either could take the form of punting or placekicking. The Packers have had a number of triple-threat backs over the years, but the last one was probably Donny Anderson, since that versatility is not greatly desired in today's more specialized game.

Besides Lewellen, Packer runners who were triple threats included:
Johnny Blood—1,272 yards rushing, 1 touchdown pass, and a 36.6 punting average all unofficially.
Bo Molenda—1,415 yards rushing, 5 touchdown passes, and 10 extra points.
Clarke Hinkle—3,860 yards rushing, 26 of 54 passing, a 40.8 punting average, 28 field goals and 31 extra points.
Swede Johnston—101 yards rushing, 3 of 4 passing, and 38.5 punting average.
Hank Bruder—1,114 yards rushing, 1 touchdown pass, and a 37.8 punting average.
Roger Grove—283 yards rushing, 2 touchdown passes, and 16 extra points.

Bob Monnett—1,488 yards rushing, 28 touchdown passes, five field goals and 27 extra points.

Hal Van Every—281 yards rushing, four touchdown passes, and a 37.5 punting average.

Lou Brock—800 yards rushing, seven touchdown passes, and a 37.2 punting average.

Tony Canadeo—4,197 yards rushing, 16 touchdown passes, and a 37.1 punting average.

Roy McKay—288 yards rushing, six touchdown passes, and a 41.9 punting average.

Paul Hornung—3,711 yards rushing, five touchdown passes, 66 field goals and 190 extra points.

Donny Anderson—3,165 yards rushing, two touchdown passes, and a 39.6 punting average.

The best combination of skills was Paul Hornung, but the widest was Clarke Hinkle, who was skilled at both forms of kicking. Joe Laws and George Sauer were also versatile Packer runners who could throw a pass, but their punting was never officially tabulated. Ted Fritsch rushed for 2,200 yards, punted for a 38.6 average, and kicked 36 field goals and 62 extra points, but threw one only pass and it went incomplete.

Packer passers who were triple threats include:

Curly Lambeau—24 touchdown passes, eight touchdown runs, six field goals and 19 extra points.

Charles Mathys—10 touchdown passes, 1 rushing touchdown, and 1 field goal.

Red Dunn—48 passing touchdowns, 290 yards rushing unofficially, a 31.6 punting average, two field goals and 48 extra points.

Arnie Herber—66 touchdown passes, 201 yards rushing, and a 39.1 punting average.

Cecil Isbell—61 touchdown passes, 1,522 yards rushing, a 32.7 punting average and three extra points.

Irv Comp—28 touchdown passes, 519 yards rushing, and a 37.8 punting average.

Jack Jacobs—21 touchdowns passes, 137 yards rushing, and a 42.1 punting average.

Jug Girard—five touchdown passes, 283 yards rushing, and a 39.2 punting average.

Babe Parilli—31 touchdown passes, 375 yards rushing, and a 39.6 punting average.

Cecil Isbell had the best combination of talents from this group. Tobin Rote had 89 touchdown passes and 2,205 yards rushing, but punted only twice (for 112 yards). Bart Starr and Zeke Bratkowski were both star punters in college, but never had the opportunity to punt with the Packers.

All good things must end, and in 1933 Lewellen lost both his jobs. Lambeau urged him to retire from football, just as the voters had urged him and many other Republicans throughout the nation to retire from political office in November 1932. He focused on his law practice and then took a position as personnel manager for Standard Oil in town. For a brief time he coached the Long Island Indians of the American Association, a minor league team with whom the Packers had an arrangement. In 1950 he was asked to join the Packer executive committee. Four years later, he was hired as the first general manager of the team. When he took over, the Packers were operating at a deficit, but within a few years the team

While he was a triple-threat player worthy of the Hall of Fame, Verne Lewellen never wore number 32 in a league game or in court as Brown County District Attorney. *Courtesy of the Stiller-Lefebvre Collection.*

had accumulated a surplus that would continue to grow year by year. In addition, he was instrumental in the campaign for a new stadium. In 1956, he spoke before the local Kiwanis Club regarding the necessity of a new stadium in Green Bay and presciently said, "I firmly believe the golden era is going to be in the 1960s." (Names, IV, 196) The bond measure passed easily and City Stadium II (now Lambeau Field) was built. With scout Jack Vainisi steadily assembling talent, imperceptible progress was made on the field as well. Vince Lombardi was hired in 1959 as coach and general manager, and Lewellen was shifted to business manager. While Lombardi took that accumulated unfocused talent and molded a champion on the field, Lewellen continued making the team a success financially. He retired in 1967 and died in 1980. When he left the game in 1932 he was the leading touchdown maker in NFL history with 51 and was the leading Packer scorer with 307 points. He is still ninth on the list of scorers in team history. He was elected to the Packer Hall of Fame in 1970 and remains one of the most qualified players not elected to the Pro Football Hall of Fame.

FOR FURTHER INFORMATION

Johnson, Chuck. *The Green Bay Packers: Pro Football's Pioneer Team.* New York: Thomas Nelson and Sons, 1963. (54-5)

Names, Larry. *The History of the Green Bay Packers: Book I: The Lambeau Years Part One.* Wautoma, WI: Angel Press of WI, 1987.

———. *The History of the Green Bay Packers: Book II: The Lambeau Years Part Two.* Wautoma, WI: Angel Press of WI, 1989.

———. *The History of the Green Bay Packers: Book III: The Lambeau Years Part Three.* Wautoma, WI: Angel Press of WI, 1990.

———. *The History of the Green Bay Packers: Book IV: The Shameful Years.* Wautoma, WI: Angel Press of WI, 1995.

Packers of the Past: A Series of Articles Reprinted from the Milwaukee Journal Sept. 28–Dec. 9, 1965. Milwaukee, WI: Milwaukee Journal, 1965. (43-5)

Porter, David L., ed. *Biographical Dictionary of American Sports: 1989-1992 Supplement for Baseball, Football, Basketball, and Other Sports.* New York: Greenwood Press, 1992. (440-1)

Ward, Arch. *The Green Bay Packers.* New York: Putnam, 1946. (87-8)

GIANT RIVAL
JESSE WHITTENTON • CORNERBACK 1958–64

WHO'S WORN THE NUMBER Gantenbein 1933, Bruder 1934, A. Rose 1935–36, L. Gordon 1937, Berezny 1942–44, Lipscomb 1945–49, Szafaryn 1950, Martinkovic 1951, Moselle 1952, V. Walker 1953–56, Whittenton 1958–64, Rule 1968–69, D. Davis 1971–72, Petway 1981, J.B. Morris 1987, R. Mitchell 1991–94, S. Galbraith 1998, T. Bell 1999.

ORIGINATOR End Milt Gantenbein 1933 (see top 22).

LONGEST TENURE Jesse Whittenton 1958–64.

NUMBER CHANGES End Milt Gantenbein wore 21 in 1931–32, 30 in 1933, 46 in 1933–34, and 22 from 1935–40; blocking back Hank Bruder wore 13 in 1931–33, 55 in 1933, 27 in 1935–36, 18 in 1935–38, and 5 in 38–39; end Al Rose wore 37 and 52 in 1932, 34 in 1933, and 49 in 1934; tackle Lou Gordon wore 53 in 1936; tackle Ben Szafaryn wore 51 in 1950 and 68 in 1953–56; defensive end John Martinkovic wore 39 in 1951 and 83 from 1952–56; halfback Dom Moselle wore 93 in 1951; replacement Jim Bob Morris also wore 30 in 1987.

OTHER NOTABLES End Milt Gantenbein (see top 22); blocking back Hank Bruder (see 27); tackle Paul Lipscomb played 10 years in the NFL and was once called "one of the dirtiest players in the league" (see 83); John Martinkovic (see 83).

ONE TO FORGET Defensive back David Petway played his entire six game career in Green Bay.

JESSE WHITTENTON In his book, *Run to Daylight*, Vince Lombardi, a man not given to extravagant public praise of his players, called Jesse Whittenton, "as close to being a perfect defensive back as anyone in the league . . . He can run with any halfback or receiver in the league and . . . he is a great student of opponents. He has studied everything about all of them, including the expressions on their faces that, when they come up to the line, may tell him something about what they are going to run." (Lombardi, 82) Along with fellow defensive backs Hank Gremminger and Johnny Symank, the three were known as "Hecker's Wreckers" after secondary coach Norb Hecker. Hecker himself referred to them as the "Katzenjammer Kids" because of the way they kept things happening. And Hecker agreed with Lombardi that Whittenton was the top man of the unit.

The Packers were fortunate to come up with Whittenton. He was originally signed by the Rams and spent two anonymous years in Los Angeles before being traded to the Bears. The Bears released him, and the Packers grabbed him early in 1958 to join the rest of the underutilized talent that Vince Lombardi would discover when he arrived in 1959. In Green Bay, Jesse blossomed into a topflight cornerback. He made All Pro in 1961, after making second team in 1960, and played in two Pro Bowls. It was New York, though, that made him a star.

The small-town Packers had a strong rivalry going with the big-city Giants since the 1920s. The teams first played in 1928 when they traded a pair of shutouts—6-0 Giants and 7-0 Packers. In the following year the Packers handed the Giants their only loss of the season to win their first championship, signaling to the rest of the league that the team from the small town in Wisconsin could play with anyone. Curly Lambeau and Giants' coach "Stout" Steve Owen would go head-to-head 28 times from 1928 through 1949 and ended up 13-13-2 against each other. Curly's teams were known for their passing offense, and Owen always featured one of the toughest defenses in the league. Three times they met in the title game, and the Packers won twice. The 1944 season brought some particularly bad blood to a boil between the two. The Giants were quarterbacked by Arnie Herber, the former Packer, and employed Red Smith as assistant coach—he had been Lambeau's line coach for many years until they had a bad parting of the ways. The teams met in the penultimate game of the regular season in New York, and, amidst Lambeau's accusations of the Giants spying on his practices, the Packers were trampled 24-0. Four weeks later in the championship match, Lambeau had his revenge as the Packers hung on to win a tough 14-7 battle.

The Packers went into decline after that and the rivalry started to disintegrate. With the Packers hiring New Jersey-bred Giants offensive coach Vince Lombardi, however, the rivalry heated up again. Lombardi was an intense competitor and wanted to prove himself most of all to all his hometown friends. When the Giants gave permission for the Packers to speak with Vince, they did so with the proviso that they might want to hire him back within a couple of years. Coach Jim Lee Howell retired earlier than expected at the end of 1960. The Giants then did as they said and requested permission to talk to Lombardi about the head job in New York. Vince was very interested, but the Packers were not about to give Lombardi permission to leave after he'd rescued the franchise from complete ineptitude and brought it to the championship game in only his second year. The Giants weren't happy, but hired Allie Sherman who turned out to be a big success at the start by winning three straight Eastern Division crowns with a popular team highlighted by an explosive, imaginative offense. As the team aged, though, Sherman would be out of his depth in trying to rebuild it.

The Giants won the first meeting of the two teams in 1959 while Lombardi was still sorting out his squad, but he never lost to New York again in Green Bay, beating them the next four times, including two title games. The next time they met was in the 12th game of the 1961 season, and Jesse Whittenton was the key performer. He was assigned to cover his former roommate on the Rams, Del Shofner, man-to-man. Shofner was perhaps the premier deep threat in the game at the time and the focal point of the Giants attack. Whittenton covered Shofner all over the field and held him to one catch all day. Still the Packers trailed 17-13 in the fourth quarter when Giants fullback Alex Webster took off on a twenty yard run from his own eight yard line. Jesse gambled and went for the ball at the 30 and stole it right out of Webster's hands in a spectacular play reminiscent of Charley Brock's strip plays in the 1940s. In five plays Green Bay converted the turnover into six points and hung on to win 20-17.

Four weeks later, the rivals met for the championship. Shofner and Whittenton had dinner the night before the game, and Shofner told his friend, "Jesse, I'm going to do everything you do and go everywhere you go and have fun and then tomorrow I'm going to run your legs off." (Hornung, 194) Whittenton responded to the challenge the next day, and Shofner caught only three balls for 41 yards. The lone time Giant quarterback Y.A. Tittle tried to find Shofner deep, Jesse picked it off. The Packers won handily, 37-0. In the final matchup of these two players in the 1962 title tilt, Shofner's longest of his three catches for the day was for 21 yards. The way Lombardi put it was, "the way Jesse covers him now, he must have made a book on the way Shofner does everything from brushing his teeth to putting on his socks." (Lombardi, 83)

After 1962, the rivalry with the Giants died out. They rarely played and within a half-dozen years both teams would be mired in a morass of mediocrity for the next twenty or more seasons. Moreover, with television money being pooled, the small town franchise was secure in its equal financial footing with the large-market teams. Through 1962 the Packers and Giants played 29 regular season games in 35 years with the Packers winning 13 and the Giants 14, with two ties. The Packers also won four of five title games. Since then, in the last 39 years, they have met only 17 times with the Packers leading 11-6. The Packer-Giant rivalry was effectively replaced by the Packer-Cowboy rivalry in the mid-1960s.

Jesse Whittenton played two more years and then retired at age 30 after the 1964 season when he took the opportunity to run a golf course in his native Texas. That turned out to be a lucrative move. Jesse befriended a young, unknown Lee Trevino in 1966 and helped sponsor him when he first went on the pro golf tour. They remained good friends for decades. Whittenton, like Trevino, is an amusing storyteller and a polished banquet speaker. Whittenton himself played briefly on the tour, as well, and later joined the Seniors tour, even winning the 1988 Seniors championship. He was inducted into the Packers Hall of Fame in 1976.

FOR FURTHER INFORMATION

Hornung, Paul, as told to Al Silverman. *Football and the Single Man.* Garden City, NY: Doubleday, 1965. (194)

Lombardi, Vince, with W.C. Heinz. *Run to Daylight.* Englewood Cliffs, NJ: Prentice-Hall, 1963. (82-4)

Pave, Marvin. "One Club to Another: Ex-Packer Whittenton Is Taking Shots with Seniors," *Boston Globe.* 7/9/89. (58)

Poling, Jerry. *Downfield! Untold Stories of the Green Bay Packers.* Madison, WI: Prairie Oak Press, 1996. (218-19)

Wagner, Len. "The Big Steal," *Green Bay Packers 1962 Yearbook.* (3)

———. "Katzenjammer Kids," *Green Bay Packers 1961 Yearbook.* (31-2)

THE PACKER
HALL OF FAME
KEN ELLIS • CORNERBACK 1970–75

WHO'S WORN THE NUMBER Hinkle 1934, F. Butler 1935–36, C. Miller 1938, Jacunski 1939–44, D. Perkins 1945, Nussbaumer 1946, T. Cook 1948–49, Loomis 1953, Psaltis 1954, Carmichael 1955–58, Pesonen 1960, K Ellis 1970–75, N. Simpson 1977–79, L. Morris 1987r, Levens 1994, Bartrum 1995, Kitts 1998.

ORIGINATOR Clarke Hinkle 1934 (see 30).

LONGEST TENURE End Harry Jacunski 1939–44 (see Notables below) and Ken Ellis 1970–75.

NUMBER CHANGES Clarke Hinkle wore 27 and 33 in 1932, 30 in 1933, 1935, and 1937–41, 39 in 1933, 45 in 1934, and 41 in 1936; center Frank Butler wore 26 and 60 in 1934, 59 in 36, and 35 in 1938; back Don Perkins wore 53 and 58 in 1943 and 23 in 1944; defensive back Bomber Nussbaumer wore 23 in 1951; end Ted Cook wore 48 in 1950; halfback Ace Loomis wore 7 in 1951 and 43 in 1952; halfback Al Carmichael wore 42 from 1953–54; replacement Lee Morris also wore 81 and 85 in 1987; running back Dorsey Levens wore 25 from 1995–2001.

OTHER NOTABLES Harry Jacunski played under coach Jim Crowley at Fordham with teammate Vince Lombardi. He got his chance to play opposite Don Hutson when Carl Mulleneaux went into the service. He caught the only TD pass that Hutson ever threw and was elected to the Packers Hall of Fame in 1991 He was an assistant coach at Yale for 32 years; Al Carmichael (see top 42); Dorsey Levens (see 25).

ONE TO FORGET Running back Nate Simpson averaged 3.2 yards per carry and fumbled 7 times in 153 carries, but lasted three years in Green Bay.

KEN ELLIS Ken Ellis was not a Hall of Famer, but he deserves to be remembered. He came to the Packers as an unheralded 1970 fourth-round draft pick out of Southern University, a small black school in Louisiana. In college, Ellis was a wide receiver and punt returner—he led the nation with a 33-yard punt return average in 1968. Among his teammates on that 1968 team were future Hall of Fame Steeler Mel Blount and future Eagle All Pro Harold Carmichael, yet they still finished 3-7.

In his first training camp with Green Bay, he was slotted behind Carroll Dale and figured to ride the bench. However, Herb

NUMBER 48

Adderley was a holdout, and second-round pick Al Mathews was with the College All Star team, so coach Phil Bengtson asked Ken if he wanted to try playing cornerback with a possibility of starting. Ellis agreed, and soon Adderley was traded to Dallas. With help from Willie Wood, Bob Jeter, and Doug Hart, Ken made such strides that he found himself in the starting lineup on opening day in Lambeau Field. He still considers that to be his biggest memory of his Packer career, despite the Pack being crushed 40-0 by the Lions in a game that signaled, once and for all, that Bengtson was not "bringing the Pack Back."

Ellis would remain a starter for the next six years. He would lead the team in interceptions three times and would score five touchdowns, three on interceptions, one on an 80-yard punt return, and one on the first missed field goal returned for a touchdown in NFL history. He was All Pro twice and went to two Pro Bowls. Ken was a bump-and-run cornerback known for his speed, once even catching the legendary Bob Hayes from behind. He led the league in punt returns in 1972 with a 15.4 yard average, but strangely never averaged more than 5 yards a return in any other year.

Ken was also a tough and dedicated teammate. In that lone winning season of 1972, Ellis dislocated his shoulder late in the season, but insisted on playing the next game on December 3 against the arch division rival Lions in a battle for first place. Ellis picked off two Greg Landry passes deep in Lion territory to set up two Packer touchdowns and then recovered a Lion fumble in Packer territory to help Green Bay roll to a 33-7 victory. His teammate Bob Brown said at the time, "He inspired us all." (Rubin, 130)

In 1976, Ellis himself was a holdout, demanding more money than Bart Starr was willing to pay him. He walked out of training camp twice, was suspended, and then was included in the trade to Houston that brought Lynn Dickey to Green Bay. He would play in five cities in the last four years of his career, but would end on the high note of playing on the 1979 Rams who lost to the Steelers in Super Bowl XIV.

During his career, Ellis had earned his master's degree from Southern and become a committed Christian. After retiring, he became increasingly involved with his church, especially by working with troubled youth, and eventually he became ordained as a minister in 1991. Once again he is inspiring people.

While Ellis will not be enshrined in Canton, he should not be forgotten. The Packers ensured that he would not be, when they inducted him into the Packer Hall of Fame in 1998. The Packer Hall of Fame is the perfect place for men like Ken Ellis, the good to very good players who are the foundation of the great success the team has had for more than 80 years in the NFL. The Packers were the first team to have a Hall of Fame museum devoted to their history, and the only other team to follow suit were the New Orleans Saints, whose tradition is not quite as rich as Green Bay's, and whose museum is basically a single room. Other teams have different ways to commemorate their greatest names, such as a Ring of Honor in their home stadium, but the Packers have a museum building with regular and changing exhibits and displays in addition to annual induction ceremonies.

The Packer Hall of Fame had its beginnings as a handful of exhibits in the concourse of the Brown County Veterans Memorial Arena in May 1967. After receiving 60,000 visitors that first summer, plans were made for a permanent building. While fundraising and construction activities went on, formal inductions began in 1970. The plan for the first five years was to take 10 players per decade each year for five years, i.e., 10 from the 1920s were inducted in the fall of 1970, 10 from the 1930s in January 1972, and so on. For the next four years, five names were selected—one oldtimer, three other players, and one contributor. In the 1980s, the oldtimer requirement was dropped, and by the 1990s there were no formal requirements of the makeup of any induction class.

The brick building itself was opened in 1976 across the street from Lambeau Field, and was dedicated by then-President Gerald Ford, who noted that Curly Lambeau had offered him a contract to join the Packers in 1935, but instead Ford opted for Yale Law School and politics. The 10,000-square-foot building was expanded to 17,000 in 1980 and has a steady attendance flow each year. In 1997, more people came to the Packer Hall of Fame than went to the Pro Football Hall of Fame in Canton. What they find in Green Bay is an Inductee Hall with plaques honoring the more than 120 former Packers and team contributors enshrined here, several videos on the history of the team, team photos of each Packer squad, exhibits devoted to each Super Bowl Championship, and the Locker Room with displays of the memorabilia of every Packer inducted in the Pro Football Hall of Fame in Canton. As part of the Lambeau Field renovations in the new century, the Packer Hall moved into the stadium's new atrium, where it will continue to ensure that the memory of past Packers will live on.

FOR FURTHER INFORMATION

Bledsoe, Terry. "Mike McCoy, Ken Ellis, Jim Carter: An Extra Season of Youth," *Green Bay Packers 1971 Yearbook.* (26-8)

Karbon, Dick. "A Permanent Hall of Fame in Green Bay," *Green Bay Packers 1975 Yearbook.* (41-2)

Poling, Jerry. *Downfield! Untold Stories of the Green Bay Packers.* Madison, WI: Prairie Oak Press, 1996. (89-92)

Remmel, Lee. "The All-New Packer 'Hall,'" *Green Bay Packers 1990 Yearbook.* (58-9)

Rubin, Bob. *Green Bay's Packers: Return to Glory.* Englewood Cliffs, NJ: Prentice-Hall, 1974. (130)

Schiefelbein, Joseph. "Dream Comes True for Ellis," *Baton Rouge Sunday Advocate.* 6/18/00. (4C)

THE UNDESERVING
WALT KIESLING • GUARD 1935–36

WHO'S WORN THE NUMBER Fitzgibbon 1932, A. Rose 1934, Kiesling 1935–36, Howell 1938, Orlich 1949–51, Wicks 1974, West 1984, Greenwood 1986, Sutton 1989, Wilner 1995, K. Smith 1996, L. Hall 1999, T. Franz 2002.

ORIGINATOR Backup back Paul Fitzgibbon 1932 scored three TDs in Green Bay.

LONGEST TENURE End Dan Orlich 1949–51 became a champion trap shooter after football, setting an American Trapshooting Association record average of .9982 and going into the Trapshooting Hall of Fame in 1979.

NUMBER CHANGES Back Paul Fitzgibbon wore 18 in 1930 and 14 in 1931–32; end Al Rose wore 37 and 52 in 1932, 34 in 1933, and 47 in 1935–36; Walt Kiesling also wore 60 in 1936; Den Orlich also wore in 19 in 1951; tight end Ed West switched to 86 in 1984 and wore it through 1994; tight end Jeff Wilner also wore 83 in 1994; tight end Lamont Hall also wore 88 in 1999.

OTHER NOTABLES None.

ONE TO FORGET All of them.

WALT KIESLING While there are 20 Packers in the Pro Football Hall of Fame, 25 of the 200+ inductees from all teams had some connection to Green Bay sometime in their careers. Of the other five, Giant Emlen Tunnell spent the last three years of his career in Green Bay tutoring his successor Willie Wood, Jan Stenerud kicked for the Green and Gold for three years after the Chiefs cut him, Raider Ted Hendricks spent a year of his prime with the Packers, and Cleveland Brown Len Ford spent his last year in Wisconsin. Stenerud is the only one who was considered enough of a Packer to be elected to the Packer Hall of Fame. Walt Kiesling is the last of the five and the only one who doesn't belong in either Hall.

Kiesling was a large and well-traveled guard and later coach for a series of teams. He is listed as a Steeler in Canton, since he both played and coached there. He played longest for the Cardinals, five years, and made All Pro there for the only time in his career. He also played two years for the Duluth Eskimos who then ceased operations, one for the Pottsville Maroons who then went out of business, one for the Chicago Bears, two for the Packers, and three for Pittsburgh. Despite playing for the 13-0 Bear team that lost the "Sneaker Game" for the 1934 title and the 1936 10-1-1 champion Packers, the record of the teams for whom Kiesling played was 66-82-11.

PACKERS BY THE NUMBERS

After retiring from playing, Walt coached Pittsburgh from 1940–42 and from 1954–56. For most of the intervening years, he spent as a line coach either with the Steelers or the Packers. The high point of his coaching career was the 1942 season when he led Pittsburgh to its first-ever winning year with a second-place 7-4 record. It would be the only winning year he would ever have as a coach; his lifetime coaching record in 30-55-6.

According to Art Rooney, coach Kiesling thought everyone was "dumb." Rooney said that whenever there was a problem, Kiesling said it was because said player was dumb. Kiesling himself is most vividly recalled today as the Pittsburgh coach who cut Johnny Unitas when he was in the 1955 Steelers' training camp. Unitas could not remember the plays and Kiesling thought he must be too dumb for the pro game. In Walt's defense, Jim Finks was the starter, Ted Marchibroda the backup, and Unitas was competing for the number-three job with Vic Eaton, who could also punt, return kicks, and play defense. However, to use Walt's term, it was a dumb move.

How do you judge the career of a player who retired 65 years ago and who played a position completely lacking any statistical framework? It's a matter of piecing together lots of bits of information and using your intuition to form an opinion. As to anecdotal evidence, there are few comments from Kiesling's contemporaries that I have found regarding his playing ability. On the plus side he did have a lengthy career, but he bounced around a lot. No Hall of Famer whose career began after the formation of the NFL in 1921 played for as many teams as Kiesling—although his partner in Green Bay and Pittsburgh, Johnny Blood, played for five. Jim Thorpe, Guy Chamberlain, Joe Guyon, and Jimmy Conzleman are the only ones who played for six teams, and they all began playing prior to the time when the NFL imposed some sense of order on professional football. In addition, over his long career he was only a first-team All Pro once and a second-teamer once. All of which seems to indicate that he was a good player, but not a great one worthy of Canton.

In *The Hidden Game of Football* the authors did a study on what the parameters are for inclusion in the Pro Football Hall of Fame. Since most positions generate little or no supporting statistics, they went to a weighted system of counting All Pro and Pro Bowl selections. Among two-way guards, Kiesling was by far the least qualified of the four enshrinees. In fact, there were nine others whose qualifications were stronger than his and who were not members. Instead, Kiesling made the overall list of the 10 inductees least deserving of the honor. Two other Packers to make this list were Johnny Blood and Paul Hornung, but there are a host of mitigating factors for both of those that make it clear why they were chosen and why they belong.

Art Rooney told the story of when Kiesling's Steelers were revolting against his coaching and went to Rooney in mutiny. Rooney calmed them by telling them what a fine fellow Walt was and how they would never find a more loyal man. It's likely that is how he made it into the Hall of Fame. He was a decent enough player who continued to serve as a coach in the league for most of his life, but of more importance he was a loyal friend. The Baseball Hall of Fame has practically an entire wing of this kind of member: Fred Lindstrom, George Kelly, Jess Haines, and so on. Kiesling was elected to the Hall posthumously in 1966; he was represented by his friend Johnny Blood and presented for induction by Supreme Court Justice Byron "Whizzer" White. His bust will remain one of the most quizzical in Canton, lit only by the reflected glory of such teammates and coaches as Fats Henry, Ernie Nevers, George Halas, Link Lyman, George Musso, Bill Hewitt, Red Grange, Bronko Nagurski, Curly Lambeau, Arnie Herber, Clarke Hinkle, Cal Hubbard, Mike Michalske, Don Hutson, Art Rooney, and Johnny Blood.

FOR FURTHER INFORMATION

Carroll, Bob, Pete Palmer, and John Thorn. *The Hidden Game of Football: The Next Edition.* New York: Total Sports, 1998. (208)

Cope, Myron. *The Game That Was: An Illustrated Account of the Tumultuous Early Days of Pro Football.* New York: Crowell, 1974. (117-18)

Daly, Dan, and Bob O'Donnell. *The Pro Football Chronicle: The Complete (Well Almost) Record of the Best Players, the Greatest Photos, the Hardest Hits, the Biggest Scandals, and the Funniest Stories in Pro Football.* New York: Collier Books, 1990. (155-56)

Porter, David L., ed. *Biographical Dictionary of American Sports: Football.* New York: Greenwood Press, 1987. (314-15)

REPLACING THE LEGENDS

JIM CARTER • LINEBACKER 1970–78

WHO'S WORN THE NUMBER C. Perry 1934, Schwammel 1935–36 and 1943, Monnett 1938, C. Thompson 1939, B. Johnson 1941, Roskie 1948, Rhodemyre 1952, B. Curry 1965–66, Hyland 1967–69, J. Carter 1970–75 and 1977–78, Wingo 1979, 1981–84, J. Holland 1987–93, Rafferty 1987r, M. Arthur 1995–96, A. Davis 1999, K.D. Williams 2000–01.

ORIGINATOR Tackle/guard Claude Perry 1934 (see top 26).

LONGEST TENURE Jim Carter 1970–75 and 1977–78.

NUMBER CHANGES Claude Perry wore 26 from 1927–30, 37 in 1929 and 1933, 27 in 1931, 24 in 1932, and 32 in 1935; tackle Ade Schwammel wore 53 in 1934, 57 in 1936, 40 in 1943 and 58 in 1944; back Bob Monnett wore 18 in 1933, 42 and 66 in 1934, 12 and 3 in 1935, 12 and 5 in 1936, and 5 in 1937; back Ken Roskie also wore 34 in 1948; center Jay Rhodemyre wore 22 in 1948–49 and 85 in 1951; center Bob Hyland wore in 55 in 1976.

OTHER NOTABLES Tackle Ade Schwammel made All Pro in 1935; Bob Monnett (see top 3); center Bill Curry became a star with the Colts and has been a successful college coach; linebacker Johnny Holland was a tackling machine until his career was ended by neck injury, and he was elected to the Packer Hall of Fame in 2001.

ONE TO FORGET Center Bob Hyland wasn't awful, but wasn't worthy of a high first round draft choice in 1967 either. He was traded to the Giants after three years and is most remembered for barreling into new Packers coach Dan Devine on the sideline in his coaching debut and breaking Devine's leg.

JIM CARTER Replacing a legend in sports is never easy, and it is even more difficult when the legend hasn't yet left the stage. Jim Brown retired as the greatest ball carrier of all time in 1965, and was replaced by unknown Leroy Kelly who, while not quite measuring up to Brown, went on to his own Hall of Fame career. Aging Joe Montana got seriously hurt and was replaced by Steve Young. Young played well, but when Montana returned two years later, the 49ers had to trade him out of town so they could move on with the younger man. Trading Montana could not erase the bitterness, and Young was never fully embraced in San Francisco, even after winning a Super Bowl. (Joe won four, after all.) Young will eventually join Joe in Canton, but Joe will always be king in the Bay area. To use a baseball example, it took Yankee fans 10 years to accept Mickey Mantle as Joe DiMaggio's replacement, and they were in the midst of winning 12 pennants in Mantle's first 14 years. Not to mention that Mantle was a better player than DiMaggio, anyway.

The first example is the ideal situation. The legendary Jim Brown took his bows and left the stage. The understudy, Kelly, was a talented unknown that fans did not expect to be as good as Brown, so they were delighted when he showed just how talented he was. He may have felt pressure in taking the place of a legend, but he was greeted warmly by fans. However, the Montana/Young example is closer to the experience of Jim Carter in pushing aging Ray Nitschke to the bench in 1971. What made it even worse was that while Carter was a good, solid player, he certainly was not a Hall of Famer. In addition, sophisticated quarterback Steve Young handled himself in public better than gruff linebacker Jim Carter. If circumstances had been different, Carter may have had a more successful career; he surely would have had a happier one.

Jim Carter was from Saint Paul and played fullback at the University of Minnesota. He came to the Packers in the third round of the 1970 draft and was also drafted by the World Hockey League's Minnesota Fighting Saints. He was shifted to linebacker in training camp and when Dave Robinson was injured early in the year, Jim replaced him as starting outside linebacker. When Robinson returned the next season, new coach Dan Devine moved Carter to middle linebacker and gave him the tougher job of replacing 14-year vet Ray Nitschke, the man voted best middle linebacker of the first 50 years of the NFL just the year before. The trouble was that Nitschke didn't feel that he'd been beaten out for his position on the field, but that his job was simply handed to Carter.

When you factor in that Carter was learning still another new position, that Nitschke was still on the roster, and, despite being a bit slower, was still a serviceable player, that Nitschke was beloved by the fans, and that Nitschke and Starr (who was ailing and failing in his final year) were the last links to the glory years of the 1960s, then it is not too surprising that the transition was not smooth. Fans were chanting "We want Nitschke" throughout the 1971 season. The fans got their wish in the next-to-last game of the year against the Bears. For Ray Nitschke Day, Devine moved Carter to the outside and started Ray in the middle one last time, and the Packers won, 31-10.

Nitschke returned in 1972 to warm the bench again. The chants had stopped, and the improved Packers featured the best defense in the NFC, giving up only 226 points on their way to winning the Central Division crown. Carter would be a second-team All Pro that year and go to the Pro Bowl the next. There was a disturbing incident in the sixth game of the 1972 season against Atlanta, though. Carter got hurt and had to be helped off the field. As he was leaving, Nitschke came in and the fans rewarded Ray with a big cheer. After his experience of the previous year, Carter interpreted that as fans being glad he was injured and took it as a personal insult. Through all of this, Carter says that Nitschke and his wife always treated him well and the two players were not personal enemies.

Of all the difficult transitions taking place as the stars of the 1960s retired or were traded away, this was by far the toughest. Willie Davis retired and Clarence Williams replaced him without incident. Herb Adderley was traded and Ken Ellis replaced him, again without incident. Bart Starr retired and rag-armed Scott Hunter replaced him, and there were no recriminations for Hunter. Nitschke-Carter was a different ballgame, though. Carter takes some of the blame himself. He made some improper gestures to the fans and some ungracious comments about Nitschke. He drank too much and hung around in bars too long. His marriage ended. His career ended. Finally, in 1983, his drinking ended.

In retirement, Carter has built a very successful car dealership chain in Wisconsin. Unlike so many former Packer players, though, Jim makes it a point not to come back to Green Bay to bask in the fans' fond remembrances. He fears their reaction would be similar to that of 30 years ago.

He played in a turbulent and mostly unsuccessful era. There was the undisciplined disorganization of Dan Devine, the players' strike of 1974 during which he crossed the picket line to report to training camp, and the on-the-job training of Bart Starr. He played for only two winning clubs and one playoff team in his eight years as a Packer, and lost another whole season to injury. Yet his fear seems unreasonable because the other problem in following a legend is that, unless you are a great player, too, you are quickly forgotten. Jim always was a proud man, not afraid to voice his opinion. He now says of Nitschke that "I probably knew then but just wouldn't admit what a great player he was. The fans loved him. He deserved the accolades. I was jealous." (Poling, 36) He was quick to add that Butkus was a better linebacker.

FOR FURTHER INFORMATION

Echternacht, Jon. "The Jim Carter Story," *Green Bay Packers 1977 Yearbook.* (34-6)

Poling, Jerry. *Downfield! Untold Stories of the Green Bay Packers.* Madison, WI: Prairie Oak Press, 1996. (33-40)

Rubin, Bob. *Green Bay's Packers: Return to Glory.* Englewood Cliffs, NJ: Prentice-Hall, 1974. (138)

ORAL MYSTERY
JIM RINGO • CENTER 1953–63

WHO'S WORN THE NUMBER Goldenberg 1934, Hubbard 1935, L. Evans 1936, Schneidman 1938–39, Lawrence 1939, Frutig 1941, Stonebreaker 1942, Comp 1943–49, Szafaryn 1950, Faverty 1951, Ringo 1953–63, Hayhoe 1969, Hefner 1972–75, Gueno 1976–80, Prather 1981–85,Weishuhn 1987, Monaco 1987r, Simpkins 1988, Bush 1989–91, Brady 1992, Morrissey 1993, M. Williams 1994, B. Williams 1995–2000, Marshall 2001–02.

ORIGINATOR Quarterback/guard Buckets Goldenberg 1934 (see 43).

LONGEST TENURE Jim Ringo 1953–63.

NUMBER CHANGES Buckets Goldenberg wore 21 in 1933, 44 in 1935–37, and 43 from 1938–45; Cal Hubbard wore 39 in 1929 and 40 in 1930; guard Lon Evans wore 17 in 1933, 25 and 65 in 1934, 46 in 1935, and 39 in 1937; Herm Schneidman wore 4 from 1935–37; back Jim Lawrence also wore 59 in 1939; end Ed Frutig wore 80 in 1945; tackle Len Szafaryn also wore 47 in 1950 and 68 from 1953–56; tackle Bill Hayhoe wore 77 from 1969–73; linebacker/fullback Torrance Marshall also wore 41 in 2002.

OTHER NOTABLES Buckets Goldenberg 1934 (see 43); Hall of Fame Tackle Cal Hubbard (see 39); Lon Evans (see top 39); Irv Comp was the last of Lambeau's passing single-wing tailbacks, and while he directed the Pack to the championship in 1944, he was no Isbell or Herber. He was prone to interceptions, and once Hutson left, he had an unbelievably low passer rating of 9.9 in 1946. He was, however, a fine defensive back who intercepted 33 passes in his career and went into the Packer Hall of Fame in 1986.

ONE TO FORGET The Packers were the second of seven teams Jeff Brady would play for in his nine-year career. The only team he stuck with for more than a year was the hated Vikings (see 93.) In his three years with Minnesota he was a continual annoyance to Packer fans. He was a small, fast, trash-talking linebacker who seemed to hold a grudge against the Packers, and his boasts and grumbles frequently made the newspaper. Unfortunately, he also made some big plays against the Packers. Most notably, in 1995 when the Packers were driving for the winning score with third-string quarterback T.J. Rubley at quarterback, Brady intercepted Rubley's ill-advised, audibilized third-and-short pass. The Vikings then kicked the winning field goal and Rubley was cut the next week. As a Panther in 1998, Brady also intercepted Favre, but the Packers won that game. Brady was not a bad player, but to Packer fans he was a thoroughly obnoxious guy.

NUMBER 51

PACKERS BY THE NUMBERS

JIM RINGO In the 1962 John Ford Western, *The Man Who Shot Liberty Valance*, Jimmy Stewart plays a mild-mannered senator who was originally elected to office due to the renown he received from his killing of notorious outlaw Liberty Valance. Years later he returns for the funeral of his old friend John Wayne, an ordinary cowboy who actually did the celebrated shooting. At long last, Stewart attempts to clear up the record by telling the true story of his friend's quiet heroism to a journalist, but the newspaper man's conclusion is "When the legend becomes fact, print the legend." This perspective is worthwhile to keep in mind when confronted with the plenitude of oral history recollections of past events, sporting and non-sporting. A good example of this is the story of Packer Hall of Fame center, Jim Ringo.

Ringo was a seventh-round draft choice out of Syracuse in 1953. At 6'1" and 230 pounds (at the most), he was so small that he even left training camp after two weeks because he felt he wasn't big enough to compete. Prompted to return by his wife and father, he of course made the team and began a 15-year career in which he was All-Pro seven times, played in 10 Pro Bowls, set a then-NFL record for consecutive games played with 182, and was elected to the Hall of Fame in 1981. He relied on his intelligence, intensity, and quickness to become the best center of his era. He was fortunate also that he joined the league just as the position of middle guard was being phased out by the advent of the middle linebacker. Thus, there was no behometh defensive lineman lined up directly on the center in his day. Instead, Ringo's quickness and smarts were great assets in going after the faster, more active middle linebacker.

Ringo played in Green Bay for 11 years until he was traded in 1963 to Philadelphia for the last four years of his career. The trade broke up Green Bay's Ringo-Starr center snap connection and freed the way for the Beatles' Ringo Starr to make a name for himself in 1964. Jim Ringo's last year as a pro, 1967, was also the last year of Lombardi's Packer dynasty. That season and the Lombardi Era as a whole were commemorated in Jerry Kramer's season-long diary published as *Instant Replay*. Among the abundance of stories Kramer tells of his teammates is the one that became Jim Ringo's ticket to immortality. In essence, the story goes that Ringo brought in an agent to negotiate his 1963 contract with Vince Lombardi. Lombardi's reaction to being introduced to a player's agent for the first time was to ask the agent to step outside for five minutes. When the agent returns, Lombardi tells him that he is negotiating with the wrong team—Ringo has been traded to Philadelphia.

Ever since the story's appearance in *Instant Replay*, whenever anyone wanted to show how tough Lombardi was and how he held total control over his team, the Ringo story is repeated. It has turned up in countless books and articles over the past 30 years, which is rather amazing because the story is patently false. Ringo was traded along with former first-round draft choice fullback Earl Gros to the Eagles for linebacker Lee Roy Caffey and the Eagles 1965 first-round draft choice (which would be used for All-American Donny Anderson). A deal of this magnitude and involving this much talent is not spontaneously thrown together in a five-minute phone call. Lombardi himself was later quoted as saying as much—"that's no way to general manage a football team." In general, though, Lombardi let the story stand because it suited his purposes by telling all interested parties that his authority would not be challenged.

As for Ringo, himself, when being interviewed in the late 1980s for the oral history compilation *Iron Men*, he relates that he actually negotiated with Pat Peppler, the assistant GM, and demanded either a raise or to be traded. At a later date, Peppler called Ringo to inform him he had been traded. Five years later, Ringo says he ran into Lombardi when Vince was coaching in Washington and they had an emotional reunion. There are other accounts indicating further that Ringo actually requested a trade to the East Coast, where he lived, to be closer to his family and business interests.

OK, case closed. The Ringo/agent story is simply an entertaining legend repeated so many times that the truth doesn't have a chance. Evidently even Ringo came to this conclusion. In September 1996, he was interviewed in the *Milwaukee Journal-Sentinel* and repeated the original apocryphal agent story as gospel as well as adding that he never spoke to Lombardi again. So much for that emotional reunion. The interviewer does not question why Ringo has foregone history to become a storyteller himself, but simply prints the legend as fact.

In 2002, the story took one more, perhaps final, twist. Ringo was interviewed by a different *Journal-Sentinel* reporter and relates that actually he didn't even have an agent at the time because they were only for elite players then. Whether that story will enable the truth to filter through the legend at long last is highly unlikely.

FOR FURTHER INFORMATION

Berghaus, Bob. "Ringo Was Told to Take a Hike," *Milwaukee Journal-Sentinel.* 9/26/96. (5)

Daly, Dan, and Bob O'Donnell. *The Pro Football Chronicle: The Complete (Well Almost) Record of the Best Players, the Greatest Photos, the Hardest Hits, the Biggest Scandals, and the Funniest Stories in Pro Football.* New York: Collier Books, 1990. (193)

Johnson, Chuck. *The Greatest Packers of Them All.* New York: Putnam, 1968. (128-30)

Leuthner, Stuart. *Iron Men: Bucko, Crazy Legs, and the Boys Recall the Golden Days of Professional Football.* New York: Doubleday, 1988. (14-25)

Maraniss, David. *When Pride Still Mattered: A Life of Vince Lombardi.* New York: Simon and Schuster, 1999. (354-5)

Porter, David L., ed. *Biographical Dictionary of American Sports: Football.* New York: Greenwood Press, 1987. (495-6)

Reischel, Rob. "Ringo Brings Ring of Truth to Old Lombardi Tale," *Milwaukee Journal-Sentinel.* 01/30/02. Available online at www.jsonline.com/packer/news/jan02/16510.asp

Schaap, Dick, ed. *Instant Replay: The Green Bay Diary of Jerry Kramer.* New York: World Publishing, 1968. (272)

1938
CHAMPIONSHIP GAME
TINY ENGEBRETSEN • GUARD 1936

WHO'S WORN THE NUMBER A. Rose 1932, Bultman 1934, Engebretsen 1936, Buhler 1939–41, Snelling 1945, Kuusisto 1946, Skoglund 1947, C. Walker 1970, Winther 1971, Schmitt 1974, Weaver 1975–79, Cumby 1980–85, Weddington 1986–90, Melka 1987r, Winters 1992–2002.

ORIGINATOR End Al "Big Un" Rose caught 13 of 21 passes and scored all five TDs with Green Bay before Don Hutson arrived in 1935.

LONGEST TENURE Center Frank Winters 1992–2002 (see Notables below).

NUMBER CHANGES Al Rose wore 37 in 1932, 34 in 1933, 49 in 1934, and 47 in 1935–36; center Red Bultman wore 45 in 1932–33, 33 and 38 in 1933, and 17 and 32 in 1934; Tiny Engebretsen wore 69 in 1934 and 34 in 1935–41; Bill Kuusisto wore 45 from 1941–45; center Wimpy Winther also wore 54 in 1971.

OTHER NOTABLES Linebacker George Cumby was an active, undersized, and underappreciated linebacker who was a second-team All Pro one year; chippy Frank Winters was never very popular among opposing linemen, but had a long successful run as the leader of Bret Favre's line and went to one Pro Bowl.

ONE TO FORGET Fullback Ken Snelling was a fifth round pick who lasted two games, running for 10 yards in three carries and fumbling once.

TINY ENGEBRETSEN The circumstances that brought Paul (Tiny) Engebretsen to Green Bay were circuitous indeed. He was a year behind Hank Bruder at Northwestern, but would not join him on the Packers for three years. In 1932, Tiny was signed by George Halas to play for the local pro team, the Bears, and helped beat the Packers 9-0 in December by kicking a fourth-quarter 14-yard field goal in the snow. He spent the entire season with Chicago as they won the championship in the first-ever NFL playoff against the Portsmouth Spartans, also by a 9-0 score. It was also the first NFL game played indoors; because of bad weather the game was played on a shortened field within Chicago Stadium. Meanwhile, in Green Bay, Curly Lambeau made a trade with Brooklyn at the end of 1932, sending veteran end Tom Nash to the football Dodgers for a "player to be named later."

NUMBER 52

In 1933, Nash played for Brooklyn, and Tiny Engebretsen moved from the Bears to Pittsburgh, where he played nine games and then came back to Chicago where he played two games for the cross-town Cardinals. In 1934, he traveled on again, this time to Brooklyn where Tom Nash was playing the last three games of his career. All this rambling was mirrored in Engebretsen's off-season activity at the time, prospecting for gold out West. At midseason, Curly Lambeau called in his marker and collected that player to be named later. Tiny joined the Packers after playing five games with Brooklyn. He would remain in Green Bay until his career ended in 1941.

In Green Bay, the 6'1" 240-pound Engebretsen became a solid starting guard and part of the placekicking committee that the Packers employed. In that era, teams did not carry a separate placekicker; the job was handled along with a player's regular duties. Due to injuries, inconsistencies, and varying skill levels, it made sense to use more than one kicker at a time. Each year, the mix for the Packers was a little different. In 1934, the duties were split between backs Bobby Monnett, Clarke Hinkle, and Hank Bruder. During 1935 and 1936, Ernie Smith handled most of the extra-point tries, while Hinkle and Ade Schwammel attempted field goals in the former year and Smith and Engebretsen tried them in the latter. By 1937, Tiny was helping Smith with the points after touchdown as well as trying his share of field goals. For the remainder of his time in Green Bay, Tiny was the primary extra-point man and tried his share of field goals as well.

Amongst the 300-pound linemen of today, his nickname would be meant literally, but at the time it was said with irony. Tiny was a big man for the 1930s. In the New York Times preview of the 1938 championship game against the New York Giants, much fanfare was given to the advantage of the larger Green Bay line—bigger by an average of 10 pounds per man. One reason the Packers were favored was that they had four behemoth tackles around 250 pounds each, together weighing "almost half a ton." (Daley, "Green...") This perspective would be echoed 59 years later in Super Bowl XXXII, and, alas, so would the result of the game. One constant in football is that size matters, but it isn't everything.

The title game itself was reminiscent of the last game of the 1938 regular season when the Packers racked up 20 first downs to the Giants 6, but lost the game 15-3 in the Polo Grounds. Three weeks later in the championship match, again in the Polo Grounds, the Packers accumulated 378 yards to the Giants 212, outgaining New York both on the ground and through the air, but still lost the game 23-17. In the *New York Times*, Arthur Daley opined, "Perhaps there have been better football games since Rutgers and Princeton started this autumnal madness 69 years ago, but no one in that huge crowd would admit it. This was a struggle of such magnificent stature that words seem such feeble tools for describing it." (Daley, "Record...")

The game was a vicious, hard-hitting affair in which teams moved up and down the field, and many players sustained injuries. Mel Hein, at 225 pounds the largest Giants lineman, sustained a concussion, Johnny Dell Isola hurt his back, and Ward Cuff injured his chest. Of most significance for Green Bay, Don Hutson, who had missed the previous game against New York with a knee injury, reinjured the knee and limped off early in the second quarter. The Giants blocked punts by both Hinkle and Isbell in the first quarter, leading to a field goal and a touchdown and a 9-0 Giants lead.

Tiny Engebretsen helped lead the Packers back. His second-quarter interception led to a 40-yard touchdown pass from Arnie Herber to Carl Mulleneaux. The Giants countered with another touchdown, and the Packers matched it on a Clarke Hinkle short run after a 66-yard pass play to Wayland Becker. In the third quarter, the Packers drove down to the Giants five, but had to settle for a Engebretsen field goal to take their first and only lead of the day. The Giants answered with a touchdown drive to retake the lead. The final quarter was scoreless, with the Packers' frantic attempts to come back thwarted by turnovers and crucial penalties. Lambeau was livid about the calls that went against Green Bay, "It isn't fair for us to lose a game on account of incompetent officiating." Despite Curly's complaint, what beat the Packers were blocked punts, turnovers, and losing Don Hutson.

As to Engebretsen, he would return to help the Packers win another title in 1939 when he would once again score five points with a field goal and two extra points as the Packers main kicker. He would spend just one more full year in Green Bay, leaving after one game in 1941 to spend most of the year coaching the Buffalo Tigers in an early version of the American Football League. Despite the presence of his old Packer teammate, 38-year-old Johnny Blood, the team finished 2-6. Tiny was elected to the Packer Hall of Fame in 1978.

FOR FURTHER INFORMATION

Daley, Arthur J. "Green Bay Favored Over Giants Today," *New York Times.* 12/11/38. (V, 1,3)

———. "Record Play-Off Throng of 48,120 Sees Giants," *New York Times.* 12/12/38. (22)

"1938 NFL Championship Game," *The Coffin Corner.* 1998. Available online at www.footballresearch.com/articles/frpage.cfm?topic'champ38.

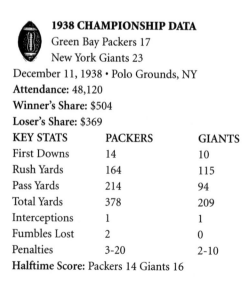

1938 CHAMPIONSHIP DATA
Green Bay Packers 17
New York Giants 23
December 11, 1938 • Polo Grounds, NY
Attendance: 48,120
Winner's Share: $504
Loser's Share: $369

KEY STATS	PACKERS	GIANTS
First Downs	14	10
Rush Yards	164	115
Pass Yards	214	94
Total Yards	378	209
Interceptions	1	1
Fumbles Lost	2	0
Penalties	3-20	2-10

Halftime Score: Packers 14 Giants 16

ADDITIONAL FACTS

•The Packers were favored in the game.

•The Giants allowed only 79 points in the regular season.

•The Giants allowed Bud Svendsen to be eligible for the game.

•If the game were to end in a tie, the team presidents and the commissioner would meet after the game to determine whether the teams would play again the following week or be declared co-champions.

END OF THE DYNASTY
FRED CARR • LINEBACKER 1968–77

WHO'S WORN THE NUMBER McCrary 1933, Schwammel 1934, L. Gordon 1936, E. Svendsen 1939, D. Evans 1940, Ingalls 1942, Don Perkins 1943, Stephenson 1953–55, Timberlake 1955, Palumbo 1955, Iman 1960–63, Carr 1968–77, Chesley 1978, M. Douglass 1979–85, Leopold 1986, Turpin 1986, A. Anderson 1987r, Corker 1988, Koonce 1992–99, M. Morton 2000, A. O'Neal 2001, Lenon 2002.

ORIGINATOR Fullback Herdis McCrary 1933 backed up Bo Molenda for three consecutive championships, finishing third on the team in rushing in 1930 and third in 1931. He then backed up Clarke Hinkle for two years.

LONGEST TENURE Fred Carr 1968–77.

NUMBER CHANGES Fullback Herdis McCrary wore 29 in 1929, 28 in 1929–30, 19 in 1931, 43 in 1932, and 38 in 1933; tackle Ade Schwammel wore 50 in 1935, 50 and 57 in 1936, 40 and 50 in 1943 and 58 in 1944; tackle Lou Gordon wore 47 in 1937; center Earl (Bud) Svendsen wore 7 in 1937 and 66 in 1939; end Dick Evans wore 22 in 1943; back Don Perkins wore 58 in 1943, 23 in 1944, and 48 in 1945; guard Dave Stephenson wore 44 in 1951 and 69 in 1952; linebacker Mike Douglass wore 65 in 1978.

OTHER NOTABLES Center Earl (Bud) Svendsen (see top 7); linebacker Mike Douglass was like his teammate George Cumby — active, undersized, underappreciated and a one-time second-team All Pro; George Koonce was a sturdy strongside and middle linebacker throughout the 1990s.

ONE TO FORGET Linebackers Francis Chesley and Miles Turpin each played one game for the Packers; Turpin extended his NFL career with three games in Tampa.

FRED CARR Although Vince Lombardi was still the general manager, 1968 began the short Phil Bengtson era in Green Bay as Lombardi's longtime loyal assistant became head coach of the team. Fred Carr was his first draft choice, and Phil felt, "Carr had the potential to play defensive end, linebacker, tight end, or safety. Getting him was like drawing the wild card in poker." (Bengtson, 156) And he was right: Carr had an amazing amount of talent and was a very good player for 10 years in Green Bay. The sad thing was he could have been even better and played even longer if the team had not deteriorated around him.

NUMBER 53

NUMBER FIFTY-THREE

At the University of Texas-El Paso, he was an All American linebacker and a member of the UTEP basketball team. He came to the Packers just as they were coming off their third consecutive world championship year; some players just have miserable timing. Ten years earlier, linebacker Wayne Walker joined the World Champion Lions in 1958 and he would make All Pro and Pro Bowl teams during his career, but would never play in a Super Bowl. Likewise, future All Pro Carr was coming in just as the 1960s dynasty was ending. If the team had had a few more replacements like Fred, perhaps things would have been different for Phil Bengtson and for the Packers in the 1970s.

As the core of the Packers aged each year, more stars needed replacing. Too often, lesser players took their place. In 1967, former number-one draft choices Donny Anderson and Jim Grabowski took their expected places at halfback and fullback. Anderson was a good, solid ballplayer, but did not have the touchdown-making flair that Hornung did; Grabowski showed promise but kept getting injured so he would never approach the level of Jim Taylor. In a rare positive development, another former number-one pick, Gale Gillingham, took over for the beloved Fuzzy Thurston in 1967 and was better than the original. In 1968 the defense was still fourth in points allowed, but the declining offense started to slip further, scoring 50 fewer points. It didn't help that Bart Starr missed half the year due to injuries. Making it even tougher to score was the lack of a reliable kicker. Don Chandler left and was replaced by Jerry Kramer, Chuck Mercein, and Mike Mercer. Better field goal kicking than the 13 of 29 that trio managed could have put the Packers in the playoffs.

In 1969, the kicking situation got even worse as Mike Mercer and Booth Lusteg combined for a 6-of-22 field goal performance. On defense, Ron Kostelnik was traded and Rich Moore was drafted. Moore flopped, but Bob Brown could take up the slack. Tommy Brown was replaced by veteran Doug Hart. The defense was still solid, finishing third in points allowed. The offense worsened from ninth in points scored to 12th, out of 16 teams. Jerry Kramer was replaced at right guard by second-year man and former number-one pick Bill Lueck, while Bob Skoronski was replaced by Francis Peay—a former number-one pick of the Giants who had flopped and was acquired in a trade.

The 1970 season truly spelled the end of the dynasty. The year was bookended by shutout losses to the Lions—40-0 at home and 20-0 on the road. Willie Davis and Henry Jordan retired and were replaced by Clarence Williams and number-one pick Mike McCoy. Lee Roy Caffey and Herb Adderley were traded and effectively replaced by Carr and rookie Ken Ellis. Dave Robinson suffered an injury and was replaced by rookie Jim Carter. The defense dropped to 19th of 26 teams in points allowed. Offensively, things continued to deteriorate as the team fell to 24th in points scored. Marv Fleming left for Miami and was replaced by has-been John Hilton and never-was Rich McGeorge. Likewise, Boyd Dowler retired to be replaced by has-been Jack Clancy and never-was John Spilis. The effects of age severely hampered the play of Bart Starr, Forrest Gregg, Ray Nitschke, Willie Wood, and Bob Jeter. It was all too much change at once; time had caught up to the Packers.

The 6'5" 235-pound Carr didn't break into the starting lineup immediately because linebacker was one position that was well stocked. The Packers experimented with him at defensive end and tight end, but found him best suited to play linebacker with skills similar to All Pro Dave Robinson. Fred was big, strong, and fast, and had a penchant for making big plays. He was All Pro in 1975 and made second team All Pro in four other seasons. He played in three Pro Bowls and was Most Valuable Lineman for the game played in 1971.

Stories told of Carr depict him as a hard liver and a party animal. In 1974, wild man Ted Hendricks joined the Packers and hit it off with Fred in training camp. Every morning Carr would pick up Hendricks, put him in the back seat, hand him a newspaper, and drive to camp. One morning Carr made one change to the ritual—he drove the entire way down Lombardi Avenue backwards. Naturally, a policeman followed them into the parking lot, so Hendricks jumped out of the car saying they were late for practice and placated the cop with some free game tickets. In another training camp story, Coach Starr was pushing the team hard with grass drills and sprints in 1977 when one draft pick, Rick Scribner, threw up on the field. Carr's reaction was to stand over the rookie screaming, "Look at me! I smoke three packs of cigarettes a day. I drink whiskey all day. And here's this 21-year-old rookie barfin' peas." (Christl)

Carr's career ended as suddenly and as badly as the team's glory years. Carr hurt his knee and told trainer Dom Gentile that he thought he was finished. Gentile claimed that it was only a cyst that needed draining and perhaps minor surgery. Much acrimony between Carr and the team followed. Eventually he was cut and then hired an attorney to file a grievance, saying that he was injured and was owed money. Ultimately there was a settlement for an undisclosed amount that Gentile later reported as being $10,000, and Fred never played again in the NFL. Despite the bad ending, there is no denying the quality of his play; he was inducted into the Packer Hall of Fame in 1983. Not only Wisconsin still remembers him. In 1999 *Sports Illustrated* ran a feature listing the best 50 athletes all time from each state, and Fred was number 26 on the Arizona list.

FOR FURTHER INFORMATION

Bengtson, Phil, with Todd Hunt. *Packer Dynasty.* Garden City, NY: Doubleday, 1969. (156)

Christl, Cliff. "Past Camps Were Character Builders," *Milwaukee Journal Sentinel.* 07/20/1997. (1 sports)

Gentile, Domenic, with Gary D'Amato. *The Packer Tapes: My 32 Years with the Green Bay Packers.* Madison, WI: Prairie Oak Press, 1995. (78-9)

Hoffman, Dale. "Fred Carr: Start with Optimism," *Green Bay Packers 1977 Yearbook.* (7-9)

Lea, Bud. "Linebackers: No Soft Spots," *Green Bay Packers 1972 Yearbook.* (17-8, 44)

Rubin, Bob. *Green Bay's Packers: Return to Glory.* Englewood Cliffs, NJ: Prentice-Hall, 1974. (132)

BROADCASTING
LARRY MCCARREN • CENTER 1973–84

WHO'S WORN THE NUMBER Culver 1932, C. Jorgenson 1934, S. Johnston 1936, Craig 1939–49, Schmidt 1952, M. Walker 1970, Winther 1971, McCarren 1973–84, J. Schuh 1986, Stephen 1987–91, G. Jensen 1987r, Malancon 1987r, K. Coleman 1993, B. Harris 1995, Cox 1996, Joyner 1997, Waddy 1998–99, Wayne 2000–02.

ORIGINATOR Tackle Al Culver 1932 played on Rockne's last Notre Dame team and was part of the honor guard that stood watch over the coach's body as it lay in state before the funeral. He lasted only one week in Green Bay, but his release was the first player release ever publicly announced in the *Green Bay Press Gazette*.

LONGEST TENURE Larry McCarren 1973–84.

NUMBER CHANGES Fullback Chester (Swede) Johnston wore 37 in 1934 and 15 in 1935–38; center Wimpy Winther also wore 52 in 1971; replacements Rydell Malancon and Greg Jensen both also wore 60 in 1987; linebacker Bernardo Harris wore 55 from 1996–2001.

OTHER NOTABLES Swede Johnston (see top 15); Larry Craig was a two-time All Pro blocking back and defensive end who was elected to the Packer Hall of Fame in 1973. His ability to play defensive line allowed Don Hutson to move to safety on defense and prolong his career.

ONE TO FORGET Former All Pro linebacker Seth Joyner came to Green Bay in 1997 to win a Super Bowl ring with old teammate Reggie White. He was of no help and was released after the Pack lost to the Broncos. He signed with the Denver, didn't do much there either, but won his ring the following year.

LARRY MCCARREN The Packers have had a long tradition of solid centers: Jug Earp, Nate Barrager, George Svendsen, Charley Brock, Jim Ringo, Ken Bowman, Larry McCarren, and Frank Winters. However, Larry McCarren started more games at center for the Packers than anyone else on that illustrious list, more than 150. In his 12-year career, he played in 162 consecutive games and that is second only to Hall of Fame tackle Forrest Gregg's team record of 187. McCarren was known as "Rock," as in "rock steady, " and that sums him up perfectly. In 1980 he had a hernia operation during training camp, but was ready for opening day against the Bears less than four weeks later. Coach Starr intended that Larry only take the first snap to keep his streak alive, but when he sent out a substitute for the second play McCarren waved him off and played the whole game. In that same year, he broke his hand, but had trainer Dom Gentile rig up a special apparatus so he could keep playing. Then in 1983, Larry spent Sunday morning in the hospital after he and his family suffered carbon monoxide poisoning Saturday night, but again started that afternoon.

He was a 240-pound 12th-round draft pick out of Illinois given little chance to make the squad in 1973, but through hard work and perseverance he fashioned a solid career. He built himself up to 270 pounds in the weight room, and rumors circulated about possible steroid use on his part, but he refuses to comment on that even today. There is no disagreement about the result, though. He won the starting job in his second year and set his goal on being one of the best centers in the league. Twice he made All Pro teams, two other times he was a second-team selection, and twice he played in the Pro Bowl. Quarterback Lynn Dickey called him, "the toughest guy I ever played with. Anybody who'd ever question his heart was nuts." (Reischel) He was added to the Packer Hall of Fame in 1992.

After his playing career ended, McCarren became a sportscaster in 1988 and again struggled at first. He looked at broadcasting as just another challenge to be overcome by hard work and dedication. By 1995 he was named Wisconsin Sportscaster of the Year and began doing Packer radio broadcasts with veteran announcers Jim Irwin and Max McGee. When those two retired in 1998, McCarren was joined by new play-by-play man Wayne Larivee to take Packer broadcasts in a new direction.

As with everything else, the Packers have a long history of game announcers. In October 1923 a crowd gathered in a gymnasium in Green Bay for the "broadcast" of the Packer-Bear game from Chicago. Telegraph updates were handed to Packer Public Address announcer Jim Coffeen, who would announce them over the loudspeaker while a large football was moved along the replica of a football gridiron on stage to show ball placement. The first radio broadcasts of Packer games were made in 1931 by WHBY and WTMJ, but regular commercial broadcasts weren't initiated until 1943 on WTMJ with Russ Winnie being the first "Voice of the Packers" for both home and road games. He was later succeeded by Bob Heise, who was followed in turn by Wisconsin broadcasting legend Earl "the Lip" Gillespie in 1952. Gillespie would be supplanted in later years by Tony Flynn and then Blaine Walsh. Ted Moore had the best timing, as he got to serve as the radio man for the Lombardi years. Finally in 1969 Jim Irwin came on board, and he would stay for almost 30 years. Irwin just missed the glory years, but he was joined by color men who remembered it well. Lionel Aldridge worked the games with Irwin for a few years, starting in 1975, and more memorably Max McGee joined Jim in 1979. Irwin and McGee covered a lot of weak Packer teams with an enjoyable style that mixed Irwin's affability with McGee's dry wit. They were a tough act for Larivee and McCarren to follow, but Wayne and Larry have their own style that tends to be more informative and attentive to the game's X's and O's.

While the first games presented on television occurred on the Dumont Network in 1953, regular coverage didn't begin until CBS acquired the NFL package in 1956. CBS assigned little-known Ray Scott to broadcast the Packer games over the more well-known Earl Gillespie, largely because Hamm's Beer was a significant sponsor, and they didn't want Gillespie since he was closely associated with rival Miller Brewing's broadcasts of Milwaukee Braves games. Scott worked for a couple of years with former Bears Johnny Lujack and George Connor before Packer legend Tony Canadeo joined the broadcasts in 1959 after Lombardi arrived; Vince did not want ex-Bears broadcasting Packers games. Aside from 1964, when Scott had a dispute with the network, Ray and Tony would spend Lombardi's entire nine years together as a cohesive and complementary team that was a pleasure to listen to. Scott in particular had a distinctive succinct style spoken in a resonant baritone that forever will be matched to the austere brilliance of Lombardi's Packers.

More than once the call went, "Starr back . . . Dowler . . . *Touchdown!*" Ray Scott never forgot he was announcing a game that viewers could follow on the screen themselves. Years later he would say, "My philosophy has always been let the action speak for itself. It doesn't need me getting in the way." After 1967, CBS stopped assigning each team its own regular announcers, and anyone could end up at Lambeau broadcasting the game. The result of that is reminiscent of a joke popular when President Nixon was embroiled in Watergate troubles—*My mother told me anyone could grow up to be President of the United States and now unfortunately I see it's true.* When that "anyone" shows up at Lambeau to broadcast the Packers' game, it is good to have the option of muting the TV and switching on the radio for the hometown voices of Larivee and McCarren.

FOR FURTHER INFORMATION

Hoffman, Dale. "Larry McCarren: The Strong Silent Type," *Green Bay Packers 1978 Yearbook.* (19-21)

Paustian, John L. "A Tradition at Center," *Green Bay Packers 1979 Yearbook.* (29-31)

"Ray Scott, 78, Voice of the Packers," *New York Times.* 3/29/98. (sec.1 p.43)

Reischel, Rob. "McCarren Stars in the Booth," *Milwaukee Journal Sentinel Packer Plus.* Available online at www.jsonline.com/packer/news/sep01/larry27092601.asp.

Shropshire, Mike. *The Ice Bowl: The Green Bay Packers and Dallas Cowboys Season of 1967.* New York: Donald I. Fine Books, 1997. (51-5)

Torinus, John. *The Packer Legend: An Inside Look.* Revised ed. Neshkoro, WI: Laranmark Press, 1982. (83-9)

Zimmerman, David. *In Search of a Hero: Life and Times of Tony Canadeo Packers' Grey Ghost.* Hales Corner, WI: Eagle Books, 2001. (206-8)

THE GREAT UNMADE FOOTBALL MOVIE
JOHNNY BLOOD MCNALLY • HALFBACK 1936

WHO'S WORN THE NUMBER Franta 1930, Bruder 1933, Bob Jones 1934, Blood 1936, A. Moore 1939, B. Adkins 1940–41, Ecker 1950–51, J. Flanigan, Sr. 1967–70, Jenke 1973–74, Hull 1975, Hyland 1976, Cheyunski 1977, M. Hunt 1978–80, R. Scott 1981–86, Jordan 1987r, G. Clark 1991, Burnette 1991, B. Collins 1992–93, Mott 1993, Strickland 1994–95, B. Harris 1996–2001, M.Wilkins 2002.

ORIGINATOR Lineman Herb "Chief" Franta 1930 followed Walt Kiesling to St. Thomas College and to the pros, but not to the Hall of Fame.

LONGEST TENURE Linebacker Bernardo Harris 1995–2001 (see Notables below).

NUMBER CHANGES Back Hank Bruder wore 13 in 1931–33, 47 in 1934, 27 in 1935–36, 18 in 1935–38 and 5 in 1938–39; Johnny Blood wore 24 in 1929–30, 20 in 1931–32, 14 in 1933, and 26 in 1935; back Bob Adkins wore 79 in 1945; Bob Hyland wore 50 from 1967–69; Bernardo Harris wore 54 in 1995.

OTHER NOTABLES Hank Bruder (see 27); Bernardo Harris grew into the middle linebacker post after joining the team as a free agent in 1995.

ONES TO FORGET Linebackers Greg Clark and Reggie Burnette shared number 55 in 1991, each playing a couple of games as they bounced in and out of town quickly.

JOHNNY BLOOD John Victor McNally was born into wealth—his father ran a flour mill and his uncle published the *Minneapolis Tribune*—but he took no notice of it. Instead he lived the life of an unpredictable gadfly for whom freedom was his very lifeblood. As he once said, "When I look back on it, I can see that some of my unorthodox behavior came out of my upbringing in Wisconsin and had nothing to do with the zodiac. Some of the Blood stories you hear talk of me as though I were some kind of society football player. I did get money from my family later, but they never trusted me with it until I was 55. My mother was a school teacher who got hold of me early and pumped a lot of myths into me. Grecian myths, Irish myths, King Arthur stuff. That part of me was going to be adventure. My father was a small town businessman and athletic fan, but a left-handed, curly-haired Irishman, which explains a lot." (Klobuchar, 101)

NUMBER 55

His life was a remarkable celebration of the joys of hearty drinking, convivial women, and late-night fun. Paul Hornung, Joe Namath, and any other subsequent colorful playboys of note are only pale imitations of the Vagabond Halfback. He was truly a multifaceted character. Clarke Hinkle found him oddly literate—reading Chaucer and Shakespeare sometimes, and cheap pornographic fiction others. McNally graduated from high school at age 14 when he wrote in his yearbook, "Dear God, how sweet it is in spring to be a boy." (Daley, 81). He would not finish college till he reached 46. In between, he played football.

On the playing field, he was a man before his time. He was the best receiver and defensive back of the early days of the NFL. Moreover, he was a touchdown maker in a low-scoring era. When he retired in 1939, he had scored more touchdowns (49—38 with Green Bay) than any other NFL player, except his Packer teammate Verne Lewellen, who had scored 51. The 38 touchdown passes he caught (29 with the Pack) were then the league record, but that would be broken within two years by Don Hutson. Unofficial counts of interceptions list Blood as the league record holder with 40 until Emlen Tunnell passed him in 1953. He was perhaps the fastest player of his day, with sure hands and great leaping ability. Once he got the ball, he was an elusive runner with a nose for the goal line. On defense he was a hard and certain tackler. Overall, he was a vibrant, adventurous leader other players would gladly follow both on and off the field.

"I wanted a life in which I could do something I enjoyed and still have leisure to do other things I enjoyed. Football was an escape, certainly, but an escape into something I enjoyed. In the off-season I would ship out to the Orient as an ordinary seaman and enjoy the beauty of the Pacific Islands. Or I would winter on Catalina Island off the coast of Los Angeles. Understand, I was not afraid of work. I had sufficient energy that work did not bother me at all. I was a hard worker. To me, freedom did not mean being able only to do the non-difficult but, rather, to do what I chose to do. One winter in Catalina I worked three shifts. I worked in the brickyard all day, making bricks. I worked the next eight hours in a gambling hall as a bouncer. And the next eight hours I 'honeymooned' with a redhead." (Cope, 52)

He fought authority at every turn, but always with a smile and not in anger. He was 6'2" and 190 pounds in his prime with jet black hair, a handsome face, and a winning attitude. Furthermore, he was extremely intelligent, ever charming, and never lacking female companionship. To put this in cinematic terms, he was the classic antihero rebelling against societal norms who is so often seen on the silver screen. As he himself put it, "I've always seen myself as an outsider. You've seen the movies where a guy goes out by himself and hits the bush, a little away from the crowd. Well I think that was me." (Klobuchar, 103) Perhaps the best way to view Johnny Blood then is to look at his life as a movie treatment. Consider the scenes that Hollywood could stage:

"The Vagabond Halfback:" Key Scenes
1) Young John McNally is having a conversation with his aunt when she asks him, "John, what are your really interested in?" He replies, "I guess I'm really interested in the theory of morals and the theory of money." At this his aunt breaks into hysterical laughter, saying, "Well isn't that funny! You'll never have any of either!" (Cope, 50)

2) Upon finishing at the then-two-year St. John's College in Minnesota where he lettered in four sports and edited the school newspaper, McNally enrolls at Notre Dame in 1924 while the Four Horsemen are Coach Knute Rockne's stars. Rockne tries to make a tackle of Johnny, but he refuses and is thrown off the team. In the spring, he is suspended from school for 60 days for curfew violations and other transgressions and takes off on an adventurous motorcycle trip to the East Coast with an attractive coed sitting right behind him. She's the wife of a sailor, and Johnny takes her to Norfolk from where her husband has already departed. He leaves her at the local YWCA and continues up the coast to visit his sisters. He later sends the coed money.

3) Upon his eventual return to the Midwest, McNally begins setting type for his uncle's newspaper and joins a local semipro football team with a friend, Ralph Hanson. In order to preserve their collegiate eligibility, they must play under assumed names. The two are passing by a movie marquee for the current Rudolph Valentino vehicle, "Blood and Sand," when McNally says to Hanson, "That's it. I'll be Blood and you be Sand." When Johnny joins the NFL Milwaukee Badgers in 1925, he remains then and forevermore Johnny Blood, a name fully fitting his swashbuckling personality.

4) When playing for the professional Duluth Eskimos in 1927, the well-read and well-oiled Blood is found by the team owner reciting poetry on a street corner late at night. The owner escorts Blood to his sixth floor hotel room and locks him in for the night.

Out the window goes Blood and drops onto the window ledge one floor down. He taps on the window and is let in by an attractive female occupant. When the team owner comes into the same room a few minutes later to visit his girlfriend, he finds Blood reciting poetry to her.

5) After spending 1928 with the failing Pottsville Maroons franchise, Blood is approached by Green Bay coach Curly Lambeau to join the Packers. Lambeau offers him $110 per game as long as he doesn't drink. Blood counters with $100 per game and no drinking after Wednesday. Blood joins the team along with fellow future Hall of Famers Cal Hubbard and Mike Michalske, and the team wins its first championship. At the celebration banquet after the season, when each player is presented with a pocket watch, a wallet, and a check for $220, Blood thanks the fans, saying, "I'm especially grateful for the check. I was reading in a Chicago paper the other day where they shot 14 wolves at Rhinelander. It's going to be a long, hard winter." (Names, 173)

Johnny Blood – Hall of Fame player and world-class raconteur—lived his life as if he were a fictional character. *Courtesy of the Stiller-Lefebvre Collection.*

6) In 1930 the team will repeat as champions. In one memorable play, quarterback Red Dunn throws a pass in the flat to Blood, who races for a long score. In another game, Dunn repeats the same play, but this time Blood laterals the ball back to Dunn who is quickly tackled for a loss. Blood later tells Dunn, "I just wanted to see what you would do with it." During a timeout at still another game, Blood passes the time dancing a jig in the middle of the field to music playing over the loudspeakers.

7) Having missed the team train to an away game because he was too busy dallying with a young lady friend, Blood drives his car ahead of the train and parks it on the tracks at a crossroads. He and the girl stay in the car as the train approaches and at last screeches to a halt. At which point, Blood gets on board, and the girl drives off. On another train trip, Blood gets a little too rambunctious in a towel fight with hulking All Pro end Lavvie Dilweg, and the angry Dilweg starts chasing Blood from car to car throughout the train. Blood finally escapes by climbing up onto the roof of a car and racing away safely because Dilweg will not follow. Johnny spends the rest of the trip conversing with the engineer.

8) In another unusual train trip, Blood runs out of money on his way to report to training camp for the 1931 season. Blood hops on a freight and passenger train from his hometown of New Richmond that will take him to Amherst Junction where he will need to hop on another train to travel to Green Bay. However, that train is scheduled to leave before the New Richmond train will arrive. So Blood wires ahead to hold the Green Bay train for a transferring passenger. The Green Bay train is waiting when Blood's train arrived and he slips onto the blinds of the second train. After no passenger transfers, the Green Bay train takes off. On the trip, the baggage man spots Blood and says, "Aren't you Johnny Blood? Did you wire ahead and have us hold the train?" Blood confesses, and the baggage man invites him into his car for lunch. Blood will later tell this story to Milwaukee reporter Ollie Kuechle, and Kuechele will write an article about it. The article is originally entitled "The Hobo Halfback," but when Lambeau hears that title he objects, so Kuechle changes it to "The Vagabond Halfback."

9) Lambeau withholds most of Blood's pay throughout the season in an attempt to keep him sober. Blood has his greatest year, scoring 14 touchdowns for the third straight Packer championship team. In one game, Blood calls signals and calls a familiar play but adds an X to the end of the play call. The fullback angrily questions what that play means, but Johnny tells him that he will take care of the X, and indeed Blood keeps the ball on that play. After the season, Blood receives the rest of his withheld pay and immediately goes on a bender.

10) During the 1932 season, Blood gets the idea for the Packers to play some sponsored exhibition games in Hawaii. Blood makes an arrangement with some Hawaiian promoters for the Packers to receive either a $10,000 guarantee or 50% of the gate, whichever is greater. He tells Lambeau only of the guarantee. After the regular season, the Packers travel to California and take a boat to Hawaii. They play two exhibition games there and earn $11,500 of which Blood pockets $1,500 off the top and gives the $10,000 guarantee to the unsuspecting and satisfied Lambeau. On the boat trip home,

Blood gets so looped on Hawaiian booze that he climbs onto the flagpole on the ship's stern one night and is seen dangling in the wind, overhanging the dark ocean.

11) Upon returning to California, the Packers play more exhibition games on the coast. At one point on the trip, Blood runs out of money and is refused an advance by Lambeau. Curly retires to his eighth-floor room for the night. Blood also goes to the eighth floor, but climbs out on to the fire escape, steps onto the window ledge, and inches along until Lambeau's ledge is five feet away, across an expanse of open air eight stories up. Blood leaps and lands on Lambeau's ledge, lifts open his window and drops into Curly's room, saying, "About that advance . . ." Lambeau falls back in shock, clutching his heart and shouting, "Take it. Take it! Take it and go. Go where you want, Johnny Blood." Blood takes the money, thanks his coach, and leaves.

12) Further along on the California trip all-star opponent Red Grange is with Blood when he is asked for his autograph. He cuts his wrist with a knife and signs "Johnny Blood" in his own blood.

13) Johnny, who has been known to rent out any of Green Bay's thriving houses of prostitution for himself for a night, enters a game and tells quarterback Arnie Herber to throw him the long ball. "Throw it towards Mother Pierre's whorehouse, Arnie," Blood explains.

14) On a trip to New York, Blood gets so drunk from a night on the town that he can barely stand. At practice the next day, he goes to punt a ball and falls flat on his backside as soon as he lifts his leg. Prompted by too many incidents like these, Lambeau fires Blood in 1934 and he spends the year with the NFL's Pittsburgh Pirates. He returns to Green Bay in 1935. At age 31, he just barely loses a footrace in training camp to rookie Don Hutson who is the fastest man in football. Blood experiments with drugs in this year, trying the same Benzedrine pills that truckers use to stay awake.

15) In a game in 1936 against the defending champion Lions, Lambeau decides he is going to grind it out and not pass at all throughout the game. Blood gets pulled early when he calls a pass play, but Lambeau sends him back later with the Packers behind. Lambeau's only orders are, "Don't pass." Blood calls a pass play, and Herber throws a pass 40 yards into the end zone where Blood leaps between defenders to grab the touchdown. The Packers will win the game and will go on to another title.

16) Blood is hired again by Pittsburgh in 1937, but this time as a player-coach. Instead of having his players count off jumping jacks "1-2-3-4," he has them shout out "Pirates never quit" for each one. In his first game he returns a kickoff 100 yards for the go-ahead touchdown in a Pittsburgh victory.

17) In 1938, Blood convinces studious Colorado football star Byron "Whizzer" White to sign a pro football contract with lowly Pittsburgh. White stays for only one year before leaving to further his education in Oxford, England, but he will maintain a lifetime friendship with the rakish Blood. Blood was present for White's swearing-in as a Supreme Court Justice, and White acted as Blood's presenter on Johnny's induction into the Pro Football Hall of Fame in 1963. In 1972, while White was still a Supreme

Court Justice, Blood campaigned for him to be drafted as the presidential nominee for the Democrats, but that quixotic quest came to nothing.

18) Unsurprisingly, Blood is a spectacular failure as a coach. One Sunday in 1938, he is seen watching the Packers play the Bears in Chicago, and is questioned why he isn't with Pittsburgh. He replies that they aren't playing that week, only to have the Eagles-Pirates score posted on the scoreboard in the next minute. When players reported to training camp in 1939, Blood was not there. He had sent a telegram to assistant coach Walt Kiesling stating, "Look up Cook and Start practice." Three days later when Johnny arrived, he explained to Kiesling, who had been searching for a person named Cook, that the wire meant to find someone to cook for the team. Team owner Art Rooney said that, "On most teams the coach worries about where the players are at night. Our players worry about the coach." (Berkow, 5) Blood's coaching record with Pittsburgh when he is fired after three years is 6-19.

19) In his own words, "One question we discussed has been on my mind for years. It was posed to me when I was coaching the Steelers. Just before the start of the season it became necessary to cut four men from the squad. I hated to do it. But I told the boys that I had heard of an independent pro team being organized in St. Louis. I suggested they go there and try out. I persuaded Art Rooney, owner of the Steelers, to advance the money enough to get them to St. Louis. Well, the boys went out, worked hard to make the team, but all four failed. They sent me a wire after their release. It read simply, 'Where to now, Coach?' I didn't know the answer. In a larger sense, does anybody?" (Holland, 24)

20) After serving as a cryptographer in Asia during World War II, Blood returns to the States and tries out for the Packers again. He realizes an epiphany when he catches a punt and is buried immediately under several hundred pounds of flesh. "Among the things that hit me were not only two big tackles, but that this was no game for a 42-year-old." (Daley, 92)

How much the tales in these scenes have been embellished varies. They all are hard to confirm with complete surety, but all have some factual basis. Clear corroborating evidence can be found for some. Blood himself disavowed some stories, of his reading Shakespeare with John Barrymore, or going to a club and being so disgusted with the performer that he got up on stage himself and put on an impromptu show. However, mere factual reality is beside the point with someone larger than life like Blood. "Football had more spontaneity on the field in our years, which could have meant more fun, I suppose. But I remember the exhilaration they talk about. I remember it from a play where I caught a pass near the goal line. I don't know who we were playing. I think Herber threw it. I just remember going up for it with another guy, and I jumped a little higher. It was an important game, and I knew I had the touchdown when I caught the ball. I was floating, really. It was like the slow motion you see in the television highlights today. I could hear the crowd roaring and it seemed like I'd never come down. The goal posts were in front of me and this is the God's truth: I actually believed I could have jumped over the cross bar. I just felt elevated, all through me. No matter what the ball player tells you, he just doesn't feel that very often." (Klobuchar, 103)

With his playing career ended, McNally got married and attained first his Bachelor's Degree and then, according to some accounts, his Master's Degree in Economics at St. John's, where he became a lecturer in that subject as well as the football coach for the following three years. The team finished 13-9 over that time, and McNally's replacement in 1953, John Gagliardi, was still there 49 years later, having won more games than any other college coach at any level. In the ensuing years, McNally ran a couple of small businesses, wrote an unpublished economics tract called *Spend Yourself Rich*, and ran unsuccessfully for county sheriff on the platform of "Honest Wrestling." He got divorced after 10 years and married for a second and final time six years later.

While some felt he became tedious in his middle years as a dated raconteur, ever willing to spin the same yarns about his wild youth to whomever asked, this charter member of the Hall of Fame grew past that and became an advocate for better pensions for old-time football players less well off than himself. In his later years, he spent his time, "Reading, studying, writing. Meditating. Once meditating was an honorable occupation. Today, it would appear on a police blotter as a form of vagrancy, I suppose." (Holland, 25) John Victor McNally died in 1985 in Palm Springs, California. His first wife summed him up best when she said, "Even when John does the expected, he does it in an unexpected way." (Henry)

FOR FURTHER INFORMATION

Berkow, Ira. "When Johnny Blood Rode," *New York Times*. 7/11/82 (sec. 5 p. 5)

Christl, Cliff. "Years Ago, Wisconsin Was Truly the 'Big Cheese,'" *Milwaukee Journal Sentinel*. 7/30/00.

Coen, Ed. "Still Another Look at Early Interceptions," *The Coffin Corner* XVII. Available online at www.footballresearch.com/articles/frpage.cfm?topic'intercep.

Cope, Myron. *The Game That Was: An Illustrated Account of the Tumultuous Early Days of Pro Football*. New York: Crowell, 1974. (46-56, 81-2, 113-4)

Daley, Arthur. *Pro Football's Hall of Fame*. New York: Grosset and Dunlap, 1968, c1963. (78-92)

Daly, Dan and Bob O'Donnell. *The Pro Football Chronicle: The Complete (Well Almost) Record of the Best Players, the Greatest Photos, the Hardest Hits, the Biggest Scandals, and the Funniest Stories in Pro Football*. New York: Collier Books, 1990. (42, 52-3)

Henry, Jack. "Johnny Blood: The Vagabond Halfback," *Pittsburgh Steelers Weekly*. Available online at www.footballresearch.com/articles/frpage.cfm?topic'blood.

Herndon, Booton. "Football's Finest Halfback," *Coronet*. 10/53 (77-83)

Holland, Gerald. "Is That You Up There, Johnny Blood?" *Sports Illustrated*. 9/2/63. (18-25)

Johnson, Chuck. *The Greatest Packers of Them All*. New York: Putnam, 1968. (83-4)

Klobuchar, Jim. "Believe Everything You Hear," in Wiebusch, John, ed. *More Than A Game*. Englewood Cliffs, NJ: Prentice-Hall, 1974. (100-103)

Maule, Tex. *The Game: The Official Picture History of the NFL and AFL.* New York: Random House, 1967. (115)

Names, Larry. *The History of the Green Bay Packers: Book I: The Lambeau Years Part One.* Wautoma, WI: Angel Press of WI, 1987.

Olderman, Murray. *The Running Backs.* Englewood Cliffs, NJ: Prentice-Hall, 1969. (147-51)

Packers of the Past: A Series of Articles Reprinted from the Milwaukee Journal Sept. 28 - Dec. 9, 1965. Milwaukee, WI: Milwaukee Journal, 1965. (3-5)

Peterson, Robert. *Pigskin: The Early Years of Pro Football.* New York: Oxford University Press, 1997. (104-5)

Porter, David L., ed. *Biographical Dictionary of American Sports: Football.* New York: Greenwood Press, 1987. (374-5)

Torinus, John. *The Packer Legend: An Inside Look.* Revised ed. Neshkoro, WI: Laranmark Press, 1982 (33, 37-9)

Ward, Arch. *The Green Bay Packers.* New York: Putnam, 1946. (95-6, 120, 173-4)

Whittingham, Richard. *What a Game They Played.* New York: Harper and Row, 1974. (29-41, 166)

CAMEOS
TED HENDRICKS • LINEBACKER 1974

WHO'S WORN THE NUMBER Pape 1930, Barragar 1932, Wunsch 1934, Greenfield 1939–41, Crutcher 1965–67, 1971–72, MacLeod 1973, T Hendricks 1974, Perko 1976, Blane Smith 1977, Nuzum 1978, E. O'Neil 1980, C. Lewis 1981–84, Dent 1986–92, Pointer 1987r, J. Willis 1993–94, Hollinquest 1996–98, K. Mays 1999, McCaslin 2000, Holmberg 2001, Nickerson 2002.

ORIGINATOR Back Oran "Nanny" Pape 1930 was declared ineligible at Iowa for borrowing money from a trust fund, then played for five teams in three years, including two games in Green Bay. After football, he became one of the original 50 Iowa Patrolmen and sadly was the first to die in the line of duty when he was murdered in 1936.

LONGEST TENURE Linebacker Burnell Dent 1986–92 started only 11 of 95 games over seven years in Green Bay, but was such a special teams demon that he held out for 44 days in 1991 (still pretty cheeky for a bomb squader).

NUMBER CHANGES Center Nate Barragar wore 31 in 1931 and 1935, and 30 and 64 in 1934.

OTHER NOTABLES Nate Barragar (see top 31).

ONE TO FORGET As if the Packers didn't have enough ineffective players named B. Smith in the 1970s, they added linebacker Blane to Barry and Barty for one game in 1977.

TED HENDRICKS Ted Hendricks was a wild character known for such stunts as coming to a Halloween practice session wearing a hollowed-out pumpkin on his head. Another time he charged onto the practice field in full football gear on the back of a horse. Still another time he was shown sitting on the bench during a Monday Night Football game wearing a harlequin's mask. He was also a great player—fast, agile, intelligent, strong, and an expert blitzer. He was a freelancer in many ways.

Called the "Mad Stork" ever since his college days at Miami for his unusual build (6'7", 220 pounds), Hendricks was a second-round pick of the Baltimore Colts in 1969. He moved right in as a starting linebacker in his rookie year. He made All Pro three times and played in three Pro Bowls in five years with the Colts. He also won a Super Bowl ring with Baltimore in 1971. In 1974, Hendricks signed with the Jacksonville Sharks of the fledgling, ill-fated World Football League for the 1975 season. Within a week, he was traded to Green Bay for an eighth round pick.

Under Dan Devine in Green Bay, he would have perhaps the finest year of his 15-year career. He led the team with five interceptions and blocked an NFL record seven kicks (three punts, three field goals, and one extra point.) Again, he made All Pro and went to the Pro Bowl. When Jacksonville defaulted on his first payment, it looked like Green Bay had a future Hall of Famer long-term. However, the one-year contract Hendricks had signed with Devine had no option year, making Hendricks a free agent. In 1975, that made him a rare bird in more ways than one.

New coach Bart Starr would not meet Hendricks' contract demands—chiefly that his contract be guaranteed. Starr could not see what a special talent Hendricks was and how it was worthwhile to go to unusual lengths to keep him. So Bart did the best thing he could think of and traded Ted to the Raiders for two number one picks. The picks would turn out to be Ezra Johnson, a good defensive end, and Mark Koncar, a mediocre lineman. Perhaps, if Starr had made better picks in 1976 and 1977, the loss of Ted Hendricks wouldn't have been so devastating.

For the Oakland Raiders, Ted would wear 83, the number of another one-year Packer, Ben Davidson. Ted would play linebacker nine more years for the Raiders and be known as "Kick 'em in the head, Ted" or "Kick 'em" for short. He would play on three more winning Super Bowl teams, make two more All Pro teams, and go to four more Pro Bowls. Neither Ezra Johnson nor Mark Koncar would ever make an All Pro team and Johnson would play in only one Pro Bowl.

Ted Hendricks is one of two Hall of Famers who made a one-year stop in Green Bay; the other was Cleveland Brown defensive end Len Ford. However, over the years many prominent players have made a final one-season cameo in Green Bay. They include: Beattie Feathers, 1940; Ward Cuff, 1947; Paul Christman, 1950; Ray Bray, 1952, Jim Keane, 1952, John Sandusky, 1956; Len Ford, 1958; Lou Michaels, 1971; Dave Kopay, 1972; Pete Lammons, 1972; Carleton Oats, 1973; Harry Schuh, 1974; John Schmitt, 1974; Ernie McMillan, 1975; Dave Osborn, 1976; Randy Vataha, 1977; Bobby Douglass, 1978; Preston Dennard, 1985; Vince Ferragamo, 1986; Dan Ross, 1986; Ross Browner, 1987; Mark Clayton, 1993; Bill Maas, 1993; John Stephens, 1993; Steve McMichael, 1994; and Mark Collins, 1997. Three others (Dick Gordon, 1973; Jim Zorn, 1985; and Keith Millard, 1992) briefly tried one other team after the Packers before retiring. That is a long list of faded talent with the largest concentration being in the 1970s, when a new has-been was hanging on in Green Bay every year but 1970 and 1979.

On the flip side, a handful of prominent players spent their one season cameo as rookies with the Packers. The Packers missed out on: Walt Michaels, 1951; Art Hunter, 1954; Tim Brown, 1959; Ben Davidson, 1961; Errol Mann, 1968; and Joe Danelo, 1975. Aside from Ted Hendricks, there is only one other notable player who had a one-season cameo in Green Bay in the middle of his career, and that was defensive lineman Keith Traylor, who came from Denver to spend his third year with the Packers before moving on to Kansas City, back to Denver, and then on to the Bears. Traylor has had a fairly solid career, but Ted Hendricks was among the best of all time.

PACKERS BY THE NUMBERS

FOR FURTHER INFORMATION

Fimrite, Ron. "Concoctions for the Defense," *Sports Illustrated.* 1/26/81. (20-28)

Porter, David L., ed. *Biographical Dictionary of American Sports: Football.* New York: Greenwood Press, 1987. (258)

Reid, Ron. "A Mad Stork Stirs Up His New Nest," *Sports Illustrated.* 9/15/75. (68-71)

Smith, Ron. *The Sporting News Selects Football's 100 Greatest Players: A Celebration of the 20th Century's Best.* St. Louis, MO: Sporting News, 1999. (141)

Zimmerman, Paul. "Who Is This Mad Hatter?" *Sports Illustrated.* 10/17/83. (92-105)

VIDEO AGE
KEN BOWMAN • CENTER 1964–73

WHO'S WORN THE NUMBER Van Sickle 1932, Seibold 1934 and 1939–40, Schwammel 1936, Zoll 1939, Wehba 1944, K. Bowman 1964–73, Acks 1974–76, Gofourth 1977–82, Parlavecchio 1983, Curcio 1983, Moran 1985–93, Choate 1987r, J. Kelly 1995, London 1998, J. Nelson 1998–99, Gizzi 2000-01.

ORIGINATOR Guard Clyde Van Sickle 1932 later was a successful high school coach in Little Rock, Arkansas.

LONGEST TENURE Ken Bowman 1964-73.

NUMBER CHANGES Clyde Van Sickle also wore 31 in 1932 and 26 in 1933; tackle Ade Schwammel also wore 53 in 1934, 50 in 1935–36 and 1943, 40 in 1943, and 58 in 1944; tackle Champ Seibold wore 37 in 1935–36, 58 in 1936, and 41 in 1937–38; end Ray Wehba also wore 17 in 1944.

OTHER NOTABLES Ade Schwammel (see top 50); Champ Seibold was a solid tackle throughout the 1930s; guard Rich Moran made All Pro once, but saw his promising career chewed up by injuries.

ONE TO FORGET Ron Wolf had always liked linebacker Antonio London and brought him in as a free agent in 1998 when he promptly tore up his knee and ended his career.

KEN BOWMAN Kenny Bowman was the quintessential offensive lineman: tough, battered, reliable, and invisible. To take it even a step further, he teamed up to make perhaps the most famous block in NFL history and received almost no credit for it at the time.

His teammates knew about Ken Bowman, though. He was an eighth-round draft pick as a center out of the University of Wisconsin in 1964, the year that All Pro Packer center Jim Ringo was traded to Philadelphia. He would play for 10 years in Green Bay, most of them as the starter. He never made All Pro or played in a Pro Bowl like his linemates (Jerry Kramer, Fuzzy Thurston, Gale Gillingham, Forrest Gregg, and Bob Skoronski) from the first few years did. However, he was a solid player and a respected warrior. Running back John Brockington thought highly of Ken: "He wasn't the biggest guy, but he was very sound, very aggressive, and always fired up. He had those pale blue eyes and he was a bleeder . . . His face would become red, and you could see those cold blue eyes staring up from behind that red. He was all fired up and breathing hard. He loved it, man. He was a great competitor." (Biever, 117)

Both his shoulders had been separated and were a constant threat to go out again at any time, so Bowman wore a shoulder harness that sounds similar to what Cecil Isbell wore 30 years before. Defensive tackle Mike McCoy described Bowman in his gear: "They called Ken Bowman Frankenstein. Big solid forehead, long hair, and this brace with chains from his arm to his shoulder. His shoulder was really bad, so he had a chain attached to a piece of material wrapped around his bicep, and it was hooked onto his shoulder pad so his arm wouldn't go above 90 degrees." (Biever, 117)

Strangely, despite earning the rare achievement of starting as a rookie on a Lombardi team, Ken was one of Lombardi's whipping boys, often coming in for harsh criticism from the coach and having to share playing time, first with Bill Curry in 1966 and then with Bob Hyland in 1967. Curry would develop into an excellent center with the Colts, but neither he nor Hyland were as good as Bowman while Vince was coaching the team. Bowman was going to law school while he played for the Packers and eventually got his degree after six years, setting up a legal practice after retirement. He especially resented Lombardi calling him "stupid" and questioning why he was "wasting his time going to law school." "I thought that was sour grapes on his part. I think he really wanted to be a lawyer, but he only went to law school for one year," Bowman said years later. (Kramer, 138)

At the culmination of the Ice Bowl, it was Bowman and Jerry Kramer delivering the block on Cowboy defensive tackle Jethro Pugh that allowed Bart Starr to score the winning touchdown with 16 seconds left. There are two funny things about that block. The first is that Jethro Pugh for years asserted that Kramer was offside on the play and that Pugh was looking around for a penalty flag after the play. Checking the film of the game years later, we find what Pugh claimed is true, but it can only be seen with the aid of the slow-motion replay camera. Lombardi's Packers were a well-oiled machine that had practiced together for many years. Kramer even said in his book *Instant Replay* that "I wouldn't swear that I didn't beat the center's snap by a fraction of a second." (Kramer, 217) Jerry was right in his intuition. He knew when the ball should be snapped, and he beat Bowman by a fraction of a fraction of a second, undetectable in real time. Pugh never had a chance.

The second strange thing is that Bowman never really had a chance, either, a chance for the fame that Jerry Kramer found after delivering that block. Kramer did not share the credit during post-game locker room interviews. At the same time, though, why didn't the broadcasters give Ken his due? Why did CBS interviewer Tom Brookshier not talk to Bowman, too? They could see the double-team block on the replay. Television broadcasts often go for the simplest approach, and this is what they took by sticking solely with Kramer. Kramer told Bowman that he was young and would have another 10 years for fame, but Bowman only had six years left for a team whose glory years were about to end. And he was an anonymous offensive lineman.

Oddly enough, though, Bowman is still remembered today for the block, and it's not just because so much has been written about that team and that game. It is also because there is so much electronic media available today to actually relive past Packer events. NFL Films produced a video series called "The NFL's Greatest Games" a few years back which shows entire past games accompanied by player commentary, and the first video in the series was the Ice Bowl. There was Ken Bowman helping out Jerry Kramer on video. Thirty years later, fans could watch it again and again.

And there has been so much more for Packer fans. The half-hour highlight films of the 1961, 1962, and 1965 Championship games were re-released on one video, and the 1966 and 1967 title game films were released on another video. The video "Three in a Row" compiled the three 40-minute season highlight films of the Packers 1965, 1966, and 1967 seasons onto one videotape. The 20-year reunion of the first Super Bowl team was chronicled in a Kramer and Schaap book (*Distant Replay*) and filmed for a video of the same name. Fifteen years later, an even larger reunion of anyone who played in Green Bay under Vince was chronicled by the video "With Love and Respect." For a Packer fan, the video reunions are sort of like attending your own high school reunion and watching the transitions people must make as they age. The hair gets thinner and whiter, the stomach gets paunchier, the gait gets stiffer, and the number of attendees starts to dwindle.

In the wake of the Packers winning Super Bowl XXXI, a number of videos were released: "The Ice Bowl" as noted above, and the Super Bowl XXXI highlight video, of course, and the annual team highlight videos (these date back to at least 1986). In addition, an hour-long "History of the Green Bay Packers" and "Connie Gomper and the Pack," an offbeat salute to Packer fans, were also produced. Lombardi himself lives on in an NFL Films production called "Lombardi." He can also be found in "A Man Named Lombardi," narrated by George C. Scott, and an out-of-print 12-video series, "Vince Lombardi on Football," that can be found on the internet. Other videos are harder to come by, such as the hour-long Public Broadcasting production, "The Green Bay Packers: The Grandstand Franchise." In an electronic age, Kenny Bowman has achieved a kind of immortal fame, after all.

FOR FURTHER INFORMATION

Biever, Vernon J., photography, Peter Strupp ed. *The Glory of Titletown: The Classic Green Bay Packers Photography of Vernon Biever.* Dallas, TX: Taylor Publishing, 1997. (117)

Christopulos, Mike. "Ken Bowman: The Offensive Line's Elder Statesman," *Green Bay Packers 1970 Yearbook.* (7-8)

Kramer, Jerry, with Dick Schaap. *Distant Replay.* New York: G.P. Putnam, 1985. (136-9)

Paustian, John L. "A Tradition at Center," *Green Bay Packers 1979 Yearbook.* (29-31)

Schaap, Dick, ed. *Instant Replay: The Green Bay Diary of Jerry Kramer.* New York: World Publishing, 1968. (217-8)

BIG GUYS
ED NEAL • DEFENSIVE GUARD, DEFENSIVE TACKLE 1945–51

WHO'S WORN THE NUMBER Kurth 1934, Seibold 1936, Kilbourn 1939, Ray 1940, J. Carter 1942, D. Perkins 1943, Schwammel 1944, Neal 1945–51, Tonnemaker 1953–54, Bettis 1955, Lauer 1956–57, Currie 1958–64, F. Winkler 1968–69, Withrow 1971–73, Cooney 1974, McCaffrey 1975, D. Hansen 1976–77, Lally 1976, D. Johnson 1978, S. Stewart 1979, Rudzinski 1979, Beekley 1980, Rubens 1982–83, Cannon 1984–89, D'Onofrio 1992, R. Hamilton 1994, Flanagan 1998–2002.

ORIGINATOR Tackle Joe Kurth 1934 was a Wisconsin native who transferred from UW to Notre Dame where he played under Rockne and Hunk Anderson and made All American. After football he worked as an electrical engineer.

LONGEST TENURE Ed Neal 1945–51 and linebacker Dan Currie 1958–64 (see Notables below).

NUMBER CHANGES Tackle Joe Kurth wore 28 in 1933 and 31 in 1934; tackle Champ Seibold wore 57 in 1934 and 1939–40, 37 in 1935–36, 58 in 1936, and 41 in 1937–38; tackle Baby Ray wore 44 in 1938–48; back Don Perkins also wore 53 in 1943, 23 in 1944, and 48 in 1945; tackle Ade Schwammel also wore 53 in 1934, 50 in 1935–36 and 1943, and 40 in 1943; linebacker Clayton Tonnemaker wore 35 in 1950; linebacker Tom Bettis wore 65 from 1956–61; center Cal Withrow also wore 74 in 1971; linebacker Paul Rudzinski wore 66 in 1978 and 70 in 1980.

OTHER NOTABLES Champ Seibold (see top 57); Baby Ray (see top 44); Ade Schwammel (see top 50); Clayton Tonnemaker (see 35); Tom Bettis (see 65); Dan Currie was a three-time All Pro who went to one Pro Bowl and was elected to the Packer Hall of Fame in 1984.

ONE TO FORGET Many have passed through this number; it was worn by 10 guys in 14 years from 1969 through 1982. Linebacker Bob Lally's NFL career lasted all of two games in the middle of that stretch.

ED NEAL The stories that are told about Ed Neal all revolve around his strength and toughness. Bear Hall of Fame center Bulldog Turner said of Neal, "His arms was as big as my leg and just as hard as that table." (Cope, 177) Each time Turner would snap the ball against the Packers, Neal would swing his forearm into Turner's face.

NUMBER 58

Bulldog claims Neal broke his nose five times with that forearm. In response, Neal claimed that Bulldog broke his nose three times, as well. Packer quarterback Tobin Rote insisted he saw Neal break beer bottles over his forearms. To make it even worse, Neal would cover his forearms with shin pads, making them even harder. Turner said that he adjusted by ducking his head as he snapped the ball. Neal reacted to that by smashing him over the top of the head, regularly smashing Turner's plastic helmet. Bulldog said he would bring a couple extra helmets to Packers games because of this. Neal said of Bulldog, "That was the meanest man I have ever played against." (Christl, 17)

Ed Neal came out of Wichita Falls, Texas. In high school he lettered in track, boxing, wrestling, and football—playing fullback and defensive tackle. He attended three different colleges: Tulane, Louisiana State, and Oachita Baptist before being signed by Philadelphia in 1942 where he spent one season. Coming to the Packers as a free agent in 1945, he settled in at middle guard in the 5-4 defense common at the time. The middle guard's function in that defense was similar to that of the nose tackle today—clog up the middle. It was an ideal spot to put a big, tough guy, and Neal was bigger and tougher than most players at the time. He was 6'4" and his weight generally ran between 290 and 300 pounds. After seven years of battling in the trenches for the Packers, Ed went over to the Bears in 1952 on Bulldog Turner's urging. He was injured in mid-season, though, and his career ended. After football, he returned to Wichita Falls and worked as a blacksmith in the oil fields for several years before landing a job with the city's water department, where he worked until he died at age 65.

Ed Neal was not the first 300-pounder who played for the Packers. The first was tackle Milburn "Tiny" Croft, who joined the team in 1942. After Neal, the team wouldn't have another 300-pound player until 1986 when tackles Greg Feasel and Tom Neville both passed that weight benchmark. In the following year, replacement player Steve Collier weighed in at 342 pounds and was given an opportunity to make the regular club after the strike. The only other player to reach that level in the 1980s was Tony Mandarich, who originally weighed in 315, but was listed at 295 in his second year as the steroids wore off.

In the 1990s, of course, 300-pound lineman became commonplace. Of the nine offensive and defensive starting linemen on the 1997 NFC Champion Packers, only Santana Dotson was under 300 pounds, a shrimp at 285. Unfortunately, the Broncos showed in Super Bowl XXXII that technique and quickness are just as important as size. The prevailing image of that game was of the Packers' wide-load defensive linemen sucking air on the sidelines, thoroughly winded by the Broncos relentless rushing attack. Gilbert Brown was probably the heaviest Packer in 1999 when he bulked up to somewhere over 360 on his way to 400 in 2000, at which point he became an ex-Packer. He came back a comparatively trim 335 pounds in 2001.

As to height, the first Packer at least 6'4" was end Tillie Voss in 1924. The first to reach 6'5" was Hall of Fame tackle Cal Hubbard in 1929. Tackle Buford "Baby" Ray was the first at 6'6" in 1938. Another tackle, Ed Ecker, was the first 6'7" Packer in 1950. Other 6'7" players who joined the Packers include: Jim Weatherwax in 1966, Leo Carroll in 1968, quarterback Frank Patrick in 1972, linebacker Ted Hendricks in 1974, defensive tackle Earl Edwards in 1979, tackle Gary Hoffman in 1984, tackle Greg Feasel in 1986, defensive tack-

PACKERS BY THE NUMBERS

le Steve Collier in 1987, tackle Lou Cheek in 1991, defensive end Sean Jones in 1994, and tackle John Michels in 1996. The tallest Packers ever were 6'8": defensive end Ben Davidson in 1961, tackle Bill Hayhoe in 1970, and defensive tackle Vernon Vanoy in 1972.

FOR FURTHER INFORMATION

Christl, Cliff. "The Packers...A Gold Mine of Lore, Trivia and Tradition." *Green Bay Packers 1977 Yearbook.* (16-20)

Cope, Myron. *The Game That Was: An Illustrated Account of the Tumultuous Early Days of Pro Football.* New York: Crowell, 1974. (177-78, 183)

D'Amato, Gary, and Cliff Christl. *Mudbaths and Bloodbaths: The Inside Story of the Bears-Packers Rivalry.* Madison, WI: Prairie Oak Press, 1997. (112-13)

1980s IN A BOX
JOHN ANDERSON • LINEBACKER 1979–89

WHO'S WORN THE NUMBER
F. Butler 1936, Lawrence 1939, R. Kuechenberg 1970, Toner 1973, 1975–77, J. Anderson 1979–89, K. Larson 1991, W. Simmons 1993–97, Diggs 2000–02.

ORIGINATOR Center Frank Butler 1936 quit the team after four games in 1934 over an argument with Lambeau, was ejected from the 1936 title game for fighting, and left the team again in 1937 because he didn't want to shift to tackle. He returned in 1938 and was released in 1939.

LONGEST TENURE John Anderson 1978–89.

NUMBER CHANGES Frank Butler also wore 26 and 60 in 1934, 48 in 1935–36, and 35 in 1938; back Jim Lawrence also wore 51 in 1939; John Anderson wore 60 in 1978.

OTHER NOTABLES Wayne Simmons was an effective strong-side linebacker for the Super Bowl trips in the 1990s. Once he left Green Bay for greener pastures, though, he was involved in some ugly on-field incidents in Kansas City, and his career ended quickly. He died in a car crash in 2002.

ONE TO FORGET Linebacker Rudy Kuechenberg was a Bears castoff and paled in comparison to his brother Bob, the All Pro guard for the Dolphins.

JOHN ANDERSON John Anderson grew up in Wisconsin, went to the University of Michigan, then came home as a first-round draft choice of the Packers in 1978. He started as a rookie for a team that went 8-7-1 and was still starting 12 years later during another winning season, 10-6. In between, he was a mainstay as a starter, but the team had only one other winning season, strike-shortened 1982 when the Packers made the playoffs for the only time in the 1980s. Anderson was good, not great, a quietly effective strong-side linebacker who was a sure tackler, able to stop the run as well as cover the tight end. In 1979 he even kicked a field goal and an extra point as the team bounced from failing Chester Marcol to faltering Tom Birney. He was steady, but never made an All Pro or Pro Bowl team in his lengthy tenure.

At first there were questions regarding Anderson's durability. John broke his arm three times in his first couple of years as a pro and had bone graft surgery in 1980 to strengthen the bone in his arm. The graft proved to be a success, and Anderson served as a dependable player for three losing coaches in his dozen years in the green and gold. Only Bart

Starr, Ray Nitschke, Forrest Gregg, Buckets Goldenberg, and Dave Hanner had longer Packer playing careers—although Leroy Butler equaled Andy in 2001. Among linebackers, only Nitschke had as many interceptions, 25, in a Packer uniform. After retiring, Anderson spent several years as a local sportscaster and was elected to the Packer Hall of Fame in 1996.

FOR FURTHER INFORMATION

Lea, Bud. "John Anderson: A Quiet Man on the Hot Seat," *Green Bay Packers 1983 Yearbook.* (28-31)

McGinn, Bob. "Linebackers: Heart of Defense," *Green Bay Packers 1982 Yearbook.* (13-7)

JOHN ANDERSON WAS A RARE QUALITY DEFENDER IN THE DEFENSELESS DECADE OF THE 1980S:
THESE LITTLE TOWN BLUES—THE PACKERS IN THE 1980s

WHERE THEY PLAYED: Lambeau Field (known as City Stadium 1957–64), 1957–; County Stadium in Milwaukee, 1953–94.

HOW THE GAME WAS PLAYED: The passing game held sway in the 1980s. Whether it was downfield darts with San Diego's Air Coryell, bombs away with Miami's Dan Marino, or the West Coast short passing attack of San Francisco, the emphasis was on throwing the ball. Defensively, the emphasis was on getting to the quarterback as sacks finally became an official statistic, and the top defenses (Chicago's famed 46 and the Giants led by Lawrence Taylor) lived by the blitz. Led largely by Bill Walsh, coaches began to make wholesale substitutions on almost every play. Aside from the occasional use of the no-huddle offense, no quarterbacks called their own plays by the end of the decade.

DECADE WON LOST RECORD: 65-84-3 .438 + 1-1 in the playoffs.

RECORD AGAINST THE BEARS: 6-11.

RECORD AGAINST THE LIONS: 7-13.

RECORD AGAINST THE VIKINGS: 14-5.

RECORD AGAINST THE COWBOYS: 2-3 (including 0-1 in the playoffs).

PLAYOFF APPEARANCES: 1982.

CHAMPIONSHIPS: None.

UNSUNG HERO: Chairman of the Board Judge Parins for doing the distasteful and finally firing Bart Starr in 1983. Starr is as big a hero as the Packers have ever had, and in retirement has been a consistent vocal supporter of the team, but as a coach he was a disaster. He was hired with only one year's experience as an assistant coach and just seemed to be getting up to speed nine years in. Any other coach in any other town would have been fired four or five years earlier. Unfortunately, Forrest Gregg could do no better.

HEAD COACHES: Bart Starr, 1975–83, 26-29-2 for the decade; Forrest Gregg, 1984–87, 25-37-1; Lindy Infante, 1988–91, 14-18 for the decade.

BEST PLAYER: James Lofton.

HALL OF FAMERS: James Lofton, Jan Stenerud.

PACKER HALL OF FAMERS: Jan Stenerud, John Anderson, Paul Coffman, Lynn Dickey, Gerry Ellis, Johnny Gray, Johnny Holland, Ezra Johnson, James Lofton, Chester Marcol, Larry McCarren, Mark Murphy, Sterling Sharpe, and Mike Douglass.

LEAGUE LEADERS: Lynn Dickey—passing yards 1983; passing TDs 1983; passing ave. gain 1983; James Lofton—receiving avg 1983, 84; Don Majkowski—passing yards 1989; Sterling Sharpe—catches 1989.

AWARD WINNERS: Tom Flynn—Defensive Rookie of the Year 1984; Tim Harris— Defensive Player of the Year 1989; Lindy Infante—Coach of the Year 1989.

ALL PROS: James Lofton 1980, 81, 82, 83, 84, 85; Mike Douglass, 1982; Tim Harris 1988, 89; Rich Moran, 1989; Sterling Sharpe, 1989.

PRO BOWLERS: James Lofton 1980, 81, 82, 83, 84, 85; Paul Coffman, 1982, 83, 84; John Jefferson, 1982; Larry McCarren, 1982, 83; Brent Fullwood, 1989; Tim Harris 1989; Don Majkowski, 1989 (selected, but did not play); Sterling Sharpe, 1989.

BEST OFFENSIVE BACKFIELD: 1985—Lynn Dickey, QB; Eddie Lee Ivery, RB; Gerry Ellis, RB; James Lofton, FL.

BEST DRAFT CHOICE: Speed rusher Tim Harris 1986 4th round. Picking up Don Majkowski in the 10th round in 1987 might have been an even better choice had Majik stayed healthy.

BEST OVERALL DRAFT: 1985 was a solid draft, garnering linemen Ken Ruettgers and Rich Moran, linebacker Brain Noble, and wideout Walter Stanley in the first five rounds, plus journeymen Mark Lewis, Gary Ellerson, and Ken Stills in later rounds. However, 1988 brought the Packers a superstar in the 1st Round, Sterling Sharpe. Chuck Cecil, Shawn Patterson, Keith Woodside, and Scot Bolton came in later rounds.

WORST DRAFT CHOICE: Unfortunately, there are plenty of wasted number ones to choose from. Bruce Clark in 1980 refused to sign with the Packers and went to Canada; dead-armed quarterback Rich Campbell was taken instead of Ronnie Lott in 1981; Tony Mandarich, though, was the number two pick in the entire 1989 draft, a can't-miss-player who it turned out couldn't play at all.

WORST OVERALL DRAFT: 1981. In addition to taking Campbell instead of Ronnie Lott, the Packers picked such mediocrities as Gary Lewis, Ray Stachowitz, Rich Turner, Byron Braggs, and Tim Huffman, whose only claim to fame was that they were good enough to make a team that finished 5-10-1 the year before.

BEST FREE AGENT: Mark Murphy was a pure undrafted free agent off the street. Gerry Ellis was drafted by the Rams, cut, and then signed by the Packers. Both were solid players throughout the decade.

BEST TRADE: The Browns were so desperate to move up to draft Lawyer Tillman that they traded Herman Fontenot, a #1 in 1990 (Tony Bennett), a #3 in 1989 (Anthony Dilweg), and a #5 in 1989 (Vince Workman) for a high #2 in 89 (Tillman) and #5 in 1989 (Kyle Kramer). The only real player in the deal was Bennett and the Packers got him.

WORST TRADE: Desperate to rid themselves of James Lofton in 1987 after he was arrested in a sex scandal, the Packers gave him to the Raiders for a #3 (Frankie Neal) and a #4 (Rollin Putzier). Lofton would continue as a deep threat for another seven years and play in three Super Bowls with the Bills.

PACKERS BY THE NUMBERS

BIGGEST OFF-FIELD EVENT: Labor troubles hit the NFL hard in the 1980s. The first strike in 1982 cancelled seven scheduled games and led to a expanded playoff roster so that the Packers reached the postseason for a change. The second strike in 1987 was met with strong owner resistance in the form of replacement players who suited up for three games, which counted in the standings.

BIGGEST ON-FIELD DEVELOPMENT: The Packers rediscovered the go-to receiver in the tradition of Don Hutson and Bill Howton. First came James Lofton, who has been elected to the Hall of Fame, and then Sterling Sharpe, who was having a Hall of Fame career before suffering his career-ending neck injury.

STRANGEST ON-FIELD EVENT: 1) Three games with replacement players in 1987 were weird. The Packers finished 2-1 in replacement games and 3-8-1 in regular ones, but no one was pining for the replacements to return. 2) The Snow Bowl game of December 1, 1985, against a Tampa Bay Bucs team that clearly wanted to be anywhere but outside as they were pelted by the snow and pummeled by the Packers 21-0 before 19,856 hardy souls.

WORST FAILURE: The draft mistakes noted above—not being able to sign Clark; drafting Campbell not Ronnie Lott; and getting stuck with the steroid-inflated Mandarich.

HOME ATTENDANCE: 3,963,749 in 76 games for an average attendance of 52,155, down a bit from the 1970s due mostly to the labor problems. Milwaukee's average attendance was 51,831 while Green Bay's was 52,378. The only years Milwaukee's average attendance was more than Green Bay's was 1985, when the Snow Bowl's crowd of 18,000 drove down the seasonal average, and 1987 when two replacement player games in Green Bay had the same effect.

FIRST GAME: September 7, 1980, In a bizarre twist to a battle of field goals against the Bears. Bespectacled Chester Marcol lined up for the winning kick in overtime and had it blocked. However, the ball fell back in his arms and to the amazement of all he ran 25 yards untouched for the winning touchdown, 12-6 Green Bay.

LAST GAME: December 24, 1989. The Packers beat the Cowboys 20-10 in Dallas, but missed the playoffs on tiebreakers. Dallas would beat the Packers the next eight times in a row. It is still the last time Green Bay won in Texas Stadium.

BEST GAME: On October 17, 1983, the 3-3 Packers played host to the champion Redskins for a "Monday Night Football" event called by Frank Gifford, Don Meredith, and OJ Simpson. The final score was 48-47, Packers, in a night that was all offense. Lynn Dickey was brilliant, especially throwing to Paul Coffman. The Packers scored first on a turnover and kept the offensive pressure on all night. I believe that this was how the 2001 Packers envisioned their playoff game with the Rams going (nonstop excitement and scoring) except that they got bogged down in Brett Favre's six interceptions. Dickey had no such problems that night. Meredith kept saying that the first team to 50 wins, and he would have been right had Mark Mosely not missed a chip shot field goal at the end. From here the Skins would return to the Super Bowl to be whipped by the Raiders. The Packers would go 8-8.

LARGEST MARGIN OF VICTORY: 45-3 over New England 10/9/88.

LARGEST MARGIN OF DEFEAT: 61-7 to the Bears 12/7/80—the widest margin in the series.

BEST OFFENSE: 1983, they finished fifth with 429 points and second in yards.

BEST DEFENSE: 1988, they finished 10th in points allowed (315) and sixth in yards.

MOST GAMES PLAYED: 141, Mark Lee. John Anderson played in 128.

MOST POINTS: 292, Jan Stenerud.

MOST FIELD GOALS: 59 out of 73, Jan Stenerud.

MOST TOUCHDOWNS: 40, James Lofton.

MOST TOUCHDOWN PASSES: 116, Lynn Dickey.

MOST PASSING YARDS: 17,771, Lynn Dickey.

MOST RECEIVING YARDS: 7,870, James Lofton.

MOST RECEPTIONS: 430, James Lofton.

MOST RUSHING YARDS: 3,826, Gerry Ellis.

MOST INTERCEPTIONS: 30, Mark Lee.

MOST SACKS: 59, Ezra Johnson (including unofficial ones). Tim Harris had 48.

MOST KICKOFF RETURN YARDS: 1,300, Harlan Huckleby.

MOST PUNT RETURN YARDS: 819, Philip Epps.

BEST BOOKS: John Torinus, *The Packer Legend: An Inside Look*, Laranmark Press, 1982. Jerry Kramer with Dick Schaap. *Distant Replay*, Putnam, 1985. Bart Starr with Murray Olderman. *Starr: My Life in Football*, Morrow, 1987.

NOTED SPORTSWRITER: Bob McGinn of the *Green Bay Press Gazette* who has a wealth of knowledgeable sources that he draws on to write very insightful game analysis. He later moved on to the *Milwaukee Journal-Sentinel*.

BEST QUOTATION: "I really do get a little tired of people talking like we're Lower Siberia. We've found if we can just get a player to come here and visit, we're fine."—Forrest Gregg, still another besieged coach.

BUBBLEGUM FACTOID: Lynn Dickey's 1983 Topps card says Lynn's "high school field was renamed in his honor, Lynn Dickey Field." John Anderson's 1984 Topps card says, "John lists barbecuing among his favorite activities." Tim Lewis, though, according to his 1984 card, "enjoys model cars in his leisure time."

UNUSUAL NAMES: Byron Braggs, Alphonso Carreker, George Cumby, Burnell Dent, Harlan Huckleby, Kani Kauahi, Jeff Query, Blaise Winter, and Vince Workman.

NICKNAMES: Buddy Aydelette, Mossy Cade, Chubs Carreker, Paul "Hog" Coffman, John "Sack Man" Corker, Kenneth "The Temple Tornado" Davis, Automatic Al Del Greco, Preston "Magic" Dennard, Tiger Greene, Johnny "Mr. Everywhere" Holland, JJ Jeferson, Don "Majik Man" Majkowski, Tony "the Terrible" Mandarich, Charles "Too Mean" Martin, Casey "Nightlife" Merrill, Dwayne "The Dude" O'Steen, Del "Popcorn" Rodgers, Moose Sams, and Walter "Hammer" Stanley.

FASTEST PLAYER: Philip Epps, followed closely by James Lofton and Walter Stanley.

HEAVIEST PLAYER: Steve Collier 342 lbs. of the replacement players; of real players, Tom Neville at 306 lbs.

LIGHTEST PLAYER: Philip Epps, 5'10" 165 lbs and Aubrey Matthews 5'7" 165 lbs.

TOUGHEST INJURY: Eddie Lee Ivery blowing out his second knee in the 1981 opener was tough, but Tim Lewis' neck injury led to his immediate retirement.

LOCAL BOYS: Ron Pitts' father Elijah played for Lombardi and Anthony Dilweg's grandfather played for Lambeau, but neither grew up here. John Anderson was a Wisconsin boy through and through.

PACKERS BY THE NUMBERS

FIRSTS:

Overtime Victory—9/7/80 12-6 over the Bears in Green Bay. (see First Game above).

In-Season Players' Strike—1982.

Use of Replacement Players—1987.

30 TD Pass Season—Lynn Dickey, 32, 1983.

COLLEGE ALL STARS
LEE ROY CAFFEY • LINEBACKER 1964–69

WHO'S WORN THE NUMBER F. Butler 1934, Kiesling 1936, C. Schultz 1939–41, Blaine 1962, Caffey 1964–69, Knutson 1976–77, J. Anderson 1978, Allerman 1980–81, Laslavic 1982, B. Moore 1984–85, G. Jensen 1987r, Malancon 1987r, Croston 1988, Houston 1990, Zeno 1993, G. McGuire 1996, R. Davis 1997–2002.

ORIGINATOR Center Frank Butler 1934 (see top 59)

LONGEST TENURE Lee Roy Caffey 1964–69 and long snapper Rob Davis.

NUMBER CHANGES Frank Butler also wore 26 in 1934, 48 in 1935–36, 59 in 1936, and 35 in 1938; Walt Kiesling also wore 49 in 1935–36; linebacker John Anderson wore 59 from 1979–89; replacements Greg Jensen and Rydell Malancon both wore 54 also in 1987.

OTHER NOTABLES Walt Kiesling (see 49); John Anderson (see 59).

ONE TO FORGET Center Lance Zeno was a zero. He got into 10 games with three teams, half with the Packers, and eventually unsuccessfully tried to resurrect his career in NFL Europe.

LEE ROY CAFFEY Lee Roy Caffey grew up in Texas and went to Texas A&M on a basketball scholarship, but made his biggest impact on the football field as a fullback and linebacker. He was drafted in 1963 by the Eagles and played alongside another future Packer linebacker, Dave Robinson, in the College All Star Game that August. The College All Star Game was dreamed up in 1934 as a charity benefit by Arch Ward, the same Chicago sportswriter/promoter who came up with baseball's All Star Game. In a time when college football was king, it pitted the current NFL champion against a team of just-graduated college all stars. As late as 1947, the pros barely led the series by the slim margin of 7-5-2. However, by the time the game died out in 1976 due to waning fan interest, the final tally was 23-9-2, as professional football had firmly established itself as the top level of gridiron competition. The Packers as a team played in more of these games than any other team and finished with a 6-2 record; the first and last college wins in the series were against Green Bay in 1937 and 1963 respectively.

As a sidenote, Dave Robinson was one of 17 future Packers who would go directly from playing against Green Bay in the All Star Game to training camp in Wisconsin: 1937—Av Daniell, Ed Jankowski, and Bud Svendsen; 1940—Lou Brock, Dick Evans, George Seeman, and Hal Van Every; 1962—Ed Blaine and Earl Gros; 1963—Robinson; 1966—

Donny Anderson, Gale Gillingham, and Jim Grabowski; 1967—Jim Flanigan and Bob Hyland; 1968—Fred Carr and Bill Lueck. Walt Schlinkman played in the 1945 game, but did not begin his pro career until 1946.

Lee Roy Caffey went from helping beat the Packers 20-17 in the All Star Game to the Eagles training camp. On their request he had bulked up from 208 to 240 pounds, mostly by eating milkshakes fortified with eggs. He made the team, but spent just one year in Philadelphia before Lombardi traded Jim Ringo and Earl Gros for Caffey and a number one draft choice. Had the deal just been for Caffey, it would still have been a good trade, since Ringo was beginning to fade and Earl Gros would never fulfill his potential, while Lee Roy would give the Packers all-league-caliber play for several years. Adding in the number one pick (who would turn out to be fellow Texan Donny Anderson) made the deal a steal. As was the Packer custom, Lee Roy spent 1964 learning behind Dan Currie; Dave Robinson became a starter that season, having spent 1963 learning behind Bill Forester who had since retired. Currie would be traded to the Rams in 1965, and Lee Roy slid into the starting lineup.

Phil Bengtson's defense emphasized the versatility of his linebackers. They had to be big enough to stop the run, fast enough to cover offensive backs all the way down the field, and smart enough to know when to do which. Blitzing was kept to a minimum, which kept the surprise element alive; putting pressure on the quarterback was the defensive line's job. Packer linebackers were given the opportunity to shine. Of the six linebackers who were regular starters on Lombardi's teams, only Tom Bettis never made All Pro. Lee Roy Caffey was big, fast, and smart; he played in the Pro Bowl in 1965 and was named All Pro in 1966. Furthermore, like his two fellow linebackers, Robinson and Nitschke, Caffey had been an offensive star as well in college and knew what to do with the ball when he came up with a turnover. He returned interceptions for touchdowns in both 1965 and 1966.

His practice habits were not the best, however, and he served as something of a whipping boy for the coach. It was not unusual in practice for the coach to yell at him, "You should be ashamed of yourself, you big turkey." One oft-run piece of game footage shows Lombardi saying forcefully on the sidelines, "I'll tell you, Lee Roy, you're not going to get your job back unless we get a better performance." Despite the constant needling, Vince paid him well. Caffey claimed he was the best paid linebacker in football, partly because he could play both the outside and middle linebacker positions, and partly because he took so much abuse from Lombardi.

In each title contest from 1965 through 1967, one of the linebackers came up with the defensive play of the game. In 1965, Nitschke covered Jim Brown on a deep pass late in the third quarter and knocked the ball away in the end zone; in 1966, Robinson wrapped up Don Meredith on a fourth and goal in the last minute and forced a bad pass that was intercepted by Tom Brown. Lee Roy's biggest contribution to the Packers' threepeat were two crucial plays he made in the third quarter of 1967's Ice Bowl. For the first play, the Packers were up 14-10 early in the third quarter, but the momentum had shifted fully to the Cowboys. Dallas had driven to the Green Bay 22 and faced a third-and-14. Meredith started to scramble and got down to the 13 when Caffey hit him just right, causing a fumble that was recovered by Herb Adderley. Late in the same quarter, after a short punt, the Cowboys moved the ball to the Packer 30 and faced a third-and-five. On a rare blitz, Caffey shot in and nailed Meredith for a nine-yard loss and forced a 47-yard field goal attempt that fell short. Without those two big third-down plays, Dallas could very well have kicked two field goals and essentially put the game out of reach when they scored on Dan Reeves' halfback option pass in the fourth quarter.

Lee Roy was with the Packers for six years. In 1970, he was traded to the Bears along with Bob Jeter and Elijah Pitts, and he moved on to the Cowboys in 1971 where he won another Super Bowl ring along with fellow former Packers Forrest Gregg and Herb Adderley. After a year in San Diego with another fellow former Packer, Lionel Aldridge, Lee Roy retired to Texas and became a successful businessman. He started out running a car dealership, then opened a bank, and finally shifted into real estate. Sadly, he died at the young age of 52 of colon cancer.

FOR FURTHER INFORMATION

Johnson, Chuck. *The Greatest Packers of Them All.* New York: Putnam, 1968. (163-67)

Kramer, Jerry, with Dick Schaap. *Distant Replay.* New York: G.P. Putnam, 1985. (147-56)

DYNASTY AFTER DYNASTY

BRUCE VAN DYKE • GUARD 1975–76

WHO'S WORN THE NUMBER L. Dilweg 1934, Ernie Smith 1936, Ruzich 1952–54, Spinks 1955–56, J. Smith 1956, Bullough 1958, Toburen 1961–62, Breen 1964, D. Bradley 1969–71, Van Dyke 1975-76, McMath 1977, D. Simmons 1979, Ane 1981, Dreschler 1983–84, Wingle 1985, Boyarsky 1986–89, McGarry 1987r, Neville 1992, S. Curry 1999.

ORIGINATOR End Lavvie Dilweg 1934 (see 22).

LONGEST TENURE Nose tackle Jerry Boyarsky 1986–89. The Packers were the fourth and final NFL team for this hard–working, but limited player who started 10 games in four years in Green Bay.

NUMBER CHANGES Lavvie Dilweg wore 22 from 1927–34; tackle Ernie Smith also wore 45 in 1935–37 and 1939; guard Hank Bullough wore 67 in 1955; linebacker Nelson Toburen also wore 69 in 1961; guard Tom Neville wore 72 from 1986–88.

OTHER NOTABLES Lavvie Dilweg (see 22); Ernie Smith (see 45).

ONE TO FORGET Dave Dreschler was college teammate of Lawrence Taylor and a second round pick who was out of the league in two years.

BRUCE VAN DYKE In the NFL, cellar dwellers often try to get fat on the scraps left by the top teams. In the 1960s glory years of the Packers, this was one reason that Vince Lombardi was such a successful trader. His merchandise was overvalued by virtue of the overall success of his team. Just because a player was not good enough to make the Packers didn't mean he was a bad player, because the Packers were the best in the league. Branch Rickey operated from the same advantage with the St. Louis Cardinals and Brooklyn Dodgers baseball teams for years.

The Steelers were a frequent customer of the Packers' bargain bin in the 1960s. They would surrender high draft picks to acquire talent that was either on the downside, like Tom Bettis, or that never really had an upside, like Urban Henry, Gene Breen, Ed Holler, Dick Arndt, Ron Smith, Kent Nix, Dick Capp, Lloyd Voss, and Gary Jeter. The last two nobodies were swapped for a number-one pick in 1967. The Steelers even signed Lombardi's line coach, Bill Austin, as their head coach in 1966, but it did them no good since they remained in the lower regions of the league.

One sign that the Packer dynasty was over was when this situation was reversed, and the Packers became the bottom-feeders in the 1970s. One sign of changing times was the Steelers' obtaining young and talented defensive back John Rowser from Green Bay for a spent tight end, John Hilton, in 1970. The final nail in the coffin, though, was Dan Devine's giving up a third-round draft pick for Bruce Van Dyke in 1974. Van Dyke had played defensive tackle and was team captain for Devine at the University of Missouri a decade before, and the coach even had advised him at that time not to try out for the pros. Now he was picking him up for one last go-round.

Van Dyke was originally drafted by the Philadelphia Eagles in 1966 and spent a year there before he was packaged with former Packer fullback Earl Gros and sent to Pittsburgh for end Gary Ballman. Bruce was nicknamed "Moose" and had a very good seven years in Pittsburgh, twice becoming All Pro and going to a Pro Bowl. He said of himself, "I believe in the mental aspect of the game. I'm from the old school . . . I'm not extremely fast or extremely strong." (Blount, 104)

In 1973 he said of his career, "This is my eighth year and you figure an offensive lineman should have four more. And now that we're beginning to win . . . If we'd win the Super Bowl, and I had that, then I could come back and sit in the stands." Unfortunately for Moose, the Steelers won the first of their four Super Bowl titles in 1974, the year they traded him to the Packers for a third-round pick. Moose sat out the season with a knee injury before playing out the string in 1975 and 1976. The Packers' dynasty was long past, and the Steelers had just begun their run.

A number of NFL dynasties succeeded the Packers. The first was the Miami Dolphins, and there were several similarities between those teams. The Dolphins had the best offensive line in the league and a punishing ground game led by a fullback who loved contact (Larry Csonka) and a halfback who wasn't fast, but who could block and follow blocks (Jim Kiick) with even better speed and depth than Green Bay due to fast and shifty third back, Mercury Morris. Their quarterback was smart and threw the ball just enough to win, and their tight end was former Packer Marv Fleming. Their defense was a solid team defense that was fast and would swarm to the ball. But there were also dissimilarities. The Dolphins run ended after their third Super Bowl. Their receivers were small while Lombardi always favored big receivers who could throw a forceful block. Moreover, their excellent defense did not have the superstars that the Packers did. Most of all, they played in Miami, a vacation pleasure palace where it is always warm and sunny.

At the time, Fleming compared the two coaches: "Each is a disciplinarian. Each demands a lot. The difference is that Shula is more personable . . . With Lombardi you had to make an appointment." Years later, in retirement, Marv had a different perspective, suggesting that while Shula was a fine football coach, Lombardi was also a coach of life. Sometimes things are clearer in retrospect than at the moment. Ultimately, when asked which team would beat the other, Marv said simply, "Whichever one I'm on." (Anderson)

The Steelers dynasty may have followed the Packers most closely in spirit, and I always viewed them as the true keepers of the flame. They played in a Northern, working-class, small city where the climate would be anything but pleasant come December.

PACKERS BY THE NUMBERS

They were built largely through the draft. Their defense was filled with superstars, especially at linebacker where Ham-Lambert-Russell bore real similarities to Robinson-Nischke-Caffey. Neither trio blitzed a lot, and both had heavy pass coverage responsibilities. Both trios featured heavy hitters with an amazing knack for making big plays at critical junctures of important games. On the defensive line, the Packers were smaller and quicker, and featured two Hall of Famers (Davis and Jordan); the Steelers had only one Hall of Famer (Greene) but L. C. Greenwood certainly deserves consideration for induction. In the secondary, both teams had a tall, Hall of Fame corner (Herb Adderley and Mel Blount) and a heavy-hitting safety (Hall of Famer Willie Wood and Hall of Fame-eligible Donnie Shell).

On the offensive side, both teams started their runs as rush-heavy teams with question marks at quarterback (Starr and Bradshaw), but by the end of their eras they were relying on the passing talents of those former question marks. Bradshaw had the stronger arm and was more inclined to use it, while Starr would take a sack if the play wasn't there. Starr of course was known for risk-taking himself by often throwing deep on third or fourth and short plays. The Packer line was a bit better than the Steelers and was known for their pulling, while the Steelers were known more for trap blocking. The Steeler receivers were more athletic than their Packer counterparts, but both sets were known for their abilities in the clutch. In the backfield, both teams featured the fullback as the primary runner, although powerful Jim Taylor and elusive Franco Harris were as far apart in running style as two fullbacks could be. At halfback, neither Hornung nor Bleir was fast, but both were known for their blocking and ability to follow interference.

There were also many differences between the two teams, but Noll's Steelers were very reminiscent of Lombardi's Packers. While Green Bay got uglier and uglier throughout the 1970s, Pittsburgh was a pleasure to watch. Unfortunately for Bruce Van Dyke, he didn't get to play for either team at its best.

FOR FURTHER INFORMATION

Anderson, Dave. "Dolphins Better than the Packers," *New York Times.* 4/8/74.

Blount, Jr., Roy. *About Three Bricks Shy of a Load: A Highly Irregular Lowdown of the Year the Pittsburgh Steelers Were Super but Missed the Bowl.* Boston: Little, Brown and Company, 1974. (27-8, 82-5, 100-12)

Kupper, Mike. "The Offensive Line Can Be a Mighty Force," *Green Bay Packers 1975 Yearbook.* (22-3)

THE DRAFT
RUSS LETLOW • GUARD 1936

WHO'S WORN THE NUMBER Norgard 1934, Letlow 1936
Twedell 1939, Afflis 1952, W. Brown 1953–56, Amundsen 1957,
Cvercko 1960, L. Aldridge 1963, Lueck 1968–74, Havig 1977, Matson
1975, Meyer 1987r, McLaughlin 1979, Aydellette 1980, M. Merrill
1982, Laughlin 1983, Mendoza 1986, Kauahi 1988, Meyer 1988,
M. Brock 1989–93, G. McIntyre 1994, Rivera 1997–2002.

ORIGINATOR End Al Norgard 1934 was declared ineligible for
the 1934 Rose Bowl because he had played in one game for
St. Ignatius College.

LONGEST TENURE Guard Bill Lueck 1968–74 was the first player
from the University of Arizona drafted in the first round. After Jerry
Kramer retired, Lueck became a serviceable starter in his second year.
After seven years in Green Bay and one in Philadelphia, he retired
with two bad knees and became a farmer.

NUMBER CHANGES Al Norgard also wore 19 in 1934; guard Russ
Letlow switched to 46 in 1936 and wore it through 1942 and in 1946.
Dick Afflis wore 15 in 1951, 72 in 1953, and 75 in 1954; guard Andy
Cvercko also wore 67 in 1960; defensive end Lionel Aldridge wore 82
from 1964–71; Matt Brock wore 94 in 1994.

OTHER NOTABLES Lineman Dick Afflis (see 72); Lionel Aldridge
(see 82); guard Marco Rivera made the Pro Bowl in 2002.

ONE TO FORGET This number has been worn by a host of
forgettable guards and linebackers. Guard Frank Twedell's entire
career consisted of four games with the Packers in 1939, but it
least it was an NFL Championship team that cut him; guard Rubin
Mendoza who was from Milwaukee could last only six games with
the 4-12 1986 Packers. The next year in the Dolphins training camp
he told coach Don Shula that he no longer wanted to pursue a
career in the NFL.

RUSS LETLOW If all the Packers' number-one draft picks had turned
out as well as their very first one in 1936, Russ Letlow, they would have
even more championship banners than the league-leading 12 that they
have won. Until 1936, all college players were free agents who could sign
on with the highest bidder. Curly Lambeau was a born salesman and
did very well in this environment with his biggest catch coming in the
last year before the draft when he outmaneuvered Shipwreck Kelly, the
owner of the Brooklyn Dodgers football team, to sign Don Hutson in
1935. The college draft ostensibly was created to help put the weaker

teams on more equal footing with the stronger ones, not to mention staving off any bidding wars for star players.

The first draft was a far cry from today's two-day affair that is broadcast on ESPN each April. Russ Letlow, the Packers' first pick, had actually already signed with the Chicago Cardinals as a free agent before the draft. A few months after the Packers drafted him, the Cardinals notified Letlow that he was released. He became a Packer and an All Pro. At six feet and 214 pounds, Letlow was a tackle at the University of San Francisco, but moved to guard in the pros. He was a first-team All Pro twice and was named to the second team in two other seasons. In 1939, he was also selected to play in the league all star game—a precursor to the Pro Bowl where the NFL champs met a team of league all stars. In 1943, Russ went into the Navy and made the All-Service football teams in 1943 and 1944. Upon his release he returned to the Packers for his eighth and final season in 1946. Even if he hadn't been such a fine player, Russ Letlow would always be remembered for his place in Packers history, and he was inducted into the Packers Hall of Fame in 1972.

Clearly though, not all Packer number ones have fared as well. Projecting how a college player will make out against the higher level of competition in the pros is often a hit-or-miss proposition, but taking a look at Green Bay's draft history shows that some people do it better than others. To form a basis of comparison among the more than 60 drafts conducted so far, I used a simple system to rate each draft: one point for anyone who makes the team, two points for someone who becomes a regular starter, three points for a star (indicated by Pro Bowl and All Pro selections), and four points for Hall of Famers. No points are given to star players selected who were waived or traded away without appearing in a Packer uniform, such as Gordy Soltau, Bob Gain, and Ken Gray. I also counted the total number of players who made the team. This method is a quick and dirty one—the ratings are crude and the raw number of players making the team would be expected to increase over time as rosters expanded, and to be greater for poorer clubs. However, this method does allow us to see the broad patterns and overall quality of those who ran the Packer drafts.

Curly Lambeau ran the first 14 drafts and wasn't very good at it. On average, fewer than four drafted players made his team each year, and his average draft score was only six points. No one did worse on either count. Moreover, he drafted only six stars (Letlow, Isbell, C. Brock, Craig, Canadeo, and Wildung) in 14 years. In his defense, World War II was having its own draft from 1941–45, and the rival All America Football Conference was competing to sign players from 1946–49. The result, though, was a team that was near bankruptcy both on and off the field by the end of the 1940s.

In the 1950s the draft was run by the head coaches, Gene Ronzani, Lisle Blackbourn, and Scooter McLean. However, credit for this decade of wonderful drafts is usually given to the team's head scout Jack Vainisi, brought in by Ronzani in 1950 as a 23-year-old. It is because of Vainisi that the average draft score in the nine years from 1950–58 was 12, twice that of Lambeau, and 5 1/2 players per draft made the Packers. The Packers were awful on the field, but Vainisi uncovered 18 stars (Tonnemaker, T. Rote, Howton, Dillon, Hanner, Forester, Zatkoff, Ringo, McGee, Gregg, Skoronski, Starr, Hornung, R. Kramer, Currie, J. Taylor, Nitschke, and J. Kramer). Fifteen of these men were still there when Lombardi arrived in 1959, and 13 of them played starring roles in the 1960s championship run.

Tragically, Vainisi died in 1960 at only 33 years of age, and drafting players was not Vince Lombardi's forte. He was terrific at trading players for more than they were worth in draft picks, thereby accumulating 14 #1s and 24 extra picks altogether in the first eight rounds from 1960–69. But he was not good at using those picks effectively. Vince's drafts average a score of eight, with 5.3 men making the squad. He came up with six stars in 10 years (Dowler, Adderley, D. Robinson, D. Anderson, Gillingham, and Carr). His successor, Phil Bengtson worked only two drafts, one bad and one excellent, not enough to judge. He did pick two stars (Ellis and J. Carter).

Dan Devine took over the team in 1971 and his draft record was mixed, just like everything else about his tenure in Green Bay. He had one great draft in four, but sacrificed the future by trading too many high picks for has-been and never-were quarterbacks. His average score was nine, and he brought in 5 1/2 players a year. He found four stars (Brockington, Buchanan, Marcol, and McCarren), but only McCarren truly would live up to early promise.

A pair of Lombardi's stars would do no better as coaches. In Bart Starr's nine years he averaged 8 1/2 points and brought in six players a year. The only stars he picked were Ezra Johnson, James Lofton, and John Anderson. His draft record is remembered more for his failure to follow his scouts' advice, and nab Joe Montana in 1979 and Ronnie Lott in 1981, because he listened to objections by his assistant coaches. Forrest Gregg followed Starr and ran the first three drafts in his four years in Green Bay. He mirrored Bart's performance—a score of nine points and six players on average. Tim Harris was his only drafted star.

Tom Braatz took over as general manager for Gregg's last year and stayed through all four of Lindy Infante's years. He continued the mediocre pattern of an average of nine points and six players per draft for five years. He had one truly exceptional draft in 1990, and overall found four stars: Sterling Sharpe in 1988 and Tony Bennett, Leroy Butler, and Bryce Paup in the great 1990 draft.

Ron Wolf ran the draft for 10 years and on that basis is widely regarded as a draft genius. His scores averaged 11 points (which still may rise a little) and almost seven players per draft. He found only seven stars in his time, though: Brooks, Chmura, Levens, Freeman, Sharper, Rivera, and Franks. His weakness was that his first-round choices were bad; none of his stars came from the first round. His strength was in the lower rounds, especially three and five where he seemed to have a special skill in projecting the growth potential of some of college football's lesser lights. Overall, what set Ron Wolf was that not only did he draft well, but he was also very good in picking players through trades and free agency. He used every means at his disposal to acquire a depth of solid football players to produce an ongoing winning team with a future. How Mike Sherman will continue the legacy will be interesting to watch.

FOR FURTHER INFORMATION

Christl, Cliff. "The Draft," *Green Bay Packers' 1977 Yearbook.* (36-9)

————. "The Packers: A Gold Mine of Lore, Trivia and Tradition," *Green Bay Packers' 1977 Yearbook.* (16-20)

PACKERS BY THE NUMBERS

Langenkamp, Don. "Lisle Blackbourn: The Hall of Fame Drafter," *Green Bay Packers' 1978 Yearbook.* (23-5)

Porter, David L., ed. *Biographical Dictionary of American Sports: 1992–1995 Supplement for Baseball, Football, Basketball, and Other Sports.* New York: Greenwood Press, 1995. (466-67)

FIRST-ROUND SECOND GUESSING CHART

Year	Packers Pick	Also Available, Same Position	Best Available Talent
1936	Russ Letlow	Dan Fortman	Tuffy Leemans
1937	Ed Jankowski	Ace Parker	
1938	Cecil Isbell	Frank Filchock; Andy Farkas	Bruiser Kinard
1939	Larry Buhner	Marshall Goldberg	
1940	Hal Van Every	Ken Kavanaugh	
1941	George Paskvan	Paul Christman; Hugh Gallerneau	
1942	Urban Odson	Al Blozis	Frankie Albert; Jack Jacobs
1943	Dick Wildung	Al Wistert	
1944	Merv Pregulman	Bob Waterfield; Otto Graham	
1945	Walt Schlinkman	Pete Pihos	
1946	Johnny Strzylkalski	Elmer Angsman	Don Paul
1947	Ernie Case		Tex Coulter; Don Paul
1948	Jug Girard Y.A. Tittle		Dan Sandifer
1949	Stan Heath	Norm Van Brocklin; Bob Thomason	
1950	Clay Tonnemaker		Ernie Stautner; Leo Nomellini
1951	Bob Gain	Art Donovan; Bud McFaddin	Y.A. Tittle in Baltimore disbursement draft
1952	Babe Parilli		Hugh McElhenny; Frank Gifford; Gino Marchetti; Yale Lary
1953	Al Carmichael	John Henry Johnson	Doug Atkins; Bob St. Clair
1954	Veryl Switzer	Rick Caseras	
1955	Tom Bettis	Larry Morris	Dick Szymanski; Rosey Grier
1956	Jack Losch Lenny Moore		
1957	Paul Hornung	Jim Brown	Len Dawson; John Brodie; Jim Parker
1958	Dan Currie	Chuck Howley; Wayne Walker	Alex Karras
1959	Randy Duncan	Joe Kapp	Dick Bass
1960	Tom Moore		Ron Mix; Maxie Baughan
1961	Herb Adderley		Fran Tarkenton; E.J. Holub
1962	Earl Gros	Bennie MacRae	Bill Miller
1963	Dave Robinson	John Mackey; Bobby Bell	
1964	Lloyd Voss	Tom Keating; Gerry Philbin	Mel Renfro; Paul Krause

Year	Packers Pick	Also Available, Same Position	Best Available Talent
1965	Larry Elkins	Fred Bilitnikoff; Roy Jefferson	
1966	Jim Grabowski	Mike Garrett	
1966	Gale Gillingham		Diron Talbert
1967	Bob Hyland	Gene Upshaw	Alan Page
1967	Don Horn		Willie Lanier; Lem Barney
1968	Bill Lueck	Art Shell	Calvin Hill; Ron Johnson; Bill Bergey; Roger Wherli
1969	Rich Moore	Fred Dryer; Art Thom; L.C. Greenwood	Ted Hendricks; Mercury Morris
1970	Mike McCoy	Mike Reid; Cedric Hardman	
1970	Rich McGeorge	Ray Chester; Jim Mandich	Jack Reynolds; Mel Blount; Jake Scott
1971	John Brockington		Isiah Robertson; Jack Ham; Jack Youngblood; Jack Tatum
1972	Jerry Tagge	Brian Sipe; Joe Gilliam	Lydell Mitchell; Franco Harris; Cliff Branch; Reggie McKenzie
1973	Barry Smith	Golden Richards	Ron Jaworski; Dan Fouts; Greg Pruitt; Terry Metcalf; Harvey Martin; Brad Van Pelt
1974	Barty Smith	Del Williams; Mark Van Eeghen	Randy Gradishar; Dave Caspar; Lynn Swann; Danny White; Jack Lambert; John Stallworth; Mike Webster
1975	No Selection		
1976	Mark Koncar	Jackie Slater; Randy Cross	
1977	Mike Butler	A.J. Duhe; Bob Baumhower	Stanley Morgan; Wesley Walker
1978	James Lofton	John Jefferson	Ross Browner; Clay Matthews; Ozzie Newsome
1979	Eddie Lee Ivery		Joe Montana
1980	Bruce Clark	Steve McMichaels; Jim Stuckey	Joe Cribbs; Ray Donaldson
1980	George Cumby	Matt Millen	Dwight Stephenson
1981	Rich Campbell	Neil Lomax; Wade Wilson	Ronnie Lott; Hugh Green; Mark May; Russ Grimm
1982	Ron Hallstrom	Roy Foster; Bubba Paris	Mark Duper; Mike Merriweather
1983	Tim Lewis	Darrell Green; Joey Browner	Jim Kelly; Dan Marino; Roger Craig; Henry Ellard

PACKERS BY THE NUMBERS

Year	Packers Pick	Also Available, Same Position	Best Available Talent
1984	Alphonso Carreker	Keith Millard; Sean Jones	Boomer Essiason
1985	Ken Ruettgers	Jim Lachey	Jerry Rice; Al Toon; Randall Cunningham
1986	No Selection		
1987	Brent Fullwood	Christian Okoye	Rod Woodson; Jerome Brown; Bruce Armstrong
1988	Sterling Sharpe	Michael Irvin; Anthony Miller	Keith Jackson; Thurman Thomas; Randall McDaniel
1989	Tony Mandarich	Andy Heck; Steve Wisniewski	Deion Sanders
1990	Darrell Thompson	Rodney Hampton; Leroy Hoard	
1991	Vinnie Clark	Aeneas Williams; Henry Jones	Roman Phifer
1992	Terrell Buckley	Troy Vincent; Dale Carter	Bob Whitfield; Leon Searcy
1993	Wayne Simmons	Chad Brown; Michael Barrow	Robert Smith
1993	George Teague	Thomas Smith; Ryan McNeill	
1994	Aaron Taylor	Todd Steusie; Kevin Mawae	
1996	John Michels		Tony Brackens; Lawyer Milloy; Muhsin Muhammed; Amani Toomer
1997	Ross Verba	Jerry Wunsch	Marcellus Wiley; Jaime Sharper; Sam Madison; Jason Taylor
1998	Vonnie Holliday		Randy Moss
1999	Antuan Edwards	Fernando Bryant; Dre Bly	
2000	Bubba Franks	Anthony Hecht	Julian Peterson
2001	Jamal Reynolds	Marcus Stroud	Dan Morgan
2002	Javon Walker	Antwaan Randle El	Ed Reed

THE SWEEP
FUZZY THURSTON • GUARD 1959–67

WHO'S WORN THE NUMBER Michalske 1934, Zarnas 1939–40, Starret 1942–45, Odson 1946–49, Stansauk 1950–51, Bray 1952, Barry 1954, Skibinski 1955–56, Matuszak 1958, Thurston 1959–67, R. Winkler 1971, Janet 1975, T. Jones 1978–84, (C. Anderson 1987r), Hartnett 1987r, Campen 1989–93, Dukes 1994, Timmerman 1994–98, R. McKenzie 1999–2000, Ferrario 2002.

ORIGINATOR Guard Mike Michalske 1934 (see 33).

LONGEST TENURE Fuzzy Thurston 1959–67.

NUMBER CHANGES Mike Michalske wore 36 in 1929–30 and 1937, 28 in 1931, 19 and 30 in 1932, 31 in 1933, 24 in 1934 and 33 and 40 in 1935; tackle Don Stansauk also wore 66 in 1950; guard Al Barry wore 66 in 1957.

OTHER NOTABLES Mike Michalske (see 33); guard Adam Timmerman was a 7th-round draft choice who has had a solid career with the Packers and then the Rams.

ONE TO FORGET The first player to wear 63 after Fuzzy retired was guard Randy Winkler who spent the last seven games of his illustrious 27-game, three-team career as a Packer.

FRED "FUZZY" THURSTON Fred Thurston has been called "Fuzzy" since he was a baby when a sister nicknamed him that because of his dark fuzzy locks. His father died of a heart attack when Fuzzy was five, so he was one of seven children raised by a single mother in Altoona, Wisconsin. Altoona High School did not have a football team then, but Fuzzy earned a basketball scholarship to Valparaiso University. As his body filled out in college, he joined the football team and was drafted in the fifth round by the Eagles in 1956. He bounced around the league a bit, not sticking with anyone until he joined Baltimore in 1958, and he was a backup guard on the Colts team that beat the Giants in the first sudden death overtime title game in NFL history. The offensive coach of the Giants was Vince Lombardi.

When Lombardi took over the Packers the next year, one of his first moves was to trade a backup linebacker to the Colts for Thurston. Fuzzy was there for all nine of Vince's years coaching Green Bay. Fuzzy was a star at guard for Lombardi. He was first-team All Pro twice and second team three times, although he never went to a Pro Bowl. Cowboys' Hall of Fame defensive tackle Bob Lilly ranked him as one of the ten toughest linemen he ever faced. Guards were featured performers in Lombardi's offense, and Fuzzy frequently said, "There are two good reasons the Packers are world champions. Jerry Kramer is one of them, and you're looking at the other one." (Kramer, 24).

PACKERS BY THE NUMBERS

Fuzzy also was one of the freest spirits on a very free-spirited team, often joking around and singing for the rest of the team. Lombardi said of him, "You need an intelligent clown on a pro ball club and Fuzzy is also that. He has a talent for rhyming and when he bellows out calypso accounts of his heroics, he doesn't need a mike." (Lombardi, 34) Center Bill Curry noted that Fuzzy had a unique way of dealing with the coach's critiques of his work on film day, "Fuzzy would sit up front, and when he knew one of his bad plays was coming up, he'd begin to rant and rave before Lombardi could. It was really a riot . . . Fuzzy'd be saying, 'Oh, look at that! Isn't that the worst block you've ever seen! That's awful!' Lombardi, in spite of himself would have to laugh. He'd say, 'Fuzzy, you're right. That's bad. Okay, next play.' And Fuzzy could get away with it." (Curry, 18-9)

In his first year with Green Bay, though, the coaches evaluated him as, "Third guard type. Not good pulling guard for our type of offense. I believe we can improve this spot. Not quite NFL caliber. We can't win with Fred." (Wagner, 43) Four years later, Lombardi himself was writing, "He's not quite as good a pulling guard as Jerry Kramer, but he's a good short-trap blocker and he's got enough quickness, size, strength, and determination so that when he and Jerry come swinging around that corner together like a pair of matched Percherons, you can see that defensive man's eyeball's pop. Fuzzy's pass-protection blocking, though, is his big card, and he is as good as anyone in the league." (Lombardi, 33-4)

The Lombardi Power Sweep was the cornerstone of the offense, and it was led by two pulling guards. Lombardi later wrote that every team has a lead play that the opponent knows they must stop, and that for the Packers it was the sweep, "There is nothing spectacular about it, it's just a yard gainer. But on that sideline when the sweep starts to develop, you can hear those linebackers and defensive backs yelling, 'Sweep! Sweep!' and almost see their eyes pop as those guards turn upfield after them. But maybe it's my number-one play because it requires all 11 men to play as one to make it succeed, and that's what 'team' means." (Flynn, 20) The Packers practiced the play thousands of times and would run it several times a game. So, many times on television or in newspaper photographs the day after the game, what everyone would see were Kramer and Thurston clearing a path for Taylor or Hornung to make good gains. The play made them as famous as any offensive lineman could hope for. Lombardi was a guard in his playing days, and fittingly his offense made his guards stars.

The play itself dated to the single-wing era of Lombardi's college days. Lombardi simply updated it for modern football. As with everything else about him, the key was its sophisticated simplicity. A lot is made of the contrast between the "cave man" Lombardi approach and the super-technical computerized approach of his chief rival Tom Landry, but there was complexity to Lombardi's offense, as well. Packer players had to be intelligent because each play presented a great many possible options for each player, depending on what the defense was doing. In the passing game, not only did quarterback Bart Starr read the defense, but the wide receivers had to read coverages as well and could change their routes accordingly. The blocking scheme of the Packers was known as option blocking, i.e., take the defensive man in the direction he is leaning. The hole for the runner may open in a different spot than where the play is ostensibly planned to go, so the runner must the find the hole, make the right cut, and "run to daylight" as Lombardi phrased it.

The sweep itself could be run to either side, and while the sweep was designed to go around the end, the runner would cut back inside if that's was where the hole was. The ability of halfback Paul Hornung to throw an accurate pass made the play that much more effective; it was one more option the defense had to defend against. They couldn't come up too fast or Hornung would throw the ball over their heads. Then, once the defense got too comfortable defending the sweep, the Packers would hit them with the "sucker" or influence play, which looked like a sweep but was actually a fake and was run as a slant play up the middle. That is just what happened in the Packers final winning drive in the Ice Bowl. The last sweep they ran was well-diagnosed by the Cowboys, whose defensive end Willie Townes swooped by fullback Chuck Mercein's missed block to drop Donny Anderson for a nine yard loss. A few plays later, though, when the Packers got down to the Cowboy 11, Starr called the first sucker play of the game. Bob Lilly went chasing the pulling guard Gale Gillingham (Fuzzy's replacement), tackle Bob Skoronski sealed off Cowboy defensive end George Andrie, and Mercein galloped through the vacant spot in the line for eight yards. That set the stage for the finish of the Ice Bowl, the successful culmination of the Lombardi years.

Like the power sweep and like the Packers, Fuzzy fell on hard times in later years. He lost his larynx to cancer and his chain of 11 Left Guard Restaurants throughout Wisconsin went bankrupt in the early 1980s, causing him to lose his house and many prized possessions. Beyond that, there was the same realization that all former athletes must come to: that their fame departed with their youth. As Fuzzy once put it to his old partner Jerry Kramer, "Nobody wants to be Fuzzy anymore." To his credit, though, Fuzzy moved on and started anew. He has run a local taproom in Green Bay for several years, and it is a shrine to the Packers past and present. He has kept himself active with the Packer Alumni group and with Packer charities, and of course rooting for the Packers every Sunday. Through it all, Fuzzy has kept a positive attitude and demonstrated that he learned at least one very valuable lesson from Lombardi very well—never quit.

FOR FURTHER INFORMATION
Angelopolous, Angelo. "Fat Fuzz: The Man Who Makes Paul Hornung," *Sport.* 8/62. (54-)

Biever, Vernon J., photography, Peter Strupp ed. *The Glory of Titletown: The Classic Green Bay Packers Photography of Vernon Biever.* Dallas, TX: Taylor Publishing, 1997. (55)

D'Amato, Gary. "For Fuzzy, It's Still a Wonderful Life," *Milwaukee Journal Sentinel.* 10/27/96. (1 Sports)

Flynn, George, ed. *Vince Lombardi on Football.* New York: New York Graphic Society Ltd and Wallyn Inc., 1973. (19-64)

Gruver, Ed. *The Ice Bowl: The Cold Truth About Football's Most Unforgettable Game.* Ithaca, NY: McBooks Press, 1998. (71-4)

Johnson, Chuck. *The Greatest Packers of Them All.* New York: Putnam, 1968. (116-9)

Kramer, Jerry, with Dick Schaap. *Distant Replay.* New York: G.P. Putnam, 1985. (19-29)

PACKERS BY THE NUMBERS

Lombardi, Vince, with W.C. Heinz. *Run to Daylight.* Englewood Cliffs, NJ: Prentice-Hall, 1963. (33-4)

Maraniss, David. *When Pride Still Mattered: A Life of Vince Lombardi.* New York: Simon and Schuster, 1999. (222-5)

Plimpton, George. *One More July: A Football Dialogue with Bill Curry.* New York: Harper and Row, 1977. (18-19)

Riger, Robert. *Best Plays of the Year 1962: A Documentary of Pro Football in the National Football League.* Englewood Cliffs, NJ: Prentice-Hall, 1963. (19-24)

Sharnik, Morton, H. "Green Bay Blocks to Win," *Sports Illustrated.* 9/7/64. (76-85)

Shropshire, Mike. *The Ice Bowl: The Green Bay Packers and Dallas Cowboys Season of 1967.* New York: Donald I. Fine Books, 1997. (190-1)

Wagner, Len. *Launching the Glory Years: The 1959 Packers—What They Didn't Tell Us.* Green Bay, WI: Coach's Books LLC [Jay Bengtson], 2001. (43)

REPLAY MAN
JERRY KRAMER • GUARD 1958–68

WHO'S WORN THE NUMBER
Barragar 1934, H. Johnson 1940–41, Fritsch 1942–50, Danjean 1957,
J. Kramer 1958–68, K. Hunt 1972, Kitson 1980–84, S. Collier 1987,
Villanucci 1987r, Jurkovic 1993–95, Wilkerson 1996–97, A. Jackson 2002.

ORIGINATOR Center Nate Barragar 1934 (see top 31).

LONGEST TENURE Jerry Kramer 1958–68.

NUMBER CHANGES Nate Barragar wore 31 in 1931 and 1935, 56
in 1932, and 30 in 1934; tackle Steve Collier wore 70, 74, and 92 in
his three games as a replacement player; nose tackle John Jurkovic
wore 92 in 1991–92.

OTHER NOTABLES Nate Barragar (see top 31); guard Howard
(Smiley) Johnson 1940–41, went into the Marines and died at Iwo
Jima 1945; a large gregarious man, Ted Fritsch was a two-time All
Pro fullback who was the star of the 1944 title game, led the league
in scoring in 1946 with 100 points, and was elected to the Packer Hall
of Fame in 1973.

ONE TO FORGET Steve Collier was a 6'7" 342-pound replacement
player who stayed on for seven games after the strike to prove once
and for all that he couldn't play.

JERRY KRAMER Jerry Kramer has packed a lot of living and near-
dying into his time on earth. He has been a football star, best-selling
author, successful entrepreneur and businessman, and rancher. He was
also once known as "Zipper" for his frequent medical mishaps: getting
his shirt caught in a lathe, accidentally shooting himself in the side, having his groin punctured by several seven-and-one-half inch slivers of
wood, and having a colostomy as well as enduring such football injuries
as concussions, chipped vertebrae, a detached retina, a broken ankle,
broken ribs, a broken thumb, and pinched nerves. Not to mention two
marriages, two divorces, and six kids. He has had an active life

Above all else, Kramer has been the historian of a special time, a
special coach, and a special team, having had a hand in four books about
the 1960s Packers. *Instant Replay* was his diary of the historic 1967 season that culminated in the Packers' third consecutive championship. It
was edited by Dick Schaap and had a most fortuitous climax of Kramer
himself opening the hole for the winning touchdown in the Ice Bowl,
thereby becoming a household name and making this book a tremendous best seller. In 1969, he and Schaap followed that up with *Farewell
to Football*, his autobiography in the wake of his retirement after 1968.

Kramer flew solo in his third book the following year in 1970, *Lombardi: Winning Is the Only Thing*, which was a compilation of interviews with friends and former players of the coach. For *Distant Replay* in 1986, Kramer was again assisted by Dick Schaap. It told the story of the 1966 Packers on the 18th anniversary of their Super Bowl I championship. It was a brilliant idea to relay what had happened to those players in the intervening two decades, and was another best seller. As center Ken Bowman put it, "Jerry had more of a sense of history than the rest of us. He came in there in that last year that Lombardi coached and started at the beginning of training camp with his little tape recorder. We all rode him a bit about this. He was chronicling everything that was going on and we kind of teased him about it, and he took it good-naturedly." (Biever, 57)

In so doing, the Replay Man became more famous than probably any other offensive lineman. Even early in his career he and his running mate at guard for the Packers, Fuzzy Thurston, were better known than most linemen by virtue of their being the prominent pulling guards of the championship Packers' power sweep play. Add in the fact that Kramer, like so many members of that team, was an articulate, intelligent man who did not shy away from exposure on camera, and you get a true anomaly in football, a famous guard. Despite this, Jerry once said, "I've asked Vince a few times to let me play defensive tackle. I'm like everyone else, I guess. Sometimes I'd like to hear my name on the public address system or read it in the newspaper the day after the game." (Maule, 109)

During his career, he was a highly respected player. He was first-team All Pro five times, second team twice, and played in three Pro Bowls. He also scored 177 points as a kicker, stepping in when Paul Hornung was banged up in 1962 and suspended in 1963. In the 1962 title game victory over the Giants, he hit three of five field goal attempts in a swirling wind and scored 10 of the Packers 16 points. Although Henry Jordan would joke about Jerry's kickoffs that, "We're the only team that kicks off and then goes into a goal line defense." And then there is that block to win the Ice Bowl— probably the most famous block in football history. Ken Bowman, his silent partner on the block, sized up the men with whom he rubbed shoulders: "Fuzzy probably makes more blocks than Jerry, but they ain't as pretty. Jerry used to go out there and he'd just drill somebody, and you'd see the bottoms of the soles of their shoes. They'd be flying through the air and landing on their backs." (Biever, 55) Kramer was selected as the Greatest Guard of the First 50 Years of the NFL in 1969 and inducted into the Packer Hall of Fame in 1975, but he has not been elected to Canton.

Kramer has been a finalist for induction to the Pro Football Hall of Fame ten times, but never has gotten enough votes. His last close encounter was in 1997 when he was the nominee of the Veterans Committee. That committee's nominee gets elected roughly 70 percent of the time. In addition, the Packers were poised to win their first Super Bowl in 29 years the next day, so it seemed that fate and poetic justice were at work, but once again Kramer was shut out. He took the snub with equanimity and cheered on his old team to victory the next day.

There are several reasons put forth as to why Kramer is not a member of the Pro Football Hall of Fame. First, there already are 10 Packer players from that era in the Hall, plus the coach. From 1976 through 1981, 33 of the 94 Hall of Fame finalists were Packers. Jerry was nominated in five of those six years. People tire of rewarding too many from one team. This could be affecting linebacker Dave Robinson's candidacy as well. Second, guards are historically underrepresented at the Hall. Including the recent elections of Tom Mack and Billy Shaw, there are now just six and a half offensive guards in the Hall. (Jim Parker is the "half" since he spent half his career as a tackle.) Third, some question whether Jerry was really great or just good. As evidence, they cite Kramer's troubles blocking Alex Karras (another player neglected by the Hall) although when two Hall of Famers clash, someone has to lose. When Forrest Gregg went against Deacon Jones, was it always a draw? Fourth, some probably resent the celebrity Kramer achieved with his best selling books glorifying his coach and his team and the notoriety derived from that famous block.

The final reason is related to the last one. Kramer was not only overexposed, but seemed to get a little punch-drunk on his own fame. Jerry himself tells the story of being invited to a Frank Sinatra recording session in the early 1980s and afterwards telling Sinatra how his approach to the song he had just recorded was all wrong. Sinatra of course just stared at him and would not dignify Kramer's arrogance with a response. As Kramer sums it up, "Would you believe that it still took a few years before I realized that I better stop listening to the wonderful sound of my own voice?" (Kramer, 18) Even taking Jerry at his word, that he got over his cockiness, that sort of obnoxious behavior over time could grate on people. Not everyone would be able to forgive or look beyond such past history. Ultimately, it doesn't matter whether Jerry Kramer is ever elected to the Hall. He had a spectacular career on the greatest team of his time, and his books have not only kept alive that team and the teachings of his unforgettable coach, but they have given Kramer a special place in football history as well.

FOR FURTHER INFORMATION

Biever, Vernon J., photography, Peter Strupp ed. *The Glory of Titletown: The Classic Green Bay Packers Photography of Vernon Biever.* Dallas, TX: Taylor Publishing, 1997. (55, 57)

Kramer, Jerry, ed. *Lombardi: Winning Is the Only Thing.* New York: World Publishing, 1970.

Kramer, Jerry, with Dick Schaap. *Distant Replay.* New York: G.P. Putnam, 1985.

Maule, Tex. *The Players.* New York: New American Library, 1967. (109)

Porter, David L., ed. *Biographical Dictionary of American Sports: Football.* New York: Greenwood Press, 1987. (321-2)

Schaap, Dick, ed. *Instant Replay: The Green Bay Diary of Jerry Kramer.* New York: World Publishing, 1968.

Schaap, Dick, ed. *Jerry Kramer's Farewell to Football.* New York: World Publishing, 1969.

1960 CHAMPIONSHIP GAME
TOM BETTIS • LINEBACKER 1956–61

WHO'S WORN THE NUMBER L. Evans 1934, G. Wilson 1947–48, R. Collins 1951, Boerio 1952, Bettis 1956–61, Holler 1963, Wortman 1972–75, M. Douglass 1978, Wellman 1979–80, Cabral 1980, Hallstrom 1982–92, Knapp 1996, Tauscher 2000–2002.

ORIGINATOR Guard Lon Evans 1934 (see top 39).

LONGEST TENURE Guard/tackle Ron Hallstrom 1982–92 put in 11 years as a durable offensive lineman before being released in a contract dispute. While Sterling Sharpe cited Ron as being a very intelligent lineman and teammate, longtime reporter Bud Lea ranked Hallstrom as one of the five biggest jerks he ever covered (along with Sharpe).

NUMBER CHANGES Lon Evans wore 17 in 1933, 25 in 1934, 46 in 1935, 51 in 1936, and 39 in 1937; Tom Bettis wore 58 in 1955; back Rip Collins wore 88 in 1951; Mike Douglass wore 53 from 1979–85.

OTHER NOTABLES Lon Evans (see top 39); linebacker Mike Douglass (see top 53).

ONE TO FORGET Linebacker Ed Holler was nothing to shout about. He spent two games in Green Bay and a year with the Steelers, mostly as their punter.

TOM BETTIS Tom Bettis was an All American guard and linebacker at Purdue, where he was two-time team MVP and was selected in the first round of the 1955 draft by Green Bay. He was 6'2" and weighed from 215–225 pounds during his career in the NFL. He was known for his intelligence and speed and had started for four years at outside linebacker when Lombardi arrived in 1959. With Dan Currie moving into a starting spot, Bettis was shifted to the middle in 1959 and began calling defensive signals. His coaches were generally pleased with his performance, calling him, "A fine leader and only limited by his lack of weight . . . Hits hard and plays it smart. Has had a real good year at middle linebacker." (Wagner, 58)

Bettis, who was called Buddha by his teammates, had grown up in Chicago not far from another linebacker on the team who was impatiently waiting for his chance to play. Ray Nitschke would walk around yelling, "Just call me the judge because I'm always on the bench." Although the coaches questioned Nitschke's stability and intelligence, it became clear during the 1960 season that

NUMBER 65

Nitschke was a better middle linebacker than Bettis. Nitschke later said that Bettis was his best friend on the club, but by Thanksgiving of 1960 he had taken Tom's starting job. The Packers linebacking corps of Bettis, Nitschke, Currie, and Bill Forester was known as the "Fearsome Foursome" several years before the Rams defensive front four appropriated the term.

The Packers went on to win the Western Conference title for the first time in 16 years in 1960 and they met the Eagles for the championship on Monday, December 26, in Philadelphia. The Packers were young and inexperienced, but were favored. Looking back on the 17-13 defeat, there are a number of turning points that could have affected the outcome. On the game's first offensive play, Packer defensive end Bill Quinlan intercepted a botched pitchout at the Eagles' 14. Three running plays left a fourth and two at the six. Lombardi decided to go for it with another running play, but Jim Taylor slipped on the slick turf and was unable to hit the hole. The Eagles took over on downs. On the following third down play, Eagle runner Bill Barnes fumbled at the 22 and linebacker Bill Forester recovered. Once again the Eagles stopped the Packers offense, and Hornung kicked a 20-yard field goal. Later in the first quarter, the Packers drove the length of the field only to be forced to settle for a 23-yard field goal after Hornung's bad pass to an open Boyd Dowler on the halfback option play was batted down. Meanwhile, Eagle quarterback Norm Van Brocklin led the Eagles to 10 points via his passing arm. The Packers drove down the field with time running out and missed a last-second 12-yard field goal to close the first half.

In the third quarter, the Packers drove the field again, but Hornung injured his shoulder and the Eagles took over on downs at their own 25. The Eagles made their own drive to the Packer five, but were stopped by a Johnny Symank interception. Aided by a 35-yard run on a fake punt for a first down by Max McGee, the Packers finally reached the end zone on a seven-yard pass from Starr to McGee early in the fourth quarter. On the ensuing kickoff, Eagle returner Ted Dean went 58 yards to the Packer 38. The Eagles moved down to the Packer five and Dean scored on a sweep. After several exchanges of punts, the Packers got the ball on their own 35 with 1:15 left, and quickly moved to the Eagle 22. On the famous last play of the game, Starr found no one open deep so he hit Taylor underneath, and Taylor was brought down on the nine by 60-minute-man Chuck Bednarik as time ran out. Lombardi told his team after the game that this would never happen to them again. And he was right, it wouldn't. As he later summed it up, "Losing that game hurt like hell. Losing is never acceptable. But that Eagle team was a great example. They taught us lessons that day that never needed to be discussed. There were so many chances for us to win that game, but we were denied by them. In the years following, my teams were very good at turning the other team's mistakes into points and victories. That day we were denied." (Strother, 57)

So many critical opportunities in this game could have gone a different direction, but ultimately the more experienced team won. Van Brocklin told reporters after the game that he took advantage of Nitschke being out of position on several occasions to hit on big plays. Could the more experienced Bettis have made a difference? Maybe, but the Packers would make up for their disappointment in this game by winning five of the next seven championships.

PACKERS BY THE NUMBERS

One interesting sidelight to this story is that at the post-game celebration, Eagles defensive back Tom Brookshier took a call from a *Denver Post* reporter who said that a former University of Colorado teammate of Brookshier's was claiming that Brookshier had called him to say that the fix was in because Brookshier had arranged with Bart Starr for the Packers to throw the game. Brookshier lived at the hotel during the season, so he could prove he had made no outgoing call to the former teammate. He got Pete Rozelle to take the reporter's call and Rozelle threatened the reporter with a lawsuit if they ran with the unsubstantiated claim. The report never ran, and the teammate who had concocted the story because he was in-deep with gamblers was given a good going-over by those same gamblers when they found out. Years later, Brookshier told the story to Starr while they were playing golf, and Bart was shocked. If that report had been made public at the time, it would have unfairly put a shadow on Starr's career, just like the badly reported misinformation that slurred Len Dawson during Super Bowl IV.

Bettis alternated with Nitschke during the 1961 season when Ray was called up to the Army Reserves and could not practice with the team. After supposedly having words with Lombardi that year, Tom was traded to the Steelers, where he spent one season before returning home to Chicago. With the Bears in 1963, Bettis was a reserve linebacker for the team's championship season. One key to that championship season was the Bears' two victories over the Packers. If the Packers had won either of those games, they would have repeated as Western Conference champs. Bettis himself was full of information for Halas. "I knew the Packers like a book, having played there. So I gave him a pretty good rundown on their personnel and the things they would go to: different plays, their system. It helped, no question about it. Halas even told me that later." (D'Amato, 158) Tom retired and eventually went into coaching. In his first year as defensive backs coach for Kansas City in 1966, he met up with his old team again in the first Super Bowl when the Packer receivers, especially Max McGee, tore apart the Chief secondary en route to an easy win. Bettis would have a successful second career as a respected assistant coach for several teams over the next 25 years, even going 1-6 in a brief stint as head man of the Chiefs in 1977.

FOR FURTHER INFORMATION

Brookshier, Tom, and Mike Mallowe. "When the Eagles Beat Green Bay," *Philadelphia Magazine.* 12/88. (31-40)

D'Amato, Gary, and Cliff Christl. *Mudbaths and Bloodbaths: The Inside Story of the Bears-Packers Rivalry.* Madison, WI: Prairie Oak Press, 1997. (158)

Nitschke, Ray, as told to Robert W. Wells. *Mean on Sunday: The Autobiography of Ray Nitschke.* 2nd ed. Madison, WI: Prairie Oak Press, 1999. (58, 60)

Remmel, Lee. "A Fearsome Foursome: The League's Best Linebackers, Bettis, Forester, Currie, Nitschke," *Green Bay Packers 1960 Yearbook.* (40-1, 56, 63)

Strother, Shelby. *NFL Top 40: The Greatest Football Games of All Time.* New York: Viking, 1988. (56-9)

Wagner, Len. *Launching the Glory Years: The 1959 Packers—What They Didn't Tell Us.* Green Bay, WI: Coach's Books LLC [Jay Bengtson], 2001. (58)

 1960 CHAMPIONSHIP DATA
Green Bay Packers 13
Philadelphia Eagles 17

December 26, 1960 • Franklin Field, Philadelphia

Attendance: 67,325

Winner's Share: $5,116.55

Loser's Share: $3,105.14

Weather: Sunny day, frozen field melted into a slippery surface

KEY STATS	PACKERS	EAGLES
First Downs	22	13
Rush Yards	223	99
Pass Yards	178	197
Total Yards	401	296
Interceptions	1	0
Fumbles Lost	1	2
Penalties	0	4-27
Third down conversions	7/17	4/11
	1/3 (fourth down)	

Halftime Score: Packers 6 Eagles 10

LEADERS

Rushing: Jim Taylor 24-105   Ted Dean 13-54

Passing: Bart Starr 21-34-0   178 yds. Norm Van Brocklin 9-20-2 204 yds.

Receiving: Gary Knafelc 6-76   Tommy McDonald 3-90

ADDITIONAL FACTS

•The Packers turned the ball over on downs twice in Eagle territory: at the 5 in the first quarter and at the 25 in the third quarter.

•Paul Hornung missed a 13-yard field goal to end the first half.

•Hornung was forced to leave the game midway through the third quarter with a pinched nerve from a jarring tackle by Chuck Bednarik.

•Eagle assistant Charlie Gauer noticed that the left side of the Packers' kickoff team was slower than the right, and set up a special return to capitalize on that. Ted Dean returned that kick 58 yards to set up the Eagles' winning score.

•Bart Starr averaged barely over five yards per attempt while Norm Van Brocklin averaged over 10.

•Bednarik played the entire 60 minutes, the last time that's been done in a championship game.

•This was also the last title game not played on a Sunday because Sunday was Christmas Day and the NFL was not bigger than Christmas, yet.

TRANSFORMATION
RAY NITSCHKE • LINEBACKER 1959–72

WHO'S WORN THE NUMBER Monnett 1934, E. Svendsen 1939, G. Svendsen 1940–41, R. Davis 1947–48, Stansauk 1950, Cone 1951, Teteak 1952–56, Barry 1957, Nitschke 1959–72 Rudzinski 1978, M. Lewis 1980.

ORIGINATOR Back Bob Monnett 1934 (see top 3).

LONGEST TENURE Ray Nitschke 1959–72

NUMBER CHANGES Bob Monnett also wore 18 in 1933, 42 in 1934, 12 and 3 in 1935, 12 and 5 in 1936, 5 in 1937 and 50 in 1938; center Earl "Bud" Svendsen wore 7 in 1937 and 53 in 1939; center George Svendsen wore 43 from 1935–37; tackle Don Stansauk wore 63 in 1950–51; Fred Cone wore 31 from 1952–57; Al Barry wore 63 in 1955; Ray Nitschke wore 33 in 1958; linebacker Paul Rudzinski wore 58 in 1979 and 70 in 1980.

OTHER NOTABLES Bob Monnett (see top 3); Earl (Bud) Svendsen (see top 7); George Svendsen (see top 43); Fred Cone was the team's leading kicker and scorer for the 1950s and was elected to the Packer Hall of Fame in 1974; Derrel Teteak was a Pro Bowl linebacker who was elected to the Packer Hall of Fame in 1987.

ONE TO FORGET Journeyman defensive tackle Mike Lewis was the last to wear 66 before it was retired in 1983.

RAY NITSCHKE The story of Ray Nitschke is the story of power, but I don't just mean raw physical power or mental toughness on the football field. Ray Nitschke's life was the embodiment of the power of love, the power of family, and the power of an individual to transform himself into a better person.

Ray grew up in Chicago and had a hard childhood. Both his parents died by the time he was 13, and he was raised by one of his brothers. Football was a great outlet for him. He played fullback and linebacker at the University of Illinois and was drafted by the Packers in the third round in 1958. He was a wild man on and off the field in college, and remained one in his early days in the pros. Ray had a great deal of hostility and a penchant for drinking that only made it worse. His coaches said of him, "Has physical ability but cannot think. Will never be able to play for us. Trade him." (Wagner, 55) When he was spotted by Lombardi violating one of the coach's rules by having a drink at the bar late in the 1960 season, Nitschke made no pretense of hiding but instead sent the coaches a round of drinks. Lombardi was furious and wanted to cut him on the spot, but defensive coach Phil Bengtson calmed him down, since the team was short on healthy linebackers. Lombardi left it up to a vote of the team, and Nitschke prevailed unanimously with that electorate.

1961 was when things began to change. Ray met his future wife Jackie at a restaurant and began to gain control over his life. In his words, he "found some unity." Soon he would quit drinking, get married, and start a family with Jackie. He would have three children, and everyone who knew him speaks of how devoted he was to his wife and kids and how much he loved spending his time with them. Any rage left in him was now solely channeled onto the football field. There he was ferocious.

"Nitschke was one of those special players who did things others didn't do. When I was with the Bears we named one of our defenses '47 Nitschke' because it was copied from the way Ray played a certain situation. Naming a defense after a player is a pretty high compliment in my book."—George Allen (Allen, 173)

"I can say playing against Ray Nitschke shortened my career dramatically. I had great respect for Nitschke. I thought he was one of the greatest linebackers to play the game. Raymond hit awfully hard, but he wasn't a dirty player."—Bear center Mike Pyle (Swain, 223)

"The toughest guy I ever played against was Ray Nitschke . . . He was a physical, tough guy and he was a great football player."—Mike Ditka

"Pound for pound, there's never been a linebacker that's come close to Ray Nitschke."—Dave Robinson (Biever, 109)

Ray was a vicious hitter and sure tackler, as noted in the above testimonials, and was a solid run stopper, but he also could cover backs in pass coverage as Bengtson's defense required. He intercepted 25 passes and recovered 20 fumbles in his years in Green Bay, and was known for making big plays at critical times. He kept up non-stop chatter when he was on the field and was the undisputed leader of the best defense in football. He was proud, intense, and feared. He was the epitome of the middle linebacker. Joe Schmidt and Sam Huff and Bill George and Willie Lanier and Jack Lambert and Nick Buoniconti and Mike Singletary were all great middle linebackers who are enshrined in Canton, but ultimately it comes down to a choice of two for the best: Butkus or Nitschke. Packer fans will give grudging respect to the great Bear backer Butkus, but Nitschke will always be their man.

Only Bart Starr played longer in a Packer uniform than Ray Nitschke. In his 15 years in Green Bay, Nitschke made All Pro three times and played in only one Pro Bowl, but was named the NFL's all-time top linebacker in 1969 and was named to the NFL's 75th Anniversary team in 1993. Of most importance to Ray himself was being elected to the Pro Football Hall of Fame in 1978. For the last 20 years of his life he would go to every annual induction ceremony to welcome his new brothers in arms. Each year there is a special inductees-only luncheon held the day before the ceremonies and that luncheon is now called the Ray Nitschke Luncheon, because year after year Ray would get up at the luncheon and give a spontaneous, emotional speech on what being elected to the Hall means. Many count Nitschke's speech among the most moving experiences of their lives. In his retirement, Ray became an unpaid ambassador for the Packers, for football and for the Hall of Fame, always happy to meet new fans and treat them with great friend-liness. When he died of a heart attack in 1998, Green Bay lost its number one citizen, and football its number one gentleman.

FOR FURTHER INFORMATION

Allen, George, with Ben Olan. *Pro Football's 100 Greatest Players: Rating the Stars of Past and Present.* Indianapolis: Bobbs-Merrill, 1982. (172-3)

Biever, Vernon J., photography, Peter Strupp ed. *The Glory of Titletown: The Classic Green Bay Packers Photography of Vernon Biever.* Dallas, TX: Taylor Publishing, 1997. (109)

Gruver, Ed. *Nitschke: The Ray Nitschke Story.* Lanham, MD: Taylor Trade, 2002.

Kramer, Jerry, with Dick Schaap. *Distant Replay.* New York: G.P. Putnam, 1985. (148-53)

Linn, Ed. "Ray Nitschke: The Hard Road to Respect," *Sport.* 11/65. (82-7)

Nitschke, Ray, as told to Robert W. Wells. *Mean on Sunday: The Autobiography of Ray Nitschke.* 2nd ed. Madison, WI: Prairie Oak Press, 1999.

Schaap, Dick. *Green Bay Replay: The Packers Return to Glory.* New York: Avon Books, 1997.

Swain, Glenn. *Packers vs. Bears.* Los Angeles: Charles Publishing, 1996. (223)

Wagner, Len. *Launching the Glory Years: The 1959 Packers—What They Didn't Tell Us.* Green Bay, WI: Coach's Books LLC [Jay Bengtson], 2001. (55)

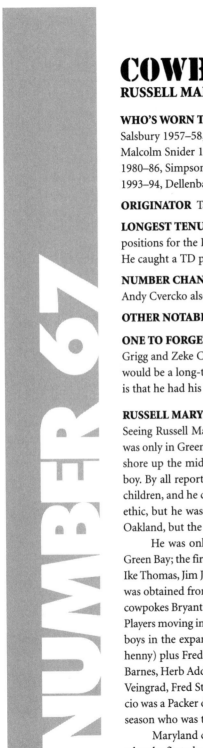

COWBOYS
RUSSELL MARYLAND • DEFENSIVE TACKLE 2000

WHO'S WORN THE NUMBER D. Logan 1952–53, Bullough 1955, Salsbury 1957–58, Cvercko 1960, Grimm 1963–65, Carroll 1968, Malcolm Snider 1972–74, Enderle 1976, Kowalkowski 1977, Swanke 1980–86, Simpson 1987r, Ard 1989–91, Barrie 1992, Hutchins 1993–94, Dellenbach 1996–98, Maryland 2000.

ORIGINATOR Tackle Dick Logan 1952–53 (see Forget below).

LONGEST TENURE Tackle Karl Swanke 1980–86 played all five line positions for the Packers before knee problems forced him to retire. He caught a TD pass in 1981 on a tackle-eligible play.

NUMBER CHANGES Guard Hank Bullough wore 61 in 1958; guard Andy Cvercko also wore 62 in 1960.

OTHER NOTABLES None.

ONE TO FORGET Dick Logan came from the Browns with Chubby Grigg and Zeke Costa for Walt Michaels in 1952. Walt Michaels would be a long-time player in the league; Logan's only claim to fame is that he had his own Bowman football card in 1952.

RUSSELL MARYLAND
Seeing Russell Maryland in a Packer uniform never seemed right. He was only in Green Bay for a year and did the job he was signed to do—shore up the middle of the defense—but he was still a stinking Cowboy. By all reports, Maryland is a fine person devoted to his wife and children, and he clearly was an on-field leader with an admirable work ethic, but he was a Cowboy. He had spent the previous four years in Oakland, but the mark of the Star would always be part of him.

He was only the seventh player to first play in Dallas and then Green Bay; the first six were Jerry Norton, Malcolm Walker, Ron Widby, Ike Thomas, Jim Jensen, and Chris Akins. In addition, Clarence Williams was obtained from the Cowboys taxi squad in a trade. In 2002, former cowpokes Bryant Westbrook and Alcender Jackson played for the Pack. Players moving in the other direction include those selected by the Cowboys in the expansion draft (Nate Borden, Bill Butler, and Don McIlhenny) plus Fred Cone, Bill Howton, Andy Cvercko, Lee Folkins, Gary Barnes, Herb Adderley, Forrest Gregg, Lee Roy Caffey, Syd Kitson, Alan Veingrad, Fred Strickland, George Teague, and Jackie Harris. Tony Liscio was a Packer draft choice cut right before the beginning of the 1963 season who was then picked up by the Cowboys.

Maryland came to Dallas out of the University of Miami, selected as the first player in the 1991 draft by his former college coach Jimmy

PACKERS BY THE NUMBERS

Johnson. In college he was a two-time All American and won the Outland Trophy as the nation's best lineman. He never quite lived up to that buildup in the pros. He went to only one Pro Bowl, but he was a solid run-stopper, very effective in the Dallas defensive scheme. He started for three Super Bowl winning teams before leaving as a free agent for big money in Oakland. After four years there, the Raiders decided they could no longer afford Maryland under their salary cap. Russell then had a good year with the Packers, plugging the middle, but the Packers made the same decision. They re-signed Gilbert Brown to perform the same function for less money. The realities of living under a hard salary cap prompt teams to make these difficult decisions every year, and players are in a continual state of movement. Maryland moved on to the Jets in 2001.

Through no fault of his own, Maryland never looked right in Green and Gold. He belonged to the team that unfortunately was the team of the 1990s, the Dallas Cowboys. In a way it is odd how an intense rivalry of teams representing such distant and disparate cities arose. The rivalries with the Bears, Lions, and Vikings are all based on geographic proximity and divisional competition. With the Bears, you can add in longevity, with both teams having met annually for roughly 80 years, in addition to the personal rivalry between coaches George Halas and Curly Lambeau. The Dallas rivalry actually comes out of New York.

Vince Lombardi and Tom Landry were intensely competitive men who ran the offense and defense respectively for the New York Giants in the late 1950s. Lombardi left in 1959 to take over the 1-10-1 Packers, and Landry left in 1960 to take over the expansion Cowboys. Lombardi quickly molded the team of the 1960s while Landry was slowly building the Cowboys, and there was a rivalry from the start when these two met, although the Packers held a big advantage in talent in the early years. As the Giants faded as an Eastern Division power, their long rivalry with Green Bay faded forever. It was replaced by The Packers' duels with the new powerhouse in the division, Dallas.

After the 1966 and 1967 seasons, the Packers and Cowboys faced off in two of the greatest championship games ever played. Both games went down to the final minute, and the Packers prevailed both times. On the first day of 1967, Green Bay intercepted a desperate fourth-and-goal Don Meredith pass to hold on and win 34-27 and go on to the first Super Bowl against the Chiefs. At that point, the mighty Packers were considered the best team in football while the inexperienced Cowboys were still youthful and improving. By the time the teams met in Green Bay on the last day of the same year, 1967, many thought the Cowboys had surpassed the Packers and were now the best team. The Cowboys themselves felt that way and were confident of victory over the Packers. As everyone knows, the Ice Bowl came down to the Packers' final 68-yard drive that culminated with Bart Starr scoring on a third-down quarterback sneak with 16 seconds left and no timeouts remaining.

Two bitter last-minute defeats took a lot out of the Cowboys, but they righted themselves and went to five Super Bowls in the 1970s while the Packers disappeared from sight. Dallas would not beat Green Bay for the first time until 1970. In that decade, the two-time champion Cowboys proclaimed themselves "America's Team," and that grated on players and fans throughout the league, especially in Green Bay, as a demonstration of the Texas team's arrogance. After all, Green Bay did not proclaim themselves America's Team in the 1960s despite winning five of six title games. All things must pass, though, and Dallas itself withered slowly in the 1980s until reaching their low point in Jimmy Johnson's first year as coach, 1989, when they finished 1-15, including two losses to the Packers. At that point, the record between the two teams stood at 10-5, Packers, including a 2-1 Green Bay advantage in the playoffs. And there was a great deal of mutual respect between the former players of the two teams. Dallas tackle Ralph Neely asserted that, "Old Cowboys and Packers migrate to each other at alumni affairs . . . There is a shared respect." (Eisenberg, 194)

Everything changed under Jimmy Johnson. Not only did he rebuild the Cowboy team, but its attitude as well. "How 'bout them Cowboys!" Johnson would shout in the locker room to his team after a victory. The Cowboys became not only the best but also the most obnoxious and classless team in the NFL. Meanwhile, Mike Holmgren and Ron Wolf were building a great team in Green Bay, step by step. However, each year they would get frustrated, losing twice to the Cowboys in Texas Stadium, once in the regular season and once in the playoffs. It happened in 1993 and in 1994 and in 1995. The Packers' two leaders viewed this situation from differing perspectives. Reggie White had been tormented by an inability to beat Dallas since his days as an Eagle, and the Cowboys' tactics and attitude angered him. Brett Favre, to his credit, simply looked on the dispiriting record of losses as evidence that the Packers needed to improve. All told, the Packers lost eight in a row (seven of them played in Dallas) before rising up and crushing Dallas 45-17 in Green Bay in 1997. In the new millennium, the record stands 14-11, Cowboys, including a 4-2 advantage in the playoffs.

Russell Maryland was part of that 1990s Cowboys team. The team whose dirty-play specialist tackle, Erik Williams, took a diving cut block at the back of John Jurkovic's knee and ended his Packer career. The team that called a timeout in the last minute of an easy victory over the Packers in 1996 so that their kicker could tie a record by kicking a seventh field goal in one game. A team with several talented, arrogant, ignorant players like Michael Irvin, who were in constant trouble with the law and were often a disgrace to the game. Russell Maryland was nothing like that, himself, but he was part of that braggadocios, undisciplined team. Seeing him playing for the home team in Lambeau only brought back bad memories, and it is good that he moved on, because Cowboys have never been heroes in Wisconsin.

FOR FURTHER INFORMATION

Eisenberg, John. *Cotton Bowl Days: Growing Up with Dallas and the Cowboys in the 1960s.* New York: Simon and Schuster, 1997.

Golenbock, Peter. *Cowboys Have Always Been My Heroes: The Definitive Oral History of America's Team.* New York: Warner Books, 1997.

Gruver, Ed. *The Ice Bowl: The Cold Truth About Football's Most Unforgettable Game.* Ithaca, NY: McBooks Press, 1998.

Landry, Tom, with Gregg Lewis. *Tom Landry: An Autobiography.* Grand Rapids, MI: Zondervan Publishing, and New York: Harper Collins, 1990.

PACKERS BY THE NUMBERS

Shropshire, Mike. *The Ice Bowl: The Green Bay Packers and Dallas Cowboys Season of 1967*. New York: Donald I. Fine Books, 1997.

Sugar, Bert Randolph. *I Hate the Dallas Cowboys: And Who Elected Them America's Team Anyway*. New York: St. Martin's Griffin, 1997.

THE UNHERALDED
GALE GILLINGHAM • GUARD 1966–74, 1976

WHO'S WORN THE NUMBER Herber 1934, Seeman 1940, Paskvan 1941, Szafaryn 1953–56, Dittrich 1959, Gillingham 1966–74, 1976, Koch 1977–85, Konopasek 1987r, B. Winter 1988–90, Singletary 1991, Sims 1992–95, Gary Brown 1996, Wahle 2000–02.

ORIGINATOR Tailback Arnie Herber 1934 (see 16).

LONGEST TENURE Gale Gillingham 1966–74, 1976.

NUMBER CHANGES Arnie Herber wore 12 in 1930, 26 in 1931, 41 in 1932–33, 16 in 1933, 45 in 1934, 38 from 1935–40, and 19 in 1937; tackle Len Szafaryn wore 47 and 51 in 1950.

OTHER NOTABLES Arnie Herber (see 16).

ONE TO FORGET Tackle Gary Brown was given every opportunity to win the left tackle position and solidify the line in 1996, but could not win the job.

GALE GILLINGHAM Cowboy Hall of Fame defensive tackle Bob Lilly called Gale Gillingham the second toughest offensive linemen he ever faced. All Pro linebacker Bill Bergey said, "When you're playing football and you're concentrating and you get hit, it never hurts. When Gillingham hit me, it hurt." (Kramer, 142) Both Bart Starr and Hawg Hanner claimed he was the best lineman they ever had on the Packers in their time. Those linemen inferior to Gillingham would include Hall of Famers, Forrest Gregg and Jim Ringo, All Pro pulling guards Jerry Kramer and Fuzzy Thurston, and Pro Bowler Bob Skoronski.

Gillingham was an immensely strong 6'2", 265-pound drive-blocker supreme. He also had amazing speed and agility for such a big man so that he would pull out on the Packer sweep just as well as Kramer and Thurston. He was a good teammate and a fierce competitor who fit right in as a rookie in 1966, and he was groomed to replace the aging Fuzzy Thurston by the ultimate team player, Fuzzy Thurston himself. "Everybody was helpful in those days. It was kind of like family," Gilly would comment years later. (Poling, 151)

Gilly would be selected as an All Pro five times and would make the Pro Bowl in each of those seasons, too. He was a second-team All Pro in still another year. He of course played in the first two Super Bowls before the team began to decline. Unfortunately, the only other year the Packers made the playoffs was in 1972, and Gilly was out all year with an injury. In an imbecilic and incompetent move, Coach Devine asked the best guard in the league to move to defensive tackle that year in training camp, because starter Mike McCoy was hurt. Learning a new position, team player Gillingham blew out his knees and was lost for the year. Maybe he would have gotten hurt, anyway, but Gilly always attributed the injury to the position shift.

He came back and had two more All Pro years in 1973 and 1974, but he was not happy under Devine. When Bart Starr became coach in 1975, Gale surveyed the scene and sat out the season. His assessment was that the inexperienced Starr did not know how to be a head coach at that time, and that the assistants he hired were terrible. Gillingham was a prescient and perceptive observer. When the Packers refused to trade him to another team, Gilly returned in 1976 for one final year, but then retired for good, still unhappy with the coaching staff. He was still able to play, but had no desire to go on losing.

Another of Gilly's former teammates, the late Ray Nitschke, was a regular attendee at Pro Football Hall of Fame inductions where he would openly welcome new members, telling them to appreciate what an exclusive club they were joining. And Canton is that. So many things over which a player has no control have to break right for him to be elected to the Hall of Fame. Former Packer players are well represented in the Hall, with 20 members, as befits a team with such a long and successful history. However, there are a half-dozen or so other Packers who belong in Canton, as well: Dave Robinson, Jerry Kramer, Bobby Dillon, Bill Howton, Lavvie Dilweg, Verne Lewellen, and Gale Gillingham.

Dave Robinson's name is batted around by the Veteran's Committee each year, and he may make it eventually. Jerry Kramer has been a Veteran's Committee nominee in the past, so it is doubtful he will be put forward again, although two of the eight unsuccessful Veteran's Committee nominees were put forth a second time, and gained approval. Both Kramer and Robinson have been hurt by the success of their team, since so many Packers from that time are already in the Hall. Bobby Dillon and Bill Howton were both picked for four Pro Bowls and were made All Pro four and two times respectively. They both amassed impressive statistics. However, neither is likely to ever be elected to the Hall because they played for mostly bad teams, which is a good way to be forgotten. Old-timers Dilweg and Lewellen were All Pros five and four times respectively for the three-time champion Packers of the 1920s and early 1930s. Both were especially noted for their defensive prowess in those days of two-way players, and Lewellen scored more than 300 points in an era when points were scarce. Since both are dead and from football's own ancient "dead ball era," it's highly unlikely they will ever be elected.

Gale Gillingham paradoxically suffers from the same sorts of drawbacks all of the other five have. He was briefly part of the glorious Lombardi era, but then spent most of his time with bad teams in a largely forgotten era. He may very well have been the best offensive lineman of his time, and the best ever to wear the green and gold, but he will remain largely unheralded everywhere but in Green Bay where he always will be appreciated and will never be forgotten. As proof of this, he was inducted into the Packer Hall of Fame in 1982.

FOR FURTHER INFORMATION

Christopulos, Mike. "Gale Gillingham: Just Another Famer?" *Green Bay Packers 1969 Yearbook.* (26-7)

Gentile, Domenic, with Gary D'Amato. *The Packer Tapes: My 32 Years with the Green Bay Packers.* Madison, WI: Prairie Oak Press, 1995. (88-90)

Kramer, Jerry, with Dick Schaap. *Distant Replay.* New York: G.P. Putnam, 1985. (140-6)

Poling, Jerry. *Downfield! Untold Stories of the Green Bay Packers.* Madison, WI: Prairie Oak Press, 1996. (149-52)

Rubin, Bob. *Green Bay's Packers: Return to Glory.* Englewood Cliffs, NJ: Prentice-Hall, 1974. (123)

BENGTSON FOR THE DEFENSE
BILL FORESTER • LINEBACKER 1953–59

WHO'S WORN THE NUMBER Engebretsen 1934, Stephenson 1952, Forester 1953–59, Toburen 1961, Bain 1975, L. Harris 1978–83, Cherry 1986–87, Gruber 1987r, Blackshear 2002.

ORIGINATOR Guard Tiny Engebretsen (see 52).

LONGEST TENURE Bill Forester 1953–59.

NUMBER CHANGES Tiny Engebretsen wore 34 from 1935–41 and 52 in 1936; guard Dave Stephenson wore 44 in 1951 and 53 in 1953–54; Bill Forester wore 71 from 1960–63; linebacker Nelson Toburen wore 61 in 1961–62.

OTHER NOTABLES Tiny Engebretsen (see 52).

ONE TO FORGET Guard Bill Bain was a number two draft pick who was gone from Green Bay in a year although he lasted in the league for another decade. He stormed out of his second training camp after a film session, demanding to be traded, and his wish was granted the next day. He eventually made All Pro in 1984 with the Rams, but lost his starting job the next year. He asked for his release and moved on to the Chiefs in 1986, but suddenly quit 10 days into training camp because it was too hot. He finished his career that year with the Jets and Patriots.

BILL FORESTER Captain of the defense, Bill "Bubba" Forester's career came alive when Lombardi and his defensive coach Phil Bengtson arrived in 1959. During that year the coaches evaluated Bubba as, "A big strong boy who has done very well this year. At times his tackling has been poor . . . Not as good on passes as we would like to have. Should improve next year." (Wagner, 57) Forester was the left outside linebacker, normally, but with the Packers' four-man linebacking rotation, Bubba would move into the middle when Ray Nitschke came in to spell Tom Bettis. Bubba had good size and was quick, smart, and a leader. He would make the Pro Bowl from 1959 through 1962 and be named All Pro 1960 through 1963. Lombardi would say this about him in 1963: "There is no one on this club who is more quiet and self contained . . . He is highly intelligent and steady on and off the field and his leadership is one of action rather than words. There is an aura of efficiency about him that the others respect and rise to." (Lombardi, 140) Was it coaching?

Lombardi remembered Phil Bengtson from a game in 1957 when Bengtson's 49er defense unleashed a new tactic on Lombardi's

NUMBER 69

Giant offense, blitzing linebackers. The 49ers called it the Red Dog defense, and they hit Giant quarterback Charlie Connerly repeatedly, causing him to fumble five times and helping San Francisco beat New York that day. So in 1959, when Vince got the job in Green Bay, he hired Bengtson right away and never regretted it. Bengtson ran the Packer defense for nine years while Lombardi was head coach and then for three more years after Phil became head coach. In those 12 years, the Packers gave up an average of 15.9 points a game. During that time, they finished first in fewest points allowed three times, second four times and third twice. They finished first in fewest yards allowed twice, second twice, and third four times. His pass defense was especially effective, allowing the fewest yards in the league six times (1962 and from 1964–68). The combination of a consistent offense and a ball-hawking defense allowed the Packers of those 12 years to be a plus-124 in turnover ratio. Over those dozen years, the defense also scored 20 touchdowns on interceptions and six on fumble recoveries. Bengtson believed, "In the modern game of football, the defense attacks. The defense has plays, formations, strategies, and it can even produce points by making touchdowns and safeties. Most important, the aggressive defensive squad must have a morale of its own." (Bengtson, 197) Phil put a great deal of emphasis on pride, and his defenses responded.

Bengtson's first Packer defenses featured a lot of blitzing, but as Lombardi brought in more quality players in the first couple of years, the blitzes decreased dramatically. Once he had the personnel in place that he wanted, Phil played a much more patient game. He felt, "The defense's job is to prevent a score, not necessarily to prevent a gain . . . We have a defense that permits short gains and tries to deny the long ones. The main objective is to minimize the gains, forcing the opponent to play our slow game rather than his fast game. Make him run lots of plays, and when he makes his share of mistakes, capitalize on them." (Bengtson, 199)

Overall, Bengtson's defense reflected Lombardi's offense. His defense was basic and relied on simplicity. The defense was a 4-3 arrangement that relied on man-to-man coverage. The defensive tackles were pinched toward the center to allow middle linebacker Nitschke the freedom to pursue the ball. As noted above, blitzing was done rarely and was that much more effective because of the element of surprise and the skill of the blitzers: Forester, Currie, Robinson, Caffey, and sometimes Nitschke. Usually, the pass rush was generated by the small and quick front line, and in particular by defensive end Willie Davis on the left side and defensive tackle Henry Jordan on the right. Left defensive tackles Hawg Hanner and Ron Kostelnik and right defensive ends Bill Quinlan and Lionel Aldridge had greater responsibilities defending the run. The big, fast, athletic linebackers were expected to cover short passes underneath and to stay with backs coming out of the backfield all the way down the field. The inside deep passing game was funneled to safety Willie Wood in "centerfield," while the quick and rangy cornerbacks took the outside routes.

Bengtson later said, "It's not the plays you use, it's the players you have." That is certainly true, but it is also true that talented players will languish if they are not used correctly. Bengtson taught his players how he wanted them to perform, and his defense allowed them to succeed. His calm personality was diametrically opposed to that of the volatile Lombardi, but he got results his own way. While the offense was berated and yelled at by Lombardi during the weekly film review of the previous game, the defense was gently corrected by Bengtson and his defense loved and respected him for it. Both Ray Nitschke and Willie Wood had Phil present them for induction into the Pro Football Hall of Fame. In becoming head coach, though, there were two problems: 1) following a legend is a near impossible task, and 2) it was the Peter Principle in action. Phil had the personality of a trusted assistant coach, not a head man.

Bengtson's defense allowed Bill Forester to shine in the second half of his career, and Bubba got a great deal of recognition in the early 1960s. He is not much remembered these days because he was replaced in 1964 by an even better linebacker, Dave Robinson, and Robinson's Packers achieved the threepeat that Forester's team fell just short of by losing the 1960 title game and by not beating the Bears in 1963. Bill Quinlan, who played defensive end in front of Forester, called him, "the smartest linebacker I ever knew." (Johnson, 166) Bubba never missed a game in 11 years in Green Bay and was inducted into the Packer Hall of Fame in 1974.

FOR FURTHER INFORMATION

Bengtson, Phil, with Todd Hunt. *Packer Dynasty.* Garden City, NY: Doubleday, 1969.

Biever, Vernon J., photography, Peter Strupp ed. *The Glory of Titletown: The Classic Green Bay Packers Photography of Vernon Biever.* Dallas, TX: Taylor Publishing, 1997. (97, 113)

Gruver, Ed. "Green Bay's Defensive Genius," *The Coffin Corner.* 1995. Available online at www.footballresearch.com/articles/frpage.cfm?/topic'bengsten.

Johnson, Chuck. *The Greatest Packers of Them All.* New York: Putnam, 1968. (166)

Lombardi, Vince, with W.C. Heinz. *Run to Daylight.* Englewood Cliffs, NJ: Prentice-Hall, 1963.

Maule, Tex. "A Perfect and Balanced Defense," *Sports Illustrated.* 11/19/62. (30-40)

Wagner, Len. *Launching the Glory Years: The 1959 Packers—What They Didn't Tell Us.* Green Bay, WI: Coach's Books LLC [Jay Bengtson], 2001. (57)

MILITARY SERVICE
DICK WILDUNG • TACKLE 1953

WHO'S WORN THE NUMBER S. Dowden 1952, Wildung 1953, A. Hunter 1954, Don King 1956, R. Marshall 1965, Crenshaw 1968, R. Moore 1969–70, Nystrom 1974, E. McMillan 1975, B. Barber 1976–79, Rudzinski 1980, Sams 1983, Uecker 1984–85, 1987–88, 1990–91, S. Collier 1987r, Grant 1993, Hope 1994, Andruzzi 1998–99.

ORIGINATOR Tackle Steve Dowden 1952 somehow appeared on his own bubblegum card as a rookie despite being a 10th-round draft pick. He lasted only a year.

LONGEST TENURE Guard Keith Uecker 1984–85, 1987–91, the oft-injured, very courageous player who formed a strange bond with Tony Mandarich (see 77) that involved them spitting on each other and other linemen.

NUMBER CHANGES Dick Wildung wore 45 from 1946–51; linebacker Paul Rudzinski wore 66 in 1978 and 58 in 1979; tackle Steve Collier also wore 74 and 92 in his three games as a replacement player and 64 after that in 1987.

OTHER NOTABLES None.

ONE TO FORGET Defensive tackle Rich Moore, Phil Bengtson's first number-one pick, was out of the league in less than two years. He would have been gone sooner, but he couldn't move that fast.

DICK WILDUNG Dick Wildung was drafted number one by two entities in 1943: the Packers and Uncle Sam. Green Bay would have to wait. Wildung was a two-time All American tackle at the University of Minnesota. The Golden Gophers were undefeated National Champions in 1940 and 1941 and lost only one game in 1942—to their former coach Bernie Bierman's Iowa Pre-Flight School team. Also on the Minnesota team was Bruce Smith, who won the Heisman Trophy in 1941, and would join the Packers in 1945, a year before Wildung. Dick finished seventh in the Heisman voting in 1942, the highest of any lineman that year, and then went into the Navy for the duration of World War II.

After the War, Wildung joined the Packers in 1946. In his seven-year career, Dick played mostly offensive and defensive tackle, but he also spent some time at guard. Two times he made All Pro, once was named a second team All Pro, and played in one Pro Bowl. He took off the 1952 season to take care of some personal business concerns, but returned for a final season in 1953. When Gene Ronzani was fired as coach that year, Wildung along with teammate Bob Forte could say that they had the unique distinction of being present for the demise of the only two coaches that the Packers had ever had.

Wildung had the bad luck to enlist with the Packers just as the team began to crumble under Lambeau. Curly did not weather the 1940s well. The Packers lost a lot of talent to the war effort and then had to compete with teams from a new league who were on steadier financial footing than Green Bay. Besides these difficulties, Lambeau had not stayed current: the Packers and Steelers were the only teams not running the T formation after the war. The Packers would convert before Pittsburgh, but even then Lambeau was no expert at it. The best teams that Wildung played for were the first two. The Packers finished 6-5 in 1946 and 6-5-1 in 1947. Through it all, however, Wildung was one bright light, and he would be elected to the Packer Hall of Fame in 1973.

Dick Wildung was one of several players drafted by the Packers during World War II who would fulfill their armed services commitments before continuing their football careers. From the 1942 draft, Bruce Smith and Ray Frankowski would not report to Green Bay till 1945; Urban Odson would not show up till 1946. From the 1943 draft, Roy McKay would not show up till 1944; Ken Snelling and Solon Barnett would be away until 1945; Bob Forte, Les Gatewood, Ace Prescott, and Earl Bennett would not report till 1946. From the 1944 draft, Merv Pregulman would miss two years and not report until 1946. From the 1945 draft, Walt Schlinkman and Don Wells would not come to Green Bay until 1946.

Of players already under contract to Green Bay when the war started, 32 missed at least one year in the service of our country. Players who missed one season include: Tony Canadeo, Joe Carter, Bob Kahler, and Ray Wehba. Players who missed two seasons include: Dick Evans, Sherwood Fries, Jim Lankas, Ernie Pannell, Charlie Sample, Andy Uram, and Alex Urban. Players who missed three years include: Bob Adkins, Ed Frutig, Tom Greenwood, Bob Ingalls, Bill Lee, Russ Letlow, Carl Mulleneaux, Ray Riddick, Fred Vant Hull, and Dick Weisgerber. Players who missed four seasons include: Ed Jankowski, Bill Johnson, Lee McLaughlin, George Paskvan, Herm Rohrig, Charlie Schultz, George Svendsen, and Hal Van Every. Clarke Hinkle had retired, but spent four years in the service. Gus Zarnas spent five years in the military.

Howard "Smiley" Johnson spent three years in the Marines and was killed in action at Iwo Jima, the only Packer to be killed in the war. Smiley was a very well liked backup guard who had gotten married just a month before enlisting in the Marines. He rose to the rank of lieutenant and won two Silver Stars for bravery in hand-to-hand combat in the Pacific. Of course, there were other former Packers like Johnny Blood and future Packers like Jack Jacobs who also spent years overseas, although they were not connected to Green Bay during the war.

During the Cold War in the 1950s and '60s, military service interrupted the early part of football careers of several prominent Packers. Someone was missing from the squad almost every year of the 1950s. Bob Forte and Wally Dreyer were called up in 1951 and thus were two Packers who were in the service during both WWII and Korea. Dreyer had been with the Bears in the 1940s. Larry Coutre, Ben Szafaryn, and Clay Tonnemaker all had military duty in 1951–52. Clarence Self missed 1953. Dick Logan and Don Barton missed 1954, Art Hunter, Bob Garrett, and Steve Knutson missed 1955, and Babe Parilli missed 1954 and 1955. Al Barry and Max McGee missed 1955 and 1956. Hank Bullough, Doyle Nix and Veryl Switzer missed 1956 and 1957.

Future Lombardi stars also did their duty. Forrest Gregg missed 1957, Bob Skoronski missed 1957 and 1958, and Ron Kramer missed 1958. When the Berlin Crisis flared up in 1961, Paul Hornung, Ray Nitschke, and Boyd Dowler were called up to the Reserves. For a good portion of that championship season, those three players would miss practice during the week while they were on duty and would get a one-day pass to show up for the game on Sunday. Hornung still led the league in scoring, but Ben Agajanian was signed to do the kicking for a few weeks during the season. Hornung did the place-kicking in the title game, though, and scored a record 19 points.

Future Packers who first served in the military are harder to trace, but there have been several, including one-time Marines Al Carmichael, Mike Mercer, and Macarthur Lane. In recent years, the main Packers connections to the military have been the players Ron Wolf brought in from the service academies, although Vaughn Booker did sandwich a tour in the Army between his college football days. Bob Kuberski and Mike Wahle from Annapolis, and Chris Gizzi from the Air Force Academy, all have played for the Packers. In the first game after 9/11, in 2001, the sight of Air Force Reservist Chris Gizzi leading the team on the field wearing his Packer gear and waving the Stars and Stripes was a stirring moment that makes one reflect back on so many players like Dick Wildung—and especially Smiley Johnson—who came through in the clutch for this nation.

FOR FURTHER INFORMATION

Barnett, Bob. "When the Packers Went to War," *The Coffin Corner*. 1983. Available online at www.footballresearch.com/articles/frpage.cfm?topic'packwar.

Poling, Jerry. *Downfield! Untold Stories of the Green Bay Packers*. Madison, WI: Prairie Oak Press, 1996. (177-9)

Porter, David L., ed. *Biographical Dictionary of American Sports: Football*. New York: Greenwood Press, 1987. (651-2)

THE WOLF ERA
SANTANA DOTSON
DEFENSIVE TACKLE 1996–2001

WHO'S WORN THE NUMBER Lucky 1955, Forester 1960–63, Voss 1964–65, Peay 1968–72, Branstetter 1973, Fanucci 1974, Basinger 1974, M. Jackson 1976–80, Arland Thompson 1981, B. Jones 1984, Shumate 1985, Ploeger 1986, Drost 1987r, Scott Jones 1991, C. Gray 1992, Gil Brown 1993, Gary Brown 1994–95, S. Dotson 1996–2001, K. Barry 2002.

ORIGINATOR Defensive tackle Bill Lucky 1955 was a former Baylor teammate of Steve Dowden (see top 70). He also lasted one year before becoming a successful high school coach.

LONGEST TENURE Santana Dotson 1996–2001.

NUMBER CHANGES Linebacker Bill Forester wore 69 from 1953–59; defensive tackle Gilbert Brown wore 93 from 1994–99 and 2001–02; tackle Gary Brown wore 68 in 1996.

OTHER NOTABLES Bill Forester (see 69).

ONE TO FORGET 1964 number one-pick Lloyd Voss was a big disappointment on the defensive line. He was packaged to Pittsburgh for another number one pick which was squandered on Bob Hyland. Voss would spend seven more years in the league.

SANTANA DOTSON In 1964, defensive tackle Alphonse Dotson was the initial first-team All American from Grambling, a small, historically black college in Louisiana that was long a football powerhouse. On the recommendation of Packer defensive end and Grambling alumnus Willie Davis (originally a 15th-round pick of the Browns), Vince Lombardi selected Dotson with the second pick of the 1965 draft. Dotson, however, elected to sign with the Kansas City Chiefs of the rival American Football League. Dotson made the Chiefs' squad, but moved to the Dolphins in 1966 and the Raiders in 1968. The Raiders had drafted their own defensive tackle, named Carleton Oats, in 1965. Oats was taken in the 21st round by Oakland and was the first draft pick chosen on the advice of Raider scout and front office assistant Ron Wolf. Oats would play eight years for Oakland and finish his career with a final season in Green Bay in 1973.

As for Al Dotson, he would never be as good a pro player as he was in college, and he finished his career with the Raiders in 1970. His time in Oakland did prove productive, however. He and his wife had a son in 1970 that they named Santana, for the famous Indian Chief noted for his philosophy of "with unity comes strength." Santana Dotson became a star defensive tackle in college just like his father, and was drafted in the fifth round by Tampa Bay in 1992. Santana spent four uneventful years with the Bucs before being signed as a free agent by Ron Wolf for the Green Bay Packers Super Bowl run in 1996.

Santana Dotson was tall and rangy with the ability to stop the run and rush the passer, and he fit into defensive coach Fritz Shurmer's scheme immediately. He has never made an All Pro team or played in a Pro Bowl, but is an intelligent man and player and has been a leader on the field. In 2000 he suffered a serious leg injury on the field and missed the whole year, but worked hard to come back and contribute to the playoff run in 2001, his last year in Green Bay.

Ron Wolf left Green Bay the year before, but his impact on the franchise was so immense that he was inducted into the Packer Hall of Fame in that same year of 2000. Wolf left Oakland in 1976 to run the new, expansion Tampa Bay Buccaneers. Within a few years, he had brought in enough talent for the Bucs to reach the playoffs, but he and Coach John McKay did not get along. Wolf returned to Oakland for several years, and then moved on to the Jets, but never had the absolute authority over an organization that he craved. Then Bob Harlan came calling and Wolf took over complete control of running the Packers in November, 1991. Friends cautioned him against going to Green Bay which was considered a dead-end franchise at the time, like the Cardinals—a place where no one can ever win. In the 24 years between Lombardi and Wolf, the Packers had won only 42% of their games, fourth worst in the league. They had made the playoffs only twice in that time, the worst in the league, and not once did they have back-to-back winning seasons.

In the ten years of the Wolf Era, Green Bay's won-lost record of 92-52 was second only to San Francisco's, and the Packers made the playoffs six times, the Super Bowl twice, and won a world championship. How did Wolf turn it around? He set up a stable organization of talented people. He made the correct crucial decisions of hiring Mike Holmgren to coach, trading for Brett Favre, and signing free agent Reggie White. With his scouting background, he proved himself to be among the very best on the NFL's annual draft day. His trading skills were a throwback to Lombardi; while every Wolf deal was not a home run, he never made a bad trade in Green Bay. His record on free agents, both resigning his own and signing those from other teams, was mixed but positive overall. Above all, he showed himself to be a throwback to Lombardi in one other critical area, understanding the urgency of winning, "My entire previous work experience has taught me that winning was the only thing that mattered, yet the Packers were finishing off a horrible 4-12 season and the prevailing atmosphere was, inconceivably, as pleasant as could be. No one really seemed concerned, no one reflected a sense of urgency. Having spent most of my career with the Raiders, I had learned that anything less than winning was failure. But not with the Packers. Losing had become acceptable." (Wolf, 29)

Wolf could be brutally honest in his pursuit of excellence. As he early on told Brian Noble, a veteran linebacker whom he regarded as a good player, "You're only here until I can replace you." It was that attitude that brought Santana Dotson to Green Bay to replace the popular John Jurkovic, and it was that attitude—from Wolf's hand-picked successor Mike Sherman—that bid Santana farewell six years later. Winning games has been paramount, but there have been other effects in addition to the victories on the field. All home games are sold out and no-shows are hard to find in Lambeau. Packer tradition is embraced by the organization as a blessing and not seen as a burden impossible to live up to. Green Bay moved to the top echelon in NFL licensed merchandise sales. It became easier to attract talented people to work for the Packers. A $295-million renovation to aging, venerated Lambeau Field was approved by voters.

Perhaps the most difficult time for Wolf was in his last few years as he attempted to put the pieces in place so that the success could continue. His first move in that regard was a disaster, hiring Ray Rhodes who had failed in Philadelphia to replace Seattle-bound Mike Holmgren. The 1999 Packers reflected the same weaknesses that plagued Rhodes' Eagles: their special teams stunk, their defense gave up too many yards and too many points, and the whole team was infected by a lack of discipline. Just as in Philadelphia, Rhodes would continually promise that he would fix the problems, but nothing was ever done. Wolf thought he was getting a tough guy, but a little research would have shown that Rhodes' tough guy image was all bluster and players could do as they pleased. I am personally convinced that Rhodes was hired partially for racial reasons, although Wolf denies this. The Packers had been complaining for years that their talented black offensive coordinator, Sherman Lewis, was being ignored as a head coaching candidate. Wolf did not want to hire Lewis himself, though, probably because he did not want to repeat Lombardi's mistake of hiring a quiet, mild-mannered, able assistant to follow a fiery disciplinarian. However, after all the Packers complaints in behalf of Lewis, if they were to hire an anonymous white coach, the black players on the team would understandably be upset that the popular Lewis was ignored. Rhodes was available, Wolf knew him from his days as defensive coordinator in Green Bay, and convinced himself that Ray would be the tough guy he wanted. To his credit, Wolf quickly fired Rhodes after one year— you're only here till I can replace you. At that point, Jesse Jackson himself tried to involve himself in the process in Green Bay, but backed off after a phone conversation with Wolf. In a surprise move, Wolf hired an anonymous white coach, Mike Sherman of Mike Holmgren's Seattle staff. Wolf was so pleased with Sherman's first year as coach that he made him general manager in his final and most important move for the future of the Packers. Sherman has big shoes to fill.

FOR FURTHER INFORMATION

Hollenback, Chris. "A Quiet Leader," *Packer Insider.* Available at www.packers.com/team/insider/dotson.html

Wolf, Ron, and Paul Attner. *The Packer Way: Nine Stepping Stones to Building a Winning Organization.* New York: St. Martin's Press, 1998.

DICK THE BRUISER
DICK AFFLIS • GUARD AND DEFENSIVE TACKLE 1953

WHO'S WORN THE NUMBER R. Kahler 1942, McPherson 1943–45, S. Barnett 1946, Kekeris 1948, T. Johnson 1952, Afflis 1953, Helluin 1954–57, Kimmell 1958, J. Miller 1960, Davidson 1961, S. Wright 1964–67, Himes 1968–77, Lathrop 1979–80, B. Oates 1981, G. Boyd 1983, Neville 1986–88, Auer 1987r, Bone 1987r, M. Hall 1989–90, Gabbard 1991, Salem 1992, E. Dotson 1993–2002.

ORIGINATOR Tackle Royal (King Kong) Kahler, 1942, the brother of back Bob Kahler. The brothers teamed with Herman Rohrig (see top 80) both at Nebraska and Green Bay.

LONGEST TENURE Tackle Dick Himes 1968–77, a long-time starter known for being grumpy to reporters. He was one of 14 picketing Packers arrested outside Lambeau Field during the 1974 players' strike.

NUMBER CHANGES Guard Solon Barnett wore 27 in 1945; guard Dick Afflis wore 15 in 1951, 62 in 1952, and 75 in 1954; guard Tom Neville wore 61 in 1992; replacement Todd Auer also wore 98.

OTHER NOTABLES Defensive end Ben Davidson would eventually become a star with the Raiders and face the Packers in the second Super Bowl; Steve Wright was a quirky oddball on Lombardi's Packers, but the tackle's legacy as the common man in the NFL lives on in two ways. First, is his amusing memoir, *I'd Rather Be Wright.* Second, when he played for New York, Steve was the model for the gladiator trophy awarded each year to the NFL Man of Year—now called the Walter Payton Award. The award is presented to the player who best combines excellence on the field with community service off it. Ironically, in its 31 years, it has never been given to a Green Bay Packer, although Jim Flanigan, Jr. won it when he was on the Bears; tackle Earl Dotson was the Packers' best lineman throughout the 1990s.

ONE TO FORGET Guard Tom Neville was a 300-pound gentle giant who had two tours in Green Bay as he bounced from team to team until his career ended in 1993. After football, he lived in Fairbanks, Alaska, with his wife and child. He became emotionally troubled and in 1998 traveled for unknown reasons to Fresno, California, where he had attended college. There, police received calls that he was acting bizarrely and out of control at a hotel near the Fresno State campus. He voluntarily surrendered a loaded rifle to them and was admitted to a mental hospital. After two days in the facility, Neville burst through a locked steel door and escaped. Police tried to subdue him, but he tossed several of them aside and reached for an officer's gun.

PACKERS BY THE NUMBERS

At that point, police opened fire and killed him. Various explanations were put forth as to why Neville exploded: bad medication, the death of his parents in 1994, the loss of his playing career, the inability to find a coaching job. Ultimately, it will remain a tragic mystery.

DICK AFFLIS Dick Afflis played guard, tackle, and defensive line in his four years with Green Bay and wore a higher uniform number each year. He was a credible performer, but will never be inducted into the Pro Football Hall of Fame. However, his chances of being selected for the Professional Wrestling Hall of Fame that opened in the spring of 2002 would have to be pretty good since he had a 35-year career within the scripted ring as "Dick the Bruiser."

Dick wasn't the greatest lineman the Packers ever had, but he was one of the most interesting characters. In college he moved around a lot. He left Purdue after punching one of the coaches and departed Miami after being caught making book. He lasted only two weeks at Notre Dame and also passed through Alabama before landing in the desert at Nevada-Reno. He was drafted in the 16th round by the Packers and was most noteworthy for his strength. He was an early proponent of bodybuilding and looked odd in his football uniform with his 52-inch barrel chest and 30-inch wasp waist.

Afflis was not someone to make angry. In the early 1950s, many Packer fans would take the train to Chicago and back for the Bears game, and sometimes they would run into players in the dining car. Once a fan got in Afflis' face about the game on the trip home, and Dick broke off a beer bottle on the bar and invited the fan to do something about it. The sight of an angry Dick the Bruiser holding a broken beer bottle was enough to quell the disturbance.

He made an impression when he arrived in Green Bay for his first training camp in 1951, fresh from working as a bouncer in Las Vegas. He was packing two .45s in shoulder holsters and asked to check them at the Northland Hotel front desk. Another time, Hawg Hanner attempted to instigate some trouble when he told Afflis that fellow lineman Jerry Helluin considered himself stronger than Dick. Dick went and found Helluin and they engaged in a series of feats of strength, smashing beer cans with their hands and so forth, until Afflis smashed a beer can on his face causing the blood to run down his contorted visage. At that, Helluin grasped that discretion truly is the better part of valor and said simply, "You win." Dick was a good man to have on your side. The Packers' first black player, Bob Mann, once hailed a cab in Baltimore, but the driver would not let him in the car. Dick took matters in his own large hands by opening the passenger door and dragging the driver out on to the sidewalk. At that point the cabbie decided to cease his discriminatory business practices, and Mann got his ride.

Afflis left the game after the 1954 season to go into professional wrestling, from which he made a lucrative living for the next 35 years. Reminiscent of his altercation with Jerry Helluin, Dick's trademark was blood streaming down his face from a hidden patch on his head, and his billing was the "World's Most Dangerous Wrestler." He was obviously a difficult man to get along with, and was married four times. One time in the ring, he slugged the referee, earning himself a suspension. Another time he went to the Indiana restaurant of his rival Cowboy Bob Ellis and turned over tables and broke windows.

He continued to cross paths with football from time to time. He and his new bride were sitting on the Packers bench for a Bears game in Wrigley Field one year. When a Packer broke off a long return, Dick's wife got so excited that she followed the player into the end zone. A fight ensued with Wrigley ushers about this, and both Dick and his wife were thrown out of the park.

During Alex Karras' gambling suspension in 1963, the banished Lion did some wrestling and arranged for a bout with Dick. The week before the match Afflis showed up at Karras' tavern as a staged publicity stunt to hype the fight, but the faux trash-talking session turned serious, as Afflis lost his temper and police were called. Afflis was found swinging a pool cue, and it took eight policemen to subdue him, dragging Dick out with hands and feet bound. One policeman's wrist was broken in the scuffle and Dick took a thumb to the eye. The match itself was held at the Olympia in Detroit. At first it went according to script, and Karras even managed to hit Afflis' patch, causing the fake blood to flow. Once again, for whatever reason, the script was abandoned, and Afflis grasped Karras around the Adam's apple and pinned him to the mat. Afflis' comment on all this was that, "Football players should leave wrestling to wrestlers and go back to their betting." Other Packers who dabbled in wrestling include Hank Bruder and Buckets Goldenberg in the 1930s and Steve McMichael and Reggie White in the 1990s. In addition, Larry Pfohl, who spent a year on injured reserve for Green Bay in the 1980s, became much better known as Lex Luger of the WWF in the 1990s.

Dick spoke in a distinctive gravelly voice that was caused by a football injury to his larnyx. During his wrestling career, he broke both ankles, several ribs, and his nose on his way to being called the most disliked and feared man of the profession. For what it's worth, he won the 1966 American Wrestling Association title and was a five-time tag-team champion with "The Crusher." In his second career, he was among the wealthiest of wrestlers and also had a construction business and an Indianapolis tavern called the Harem Athletic Club. He died at he age of 62 lifting weights in his Florida home when a blood vessel in his esophagus burst, causing extensive internal bleeding. Although he died relatively young, he lived just as he chose, a full and contentious life.

FOR FURTHER INFORMATION

Cameron, Steve. *The Packers! Seventy-Five Seasons of Memories and Mystique in Green Bay.* Dallas, TX: Taylor Publishing, 1996. (162-3)

D'Amato, Gary, and Cliff Christl. *Mudbaths and Bloodbaths: The Inside Story of the Bears-Packers Rivalry.* Madison, WI: Prairie Oak Press, 1997. (192-3)

"Dick the Bruiser: Uncontrolled Fury," *Wrestling World.* 1/63. (34+)

Karras, Alex, with Herb Gluck. *Even Big Guys Cry.* New York: Holt, Rinehart and Winston, 1977.

Murray, Jim. "Wrestling's Resident Rat Fink," *Los Angeles Times.* (date unknown)

Plimpton, George. *Paper Lion.* New York: Harper and Row, 1966. (315-6)

Weinstein, Marc. "Dick the Bruiser Takes a Licking and Keeps on Ticking," *Indianapolis Business Journal.* 4/1/85 (10A)

COLLEGE HEROICS
AARON TAYLOR • GUARD 1995–97

WHO'S WORN THE NUMBER Serini 1952, Cifelli 1953, K. Beck 1959–60, Gassert 1962, J. McDowell 1964, Weatherwax 1966–67, 1969, Hardy 1970, Vanoy 1972, Oats 1973, Okoniewski 1974–75, Skinner 1978, Edwards 1979, Braggs 1981–83, Veingrad 1986–87 and 1989–90, Caldwell 1987r, Robbins 1992–93, A. Taylor 1995–97, K. McKenzie 2002.

ORIGINATOR Guard Washington Serini 1952. After four unbearable years in Chicago, Wash spent his final year as a pro in Green Bay. The University of Kentucky retired his jersey in 1992.

LONGEST TENURE Tackle Alan Veingrad 1986–90. After five years in Green Bay, Veingrad moved to Dallas as a Plan B free agent for the last two years of his career and won a Super Bowl ring. After retiring, he spoke of the alienation and pressures of being a Jewish football player.

NUMBER CHANGES Defensive end Keith McKenzie wore 95 from 1996–99.

OTHER NOTABLES None.

ONE TO FORGET Defensive tackle Kevin Hardy came out of Notre Dame with unlimited potential and knee problems. He was the number-one draft choice of New Orleans, but was given to the 49ers by Commissioner Pete Rozele as partial ompensation for Dave Parks, who signed that year with the Saints as a free agent. Hardy was in San Francisco for one year before they traded him to Green Bay for a number-two pick. He spent a year with the Packers before being traded to San Diego for another number one (who turned out to be Jerry Tagge). How he was still seen to be worth a number one after washing out of three cities in two years is a testament to his unused talent.

AARON TAYLOR Injuries are a sad fact of life in the NFL. Careers are commonly diminished, shortened, and ended by one misstep, one slip, one bad twist, or one wrong turn. Broken legs slowed Willie Buchanon; a broken leg coupled with hip and shoulder injuries altered the arc of Lynn Dickey's career; Gale Gillingham and Rich Moran blew out their knees, Eddie Lee Ivery blew out his knee in his first game and then reinjured it two years later; Nelson Toburen, Tim Lewis, and Sterling Sharpe injured their necks and had to retire immediately; Don Majkowski ruined his shoulder;

Mark D'Onofrio tore up his hamstring after two games; Robert Brooks and Craig Newsome tore the anterior cruciate ligaments in their knees; Mark Chmura severely hurt his back.

Aaron Taylor came out of college a two-time consensus All American and the winner of the Lombardi Award as the best college lineman in the nation in his senior year at Notre Dame. The Packers grabbed him with the 13th pick in the first round of the 1994 draft. At 6'4" 300 pounds, he was big and strong and fast, and the Packers thought they had an anchor for their offensive line for years. Like Ivery and D'Onofrio, though, Taylor got hurt before his career even got started. He tore up his knee in training camp and sat out his rookie year on the injured reserve list.

He fought back from the first knee injury and started at right guard throughout the 1995 season until he tore up his other knee in the first game of the playoffs. Again he fought his way back, rehabilitating the other knee and playing in 1996 and 1997 with braces on both knees. He got to two Super Bowls and was a decent player, but was probably only the fifth best starter on the team's offensive line. As the Packers watched Taylor sign a four-year, $10.8-million free-agent contract with the Chargers in 1998, Ron Wolf said of him, "He came back and he started, which is a great credit to him and the job that he did. He's a pretty good player. He's got to feel proud of his accomplishments here. He's just not the player he was before he had those injuries. It was most noticeable in the passing game. He's not as flexible as he was, and he doesn't have the mobility he once had." (McGinn)

Taylor had that flexibility and mobility at Notre Dame. He was the third Lombardi Award winner to be drafted by the Packers, but was the first to sign with them. The award, named after the famous Green Bay coach, was instituted in 1970 and was first given to an undersized middle guard from Ohio State named Jim Stillwagon, who was drafted in the fifth round, appropriately by the Packers. Stillwagon instead headed for Canada. The 1978 winner, Bruce Clark of Penn State, did the same thing after being selected first by Green Bay in the 1980 draft. Notre Dame's Ross Browner and Texas' Tony Degrate were two other Lombardi winners who started with the Bengals and played briefly with the Pack, and current Packer Jamal Reynolds of Florida State won the award in 2001. In addition, Stillwagon won the Outland Trophy, also given to the top lineman in college ball, as did Kentucky's Bob Gain, who also went to Canada rather than sign with Green Bay. Ross Browner and Miami's Russell Maryland were two other Outland winners who spent brief time with the Packers.

Packer players have won other major college awards. Green Bay Heisman Trophy winners include: Minnesota halfback Bruce Smith, Notre Dame quarterback Paul Hornung, Brigham Young quarterback Ty Detmer, Michigan receiver Desmond Howard, and Florida quarterback Danny Wuerffel. Colorado running back Rashan Salaam was signed as a free agent at the end of the 1998 season by the Pack, but was never activated. Packer Maxwell Club Award winners include: Notre Dame lineman Ross Browner, Penn State quarterback Chuck Fusina, Ty Detmer, Desmond Howard, and Danny Wuerffel. Brigham Young's Jim McMahon, Ty Detmer (twice), and Danny Wuerffel (twice) all won the Davey O'Brien Award as the best quarterback in the country. Florida State's Terrell Buckley won the Jim Thorpe Award as the best defensive back, Terry Glenn nabbed the Fred Biletnikoff Award as the finest wide receiver, and non-Packer Rashan Salaam won the Doak Walker Award for best running back.

The list of consensus All Americans who later played, sometimes only briefly, with Green Bay is lengthy. Jim Crowley, 1924; Larry Bettencourt, 1927; Tom Nash, 1927; Elmer Sleight, 1929; Milo Lubratovich, 1930; Jess Quatse, 1931; Joe Kurth, 1932; Ernie Smith, 1932; Beattie Feathers, 1933; George Sauer, 1933; Don Hutson, 1934, Bill Lee, 1934; Av Daniel, 1936; Paul Christman, 1939; Urban Odson, 1940; Bruce Smith, 1941; Dick Wildung, 1941–42; Buddy Burris, 1948; Clayton Tonnemaker, 1949; Babe Parilli, 1950–51; Carlton Massey, 1953; Art Hunter, 1953; Ron Kramer, 1955–56; Norm Masters, 1955, Paul Hornung, 1955; Lou Michaels, 1956–57; Dan Currie, 1957; Donny Anderson, 1965; Jim Grabowski, 1965; Aaron Brown, 1965; Kevin Hardy, 1967; Ted Hendricks, 1967–68; Mike McCoy, 1969; Ed O'Neil, 1973; Dave Brown, 1973–74; Derrell Gofourth, 1976; Ross Browner, 1976–77; John Jefferson, 1977; Chuck Fusina, 1978; Bruce Clark, 1978–79; Steve McMichael, 1979; George Cumby, 1979; Ray Stachowitz, 1980; Jim McMahon, 1981; Dave Drechsler, 1982; Reggie White, 1983; Mossy Cade, 1983; Tony Degrate, 1984; John Holland, 1985; Brent Fullwood, 1986; Keith Jackson, 1986–87; Chuck Cecil, 1987; Tony Mandarich, 1988; Leroy Butler, 1989; Russell Maryland, 1990; Ty Detmer, 1990–91; Desmond Howard, 1991; Santana Dotson, 1991; Terrell Buckley, 1991; Aaron Taylor, 1992–93; LeShon Johnson, 1993; Ki–Jana Carter, 1994; Terry Glenn, 1995; Jared Tomich, 1995–96; Danny Wuerffel, 1996; Jamal Reynolds, 2001. Several Packers have been Division 1-AA All Americans as well: Mark Cannon, 1984; Tony DeLuca, 1983; John Dorsey, 1983; John Jurkovic, 1989; Tim Hauck, 1989; Billy Lyon 1996; and Darren Sharper, 1996.

Of that long list, only Don Hutson, Dick Wildung, Ron Kramer, Paul Hornung, Dan Currie, Donny Anderson, and John Holland have been elected to the Packer Hall of Fame, although Reggie White, Keith Jackson, and Leroy Butler likely will be elected when they become eligible. The Big Man on Campus does not necessarily assume unqualified success in the pro ranks. Fate sometimes intervenes, as happened with Aaron Taylor. With San Diego he lasted only two years before walking away and retiring as a battered hulk, a long distance from his college heroics.

FOR FURTHER INFORMATION
McGinn, Bob. "Chargers Sign Taylor," *Milwaukee Journal Sentinel.* 3/7/98. (1 Sports)

Rauen, Karen. "Taylor Develops Game Plan for Success After Football,"
Green Bay Press Gazette. 12/30/01. Available online at
http://cgi.greenbaypressgazette.com/cgi-bin/packerwrapper.pl?URL' or
http://www.packersnews.com/archives/news/pack_1865276.shtml&AFFIL'packgroup

1960s IN A BOX
HENRY JORDAN • DEFENSIVE TACKLE 1959–69

WHO'S WORN THE NUMBER Olsonoski 1948, Steiner 1950–51, Zatkoff 1953–56, Vereen 1957, H. Jordan 1959–69, Withrow 1971, D. Smith 1971, A. Brown 1973–74, Roller 1975–78, K. Brown 1980, Huffman 1981–85, S. Collier 1987r, Haley 1988, Archambeau 1990–92, Widdell 1992, Dingle 1999, Kampman 2002.

ORIGINATOR Center Larry Olsonoski 1948 was a fourth round pick from the University of Minnesota who was traded to the New York Bulldogs in his second year.

LONGEST TENURE Henry Jordan 1959–69

NUMBER CHANGES Larry Olsonowski wore 46 in 1988-89; Cal Withrow also wore 58 in 1971–73; tackle Steve Collier also wore 70 and 92 in his three games as a replacement player and 64 for the rest of 1987.

OTHER NOTABLES Defensive back Rebel Steiner was best known for returning an interception 94 yards for a TD in a 31–21 win over the Bears in 1950. That set a team record that lasted 34 years until Tim Lewis went 99 yards with a pick. Rebel was his real name; Bob "Zany" Zatkoff was a two–time All Pro linebacker and played in three Pro Bowls. He was known to drive his helmet into opponents' chests. On occasion, he took out two or more players in a single game. Dave Roller was a fan favorite in the late 1970s who once led the team in sacks.

ONE TO FORGET Center Cal Withrow was obtained from the Chargers for a 17th–round draft pick in 1971. He and fifth–round pick Donnell Smith both wore Henry Jordan's 74 that year, but neither would be mistaken for a Hall of Famer.

HENRY JORDAN Henry Jordan was a small, devastatingly quick, and intelligent pass-rushing defensive tackle. He was originally drafted by the Browns with a fifth-round pick they had obtained from the Packers for Don King and Gene Donaldson, who were both gone from Green Bay within a year. The Browns traded Jordan to the Packers for a fourth-round pick in one of Lombardi's first deals. He was named All Pro five times and played in four Pro Bowls in his Hall of Fame career. In perhaps his most memorable game, he sacked Rams quarterback Roman Gabriel four times in the 1967 playoffs to help the Packers advance to the Ice Bowl. Colts Hall of Fame guard Jim Parker said of him that, "After I play Green Bay my ankles hurt all week. I had to stay on the balls of my feet against Henry because I never know what he's going to do next. Other tackles don't have Henry's moves." Some were undoubtedly moves Henry picked up as he advanced to the NCAA finals in wrestling in 1957.

NUMBER 74

PACKERS BY THE NUMBERS

Henry was typical of the 1960s Packers in a number of ways. He was fast and smart; linemen and linebackers in particular had to be able to move and think in Lombardi's system. Henry also was articulate and witty; he was president of his class four years in a row in high school, vice-president of his class at the University of Virginia, and, like so many of his teammates, always good for a clever comment. Once, he said he was going to continue playing for "the love of the game, the love of money, and the fear of Lombardi." Another time, after a win, Jordan's elation was tempered by the thought that under Lombardi, "We'll walk into the movies Tuesday morning and we'll think we lost the game." In the 1960s, the Packers were all over magazines, newspapers, and television because they won and because they were extremely good at dealing with the media.

After retirement, Jordan, again like so many of his teammates, was very successful in business. The Packers of that era coupled their intelligence with Lombardi-like discipline to succeed in a number of arenas. Jordan unfortunately suffered a fatal heart attack while jogging in 1977. He was 42 and sadly left a wife and three children. His election to Canton was posthumous.

FOR FURTHER INFORMATION

Anderson, Dave, "A Packer in Pursuit of Football Fish," *Sport.* 38, December 1964. (52-4)

Grosshandler, Stan. "The Executives: 'We Thought Like Champs'" *The Coffin Corner.* II 1980. Available online at: www.footballresearch.com/articles/frpage.cfm?topic'gbexecs.

Johnson, Chuck. *The Greatest Packers of Them All.* New York: Putnam, 1968. (133-41)

Kramer, Jerry, with Dick Schaap. *Distant Replay.* New York: G.P. Putnam, 1985. (94-102)

Lea, Bud. "Quickness, Humor: Trademarks of Jordan, New 'Famer'" *Green Bay Packers 1995 Yearbook.* (73-5)

Porter, David L., ed. *Biographical Dictionary of American Sports: 1989–1992 Supplement for Baseball, Football, Basketball, and Other Sports.* New York: Greenwood Press, 1992. (429-30)

Smith, Don. "Henry Jordan," *The Coffin Corner.* XVII. Available online at: www.footballresearch.com/articles/frpage.cfm?topic'jordanh.

THE PACKERS IN THE 1960S—TITLETOWN USA

WHERE THEY PLAYED: Lambeau Field (known as City Stadium 1957–64), 1957–; County Stadium in Milwaukee, 1953–94.

HOW THE GAME WAS PLAYED: The wide-open passing attacks of the 1950s were countered by the Packers' emphasis on basic football, blocking and tackling. Some likened the Packers' signature play of the decade, the power sweep, to the pulling linemen in a single-wing running attack. As the decade progressed, rushing and defense were stressed more and more throughout the league. Tom Landry also started calling the plays, even using messenger quarterbacks at one point. Increasingly, teams began to use roster spots for kickers and/or punters.

DECADE WON-LOST RECORD: 96-37-5 .714 + 9-1 in the playoffs.

RECORD AGAINST THE BEARS: 15-5.

RECORD AGAINST THE LIONS: 11-6-3.

RECORD AGAINST THE VIKINGS: 11-7.

RECORD AGAINST THE GIANTS: 5-0 (including 2-0 in the playoffs).

RECORD AGAINST THE COWBOYS: 6-0 (including 2-0 in the playoffs).

RECORD AGAINST THE COLTS: 11-7 (including 1-0 in the playoffs).

PLAYOFF APPEARANCES: 1960, 1961, 1962, 1965, 1966, 1967, plus appearances in the ill-conceived Runner-Up Bowl in 1963 and 1964.

CHAMPIONSHIPS: 1961, 1962, 1965, 1966, and 1967.

UNSUNG HERO: Jack Vainisi, the team's head scout throughout the 1950s. It was his drafting acumen that accumulated the talent that Lombardi molded into a dynasty in the 1960s. Tragically, he died during the 1960 season at the age of 33.

HEAD COACHES: Vince Lombardi, 1959–67; Phil Bengtson, 1968–70.

BEST PLAYER: Lombardi's favorite, Forrest Gregg; the players' favorite, Paul Hornung; player with the greatest football intellect, Bart Starr; player with the most impact, Jim Taylor; most vocal leader, Ray Nitschke.

HALL OF FAMERS: Jim Ringo, Bart Starr, Forrest Gregg, Paul Hornung, Ray Nitschke, Jim Taylor, Vince Lombardi, Emlen Tunnell, Henry Jordan, Willie Davis, Willie Wood, and Herb Adderley.

PACKER HALL OF FAMERS: Jim Ringo, Bart Starr, Forrest Gregg, Paul Hornung, Ray Nitschke, Jim Taylor, Vince Lombardi, Emlen Tunnell, Henry Jordan, Willie Davis, Willie Wood, Herb Adderley, Lionel Aldridge, Donny Anderson, Phil Bengtson, Ken Bowman, Zeke Bratkowski, Lee Roy Caffey, Fred Carr, Don Chandler, Dan Currie, Carroll Dale, Boyd Dowler, Bill Forester, Gale Gillingham, Hank Gremminger, Dave Hanner, Bob Jeter, Gary Knafelc, Ron Kostelnik, Jerry Kramer, Ron Kramer, Max McGee, Elijah Pitts, Dave Robinson, Bob Skoronski, Fuzzy Thurston, Travis Williams, and Jesse Whittenton.

LEAGUE LEADERS: Paul Hornung—TDs 1960; points 1960, 61; Tom Moore—kickoff return avg 1960; Bart Starr passing % 1962, 68, 69; passing avg gain 1966, 67, 68; Jim Taylor—rushing yards 1962; rushing TDs 1961, 62; TDs 1962; points 1962; Travis Williams—kickoff return avg 1967; kickoff return TDs 1967; Willie Wood—interceptions 1962; punt return avg 1961; punt return TDs 1961.

AWARD WINNERS: Paul Hornung—MVP, 1960; Bart Starr—MVP 1966; Super Bowl MVP 1966, 67; Jim Taylor—MVP 1962; Vince Lombardi—Coach of the Year 1961.

ALL PROS: Bill Forester, 1960, 61, 62, 63; Forrest Gregg, 1960, 61, 62, 63, 64, 65, 66, 67; Paul Hornung, 1960; Henry Jordan, 1960, 61, 62, 63, 64; Jerry Kramer, 1960, 62, 63, 66, 67; Jim Ringo, 1960, 61, 62, 63; Dan Currie, 1961, 62; Jim Taylor, 1961, 62; Fuzzy Thurston, 1961, 62; Jesse Whittenton, 1961; Herb Adderley, 1962, 63, 65, 66, 69; Willie Davis, 1962, 64, 65, 66, 67; Ron Kramer, 1962; Willie Wood, 1963, 64, 65, 66, 67, 68; Ray Nitschke, 1964, 65, 66; Lee Roy Caffey, 1966; Bart Starr, 1966; Bob Jeter, 1967; Dave Robinson, 1967, 68, 69; Gale Gillingham, 1969.

PRO BOWLERS: Dan Currie, 1960; Bill Forester, 1960, 61, 62; Forrest Gregg, 1960, 61, 62, 63, 64, 65, 66, 67, 68; Paul Hornung, 1960; Henry Jordan, 1960, 61, 63, 66; Jim Ringo, 1960, 61, 62, 63; Bart Starr, 1960, 61, 62, 66; Jim Taylor, 1960, 61, 62*, 63, 64; Max McGee,

1961; Jesse Whittenton, 1961, 63; Jerry Kramer, 1962, 63, 67; Ron Kramer, 1962; Tom Moore, 1962; Willie Wood, 1962, 64, 65, 66, 67, 68, 69; Herb Adderley, 1963, 64, 65, 66, 67; Willie Davis, 1963, 64, 65, 67; Ray Nitschke, 1964; Lee Roy Caffey, 1965; Boyd Dowler, 1965, 67; Dave Robinson, 1966, 67, 69; Bob Skoronski, 1966; Don Chandler, 1967; Bob Jeter, 1967, 69; Donny Anderson, 1968; Carroll Dale, 1968, 69; Gale Gillingham, 1969. (* selected, but did not play)

BEST OFFENSIVE BACKFIELD: 1961—Bart Starr, QB; Paul Hornung, HB; Jim Taylor, FB; Boyd Dowler, FL.

BEST DRAFT CHOICE: Travis Williams, 4th round 1967.

BEST OVERALL DRAFT: 1963. All Pro Dave Robinson in the 1st round; starters Tom Brown #2, Lionel Aldridge #4, and Marv Fleming #11. Plus Dennis Claridge #3, Dan Grimm #5, Jan Barrett #6, Ed Holler #14, and Gene Breen #15 all made the team and Tony Liscio #3 started for the Cowboys for several years. #12 Daryle Lamonica signed with the Bills in the AFL and started for the Raiders against the Packers in Super Bowl II.

WORST DRAFT CHOICE: Defensive tackle Rich Moore, 1969 1st round, was an immobile tub.

WORST OVERALL DRAFT: 1962. Earl Gros #1, Ed Blaine #2, Gary Barnes #3, and Ron Gassert #4 all made the team and the first three played for a number of other teams in the league, but none became a star. The two stars of the draft were #14 Ernie Green who was traded to Cleveland and #17 Buck Buchanon who signed with the Chiefs (then Dallas Texans) in the AFL and became a Hall of Famer.

BEST FREE AGENT: Willie Wood, 1960, Hall of Fame safety.

BEST TRADE: 1964. Aging Jim Ringo and injury-prone Earl Gros are traded to the Eagles for future All Pro linebacker Lee Roy Caffey and 1965 #1 draft choice (Donny Anderson chosen as a future pick). Other outstanding deals included aging Dan Currie for Carroll Dale in 1965, a 3rd-rounder to the Giants for Don Chandler, also in 1965, Lloyd Voss and Gary Jeter to the Steelers in 1966 for a #1 (Bob Hyland), and Ron Rector to the Redskins also in 1966 for a #4 (Travis Williams). The Packers also received #1s in 1966 (Jim Grabowski) and 1968 (Fred Carr) respectively for Ron Kramer and Jim Taylor playing out their options.

WORST TRADE: Lombardi made no outrageously bad trades. He did give up on Ben Davidson in 1962 and traded him to the Redskins for a 5th-round pick (Jack Cvercko). He also saw that he had enough depth at running back to trade Ernie Green to the Browns for 7th-round pick (Gary Kroner).

BIGGEST OFF-FIELD EVENTS: Three things—1) The American Football League is formed and begins a war with the NFL; 2) Under Pete Rozelle's direction, NFL owners agree to pool national television money starting in 1961, allowing a small market franchise like Green Bay to compete equally; 3) Paul Hornung and Alex Karras are suspended for the entire 1963 season because of gambling. Ironically, the impact is felt strongest in 1964 when Hornung returns but has lost his touch and kicks so poorly that a number of games are literally kicked away, allowing Baltimore to take the Western Division.

BIGGEST ON-FIELD DEVELOPMENT: An expanded playoff setup arrives just in time for the Packers to take advantage to win their final Championship in 1967. If the postseason were run as in previous years, the Packers would not have gotten past the Rams and Colts in the standings to make the playoffs.

STRANGEST ON-FIELD EVENT: The 1965 Western Division playoff against the Colts, a team the Packers had beaten twice that season already. The Colts had a different quarterback each time they met the Packers that year: Unitas, then Cuozzo, and finally halfback Tom Matte in the playoff. Starr was injured on the first play of the game so Bratkowski came in for a battle of the backups. Green Bay moved the ball all day, but couldn't score. Finally, Don Chandler booted a disputed tying field goal at the end of regulation. Overtime dragged on for 13 minutes before Chandler at last won the game with another (undisputed) three-pointer, 13-10.

WORST FAILURE: The draft. Lombardi was a brilliant trader and accumulated a wealth of draft picks throughout the decade, 14 #1s and 24 extra picks altogether in the first eight rounds from 1960-69. However, he did not draft well enough for the success on the field to continue into the 1970s.

HOME ATTENDANCE: 3,157,271 in 69 games, an average attendance of 45,758. 29 Milwaukee home games averaged 47,015 while 40 Green Bay home games averaged 44,847. Green Bay had a higher average attendance from 1965 through 1969 after seating in Lambeau had been increased several times.

FIRST GAME: September 25, 1960. Green Bay loses a squeaker to Chicago at home, 17-14.

LAST GAME: December 21, 1969. The Packers ring up their highest score of the year beating the Cardinals 45-28 to clinch Phil Bengtson's only winning season.

BEST GAME: Everyone remembers the Ice Bowl, but the 1966 Championship game against Dallas was a better all-around game, and it also came down to the last few seconds. As for regular season games, Paul Hornung made the October 8, 1961, 45-7 victory over the Colts memorable by scoring a team record 33 points. Four years later, on December 12, 1965, Hornung scored five touchdowns in his last great game, beating the Colts in the fog 42-27. And beating Halas' Bears 49-0 in 1962 was sweet.

LARGEST MARGIN OF VICTORY: 56-3, 10/23/66, over the Falcons. Other wide victories included 49-0 over both the Bears and Eagles in 1962 and 55-7 over the Browns in 1967.

LARGEST MARGIN OF DEFEAT: 45-21 to the Colts, 11/5/61.

BEST OFFENSE: 1962, 415 points, the most in the league featuring the league's top rusher and scorer in Jim Taylor.

BEST DEFENSE: 1962—148 points allowed the fewest in the league. Number one in points and points allowed—no wonder they finished 13-1.

MOST GAMES PLAYED: All 138 regular-season games featured Willie Davis, Boyd Dowler, Forrest Gregg, and Willie Wood. Starr played in 133, Nitschke in 132 and Henry Jordan in 127. One of the reasons the team was so good is that the stars showed up every week.

MOST POINTS: 581, Paul Hornung.

MOST FIELD GOALS: 48 out of 83, Don Chandler; 48 out of 98, Paul Hornung.

MOST TOUCHDOWNS: 81, Jim Taylor.

MOST TOUCHDOWN PASSES: 125, Bart Starr.

PACKERS BY THE NUMBERS

MOST PASSING YARDS: 19,126, Bart Starr.

MOST RECEIVING YARDS: 6,369, Boyd Dowler.

MOST RECEPTIONS: 416, Boyd Dowler.

MOST RUSHING YARDS: 7,898, Jim Taylor.

MOST INTERCEPTIONS: 40, Willie Wood.

MOST KICKOFF RETURN YARDS: 3,080, Herb Adderley.

MOST PUNT RETURN YARDS: 1,312, Willie Wood.

BEST BOOKS: Dick Schaap, ed. *Instant Replay: The Green Bay Diary of Jerry Kramer,* World Publishing, 1968. Vince Lombardi with W.C. Heinz, *Run to Daylight,* Prentice-Hall, 1963. Paul Hornung as told to Al Silverman, *Football and the Single Man,* Double-day, 1965.

NOTED SPORTSWRITER: Chuck Johnson of the *Milwaukee Journal* wrote two books on the team during the 1960s—*The Green Bay Packers: Pro Football's Pioneer Team* and *Greatest Packers of Them All.*

BEST QUOTATIONS: "This game was our mark of distinction," —Bob Skoronski, speaking of the Ice Bowl. Henry Jordan got to the essence of Lombardi with two comments, "He treats us all alike, like dogs," and, "When he says sit, I don't look around for a chair."

BUBBLEGUM FACTOIDS: Paul Hornung's Philadelphia Gum card gets right to the point, "Paul did not play during the '63 season because of a suspension." Jerry Kramer's 1964 Philadelphia card states, "Jerry, a mountain of a man, is the NFL's top right guard. He blocks like a Mack truck." Fred Thurston's 1962 Topps card tells us that, "There's no stopping Fred when he is out to open a hole in the defender's forward wall. The power-packed center [sic] doesn't let any obstacles stand in his way."

UNUSUAL NAMES: Ben Agajanian, Lionel Aldridge, Gene Breen, Junior Coffey, Tommy Joe Crutcher, Bill Hayhoe, Urban Henry, Ed Holler, Booth Lusteg, Francis Peay, Elijah Pitts, Nelson Toburen, Phil Vandersea, Jim Weatherwax, Francis Winkler.

NICKNAMES: Titletown USA, The Frozen Tundra, "Million Dollar Babies" and "Gold Dust Twins" referring to Donny Anderson and Jim Grabowski, Donny "The Golden Palomino" Anderson, Zeke Bratkowski, Allen "Red" Brown, Babe Chandler, Dapper Dan Currie, Willie "Dr. Feelgood" Davis, Doug "Li'l Brother" Hart, Buster Hathcock, Paul "Golden Boy" or "Goat Shoulders" Hornung, Jerry "Zipper" Kramer, Ron "The Big Oaf" Kramer, Bob "Flakey" Long, Red Mack, Elijah "Gravel" or "Za Su" or "Olive" Pitts, Fuzzy Thurston, Emlen "The Gremlin" Tunnell, Jungle Jim Weatherwax, Travis "Roadrunner" Williams, and Bubba Winkler.

FASTEST PLAYER: Travis Williams.

HEAVIEST PLAYER: Rich Moore, 285 lbs.

LIGHTEST PLAYERS: Red Mack and Johnny Symank both were 180 lbs.

TOUGHEST INJURY: Nelson Toburen broke his neck on a play, was nearly paralyzed, and had to retire. Of greater importance to the play of the team on the field were Jerry Kramer's problems. His extensive medical history included a detached retina and a bro-ken ankle. Most significantly, he nearly died in1964 when some hidden slivers of wood that had been lodged in his body since he was a teenager mysteriously made him so ill that doctors expected him to die.

LOCAL BOYS: Fuzzy Thurston and Dale Hackbart were both in-staters.

FIRSTS:

Two Super Bowl Victories—1966 and 1967 seasons.

Million Dollar Gate—1961 title game.

Championship Game Highlight Film by the Company That Would Become NFL Films—1961.

176 Points in a Season—1960, Paul Hornung in 12 games.

4 Kickoff Return TDs in one season—Travis Williams 1967.

Initial Class of Pro Football Hall of Fame Inductees—1963, Cal Hubbard, Don Hutson, Curly Lambeau, and Johnny Blood.

Team to Have Its Own Hall of Fame—1967, The Hall of Fame started as a seasonal display in the concourse of the Brown County Veterans Memorial Arena.

COACHING LEGACIES

FORREST GREGG • TACKLE 1956, 1958–70

WHO'S WORN THE NUMBER Croft 1942–47, Ruetz 1951–53, Afflis 1954, Gregg 1956, 1958–70, L. Michaels 1971, Pureifory 1972–77, Barzilaukas 1978–79, R. Turner 1981–83, Ruettgers 1985–96, Heimburger 1999, J. Flanigan 2001, Tomich 2002.

ORIGINATOR Tackle Milburn "Tiny" Croft 1942–47 was the Packers first 300 pounder.

LONGEST TENURE Forrest Gregg 1956, 1958–70.

NUMBER CHANGES Guard Dick Afflis wore 15 in 1951, 62 in 1952, and 72 in 1953.

OTHER NOTABLES Dick Afflis (see 72); tackle Ken Ruetgers spent 12 years solidly protecting his quarterback's blind side only to be blind sided by knee injuries and have to retire in the very year the Packers finally won the Super Bowl. In 1995, Ruettgers cowrote a book, *Home Field Advantage: Modeling Your Life When the Score Really Counts*, on being a Christian role model for your own kids.

ONE TO FORGET The Packers book-ended the Michaels brothers, Walt and Lou, losing out on a lot of quality football. After Walt's rookie season, they traded the linebacker to the Browns in 1952 where he spent the next 12 years of his career. They obtained lineman/kicker Lou in 1971. He wore Forrest Gregg's number and finished his career booting 8 of 14 field goals for Dan Devine's first squad.

FORREST GREGG Forrest Gregg's playing career can be summed up in two words—dependable excellence. He did not play on opening day of his rookie year, but aside from the year he spent in the service he never missed another game for Green Bay. In 14 years, that adds up to 187 consecutive games played, a team record. He once said of himself as an offensive lineman, "We don't have any statistics to be remembered by so I don't want anyone to overlook the fact that I haven't missed a game since I came into the league in 1956." (Zimmerman, 28)

He wasn't just tough and durable, though, he was a great lineman. He played most of his career at tackle, but moved over to guard in 1961 when Jerry Kramer broke his leg, and he made All Pro there, too. In his career he was named All Pro nine times (each year Lombardi coached) and went to nine Pro Bowls (as a tackle, that's been surpassed only by Anthony Munoz's 11 Pro Bowl appearances). He won five championships and two Super Bowls with the Packers, and then spent his last year in Dallas earning another ring as a substitute on Tom Landry's Cowboys. He went right into the Pro Football Hall of Fame in 1977.

Lombardi said of him, "He a fine downfield blocker, too. His speed isn't great, but he's very quick off that ball and he has that mental sharpness to adjust quickly to sudden situations. He has that knack of getting in front of the runner and, with his excellent sense of timing, of making the key block." (Lombardi, 132) Vince would also call him the "best player I ever coached." Rival coach George Allen wrote, "He had size, strength, and speed—all the tools. He used his talent to the fullest. He had quick feet and hands and superior intelligence. He had the best footwork I've ever seen on an offensive lineman and the best techniques. They called him the best dancer since Fred Astaire. He did his little dance and turned people around. He never seemed to make a mistake. He seldom was beaten." (Allen, 98) In the opinion of his teammate and fellow tackle Bob Skoronski, "Forrest was the greatest tackle in the world because of his downfield blocking. He was the premier downfield blocker in the game." (Kramer, 135) Such rival players as Bob Lilly, Jim Parker, and Lenny Moore all rated Gregg as one of the best and toughest opponents they ever faced.

Gregg himself said, "No one takes delight in being hit. The pleasure is in hitting someone else . . . When you get a good downfield block and pry open a hole for a runner, it's the best feeling a lineman can experience." (Lea, 39) His battles with Hall of Famers Gino Marchetti of the Colts and Deacon Jones of the Rams were legendary for their intensity. In the 1967 playoff game against the Rams, when Deacon was at his swift and powerful peak, Gregg controlled the head slapping All Pro all day, helping the Packers to roll to a convincing victory. Jones would later complain of the icy footing in Milwaukee that day, but Gregg kept him off balance by a combination of technique and quickness, the watchwords of his entire career.

Forrest had the fiery temperament of his coach Vince Lombardi. Vince himself pointed out, "I've seen him, with that quick temper, flare at some of [his teammates] in practice." (Lombardi, 132) And so he went into coaching. After an apprenticeship of assistant coaching positions, he landed his first head coaching job with the Cleveland Browns. His tenure there would prove to be fairly representative of his coaching career. He had some success, being named NFL Coach of the Year in 1976 and successfully battling cancer, but ultimately he had a losing record and was fired. He coached Toronto in the Canadian Football League for one losing season, and then signed with Cincinnati. He took the Bengals to Super Bowl XVI, where they lost to San Francisco. After a couple of losing seasons, he resigned to return to Green Bay, where he followed up Bart Starr's crest of mediocrity with two 8-8 seasons before attempting to rebuild the team and enduring another couple of losing seasons. Again he resigned, and this time moved on to his alma mater, Southern Methodist University, which was coming back from having their football program suspended for serious NCAA violations. Later he would coach again in the CFL, with the short-lived Shreveport Pirates. His cumulative NFL coaching record was 75-85-1.

The sorry thing was that he was the most successful coach of Vince Lombardi's former players. Bart Starr, Jim Ringo, and Tom Bettis also held head coaching positions in the NFL. The combined record of all four former players was 131-187-4, with a 3-3 combined playoff record. Five of Vince's former assistant coaches also landed head jobs: Bill

PACKERS BY THE NUMBERS

Austin, Norb Hecker, Tom Fears, Phil Bengtson, and Jerry Burns. Their combined record was 110-167-7. Jerry Burns was the only one to have a winning record and the only one ever to reach the playoffs; his record was 55-46, plus 3-3 in the post-season. If you add in the 3-6 record achieved by Lombardi's personnel assistant, Pat Peppler, coaching the Falcons, the grand total for Lombardi proteges was 244-360-11, an unimpressive .406 percentage. Another former player turned coach not included here is Bill Curry, who played under Lombardi, was an assistant under Bart Starr, and spent 17 years coaching Georgia Tech, Alabama, and Kentucky, compiling an overall 79-98-4 record.

If you look at Curly Lambeau's legacy, you will find a similar story. Of Curly's players and assistants, only Cecil Isbell, Walt Kiesling, and Johnny Blood held head coaching jobs in the NFL or the AAFC. Blood and other Lambeau players such as Cub Buck and Mike Michalske also coached college football. Curly's alums combined professional record was 46-97-2, an even worse .324 percentage. Hiring Johnny Blood as head coach was akin to hiring baseball carouser Babe Ruth to manage a major league team; Ruth was bitter that he never got that chance, but his record would likely have rivaled Blood's 6-19.

Perhaps the purposeful volatility of Lombardi and Lambeau was not transferable. By contrast, the other Packer championship coach, Mike Holmgren, has a much different legacy. His former assistants who have attained head coaching positions include: Ray Rhodes, Steve Mariucci, Jon Gruden, Andy Reid, Mike Sherman, Dick Jauron, and Marty Mornhinweg. Their cumulative record through the 2002 season was 248-215-1, plus 12-14 in the playoffs. That's a solid .536 winning percentage. Having six former assistants all holding head jobs in a single year had never been accomplished before the latter six coaches did so in 2001. In 2002, all four NFC division winners were Holgren protégés. Lombardi considered himself a teacher above all, and his former players often attributed their post-football success to lessons learned from Vince. However, the coaching record of his followers would indicate that some lessons were not transmittable. Holmgren's reputation as a teacher, however, is borne out by the coaching success of his pupils. In a strange coincidence, one of those pupils, Dick Jauron, got his coaching start under Forrest Gregg as a defensive backs coach. Even stranger, he coaches the Bears with whom Gregg had a violent, heated, and unsuccessful competition as a coach. In a strange and coincidental way, the Bear coach is the connection between Vince Lombardi and Mike Holmgren.

FOR FURTHER INFORMATION

Allen, George, with Ben Olan. *Pro Football's 100 Greatest Players: Rating the Stars of Past and Present.* Indianapolis: Bobbs-Merrill, 1982. (96-8)

Kramer, Jerry, with Dick Schaap. *Distant Replay.* New York: G.P. Putnam, 1985. (43-8)

Lea, Bud. "Forrest Gregg: Guard or Tackle," *Green Bay Packers 1966 Yearbook.* (39-40)

Lombardi, Vince, with W.C. Heinz. *Run to Daylight.* Englewood Cliffs, NJ: Prentice-Hall, 1963. (132-3)

Porter, David L., ed. *Biographical Dictionary of American Sports: Football.* New York: Greenwood Press, 1987. (223-4)

Zimmerman, Paul. *The New Thinking Man's Guide to Pro Football.* New York: Simon and Schuster, 1984. (28-30)

FROZEN TUNDRA
BOB SKORONSKI • TACKLE 1956, 1959–69

WHO'S WORN THE NUMBER Crimmins 1945, T. Miller 1946, Kovatch 1947, O'Malley 1950, Dees 1952, Skoronski 1956, 1959–69, M. P. McCoy 1970–76, T. Stokes 1978–82, Carreker 1984–88, Ariey 1989, Viane 1992, H. Galbreath 1993–95, Willig 1998, Clifton 2000–02.

ORIGINATOR Guard Bernie Crimmins 1945 played and coached under Frank Leahy at Notre Dame before becoming head man at Indiana and then Purdue. Fellow Louisville resident Paul Hornung once dated his niece.

LONGEST TENURE Bob Skoronski 1956, 1959–69.

NUMBER CHANGES None.

OTHER NOTABLES End Tom Miller finished his playing career with two games for the Packers in 1946. In 1956 he began working in the front office for the team, became Lombardi's right-hand man, and stayed 32 years. He was elected to the Packer Hall of Fame in 1999; defensive tackle Mike McCoy never lived up to being the second pick in the 1970 draft, but was a presence in the middle for several seasons.

ONES TO FORGET Undersized Florida State defensive end Alphonso Carreker was a first-round pick in 1984, but produced only 18.5 sacks in five years in Green Bay. Quarterback Tom O'Malley was obtained from the Browns for a fourth round draft pick in 1950. O'Malley was disappointed to be traded to the Packers, who were so disorganized that he was not even given a playbook. On opening day 1950, after being with the team for a week, he took over for an injured Tobin Rote against the Lions. Since O'Malley didn't even know the plays, it's not surprising that he set a team record by throwing six interceptions in a 45-7 loss. He was cut the next week and went to Canada, where he led Ottawa to the Grey Cup in 1951.

BOB SKORONSKI The Packers of the 1960s featured one of the greatest offensive lines of all time. The team's four highest all-time rushing totals were achieved from 1961 through 1964, and Green Bay led the league in rushing in three of those years, despite going head-to-head with Jim Brown's Cleveland Browns. It was a disciplined group noted for their speed, strength, technique, and hustle. A famous film clip of a quick-toss play run to perfection against the Lions in 1964 shows Jimmy Taylor taking the ball 84 yards for a touchdown. The Packer player accompanying him all the way down the field is opposite-side tackle Bob Skoronski, making the final block on the play *80 yards* from the line of scrimmage.

PACKERS BY THE NUMBERS

It was the longest running play of the Lombardi years, the second longest in team history, and was immortalized on the 1965 Philadelphia Gum football card number 84, "Packers Play of the Year."

Four of the starters on the Packers' line were continually celebrated for their excellence. Hall of Famers Forrest Gregg and Jim Ringo were named All Pro and Pro Bowl teams nine and seven times respectively. Guards Jerry Kramer and Fuzzy Thurston were named All Pro five and two times respectively, and Kramer went to three Pro Bowls. Left tackle Bob Skoronski was never named to an All Pro team and made the Pro Bowl only once, in his tenth and penultimate season in the NFL. Years later he would wonder, "Was my guy the only guy who got to the quarterback? Did we always run to the right side? The captaincy of the Packers wasn't an elected position. Why did Lombardi select me?" (Kramer, 132)

One reason for Skoronski's lack of recognition was that, beginning in 1962, he alternated at left tackle with Norm Masters after Skoronski had missed time with a knee injury in 1961. Lombardi considered them to be of near equal ability, so he would start Skoronski and substitute with Masters. When Masters retired after the 1964 season, Skoronski took over the whole job. The offense itself was changing by then. Paul Hornung was not the same player and Jim Taylor was aging. They would not be replaced at the same level, and so the offense came to rely more on Bart Starr's arm and the pass-blocking skills of the line.

Bob Skoronski was a team player and did not let the lack of accolades bother him. As an ambitious child of immigrants, he was part of a family of achievers. His four brothers and sisters all went beyond Bob's bachelor's degree in marketing. Bob was the quintessential family man whose four adult children have carried on that tradition of accomplishment. He retired after the 1968 season and built several successful businesses over the next 30 years. He may be best remembered by the public though for his apt summation of the Ice Bowl: "It was our mark of distinction." (Gruver, 199) Ironically, even in that game, Bob delivered a key block that was overshadowed. On a sucker play at the Cowboy 11, he thoroughly sealed off defensive end George Andrie while defensive tackle Bob Lilly followed pulling-guard Gale Gillingham, allowing Chuck Mercein to rumble through a huge hole down to the three. If Mercein could have kept his feet, he might have scored and perhaps brought Skoronski some of the recognition that would fall to Jerry Kramer for his double-team block on Jethro Pugh four plays later.

In his comment, Skoronski was right. It was their mark of distinction. But why? Why were two entire books on just that game published 30 years later? Why is that game still remembered in the next century? Other title games have been played in bad conditions. The "Sneaker" Games between the Giants and Bears in 1934 and 1956, when the Giants gained superior footing on an icy field by wearing sneakers. The Cleveland Rams victory over the Washington Redskins in 1945, when game time temperature was three degrees and the difference in the game was the safety the Rams scored when a Sammy Baugh pass bounced off the uprights into his own end zone. The Bengals/Chargers AFC championship game in 1981 was played in a wind-chill of 59 below zero, and the Chargers were literally blown out. Several Packers still list their 1962 battle in Yankee Stadium against the Giants and frequent 30-mph wind gusts a colder experience than the Ice Bowl, but it is the Ice Bowl that achieved mythic status. Why?

First, it was played in fabled Lambeau Field, on the "frozen tundra" in the redundant phrase solemnly intoned by NFL Films voiceover announcer John Facenda. Lambeau games are frequently framed by the elements. Such primal conflict is a joy to watch. Even in the regular season, befouled soggy conditions can make for memorable moments, such as in the 1985 Snow Bowl against Tampa Bay, when quarterback Steve Young was sacked and got up with so much snow behind his face mask that he couldn't see. Or Dorsey Levens making an impossible lyrical sliding touchdown catch in the snow against the Cleveland Browns in 2001. The 1965 playoff against the Colts was played in a gloomy fog; the following week the championship game against the Browns was played on a sloppy, snowy, muddy field in which everyone's uniform was a grimy mess from the first quarter on. The 1997 playoff against the 49ers was played on a similar field with similar results. But 13 below zero and a windchill of -46 was a whole other hell on earth, and the Cowboys deserve a great deal of respect for overcoming the weather and a slow start to hold the advantage late in the fourth quarter.

Second, the Ice Bowl was a close game decided at the very end by an improbable comeback—a 12-play, 68-yard march in the final five minutes of the game in which most of the yards were accumulated by little-known journeyman Chuck Mercein. It was a great clutch closing drive: Starr to Anderson for six yards in the flat; Mercein sweeps for seven; Starr to Dowler over the middle for 13; Anderson loses nine on a sweep; Starr to Anderson on the right for 12, and then again for nine; Starr then to the left to Mercein, who chugs 19 yards to the 11; Mercein on the sucker play for eight; Anderson to the right for two, and then two more times for no gain; with 16 seconds left, Starr's sneak for the ballgame and the unprecedented third straight championship.

Third, in those pre-Namath-Super-Bowl years, the NFL title game was for the championship. This game and that drive against those brutal elements were the culmination of the Lombardi era. It was also the fullest expression of a Lombardi tenet that Skoronski has subscribed to thoughout his life—"the will to win, the will to excel, these are the things that endure." That team will never be forgotten, but neither will Bob Skoronski. He is a member of the Indiana University Hall of Fame, the Polish American Sports Hall of Fame, and, of course, the Packer Hall of Fame.

FOR FURTHER INFORMATION

Christl, Cliff. "The Packers: A Gold Mine of Lore, Trivia and Tradition," *Green Bay Packers 1977 Yearbook.* (16-20)

Gruver, Ed. *The Ice Bowl: The Cold Truth About Football's Most Unforgettable Game.* Ithaca, NY: McBooks Press, 1998.

Johnson, Chuck. *The Greatest Packers of Them All.* New York: Putnam, 1968. (120-7)

Kramer, Jerry, with Dick Schaap. *Distant Replay.* New York: G.P. Putnam, 1985. (131-6)

Lombardi, Vince, with W.C. Heinz. *Run to Daylight.* Englewood Cliffs, NJ: Prentice-Hall, 1963. (40-41)

Shropshire, Mike. *The Ice Bowl: The Green Bay Packers and Dallas Cowboys Season of 1967.* New York: Donald I. Fine Books, 1997.

Wagner, Len. "Masters and Skoronski: Starting at Left Tackle," *Green Bay Packers 1963 Yearbook.*

DRAFT BUSTS
TONY MANDARICH • TACKLE 1989–91

WHO'S WORN THE NUMBER Gatewood 1946, Tollefson 1947, Summerhays 1949–51, Hanner 1952–54, Sandusky 1956, O. Spencer 1957–58, Kostelnik 1961–68, Hayhoe 1969–73, M. Butler 1977–82, 1985, Getty 1983, Neill 1984, Feasel 1986, Robison 1987, McGrew 1987r, Mandarich 1989–91, Millard 1992, Maas 1993, Michels 1996–97, B. Brooks 2002, Wisne 2002.

ORIGINATOR Center Les Gatewood 1947 was a third team All American as a sophomore in 1943 at Tulane before transferring to Baylor.

LONGEST TENURE Defensive tackle Ron Kostelnik 1961–68 (see Notables below).

NUMBER CHANGES Les Gatewood also wore 33 in 1946–47, guard Charles Tollefson wore 46 from 1944–45 and 27 in 1946; defensive tackle Dave "Hawg" Hanner wore 79 from 1955–64; tackle Bill Hayhoe also wore 51 in 1969.

OTHER NOTABLES Ron Kostelnik capably replaced Hawg Hanner and filled the middle for the threepeat of the 1960s; Mike Butler had a couple of decent years at defensive end.

ONE TO FORGET Besides Mandarich? John Michels was a 1st-round flop at tackle as well, but with much less hype.

TONY MANDARICH In college at Michigan State, Tony Mandarich was once called "The Incredible Bulk" and appeared on the cover of *Sports Illustrated* with the tag line, "The Greatest Offensive Line Prospect Ever." He was 6'6" 320 pounds, fast, agile, and able to bench-press 550 pounds. His college line coaches created new categories to grade his games: number of "pancake" blocks where he flattened his opponent, number of players he drove out of camera range, and number of defenders who simply quit against him. Scouts likened him to Anthony Munoz, only better. He was a can't-miss prospect and seen as second only to Troy Aikman in the 1989 draft. It was the Packers bad luck that they held the second draft pick because they picked Mandarich just as any other team in that slot would do, and Tony became, arguably, the biggest flop in NFL draft history.

The number-one rumor was that Mandarich was a product of steroids, and his body appeared to be artificially pumped up. In addition, he seemed to play in the kind of maniacal rage that users of anabolic steroids sometimes do. After the Packers drafted him, Mandarich conducted a lengthy acrimonious public contract negotiation, during which he insulted Green Bay, talked of how much he wanted to stay in California where he could be a star, and threatened to sit out the football season and fight Mike Tyson for $10 million instead. He missed most of training camp, but finally signed a four-year deal worth $4.4 million. When he reported to the team, suspicions of steroid use were further aroused because he was at least 20 pounds lighter and lacked the muscle mass and definition he had previously displayed.

Once he got on the field, it was even worse. He was used to overpowering people in college, and his footwork, balance, and technique were all terrible, particularly for pass blocking. He started only 31 games in his first three years, then spent the fourth season on injured reserve. He became a gridiron joke. Bear defensive lineman Dan Hampton laughed at him, "Mandarich was all facade. The Packers got the prize, unwrapped it and saw that he wasn't the same—physically and emotionally—as what they had seen in college. He's pathetic." (Lieber, 32) Eagle nose-tackle Mike Golic said, "I can't believe how Reggie [White] was throwing Mandarich around. They're basically the same size, and Reggie treated him like a toy. I'd start to rush and I had to watch to keep from tripping over Mandarich." (Lieber, 34)

After four years, the Packers cut him and he was out of football. He claimed that he was sick of it all: practice, the game, the media, and the persona he could not live up to. Three years later he contacted his old Packers coach Lindy Infante, then coaching the Colts, and requested a tryout. He made the team and spent three years as a sometime starter at guard for Indianapolis before his career ended for good in 1999. With the Colts, he was much less of a loud-mouthed braggart, bringing to mind the old line that "too many athletes are learning to say hello just when it is time to say goodbye." To the end, when questioned about past steroid use, Mandarich would always respond accurately that he had never failed a drug test.

No matter what the reason, Tony Mandarich was a monumental bust for the Packers, but he was far from the first or last. One could make up a team of Packer draft busts covering all 22 positions, and I have taken the liberty to do so. Aside from the kicker, all are first- or second-round choices, and more weight is given for those busts picked higher in the draft.

THE ALL-TIME PACKER DRAFT BUST TEAM:

OFFENSE

WIDE RECEIVER—Barry Smith (1973, rd. 1, no. 21) 41 catches and four TDs in three years; Dave Dunaway (1967, rd. 2, no. 41) worthless bonus baby who never caught a pass in Green Bay.

TIGHT END—Rich McGeorge (1970, rd. 1, no.16) good blocker, but more was needed from 16th player taken in the draft.

TACKLE—Tony Mandarich (1989, rd. 1, no. 2.) the Captain of this team; John Michels (1996, rd. 1, no. 27) eventually traded to Eagles for another number one flop (Jon Harris) so neither team had to be embarrassed by cutting its own number one pick.

GUARD—Bill Bain (1975, rd. 2, no. 47) lasted just one year in Green Bay; Dave Drechsler (1983, rd. 2, no. 48) must have been twice as good because he lasted two years.

PACKERS BY THE NUMBERS

CENTER—Bob Hyland (1967, rd. 1, no. 9) had two tours of duty with the Packers, but the ninth player taken should be of All Pro caliber. When with the Giants, he broke Dan Devine's leg.

QUARTERBACK—Stan Heath (1949, rd. 1, no. 5) top flop completed 24% of his passes for 1 TD and 14 interceptions in only year; Randy Duncan (1959, rd. 1, no. 1) top pick flop signed with CFL instead and drifted to the AFL; Jerry Tagge (1972, rd. 1, no. 11) hometown flop completed 48% of his passes for three TDs and 17 interceptions in three years; Rich Campbell (1981, rd. 1, no. 6) rag-armed flop completed 45% of his passes for three TDs and nine interceptions in four years.

RUNNING BACK—Jack Losch (1956, rd. 1 no. 8) gained 43 yards and averaged 2.3 yards per carry in only season; Barty Smith (1974, rd. 1, no. 12) slow plodder gained 1,942 yards and averaged 3.6 yards per carry over seven years; Brent Fullwood (1987, rd. 1, no. 4) gained 1,702 yards and averaged 3.9 yards per carry over four years, also fumbled 15 times and had questionable attitude; Darrell Thompson (1990, rd. 1, no. 19) a tackling dummy who gained 1,641 yards and averaged 3.5 yards per carry over five years.

DEFENSE
DEFENSIVE END—Lloyd Voss (1964, rd. 1, no. 13) big stiff traded to Steelers after two years and lasted seven more years in NFL; Alphonso Carreker (1984, rd. 1, no. 12) never amounted to what was expected of him. Fellow FSU alum Jamal Reynolds (2001, rd. 1, no.10) belongs, too.

DEFENSIVE TACKLE—Rich Moore (1969 rd. 1, no. 12) a gigantic stiff played in 20 games in two years; Bruce Clark (1980, rd. 1, no. 4) signed with CFL, eventually came south and had a disappointing career in New Orleans.

LINEBACKER—Jim Flanigan (1967, rd. 2, no. 51) one of the better players on this team; Mike Hunt (1978, rd. 2, no. 34) played in only 22 games in three years; Mark D'Onofrio (1992, rd. 2, no. 34) suffered a catastrophic leg injury and played only two games in the league.

DEFENSIVE BACK—Vinnie Clark (1991, rd. 1, no. 19) lasted two years with the Packers and had four interceptions; Terrell Buckley (1992, rd. 1, no. 5) has lasted 10 years in the league, but was not cut out for Green Bay; Fred Vinson (1999, rd. 2, no. 47) his career ended quickly from injuries, but not before he brought Ahman Green in trade; Antuan Edwards (1999, rd. 1, no. 25) has not been able to win a starting job.

SPECIAL TEAMS
Kicker—Brett Conway (1997, rd. 3, no. 90) handed the job, but beaten out by free agent Longwell and has since bounced around the league unsuccessfully.

Punter—Jug Girard (1948, rd. 1, no. 7) flopped as quarterback, halfback, and defensive back, but was decent punter.

FOR FURTHER INFORMATION

Attner, Paul. "Second Time Around," *Sporting News.* 9/16/96. (32)

Bell, Jarrett. "Mandarich Gets Second Chance with Colts," *USA Today.* 8/22/96. (12C)

Gentile, Domenic, with Gary D'Amato. *The Packer Tapes: My 32 Years with the Green Bay Packers.* Madison, WI: Prairie Oak Press, 1995. (96-8)

Lieber, Jill. "Tony the Terrible," *Sports Illustrated.* 9/28/92. (30-4)

Telander, Rick. "The Big Enchilada," *Sports Illustrated.* 4/24/89. (40-9)

BENCH STRENGTH
BOB BROWN • DEFENSIVE TACKLE 1966–73

WHO'S WORN THE NUMBER Aberson 1946, Dahms 1955, Masters 1957–64, B. Brown 1966–73, Wafer 1974, Cooke 1975, E. Johnson 1977–78, C. Merrill 1979–83, G. Hoffman 1984, Hobbins 1987r, Cheek 1991, Verba 1997–2000.

ORIGINATOR Tailback Cliff Aberson 1946 who never went to college spent parts of three years in the major leagues with the Cubs and hit .251 with five homers (also see Forget below).

LONGEST TENURE Tackle Norm Masters 1957–64 and Bob Brown 1966–73.

NUMBER CHANGES Defensive end Ezra Johnson wore 90 from 1979–87.

OTHER NOTABLES Tackle Norm Masters was the offensive equivalent to Bob Brown—an ever reliable and ready substitute good enough to start for most teams; Ezra Johnson (see 90).

ONE TO FORGET In 1946 when tailback Irv Comp attained a 9.9 passing rating by completing 28% of his 94 passes for one touchdown and eight interceptions, the team's second passer, Cliff Aberson, was even worse, with a 9.7 rating by completing 34% of his 41 passes for no touchdowns and five interceptions.

BOB BROWN Norm Masters and Bob Brown were mirror images of each other in Packer colors. Both came to Green Bay after failing to catch on with a different team: Masters with the Cardinals and Lions and Brown with the 49ers. Each spent eight years wearing number 78 in 104 games: Masters as primarily an offensive tackle and Brown as primarily a defensive tackle. Both played for two champions and one playoff team: Masters first played for a losing playoff team and then two champs near the end of his tenure; Brown played for a champion the first two years in Green Bay and played on a losing playoff team in his next to last year. Masters was white, born in a big city, and went to a large university (Michigan State); Brown was black, born in a rural area, and went to a small school (Arkansas–Pine Bluff).

The main difference between Masters and Brown was that Bob eventually won a starting job and played well enough to earn second-team All Pro recognition twice and go to a Pro Bowl, but it was a long and circuitous trip. Brown was signed as an undrafted free agent by San Francisco in 1964, but was cut, so he played that year for the Wheeling, West Virginia, Ironmen of the Continental

League. Again in 1965 Bob went to the 49ers training camp but was cut. This time he went to Canada to play for Toronto in the CFL. From there, the Packers signed him and he made the team in 1966, filling in at both defensive end and defensive tackle. At 6'5" 275 pounds, he was an imposing figure at the time, and he would balloon much heavier on occasion.

His best attributes were toughness, quickness, and relentlessness. In one game against the Vikings he was struggling with pain in his leg for the whole game. The next day, when the leg was swollen, X-rays were taken and revealed that he had played that game on a broken leg. In the 1972 off-season, Bob was shot in the neck while driving after a dispute over a card game. He went on to play so well in the ensuing season that he went to the Pro Bowl. He played the game all out. He was known to power straight ahead on every play, ignoring all fakes, and made more than his share of big plays.

What Brown and Masters most represented was something that all championship clubs need, bench strength. No matter how good your starters are, when they tire or when they get hurt, someone else has to step in. When Jerry Kramer was injured, Forrest Gregg could move to guard and Masters could take right tackle. If Jim Ringo got dinged up, Bob Skoronski could move to center and Masters could handle left tackle. If Lionel Aldridge needed a blow, Bob Brown could take right defensive end. If Henry Jordan's back was wrenched, Brown could move inside.

Curly Lambeau's teams of the thirties and early forties were deep clubs at many positions. At fullback, Hall of Famer Clarke Hinkle was ably backed up by Herdis McCrary in 1932 and 1933, then by Swede Johnston from 1934 through 1938, and by Eddie Jankowski from 1937 to 1941. Johnston and Jankowski were so handy that they were both elected to the Packer Hall of Fame. Arnie Herber was backed up and eventually supplanted by Cecil Isbell at tailback. In addition to stars Johnny Blood and Tony Canadeo, Lambeau's backfield employed a fleet of capable men playing concurrently: Joe Laws, Bobby Monnett, Hank Bruder, Andy Uram, Larry Craig, and Lou Brock.

In the line, Lambeau's Packers were strong at tackle with Cal Hubbard, Champ Seibold, Ernie Smith, Ade Schwammel, Bill Lee and Baby Ray having overlapping careers. At guard the quality was even stronger. The careers of Mike Michalske, Tiny Engebretsen, Walt Kiesling, Buckets Goldenberg, Lon Evans, Russ Letlow, and Pete Tinsley all intersected. As the team declined in the late 1940s, it was hard enough to find quality starters, let alone depth. In the 1950s the only similar situation was when the inconsistent Tobin Rote competed with the inexperienced Babe Parilli for the starting quarterback position. In the 1960s, the Packers featured a wealth of depth: Tom Bettis and then Tommy Joe Crutcher at linebacker, Tom Moore and Elijah Pitts at running back, Johnny Symank and Doug Hart at defensive back, and of course Norm Masters and Bob Brown.

Today, with the salary cap, all is changed. It is harder to keep a team together. Players of quality bolt for larger free-agent dollars as soon as they are able. Men like Dorsey Levens and Mark Chmura began as late draft picks and slowly worked themselves into the starting lineup as the former starters left in free agency. In recent years, the Packers have stressed trying to retain their own quality players rather than signing a lot of free agents. Still, of the 53 men on the roster for the 1996 Super Bowl team, only 12 were still with the team five years later in 2001, and two of them, Gilbert Brown and Doug Pedersen, had left the team and come back. The only starters on both teams were Brett Favre, Antonio Freeman, William Henderson, Brown, Santana Dotson and Leroy Butler. By contrast, 16 of the 41 players from Vince Lombardi's first championship team in 1961 were still on the team in 1966. All were starters at one point and 14 of them were still starting for Lombardi's fourth title. Veteran raconteurs Paul Hornung and Max McGee joined with Bob Brown that year to become bench strength for Vince's fourth title team.

FOR FURTHER INFORMATION

Gentile, Domenic, with Gary D'Amato. *The Packer Tapes: My 32 Years with the Green Bay Packers.* Madison, WI: Prairie Oak Press, 1995. (73-4)

Greene, Bob. "Robert Eddie Brown Finally Found a Home," *Green Bay Packers 1971 Yearbook.* (22-3)

Kramer, Jerry, with Dick Schaap. *Distant Replay.* New York: G.P. Putnam, 1985. (207-11)

Rubin, Bob. *Green Bay's Packers: Return to Glory.* Englewood Cliffs, NJ: Prentice-Hall, 1974. (117)

Wagner, Len. *Launching the Glory Years: The 1959 Packers—What They Didn't Tell Us.* Green Bay, WI: Coach's Books LLC [Jay Bengtson], 2001. (48)

FIELD HAND
DAVE "HAWG" HANNER • DEFENSIVE TACKLE
1955–64

WHO'S WORN THE NUMBER
Adkins 1945–46, Urban 1945, Vogds 1948–49, Moje 1951, J. Spencer 1951, Hanner 1955–64, Delisle 1971, H. Schuh 1974, Koncar 1976–77, 1979–81, A. Fields 1982, Spears 1983, Humphrey 1984–86, Browner 1987, Estep 1987r, B. Nelson 1988–90, Ilkin 1993, Stokes 2000–01.

ORIGINATOR Blocking back/defensive end Bob Adkins 1945 was Larry Craig's backup. His career was interrupted by WWII and ended by a broken leg. Years later, he chuckled, "I was just a big, old hillbilly playing with the Green Bay Packers. It was nice." or incredibly shrinking defensive end Alex Urban 1945 who was said to be 6'6" as a sophomore at South Carolina in 1938, 6'4" as a senior in 1940 and 6'3" or 6'2" with Packers.

LONGEST TENURE Hawg Hanner 1955–64.

NUMBER CHANGES Bob Adkins wore 55 from 1940–41; end Alex Urban wore 23 in 1941 and 18 in 1944; tackle Joe Spencer also wore 34 in 1950–51; Hawg Hanner wore 77 from 1952–54.

OTHER NOTABLES None.

ONE TO FORGET Defensive end Dick Moje spent his entire two-game NFL career in Green Bay, highlighted by catching an 11-yard pass.

DAVE "HAWG" HANNER Curly Lambeau spent an amazing 29 years in the NFL on the field with the Packers, playing or coaching; so did beefy, ruddy-faced Arkansas farm boy Dave Hanner. No one else provided as much on-field service as those two, and their nearly overlapping careers in Green Bay took the team from its inception to its third Super Bowl title. Lambeau also played for the team for a few years before it joined the NFL, while Hanner continued as a scout for several years after his coaching career ended. When Dave arrived at Packer training camp as a fifth-round pick in 1952, no one envisioned him devoting 44 years of his life to the team—13 years as a player, 16 years as an assistant coach, and 15 years as a scout.

In that first training camp, veteran star Tony Canadeo took a liking to the amiable and hard-working Hanner and helped teach him how to be a professional. Canadeo also gave Dave the nickname "Hawg," which was fitting because he was raised on a farm, and at 6'2" 260 pounds was a big man for the time. Hanner would be known as Hawg from then on. He would experience immediate success and go to the Pro Bowl both in his second and third years and be named All Pro in 1957 and 1959.

Lombardi arrived in 1959 of course, and Vince looked on Hanner favorably, calling him by his given name "Joel." "He is thirty-two, now, and it is going to be a sad day in Green Bay when the years get him, because he has only been All Pro five times [sic] but there is nobody on this squad who is better liked than big, easy-going, quiet Dave with that chaw of tobacco in his right cheek and his constant weight problem." (Lombardi, 86) Hanner would sometimes end up in the hospital with heat prostration in training camp, as he attempted to sweat off those extra pounds in the Lombardi weight-loss plan. Lombardi liked him most of all because he had a great work ethic. "He will ask more questions of Phil Bengtson than the greenest first-year man, and when we put in a move that's unique for a game, Dave can't wait to try it . . . Jerry Kramer is always using Dave to perfect his own techniques, and they work together a lot in practice." (Lombardi, 87) In 1961, he missed the first game of his career when he had to undergo an emergency appendectomy, but he was back for the next game only 11 days after his surgery. He was a team man all the way and played a big role in training his replacement, Ron Kostelnik.

When it came time to retire, Hanner was brought right in as defensive line coach and coached under Lombardi, Bengtson, Devine, and Starr. He was a candidate for the head job when Devine left, and Devine suspected Hanner of sedition. However, the Packers hired Starr and Hawg instead became defensive coordinator. He worked for his old teammate for five years until he was abruptly fired in 1979 when the team switched to a 3-4 defense. After a year mostly out of football, he was brought back to Green Bay as a scout in 1981. What hurt Hawg most was that he found out about his firing from others before Bart ever spoke to him. The two have spoken little ever since, although Bart did rehire Hawg as a coach in 1982 to break down film.

In his 29 years, Curly Lambeau played and coached in Hagemeister Park, Bellevue Field, and City Stadium in Green Bay, and Borchert Field and the Wisconsin State Fair Park in Milwaukee. Hawg Hanner spent his 29 years in City Stadium and City Stadium II (later called Lambeau Field) in Green Bay, and Marquette Stadium and County Stadium in Milwaukee. The original City Stadium is the one field the two have in common, and it was home to the Packers for 32 years from 1925–56. It seated only 23,500 fans and was essentially a high school stadium where fans sat on wooden bleachers that were open underneath. Security guards were stationed underneath the stands to retrieve fallen handbags. There were no bathrooms and no visiting team locker room. Visitors had to get dressed in their hotel and take the team bus to the stadium in full football gear. The home team locker room consisted of a small room with concrete floors underneath the stands. Later, both teams would dress in the locker room at the adjacent East High School. The field itself was surrounded by a cinder track that was separated from the field by a four foot high wooden fence that players would frequently have to avoid when a play carried them out of bounds. The field itself still serves as the football gridiron for East High School.

It is little wonder, then, that City Stadium II, as the new field would be called from 1957 until 1965, was so eagerly anticipated and urgently needed. The opening of "Lambeau" in 1957 was attended by Vice President Nixon, Gunsmoke star James Arness, and the reigning Miss America. That game was won by the Packers over the Bears on a late touchdown pass from Babe Parilli to Gary Knafelc. At its opening, "Lambeau" seated 32,150, but was continually enlarged; seating capacity was increased to 38,600 in 1961, 42,300 in 1963, 50,800 in 1965, 56,200 in 1970, 56,900 in 1985, 59,500 in 1990, and 60,790 in 1995. The renovations undergone in 2002 brought the seating capacity to more than 71,000. Along the way, home games in Milwaukee became financially disadvantageous to those in Green Bay, and the practice of playing three home games a season in Milwaukee was halted after 1994. Today, Lambeau Field is a green bowl surrounded by a brick shell steeped in history and exuding character. It is the exclusive home of the Packers, and the finest place in the league to watch a pro football game.

It is also a place that offers an imposing home-field advantage. The Packers regular season record in Lambeau since 1992 is 68-11. In almost 70 years of playoffs, Green Bay has a 23-12 record—12-1 at home (including 1-0 in Milwaukee) and 11-11 on the road. Oddly, when the Packers played in both cities from 1933 through 1994, they went 105-61-3 for a winning percentage of .630 in Milwaukee, while they went 129-111-6 in Green Bay for a lower .537 percentage. In the years before 1933 and after 1994, the Packers home record has been 106-16-7, for a .849 percentage. Part of that advantage is the weather, but for years that weather caused the Packers to have strange scheduling. The team's first home game in December was not until the 1939 Championship game played in Milwaukee. They would not have another until another game in Milwaukee in 1942. Their first December home game in Green Bay was not until 1951. For years Green Bay would have to play an unbalanced schedule, sending them on the road for the final stretch of the season. In the 1950s and early 1960s, the team would traditionally end the season with a West-Coast trip playing the Rams and 49ers. It wasn't until the end of the decade that this whole unfair scheduling practice really began to change.

On these fields, Dave Hanner played for two championship teams and coached on three others. He retired the year that the Packers returned to the Super Bowl and got to watch some of the players he had scouted, such as Edgar Bennett and Wayne Simmons, help the Packers win a twelfth championship. Packer GM Ron Wolf said of Hanner, "It was tremendous for me personally to work with him; I've learned an awful lot." (Norris) Fellow scout and now scouting director John Dorsey added, "That man wears the Packer 'G' with more pride than anyone I've ever met." (Norris) Hanner's son Joe continued in the family business, coaching locally at the high school level.

FOR FURTHER INFORMATION

Daley, Art. "Hanner Calls It a Career After 45 Years in the Green and Gold," *Green Bay Packers 1996 Yearbook*. (46-7)

Lombardi, Vince, with W.C. Heinz. *Run to Daylight*. Englewood Cliffs, NJ: Prentice-Hall, 1963. (86-7)

Norris, Tim. "Leaving Hawg Heaven," *Milwaukee Journal Sentinel*. 4/30/96. (Sports 1)

Remmel, Lee. "Hawg," *Green Bay Packers 1961 Yearbook*. (11,48)

Wagner, Len. *Launching the Glory Years: The 1959 Packers—What They Didn't Tell Us*. Green Bay, WI: Coach's Books LLC [Jay Bengtson], 2001. (51)

1982 PLAYOFFS
JAMES LOFTON • WIDE RECEIVER 1978–86

WHO'S WORN THE NUMBER Frutig 1945, Rohrig 1946–47, Provo 1948, F. Reid 1950–51, C. Elliott 1952–54, Deschaine 1955–57, Meilinger 1958 and 1960, G. Barnes 1962, Long 1964–67, Pope 1968, Clancy 1970, Barry Smith 1973–75, D. Zimmerman 1976, Lofton 1978–86, F. Neal 1987, Didier 1988–89, J. Harris 1990–93, C. Jordan 1994–95, Mayes 1996–98, Driver 1999–2002.

ORIGINATOR End Ed Frutig 1945 wrapped two years in Green Bay around three years in the Navy before going into coaching and then advertising.

LONGEST TENURE James Lofton 1978–86.

NUMBER CHANGES Herman Rohrig wore 8 in 1941; halfback Floyd "Breezy" Reid wore 24 from 1952–56; Carlton Elliott wore 40 in 1951; Charles Jordan wore 82 in 1995 and 1998.

OTHER NOTABLES Herman "Stumpy" Rohrig was a good defensive back, but his 1946 rushing line showed only 14 carries for -23 yards. Lifetime he carried 42 times for 1 yard. He became a college and pro official and even worked the 1960 championship game that his former team lost. Breezy Reid led the team in rushing in 1953 and 1954.

ONE TO FORGET Wide receiver Barry Smith was a number-one draft choice in 1973 who was compared at the time to fellow Florida State alumnus Fred Biletnikoff. Smith, however, did not like going over the middle in the NFL, and caught 41 balls for 604 yards and four touchdowns in three years, a mere 548 catches, 8,370 yards, and 72 touchdowns behind Fred. He went to Tampa Bay in the 1976 expansion draft and then disappeared.

JAMES LOFTON At his Packers Hall of Fame induction ceremony in 1999, James Lofton said that he heard that ESPN commentator Sterling Sharpe was calling himself the greatest receiver in Packers history. Lofton responded with this comment, "Without a doubt, Don Hutson, who played here, was the greatest receiver. I hate to break the news to Sterling, but he was the third best." That line typified James Lofton—confident, intelligent, funny, and, in this instance, probably correct.

At Stanford where he graduated with a degree in industrial engineering, Lofton was a world-class sprinter and long jumper as well as a star at wide receiver under coach Bill Walsh. He was the Packers first choice in the 1978 draft and was named NFC Rookie of the Year. In addition, he played in his first Pro Bowl that year; he would appear in seven more during his career. He was the Randy Moss of his time, but one who applied himself to his craft. An early devotee of weightlifting, he was not only fast, elusive, and a great leaper, but had great strength for a wide receiver. He moved fluidly and always appeared at ease on the field. In short, he was the premier deep threat in the game— not only could he run past defensive backs, but he could out-jump them, too. During his career, more and more teams went to variations of the short passing West Coast Offense. Consequently, of those who have played since 1978 and who have caught at least 500 passes, only the Patriots' Stanley Morgan had a greater yards-per-catch average (19.2 on 557 receptions) than Lofton's 18.3 on 764 catches. At his retirement, James was the all-time leader in yards receiving, although that record has since been broken by Jerry Rice.

James said this of his style: "I don't know if I'd want to catch a hundred short passes. I'd rather come up with big plays, and I'd rather the team spread the ball around." (Johnson, 35) He was a competitor and that got him in trouble twice in his second season. One time he threw his helmet into his locker to protest Coach Bart Starr's conservative approach at the end of one losing game. The second time, the fans booed him for fumbling a pass and he responded in anger with the middle finger salute, followed by some choice post-game comments. In response, Packers public relations man Chuck Lane called him a "prima donna." Upon James' marriage in the next year, he seemed to mature and become a team leader. Five times he went over a thousand yards receiving and is still the Packers' all-time leader with a total of 9,656 yards.

The Packers of Lofton's time had an explosive offense. He described it thus: "There's an old adage, 'We'll take what the defense gives us.' Well, for really dominant receivers, you take what you want. And that's the way we approached our passing game. We're going to go deep over the middle, deep to the outside, and we're going to do it regardless whether or not the defense wanted to let us do it." (Biever, 145) On October 2, 1983, against the Buccaneers, the Packers set a record by scoring 49 points in the first half of a 55-14 win. Three other times that year they scored over forty points and still managed to lose one of those games. The problem for those Packer teams was defense.

In both 1981 and 1983, the Packers finished at 8-8, and the defense gave up more points than the offense could score. Seven games were wiped out by the 1982 strike, but Green Bay made the playoffs for the first time in 10 years with a 5-3-1 record, propelled by their three Pro Bowl receivers Lofton, John Jefferson, and Paul Coffman. Lofton was on track for a 1,500-yard season in 1982 and achieved the third-longest run from scrimmage in Packer history with an 83-yard reverse for a touchdown that would foreshadow his playoff work later that season. The playoffs were an expanded 16-team tournament that year because of the shortened season, and the Packers hosted the St. Louis Cardinals in the first playoff game in Lambeau in 15 years. Green Bay maintained Packer home playoff perfection by pounding the Cardinals 41-16. They were led by Lynn Dickey's four touchdown passes, including two to Jefferson and one to Lofton. The following week, the Packers traveled to Dallas and missed their chance to go to the NFC Championship by losing to the Cowboys 37-26. Dallas led only 13-7 with a minute left in the first half when Dickey, under pressure, forced a bad pass that was picked off and returned for a touchdown by Cowboy Dennis Thurman. Lofton had scored Green Bay's first touchdown on a six-yard reception in the second quarter; he scored their second touchdown in the fourth quarter on a 71-yard reverse. Dallas blocked the extra point to maintain a four point 23-19 lead. The teams traded two more touchdowns, the Packers scoring on Mark Lee's interception return to make the score 30-26. But then Dallas had the last word when one wide-out, Drew Pearson, threw a 49-yard option pass to the other wide-out, Tony Hill, for the closing score. Lofton caught five passes for 109 yards and ran for 71, but the team fell short. That playoff experience was the high point for his Packer years.

The following two years were his greatest personally, as he averaged over 20 yards per catch and gained over 1,300 yards each year, but the defenseless team could only manage two 8-8 seasons. After a third straight 8-8 season, coach Forrest Gregg, who had taken over from Starr in 1984, decided to blow it all up and start over. Unfortunately, James' personal life blew up, as well. He was involved in a sexual incident with a dancer in 1984, although no charges were ever filed, and then was charged with sexual assault in a second incident in 1986. Although he was acquitted of any crime, he was traded to the Raiders for the 1987 season due to the sordid nature of the whole affair. In Oakland, he never quite fit in and was released in 1989. He signed with Buffalo and had a three-year resurgence with the Bills. He went over 1,000 yards receiving for the sixth and final time in his career and appeared in two Super Bowls. After the Bills released him in 1993, he spent his 16th and final season bouncing from the Rams to the Eagles before retiring and going into television. A four-time All Pro, he finally made the Pro Football Hall of Fame in 2003. Were it not for his off-the-field misadventures, he would have been inducted sooner. He was the best receiver of his generation.

FOR FURTHER INFORMATION

Biever, Vernon J., photography, Peter Strupp ed. *The Glory of Titletown: The Classic Green Bay Packers Photography of Vernon Biever.* Dallas, TX: Taylor Publishing, 1997. (145)

Heisler, Mark. "James Lofton's Trying Times," *Los Angeles Times.* 6/21/87. (Sports 3)

Johnson, Roy S. "Sport Interview: James Lofton," *Sport.* 10/85. (31-8)

Porter, David L., ed. *Biographical Dictionary of American Sports: Football.* New York: Greenwood Press, 1987. (351-2)

Telander, Rick. "A Picture Perfect End," *Sports Illustrated.* 12/6/82. (52-8)

SUPER BOWL XXXI
DESMOND HOWARD • KICK RETURNER 1996

WHO'S WORN THE NUMBER Berrang 1952, Keane 1952, Rush 1953, G. Knutson 1954, 1956, O'Donahue 1955, Massey 1957–58, A.D. Williams 1959, Folkins 1961, Fleming 1963–69, McGeorge 1970–78, G. Lewis 1981–84, Ross 1986, Lee Morris 1987, Jay 1987r, Kemp 1988–91, C. Harris 1992, S. Collins 1992, A. Morgan 1993–95, Howard 1996, T. Davis 1997–2002.

ORIGINATOR End Ed Berrang broke in #81 on opening day 1952 against the Bears. He was then released and his jersey was given to end Jim Keane 1952, a former Bear just set free from the Chicago Zoo.

LONGEST TENURE Tight end Rich McGeorge 1970–78. McGeorge was big and could block, but wasn't much of receiver. He was a reach as a number-one pick in 1970.

NUMBER CHANGES Replacement Lee Morris wore 48 and 85 in 1987; wide receiver Corey Harris was moved to defensive back and wore 30 in 1993–94; receiver Anthony Morgan wore 84 in 1996; Desmond Howard had to switch to 82 for his brief return in 1999.

OTHER NOTABLES Tight end Marv Fleming started in Super Bowls I and II for Vince Lombardi, then went to Miami where he played in three straight for Don Shula, winning two and giving him a total of four Super Bowl rings.

ONE TO FORGET Tight end Gary Lewis was a bust as a second-round pick, catching only 21 passes in four years. He did have one special ability: he blocked several field goals and extra points for the Packers.

DESMOND HOWARD Desmond Howard had one of the most celebrated college football careers in history. At the University of Michigan, where he played with his high school quarterback, Elvis Grbac, he scored 37 touchdowns in 36 games. In his senior year he caught 19 touchdown passes and scored 138 points. He won the Heisman Trophy, the Maxwell Award, the Walter Camp Trophy, the UPI and AP Offensive Player of the Year awards, and the Dunlop Pro-Am Athlete of the Year award. Packers' GM Ron Wolf was poised to select him with the fifth pick in the 1992 draft when the Washington Redskins traded up to nab him with the fourth pick.

As a pro, though, the 5'9" Howard was too slight to get separation and spent three generally disappointing seasons as a wide receiver in Washington and one in Jacksonville which had selected him in the expansion draft. Wolf still saw Howard's breakaway speed and moves, envisioned his potential as a kick returner, and signed him as a free agent in 1996. In training camp, Howard suffered a painful hip pointer and barely played before breaking a punt return in the final exhibition game to secure a spot on the team.

The 1996 season was Howard's greatest as a professional. He set a new NFL season record by returning punts for 875 yards and led the league with a 15.1-yard return average. He returned three of his 58 punt returns for touchdowns. In that Super Bowl season, the play of the Packers special-teams units sparked the offense and defense all year, giving them favorable field position. Howard's ability to use his blockers and to make defenders miss helped impel the return units to their best efforts. In the playoffs, he went into overdrive.

The first playoff game was in the mud at Lambeau against the rival 49ers, and it displayed the best and worst elements of Desmond Howard. After the 49ers first possession, he followed his blocks and broke a tackle to return the San Francisco punt 71 yards for a touchdown, mugging like Jim Carrey from *The Mask* in the end zone. After the 49ers third possession, Howard took a short punt on the run and scooted 46 yards before being tripped up from behind at the San Francisco seven. Brett Favre followed with a four-yard touchdown pass to Andre Rison, and the Packers led 14-0 in the first quarter. They would never trail, but allowed the 49ers to come close to making a game of it when Howard took too long changing into a clean pair of pants at halftime. He did not come out of the locker room in time to make the second half kickoff, and the 49ers beat the Packers to the free ball at the four. They scored in one play to make the score 21-14 Green Bay. However, between the 49ers' five turnovers and the Packers' 139 yards on the ground, Green Bay maintained control to win, 35-14.

In the NFC Championship game at a freshly resodded Lambeau one week later, the Packers followed Dorsey Levens' 205 rushing and receiving yards and Edgar Bennett's 99 yards rushing to convincingly defeat the Carolina Panthers 30-13. Desmond Howard had no special role to play in that game, but he did two weeks later in Super Bowl XXXI, in New Orleans, against the New England Patriots.

The Patriots received the opening kickoff and were forced to punt after making only one first down. Howard caught the ball at his own 13 and brought it back 32 yards, and after the whistle got into a heated trash-talking exchange with the Patriot bench that would continue throughout the game. On the Packers' second play from scrimmage, Favre audibled and threw a 54-yard touchdown to Andre Rison for the first score of the game. Brett was so excited that he started to run to the wrong bench in celebration. Green Bay went up 10-0 and then fell behind 14-10 by the time the first quarter ended—a Super Bowl record for combined first-quarter points. Another Favre audible resulted in an 81-yard touchdown pass to Antonio Freeman—a new Super Bowl record for the longest scoring pass play—and a 17-14 lead that they would never relinquish. Howard would return another punt 34 yards to set up a Chris Jacke field goal, and Favre would culminate a long drive with a touchdown scamper to close the first half 27-14, Packers.

Green Bay started a long march on the opening possession of the third quarter, but foundered on a bizarre fourth-and-one sweep call that resulted in a seven-yard loss and Patriot ball. After an exchange of punts, New England went on a 53-yard scoring drive that brought them within six points with three and a half minutes remaining in the quarter. Momentum seemed to be swinging in the Patriots favor until Desmond

Howard caught the ensuing kickoff at the one and came right up the center of the field where Packers' special teamers Calvin Jones, Travis Jervey, Jeff Thomason, Keith McKenzie, Lamont Hollinquest, and Don Beebe all took out their men and Desmond burst through nearly untouched. He even had time to glance at the Jumbotron screen above him as he sped for the goal line where he slowed to strike some Michael Jackson dance moves as he scored the clinching touchdown. He would finish the game with 244 return yards, 154 from kickoffs and 90 from punts, a record that would win him the Super Bowl MVP award. He was the first special teams player to win it and did so deservedly over Favre's two TD passes and Reggie White's record three sacks.

Strangely, that has been the only kickoff that Howard ever took back for a score. In 10 years in the NFL, he has never done so in the regular season. After his MVP heroics in the Super Bowl, Desmond was courted by the Raiders and signed a substantial free-agent contract in 1997. His first year was forgettable, but he did run two more punts back for scores in his second year in Oakland. In 1999, Ron Wolf brought him back to Green Bay again, but the magic seemingly was gone. Howard was waived at mid-season after being tentative and ineffective on both kickoffs and punts as well as suffering from finger injuries. The next year he signed with the Lions and resumed being an effective return man—even scoring his eighth touchdown by punt return. His second coach in Green Bay, Ray Rhodes, cost the Packers the services of one of the best punt returners in NFL history. Rhodes' special teams were horrible for four years in Philadelphia and dreadful for his one year in Green Bay, masking the still-explosive talent of Desmond Howard who once claimed, "I always envision myself scoring. That makes it easier in the game. Then it's deja vu, it's like I've been there before." (Biever, 239)

FOR FURTHER INFORMATION

Biever, Vernon J., photography, Peter Strupp ed. *The Glory of Titletown: The Classic Green Bay Packers Photography of Vernon Biever.* Dallas, TX: Taylor Publishing, 1997. (239)

Carlson, Chuck. *Titletown Again: The Super Bowl Season of the 1996 Green Bay Packers.* Lenexa, KS: Addax Publishing Group, 1997.

McGinn, Bob. *The Road to Glory: The Inside Story of the Packers Super Bowl XXXI Championship Season.* Louisville, KY: AdCraft Sports Marketing, 1997.

Peary, Danny. *Super Bowl: The Game of Their Lives.* New York: Macmillan, 1997.

Porter, David L., ed. *Biographical Dictionary of American Sports: 1992–1995 Supplement for Baseball, Football, Basketball, and Other Sports.* New York: Greenwood Press, 1995. (446-8)

Titletown: The Green Bay Packers Improbable Journey to Super Bowl XXXI. [Green Bay Press-Gazette] Louisville, KY: AdCraft Sports Marketing, 1997.

PACKERS BY THE NUMBERS

 1996 SUPER BOWL XXXI DATA
Green Bay Packers 35
New England Patriots 21

January 26, 1997 • Superdome, New Orleans

Attendance: 72,301

Winner's Share: $48,000

Loser's Share: $30,000

Weather: In a dome.

KEY STATS	PACKERS	PATRIOTS
First Downs	16	16
Rush Yards	115	43
Pass Yard	208	214
Total Yards	323	257
Return Yards	244	165
Interceptions	4	0
Fumbles Lost	0	0
Penalties	3-41	2-22
Third down conversions	3/15	4/14
Fourth down conversions	0/1	0/2
Time of Possession	34:15	25:45

Halftime Score: Packers 27 Patriots 14

LEADERS

Rushing: Dorsey Levens 14-61.   Curtis Martin 11-42

Passing: Brett Favre 14-27-0 246 yds.   Drew Bledsoe 25-48-4 253 yds.

Receiving: Antonio Freeman 3-105.   Ben Coates 6-67

ADDITIONAL FACTS

•In the playoffs against the 49ers, Panthers, and Patriots, Bret Favre's passing line was 44-71-1 for 617 yards and five TDs. The Packers out-rushed their opponents 455 to 156 and held an average time of possession edge of 35:25 to 24:35. The Packers return teams held a 508 to 288 yard lead over their opponents.

•Patriots coach Bill Parcells had been offered the Packers coaching job by GM Ron Wolf before Wolf hired Mike Holmgren.

•Reggie White set a Super Bowl record with three sacks.

•Desmond Howard was the first special-teams player to win a Super Bowl MVP.

•May 20, 1997, marked the first Packers trip to the White House as President Clinton hosted a celebration for most of the team. Mark Chmura refused to go, and Desmond Howard, Andre Rison, and Chris Jacke had cut their ties with the Packers and were not invited.

TRAGIC ADVERSITY
LIONEL ALDRIDGE • DEFENSIVE END 1964–71

WHO'S WORN THE NUMBER E. Bell 1947–49, Cloud 1950–51, Temp 1957–60, Barrett 1963, Aldridge 1964–71, Tinker 1975, Hartwig 1977, Coffman 1978–85, Moffitt 1986, Paskett 1987, Harden 1987r, Bolton 1988, Affholter 1991, Beach 1992, Reggie Johnson 1994, M. Ingram 1995, Beebe 1996–97, Manning 1998, C. Jordan 1999, Howard 1999, C. Lee 2000–02.

ORIGINATOR Guard Ed Bell 1947–49, came to the Packers from the All America Football Conference. He played in both the 1945 (against the Packers) and 1946 College All Star Games.

LONGEST TENURE Lionel Aldridge 1964–71 and tight end Paul Coffman 1978–85 (see Notables below).

NUMBER CHANGES Lionel Aldridge wore 62 in 1963; tight end Reggie Johnson wore 88 in 1997; receiver Charles Jordan wore 80 in 1994–95; returner Desmond Howard wore 81 in 1996.

OTHER NOTABLES Paul Coffman is probably the best–receiving tight end in Packers' history. He was always open when fellow Kansas State alumnus Lynn Dickey was in trouble and caught 322 passes including 39 scores. He went into the Packer Hall of Fame in 1994. Wide–out Don Beebe was a super sub in 1996 and finally won a Super Bowl ring in his fifth try.

ONE TO FORGET Despite the several ineffective receivers who wore 82, let's go with All American fullback Jack "Flying" Cloud who ran the ball 47 times in two years for Green Bay, fumbled three times, and gained 113 yards, a 2.4 average. He had injured his knee in the Dixie Bowl in his senior year and never recovered. He was an assistant coach at Navy for several years.

LIONEL ALDRIDGE My favorite line from Vince Lombardi has always been, "The greatest glory is not in never falling, but in rising every time we fall." (Kramer, 158) While that is certainly true in the competitive world of professional football, it has even greater applicability in life itself. Many of Vince's players achieved a great deal of success after they left the game, but for some it did not come without intermittently experiencing failure and hardship. Many had to overcome financial setbacks and physical ailments, but Lionel Aldridge accomplished much more than any of his teammates. Aldridge came back from the snake pit of mental illness; he drove off the demons that had overrun his mind.

Lionel was a fourth-round draft pick in 1963 who arrived as a guard and was given number 62. By opening day, he was the starting right defensive end, replacing Bill Quinlan who had been traded to the

Giants. Aldridge was a rare individual, a rookie starting on a Lombardi team; Vince preferred that rookies sit for a year and learn their positions and profession. Besides Aldridge, only Boyd Dowler and Ken Bowman won starting jobs in their first years during Lombardi's rule. Lionel was fast, strong, and an able pass-rusher. He was known as the "Big Train" and would start for Green Bay for the next nine years, until Dan Devine traded him to San Diego for Jim Hill, who would turn out to be a key player for the 1972 playoff run. Even when he broke his leg in 1967 training camp, Lionel had the cast off in two weeks and was back on the field for the third game of the year.

Aldridge spent two losing seasons in San Diego while that team was in the midst of a very public and horrific drug scandal. He retired in 1973 and with his rich baritone voice and articulate manner went right into broadcasting. He was an immediate success in his new field, doing sports reports on television, then serving as Jim Irwin's analyst for Packers games, and even working for NBC on network games. However, that would all change rapidly.

Lionel's early life had not been without stress. He was born poor in segregated Louisiana and was raised in his grandfather's house along with 10 other children. His grandfather was a sharecropper, and Lionel quickly learned that field work was not for him, so he focused on his school work. When he was 15, his grandfather died and Lionel was sent to live with an aunt and uncle in California as one of 14 children raised by the couple. In that house, education was given first priority, and all the children went to college. At 16, Lionel was urged to go out for the football team, although he had never played the game before. It took some coaching for him to get up to speed, but he worked hard and mastered the game.

His high school coach took a job at Utah State and arranged a football scholarship for Lionel. It was a great opportunity, but it did not come without a price. The community was mostly white and mostly Mormon, which clearly made Lionel an outsider. At Utah State, he and a white Mormon woman fell in love. Over the objections and obstructions of her parents, they became engaged. Once Lionel was drafted by the Packers, he claimed that NFL commissioner Pete Rozelle personally urged him and his fiancé Vicky not to get married. Lombardi was in their corner, though, and told them to come to him with any problems.

After his initial success in broadcasting in 1974, Aldridge began to hear voices in his head saying that he was failing as a husband and a father and that he didn't deserve his professional success. He thought that people watching him on television could see inside him and that they were out to destroy him. His work began to suffer. Jim Irwin remembers a broadcast when Lionel stared at the 50-yard line the whole game and did not say a word. His home life suffered even more, and eventually he and his wife would divorce. He began to be hospitalized periodically for his worsening mental problems. In later years he could remember being admitted to a mental hospital at least 13 times. He was alternately diagnosed as either a manic depressive or a paranoid schizophrenic and given medication. Some reports say that he failed to take his medication, but Aldridge himself also reported that one of the problems of the medication was that it would make him feel so good that he felt he could stop taking it because he was no longer sick.

After the divorce in the 1980s, he began to drift around the country from home-less shelter to soup kitchen in Florida, Louisiana, Utah, California, and Chicago. He turned up in old teammate Willie Davis' Los Angeles office one day asking for three dollars. Willie gave him $300 and got him a hotel room, but Lionel quickly vanished again. After two years of wandering the nation homeless, he turned up at a Milwaukee rescue mission in 1983 and at last got on a regular and appropriate medication program. He began work-ing at the Milwaukee Post Office and took up public speaking on behalf of the mental-ly ill and homeless.

He lived alone but was self-sufficient and seemed reasonably content. His greatest enjoyment in his final years was silence. He described the pleasure of sitting alone in the dark of his apartment: "For so many years, I had so many sounds in my head. I love to sit there. The only things I hear are the external. The cars on the street, dogs, people." He had carried his Bible everywhere with him in his arduous, tenuous life on the road, and said of that time, "But I was living the whole time. Every moment in life is living, so I have no regrets." (Briggs) He also felt that Lombardi was always with him and helped him even-tually overcome his mental illness.

Dan Devine once said, "Willie Davis was flashier, but no one was steadier than Lionel Aldridge." This steady man on the field was inducted in the Packer Hall of Fame in 1988. He died in 1997 at the age of 56 of congestive heart failure, and weighed over 400 pounds by then. Outside the easily charted, win-or-lose atmosphere of profession-al sports, each person measures success differently. Each person must achieve his own triumph. In my book—the one you're reading—Lionel Aldridge achieved a major tri-umph in life by coming to a certain peace and being able to say, "Every day I am OK is a miracle. I worry about my kids. But nothing really makes me mad."

FOR FURTHER INFORMATION

Briggs, Jennifer. "Sounds of Silence Suit Aldridge," *Wisconsin State Journal.* 3/19/97. (1B)

Briggs, Jennifer, comp. *Strive to Excel: The Wit and Wisdom of Vince Lombardi.* Nashville, TN: Rutledge Hill Press, 1997. (70-3)

Gentile, Domenic, with Gary D'Amato. *The Packer Tapes: My 32 Years with the Green Bay Packers.* Madison, WI: Prairie Oak Press, 1995. (67-70)

Greene, Bob. "Lionel Aldridge Casts a Big Shadow," *Green Bay Packers 1970 Yearbook.* (11-3)

Kramer, Jerry with Dick Schaap. *Distant Replay.* New York: G.P. Putnam, 1985. (96-102, 234-6)

Lea, Bud. "Nitschke, Aldridge Leave Us," *Green Bay Packers 1998 Yearbook.* (88-9)

Oates, Bob. "Meaning of Thanksgiving Is Learned Hard Way," *Los Angeles Times* 11/26/87. (D1)

TRICKS OF THE TRADE

JOHN MARTINKOVIC • DEFENSIVE END 1952–56

WHO'S WORN THE NUMBER Martinkovic 1952–56, Ford 1958, Quinlan 1959–62, U. Henry 1963, Allen Brown 1966–67, Vandersea 1968–69, C. Williams 1970–77, J. Thompson 1979–80, J. Jefferson 1981–84, P. Scott 1987–88, Bland 1989–90, Clayton 1993, Wilner 1994, J. Thomason 1995–99, Wetnight 2000, D. Martin 2001, Glenn 2002.

ORIGINATOR John Martinkovic 1952–56.

LONGEST TENURE Defensive end Clarence Williams 1970–77 (see Notables below).

NUMBER CHANGES John Martinkovic wore 39 ands 47 in 1951; linebacker Phil Vandersea wore 37 in 1966; tight end John Thompson wore 87 in 1981–82; tight end Jeff Wilner wore 49 in 1995; tight end David Martin wore 87 in 2002.

OTHER NOTABLES Defensive end Len Ford concluded his Hall of Fame career with one sad year in Green Bay. Defensive end Bill Quinlan helped solidify the defensive line for Lombardi's first teams and was very good against the run. He was also a hard-living roustabout who did not cater to authority, and Lombardi got rid of him as soon as he could replace him adequately. Clarence Williams put in eight serviceable years as a pass-rusher after replacing Hall of Famer Willie Davis. Receiver John Jefferson had lost a step and never reached the heights he had attained in San Diego.

ONES TO FORGET Defensive lineman Urban Henry was something of a redneck who started a successful business with Jerry Kramer and Jim Taylor after his football career. His most memorable moment on the football field occurred after he had been traded to Pittsburgh in 1964. NFL Films has a priceless shot of him sitting on the bench as an opponent comes speeding out of bounds. Henry quickly stands up and cold cocks the ball-carrier, who goes down like a shot. Free agent receiver Mark Clayton was past his prime and held up Robert Brooks' development for one year.

JOHN MARTINKOVIC John Martinkovic was one of the better defensive ends in the league in the 1950s, twice being selected to play in the Pro Bowl. He was noted for his quickness and notorious for his toughness. In its October 24, 1955, issue, *Life* ran an expose of pro football violence with the catchy title, "Savagery on Sunday." Mar-

NUMBER 83

tinkovic was the only Packer included among the roughest players in the game—although former Packer Paul Lipscomb was called "just about the dirtiest player in the game." In response, Bucko Kilroy and Wayne Robinson of the Eagles brought a libel suit against the magazine and won the case in a Philadelphia court in 1958. Nonetheless, the 1950s were filled with brutal hits and ferocious tackling. Martinkovic could dish it out with the best, but was a handsome, popular player and a successful car dealer in town when he was traded to the Giants. He spent his final 1958 season in New York and was elected to the Packer Hall of Fame in 1974.

There's a neat symmetry to Martinkovic's career. He came in a trade from Washington for Ted Cook, who would not play in the NFL again, and left Green Bay six years later in a trade for a high draft pick who turned out to be Ray Nitschke. In a way, the Packers got 21 years of great defense for one year of declining defense. Several other Packer number 83s came via trades. Hall of Famer Len Ford was washed up when he came over from the Browns for a draft pick in 1958. The next year, Bill Quinlan also came over from the Browns, along with Lew Carpenter, for Bill Howton. In 1970, the Packers traded Herb Adderley to the Cowboys for still another defensive end, Clarence Williams, as well as center Mal Walker. Coach Bart Starr acquired holdout receiver John Jefferson from the Chargers for a bunch of draft picks in 1983. Finally in 2002, General Manager Mike Sherman traded for head-case receiver Terry Glenn and challenged coach Mike Sherman to make it work.

What follows is a table of all major Packer trades throughout their history. Trades involving only draft position exchanges and waiver deals are not included. Neither are most outright sales or purchases of players' contracts; those included are indicated with a $. Also ignored are most deals for "past considerations" and those for conditional draft choices when the player involved failed to make the team so that the draft choice reverted to its original owner. This example demonstrates how to interpret the table:

PACKERS TRADE REGISTER
HOW TO READ THIS TABLE:

| 1978 | 79-8 (Ron Cassady) | 49ers | Steve Knutson |
| 1978 | 80-5 (Browns- Paul McDonald) | Rams | Rick Nuzum |

In 1978 the Packers obtained Steve Knutson from the 49ers in exchange for an 8th-round pick in the 1979 draft which the 49ers used to select Ron Cassady. Also in 1978, the Packers obtained Rick Nuzum from the Rams in exchange for a 5th-round pick in the 1980 draft. The Rams subsequently dealt that pick to the Browns and Cleveland selected Paul McDonald with the pick.

DATE	GAVE	TO	RECEIVED
1923	Jab Murray	Racine Legion	Whitey Woodin
1923	$	Racine Legion	Butts Hayes
1924	$	Cleveland	Tillie Voss
1925	$	Duluth	Dick O'Donnell
1929	?	Giants	Cal Hubbard
1931	Bo Molenda	Giants	$
1932	Tom Nash	Brooklyn	Player Named Later
1934	See 1932	Brooklyn	Tiny Engebretsen

PACKERS BY THE NUMBERS

DATE	GAVE	TO	RECEIVED
1934	Johnny Blood	Pirates	$
1935	?	Bears	Walt Kiesling
1936	Roger Grove	Brooklyn	Wayland Becker & Bill Croft
1937	Av Daniel	Brooklyn	Bill Lee
1938	Lou Gordon	Rams	Charles Ookie Miller
1939	John Yerby	Rams	Dick Zoll
1939	Bernie Scherer	Steelers	Clarence Thompson
1939	Wayland Becker	Steelers	?
1939	39-10 (Carl Kaplanoff)	Brooklyn	Leo Disend
1940	Millard White	Eagles	Fred Shirey
1940	Bud Svendsen	Brooklyn	Beattie Feathers & Dick Cassiano
1940	Hank Bruder	Steelers	Lou Midler
1940	Fred Shirey	Rams	?
1941	?	Eagles	Mike Bucchianeri
1941	Frank Balazs	Cards	$
1947	Bob Nussbaumer	Redskins	Jack Jacobs
1947	Merv Pregulman	Lions	Damon Tassos
1947	$	Cards	Ward Cuff
1947	48-15 (Dale Schwartzkopf)	Redskins	Johnny Kovatch
1947	?	Lions	48-5 (Don Richards)
1947	48-9 (Ken Wittgen)	Giants	?
1948	49-7 (Jerry Williams)	Rams	Clyde Johnson
1948	Roy McKay	Redskins	Don Deeks
1948	Bob Rennebohm & H. Brown	Lions	Ted Cook & Frank Syzmanski
1948	Frank Syzmanski	Eagles	Jim Kekeris
1948	49-10 (Rams- George Buksar)	Lions	?
1949	50-5 (Tom Rowe)	Steelers	Bob Cifers
1949	Pat West & Jim Ford	Giants	J. Bush & E. Kelley
1950	Paul Lipscomb	Redskins	Ben Szafaryn
1950	Gordy Soltau	Browns	Joe Spencer
1950	51-4 (Bob Smith)	Browns	Tom O'Malley
1950	?	Cards	Paul Christman
1950	51-8 (Art Spinney)	Browns	Bill Boedecker
1951	Conditional 1&2	Rams	Bob Thomason
1951	Dan Orlich	Browns	Walt Michaels
1951	Ted Cook	Redskins	John Martinkovic
1951	?	Bears	52-10 (Bud Ruffler)
1952	Bob Gain & (Zeke Costa)	Browns	Dom Moselle, Ace Loomis, 52-4 Don Schroll, Dan Orlich

DATE	GAVE	TO	RECEIVED
1952	Walt Michaels	Browns	Dick Logan, Forest Chubby Grigg, Zeke Costa
1952	Al Collins	Eagles	Dan Sandifer
1952	Ace Loomis	Browns	Tony Adamle & Don Phelps
1952	$	Lions	Clarence Self
1952	Jug Girard	Lions	Ed Berrang & Steve Dowden
1952	$	Bears	Ray Bray
1953	Arnold Galifa	Giants	54-1(Veryl Switzer) & Val Joe Walker
1953	54-4 (Ralph Felton)	Redskins	Johnny Papit
1953	54-15 (Ed Gossage)	49ers	Ben Aldridge
1953	54-6 (Dacus Pence)	Browns	Gus Cifelli
1953	?	Colts	54-4 (Tom Allman)
1954	55-4 (Paul Reynolds)	Browns	Jerry Helluin
1954	Babe Parilli & Bob Fleck	Browns	Bob Garrett, John Bauer, Jack Miller, Chester Gierula
1954	John Bauer	Giants	55-20 (Bob Antkowiak)
1955	Art Hunter	Browns	Bill Lucky & Joe Skibinski
1955	Carl Elliot & 56-3 (AD Williams)	Rams	Tom Dahms
1956	57-5 (Henry Jordan)	Browns	Don King & Gene Donaldson
1956	57-6 (Joe Amstutz)	Browns	John Sandusky
1956	Tom Dahms	Cards	57-6 (John Nisby)
1956	Jack Spinks	Giants	57-12 (Glenn Bestor)
1957	Bob Garrett & Roger Zatkoff	Browns	Babe Parilli, John Petitbon, Carl Massey, Sam Palumbo, Bill Kinard, John Macerelli
1957	Tobin Rote & Val Joe Walker	Lions	Ollie Spencer, Norm Masters, Jim Salsbury, Don McIlhenny
1957	Ben Szafaryn	Eagles	Ray Bawel
1957	John Martinkovic & Dalton Truax	Giants	58-3 (Ray Nitschke)
1957	Lee Hermsen	Bears	58-19 (Bill Roehnelt)
1957	John Nisby	Steelers	$
1958	Dick Deschaine	Browns	59-8 (Bob Laraba)
1958	Dick Christy	Steelers	59-5 (Andy Cvercko)
1958	John Petitbon, Doyle Nix & 59-5 (Bob Wetoska)	Redskins	Steve Meilinger & JD Kimmel
1958	59-4 (Gary Prahst)	Browns	Len Ford
1958	Al Barry & Joe Skibinski	Giants	59-7 (Gary Raid)
1959	Bill Howton	Browns	Bill Quinlan & Lew Carpenter

PACKERS BY THE NUMBERS

DATE	GAVE	TO	RECEIVED
1959	60-4 (Johnny Brewer)	Browns	Henry Jordan
1959	Marv Matuszak	Colts	Fuzzy Thurston
1959	60-3 (Charley Elizey)	Cards	Lamar McHan
1959	$	Giants	Emlen Tunnell
1959	60-5 (Bob Jarus)	Browns	Bob Freeman
1959	Ollie Spencer	Lions	60-5 (Dale Hackbart)
1959	60-10 (Paul Oglesby)	Cards	Ken Beck
1960	A.D. Williams	Browns	Willie Davis
1960	Bob Freeman	Eagles	61-4 (Joe Lesage)
1960	Fred Cone	Cowboys	61-10 (Roger Hagberg)
1960	61-8 (Fred Cox)	Browns	Bob Jarus
1960	$	Cards	Larry Hickman
1961	Joel Wells	Giants	62-3 (Gary Barnes)
1961	Lamar McHan	Colts	62-5 (Chuck Morris
1961	Dale Hackbart	Redskins	62-6 (Joe Sutro)
1961	Steve Meilinger	Cowboys	62-12 (Joe Thorne)
1961	62-3 (John Furman)	Browns	John Roach
1962	Tom Bettis	Steelers	63-3 (Dennis Claridge)
1962	Paul Dudley	Giants	63-4 (Lionel Aldridge)
1962	Ben Davidson	Redskins	63-5 (Jack Cvercko)
1962	Ernie Green	Browns	63-7 (Gary Kroner)
1962	?	Steelers	63-7 (Olin Hill)
1962	?	Cowboys	63-8 (Keith Kinderman)
1963	Bill Quinlan & John Symank	Giants	64-3 (Joe O'Donnell)
1963	Ed Blaine	Eagles	64-4 (Bob Long)
1963	64-6 (Jim Evans)	Cowboys	Jerry Norton
1963	Ken Iman	Rams	Zeke Bratkowski
1963	Gary Barnes	Cowboys	64-5 (Duke Carlysle)
1963	?	Colts	64-3 (Ode Burrell)
1964	Jim Ringo & Earl Gros	Eagles	Lee Roy Caffey & 65-1 (Donny Anderson)
1964	Urban Henry	Steelers	65-6 (Rich Koeper)?
1964	Turnley Todd	Giants	65-7 (Jerry Roberts)
1965	Dan Currie	Rams	Carroll Dale
1965	65-3 (Bob Timberlake—from Dallas)	Giants	Don Chandler
1965	Ron Kramer (played out option)	Lions	66-1 (Jim Grabowski)
1965	66-6 (Ed Yates)	Redskins	Bill Anderson
1965	?	Browns	66-3 (Fred Heron)
1965	66-5 (Dick Arndt)	Rams	?

DATE	GAVE	TO	RECEIVED
1966	Tom Moore	Rams	67-2 (Dave Dunaway)
1966	Lloyd Voss & Tony Jeter	Steelers	67-1 (Bob Hyland)
1966	Ron Rector	Redskins	67-4 (Travis Williams)
1966	Ron Smith	Steelers	67-5 (Dwight Hood)
1966	Hank Gremminger	Cowboys	67-5 (Dick Tate)
1966	Allen Jacobs	Giants	67-7 (Bob Ziolkowski)
1967	68-2 (John Wright)	Rams	Ben Wilson
1967	Jim Taylor (played out option)	Saints	68-1 (Fred Carr)
1967	Fred Heron	Cards	68-3 (Bill Stevens)
1967	Kent Nix	Steelers	68-5 (Steve Duich)
1967	Dave Hathcock	Giants	68-10 (Rick Cash)
1967	Dick Arndt	Steelers	68-4 (Brendan McCarthy)
1968	Steve Wright & Tommy Crutcher	Giants	Francis Peay
1968	Dick Capp	Steelers	69-6 (Ron Jones)
1968	Bob Long	Falcons	Leo Carroll
1969	Leo Carroll	Redskins	70-10 (Frank Patrick)
1969	Ron Kostelnik	Colts	70-4 (Skip Butler)
1970	Herb Adderley	Cowboys	Clarence Williams & Mal Walker
1970	Lee Roy Caffey, Elijah Pitts, & Bob Hyland	Bears	70-1 (Mike McCoy)
1970	71-2 (Ernie Janet)	49ers	Kevin Hardy
1970	Tom Brown	Redskins	71-5 (Donnell Smith)
1970	Travis Williams & 71-4 (Steve Worster)	Rams	71-2 (Virgil Robinson) & 72-6 (Robert Hudson)
1970	Marv Fleming	Dolphins	Jack Clancy
1970	John Rowser	Steelers	John Hilton
1970	Francis Winkler	Falcons	Ken Mendenhall
1970	Ron Jones	Falcons	$
1970	Jacques MacKinnon	Raiders	71-7 (James Johnson)
1971	Boyd Dowler	Redskins	71-5 (Jim Stillwagon)
1971	Don Horn & 71-1 (Marv Montgomery)	Broncos	Alden Roche and 71-1 (John Brockington)
1971	Bob Jeter	Bears	72-6 (Dave Pureifory)
1971	Kevin Hardy	Chargers	72-1 (Jerry Tagge)
1971	72-3 (Bart Buetow)	Vikings	Zeke Bratkowski
1971	72-17 (Oscar Dragon)	Chargers	Cal Withrow
1971	72-5 (Bill Butler)	Saints	Wimpy Winther
1971	72-9 (Gary Hambell)	Colts	?
1972	Donny Anderson	Cards	Mac Lane
1972	Dave Hampton	Falcons	Malcolm Snider
1972	Lionel Aldridge & 74-3 (Steve Craig)	Chargers	Jim Hill

PACKERS BY THE NUMBERS

DATE	GAVE	TO	RECEIVED
1972	Vern Vanoy & 73-5 (Louis Neal)	Raiders	Carleton Oats
1972	73-4 (Terry Nelson)	Rams	Tommy Crutcher
1973	Dave Robinson	Redskins	75-2 (Bill Bain)
1973	73-2 (Golden Richards)	Cowboys	Ron Widby and Ike Thomas
1973	74-2 (Fred Solomon) & 75-2 (Andre Tillman)	Dolphins	Jim Del Gaizo
1973	74-4 (Sammy Johnson)	49ers	Al Randolph
1973	Zeke Bratkowski	Bears	74-6 (Don Woods)
1973	Francis Peay	Chiefs	Aaron Brown
1973	Len Garrett	Saints	74-8 (Ned Gullett)
1974	75-8 (Mario Cage)	Colts	Ted Hendricks
1974	Tom McLeod	Colts	75-2 (Monte Jackson in Hadl Trade below)
1974	75-1 (Mike Fanning) & 76-1 (Dennis Lick) & 75-2 (Monte Jackson) & 76-2 Pat Thomas) & 75-3 (Geoff Reese)	Rams	John Hadl
1974	Scott Hunter	Bills	Steve Okoniewski & Pete Van Valkenberg
1974	Bob Brown	Chargers	75-3 (Will Harrell)
1974	75-5 (Kyle Davis)	Cowboys	Jack Concannon
1974	75-6 (Darius McCarthy)	Rams	Harry Schuh
1974	76-3 (Ron Coder)	Steelers	Bruce Van Dyke
1975	Ted Hendricks	Raiders	76-1 (Mark Koncar) & 77-1 (Ezra Johnson)
1975	Mac Lane	Chiefs	76-3 (Mike C. McCoy)
1975	76-6 (Chiefs—Steve Taylor)	Oilers	Paul Robinson
1975	76-7 (Pete Rome)	Bengals	Pat Matson
1975	Jim Del Gaizo	Giants	76-3 (see Carlson trade below)
1975	76-3 (Gary Barbaro)	Chiefs	Dean Carlson
1975	Bill Lueck	Eagles	76-4 (Steve Largent in Dickey trade below)
1976	John Hadl, Ken Ellis, 77-3 (Tim Wilson) & 76-4 (Steve Largent)	Oilers	Lynn Dickey
1976	Perry Smith	Cards	77-3 (Terdel Middleton)
1976	Bill Bain	Broncos	77-3 (Rick Scribner)
1976	Joe Danelo	Giants	77-7 (Derrell Gofourth) & 78-10 (Mark Totten)

NUMBER EIGHTY-THREE

DATE	GAVE	TO	RECEIVED
1976	77-12 (Rod Martin)	Raiders	Ollie Smith
1976	77-4 (Ted Petersen)	Steelers	Bob Barber
1976	$	Seahawks	Don Hansen
1977	Mike McCoy	Raiders	78-1 (John Anderson) & 79-4 (to Redskins for Tim Stokes) & Herb McMath
1977	Dave Pureifory	Steelers	78-5 (Willie Wilder)
1977	Perry Smith	Cards	Terdell Middleton
1978	79-4 (Johnny Lynn) Jets & 79-5 (Stan Blinka)		Carl Barzilaukas
1978	79-8 (Ron Cassady)	49ers	Steve Knutson
1978	80-5 (Browns—Paul McDonald)	Rams	Rick Nuzum
1979	Willie Buchanan	Chargers	80-1 (George Cumby) & 79-7 (Rich Wingo)
1980	81-6 (Mel Hoover)	Giants	Randy Dean
1981	Steve Luke	Falcons	Frank Reed
1982	83-3 (Dolphins—Charles Benson)	Oilers	Angelo Fields
1982	Aundra Thompson & 82-1 (Saints—Lindsay Scott) & 83-1 (Gary Anderson) & 82-2 (Patriots—Robert Weathers) & 84-2 (Jets—Glen Dennison)	Chargers	John Jefferson & 82-1 (Ron Hallstrom)
1982	Mark Koncar	Oilers	83-10 (Byron Williams)
1983	Bruce Clark	Saints	83-1 (Tim Lewis)
1983	84-8 (Winford Hood)	Broncos	Greg Boyd
1983	84-9 (Dave Hestera)	Chiefs	Charley Getty
1983	Derrell Gofourth	Chargers	84-12 (Lenny Taylor)
1984	Jan Stenerud	Vikings	85-7 (Eric Wilson)
1985	86-1 (Gerald Robinson) & 87-5 (Nelson Jones) & rights to USFL's Tom Robison	Chargers	Mossy Cade
1985	John Jefferson	Browns	87-7 (Bill Smith)
1985	86-6 (Orson Mobley)	Broncos	Scott Brunner
1985	Scott Brunner	Cards	86-6 (Burnell Dent)
1985	86-11 (Tom Flaherty)	Bengals	Mike Obravac
1985	86-12 (Derek Christian)	Bills	Preston Dennard
1986	87-12 (Wes Dove)	Seahawks	Dan Ross
1986	Phil McConkey	Giants	87-12 (Norman Jefferson)

PACKERS BY THE NUMBERS

DATE	GAVE	TO	RECEIVED
1987	James Lofton	Raiders	87-3 (Frankie Neal) & 88-4 (Rollin Putzier)
1987	88-11 (Rick Macleod)	Seahawks	Dave Brown
1988	89-2 (Lawyer Tillman) & 89-5 (Kyle Kramer)	Browns	Herman Fontenot, 90-1(Tony Bennett), 89-3 (Anthony Dilweg) & 89-5 (Vince Workman)
1989	Jeff Graham	Redskins	Erik Affholter, 89-5 (Jeff Query) & 89-8 (Brian Shulman)
1990	Brent Fullwood	Browns	91-7 (Frank Blevins)
1991	91-1 (Antone Davis)	Eagles	91-1 (Vinnie Clark) & 92-1 (given to Falcons for Favre)
1991	Tim Harris	49ers	92-2 & 93-2 (Holmgren and Position exchange with Cowboys)
1991	Conditional draft pick	Falcons	Brad Daluiso
1992	92-2 (From Tim Harris trade)	49ers	Mike Holmgren
1992	92-1 (Cowboys—Kevin Smith)	Falcons	Brett Favre
1992	92-6 (Brian Brauninger)	Cards	Tootie Robbins
1992	Vince Workman	Bucs	93-5 (Mark Brunell)
1993	93-5 (Kenny Shedd)	Jets	Ken O'Brien
1993	Dave McCloughan	Seahawks	93-6 (Doug Evans)
1993	94-7 (Bynote Butler)	Broncos	Doug Widell
1993	94-4 (Chargers- Lewis Bush)	Patriots	John Stephens
1993	Lester Archambeau	Falcons	James Milling
1993	Vinnie Clark	Falcons	93-4 (trade to Cowboys in position exchange)
1993	John Stephens	Falcons	Eric Dickerson
1994	95-5 (Redskins—Rich Owens)	Raiders	Charles Jordan
1995	95-4 (Given back in Jackson trade)	Dolphins	Mark Ingram
1995	95-2 (Andrew Greene)	Dolphins	Keith Jackson & 95-4 (from Ingram trade)
1995	Terrell Buckley	Dolphins	Past Considerations
1995	Mark Brunell	Jaguars	95-3 (William Henderson) & 95-5 (Travis Jervey)
1995	Corey Harris	Seahawks	95-3 (Brian Williams)
1995	96-5 (Cards—Harry Stamps)	Chiefs	Lindsay Knapp

DATE	GAVE	TO	RECEIVED
1995	96-6 (Tony Johnson)	Eagles	Joe Sims
1995	Bill Schroeder & Jeff Wilner	Patriots	Mike Arthur
1996	Matt Labounty	Seahawks	Eugene Robinson
1996	Lenny McGill	Falcons	Robert Baldwin
1996	George Teague	Falcons	Conditional Draft Choice
1997	Wayne Simmons	Chiefs	98-5 (Corey Bradford)
1997	98-6 (Kevin McLeaod)	Jaguars	Paul Frase
1997	Chris Hayes	Jets	Carl Greenwood
1997	Past Considerations	Jets	Tyrone Davis
1998	Conditional 7 in 99	Lions	Glyn Milburn
1998	99-4 (Bobbie Collins)	Bills	Darick Holmes
1998	Mike Holmgren	Seahawks	99-2 (Fred Vinson)
1998	Steve Bono	Rams	99-7 (Chris Akins)
1998	Darius Holland	Chiefs	Vaughn Booker
1998	Glyn Milburn	Bears	99-7 (Donald Driver)
1998	Seth Joyner	Broncos	Past Considerations
1999	Past Considerations	Steelers	Jahine Arnold
1999	Rick Mirer	Jets	00-4 (traded to 49ers in position exchange)
1999	John Michels	Eagles	Jon Harris
1999	Derrick Mayes	Seahawks	01-7 (Ron Moore)
1999	Craig Newsome	49ers	00-5 (traded back to 49ers in position exchange)
2000	Fred Vinson & 00-6 (John Hilliard)	Seahawks	Ahman Green & 00-5 (Joey Jamison)
2000	Aaron Brooks & Lamont Hall	Saints	KD Williams & 01-3 (position exchange with 49ers)
2000	01-5 (Tony Stewart)	Eagles	Allen Rossum
2000	Mike Morton	Rams	01-7 (Seahawks- Dennis Norman)
2000	01-7 (Falcons—Kynan Forney)	Broncos	David Bowens
2000	01-4 (Ben Hamilton)	Broncos	Nate Wayne
2000	Jeff Thomason	Eagles	Kaseem Sinceno
2001	Matt Hasselbeck & 01-1 (Steve Hutchinson)	Seahawks	01-1 (Jamal Reynolds) & 01-3 (Torrance Marshall)
2001	David Bowens	Bills	Bobby Collins
2001	02-7 (Carlos Hall)	Titans	Rod Walker
2002	02-4 (Jarvis Green) & 03-4 (Bryant McNeal)	Patriots / Broncos	Terry Glenn

MID-WEST COAST OFFENSE

STERLING SHARPE • WIDE RECEIVER 1988–94

WHO'S WORN THE NUMBER
D. Wells 1946, Knafelc 1954–62, Dale 1965–72, Odom 1974–79, Nixon 1980–81, L. Taylor 1984, Franz 1986, W. Smith 1987r, Sharpe 1988–94, A. Morgan 1996, Rison 1996, Schroeder 1997–2001, J. Walker 2002–.

ORIGINATOR End Don Wells 1946 caught 2 passes for 74 yards in his four years as a Packer.

LONGEST TENURE Gary Knafelc 1954–62.

NUMBER CHANGES End Don Wells wore 43 in 1946–49; receiver Anthony Morgan wore 81 in 1993–95; receiver Bill Schroeder wore 19 in 1994.

OTHER NOTABLES End Gary Knafelc, whom the Packers plucked off the waiver wire, caught the winning touchdown pass in the first game at the new City Stadium in 1957 and later spent several years as the Lambeau Field public-address announcer. He was inducted into the Packer Hall of Fame in 1976. Wide receiver Carroll Dale came over in a great trade with the Rams for aging Dan Currie. Dale was an able deep threat for the Packers for eight years, catching 275 passes for a team record 19.7 average and 35 touchdowns. He was inducted into the Packer Hall of Fame in 1979.

ONE TO FORGET Andre "Bad Moon" Rison, as Chris Berman calls him, was a fortunate pickup for the 1996 Packers, who were decimated by injuries to their receiving corps at midseason. He didn't do much during the regular season, but he paid off in the Super Bowl, catching a 54-yard touchdown pass on the Packers' first play from scrimmage. However, the organization released him after the season, and Rison reacted with some very negative remarks about how he was going to throw his Super Bowl ring into the Flint River because he wanted no memories of Green Bay. The feeling was mutual. It was his only trip to the Big Game.

STERLING SHARPE
When *Milwaukee Journal Sentinel* columnist Bud Lea was asked who were the biggest jerks he dealt with in his nearly 50 years covering the Packers, he rated Sterling Sharpe number one. Sterling Sharpe was one of the three greatest receivers in team history, but Lea's assessment would find agreement in many quarters. For one thing, Sharpe

NUMBER 84

stopped talking to the local media early on in his career. Ironically, in retirement he became part of the media by joining ESPN as a studio analyst, a job at which he has proven himself quite capable. A second reason is that Sharpe, as evinced on ESPN, has a grating personality. He is very knowledgeable and intelligent, but his sense of humor is cutting and sarcastic. In contrast to Max McGee, another former Packer receiver who went into broadcasting, Sharpe's jokes are always outwardly directed; there is no hint of amusing self-deprecation about him. In part, that represents his strong ego and is the third reason to take exception to him: he wanted every pass to come his way. Some questioned how much of a team player he was because of that.

The final two reasons are more specific. In the last few days before the 1994 season opener, Sharpe walked out on the team and demanded to renegotiate his contract. He had signed a long-term deal a year or two before, but decided to walk out on the contract and the team in order to demand more money. It was a selfish and crass move and was resented by a number of his teammates, not to mention the fans. The team managed to mollify him in time to get him in uniform for the opener, but the whole affair left a bad taste. Finally, when Sterling became eligible for the Packer Hall of Fame in 2000, the selection committee voted overwhelmingly to induct him. Unfortunately, they were unable to get in touch with him to confirm arrangements for the ceremony. Sharpe, who works in a very visible position for a very large media outlet, did not respond to any of a series of telephone calls, letters, and emails. After the passage of months, his wife at last called the Packer Hall to accept the honor. With the induction dinner fast approaching, the Hall told her that next year would be better, and Sharpe was inducted in 2002. Lea reported that Sharpe was the first player to rudely blow off this unique team honor.

In Sharpe's defense, he said he stopped talking to local media people because, "I don't want anything to come out that may be negative or twisted that offends my teammates." (Attner) Reporters do like to dig up the dirt. Perhaps Sharpe was concerned that some of his cutting remarks taken in jest in the locker room would look different if reported in the press and would stir resentment. Or maybe he just didn't want to deal with inevitable questions about why he or the team failed in a particular game. As to wanting the ball too much, the same has been said of Jerry Rice and many others in every sport. The greatest players are supremely confident of their ability and feel with some justification that the best way for the team to win is for them to have the ball. Great players who share the ball and the credit, like Michael Jordan or Brett Favre, are rare. Regarding the last-minute holdout, football is a business, and each player must maximize his earnings potential at all times. Sharpe's side of the Hall of Fame dispute has not been reported. When he finally was inducted, Sharpe asserted that he was pleased because he never had to "kiss babies" or campaign for election, but got in solely "by being the type of player that I was."

Sharpe clearly had a dominant personality. What is lost in all that is what a magnificent player he was. He was big and strong and had good speed, but more important had great moves and could get open against anyone. He had terrific hands and did not shy away from catching the ball in heavy traffic. Once he caught the ball, he knew what to do with it and where the end zone was. In short, he was ideally suited to the San Francisco passing scheme, commonly known as the West Coast Offense, that new coach Mike Holmgren installed in Sharpe's fifth year.

Sharpe credited that offense with helping him reach new heights, "I've had a chance to line up all over the field and that makes it hard to double me. And if you get open, they will get you the ball. As a receiver, you can't help but love it." (Attner) The San Francisco passing scheme was first developed by Bill Walsh when he was the offensive coach for the Cincinnati Bengals in the early 1970s. Originally he ran a version of the real West Coast Offense first established by Sid Gillman of the San Diego Chargers in the early 1960s. That offense was wide open and relied on passing the ball deep downfield often. Branches of the real West Coast Offense include Al Davis' Oakland Raiders' vertical passing attack, the Chargers Don "Air" Coryell, the Redskins Joe Gibbs scheme, the Cowboys Norv Turner precision, timing offense, and the St. Louis Rams Mike Martz's greatest show of turf. Bill Walsh's misnamed West Coast Offense was proof that necessity is the mother of invention. Walsh was forced to come up with something different when his strong-armed quarterback Greg Cook got hurt and was replaced by Virgil Carter, who was smart and mobile, but lacked arm strength. Furthermore, the Bengals did not have a real strong running attack.

What Walsh devised was a precision, ball-control, short-passing offense. The offense was designed to have the quarterback quickly go through a progression of reads, hit the open man in stride, and let the receiver gain yards after the catch. Joe Montana and Steve Young ran it to perfection for the 49ers. Holmgren added his own twists to the offense as one must, depending on the personnel available. While he was having trouble getting a running game going in Green Bay's Mid-West Coast Offense, Holmgren ran a lot of screen passes which Walsh never did, for example. The most important common element of all the later varieties of Walsh's original scheme is that the quarterback get the ball into the hands of the open receiver quickly, and Favre was glad to comply with Sharpe in Green Bay.

Sterling led the league in receptions three times, once in yards receiving, and twice in touchdown catches. In his seven-year career he caught 595 passes for 8,134 yards and 65 touchdowns. In addition, he was tough; he was frequently called a "warrior." In those seven years he played through broken ribs, pulled hamstrings, a cervical injury, and turf toe without complaint. Often he was too hurt to practice, but he never missed a game. In his own words, he was Old School, "And to me, Lambeau Field is Old School. You play when you're hurt, you play in the cold, you play in the mud, you play when the field conditions are nowhere near their best, and you go out there and you perform because you're a professional. Every time I think of Lambeau Field, that's football to me." ("Q&A")

In the 1994 season finale, though, he hurt his neck, and his career ended in an instant. He had surgery on his neck and engaged in a bitter contract dispute with the team until they released him. He considered returning to football with another team and risking permanent paralysis, but instead wisely stayed in the ESPN studios. From there he openly rooted for the Packers to win Super Bowl XXXI, but rooted against them the following year for an understandable reason —his loquacious brother Shannon starred at tight end for the Broncos. When Denver won, Shannon gave his Super Bowl ring to his brother. Since he would later win a second with Denver and a third with the Ravens, Shannon would never miss it. If Sterling had stayed healthy, he would have earned one with his Packer teammates in 1996; a healthy Sharpe on the Green Bay side might have helped put down the Broncos in 1997, as well, but we will never know. How unstoppable would a three-receiver set of Sharpe, Brooks, and Freeman have been?

FOR FURTHER INFORMATION

Attner, Paul. "A Sterling Receiver," *The Sporting News.* 12/28/92. (12)

Bauman, Michael. "Sharpe Let's His Fingers Do the Talking," *Green Bay Packers 1993 Yearbook.* (14-7)

Castle, George. "Leader of the Pack," *Sport.* 9/93. (80-2)

Favre, Brett, with Chris Havel. *Favre: For the Record.* Garden City, NY: Doubleday, 1997. (149-50, 206-9)

Faust, Pete. "Record Breaking Rookie," *Green Bay Packers 1989 Yearbook.* (37-3)

Gentile, Domenic, with Gary D'Amato. *The Packer Tapes: My 32 Years with the Green Bay Packers.* Madison, WI: Prairie Oak Press, 1995. (101-2)

Lea, Bud. "Aloof Sharpe Goofs Up Packer Hall Plans," *Milwaukee Journal Sentinel Packer Plus.* 3/14/01. Available online at www.jsonline.com/packer/comm/mar01/leacol15031401.asp.

McGinn, Bob. "All-for-One Concept Easier Without Sharpe," *Milwaukee Journal Sentinel.* 11/26/95. (Sports 9)

Oates, Tom. "Sharpe," *Green Bay Packers 1994 Yearbook.* (10-2)

"Questions and Answers with Sterling Sharpe," Green Bay Packers Web site. Available at www.packers.com/news/stories/2002/07/13/1.

SUPER BOWL I
MAX MCGEE • WIDE RECEIVER 1954, 1957–67

WHO'S WORN THE NUMBER Deeks 1948, Ethridge 1949, Rhodemyre 1951, Wimberly 1952, Romine 1955, Jennings 1955, E. Barnes 1956, McGee 1954, 1957–67, Spilis 1969–71, D. Gordon 1973, Staroba 1973, Payne 1974–77, E. Boyd 1978, Kimball 1979–80 Epps 1982–88, Query 1989–91, Lee Morris 1987r, K. Taylor 1992, R. Lewis 1992–94, Mickens 1995–97, Bradford 1998–2001.

ORIGINATOR Tackle Don Deeks 1948—three teams, four years, 29 games (eight in Green Bay).

LONGEST TENURE Max McGee 1954, 1957–67.

NUMBER CHANGES Center Jay Rhodemyre wore 22 in 1948–49 and 50 in1952; defensive end Ab Wimberly wore 16 in 1950–51 and 43 in 1950; back Al Romine wore 23 in 1958; receiver Dick Gordon also wore 7 in 1973; replacement Lee Morris also wore 48 and 81 in 1987; wide receiver Terry Mickens wore 88 in 1994.

OTHER NOTABLES Jay Rhodemyre was second team All Pro in 1951; Ab Wimberly (see top 16).

ONE TO FORGET Third-round pick John Spilis caught 27 passes in 40 games for one touchdown, not quite living up to Max McGee's legacy.

MAX MCGEE Cool in the clutch was Max McGee. The bigger the game, the more tense the situation, the better he played. He had a remarkable ability to relax in any environment and to enjoy himself both on and off the field. He grew up in Texas and enrolled at Tulane University in New Orleans, where he not only led the team in rushing for three years while also lettering in baseball and basketball, but also took full advantage of the extracurricular advantages offered by the Big Easy. And he earned a useful degree in business, as well.

He was the Packers fifth-round draft choice in 1954 and went on to catch nine scoring passes as a rookie, in addition to holding the job as the team's punter. After two years in the Air Force, where he served with future teammate and roommate Zeke Bratkowski, Max returned to Green Bay in 1957. Over the next few years, he established himself as the struggling team's deep threat. In Lombardi's first year, 1959, McGee led the league with an average of 23.2 yards per catch.

Lombardi's assistant coaches were not impressed, though. Their assessment was unanimous—trade him. Among their comments were, "I don't think he tries all the time. No team player and bad for the team

. . . Attitude of Max is bad. I question whether Max is the type of player who can get us a championship . . . I would like to see us replace him. We need someone dependable . . . Poor attitude and a bad actor off the field." (Wagner, 31)

However, Lombardi saw other qualities in Max, qualities that would make McGee one of the coach's favorites. For one thing, he was big, and Lombardi favored large receivers because they make larger targets and tend to be better able to block. He was swift, with good moves, and was especially skilled at gaining yards after the catch. His one flaw was that he was so impassive that he would sometimes drop the easy ones, although the tough ones got his full attention.

Perhaps of most importance, Max was intelligent; he had a good sense of what would work against a particular defense in a particular situation, and gave Lombardi and Starr good suggestions as to how he could get open at any time. That intelligence was coupled with a quick wit that came in useful in a variety of situations. For instance, when Lombardi would come on too strong with the team, McGee frequently would break the tension with a sardonic crack. One time Lombardi was disgusted with the team in practice and told them they were going to have to start with the basics. He held up a ball and said, "This is a football." McGee immediately called out, "Stop, coach, you're going too fast," and that gave everyone a laugh. Vince respected those who stood up to him and seemed to understand that McGee's jokes were not said disrespectfully and were not meant to spark a confrontation, but rather to lighten the mood. On the team, McGee was well liked and respected by his teammates.

Finally, there was the simple fact that he could play. He might run around all night with his buddy Paul Hornung—and the stories those two could tell would make a whole other book—but he could still run on the field at game time. In the big games, he was at his best. In the 1960 title game against the Eagles, McGee did fumble once, but he also ran a fake punt 35 yards to convert a fourth down, which led to the Packers only touchdown eight plays later—a seven-yard pass to Max. In the 1966 championship game against Dallas, Starr threw the last of his four touchdown passes 28 yards to McGee, wide open on a corner route for what would be the clinching score. Two weeks later came the game for which he is most remembered, Super Bowl I against Kansas City.

McGee caught only four passes all year in 1966 as a backup to Carroll Dale and Boyd Dowler, so no one really expected him to play much, if at all. The buildup to the game was mostly an attempt to hype a game that most expected to be easily won by whichever team the established NFL would send against the upstart AFL champion. There were 31,000 unsold seats at the Los Angeles Coliseum, despite the top ticket price of only $12. The pressure was all on the Packers as the expected victors. Lombardi got a host of telegrams from other NFL executives, saying how much they were counting on him to uphold the standing of the league. As always, the Packer players themselves remained quiet and engaged in no inflammatory trash-talking, but Chief defensive back Fred "Hammer" Williamson was quoted extensively in the press as to how he was going to pound Packer receivers like Boyd Dowler into submission with his hammer blows. The Chiefs attempted to psych themselves up by drawing on the disrespect everyone was affording them as representatives of the "Mickey Mouse" league. Someone even brought enough sets of Mickey Mouse ears into the locker room so that every Chief player could don them and get ready to explode on the field. With so much expected of them, and with Lombardi exuding anxiety, the Packers were nervous. Except for Max, who went out on the town the night before and didn't get in until 7:30 AM to join Hornung at breakfast. Assistant coach and bed-checker Hawg Hanner disputes that McGee ever left the room, but the romantic legend will live on as a better story.

Green Bay got the ball first, and McGee sat contentedly on the bench with his best friend Hornung discussing the details of Paul's upcoming wedding. On the fourth play of the game, Dowler was hurt while blocking on a running play, and Lombardi yelled out "McGee!" At first Max said he thought that Lombardi had found out about last night and was going to fine him right there on the field. When he realized he was to go in, he couldn't find his helmet, and coach Hanner had to throw him one. In that series, Starr was sacked twice, and the two teams would exchange punts. Starting from their own 20 on their second possession, the Packers moved 43 yards on three passes and two runs. Facing a third and three from the Kansas City 37, Starr stared down a blitz and threw a pass behind McGee at the KC 23. Max reached back and grabbed the pass one-handed, shook off cornerback Willie Mitchell, and ran in for the score. McGee would get open repeatedly on this slant play. The Chiefs were blitzing right linebacker E.J. Holub because right defensive end Chuck Hurston was in a weakened state from having lost 40 pounds recovering from a virus. Thus, Mitchell had no help from the linebacker in front of him, and also got none from the free safety deep because he was covering the back flaring out of the backfield. Later in the quarter, the Chiefs Mike Mercer (a future Packer) would miss a 40-yard field goal, and the quarter ended with the Packers leading 7-0.

Kansas City tied the score on a 66-yard drive in the second quarter. Green Bay answered immediately with a 73-yard drive of its own. On the third play of the drive, a 64-touchdown pass to Dale was nullified by an offsides penalty, so the Packers took the long way and scored on a vintage power sweep by Jim Taylor from the KC 14. Kansas City came right back down the field to kick a 31-yard field goal in the last minute of the half to trail by only 14-10.

The second half was a different ball game. The Packers defense came out aggressively. On the fourth play of the half, Lee Roy Caffey and Ray Nitschke blitzed Len Dawson, who threw a bad pass off his back foot that Willie Wood picked off at his own 45 and returned 50 yards to the KC five, where Mike Garrett ran him down. Elijah Pitts ran it in on the next play, and the game was essentially over. Later in the quarter, the Packers would cap a 56-yard drive with a perfect 13-yard Starr touchdown pass to McGee, who juggled it for a second before securing the score. The Packers would score a final touchdown on another short Pitts run in the fourth quarter. More important, in that quarter the Chiefs mouthy Hammer would get hammered on a running play late in the game and be carried off the field unconscious. The final score was 35-10. Aided by cool Max McGee's seven catches for 138 yards and two scores, Green Bay overcame early nervousness to make the game a rout. Bart Starr was voted the MVP, but the award could just as easily have gone to McGee—especially considering his previous night's busy activities.

Max played one more year and caught only three passes. He did nothing memorable against the Rams or Cowboys in the playoffs, but he did make his final professional catch in Super Bowl II against the Raiders. It went for 35 yards on a third-and-one, one last big play in one last championship victory. In his dozen years in Green Bay, McGee caught 345 passes for 6,346 yards and 50 touchdowns. He averaged 18.4 yards per catch, trailing only Carroll Dale and Billy Howton among Packers who have caught at least 100 passes.

In retirement, his business acumen paid off and Max first struck it rich by investing early in the restaurant chain Chi Chi's. He has had many other successful business ventures since. McGee did not get married until he was in his 50s, and has two sons, one with juvenile diabetes. Sparked by that, he has raised over a million dollars for research into this disease. Along with his business and charity activities, Max also spent 20 years teamed with Jim Irwin in the Packers broadcast booth. The two had a natural chemistry and an easy casual style that made listening fun. With his affable charm and pass catching heroics, he personified Packer grace under pressure. Max will always seem like an old friend to Packer fans.

FOR FURTHER INFORMATION

Gutner, George. "When Max Attacked," *New Orleans.* 1/97. (116-7)

Hornung, Paul, as told to Al Silverman. *Football and the Single Man.* Garden City, NY: Doubleday, 1965. (209-16)

Kramer, Jerry, with Dick Schaap. *Distant Replay.* New York: G.P. Putnam, 1985. (58-61,64-7)

Lombardi, Vince, with W.C. Heinz. *Run to Daylight.* Englewood Cliffs, NJ: Prentice-Hall, 1963. (60-1)

Peary, Danny. *Super Bowl: The Game of Their Lives.* New York: Macmillan, 1997. (3-17)

Remmel, Lee. "Maxie the Taxi," *Green Bay Packers 1961 Yearbook.* (28-30)

Starr, Bart, with Murray Olderman. *Starr: My Life in Football.* New York: William Morrow, 1987. (81-3)

Wagner, Len. *Launching the Glory Years: The 1959 Packers—What They Didn't Tell Us.* Green Bay, WI: Coach's Books LLC [Jay Bengtson], 2001. (31)

Zimmerman, Paul. "Day One," *Sports Illustrated.* Fall 1995. (74-81)

 1966 SUPER BOWL I DATA
Green Bay Packers 35
Kansas City Chiefs 10
January 15, 1967 • Los Angeles Memorial Coliseum
Attendance: 61,946 (Top ticket price was $12, but there were 30,000 empty seats)
Winner's Share: $15,000
Loser's Share: $7,500
Weather: 72 degrees, sunny and hazy

KEY STATS	PACKERS	CHIEFS
First Downs	21	17
Rush Yards	133	72
Pass Yards	228	167

PACKERS BY THE NUMBERS

KEY STATS	PACKERS	CHIEFS
Total Yards	361	239
Interceptions	1	1
Fumbles Lost	1	1
Penalties	4-40	4-26
Third down conversions	11/15	3/13
Time of Possession	31:25	28:35

Halftime Score: Packers 14 Chiefs 10

LEADERS

Rushing: Jim Taylor 17-56   Len Dawson 3-24
Passing: Bart Starr 16-23-1 250 yds.   Len Dawson16-27-1 211 yds.
Receiving: Max McGee 7-138   Chris Burford 4-67

ADDITIONAL FACTS

•Chiefs Buck Buchanon, Chuck Hurston, and Jon Gilliam had been drafted by the Packers. Chiefs Mike Mercer and Aaron Brown would play for the Packers a few years later, and former Packer Tom Bettis was an assistant coach for Kansas City.

•As the first championship game between the rival NFL and AFL, Super Bowl I was broadcast on both NBC (by Curt Gowdy, Paul Christman and Charley Jones) and CBS (by Ray Scott, Jack Whttaker, Frank Gifford, and Pat Summerall).

•At the coin flip, Packers captain Willie Davis tried to snooker NFL referee Norm Schachter and the Chiefs when the Packers won the toss. Davis asserted that "we would like to receive at that end," pointing to one goal line. Schachter replied to Willie that he only go one choice, the ball or the location. The Packers took the ball.

•Paul Hornung was the only Packer not to appear in the game. Lombardi offered the injured Golden Boy the chance, but he declined.

•Kansas City defensive end Chuck Hurston said of Starr, "I've never seen anything like that. Once I was this close to him, and he still threw a touchdown pass. And he didn't even notice me." Starr's passing line for the playoffs was 35-51-1 for 554 yards and six TDs.

•In the playoffs against the Cowboys and Chiefs, the Packers were out-gained on the ground 259 to 235, but held a 493 to 400 edge through the air. They also held a third-down conversion edge over their opponents, 19 of 28 vs. 8 of 27. Each Packer received $9,813 for their victory over Dallas.

•When Fred "The Hammer" Williamson came to in the locker room after being knocked out, he wondered, "I don't remember a thing. Did I make the tackle?"

KING OF SIBERIA
BILL HOWTON • WIDE RECEIVER 1952–58

WHO'S WORN THE NUMBER Schroll 1951, Howton 1952–58, Dowler 1959–69, Hilton 1970, Lammons 1972, M. Donohoe 1973–74, Gaydos 1975, J. Green 1976, E. West 1984–94, Summers 1987r, Freeman 1995–2001.

ORIGINATOR Linebacker Bill "Bonk" Schroll 1951 first played in the All America Football Conference and then with the Lions before finishing his career in Green Bay.

LONGEST TENURE Wide receiver Boyd Dowler 1959–69.

NUMBER CHANGES Tight end Ed West also wore 49 in 1984.

OTHER NOTABLES Lanky Boyd Dowler never got enough recognition in Lombardi's run-oriented offense, but he caught 448 passes for a 15.4 yard average and 40 touchdowns in his 11 years in Green Bay. He was deadly in title games, catching touchdown passes in 1961, 1966, two in the Ice Bowl, and one in Super Bowl II. He was elected to the Packer Hall of Fame in 1978. Antonio Freeman's career faded too quickly, but he had some spectacular seasons as he and Favre teamed up for 57 scores in his seven years. In the playoffs he scored an additional 11 touchdowns, including three in two Super Bowls.

ONE TO FORGET This number was represented by a number of tight ends who could not play. John Hilton was good with Pittsburgh and Pete Lammons played well with the Jets, but both were washed up in Green Bay. Mike Donohoe, though, never was any good, coming over from Atlanta and catching two passes for 18 yards in two years.

BILL HOWTON From 1948 through 1958, the Packers record was 37-93-2, a winning percentage of .288. If we lop off Lambeau's last two years as coach, the record from 1950 through 1958 improves the winning percentage to .306. If we look at the entire decade of the 1950s, including Lombardi's first year of 1959, the percentage leaps to .333. The Packers won only one-third of their games throughout the decade. It was the most embarrassing decade in team history, far surpassing the prolonged mediocrity of both the 1970s and 1980s. Those decades featured disturbing winning percentages of .413 and .438 respectively. A winning percentage of .333 is a grotesque record of a club slowly going out of business, although they were only the second-worst league team of the 1950s. The Cardinals finished 33-84-3, for an all-time low full-decade winning percentage of .288. Other teams that won fewer than one third of their games over a full decade are limited to the 1960s Broncos, .293; the 1970s Saints, .306; the 1980s Bucs, .299; and the 1990s Bengals, .325. In the 1950s, opposing coaches threatened underachieving players that they would be shipped to Green Bay to finish their careers in snowy, losing oblivion. Between the weather and the hopeless performance of the Packers, Green Bay was considered the NFL's Siberia.

The facilities were substandard and the coaching was spotty, but the Packers did have some good players at the time—just not enough of them. Of the dozen hearty souls who played most of the decade in Green Bay, Al Carmichael and Howie Ferguson, two running backs, experienced the worst of the losing from 1953 through 1958. Their years as Packers produced just 20 wins and two ties in 72 games for a .292 winning percentage. The other 10 trapped players included Breezy Reid, Tobin Rote, Fred Cone, John Martinkovic, Bobby Dillon, Billy Howton, Hawg Hanner, Jim Ringo, Bill Forester, and Gary Knafelc. The three biggest stars of the group were defensive back Bobby Dillon, quarterback Tobin Rote, and wide receiver Billy Howton. With a 26-56-2 record from 1952 through 1958, Howton's Packers achieved the lowest winning percentage (.321) of those

three stars, giving him the dubious crown of the King of Siberia.

Billy Howton was a fast and shifty end who was a two-time collegiate team MVP at Rice. He was selected in the second round of the 1952 draft by the Packers and reunited in Green Bay with Tobin Rote, who had graduated two years ahead of Howton at Rice. Bill burst into the NFL with flair. As a rookie, he caught 53 passes for a league-leading 1,231 yards and 13 touchdowns. The 13 touchdown receptions in a 12-game season was a league rookie record not broken until Viking Randy Moss caught 17 in a 16-game season in 1998. Howton quickly was called the "new Don Hutson," and he would end his Green Bay career, seven years later, second only to Hutson in most team receiving categories. In 1956, he caught seven passes for 257 yards in one game against the

Now largely forgotten, Billy Howton was called the "new Don Hutson" when he set a rookie record in 1952 with 13 TD catches; the record lasted for 46 years. When he retired, he had surpassed Hutson in both total receptions and receiving yards, but had play for only one winning team in his 12-year career. *Courtesy of the Stiller-Lefebvre Collection.*

Rams. He was a master of the deep pass and would be named to two All Pro teams and four Pro Bowls in his 12-year career, but the team around him was awful.

Things would change dramatically for "Siberia" at the end of the decade, but not for its king. When Lombardi arrived, one of his first moves was to trade Howton to Cleveland for halfback Lew Carpenter and defensive end Bill Quinlan. Why was he traded? Many theories have been espoused. Howton felt it was due to his being the team's player representative, but Lombardi got along fine with New York Giants player representative Kyle Rote. A popular story told by Howton's roommate Gary Knafelc is that Howton took an aggressive attitude into his first and only meeting with the new coach and found out too late that Lombardi was fully in charge. Defensive assistant Phil Bengtson wrote that Lombardi was originally offering Howton to the Colts for Johnny Unitas' backup George Shaw because the Packers had a pressing need for a starting quarterback, but that deal fell through. Of more importance, Bengtson noted that Lombardi felt that Howton was slipping and should be traded while his value was still high. Furthermore, Howton was not that big and was not noted for his blocking, which was something at which Lombardi's ends needed to excel.

Take all those factors together and you get a situation where a player on the downside with a bit of an attitude can be used to obtain players to fill other holes. Lombardi was absolutely correct about Howton—he had averaged 18.7 yards per catch on 303 receptions in seven years in Green Bay, but would average only 14.4 on 200 receptions in his last five years in the league. He would never again be named to an All Pro or Pro Bowl team after he was traded from Green Bay. In addition, the Packers defensive line that Lombardi inherited was a sieve that Bill Quinlan would help plug for two championships, while Lew Carpenter was a capable fill-in at several positions.

Teamwise, things would not improve much for Howton after he left Wisconsin. In his one year in Cleveland, the Browns finished 7-5, the only winning season Howton would ever enjoy as a pro. He was selected in the expansion draft by Dallas, and would spend four losing years as a Cowboy. His teams' total winning percentage in those last five years was .311, even worse than his time in Green Bay. At least the native Texan ended up playing in his home state. He was still a moderately effective receiver, but not the same flashy star of his early years. He was now known as the Red Fox, for his red hair and craftiness in getting open. As he put it at the time, "When I started my first game as a rookie in Green Bay in 1952 and I stood at that line of scrimmage and looked at that defense, I knew I could beat them . . . Now, 12 seasons later, I wonder if this game isn't passing me by." (Riger, 48)

After his playing career ended in 1963, Howton was briefly the all-time league leader in both receptions with 503 and receiving yards with 8,459. As president of the NFL Players Association, he had successfully fought to have a pension plan instituted for retired players, even testifying before Congress in 1958. He moved on in retirement and did some coaching at Rice before becoming a building contractor. Years later, he became involved in financial investing and in 1981 was sentenced to five years in federal prison for a fraud case involving $8 million in misappropriated funds. He and his partner were later ordered to repay $1 million of that money to an Ohio Savings and Loan. After serving two years in jail, Howton was released. On vacation in Yugoslavia in the late 1980s, he fell in love with an employee of Iberia Airlines and moved to Madrid to retire and write his memoirs. As of 1990, he was said to have written about 600 pages on his life in the NFL and intended to shop the manuscript to publishers. At this time, though, his project has the same publishing status as Johnny Blood's rumored economics tome, *Spend Yourself Rich.* Today Howton is largely forgotten. Had he had the opportunity to play with some better teams, he might have had a Hall of Fame career and found a buyer for those memoirs. In football, as in many other endeavors, the company you keep is of vital importance.

FOR FURTHER INFORMATION

Bengtson, Phil, with Todd Hunt. *Packer Dynasty.* Garden City, NY: Doubleday, 1969. (14-5)

Blair, Sam. "Cowboys Yesterday," *Dallas Morning News.* 11/14/90. (4B)

Packers of the Past: A Series of Articles Reprinted from the Milwaukee Journal Sept. 28–Dec. 9, 1965. Milwaukee, WI: Milwaukee Journal, 1965. (39-40)

Porter, David L., ed. *Biographical Dictionary of American Sports: Football.* New York: Greenwood Press, 1987. (275-6)

Riger, Robert. *Best Plays of the Year 1963: A Documentary of Pro Football in the National Football League.* Englewood Cliffs, NJ: Prentice-Hall, 1964. (48-9)

RACE
BOB MANN • END 1952–54

WHO'S WORN THE NUMBER
B. Mann 1952–54, Borden 1955–59, W. Davis 1960–69, Amsler 1970, Roche 1971–76, Tullis 1979, B. Larson 1980, J. Thompson 1981–82, Stanley 1985–88, Redick 1987r, Weathers 1990–91, R. Brooks 1992–98, B. Collins 2001, D. Martin 2002.

ORIGINATOR Bob Mann 1952–54.

LONGEST TENURE Defensive end Willie Davis 1960–69 (see below).

NUMBER CHANGES Bob Mann wore 31 in 1950–51; wide receiver Walter Tullis wore 20 in 1978; tight end John Thompson wore 83 in 1979–80; tight end David Martin wore 83 in 2001.

OTHER NOTABLES Willie Davis was a Hall of Famer, and there's more about him and star wide receiver Robert Brooks in the essay below.

ONE TO FORGET How do you hand Willie Davis' number to Marty Amsler the very year he retired? Amsler was an ex-Bear by way of Cincinnati who finished his three-year career with nine games as a Packers defensive end in 1970. He was a high-effort guy who had started in the Continental League, but he was never going to be confused with a Hall of Famer.

BOB MANN According to the 1950 Census, 17 of the 52,375 residents of Green Bay were black. By 1960, the total population had increased to 62,888, but the black population had increased by only one to 18. In 1970, the city's population was up to 87,809 with 65 blacks; that's 98.9% white and 1.1% other races including .07% was black. In 1980 the total population was 87,899 with the black population rising to 216; that's 96.8 white and .2% black. In 1990, population was up to 96,466 including 453 blacks; that's 94.2% white and .5% black. By the last Census in 2000, Green Bay has reached 102,313 people, 1,407 of them black. The percentage white had decreased to 85.9% and the percentage black had passed one for the first time, 1.4% to be precise. Of course, blacks in Green Bay were also outnumbered by American Indians and Asians.

In the first 29 years of the Packers NFL history, the team never had a black player. The Pro Football Hall of Fame has identified 13 black players who played in the league between 1920 and 1933. Three of the best of that group, Fritz Pollard, Paul Robeson, and Duke Slater, all spent the 1922 season with Milwaukee. Curly Lambeau played and coached against all of these talented black players, but he would never have a black player on his own team—not in 29 years in Green Bay, or in two subsequent years with the Cardinals, or two final seasons in Washington. If he had been more progressive in his thinking, and signed some of the available black talent in the late 1940s, it might have saved his job with the Packers. However, he remained true to the unwritten agreement instituted in 1933 between NFL clubs, barring the hiring of blacks. This policy was most likely spurred on by an unwillingness to give scarce jobs to non-whites during the Great Depression. The color line lasted until the end of World War II, when the NFL Rams and AAFC Browns each signed two blacks for their teams.

Receiver Bob Mann ended the discriminatory practice in Green Bay when he became the first black player on a Packers' roster in the middle of the 1950 season. He wore number 31 that year and the next, but switched to 87 in 1952. Mann had been a star end for the national champion University of Michigan in 1947, and signed with the Detroit Lions in 1948 as one of their first two black players, along with Melvin Groomes. In 1949, Mann finished second in the league in catches with 66 and first in receiving yards with 1,014. In the wake of the seller's market created by the NFL's merger with the rival AAFC in 1950, the Lions offered salary cuts to all their players. Mann, the Lions top receiver, was offered a $1,500 cut from $7,500 to $6,000 and refused to sign his contract. In addition, he held an off-season sales position with team owner Edwin Anderson's Goebel Brewing Company, which at the time coincidentally was being boycotted by the black neighborhood that was Mann's sales territory. Mann was whipsawed by Anderson from two directions—he was fired from his sales job and traded from the football team to the New York Yankees football team for Bobby Layne. Mann encountered more bad luck in New York's training camp when he was cut because he was "too small." Bob believed that New York had already filled its quota of black players for the year. Unable to hook on with any other team, the reigning league leader in yards receiving complained to Commissioner Bert Bell that he was being blackballed, but Bell claimed to know nothing about it.

Finally, in November, Mann signed with the Packers and spent five years in Green Bay as a solid starter. On his first day in the clubhouse, Mann was greeted and welcomed by Tony Canadeo and Clayton Tonnemaker. In practice, Tobin Rote complimented him on his skills and Mann made good friends with teammate and future wrestler Dick "the Bruiser" Afflis. Mann's time in Green Bay was without racial incident, and Coach Ronzani tried to make Bob more comfortable by letting him travel freely to Milwaukee and Chicago and sometimes stay over in New York after the team played there. In his first full season as a Packer in 1951, he caught 50 passes for eight touchdowns. In one game against the Eagles that year, he caught three touchdown passes. His career ended abruptly in 1954 when a tackle by the Eagles Chuck Bednarik ruined his knee. His final numbers with Green Bay included 109 catches for 1,629 yards and 17 touchdowns, and he went into the Packer Hall of Fame in 1988. After his retirement, Mann eventually went to law school while in his forties and was still practicing criminal law in his late seventies.

Mann was the only black on the team until 1952, when he was joined by the first black draft pick to make the team, sixth-rounder Tom Johnson. Johnson lasted only a year, making Mann the sole black on the team again in 1953. In 1954 the Packers drafted a black person in the first round for the first time, and Veryl Switzer of Kansas State joined Mann for his final year in football. Charley Brackins of Prairie View was signed by the Packers in 1955 and became the fifth black quarterback in NFL history that year. He got into only one game as a quarterback, but did play at end and on special teams before he was summarily cut from the team after a curfew violation in midseason. As a prime example of the anguish of black quarterbacks, he never got another chance in the NFL. He was one of four blacks on the team that year along with Switzer, Jack Spinks, and Nate Borden. Spinks, Borden, and Emery Barnes were the only blacks in 1956, followed by Borden and Frank Purnell in 1957 and Borden and Len Ford in 1958.

When Lombardi arrived in 1959, the only black player still on the roster was Nate Borden, the four-year veteran defensive end (who incidentally inherited number 87 from Bob Mann). Borden had been unable to find suitable housing in all that time and was living in what was described as a shack. When Lombardi found out, he berated the landlord and got Nate a better place to live. Vince also brought in veteran safety Emlen Tunnell from the Giants to lend some experience to the porous defense, put him up in the Northland Hotel in town, and paid the tab for the three years Tunnell was on the roster. Lombardi had great sensitivity to prejudice of any kind, and refused to allow it on his team. At one of his first team meetings he told the players, "If I ever hear anyone using any racial epithets around here like nigger or dago or Jew, you're gone. I don't care who you are" (Kramer, 71-2) Throughout the turbulent 1960s while several teams had racial problems reflective of the country as a whole, the Packers were a raucous, interracial, harmonic brotherhood. The 1959 squad had only four blacks, Borden, Tunnell, A.D. Williams, and Tim Brown, out of 35 players, but on his last championship team in 1967, 13 of the 40 players were black, including most of the starters on defense.

One of those starters was number 87, Willie Davis, one of the greatest defensive ends ever to play the game. Davis had starred for Eddie Robinson at Grambling University and was one of the first of many NFL stars to emerge from that small black college in Louisiana. He was a 15th-round draft choice of the Cleveland Browns where another legendary coach, Paul Brown, switched him back and forth from offense to defense before finally trading him to Vince Lombardi for end A.D. Williams in 1960. Lombardi put him at left defensive end, where Willie's great speed, strength, quickness, and agility made him a five-time All Pro and five-time Pro Bowl selection in the 1960s. He had a knack for making the big play, and still is the career team leader in fumble recoveries with 21. He was durable, never missing a game in 12 years with the Browns and Packers, and had the effervescent personality of a natural leader, known to his teammates as "Dr. Feelgood." He was elected to the Packer Hall of Fame in 1975 and to the Pro Football Hall of Fame in 1981. In retirement he used all of those qualities to become an even bigger success in the business world. He often would say that whenever he went into a sales meeting, the words and lessons of Lombardi went with him. He became the second black member of the Packers Board of Directors in 1994. Dr. Theodore Jamison was the first in 1980.

In the 1970s and 1980s, the harmony began to deteriorate. Especially in the 1980s, a series of off-the-field incidents involving black players tarred both the team and the town. Black players reported feeling as if they were targets in the community, since it could be reasonably assumed that any black man out in public was a player. They could be targets for positive attention or targets for more negative actions. During those two decades, Green Bay became a less inviting place for black players to want to play. There were memorable incidents that demonstrated this clearly. In 1980, first-round choice Bruce Clark signed with Toronto of the CFL rather than the Packers. In 1989, Deion Sanders was televised chanting "No way Green Bay" to discourage the Packers from picking him. Black free agents would not seriously consider the Packers for years, until Mike Holmgren and Ron Wolf persuaded Reggie White to come to Green Bay.

Among Mike Holmgren's many successes in the 1990s was making the Packers an organization attuned to the concerns of black players and coaches. By hiring Sherm Lewis and Ray Rhodes as his first coordinators, Holmgren made the Packers the first NFL team with two black coordinators. Rhodes actually played a big role in getting Reggie White to sign. Holmgren did a number of little things that made black players view Green Bay in a more positive light. He brought in a black barber from Milwaukee every week for the convenience of his players. He had soul food catered in once a week. Overall, black players found they were dealt with honestly and with respect.

One of Holmgren's most popular players was Robert Brooks who wore number 87. Brooks followed Sterling Sharpe at South Carolina and also as the go-to guy on the Packers. While Leroy Butler invented the Lambeau Leap into the crowd after scoring a touchdown in 1993, Brooks perfected it two years later. He even recorded a rap song about it called "Jump in the Stands." Of course, as the lead wide receiver on the team, he had more opportunities for post-scoring leaps than Leroy. Brooks caught 32 TD passes and scored on one punt return and two kick returns in his brief career, shortened by injuries. In 1995 Robert caught 102 passes for a team record 1,497 yards and 13 touchdowns. The next year he went down early with a knee injury and missed Super Bowl XXXI. He returned to play in Super Bowl XXXII, but he was never really the same explosive, buoyant player. His former coach, Mike Holmgren, called him, "pound for pound the toughest player I ever coached." Despite his dedication and work ethic, the constant pounding on his slight 180-pound frame caused him to retire at age 29 in 1999. He returned as a backup with Denver one year later and then retired for good.

Over the past 50 years, those who have worn jersey number 87 in Green Bay have mirrored both the progress and the struggle of blacks in this country, from being segregated and invisible to integrating into a changing society. Fifty-one years after Bob Mann became the first black Packer, fully 42 of 58 Green Bay players were black, as well as several people in the front office. All is not perfect, and never will be. Even in the championship season of 1996, some black players, much to Coach Holmgren's chagrin, discussed the difficulty of living in an overwhelmingly white community for an ESPN "Behind the Lines" special on Green Bay. However, we should focus on the more prevalent positive influence that sports has had in this regard, and the astounding progress that has occurred. The very nature of the meritocracy of sports provides a model for a less color-conscious society—disparate members of a team uniting to achieve a common purpose. Had Vince Lombardi edited Thomas Jefferson, our national common purpose might have been expressed that we are all endowed with certain rights, among them life, liberty, and the pursuit of perfection. Had he collaborated with filmmaker Spike Lee, they would have emphasized that around here you don't do the right thing once in a while, you do the right thing all the time. The work goes on, of course.

FOR FURTHER INFORMATION

Ashe, Arthur. *A Hard Road to Glory: A History of the African-American Athlete.* New York: Warner Books, 1988. (Vol. 3 398, 435-8)

Berghaus, Bob. "Mann Was a Pioneer in More Ways than One," *Milwaukee Journal Sentinel.* 10/24/96. (Sports 5)

Carroll, Bob. *When the Grass Was Real: Unitas, Brown, Lombardi, Sayers, Butkus, Namath and All the Rest: The Ten Best Years of Pro Football.* New York: Simon and Schuster, 1993. (55-60)

Chalk, Ocania. *Pioneers of Black Sport: The Early Days of the Black Professional Athlete in Baseball, Basketball, Boxing, and Football.* New York: Dodd Mead, 1975. (242-4)

Dow, Bill. "Mann Pioneer Player in NFL," *Detroit Free Press.* 1/11/02. Available online from www.freep.com/sports/lions/mann11_20020111.htm.

Kramer, Jerry, ed. *Lombardi: Winning Is the Only Thing.* New York: World Publishing, 1970. (69-78)

McGinn, Bob. "Pain Catches up to Brooks," *Milwaukee Journal Sentinel.* 8/3/99. (Sports 1)

Porter, David L., ed. *Biographical Dictionary of American Sports: Football.* New York: Greenwood Press, 1987. (131-2)

Ross, Charles K. *Outside the Lines: African Americans and the Integration of the National Football League.* New York: New York University Press, 1999. (123-5, 133)

Smith, Don. "Willie Davis: Speed, Agility, and Size," *The Coffin Corner.* Available online at www.footballresearch.com/articles/frpage.cfm?topic'davis-w.

THE LIONS
RON KRAMER • TIGHT END 1957, 1959–64

WHO'S WORN THE NUMBER R. Collins 1951, Hays 1953,
G. White 1954, R. Kramer 1957, 1959–64, B. Anderson 1965–66,
Capp 1967, R. Jones 1969, Garrett 1971–73, Askson 1975–77,
Cassidy 1979–81, 1983–84, Dennard 1985, McConkey 1986, A.
Bell 1988, A. Matthews 1988–89, C. Wilson 1990–91, D. Ingram
1992–93, Mickens 1994, K. Jackson 1995–96, Reggie Johnson 1997,
Preston 1997–98, Arnold 1999, L. Hall 1999, Franks 2000–02.

ORIGINATOR Albin "Rip" Collins 1951 came to the Packers
from Baltimore, where he had averaged 1.5 yards per carry on
69 rushing attempts in 1950. With Green Bay he carried five
times for four yards, an average of 0.8.

LONGEST TENURE Ron Kramer 1957, 1959–64

NUMBER CHANGES Halfback Rip Collins also wore 65 in
1951; wide receiver Terry Mickens wore 85 in 1995–97; tight end
Lamont Hall also wore 49 in 1999.

OTHER NOTABLES Tight end Keith Jackson spent only a season
and a half in Green Bay, but he was still an impact player whose
offensive talents helped the team win Super Bowl XXXI.

ONES TO FORGET This number has been worn by a long
list of retread receivers: Bill Anderson, Bert Askson, Preston
Dennard, Phil McConkey, Aubrey Matthews, Mark Ingram,
Roell Preston, and Jahine Arnold.

RON KRAMER At the University of Michigan, Ron Kramer was
known as the 'Terror of the Big Ten." He caught passes, placekicked,
punted, and blocked on offense; on defense he played defensive end
in a bruising style that got him thrown out of the Ohio State game
as a senior for unnecessary roughness. In addition to being a two-
time All American in football, he played center on the basketball
team where he was three-time team MVP, and also lettered three
years in track.

Drafted in the first round by the Packers in 1957, his pro
career fell into three equal phases. In his first four years, he looked
like a flop. As a rookie, he caught 28 passes, but then missed more
than a year in the military. By the time he reported to the team in
1959, he had missed training camp and was out of shape. He did
not catch a pass all year. In the following year, he won the starting
tight-end job in training camp. However, Lombardi sent him back
to the bench after he ran the wrong pass pattern in the opener,

causing a crucial pass interception in the loss to the Bears. He caught only four passes all year while being stuck on the pine.

Kramer rededicated his effort the next year and began the second phase of his pro career. From 1961 through 1964, he was the prototypical tight end, a true blend of lineman and receiver. As Kramer described it, the tight end is "a loose tackle." When *Sport Magazine* covered the tight-end position in its 1960s series, "The Specialist in Pro Football," Kramer is the tight end they chose to profile. In those four years, he caught 138 passes for 2,202 yards and 15 touchdowns. In the 1961 37-0 demolishing of the New York Giants in the title game, Kramer caught four passes including two for touchdowns. In addition, Ron was a leveling blocker at 6'3" and 240 pounds, and that was even more important to the Packers' attack. In that same 1961 title game, the Giants Sam Huff remarked to Paul Hornung, "Every time I reach for you, I end up with Kramer in my chest." (Schaap, 79) The Bears' Mike Ditka and the Colts' John Mackey were more central to their teams' passing offenses and caught more passes, but Kramer was a powerful force at the line of scrimmage for Green Bay. His ability to handle a defensive end by himself freed the Packer interior lineman to expand their own blocking range.

Kramer was one of the first NFL players to play out his option. When he did so, to move closer to home by playing with the Detroit Lions in 1965, he embarked on the last phase of his career. The Packers received a number-one pick in 1966 for Kramer and would use it to nab fullback Jim Grabowski. As it turned out, though, the exchange did not work out very well for either team. Because of injuries, Grabowski never developed into a star for the Packers, and Kramer was finished by the time he got to the Lions. In three years he caught only 59 passes for a single touchdown.

Dealings between the Packers and Lions never seem to work out quite as expected. This lengthy rivalry extends back to the origins of the Lions as another small Midwestern town team, the Portsmouth Spartans. When the Spartans came into the league in 1930, the defending champion Packers won the first game between the two franchises 47-13. By the second meeting that year, the Spartans closed a lot of ground and tied the Packers 6-6. The next year was the completion of the first Green Bay threepeat, and the one black mark on that achievement is that the Packers ducked the Spartans that year. The teams were tentatively scheduled to meet late in the season, but when that tentative game got closer, Green Bay backed out of the contest and claimed the title. Portsmouth players and fans were incensed and took it out on the Packers in December, 1932, when the Spartans pummeled the Packers 19-0. The game was played before a raucous and insulting crowd that threw oranges and eggs at the Packers as they got off their team bus. Today, the records of the Bears (6-1-6), Spartans (6-1-4), and Packers (10-3-1) would result in Green Bay being declared champions. However, ties did not count at all in those days, so the Bears and Spartans met in the first NFL playoff game. The Bears won that game and the championship.

The Spartans moved to the big city in 1934 and became the Lions, but their rivalry with the Packers continued. The Lions mostly finished third behind the Packers and Bears throughout the rest of the decade, but the three teams were pretty evenly balanced. In the 1940s, the bottom fell out in the Motor City and the Lions had the worst record in the league over that ten year period, attaining a winning percentage of only .336. The

PACKERS BY THE NUMBERS

Packers beat them nine straight times from 1940 through 1945. That streak began with a 50-7 pasting of the Lions in Detroit on November 24, 1940, and ended with a 57-21 crushing of Detroit in Milwaukee on October 7, 1945. In the latter game, Don Hutson caught four touchdown passes in the second quarter to go with five extra points, totaling a one-quarter record of 29 points scored by a single player. He would kick two more extra points in the second half to finish with 31 points for the day. After losing the second Lions game of 1945, the Packer won the next five between 1946 and 1948.

The positions were reversed in the 1950s. Starting with the last Lions-Packers game of 1949, the Lions won 11 straight meetings of the two teams. The 1950s were the Lions golden decade, with four title games and three championships, while the Packers were the second-worst team in the league during this time. The 1950s were also the beginning of Thanksgiving football from Detroit as the Lions instituted an annual Turkey Day game beginning in 1951. Unfortunately, the Packers were the annual opponents from 1951-63 and were usually carved up like roasted fowl, going 3-9-1 in those games against the Lions. The most memorable game was in 1962, when the Packers went into the game 10-0 for the year. The Lions were 8-2, and the loss they suffered to Packers in the fourth game of the year was a particularly bitter one. Detroit had been leading 7-6 with time running out when quarterback Milt Plum threw a pass in the flat on third and eight. Intended receiver Terry Barr fell down, and Herb Adderley intercepted the ball and returned it 30 yards to set up a winning field goal by Paul Hornung at the gun. The proud Lion defense was always suspicious of the offense and wanted to kill their own quarterback that day. The Lions looked forward to the Thanksgiving rematch for six weeks, stoking their anger.

Detroit erupted right from the start. Employing a series of blitzes and line stunts, the Lions stormed the acclaimed Packer offensive line and literally overran it. Fuzzy Thurston would later joke that he invented the "lookout block" that day. As 300-pound defensive tackle Roger Brown would blow by him, he would turn and yell, "Look out, Bart!" Quarterback Bart Starr was sacked 11 times for 112 yards by the Lions and the Lion defensive line twice scored, once on a fumble recovery for a touchdown and once on a sack for a safety. The Lions were up 23-0 at the half and won easily 26-14. However, the Packers won their last three games to finish 13-1 for the season while the Lions won only two of their last three to end up 11-3 in second place.

The Lions finished second to the Packers in 1960, 1961, and 1962. In those three frustrating years, the Lions split the six Packer games, but could not outplay the Packers against the rest of the league. The Team of the 1950s (the Lions) had been surpassed by the Team of the 1960s (the Packers), and the Lions really seemed to despise and resent the Packers' success. It was reminiscent of the Team of the 1930s (the Packers) being supplanted by the Team of the 1940s (the Bears). While the superceded team could get itself fired up enough to play competitively against the new rival, it could not compete as well over the length of the season.

Later, the Lions did have the satisfaction of putting the final nails in the coffin for the Packer dynasty by bookending the 1970 season with a pair of shutouts over Green Bay—40-0 on opening day and 20-0 in the last game of the year. By then, however, the Lions were futilely chasing another divisional rival, the Vikings. Lombardi had pulled the Packers out of the annual Thanksgiving appearance the year after the 1962 disaster, but the two teams did meet on Thanksgiving twice in the 1980s. The Lions winning 31-28 in 1984 and the Packers winning 44-40 in 1986 on a thrilling 83-yard punt return by Walter Stanley with less than a minute left in the game. The rivalry heated up again in the mid-1990s when the two teams met two years in a row in the opening game of the playoffs. The Packers took both games—28-24 in Detroit in January, 1994, on a 40-yard last-minute bomb from Favre to Sharpe, and 16-12 in Green Bay in December, 1994, when the Pack defense held Barry Sanders to -1 yard in 13 carries.

The two teams have shared many things in their long history. Both teams originated in small towns in the Midwest, had a fan base in the Upper Peninsula of Michigan, and had the same player break the color line for them (Bob Mann). Among the many players who played for both franchises, these played for the Lions first: Byron Bailey, Ed Berrang, Carl Bland, Lew Carpenter, Bob Cifers, Ted Cook, Aldo Forte, Roger Harding, Dave Kopay, Bob Kowalkowski, Jim Laslavic, Antonio London, Don McIlhenny, Bob Mann, Ed O'Neil, Lindy Pearson, Jim Salsbury, Dan Sandifer, Clarence Self, Ollie Spencer, and Damon Tassos. The following played first in Green Bay: Jessie Clark, Jack Concannon, Gary Ellerson, Ken Ellis, Ed Frutig, Jim Gillette, Jug Girard, Maurice Harvey, John Hilton, Desmond Howard, Ron Kramer, Errol Mann, Aubrey Mathews, Merv Pregulman, Dave Pureifory, Bill Quinlan, Tobin Rote, Bill Schroeder, Walter Stanley, Val Joe Walker, and Roger Zatkoff. Ron Kramer was one of the best. Rival coach Norm Van Brocklin called him the "big oaf" from his frustration in trying to deal with such a big load at end. For a few years, the Big Oaf was a force for Green Bay, whether blocking or receiving. Ron only made one All Pro team in his career, but for a short four-year period he was as good as any tight end in the league and a perfect soldier for the Lombardi offense. He was elected to the Packer Hall of Fame in 1975.

FOR FURTHER INFORMATION

Becker, Carl M. *Home and Away: The Rise and Fall of Professional Football on the Banks of the Ohio, 1919–1934.* Athens, OH: Ohio University Press, 1998. (274-5, 282-3)

Hornung, Paul, as told to Al Silverman. *Football and the Single Man.* Garden City, NY: Doubleday, 1965. (223-4)

Lombardi, Vince, with W.C. Heinz. *Run to Daylight.* Englewood Cliffs, NJ: Prentice-Hall, 1963. (125-6)

Paxton, Harry T. "Terror of the Big Ten," *Saturday Evening Post.* 10/20/56. (31+)

Porter, David L., ed. *Biographical Dictionary of American Sports: Football.* New York: Greenwood Press, 1987. (322-3)

Schaap, Dick. "Ron Kramer, Tight End," *Sport.* 12/62. (12+)

Wagner, Len. *Launching the Glory Years: The 1959 Packers — What They Didn't Tell Us.* Green Bay, WI: Coach's Books LLC [Jay Bengtson], 2001. (35)

THREEPEAT II
DAVE ROBINSON • LINEBACKER 1963–72

WHO'S WORN THE NUMBER
D. Robinson 1963–72, Wade 1975, O. Smith 1976–77, W. Taylor 1978, A. Thompson 1979–81, Childs 1984, M. Lewis 1985–87, Hackett 1987–88, Fitzgerald 1987r, Spagnola 1989, W. Harris 1990, Chmura 1993–99, Ferguson 2001–02.

ORIGINATOR Dave Robinson 1963–72.

LONGEST TENURE Dave Robinson 1963–72.

NUMBER CHANGES Wide receiver Aundra Thompson wore 43 in 1977–78.

OTHER NOTABLES Tight end Mark Chmura was a powerful blocker and Brett Favre's favorite sure-handed safety valve receiver who went to the 1995 and 1997 Pro Bowls.

ONE TO FORGET Mark Chmura embarrassed his family, his team, and his town by getting caught up in a sex scandal that ended his career. While he was acquitted of sexual assault charges, he was caught playing drinking games in a hot tub with high school coeds, and that should not be a proud moment for anyone.

DAVE ROBINSON Dave Robinson played at Penn State while Joe Paterno was still an assistant coach and before the university became known as Linebacker U., for all the talented professional linebackers the school produced. On the football field, he was an All American two-way end. On offense he caught passes and blocked, and on defense he was active and ferocious with a propensity for making the big play. Robinson also starred as a forward on the basketball team and graduated with a degree in Engineering. The Packers drafted him number one in 1963 as a defensive end and moved him to linebacker, where consistently he would make more than his share of key plays for the best defense in the league.

Green Bay outbid the AFL San Diego Chargers to sign Robinson, but he spent his rookie year on the bench learning from the team's three All Pro linebackers—especially Bill Forester on the strong side. When Forester retired at the end of the season, Robinson moved into the starting lineup in 1964 as the left outside linebacker. Hall of Famer Willie Davis was in front of him at defensive end, and Hall of Famer Herb Adderley was behind him at cornerback. Dave himself missed election to Canton by only two votes in 1989, and is still a viable candidate for the Hall. That's good, because he may have been the best player of those three greats. He was about the same size as Davis, at 6'3" 240 pounds, with long arms and springs in his legs. With his size, quickness, and anticipation, he would excel at linebacker in today's game as well.

The 1960s Packers were obviously a great team and the threepeat championship they won from 1965 through 1967 was their crowning achievement. The only other team in NFL history to win three straight titles was the 1929-31 Packers, who played in the early days before there was a playoff structure. At that time, the team with the best won-lost record at the end of the year was the champ. That those early Packer teams were able to win three in a row was quite an accomplishment, but winning three straight in a playoff environment, when a whole season can hang on one play or drive, is even more impressive. Thirteen times in NFL history there have been repeat champions, most recently the 1997–98 Broncos. Three franchises have done so multiple times—the 1932–33 and 1940–41 Bears, the 1974–75 and 1978–79 Steelers, and the Packers with their two threepeats and the 1960–61 back-to-back. Other sports have had fewer repeats, but more threepeats-and-beyond. In baseball, there have been eight repeaters, two threepeaters (the 1998–2000 Yankees and the 1972–74 Athletics), one streak of four (the 1936–39 Yankees) and one streak of five (the 1949–53 Yankees). The NHL has had nine repeaters, two threepeaters (Toronto in 1947–49 and 1962–64) two streaks of four (the 1976–79 Canadiens and the 1980–83 Islanders) and one streak of five (the 1956–60 Canadiens). The NBA has had six repeaters, four threepeaters (the Lakers in 1952–54 and 2000–02 and the Bulls in 1991–93 and 1996–98) and one incredible unsurpassable streak of eight (the 1959–66 Celtics).

Three in a row was an achievement Lombardi aimed for all along. He fell just short in Robinson's rookie year when the Packers inability to beat the Bears kept Dave from being part of two threepeat experiences. Like many Packers, Robinson lost his father early in his life, and Dave looked on Lombardi as a second father for whom he would do anything to gain approval. Lombardi's desire to win three in a row became the team's mission. It was a nearly impossible mission that often came within a play of being derailed.

With his talent for big plays, Robinson was often the difference between victory or defeat for the Packers. In 1965 the Packers played the Colts in Baltimore in the next-to-last game of the season. At the end of the first half the Packers were leading 14-13, but Colts' backup quarterback Gary Cuozzo tried a swing pass from the Packers' two-yard line. Robinson leaped and tipped the ball to himself and returned it 87 yards to the Colt 10. The Packers scored a touchdown to close the half, up 21-13 rather than down 20-14. That crucial 14-point swing at the end of the half enabled them to go on to win 42-27. The next year, again in the penultimate game in Baltimore, Johnny Unitas was driving the Colts on one of his deadly two-minute drills. He was deep in Packer territory, trying to take the lead, when Willie Davis stripped Unitas of the ball, Robinson recovered the fumble, and the Packers clinched a 14-10 win and a divisional title. Robinson's most famous play, though, was that same year in the title game against Dallas. The Cowboys were down 34-27 and faced a fourth-and-goal from the Packers' two. Quarterback Don Meredith rolled out as Robby knocked aside Bob Hayes and sped to Meredith. Robinson crashed into Meredith's left side, causing the pass he threw to wobble safely into the hands of Packer safety Tom Brown for the ball game. Robinson berated himself for not wrapping up Meredith's throwing arm and preventing the throw altogether. Lombardi later told Robinson that he was graded poorly on the play because he had ignored the run, which was his first responsibility. To win three in a row you have to strive to excel, and the Packers were a team of perfectionists, driven by a demanding, unyielding coach.

As an engineer, Robinson was a natural at using film study to improve his game. One of the things he took note of was how high he could leap versus the trajectory of passes thrown by the quarterback he would be playing against. Comparing these two factors, he could determine how deep his drop should be on pass plays. He intercepted 27 passes in his career, 21 in his ten years as a Packer. In his last year in Green Bay, in 1972, the Packers made the playoffs for the only time in the decade of the 1970s. They lost to Washington in the first game. The next year, Coach George Allen acquired Robinson. Although Robby at first tried to retire, Allen was able to persuade him to play in Washington for two more years. The Redskins went to the playoffs both years but made a first-round exit each time. Those three consecutive first-round playoff defeats serve to emphasize just how special and difficult an accomplishment the 1965–67 threepeat championships were. Robinson retired for real in 1975 and began a successful second career as an independent beer distributor.

Robinson was boisterous, bright, and a leader. He was the Packers' player representative, a three-time All Pro, and a three-time Pro Bowler. He remains a Packers fan and a fan of Green Bay. "When I got here, it was the fans. The fact that it was a real family-type atmosphere. We weren't players on a team. We were just members of the community who happened to play football." (Rauen) His one regret was that Dan Devine traded him to Washington and he didn't play his entire career in Green and Gold. Inducted to the Packer Hall of Fame in 1982, Dave Robinson is forever a Packer.

FOR FURTHER INFORMATION

Hartnett, Ken. "Doubting Dave," *Green Bay Packers 1967 Yearbook.* (35)

Johnson, Chuck. *The Greatest Packers of Them All.* New York: Putnam, 1968. (158-63)

Kramer, Jerry, with Dick Schaap. *Distant Replay.* New York: G.P. Putnam, 1985. (148, 156-9)

Porter, David L., ed. *Biographical Dictionary of American Sports: Football.* New York: Greenwood Press, 1987. (502-3)

Rauen, Karen. "Robinson Made Winning Choice with Green Bay," *Green Bay Press Gazette.* 9/9/01. Available online at www.greenbaypressgazette.packernews.com site.

Reischel, Rob. "Standing Out in a Crowd," *Milwaukee Journal Sentinel Packer Plus.* 3/13/02. Available online at www.jsonline.com/packer/news/mar02/26987.asp.

Zimmerman, Paul. *The Linebackers: The Tough Ones of Pro Football.* New York: Scholastic Books, 1973. (79-88)

DISCIPLINE
EZRA JOHNSON • DEFENSIVE END 1979–87

WHO'S WORN THE NUMBER
Manley 1950–51, E. Johnson 1979–87, N. Hill 1988, T. Bennett 1990–93, McMichael 1994, D. Holland 1995–97, Holliday 1998–2002.

ORIGINATOR Guard Leon Manley 1950–51, the first Packer to wear a number in the 90s, was a high school and college teammate of Darrell Royal. Manley coached under his close friend for many years at Texas.

LONGEST TENURE Ezra Johnson 1979–87.

NUMBER CHANGES Ezra Johnson wore 78 in 1977–78.

OTHER NOTABLES Speed-rushing linebacker Tony Bennett had a couple of sack-happy years in the early 1990s.

ONE TO FORGET Darius Holland had a world of potential and the opportunity to use it, but ended up being fat and useless in Green Bay. He has continued to bounce around the league collecting a paycheck.

EZRA JOHNSON During the 1976 season, the Packers finished 21st in points allowed with 299. Bart Starr used his two 1977 first-round choices for a pair of defensive ends: Mike Butler of Kansas and Ezra Johnson from the tiny black college of Morris Brown, in Atlanta. With this influx of talent, the defense gave up 80 fewer points and moved up in rank to tenth despite their sack total going down and their opponents pass completion percentage going up. Thus the reason for the significant decrease in points allowed remains a mystery of life. Perhaps the opponents' offenses were lulled into a comatose state from watching the plodding Packer offense that generated only 134 points that year, less than 10 a game.

Because he came from a small school, it was no surprise that Ezra Johnson was a rough diamond in his rookie year. He did not even know how to get into a three-point stance at first. He was also very small, at 230 pounds, although he would bulk up by 30 pounds in the next few years. In spot duty as a speed-rusher he got 3.5 sacks in his rookie year. In his second year, he pumped up that total to 20.5 sacks and made the Pro Bowl team as an alternate selection. Opposing linemen could not handle his speed and moves. He got five sacks against Detroit in the season opener and kept up the pressure all year. He was the team's sack specialist and outsacked his major college draft-mate Mike Butler every year but 1980 and 1981 in their seven years together as Packers. For most of those years, Ezra's sack totals are unofficial, because the league didn't start counting sacks until 1982. Thus his official lifetime sack total for Green Bay is only 41.5. If you add in unofficial counts, you get a total of 89. Of course, for older players like Hall of Fame defensive end Willie Davis, we don't even have unofficial numbers. I mean no disrespect to Johnson, but it would not be a shock if Davis accumulated more than 89 sacks in his ten years in Green Bay.

Ezra was a popular, productive, and hard-working member of the team, and he underwent surgery 12 times during his career—mostly to his back and knees. However, he will always be remembered for the "hot dog incident." In the 1980 exhibition season, Bart Starr was under fire for the team's performance. The Packers had their first winning season under him in 1978, but had fallen back to 5-11 in 1979, and the outlook for 1980 was not good. In the fifth and final exhibition game against Denver at home, the Packers were in the midst of losing for the fourth time and enduring their third shutout when a fan handed Johnson a hot dog on the sideline. Despite the 38-0 score, Johnson was caught eating the hot dog during the game. In the next week, Starr fined Johnson $1,000 and had him apologize to the team. However, Johnson's position coach Fred vonAppen resigned, apparently feeling that he could not coach in an atmosphere so lacking in discipline.

Discipline is a vital element for successful football teams. In the Packers' early days, of course, Lambeau ran the team with an iron fist and full-throated fury. Long-time team photographer Vern Biever said, "People talk of Vince Lombardi, but Curly Lambeau did his share of yelling, too. If anything, I think Lambeau did more of it." (Vecsey) One of Lambeau's own assistant coaches, Bob Snyder, spoke of the fear he generated: "A lot of guys didn't like Paul Brown. A lot of guys didn't like Vince Lombardi. But they respected them. I think they were just scared of Curly." (Christl) Lambeau controlled the players by virtue of his total authority over everything related to the team—especially their paychecks. When the team's talent and performance began to slip in the late 1940s, so did Lambeau's control. The final straw came in 1948 when Curly fined each player half his game salary for their performance against the Cardinals in the fourth game of the year. The team went out the next week and shut out the Rams to bring their season record to 3-2. The players expected the previous week's fine to be rescinded, since the motivational tool had delivered an impressive victory. When Lambeau kept the fines, the players were shocked and lost all seven remaining games. Lambeau would never have a winning record again in Green Bay and was pushed out a year later.

The 1950s were marked by the Packers' coaches consistently being undermined by the team Board of Directors' meddling in on-field affairs. This culminated in the one-year reign of Scooter McLean in 1958. McLean was a friendly, easy-going coach who the players treated as a doormat on their way to the worst record in team history. Then, Lombardi arrived and there was no longer any question as to who was in charge. All discipline problems ceased. If you weren't with the program, Lombardi told them at the outset that "there are planes, trains, and buses leaving town every day, and you're going to be on one." Under Lombardi's laid-back successor Phil Bengtson, the problems involved age and motivation more than discipline.

Dan Devine never really earned the total respect of the players in his four years as coach, and when he left, the team was split in at least two factions. There was fairly open talk of a boycott before the final game of the 1974 season against Atlanta, and one player even was reportedly drinking during the game. Bart Starr was an inexperienced coach walking into a deteriorating situation during challenging times. There were incidents almost every year on his watch. Veterans Ken Ellis and Bill Lueck demanded to be traded and Ellis walked out of training camp in 1975. Bill Bain walked out of training camp in 1976. Ken Payne was fined, suspended, and then waived after responding obscenely to a coach's order to move back on the sideline in 1977. James Lofton showed disrespect to Starr one week and made an obscene gesture to the fans another week in 1979. The 1980 season brought the "hot dog incident," and 1981 saw Mark Koncar walking off the team in anger after being criticized by Starr in a team meeting. In Starr's final year of 1983, he waived starter Maurice Harvey during the season for a "lousy attitude."

Forrest Gregg's tenure was pockmarked by a series of off-field sexual incidents involving Eddie Lee Ivery, James Lofton, and Mossy Cade, and he never seemed to gain the trust or respect of his players. Lindy Infante ran a lax program that appalled Ron Wolf when he was brought in as General Manager in 1991. Wolf hired Holmgren, and both discipline and winning were once again established in Green Bay. Holmgren was followed briefly by Ray Rhodes, but his lax attitude toward discipline and the resultant lack of results on the field got him fired in one year. Mike Sherman credibly handled the first threat to his control of the team—the Chris Akins mutiny in 2001. In order for his early coaching success to continue, team history indicates that Sherman would be well advised to lead decisively and firmly.

Ezra Johnson survived the hot dog incident and played eight more years in Green Bay, under both Starr ,whom he greatly admired, and Forrest Gregg. After being released in 1988, he caught on with the Colts for two years and then finished his career with two more years in Houston. He attained an additional 14 sacks in those last four years to give him an unofficial pro career total of 103 in 15 years spread over three decades. In 1995, Ezra returned to Green Bay to serve as honorary captain before a game at Lambeau, and then came back in 1997 to be inducted into the Packer Hall of Fame as one of the best pass rushers and biggest frankfurter aficionados in team history.

FOR FURTHER INFORMATION

Christl, Cliff. "Curly Lambeau: Loved, Hated Equally," *Milwaukee Journal Sentinel.* 10/18/98. (Sports 1)

Gentile, Domenic, with Gary D'Amato. *The Packer Tapes: My 32 Years with the Green Bay Packers.* Madison, WI: Prairie Oak Press, 1995. (93-4)

Langenkamp, Don. "Thunder and Lightning at Defensive End," *Green Bay Packers 1979 Yearbook.* (23-5)

Lea, Bud. "Packer 'Hal' Inducts Cochran, Ezra Johnson and Travis Williams," *Green Bay Packers 1997 Yearbook.* (93)

Poling, Jerry. *Downfield! Untold Stories of the Green Bay Packers.* Madison, WI: Prairie Oak Press, 1996. (52-5)

Reischel, Rob. "Johnson feels NFL sacking His Achievements," *Milwaukee Journal Sentinel Packer Plus.* 10/31/01. Available online at www.jsonline.com/packer/news/oct01/flash01103101.asp.

Starr, Bart, with Murray Olderman. *Starr: My Life in Football.* New York: William Morrow, 1987. (182-3)

Vecsey, George. "The Man Who Shot Curly Lambeau Still Shoots the Packers," *New York Times.* 1/26/97. (sec. 8, p. 11)

TRADING CARDS AND MEMORABILIA
BRIAN NOBLE • LINEBACKER 1985–93

WHO'S WORN THE NUMBER Skaugstad 1983, Noble 1985–93, Clavelle 1995–97, J. Brown 1998, Thierry 2000–01, J. Johnson 2002.

ORIGINATOR Nose tackle Daryle Skaugstad, appeared in only nine games in 1983, starting five of them on his way out of the NFL.

LONGEST TENURE Brian Noble 1985–93

NUMBER CHANGES None

OTHER NOTABLES None

ONE TO FORGET Although there's not a lot to report in this group, DE Jonathan Brown was a third-round draft choice for whom there were some high hopes in the wake of Reggie White's retirement. However, Brown's pass-rushing talents were never demonstrated on the playing field.

BRIAN NOBLE Brian Noble was a solid, active linebacker for the Packers until he blew out his knee early in 1993, just as the team was beginning to rise under Mike Holmgren. A fifth-round draft choice out of Arizona State, he led the team in tackles four times (averaging over 100 a season for his career) and made the All-Madden tough-guy team in 1990, although he never made the Pro Bowl. Ray Nitschke once said of him that, "Brian Noble was a very physical player. A great run stopper." One time, Brian single-handedly stopped the 350-pound "Refrigerator" Perry for a loss at the goal line. Noble would say of Nitschke, "He's talked to me about leadership and has critiqued my play. He's instilled in me what it used to be and what it should be like around here." (Froberg, 47) Noble got to play on only two winning teams in his years with the Packers, but he was the prototypical Packer. "I think I fit the Green Bay Packers image of mud, snow, and ice, or a perfectly clear fall day where you love to watch football." ("Holland. . .", 71) An avid outdoorsman, Brian went into broadcasting after his playing career and has been a local TV sports reporter and hosted his own weekly outdoors show in Wisconsin.

Brian Noble's career coincided with the explosive growth of the trading card and memorabilia industry. The aforementioned Ray Nitschke, Hall of Fame linebacker from the 1960s, played for 16 years and was featured on eight regular-issue trading cards during that time. Brian Noble played for nine years and was featured on, at least, 48 cards. As Brian himself says:

NUMBER 91

Most present day football cards are action photos, or if they take a shot of you it's on the sidelines without your helmet on. I posed for a couple of cards, but nothing like the swinging through the air they did then. Nowadays, I don't know how many athletes would do that.

The thing that bothers me today is that back when those old football card photos were done, they were collectibles not because of their dollar value but because kids just liked to say they had one of those cards. Now it's gotten to the point that there's such a large value placed on those things that it's really spoiled for the kid that just wants to have a Reggie White autographed football card or a Brett Favre autographed football. It's upsetting to the extent that the days of Reggie and Brett walking to camp are over, because you have people paying young kids to run up there and get their autograph and they pay kids five, ten bucks, then turn around and sell the thing for sixty, seventy dollars. It's ruined something very memorable for a kid. (Biever, Vernon, 25)

While football cards and collectibles have always run second to those for base-ball, they have a long history. The first card-like collectible featuring professional foot-ball players were Diamond matchbooks, starting in 1933. One side of the matchbook exhibited the player's colorized photograph and the other side a written description. Packer players of the time, such as Arnie Herber and Joe Laws, were featured in 1933 and 1934 issues. The first actual card set was the 1935 National Chicle set, which was a mix of college and professional players and included Clarke Hinkle, Swede Johnston, and Ernie Smith. Thirteen years later, two gum companies tried again. In 1948, Leaf produced another mixed college and professional set, and Bowman produced the first all-professional player football card set. It was in black and white. The following year, Leaf reran a number of the same cards with new write-ups on the back. Packers' star running back Ted Fritsch was included in both years. In the early 1970s, his nephew Larry Fritsch became the first sports card dealer in the nation to open his own shop.

Bowman skipped 1949, but from 1950 through 1955 they produced beautiful full-color sets each year. On the backs of Bowman's cards, collectors could learn such fasci-nating facts as: Bill Howton was called the number one softball pitcher in Texas in 1950; Dick Wildung was a member of the Phi Delta Theta Fraternity; Tom Johnson's hobby is music and "he toots a mean trumpet;" Jim Ringo majored in geography; Dave Hanner worked in a Green Bay fertilizer plant; Bob Fleck is the "type of lineman that the coach dreams about;" and so forth. Topps bought out Bowman and has produced cards for pro-fessional football ever since. Topps gave second-class status to football cards, often using obviously dated photographs in its sets. They frequently used cartoons to fill space on the back of the card. They were challenged by Fleer, Post, and Philadelphia in the 1960s, but starting in the late '60s Topps held a monopoly on regular-issue football player cards for 20 years until 1989, when Fleer, Score, and Pro Set all got into the game.

Since the Packers were so dominant in the 1960s, they were exceedingly well rep-resented on the cards of that time. Almost all starters from the Lombardi era were on at least one regular issue card—including all five offensive linemen, which is particularly remarkable for an era when entire football card sets consisted of fewer than 200 cards in most years. Specialty sets were also produced. A particular favorite is the green-tinted 1961 Lake-to-Lake Packer set distributed via the milk cartons of the Midwestern Lake-to-Lake Dairy. Among the most valuable regular-issue cards are the 1957 Bart Starr and Paul Hornung rookie cards, both picturing them when they had hair. Both are worth several hundred dollars today in excellent condition. The Starr rookie card is notable in that he is pictured as wearing a number he never wore in a game, 42. As a 17th-round draft choice, he was originally assigned a high number for his first picture day. Errors abound throughout these sets, as well. How is it that the 1956 and 1957 sets feature Packers in uniforms they stopped wearing in 1950—blue jerseys with gold shoulders? The strangest is the Jim Taylor 1959 rookie card that displays a picture of the moderately handsome Cardinals' linebacker with the same name as the more rugged-looking Packer fullback. Unbelievably, Topps repeated this mistake by reusing the same incorrect photo in its 1960 set.

Of the roughly 100 men who played for Vince Lombardi, only 11 (Jan Barrett, Ken Beck, Nate Borden, Gene Breen, John Dittrich, Ron Gassert, Ed Holler, John Miller, A.D. Williams, Howie Williams, and Paul Winslow) never appeared on a card or bottle cap or sticker. Among the oddities that collectors search out for the players and coaches of that time are Tom Brown on a 1964 Topps Baseball card, Gale Gillingham on a 1971 Bazooka Gum Box Panel, Travis Williams on a 1970 Kellogg's 3D card, Rich Marshall on a 1965 Coke bottle cap, Bob Jeter on a 1962 Canadian Post Cereal Card, John McDowell on a 1968 Topps Canadian card, Bob Hyland on a 1976 RC Cola can, coach Norb Hecker on a 1960 Washington Redskins Matchbook, coach Tom McCormick on a 1955 Los Angeles Rams team-issued set, and Phil Bengtson on a 1993 Packer Hall of Fame set. Retrospective sets also have multiplied in recent years. Colleges in particular have produced sets of their football greats. Ray Nitschke, Bart Starr, Jim Taylor, Paul Hornung, Ron Kramer, Dave Robinson, Tom Bettis, Norm Masters, Jim Grabowski, and Zeke Bratkowski can all be found on such supplemental, oddball sets that have much smaller printing runs.

In the 1990s, companies proliferated for several years until bankruptcies and mergers decreased the number of companies producing regular-issue cards, but each company produces several different sets each year. Not to mention specialty sets. Upper Deck produced special 90-180 card Packer team sets for Wisconsin Shopko stores from 1996–98. Card stock and graphics quality improved radically in the 1990s and color photographs were included on both sides of the card, but scarcity had to be artificially introduced with insert cards—cards deliberately produced in lesser quantities to create a seller's market. Most rookie cards are insert cards. Inserts, rookies, and autographed cards have the highest value and are listed prominently on online auction web sites such as eBay. Collectibles themselves can run the gamut from action figures to bobble heads to drinking glasses to magnets to matchbooks to magazines to cereal boxes to soda cans to labeled bottles, and on and on. Vintage items come with built-in scarcity and command a premium.

Once, football cards reeking of bubblegum were purchased solely through single packs by kids at corner stores. Now the industry is a big business, selling primarily to collectors and dealers. Kids today have more sophisticated interests and tastes; there are a host of other sports, cable television channels, web sites, video games, and other high technology toys to divert their attention. More honest journalistic practices also make current players appear less heroic than their predecessors. When these kids become adults, they will not have the pleasant memory of going to the corner candy store and buying their packs of five cards for a nickel to collect pictures of their sports heroes. If they invest in a pack of cards, they may find a copy of one of a hundred or so Brett Favre cards produced that year—maybe it's even an insert card that they can sell on eBay. They will not get the thrill of finding Bart Starr's only card that year. Yes, it's a different world, and progress has brought many improvements, but Brian Noble is right. Something's been spoiled in the process.

FOR FURTHER INFORMATION

Berghaus, Bob. "Playoffs Eluded Noble" *Milwaukee Journal-Sentinel.* 10/17/96. (5)

Biever, Vernon J., photography, Peter Strupp ed. *The Glory of Titletown: The Classic Green Bay Packers Photography of Vernon Biever.* Dallas, TX: Taylor Publishing, 1997. (25, 153)

D'Amato, Gary. *Mudbaths and Bloodbaths: The Inside Story of the Bears-Packers Rivalry.* Madison, WI: Prairie Oak Press, 1997. (228)

Froberg, Tim. "Converted Californian Noble Finds Green Bay a Great Fit," *Green Bay Packers 1992 Yearbook.* (46-9)

"Holland and Noble Bow Out with Class," *Green Bay Packers 1994 Yearbook.* (70-1)

Reischel, Rob. "Noble Excelled During Down Years," *Milwaukee Journal-Sentinel Packer Plus.* Available at www.jsonline.com/packer/news/jul02/59565.asp.

Sauerberg, George. "Brian Noble—Tenacious, Strong," *Green Bay Packers 1986 Yearbook.* (59-61)

1995 PLAYOFFS
REGGIE WHITE • DEFENSIVE END 1993–98

WHO'S WORN THE NUMBER Dimler 1980, Koart 1986, B. Thomas 1986, S. Collier 1987r, Jurkovic 1991–92, White 1993–98.

ORIGINATOR 6'6" 260 pound defensive tackle Rich Dimler spent one season in Cleveland and 1980 in Green Bay. He appeared in only three games and later resurfaced in the USFL. He died at 44 of pancreatis. Larry McCarren once recalled him as the craziest guy he ever played with.

LONGEST TENURE Reggie White 1993–98.

NUMBER CHANGES Steve Collier wore 70 and 74 as a replacement player and 64 on the regular roster in 1987; John Jurkovic switched to 64 when Reggie came in 1993.

OTHER NOTABLES None, and there will be no more; Reggie's jersey was retired in 1999.

ONES TO FORGET None of the four humps who wore 92 before John Jurkovic lasted one full season with the team.

REGGIE WHITE When Hall of Famers Herb Adderley, Lance Alworth, Ronnie Lott, Lenny Moore, Merlin Olsen, Jim Parker, Paul Warfield, and Kellen Winslow were asked to name the 10 best football players they had ever seen, Reggie White was on everyone's list. The NFL's all-time leader in sacks is expected to be elected to Canton the first year he is eligible, which is befitting the man that many consider the finest defensive end ever to play the game.

Reggie was born and raised in Tennessee and went to the University of Tennessee, where he was an All American and the Southeastern Conference Player of the Year in his senior year. He signed with the Memphis Showboats of the rival spring football league, the USFL, before the NFL draft in 1984, and spent two seasons in Memphis. In his second season, before the league folded, he was named USFL Defensive Player of the Year. Reggie was one of two future Hall of Famers to come out of the USFL supplemental draft held by the NFL in 1984; the Eagles selected him fourth overall behind Steve Young, Mike Rozier, and Gary Zimmerman. After having played 18 USFL games in the spring of 1985, he played in 13 games for the Eagles that fall and attained his first 13 NFL sacks. He was chosen NFL Rookie of the Year. The next season, on the strength of 18 sacks and 83 solo tackles, Reggie made the Pro Bowl for the first of 13 consecutive times from 1986–98. The best thing about White was that he wasn't just a speed-rush-

NUMBER 92

ing sack artist, but a 290-pound lineman equally skilled in defending against the run, and he took great pride in being a complete player.

Reggie became famous in Philadelphia as the leader of a ferocious pressure defense coached by Buddy Ryan, originator of the Bears 46 defense from their 1985 Super Bowl run. Ryan moved White around in the line, so opposing offenses were never sure where he was coming from. White was consistently double- and even triple-teamed, making it possible for a decent defensive end like Clyde Simmons to lead the NFL in sacks one year with 19. White was known as "the Big Dawg" for his talent, and as the "Minister of Defense" in recognition of the pavement preaching he did in some of the worst neighborhoods in Philadelphia. White, indeed, was an ordained minister and not shy about sharing his faith. In eight years in Philadelphia, Reggie accumulated 124 sacks, but won only one playoff game, that one over the New Orleans Saints in 1992. Perhaps of greater significance in 1992, White's was the lead name in a class-action antitrust suit several players filed against the NFL. The suit led to a collective bargaining agreement in 1993 that instituted free agency in pro football.

Eagles owner Norman Braman was adamant that he would not overpay to retain Reggie White, asserting that White's best years were behind him. Reggie went on a well publicized 37-day free agency tour before shocking the sports world by signing with Green Bay. Reggie said that God told him to go to Green Bay; cynics figured that money had more to do with the decision. In reality, the Packers made a very competitive offer, had an improving team with an impressive young quarterback in Brett Favre, and a persuasive and positive negotiating team of GM Ron Wolf, Coach Mike Holmgren and Defensive Assistant Ray Rhodes. As it would turn out, Braman was right, Reggie's was not as good a player as he was in Philadelphia, but he was still among the best linemen in the game, would still make big plays that no one else could, and was an unquestioned, respected leader in the clubhouse and on the field. Braman was penny-wise and pound-foolish. He saved some money, but his football team never went to the Super Bowl.

Reggie had a multitude of moves to get to the passer. He could simply bull-rush right through the lineman who was trying to block him, or use his forearm like a club to beat his way through the line, or swing his arm in a swimming motion to toss the opposing lineman aside like a toy. Buoyed by Reggie, the Packer defense would improve its rank in points allowed each year in their quest for the championship, going from 15th in 1992 to 9th in 1993, 5th in 1994, 4th in 1995, and finally 1st in the Super Bowl season of 1996.

Reggie's third year in Green Bay would prove to be crucial for Mike Holmgren's program. On the one hand, the team had made steady progress. Holmgren had led them to an improbable 9-7 finish in 1992 and had installed the quarterback of the future in Brett Favre. In 1993 they went 9-7 again, but made the playoffs where they went 1-1. In 1994 they went 9-7 still again, but earned a home playoff game which they won before ending another season disappointed in Dallas. On the other hand, they had gone 9-7 three years in a row, had lost their main offensive weapon in receiver Sterling Sharpe to injury, had lost All Pro linebacker Bryce Paup in free agency, had not adequately replaced tight end Jackie Harris who had left the year before, and had waved good bye to first-round flop Terrell Buckley. Some were predicting a step backwards in 1995. So what happened? Robert Brooks, Mark Chmura, Wayne Simmons, and Craig Newsome stepped up, Keith Jackson gave the offense another boost when he signed in mid-season, and the Packers won the Central Division for the first time in 23 years with an 11-5 record.

There was something almost miraculous about that result. In December, Reggie severely injured his hamstring and was declared out for the season. The next game, the Packers lost to the lowly Buccaneerss in overtime, 13-10. At that point, their record was 9-5 and another 9-7 season was still possible. White began to heal at a miraculously rapid clip and played about 20 snaps in the next game, a win over the Saints. In the final game of the season against Pittsburgh, Reggie was on the field for 51 snaps. In that see-saw battle, the Packers hung on to win 24-19, as star Steeler receiver Yancey Thigpen dropped a last-minute fourth-down pass in the end zone to preserve the Packer victory. The next week brought a home playoff game against the Falcons, and the Packers won easily, 37-20, with Favre throwing three touchdown passes and Antonio Freeman returning a punt 76 yards for another score.

The following week was a homecoming for Bay Area native Coach Mike Holmgren. Green Bay was a 10-point underdog to the 49ers, but delivered a stunning 27-17 whipping of the defending champions in San Francisco in a game that wasn't really that close. Wayne Simmons caused a fumble on the 49ers first possession that Craig Newsome ran in for a touchdown. Brett Favre hit on 15 of 17 passes for 222 yards in the first half, and Keith Jackson caught four passes for 101 yards. 49ers' quarterback Steve Young threw 65 passes in trying to rally San Francisco, but the Packers hit both Young and the 49er receivers hard and often to control the game.

The annual losing trip to Dallas came a week later, and while it was as frustrating as usual, there was a bright side this time. The Packers had taken another step by advancing to the NFC Championship game. They were clearly gaining on the Cowboys, as they lost only 38-27 and were leading in the fourth quarter before an ill-advised Favre pass led to the clinching Dallas score. The feeling after that game was that the Packers needed to bring the Cowboys to Lambeau for their next meeting, and that forged a whole new determination for the next season.

The Packers would go on to win the Super Bowl in 1996 and one of the enduring images of that victory is of Reggie White running laps around the New Orleans Superdome after the game, holding high the Vince Lombardi trophy, a champion at last. The following season, the team made the Bowl again, but Reggie suffered from back troubles all year and struggled throughout the title game loss to the Broncos. In the off-season, he announced his retirement and then rescinded it a week later. He worked on reconditioning his back and came back fiercely with 16 sacks in 1998. However most were in the first half of the year—only one came in December. Reggie was clearly wearing down, as was the team that went 11-5 and lost in the first round of the playoffs. Reggie retired for 1999, and his jersey was retired at halftime of a dismal, nationally televised Monday night loss to Mike Holmgren's Seattle Seahawks. He wanted to come back again in 2000 for the camaraderie, for the glory, and for the money. Ron Wolf gave him his release and he signed to play one last, uneventful season with the dreary Carolina Panthers before retiring for good.

The 11-time All Pro made headlines of a different sort in 1998 when he was invited to address a session of the Wisconsin State Assembly and made some very politically incorrect statements regarding different ethnic groups. That speech probably cost him any chance of becoming a broadcast analyst for NFL telecasts. Packer fans had shown their appreciation of the player and the man in 1996 when his Tennessee church was burned down, and Wisconsinites sent White a quarter of a million dollars to help rebuild it. However, the church was never rebuilt, and Reggie's partner in the institution went to prison on drug and weapons charges after all the money was spent. Recently, Reggie was shown in a broadcast on Fox Sports as disavowing interest in the Christian Church because it does not forcefully address sin. Instead, he continues to strive to follow the Bible and to explore "what I need to do to be holy." His off-field activities often seem curious, but his football performances never were. When he is inducted into the Pro Football Hall of Fame, White has said he will go in as a Packer. That will make Packer fans proud, because he was the cornerstone in the reviving of the franchise in the 1990s.

FOR FURTHER INFORMATION

Porter, David L., ed. *Biographical Dictionary of American Sports: 1992–1995 Supplement for Baseball, Football, Basketball, and Other Sports.* New York: Greenwood Press, 1995. (553-4)

White, Reggie, with Jim Denney. *In the Trenches: The Autobiography.* Nashville, TN: T. Nelson, 1996.

White, Reggie, with Terry Hill. *Reggie White: Minister of Defense.* Brentwood, TN: Wolgemuth and Hyatt, 1991.

White, Reggie, with Steve Hubbard. *God's Playbook: The Bible's Game Plan for Life.* Nashville, TN: T. Nelson, 1998.

"White, Reggie" in *Current Biography Yearbook 1995.* New York: H.W. Wilson, 1996. (587-90)

Wolf, Ron, and Paul Attner. *The Packer Way: Nine Stepping Stones to Building a Winning Organization.* New York: St. Martin's Press, 1998. (95-111)

Zimmerman, Paul. "White Heat," *Sports Illustrated.* 11/27/89. (64-8)

VIKINGS RIVALRY
GILBERT BROWN • DEFENSIVE TACKLE
1994-99, 2001-02

WHO'S WORN THE NUMBER
Moselle 1951, R. Brown 1982–92, C. Wallace 1987r,
Gil Brown 1994–9, 2001–02.

ORIGINATOR Halfback Dom Moselle 1951 was acquired
from Cleveland and was best as a kick returner, averaging
27.4 yards per return in 1951. He later coached basketball
at UW—Superior.

LONGEST TENURE Defensive end Robert Brown
1982–92 (see Forget below).

NUMBER CHANGES Dom Moselle wore 47 in 1952.

OTHER NOTABLES None.

ONE TO FORGET The fact that hard-working but nondescript
defensive end Robert Brown II lasted 11 years with the Packers,
mostly as a starter, says all you need to know about the sorry
state of their defense in the 1980s.

GILBERT BROWN Who can forget Gilbert Brown's strutting
entrance onto the field for Super Bowl XXXI? Flexing his powerful
upper body while his massive middle shook like jelly, he was probably the biggest man ever to play for Green Bay. While his most effective playing weight was at 335-340 pounds, he would eventually
expand to over 400 pounds and be dropped from the roster. Since
no other team was interested in an immense, immobile barrel of
blubber, it can be said that Gilbert ate himself out of football. Fortunately for Packer fans, though, he had the determination to recon-
dition himself at that point and return to the team at his old weight
a year later. While he was not quite the player he once was, he still
was one of the best run-stuffers in football.

Gilbert played his college ball at the University of Kansas,
where he teamed with future 49er Dana Stubblefield to form one of
the toughest defensive lines in the college ranks. He was selected by
the Vikings in the third round of the 1993 draft, but didn't make it
out of his first training camp. He was cut in August when the pre-
Slimfast Vikings Coach Dennis Green told Brown he needed to lose
weight. The Packers had thought highly of Brown going into the
draft that year, and picked him up off waivers. He spent 1993 learning Fritz Shurmur's defense and got into only two games. Over the
next two years, Gilbert got into the defensive line rotation and was

on the field more and more. When John Jurkovic left as a free agent after the 1995 season, Brown became the full-time starter at nose tackle.

In the Super Bowl year of 1996, Brown was at his peak. He was the best run-stuffer in the league and was called the "Gravedigger" for his signature shoveling move to punctuate his tackles. With his broad chest and sloppy stomach filling out an XXX-large Green jersey and his shaded helmet visor, he was quite a site on the field: a rumbling, jiggling, dominant warrior Buddha in pads. At 340 pounds, he was almost impossible to move in the middle of the line and often occupied two blockers, allowing his teammates on the defensive line to break free to the ball more easily. The Packers had the top defense in the league that year, and Gilbert had his best year statistically, with 51 tackles. After winning a Super Bowl ring, Brown became a free agent and surprised everyone by staying in Green Bay for a bit less money than the Jaguars were offering him to come to Jacksonville. He signed a three-year deal for $8.25 million to stay in Wisconsin because he had formed a tight bond with his teammates and the fans, and he was popular with both. At the local Burger King, they even served "Gilbertburgers" which were what Gilbert always ordered—basically a Whopper times two—double meat, double cheese, double tomato, double lettuce, a whole onion, no pickle, slathered in mayonnaise, and cut in half. The local kids loved him because he was clearly still a big kid himself. As he put it, "It comes down to being happy or just getting a paycheck. It's fun to come to work here."

He would not be able to maintain his body size, health, or level of play consistently beyond 1996, but would still be an effective player for the next few years. In 1997, he missed four games and was slowed by a series of nagging injuries that limited his ability in the middle of the season and the Packers run defense disappeared. Opposing teams ran on them at will. As his waistline got larger, his wind got shorter, and his knees began to ache. He lost quickness and was less effective at clogging the middle. He was well over 370 pounds when the Packers released him after the 1999 season. At 400 pounds and out of football, Gilbert missed the game and his teammates terribly and decided to try to turn things around. He returned to Lawrence, Kansas, at Thanksgiving and moved in with his conditioning coach from college. In eight months, he dropped 65 pounds and earned a spot back in the middle of the Packer defensive line for the 2001 season. He started 12 games and was once again a force against the run. That was made even more evident by the four games he missed to injury when the Packers run defense began to give up over 150 yards a game. He came back for the stretch run, and on the first play of the first playoff game against the 49ers, set the tone for the Packers victory by sacking and bloodying quarterback Jeff Garcia. Gilbert drove Garcia into the turf and fell on him. The Gravedigger was back.

While Brown never actually played for the Vikings, many Packers have. The 1961 expansion draft sent Ken Beck, Paul Winslow, and Dick Pesonen to the Vikings, but only Pesonen made the team. In ensuing years, others who first played with the Packers before joining the Vikings include: Jeff Brady, Bill Butler, Jesse Clark, Paul Coffman, Carroll Dale, Dale Hackbart, John Hilton, Bob Houston, Greg Koch, Jim Nelson, Bryce Paup, Kurt Ploeger, Al Randolph, Dave Roller, Jeff Schuh, Bucky Scribner, Matt Snider, Jan Stenerud, Ken Stills, Esera Tualo, and A.D. Williams. Those going in the opposite direction from Minnesota to Green Bay include: Steve Bono, Kerry Cooks, Dan Hansen, Rob Holmberg, Jim McMahon, Mike Merriweather, Keith Millard, Andre O'Neal, Dave Osborn, Allen Rice, Rod Smith, Fred Strickland, Keith Thibodeaux, and Maurice Turner.

The rivalry between the teams is certainly not as intense as that of the Bears-Packers, but it is serious stuff in the Great White North. The bordering states of Minnesota and Wisconsin have had a longer football history than that involving the Vikings. Indeed, Minnesota hosted a handful of teams in the first decade of the NFL. The Minneapolis Marines lost to the Packers four times from 1921–24, including in the Packers very first NFL game; the Minneapolis Red Jackets lost four games to Green Bay in 1929–30. The Duluth Kelleys lost three of four from 1922–24 and the Duluth Eskimos tied one game and lost the other to the Packers in 1926–27. The Packers maintained a following in their neighboring state for years after that and drew many players from Minnesota colleges. The 1961 season brought the expansion Vikings to the NFL and Vince Lombardi's commanding Packers beat them repeatedly until Fran Tarkenton's freelancing solution to a fourth-and-22 from his own 35 with a minute left led to a game-winning field goal at the gun on October 4, 1964. That gave the Vikings their first win of the series by a 24-23 score. Lombardi would finish 11-3 against the Vikings, but his successor Phil Bengtson ran into the beginning of the Bud Grant era in Minnesota, and the fortunes of the two teams reversed for the decades to come.

Bud Grant would compile a 22-12-1 record against Green Bay in his 18 years as head coach, while the Vikings regularly won the division in those years. One exception was 1972, when Dan Devine's Packers clinched Green Bay's sole divisional title of the 1970s by beating the Vikings 23-7 on December 10 in Minnesota. The Packers scored all their points in the second half and just wore down the Vikings with a relentless ground game that amassed 214 yards. On defense, the Pack intercepted Tarkenton three times. However, the Vikings would win seven games in a row from 1975 through 1978, then play the only tie in the series before beating Bart Starr's Packers for the eighth time in nine tries in 1979. Starr would win his first game against Minnesota in the second meeting of 1979, 19-7, on November 11. The Packers scored three touchdowns but had two extra-point tries blocked. The 1980s were not a magical decade for the Packers, but they did hold control of the Vikings series, winning 14 of 19 games during the decade, including five in a row from 1983–85. Highlights included scoring two fourth-quarter touchdowns on Lynn Dickey passes to win 16-3, on 10/26/80, in Lambeau coming from behind on a 72-yard, 10-play drive to win 16-10 on 12/13/87 in Milwaukee, and holding off a Viking comeback with two Dave Brown interceptions to win 20-19, again in Milwaukee, 11/26/89.

Dennis Green and Mike Holmgren, friends and rivals from their days coaching together in San Francisco, brought the rivalry some of its most competitive games during their tenures in Minnesota and Green Bay respectively. Green would ultimately hold a 9-5 edge in the series between the two, and some of Holmgren's defeats—particularly in the cursed Metrodome—were very bitter. In their first game, 9/6/92, in Lambeau, a 45-yard draw play by Viking running back Terry Allen to the Packer 11 in the closing minute led to a Viking field goal and a 23-20 victory. A year later, trash-talking Packer cornerback Terrell Buckley let Viking receiver Eric Guliford get so far behind him that weak-armed Minnesota quarterback Jim McMahon was able to hit Guliford for a 45-yard gain with 14 seconds left. That 9/26/93 game ended 15-13 on another game-winning Viking field goal. The following September, Sterling Sharpe walked out on the team before the opener and demanded a new contract. Holmgren held the team together, Sharpe came back to catch a touchdown pass, and the Packers hung on to beat Minnesota for the first time, 16-10, in Lambeau on 9/4/94. But later that year in the Metrodome, Minnesota quarterback Warren Moon led the Vikings to still another last-second field goal, this time to tie, and then won the game in overtime 13-10 on 10/20/94. The game on 11/5/95 brought perhaps the biggest heartbreaker with Minnesota, the T.J. Rubley game. Both Favre and his backup Ty Detmer got hurt, leaving the quarterbacking to journeyman Rubley in a tie game late in the fourth quarter. The Packers had moved to the Viking 38 and faced third and about a foot. Holmgren called for a quarterback sneak, but Rubley audibled to a pass play. T.J. rolled out and then threw back across his body and was intercepted by former Packer Jeff Brady at the 28. The Vikings then drove for one more last second winning field goal, 27-24 Minnesota. Rubley was cut the next week.

The Super Bowl year of 1996 delivered another loss in Minnesota, but also brought a very satisfying defeat of the Vikings in the final game of the season in Lambeau, 38-10. The Packers outscored the Vikings 28-0 in the second half and ran for 233 yards. In 1997 the Packers would win both games in the series, including Holmgren's only victory in the Metrodome by the comfortable margin of 27-11. Monday night, October 5, 1998, delivered a shocking blow to the Packers. It was Randy Moss' coming out party and it came in Lambeau on national TV. The Vikings won 37-24 and it was the first home loss by the Packers in 25 games. Quarterback Randall Cunningham threw for over 400 yards, including five passes to Moss for 190 yards and two touchdowns. Moss appeared to be covered on several instances, but simply out-leaped the defenders, displaying a new devastating weapon for the long-ball Vikings. Moss would later catch eight passes for 153 yards in the second contest of the rivals that year, a 28-14 Viking win.

The Packers would respond in the off-season by drafting three new, big, defensive backs and all three would play in the opening Minnesota matchup on 9/26/99 in Green Bay. First-round pick Antuwan Edwards even returned an interception for a touchdown, but ultimately the game belonged to Brett Favre, who completed six of seven passes for 77 yards on a final drive that concluded with a 23-yard touchdown toss to Corey Bradford with 14 seconds left, 23-20 Packers. On a rainy Monday night, November 6, 2000, perhaps the strangest game of the 40-year series took place. The game was tied in the closing minutes, but Minnesota lined up on third down for a potential game-winning 33-yard field goal with eight seconds left. The snap was bad, but rather than simply throwing the ball away and trying again on fourth down, holder Mitch Berger tried to force a bad pass that was picked off by Tyrone Williams, and time expired. The Packers won the coin flip in overtime and moved to the Viking 43. On third-and-four, Favre tried a deep lob to Antonio Freeman, who was well covered by Viking defensive back Chris Dishman. Freeman fell down and Dishman tried to bat the wobbling ball away, but it bounced off of him onto Freeman who was lying on his stomach. Somehow, Antonio juggled the ball in the air as he turned over and then finally grabbed it. While Dishman celebrated what he took to be an incomplete pass, Freeman got up and raced to the end zone. The Packers won 26-20 to provide a positive memory to erase all those hard-luck losses in this evenly-matched rivalry. Like T.J. Rubley before him, Dishman was cut the next week. The Packers would win both games against the Viking in 2001 to even up the series standings. For the first 42 years, the series stands dead even at 41-41-1.

FOR FURTHER INFORMATION

Anderson, Dave. "The Packer Who Packs the Middle," *New York Times.* 1/21/98. (C1)

Dougherty, Pete. "Failure Lit Fire for Gilbert Brown," *Green Bay Packers 1997 Yearbook.* (80-1)

Kessenich, Tom. "Little Son Big Motivator for Gilbert Brown," *Green Bay Packers 1995 Yearbook.* (48-9)

Murphy, Austin. "What's Eating Gilbert Brown?" *Sports Illustrated.* 1/26/98. (34-8)

BEARS RIVALRY II: UNNECESSARY ROUGHNESS
CHARLES MARTIN • DEFENSIVE TACKLE 1984–87

WHO'S WORN THE NUMBER
C. Martin 1984–87, D. Logan 1987, Matalele 1987r, M. Brock 1994, Kuberski 1995–98, Barker 1999, Gbaja–Biamila 2000–02.

ORIGINATOR Charles Martin 1984–87.

LONGEST TENURE Charles Martin 1984–87 and defensive tackle Bob Kuberski 1995–98—Scooby was a high-effort back-up.

NUMBER CHANGES Defensive end Matt Brock wore 62 from 1989–93.

OTHER NOTABLES Nigerian Kabeer Gbaja-Biamila is a pass rushing force.

ONE TO FORGET No one as embarrassing as Martin. Picking up defensive tackle Dave Logan for the last two games of his nine-year career is nothing worth remembering.

CHARLES MARTIN In high school, defensive tackle Charles Martin became known as "Too Mean," and he lived up to that nickname as a Green Bay Packer. He went to tiny Livingston College and played with Birmingham in the USFL before joining Forrest Gregg's first Packer team in 1984. Gregg's teams were short on talent, and he tried to make up for that by having them play aggressively, especially against the hated Bears. For some reason, there was very bad blood between Gregg and Bear Coach Mike Ditka, probably going back to their playing days in the 1960s. Ditka had a vast advantage in talented players and that allowed him to beat the Packers at will. With Gregg, his foe, as the opposing coach, Ditka took to rubbing Forrest's nose in it. In their 1985 championship season, the Bears won both games against the Packers so easily that they had 300-pound defensive tackle William "Refrigerator" Perry score a touchdown in each game. One came on a run and one on a pass reception off of play action.

One of Gregg's oddest players was Charles Martin, 6'2" and 285 pounds, with a modicum of talent and an abundance of belligerence. He was known for frequenting bars and becoming extremely antagonistic after having a few drinks. A few years later, he would check into an alcohol treatment center. Some teammates also suspected that he used steroids. As an example of his troubled behavior, there was a sexual incident in a bar in 1986 that got Charles a two-game suspension by the team. The first game against the Bears that year was very hard-hitting. Mark Lee was thrown out of the game for tussling with Walter Payton on the Packers' second possession. On the next possession, Martin dropped Walter Payton on a running play. The whistle blew, and the Packers safety Ken Stills came charging in and drilled Bear fullback Matt Suhey from behind as he was walking back to the huddle. The Packers were penalized and defensive coach Dick Modzelewski began yelling at Stills from the sideline, but Gregg told Modzelewski to lay off. He liked the aggressive attitude. The Bears went on to win again, 26-12. The 1986 rematch at Soldier Field is noted for the one play for which Charles Martin is remembered today. That day, Martin wore a towel at his waist with five uniform numbers he was gunning for: McMahon, Payton, Dennis Gentry, Willie Gault, and Jay Hilgenberg. In the second quarter, Bear quarterback Jim McMahon threw a pass that was picked off by Mark Lee. After the pass was picked off, Martin headed right for McMahon. However, instead of blocking him, as was his right, Martin grabbed McMahon from the blind side, picked him up off the ground, and body-slammed him onto the hard ground as if the two were in a World Wrestling Federation grudge match. McMahon landed on his shoulder and would be out the rest of the year. Martin was thrown out of the game and came off the field getting high fives from some teammates; he would be suspended by the league for two games. Once again, the Bears prevailed, winning 12-10 in the fourth quarter.

It was an embarrassing moment to be a Packer fan. To his credit, second-year linebacker Brian Noble went over to the Bears' locker room after the game and apologized personally to Ditka for his teammates' actions. Martin apologized through the media and unsuccessfully appealed the suspension. It was a low point in a rough, tough rivalry that has had its ups and downs for more than 80 years.

The 1920s were especially noted for the fierce battles between Packer center Jug Earp and Bear center George Trafton. In the very first game between the Packers and the then-Chicago Staleys, Bears' guard Tarzan Taylor sucker-punched the mild-mannered giant Packer tackle, Cub Buck, and broke his nose. Another Bear would try to break Buck's nose again in 1925, but Cub broke the Bear's arm instead. In 1926, ends Dick O'Donnell of the Packers and Frank Hanny of the Bears were ejected from the game for fighting. The Packers' Cal Hubbard got into dustups with a variety of players and officials in his career, and was later compared to Dick Butkus in his verve for the game. Against the Bears, Hubbard tangled with Bill Fleckenstein in 1929 and knocked the Bear out near the end of the game. The 1930s were marked by the epic duels between Clarke Hinkle and Bronko Nagurski that are celebrated in chapter 30. But first, Hubbard tested Nagurski's mettle on a punt. Cal made a deal with the Bears' Red Grange not to block the punt if Grange let him through to take a shot at Nagurski. Bronko knocked Hubbard back off his feet, and Cal was satisfied that the hype about the Bear fullback was true.

Tony Canadeo would remember his first Bears game in 1941 as one where he was spitting teeth and blood from the very first play. In 1944, he and fellow Italian-American, the Bears' Gary Famiglietti, got into a fist fight after an exchange of ethnic slurs. That year also marked the hiring of former Bear George Trafton as the Packers' line coach, and the hardened Packer line would lead the team to Lambeau's last championship that year. Trafton clashed with Lambeau and was released at the end of the year.

Former Bears never seem to last long in Green Bay. The post-war era ushered in a particularly violent period between the two teams. Villains on the Bears' side were Ed Sprinkle, Lee Artoe, Ray Bray, and Bulldog Turner, while on the Packers' side the rogues included Ed Neal, Paul Lipscomb, and Larry Craig.

In 1945, Artoe would sucker-punch Craig on one play and later in the game would receive a forearm shiver from Packer Ken Keuper that would break Lee's jaw. In the next decade, fistfights were frequent, as were thrown elbows, head butts, eye gouges, biting, and blind-side hits. Roy McKay had his nose broken. Carl Mulleneaux suffered five dislocated vertebrae, three missing teeth, a broken nose, and concussion on one blind side hit by John Schiechl; Mulleneaux would never play again. In the second matchup of 1950, the Bears' Paul Stenn was ejected for fighting with Dick Wildung, and the Bears' Fred Davis was thrown out after he knocked Clayton Tonnemaker out cold. Afterwards, the Bears' Ed Cody found himself in the hospital with a dislocated jaw from a Tony Canadeo blow in that same game. Bulldog Turner gave out plenty of punishment himself, but also suffered a broken nose several times at the swinging forearm of Ed Neal. Sprinkle added his patented hook tackle, which was basically a then-legal clothesline tackle by the neck. Lipscomb was said to have stepped on players' backs and kicked opponents. All of the above players were noted for delivering shots to the faces of rivals not wearing face masks. At the time, most players did not wear the protective face guards and their visages presented unhindered targets. There were too many broken noses to list in these years. Play in the interior line scrum was sadistic and unrestrained. Pileups were uncivilized places where bites and gouges could be perpetrated without detection or penalty.

The brutal, ruthless play reached its climax when George Connor uncorked a legendary legal hit on Packer kick-returner Veryl Switzer in 1955. Connor raced downfield unblocked and ran right through Switzer's chest. The ball flew one way and Switzer went the other. Switzer's helmet popped off his head with the chin strap still fastened. Switzer suffered a severely bruised sternum that would cause him to bleed internally for several weeks, but he missed only a few minutes of action that day. The 1950s were a violent decade in general, but as face masks became universal and as rules were changed to outlaw certain types of nasty behavior, play became less vicious. From then on, the rivalry remained hard-fought and bitter, but not so brutal. Jim Taylor and Mike Ditka would struggle and strain and push and shove to gain every inch they could, but they weren't dirty players. Ray Nitschke and Dick Butkus were intense, savage hitters, but played within the rules. The rivalry would continue that way until the aforementioned Forrest Gregg era.

After Gregg left, the rapidly boiling rivalry returned to a simmering feud. Incidents like those previously noted don't occur without encouragement from the coach. George Halas was known to strive to intimidate at all times. Packer receiver Bob Mann remembered scoring a touchdown in the 1950s and from the end zone seeing Halas running down the sideline, still yelling at his players to deck Mann. Charles Martin was involved in another bar incident in 1987—this time involving a bouncer, and was waived from the Packers. He was picked up by the Oilers and spent a year there and another year in Atlanta before drifting out of the league. His violent take-down along with other sacks not quite as heinous led to 1987 rule changes outlawing body slams and the taking of more than one step toward the passer after the ball has been thrown. As a Packer, Martin will remain an embarrassment and a reminder of the time when competitiveness was overrun by barbarism and a great rivalry was turned into a blood sport.

FOR FURTHER INFORMATION

Anderson, Dave. "Two Games Too Lenient," *New York Times*. 11/26/86. (D23)

Daly, Dan, and Bob O'Donnell. *The Pro Football Chronicle: The Complete (Well Almost) Record of the Best Players, the Greatest Photos, the Hardest Hits, the Biggest Scandals, and the Funniest Stories in Pro Football*. New York: Collier Books, 1990. (142-52)

D'Amato, Gary, and Cliff Christl. *Mudbaths and Bloodbaths: The Inside Story of the Bears-Packers Rivalry*. Madison, WI: Prairie Oak Press, 1997.

Lieber, Jill. "Too Mean and Also Too Lenient," *Sports Illustrated*. 12/8/86. (24-5)

Swain, Glenn. *Packers vs. Bears*. Los Angeles: Charles Publishing, 1996.

1993 & 1994 PLAYOFFS
BRYCE PAUP • LINEBACKER 1990–94

WHO'S WORN THE NUMBER Degrate 1985, C. Sullivan 1987r, Paup 1990–94, K. McKenzie 1996–99, 2002, S. Warren 2000, R. Walker 2001–02.

ORIGINATOR Nose tackle Tony Degrate 1985 (see Forget below).

LONGEST TENURE Bryce Paup 1990–94.

NUMBER CHANGES Nose tackle Steve Warren switched to 96 while on injured reserve in 2001.

OTHER NOTABLES None.

ONE TO FORGET Tony Degrate was not so grate [sic]. The 1984 Lombardi Award winner as the best college lineman was drafted by the Bengals in the fifth round and then cut in training camp. Green Bay picked him up for one week. The next year, Tampa cut him in training camp. This consensus All American had a one-game NFL career.

BRYCE PAUP Some players have no sense of timing. Bryce Paup played for teams that went to six Super Bowls during his eleven years in the NFL, but he never went to even one. He left Green Bay in 1995 and just missed three straight division titles, three straight conference championship games, and two straight Super Bowl appearances. He signed that year with Buffalo, which was just coming off four straight Super Bowl appearances but would not be returning to the big game for the rest of that decade. By contrast, Don Beebe came into the league the year before Paup, lasted nine years, and played on all six of those Super Bowl teams in that time.

Bryce Paup made himself into a player through hard work and dedication. He grew up a lanky, muscular Iowa farm boy who was part of a high school graduating class of 19 students. It's a wonder that Bryce made it off the farm at all, because in that high school only 19 boys went out for the football team. Paup's girlfriend was attending Northern Iowa and spoke to an assistant football coach about her boyfriend. After further prompting by Paup's high school coach, the Northern Iowa assistant looked at a homemade game tape of Paup and offered him a scholarship. Paup worked hard and became a third-team All American in his senior year. The Packers selected him in the sixth round of the 1990 draft and he made the team, although he saw little action as a rookie. In 1991, he replaced holdout Tim Harris and ripped off six sacks in his first three games before the offenses adjusted and Paup got hurt so he registered only one more sack that year.

He was 6'5" 250 pounds, and could play inside and outside linebacker as well as pass-rushing defensive end. In his five years in Green

PACKERS BY THE NUMBERS

Bay he would do all of that, but primarily would serve as a pass-rusher who attained 32.5 sacks in 64 games as a Packer. He was strong against the run, but his pass coverage skills were suspect at first, so he spent hours drilling to get the footwork right for dropping into coverage. Defensive coach Fritz Shurmur valued Paup's versatility overall, using him as an outside linebacker who would move to defensive end on passing downs, with Reggie White moving to defensive tackle. In 1994 he was named All Pro and went to the Pro Bowl. Coach Holmgren would say of him, "He has proven to me that he is the total package as a linebacker. In this day of situational substitutions, often times a linebacker comes in and out of the game. And while we still do that, Bryce has exhibited the ability to play the whole game." (Youngblood)

Paup was a valuable contributor to Mike Holmgren's first two playoff teams in 1993 and 1994. While Reggie White was the biggest factor in pushing the improving team over the hump, the presence of more and more solid performers like Bryce Paup made the team good enough for White to lead them to the post-season. The 1993 and 1994 seasons were good news/bad news kinds of years in which the Packers played the same two teams with the same results both years. In 1993, the team made the playoffs for the first time since 1982, but the playoffs really started the week before when they played the Lions in Detroit to see who would win the Black and Blue Division (the Central) and host the following week's playoff game between the same two teams. Third-string quarterback Erik Kramer led the Lions to a 30-20 victory over the Packers, greatly assisted by Brett Favre's four pass interceptions.

The next week, the two teams met again in Detroit to start the playoffs, and it looked as if Favre might turn out to be the goat again when he had a pass intercepted at his own 15 by Melvin Jenkins, who returned it for a touchdown, putting the Lions up 17-7 in the third quarter. Brett led the team down the field and threw a touchdown pass to Sterling Sharpe to make it 17-14. The Lions countered with a long drive to the Packer five, but Packer safety George Teague intercepted an Erik Kramer pass and took it 101 yards for the go-ahead touchdown late in the third quarter. The Lions regained the lead 24-21 with eight minutes left in the game when they drove 89 yards and scored on a five-yard run by Derrick Moore. The Packers got the ball for the last time at their own 29 with 2:26 left. Four plays and 1:31 later they were on the Lions' 40 when Favre uncorked one of the most impressive plays of his career. Scrambling to his left he spotted Sterling Sharpe breaking free down the right sideline. Brett turned and threw in the opposite direction across the field, 40 yards downfield to hit the streaking Sharpe for his third touchdown reception of the day and a 28-24 Packer victory. What that great game won the Packers was a chance to go to Dallas to face the defending champions in a divisional playoff game. Not surprising, the vastly superior Cowboys won 27-17. They had held only a 7-3 lead until a field goal, a fumble recovery, and an Aikman touchdown pass in the last 23 seconds of the half made the score 17-3 at the intermission. The Packers would not recover.

The 1994 season signaled a small step forward. The Packers got a home game for the wild card round of the playoffs. Once again the opponents were the Lions, but the character of this game was entirely different. Sterling Sharpe was gone, having suffered a career-ending neck injury the week before. The game was played in Lambeau on a moderately cold 33-degree day, and the Packer defense was king. The Packer offense out-gained the Lions 336-171. More significantly, they held the great Barry Sanders to his worst day as a pro running back, 13 carries for -1 yard. His longest run of the day was for seven yards. Despite the wide disparity in yards, the game was close right to the end. The Lions had a third-and-eight at the Packer 11 at the two-minute warning when Paup sacked Lions' quarterback Dave Kreig for a six-yard loss. On fourth down, Kreig's pass to Herman Moore went out of the end zone, and Green Bay took over. Once again, a victory over Detroit only set them up for defeat in Dallas a week later. This time the disappointment was greater, as they were buried by the Cowboys 35-9. With the loss of Sharpe, they seemed to have fallen even farther behind Dallas in the chase for a championship.

Paup became a victim of the salary cap in 1995, when the Packers elected not to resign him. Reports were that the team felt that Paup's sacks were a result of the extra attention that opposing offenses would devote to Reggie White. In addition, while Paup gave all-out effort at all times, he didn't have the exceptional skill level the Packers were looking for. Paup went to Buffalo, lined up on the opposite side from Bruce Smith, and had a career year with a league-leading 17.5 sacks, three forced fumbles, and two interceptions. It came as no surprise that he was voted NFL Defensive Player of the Year in 1995. Packer GM Ron Wolf later would term Paup's departure as a "miscalculation."

Bryce Paup was a quiet, religious, family man who continued to live in Green Bay after signing with Buffalo because he thought the area had a nice small-town atmosphere and was a good place to raise a family. He even floated the prospect of returning to the Packers when he became a free agent again in 1998 and in 2000, but the team had no interest. Wolf was right on both those occasions, because Paup was finished as an impact player by that point. He ended his career with two years in Jacksonville and one in Minnesota, going to two more conference championship games, but losing badly both times. In 2002, he requested that the Packers sign him and cut him the next day, so he could go out as a Packer.

FOR FURTHER INFORMATION
Froberg, Tim. "Paup Comes into His Own," *Green Bay Packers 1994 Yearbook.* (44-7)

Ledbetter, Orlando. "Paup in Spotlight," *Milwaukee Journal Sentinel.* 12/16/94. (C1)

Murphy, Austin. "Paup Fiction," *Sports Illustrated.* 3/4/96 (64-8)

Silverstein, Tom. "Paup at Home in Green Bay," *Milwaukee Journal Sentinel.* 2/3/96. (Sports 1)

Youngblood, Kent. "Paup Playing at a Higher Level," *Wisconsin State Journal.* 11/10/94. (1C)

BIOGRAPHICAL TRIVIA

SEAN JONES • DEFENSIVE END 1994–96

WHO'S WORN THE NUMBER Leiker 1987r, Patterson 1988–91, 1993, S. Jones 1994–96, G. Williams 1997, Booker 1998–99, D. Bowens 2000, Warren 2002.

ORIGINATOR Tony Leiker in 1987 had been drafted in the seventh round by the Packers and was cut in training camp before being brought back as a replacement player during the 1987 players' strike. He later sued the team over an injured knee.

LONGEST TENURE Sean Paterson 1988–91 and 1993.

NUMBER CHANGES Defensive tackle Steve Warren wore 95 in 2000.

OTHER NOTABLES None.

ONES TO FORGET Sean Patterson was disappointing as a number-two draft pick; defensive end Vaughn Booker was disappointing as a free-agent pickup; defensive end David Bowens was disappointing as a trade acquisition.

SEAN JONES Born in Kingston, Jamaica, Sean Jones grew to alarming size according to opposing quarterbacks. The 6'7" 270-pound long-armed defensive end graduated from Northeastern University in Boston and was drafted in the second round by the Super Bowl champion Raiders in 1984. He spent four seasons in LA and had an AFC high of 15.5 sacks in 1986. In 1988, he signed with the Oilers as a free agent and began a six-year stretch of solid play in Houston for a team that never reached its goals. After the continual frustration of always losing the pressure-cooker games to Elway's Broncos, Joe Montana's Chiefs and the Buffalo Bills, Jones was looking for a chance to get to the Super Bowl when he became a free agent again in 1994. At that time, he considered signing with the Cardinals, who were coached by his former defensive coach at Houston, Buddy Ryan, but in a smart move opted for Green Bay after having a productive talk with Coach Mike Holmgren.

Jones came to Wisconsin with 88.5 sacks in 10 years and would lead the Packers in that category in 1994 with 10.5. The next year, he became the ninth player to accumulate more than 100 sacks since the NFL began officially counting them in 1982. Besides his pass-rushing skills, he was tough against the run. Jones was a savvy veteran who his teammates looked up to both for his football knowledge and for his financial acumen—he worked as a stockbroker at Dean Witter, began a financial services company of his own, and would begin serving as a player agent once his playing career ended. Jones was always good for a quote, and was outspoken and not afraid to challenge authority figures. Nonetheless, he got along well with Holmgren, who respected stong-minded, intelligent players like Jones and Leroy Butler. Sean began to slip a bit in 1996 and recorded only five sacks that year, but he won his Super Bowl ring. In the off-season, Wolf and Holmgren decided it was time to move on with the younger Gabe Wilkins. Holmgren felt that Sean did not have the disposition of a backup defensive end, so Jones was released, but he moved smoothly into his post-playing career without regret. In 201 professional games, he had recorded 113 sacks, one interception, and one fumble recovery for a Green Bay touchdown. He was missed in the next Super Bowl when Wilkins came up lame while the Broncos ran free.

There have been 14 Packers other than Sean Jones who were born outside the United States: Dean Dorsey, Paul Duhart, Tony Mandarich, and Lyle Sturgeon were born in Canada.

Two players were born south of the border, Max Zendejas in Mexico and Ted Hendricks in Guatemala. European-born Packers include John Jurkovic and David Whitehurst from Germany, Jan Stenrud from Norway, Buckets Goldenberg from Odessa, Ukraine, and Tunch Ilkin from Istanbul, Turkey. Two Packers hailed from the South Pacific island of Tonga— Vai Sikahema and Stan Mataele. Bhawoh Jue emigrated with his family from Monrovia, Liberia, when he was only one year old.

As near as I can tell only one former Packer died outside the U.S.—Howard "Smiley" Johnson, a Marine who died on Iwo Jima in World War II.

Some of the hometowns of Packer players have an interesting ring. There are hometowns that have names with literal meaning. My favorite is Cando, SD, where former Viking and Packer Dave Osborn started out. Osborn was infused with the "can do" spirit. Some others: Birthright, TX (Forrest Gregg); Buckeye, AZ (Bill Lueck); Burnt Ranch, CA (Ben Starrett); Clover, SC (Lamont Hall); Coffee Springs, AL (Jim Bowdoin); Ducktown, TN (Brian Satterfield); Hominy, OK (Bob Hudson); Mayflower, AR (Elijah Pitts); Muleshoe, TX (Elmo Boyd); Oilton, OK (Charlie Mitchell); Pineapple, AL (Fred Cone); Spearfish, SD (Ernie Smith); Sweatman, MS (Frank Purnell); and Wise, VA (Carroll Dale).

Other hometowns seem to belong somewhere else. Florence, AL (Al Romine); Norway, MI (Rudy Rosatti); Palestine, TX (Keith Crawford); Paris, TX (Bobby Jack Floyd); and Thebes, AR (Jessie Clark).

Still other hometown names are wholly unique. Brazonia, TX (Clarence Williams); Bucyrus, OH (Bob Monnett); Chickasha, OK (Jonathan Brown); Cokato, MN (Earl Ohlgren); DeFuniak Springs, FL (Dexter McNabb); Goodlettsville, TN (Tom Moore); Hamtramack, MI (Roger Zatkoff) Natchitoches, LA (Steve Dowden); Oconta, WI (Red Mack, Jab Murray, and others); Puxico, MO (Russ Mosley); Tippah County, MS (Michael Haddix); and Tulahoma, TN (Antonio London).

Packers Marion Ashmore, Tom Birney, and Gil Skeate all went to J. M. Weatherwax High School in Aberdeen, WA, but fellow Packer Jim Weatherwax went to Redlands High in California. Charley Brock went to Kramer High School in Columbus, NE, before future Packers Ron or Jerry Kramer were even born.

PACKERS BY THE NUMBERS

Three Packers went to Marshall High in Minnesota (Andy Uram, George, and Bud Svendsen) and to St. Ignatius High in Cleveland (Ed Ecker, Brian Dowling, and Chris Gizzi). Four Packers went to Temple High in Texas (Ken Davis, Bobby Dillon, Bill Lucky, and Mike Weddington) and Phoenix Union in Arizona (Fred Carr, Carl and Lee Mulleneaux, and Hal Prescott). Topping the tally, five Packers went to Marinette High in Wisconsin (Jug Girard, Eddie Glick, Jab Murray, Sammy Powers, and Buff Wagner).

Several players went to Thomas Jefferson High School: John Brockington in Brooklyn, Joe Kelly in Los Angeles, Carl Bland and Lee McLaughlin in Richmond, VA, Tim Huffman in Dallas, Damon Tassos in San Antonio, and K.D. Williams in Tampa.

Green Bay East High alumni include: Nate Abrams, Wayland Becker, James Cook, Jim Crowley, Les and Tom Hearden, Curly Lambeau, Russ Saunders, and Dave Zuidmulder. Green Bay West alumni include: Art Bultman, Butts Hayes, Arnie Herber, Fee Klaus, Wes Leaper, Herm Martell, Dave Mason, Charlie Mathys, Ray McLean, Ken Radick, Joe Secord, Jerry Tagge, Cowboy Wheeler, and Carl, Marty and Dick Zoll. Bob Kroll and Jim Hobbins went to Preble High in Green Bay.

In Milwaukee, Buckets Goldenberg went to West, Ed Jankowski went to East, Derrick Harden and Roy Schoeman went to South, and Lavvie Dilweg and Wally Dreyer went to Washington. In Minneapolis, Joe Fuller, Dewey Lyle, and Marty Norton went to Central, Pat Dunnigan and Bob Tenner went to West, Ken Haycraft went to East, and George Tuttle went to South. In Des Moines, Paul Minick went to West and Harry O'Boyle went to East. In Fort Wayne, Herb Banet went to South Side and Bill Boedecker went to North Side. In Memphis, Lew Carpenter went to West and Terdell Middleton and Cliff Taylor went to South Side.

Three Packers went to Notre Dame High: Dave Kopay in Los Angeles, Steve Broussard in Biloxi, MS, and Norm Barry in South Bend, IN. None of them went to the University of Notre Dame.

Twelve Packers went to Military Prep Schools including Don Barton, Ed Berrang, Ron Gassert, Jim Keane, Lou Michaels, Steve Pritko, and George Vergara. Tyrone Davis, Antonio Dingle, Don Majkowski, Steve Meilinger, and Tom Miller all attended Fort Union Military Academy in Virginia.

In college, Dale Livingston attended both Eastern Michigan and Western Michigan.

More than 130 Packers attended two colleges, including community colleges. These 18 players went to three colleges: Bill Bain, Don Beebe, Dirk Borgognone, Steve Broussard, Leo Carroll, Steve Collier, Boob Darling, Mike Douglass, Don Horn, Tubby Howard, Johnny Blood, Ed Neal, Steve Okoniewski, Francis Peay, Allen Rice, Rosey Rosatti, Keith Traylor, and Blake Wingle. Four Packers went to four institutions of higher learning: Dutch Hendrian (Depauw, Detroit Mercy, Pittsburgh, and Princeton), Mike Mercer (Minnesota, Florida State, Hardin-Simmons, and Arizona State), Dan Orlich (Compton Community College, Northwestern, Penn State, and Nevada-Reno), and Elbert Watts (East Los Angeles College, Santa Monica College, Oklahoma, and USC). Dick Afflis claimed to have passed through five universities: Purdue, Miami, Notre Dame, Alabama, and finally Nevada.

Twenty-three Packers never went to college at all, including: Cliff Aberson, Nate Abrams, Walt Buland, Billy Dumoe, Gus Gardella, Buck Gavin, Jack Gray, Fee Klaus,

Adolph Kliebhan, Wally Ladrow, Herm Martell, Ray McLean, Marty Norton, Dick O'Donnell, Sammy Powers, Art Schmaehl, Joe Secord, and Carl and Marty Zoll. Only four Packers since 1950 did not attend college: Howie Ferguson (1953–58), Dick Deschaine (1955–57), Charlie Leigh (1974) and replacement player Greg Jensen (1987).

Five Packers played major-league baseball: Cliff Aberson, Larry Bettencourt, Tom Brown, Pid Purdy, and Red Smith. None was a candidate for Cooperstown, although Cal Hubbard is there as an umpire.

At least six Packers played professional basketball. Connie Berry, Ted Cook, Len Ford, Ted Fritsch, and George Svendsen played in the National Basketball League in the 1930s and 1940s. Ron Widby played in the ABA in the 1960s.

Five Packers became NFL officials: George Vergara, Verne Lewellen, Lon Evans, Herman Rohrig, and Steve Pritko.

Six Packers played under four different head coaches. Forrest Gregg (Blackbourn, McLean, Lombardi, and Bengtson), Ray Nitschke (McLean, Lombardi, Bengtson, and Devine), Gale Gillingham (Lombardi, Bengtson, Devine, and Starr), Robert Brown and Ron Hallstrom (Starr, Gregg, Infante, and Holmgren), and Leroy Butler (Infante, Holmgren, Rhodes, and Sherman). Only Bart Starr played under five Packer head coaches (Blackbourn, McLean, Lombardi, Bengtson, and Devine).

Both Curly Lambeau and Vince Lombardi finished their coaching careers with a winning season in Washington.

Vince Lombardi played college football at Fordham in the 1930s as one of the famous "Seven Blocks of Granite" under Coach Jim Crowley. Jim Crowley was famous for being one of Notre Dame's "Four Horsemen" in the early 1920s. He had gone to Green Bay's East High School and was coached there by Curly Lambeau, who was helping out his old school in 1919 and 1920. Crowley also played a few games for the Packers after graduating from Notre Dame. Sleepy Jim is one connection between the Packers' two Hall of Fame coaches. Another connection is end Harry Jacunski, who played alongside Lombardi for two years at Fordham and then played for the Packers for six years from 1939 through 1944 under Lambeau.

There are six degrees of separation between Sean Jones and the team's co-founder, Nate Abrams. Jones played with tackle Ken Ruettgers, who started out in 1985 under coach Forrest Gregg, who played with Tobin Rote in 1956, who played with Tony Canadeo, who played under Curly Lambeau, who played with Nate Abrams in 1921, the Packers first year in the NFL. All Packers are part of a long tradition.

FOR FURTHER INFORMATION

McClain, John. "The Word on Sean Jones," *The Sporting News.* 1/10/94. (17)

"Off-Season Professionals," *Black Enterprise.* 10/92. (162-6)

Raboin, Sharon. "Sean Jones," *Green Bay Packers 1996 Yearbook.* (62-3)

LEADERS
TIM HARRIS • LINEBACKER 1986–90

WHO'S WORN THE NUMBER
T. Harris 1986–90, J. Miller 1987r, Noonan 1992, Traylor 1993, Merriweather 1993, LaBounty 1995, Frase 1997, C. Hunt 1999–2002.

ORIGINATOR Tim Harris 1986–90.

LONGEST TENURE Tim Harris 1986–90.

NUMBER CHANGES None.

OTHER NOTABLES None.

ONE TO FORGET Keith Traylor started with Denver as a 260-pound linebacker, came to the Packers as a 290-pound defensive tackle, and lasted for five games. He then traveled on to Kansas City and back to Denver before finally landing in Chicago, fully grown as a 350-pound nose tackle eight years later.

TIM HARRIS Tim Harris was a flashy motor-mouth. He would spout a non-stop stream of trash-talk throughout a game, trying to distract opponents and gain an advantage. In his prime, though, he didn't need much of edge. He was 6'5" 250 pounds with long arms, quick acceleration, speed, and moves. He had all the key attributes to play the Elephant position in the modern defense, a pass-rushing defensive end/outside linebacker. But any particular position was a misnomer for Tim. He would line up as linebacker, at times, at other times as a defensive end on either side of the line, and sometimes he would line up directly over the center. He was not one for playbooks or film study; he was at his best as a free-lancer, and the Packers would design defenses around that ability. His love of playing the game showed in his peripatetic, perpetual pursuit on each play. He might make the play behind the line of scrimmage or he might chase down the ball carrier from behind several yards downfield. One thing was certain—he was always around the ball.

He would celebrate a sack whether the Packers were winning or being blown out, and this brought him criticism for being more interested in his own statistics than the success of the team. Harris answered, "I never can hold something back on myself. I'm not that type of person. I need to play with emotions. I need to talk loud and have a good time. As long as I do that, I can be out there enjoying myself. If other people see it as hot-doggish, I just think they're seeing it from a wrong point of view." (Oates, 12)

Harris was drafted in the fourth round of the 1986 draft and made the starting lineup as an outside linebacker by mid-season.

He recorded eight sacks as a rookie and seven the next year, and he would celebrate his sacks by drawing imaginary six-shooters from his belt until the league made him stop. "When I make a sack or shoot my guns, a lot of guys on the team may get fired up. It fires me up, too." (Oates, 11)

His guns exploded in his third year, with 13.5 sacks, two safeties, and a touchdown. The 1989 season was even better, with 19.5 sacks. He was named All Pro for both those years and went to the Pro Bowl after the 1989 season. In 1989, he was named Defensive Player of the Year by the NEA. His numbers fell off to only seven sacks in 1990, as his pistols stayed in their holsters, and the following year began with a protracted, bitter contract holdout that ended with Harris being traded to the San Francisco 49ers for draft picks. In San Francisco, he found himself playing behind a resentful Charles Haley. According to some reports, Haley even urinated on Harris' car to show his contemptuous feelings for his teammate, but Tim later denied that story. Haley was traded in 1992 and went to the Super Bowl while with Dallas. Harris revived his career with 17.5 sacks in Frisco. Tim would sign with the Eagles as a free agent in 1993, but because of injuries he would play in only four games, record no sacks, and then drop out of football. Late in 1994, 49ers' defensive coach Ray Rhodes brought Harris back to San Francisco for the stretch run, and he would earn his only Super Bowl ring that year as a part-time pass-rush specialist. He finished his career the following year with the 49ers, although he would try another comeback in 1998 with Montreal in the Canadian Football League, but did not make the team.

Tim Harris' award as the 1989 Defensive Player of the Year was the first time a Packer had won that honor. Reggie White won the same title in 1998, his final year in Green Bay. Brett Favre won the Offensive Player of the Year award in both 1995 and 1996. Of course, Favre was league MVP an unprecedented three consecutive seasons, from 1995–97. He joined previous Packer league MVPs Don Hutson in 1941 and 1942, Paul Hornung in 1960 and 1961, Jim Taylor in 1962 and Bart Starr in 1966. Boyd Dowler was Rookie of the Year in 1959. John Brockington was NFC Rookie of the Year in 1971. In 1972, Chester Marcol was NFC Rookie of the Year, according to UPI and the Sporting News, while Willie Buchanon was NFC Rookie of the Year according to the NEA. Coach of the Year was won by Vince Lombardi in 1959 (AP and UPI) and again in 1961 (Sporting News); Lindy Infante won that honor in 1989. Bart Starr was Super Bowl MVP for I and II, while Desmond Howard won for XXXI. John Jefferson was Pro Bowl MVP in 1982.

The only time a Packer won the NFL rushing title was when Jim Taylor beat out Jim Brown in 1962. Oddly, only two Packer passers have led the league in average yards per carry—tailback Cecil Isbell in 1938 and quarterback Tobin Rote in 1951. Bart Starr led the league in passing three times—1962, 1964, and 1966. Among individual passing categories, we can see the traditional Packer emphasis on the air game. Passing yards leaders include Arnie Herber in 1932, 1934, and 1936, Cecil Isbell in 1941 and 1942, Irv Comp in 1944, Lynn Dickey in 1983, Don Majkowski in 1989, and Brett Favre in 1995. Leaders in average gain per attempt were Starr in 1966 through 1968, and Lynn Dickey in 1983. Starr led in completion percentage in 1962, 1968, and 1969, and in fewest interceptions in 1963, 1966, 1968, and 1969. Tobin Rote also led in fewest interceptions in 1952. Touchdown pass leaders include Arnie Herber in 1932, 1934, and 1936, Cecil Isbell in 1941 and 1942, Tobin Rote in 1955 and 1956, Lynn Dickey in 1983, and Brett Favre in 1995 through 1997.

Undeniably, Don Hutson dominated the league receiving statistics on a yearly basis. He led in receptions in 1936, 1937, 1939, and in 1941 through 1945. Sterling Sharpe led in 1989, 1992, and 1993. Hutson led in receiving yards in 1936, 1938, 1939, and in 1941 through 1944. Bill Howton led this category in 1952 and 1956, while Sharpe led in 1992. Hutson led in touchdown catches in 1936 through 1938 and in 1940 through 1944. Howton led in 1956 and Sharpe led in 1992 and 1994. James Lofton led in average gain per catch in 1983 and 1984.

Hutson also was dominant in scoring, leading the NFL in points scored in 1938 and in 1940 through 1944. Johnny Blood led in 1931, Ted Fritsch in 1946, Paul Hornung in 1959 through 1961, Jim Taylor in 1962, and Chester Marcol in 1972 and 1974. League touchdown leaders include Blood in 1931, Buckets Goldenberg in 1933, Hutson in 1935 through 1938 and in 1941 through 1944, Fritsch in 1946, Hornung in 1960, and Taylor in 1962. Marcol led in field goals in 1972 and 1974.

Green Bay NFL punt return average leaders have been Veryl Switzer in 1954, Willie Wood in 1961, Ken Ellis in 1971, and Desmond Howard in 1996. Punt return yardage leaders were Billy Grimes in 1950, Switzer in 1954, and Howard in 1996. Punt return touchdown leaders were Grimes in 1950, Wood in 1961, and Howard in 1996. League leaders in kickoff return average have been Al Carmichael in 1955, Tom Moore in 1960, Travis Williams in 1967, Steve Odom in 1978, and Robert Brooks in 1993. Dave Hampton led in total yards in 1971, and Travis Williams led in touchdowns in 1967.

Defensively, Don Hutson (1940), Willie Wood (1961), and Darren Sharper (2000) have led the NFL in interceptions. Charley Brock (1945), Herb Adderley (1965), and Bob Jeter (1966) led the league in interceptions returned for touchdowns. No Packer, even sack artist Tim Harris, has ever led the NFL in sacks, although Reggie White paced the NFC in 1993 and 1998. Ironically, while Harris was replaced by Tony Bennett and then Bryce Paup, and eventually Reggie White in Green Bay, Harris was signed by Philadelphia in 1993 to replace Reggie. Tim's star faded quickly, though, and the Packers got the better of that indirect exchange. With Harris, it was all or nothing. "Nothing's going to ever cool me out to where I'll be that wise old linebacker where I'm real quiet and just do my job and can't get back up, because that's not me." (Oates, 13)

FOR FURTHER INFORMATION

Biever, Vernon J., photography, Peter Strupp ed. *The Glory of Titletown: The Classic Green Bay Packers Photography of Vernon Biever.* Dallas, TX: Taylor Publishing, 1997. (155)

Cohn, Lowell. "The Truth Finally Trickles Out," *San Francisco Chronicle.* 9/25/92. (E5)

King, Peter. "Green Bay Sacker," *Sports Illustrated.* 10/16/89. (70-2)

Oates, Tom. "Tim Terrific: Harris Is Green Bay's Shooting Star," *Green Bay Packers 1989 Yearbook.* (11-3)

SUPER BOWL XXXII
GABE WILKINS • DEFENSIVE END 1994–97

WHO'S WORN THE NUMBER DeLuca 1984, B. Moore 1987, Auer 1987r, Tualo 1991–92, Oglesby 1992, Wilkins 1994–97, Lyon 1998–2002.

ORIGINATOR Nose tackle Tony DeLuca, 1984, was a Division 1-AA All American who had a one-game NFL career. Sadly, he died of a heart attack at the age of 38.

LONGEST TENURE Gabe Wilkins 1994–97 and backup defensive lineman Billy Lyon 1998–2001, who was a Division 1-AA All American at Marshall . He was a teammate of Randy Moss there.

NUMBER CHANGES Replacement Todd Auer also wore 72 in 1987.

OTHER NOTABLES None.

ONE TO FORGET Esera Tualo sang the national anthem before the October 17, 1991, game against the Bears. The Packers lost 10-0; Tualo was a better singer than tackle.

GABE WILKINS In his fourth season, Gabe Wilkins made one great play that would leave Packer fans wondering later just how good he could have been. But in that year's Super Bowl, Gabe sat while his teammates needed him.

Wilkins played his college ball at the obscure college of Gardner Webb, an NAIA school located in Boiling Springs, North Carolina. He was picked in the fourth round of the 1994 draft by Ron Wolf, who liked his 6'5" 300-pound size, his quickness, and his versatility. He began as a defensive end, but Green Bay moved him to tackle. In his first year, he played behind Steve McMichael at tackle and Sean Jones at end, but when McMichael was let go in 1995, Wilkins won his starting defensive tackle spot. Unfortunately, Wilkins tore the medial collateral ligament in his knee in the first half of that season. When he came back, four weeks later, Gilbert Brown was the starting tackle and the Packers began practicing Wilkins at end. In 1996, the Packers signed Santana Dotson to replace the departed John Jurkovic, and Wilkins backed up Sean Jones at end again as the team won the Super Bowl. When Jones was let go the next year, Wilkins was handed the starting defensive end job opposite Reggie White.

Wilkins had an adequate year in 1997. He was solid against the run and accumulated 5.5 sacks, which was half a sack more than the aging Jones had recorded in his final year. He also made that one truly remarkable play in a key divisional game against the Bucs in October, at Lambeau. The Pack led only 7-3 in the second quarter when Tampa recovered a Brett Favre fumble at the Green Bay 18. On the next play, quarterback Trent Dilfer tried a swing pass to Mike Alstott, but Wilkins made a strong rush, got in the path of the pass, and intercepted it. Dilfer tried to cut Wilkins low, but Gabe hurdled the grounded quarterback and rumbled 77 yards untouched for a touchdown and a 14-3 lead. It was a play that displayed the very best of Wilkins—his power, his quickness, his agility, and his speed. The Packers won the game 21-16 and got back in the race for the 1997 divisional title.

The team strove unsuccessfully all year, trying to dominate as it had in 1996. The offense was inconsistent, but the defense really struggled. Cornerback Craig Newsome went down to injury in the first game, Gilbert Brown suffered a series of nagging injuries that sapped his productivity, and Reggie White had back problems that would cause him to want to retire by the end of the year. The top-ranked defense of 1996 sank to fifth in points allowed and seventh in yards. The good news was that everything seemed to come together for the stretch run, and Green Bay won its last five games of the regular season. In the first game of the playoffs, they faced the Bucs again at Lambeau and won unimpressively, 21-7, on a dreary, muddy day. The defense played well, pressuring Dilfer and holding him to 11 completions in 36 attempts, but Favre was out of sync, throwing two interceptions and only one touchdown. Dorsey Levens was the hero of the game, gaining 112 yards on 25 carries to lead the Packers into the next round.

The 49ers had earned home field advantage, so the next week's conference championship took place in rainy, muddy San Francisco. Perhaps inspired by facing their West Coast rivals, coached by former Packer quarterbacks coach Steve Mariucci, Green Bay brought their "A" game to the coast and dominated the 49ers. Favre was sharp, the defense was unrelenting, and the Pack won 23-10 to return to the Super Bowl. Taking into account the NFC's 13-game Super Bowl win streak, and the Packers' powerful title game performance, Green Bay was a double-digit favorite over the Denver Broncos in San Diego.

But that's why they play the games. Super Bowl XXXII was marvelous to watch, as long as you weren't a Packer fan. The Packers drove right down the field on their first possession and scored quickly on a 22-yard pass to Freeman to go up 7-0. The Broncos came back to tie the score, aided by a critical third-down holding penalty against cornerback Doug Evans. Favre made a couple of mistakes in the second quarter, an interception and a fumble, that led to 10 Bronco points. Favre answered with a 90-yard drive and a touchdown pass to Mark Chmura to close the first half down 14-17. A Terrell Davis fumble in the third quarter quickly led to a tying Packer field goal. Denver took back the lead late in the third quarter, 24-17, and the Packers countered early in the fourth quarter with another touchdown pass to Freeman to tie the game at 24. With less than two minutes to play, the Broncos climaxed a 51-yard drive with a two-yard touchdown run by Davis—the last of his 157 yards rushing for the day. Coach Mike Holmgren had instructed his defense to let Davis through, so that the Packers would get the ball back with time remaining. Favre moved the team to the Denver 31. On fourth-and-six, Favre's pass to Chmura fell incomplete, and John Elway had finally won a Super Bowl.

So what happened to the new Packer dynasty? Simply put, Denver outplayed and outcoached Green Bay.

The Broncos focused on Leroy Butler in its game plan in two ways: 1) they consistently put Shannon Sharpe in the slot, expecting Butler to cover him, and then ran the other way; and 2) they made sure that he was always accounted for in their blocking scheme. Defensive coach Fritz Shurmur never adjusted.

The Bronco defense blitzed Brett Favre from every angle at all times. Mike Holmgren never adjusted.

Favre was good that day, but not great. His last pass to Brooks around the 10-yard line in the final drive just missed. Maybe a younger Brooks could have reached it.

The defensive line of the Packers collapsed. Gabe Wilkins went out with knee problems in the first quarter, to be replaced by the ineffectual Darius Holland. Both Holmgren and Butler exhorted Wilkins to get back into the game because it was the Super Bowl, but Wilkins sat the game out. Meanwhile, Gilbert Brown got winded and Reggie White's sore back flared up. The Pack could not stop Davis. The interesting question was, if Green Bay had scored on that last drive, would they have kicked the extra point to go to overtime, or tried to win the game with a two-point conversion in regulation? The Packers defense was exhausted.

Ron Wolf thought that the team came in overconfident and not hungry enough.

One other little-reported story was the Broncos' intelligence-gathering. The Packers had carried a very bright linebacker named Jon Hesse on their practice squad all year, until he was signed by the Broncos to their active roster one week before the playoffs. Hesse fed the Broncos details about the Packers formations, plays, and tendencies. He also told them about Gilbert Brown's unreported sore knee that would wear down quickly if the Broncos went right at him. So many factors go into any big game. The ultimate point is that Green Bay lost because it was outplayed and out-coached, and no second guessing can change that.

Wilkins would sign a five-year, $20 million dollar deal with the rival 49ers a couple of weeks after the Super Bowl loss, despite his knee problems. San Francisco felt the signing would improve their line and weaken Green Bay's in one smooth, smart move. The Packers believed Wilkins suffered from patellar tendonitis, but Gabe underwent arthroscopic surgery and the 49ers' surgeons determined that he actually was missing cartilage in his knee. Wilkins would not get back on the field until mid-season 1998, though, and would not start until the last four games of the season, when he moved in at defensive tackle to replace the injured Bryant Young. He did play in the 1998 49er/Packer playoff game won by San Francisco. The following season, he started 15 games at defensive end, but rang up only one sack—in the next-to-last game of the season.

In January 1999, the 49ers waived him and his football career was over, leaving a wake of questions. Was it injuries that kept him from fully developing his potential? Could he have played in Super Bowl XXXII? Should he have? Would it have made a difference in the outcome of the game? Would it have made a difference in his earning capacity? These questions have no definitive answers, but they reflect the common reaction to a disappointing player and a frustrating game.

FOR FURTHER INFORMATION

Anderson, Lars. *The Proving Ground: A Season on the Fringe in NFL Europe.* New York: St. Martin's Press, 2001. (218-20)

Murphy, Brian. "Neutralizing a Nemesis," *The Sporting News.* 3/2/98. (51)

PACKERS BY THE NUMBERS

Silver, Michael. "Power Pack," *Sports Illustrated*. 10/13/97. (62-7)

————. "Seven Up," *Sports Illustrated*. 2/2/98. (50-63)

Wilde, Jason. "Wilkins Offers His Side," *Wisconsin State Journal*. 10/29/98. (3B)

Wolf, Ron, and Paul Attner. *The Packer Way: Nine Stepping Stones to Building a Winning Organization*. New York: St. Martin's Press, 1998. (235-9)

Zimmerman, Paul. "Marked Man," *Sports Illustrated*. 2/2/98. (62)

1997 SUPER BOWL XXXII DATA
Green Bay Packers 24
Denver Broncos 31

January 25, 1998 • Qualcomm Stadium, San Diego
Attendance: 68,912
Winner's Share: $48,000 (+ $55,000 from previous playoff games)
Loser's Share: $30,000 (+ $60,000 from previous playoff games)
Weather: 73 degrees.

KEY STATS	PACKERS	BRONCOS
First Downs	21	21
Rush Yards	95	179
Pass Yards	255	123
Total Yards	350	302
Interceptions	1	1
Fumbles Lost	2	1
Penalties	9-59	7-66
Third down conversions	5/14	5/10
Time of Possession	27:35	32:25

Halftime Score: Packers 14 Broncos 17

LEADERS
Rushing: Dorsey Levens 19-90.   Terrell Davis 30-157
Passing: Brett Favre 25-42-1 256 yds.   John Elway 12-22-1 123 yds.
Receiving: Antonio Freeman 9-126.   Shannon Sharpe 5-38

ADDITIONAL FACTS
•The three Packer coaches who have won titles, Curly Lambeau, Vince Lombardi and Mike Holmgren, each lost one title game as well. In all of the three losses, the Packers were the favored team, but lost in a close, exciting games. The Packers always trailed at the half, always outgained their opponent, and always were moving the ball in the opponent's territory in the last minute with a chance to pull the game out.

•Denver was the first AFC team to win a Super Bowl in thirteen years.

•Like Reggie White the year before, John Elway was the sentimental favorite of many, because he was a solid pro who had never won a title in his long career.

•This was the first Super Bowl to pit two Bill Walsh offense devotees from San Francisco against one another, in Mike Holmgren and Mike Shanahan.

•In the playoffs against the Buccaneers, 49ers, and Broncos, the Packers outgained their opponents on the ground 319 to 302 and through the air 645 to 520. Unfortunately, they were penalized more frequently as well, 25-211 yards against 16-167 yards.

WISCONSIN BOYS
DON DAVEY • DEFENSIVE END 1991–94

WHO'S WORN THE NUMBER C. Johnson 1979–80, 1983, J. Dorsey 1984–88, Davey 1991–94, J. Smith 1997, 1999, A. Robbins 2000, J. Reynolds 2001–02.

ORIGINATOR Nose tackle Charles Johnson 1979–80, 1982 (see Forget below).

LONGEST TENURE Linebacker John Dorsey 1984–88, a Division 1-AA All American who became director of college scouting with the Packers.

NUMBER CHANGES None.

OTHER NOTABLES None.

ONE TO FORGET Charles Johnson was drafted instead of Joe Montana in the third round of the 1979 draft. He was an undersized nose-tackle who lasted until the end of Bart Starr's coaching career as a constant reminder of the consequences of making bad decisions.

DON DAVEY The first four-time Academic All American at the University of Wisconsin was Don Davey who majored in mechanical engineering while starring at defensive end for the Badgers. The Manitowoc, Wisconsin, native grew up as a Packer fan and was chosen in the third round of the 1991 draft. He was a popular, high-energy, high-effort, local favorite who lasted four years as a sometime-starter in Green Bay.

Football in Green Bay dates to the town teams that formed annually almost every year from 1895 through 1918 to battle other local town teams on the gridiron. The Packers emerged from that environment in 1919 with local stud back, Earl "Curly" Lambeau, as the team leader and procurer of talent. As the town team evolved into the professional one, it retained a college-like parochial flavor. Most of the players in the early years were local boys from Wisconsin or its neighboring states. Lambeau's first big signing was Cub Buck, a University of Wisconsin alumnus who had previously blocked for Jim Thorpe on the Canton Bulldogs. Many players also came from Notre Dame, where Curly had a connection, having played briefly under Rockne for the Fighting Irish. As both professional football and the Packers grew in importance and ability, Lambeau began casting a wider net in finding players for the team. Soon enough, Curly was taking annual postseason scouting trips to the West Coast and signing players from every region of the country. However, a large proportion of the team remained Midwestern into the late 1940s.

The state whose colleges have sent the most players to Green Bay is Texas, with 121, followed closely by California with 118. Since those states have climates conducive to outdoor winter sports, it is not surprising that they became football hotbeds. It is a little surprising that Florida, whose schools have recently become so dominant in football, has only sent 25 players to the Packers.

The Midwestern basis of the Packers is shown by the next states on the list. Wisconsin is third, having sent 87 of its collegians to Green Bay, followed by Indiana with 84, Michigan with 62, and Minnesota with 51. The University of Minnesota, incidentally, is the school with the most Packer number-one draft choices, with seven: Larry Buhler (1939), Hal Van Every (1940), Urban Odson (1942), Dick Wildung (1943), Clayton Tonnemaker (1950), Gale Gillingham (1966), and Darrell Thompson (1990). Considering that the Golden Gophers were a national powerhouse in the 1940s, that preponderance of high picks is not surprising. Rounding out the top ten of states, Alabama and Pennsylvania are tied for seventh with 46 players, Oklahoma is ninth with 37, and Louisiana is tenth with 34.

As for specific colleges, Notre Dame alumni are more populous than any others. Forty-eight former Fighting Irish have played for Green Bay. Right behind Notre Dame is the University of Wisconsin system, which has sent 45 players on to the Packers. Third is the University of Minnesota with 44 alumni. Other colleges prominent on the alumni list are the University of Southern California with 32, Nebraska with 28, the University of Michigan with 25, Alabama with 24, and both Oklahoma and Michigan State with 20.

Of course, the major universities don't tell the whole story. Many important Packer contributors through the years have come from small local colleges. Eddie Kotal came from Lawrence, Tiny Croft from Ripon, Boob Darling from Beloit. Ted Fritsch came from Stevens Point Teachers' College. All those were Wisconsin schools. Irv Comp came from Benedictine in Kansas, Jug Earp from Monmouth in Illinois, Chester Marcol from Hillsdale in Michigan. Green Bay native Arnie Herber went to Regis in Colorado. Moreover, 18 Packers in the 1920s never attended college at all; they were just local talent.

While the professional game quickly outgrew local town footballers with no college experience, Green Bay maintained a special affection for players with a local connection. Even today, Packer fans keep an eye on talented Badgers. Fans were rightfully disappointed when Ron Wolf took Terrell Buckley rather than Badger cornerback Troy Vincent with his first Packer draft pick. Fans also hoped that he would consider Badger receiver Chris Chambers in his last Packer draft, to no avail.

Don Davey was drafted the year before Ron Wolf arrived. He got into every game as a rookie, and then was cut from the team by Mike Holmgren in 1992. For six weeks, Davey was out of football until the Packers brought him back in mid-season. He played occasionally that year and the next, and made a couple of big plays that helped set up game-winning field goals against Philadelphia and New Orleans in 1992. When Fritz Shurmur took over the defense in 1994, Davey began to see more playing time because Shurmur liked Davey's versatility. Fritz used him that year at defensive end and both defensive tackle spots, especially after Gilbert Brown went down to a knee injury in December. Don started two games and even fulfilled a childhood dream by recording a sack in a 40-3 thrashing of the Bears at Lambeau.

As a free agent in 1995, Davey signed with the expansion Jacksonville Jaguars, whose defensive coordinator was former Packer assistant coach Dick Jauron. With the Jags, Davey at last became a starter at defensive tackle for three years, until he tore his ACL in the 10th game of the 1997 season. In 1998, he spent the entire year on the injured reserve list and was released after the season. In Jacksonville, he started 38 games and had 6.5 sacks. While he was at the University of Wisconsin, Davey wasn't even sure if he would be drafted by the pros, but he played professionally for seven years. Although the Badger scholar had originally planned on going into biomedical engineering to design artificial limbs and heart and lung machines, his football career took him far beyond that, and he started his own investment company in retirement.

FOR FURTHER INFORMATION

Looney, Douglas S. "Gee, It's Great to Be a Badger," *Sports Illustrated.* 9/5/88. (70-81)

Thomas, Howard. "A Survivor," *Capital Times.* 9/1/94. (1F)

BIBLIOGRAPHY

Allen, George, with Ben Olan. *Pro Football's 100 Greatest Players: Rating the Stars of Past and Present.* Indianapolis: Bobbs-Merrill, 1982.

Anderson, Lars. *The Proving Ground: A Season on the Fringe in NFL Europe.* New York: St. Martin's Press, 2001.

Ashe, Arthur. *A Hard Road to Glory: A History of the African-American Athlete.* New York: Warner Books, 1988. 3v.

Barber, Phil. *Football America: Celebrating America's National Passion.* Atlanta, GA: Turner Publishing, 1996.

Barra, Alan. *That's Not the Way It Was: (Almost) Everything They Told You About Sports Is Wrong.* New York: Hyperion, 1995.

Becker, Carl M. *Home and Away: The Rise and Fall of Professional Football on the Banks of the Ohio, 1919–1934.* Athens, OH: Ohio University Press, 1998.

Beebe, Don, with Bob Schaller. *More than a Ring.* Neshkoro, WI: Angel Press of Wisconsin, 1998.

Benedict, Jeff, and Don Yeager. *Pros and Cons: The Criminals Who Play in the NFL.* New York: Warner Books, 1998.

Bengtson, Phil, with Todd Hunt. *Packer Dynasty.* Garden City, NY: Doubleday, 1969.

Biever, John, with George Vecsey. *Young Sports Photographer with the Green Bay Packers.* New York: Norton, 1969.

Biever, Vernon J., photography, Peter Strupp ed. *The Glory of Titletown: The Classic Green Bay Packers Photography of Vernon Biever.* Dallas, TX: Taylor Publishing, 1997.

Blount, Jr., Roy. *About Three Bricks Shy of a Load: A Highly Irregular Lowdown of the Year the Pittsburgh Steelers Were Super but Missed the Bowl.* Boston: Little, Brown and Company, 1974.

Bradshaw, Terry, with David Fisher. *It's Only a Game.* New York: Pocket Books, 2001.

Briggs, Jennifer, comp. *Strive to Excel: The Wit and Wisdom of Vince Lombardi.* Nashville, TN: Rutledge Hill Press, 1997.

Bynum, Mike, ed. *Vince Lombardi: Memories of a Special Time.* [United States]: October Football Corp., 1988.

Cameron, Steve. *The Packers! Seventy Five Seasons of Memories and Mystique in Green Bay.* Dallas, TX: Taylor Publishing, 1996.

Campbell, Jim. *Golden Years of Pro Football.* Avenel, NJ: Crescent Books, 1993.

Carlson, Chuck. *Green Bay Packers Pocket Primer.* Lenexa, KS: Addax Publishing Group, 1997.

————. *Titletown Again: the Super Bowl Season of the 1996 Green Bay Packers.* Lenexa, KS: Addax Publishing Group, 1997.

Carpentier, John. *Price Guide to Packers Memorabilia.* Iola, WI: Krause Publications, 1998.

Carroll, Bob. *When the Grass Was Real: Unitas, Brown, Lombardi, Sayers, Butkus, Namath and All the Rest: The Ten Best Years of Pro Football.* New York: Simon and Schuster, 1993.

Carroll, Bob, Michael Gershman, David Neft, and John Thorn. *Total Football: The Official Encyclopedia of the National Football League.* New York: Harper Collins, 1999.

————. *Total Packers: The Official Encyclopedia of the Green Bay Packers.* New York: Harper Perennial, 1998.

Carroll, Bob, Pete Palmer, and John Thorn. *The Hidden Game of Football: The Next Edition.* New York: Total Sports, 1998.

Chalk, Ocania. *Pioneers of Black Sport: The Early Days of the Black Professional Athlete in Baseball, Basketball, Boxing, and Football.* New York: Dodd Mead, 1975.

Clary, Jack. *Pro Football's Great Moments.* New York: Bonanza Books, 1983.

Cohen, Richard M., Jordan A. Deutsch, Roland T. Johnson, and David S. Neft. *The Scrapbook History of Pro Football.* Indianapolis, IN: Bobbs-Merrill, 1976.

Cope, Myron. *The Game That Was: An Illustrated Account of the Tumultuous Early Days of Pro Football.* New York: Crowell, 1974.

Crothers, Tim. *The Greatest Teams: The Most Dominant Powerhouses in Sports.* New York: Sports Illustrated [Time-Life], 1998.

Curran, Bob. *Pro Football's Rag Days.* Englewood Cliffs, NJ: Prentice-Hall, 1969.

Daley, Art, and Jack Yuenger. *The Lombardi Era of the Green Bay Packers.* Green Bay, WI: The Jaycees, 1968.

Daley, Arthur. *Pro Football's Hall of Fame.* New York: Grosset and Dunlap, 1968, c1963.

Daly, Dan, and Bob O'Donnell. *The Pro Football Chronicle: The Complete (Well Almost) Record of the Best Players, the Greatest Photos, the Hardest Hits, the Biggest Scandals, and the Funniest Stories in Pro Football.* New York: Collier Books, 1990.

D'Amato, Gary, and Cliff Christl. *Mudbaths and Bloodbaths: The Inside Story of the Bears-Packers Rivalry.* Madison, WI: Prairie Oak Press, 1997.

Dowling, Tom. *Coach: A Season with Lombardi.* NY: Norton, 1970.

Eckstein, Dan. *The 41st Packer: A Rookie's Diary.* Clinton, SC: Jacobs Press, 1970.

Eisenberg, John. *Cotton Bowl Days: Growing Up with Dallas and the Cowboys in the 1960s.* New York: Simon and Schuster, 1997.

Eskenazi, Gerald. *There Were Giants in Those Days.* New York: Grosset and Dunlap, 1976.

Everson, Jeff. *This Day in Green Bay Packers History.* Wautoma, WI: Angel Press of WI, 1997.

The Fabulous Green Bay Packers. Milwaukee, WI: Milwaukee Journal, 1968.

Favre, Brett, with Chris Havel. *Favre: For the Record.* Garden City, NY: Doubleday, 1997.

50 Years of Professional Football 1919–68: A Complete Picture History of the Green Bay Packers. Green Bay, WI: Green Bay Packers Alumni Association, 1968.

Flynn, George, ed. *Vince Lombardi on Football.* New York: New York Graphic Society Ltd and Wallyn Inc., 1973.

———. *The Vince Lombardi Scrapbook.* New York: Grossett and Dunlap, 1976.

Fowler, Scott, and Charles Chandler. *Year of the Cat: How the Carolina Panthers Clawed Their Way to the Brink of the Super Bowl.* New York: Simon and Schuster, 1997.

Freund, Carl, Louis Hulme, D. Kent Pingel, and Kitty Evans Loveless eds. *The Purple Lawman: From Horned Frog to High Sheriff: The Story of Lon Evans.* Fort Worth, TX: the Summit Group, 1990.

Garraty, John A., and Mark C. Carnes, general editors. *American National Biography.* New York: Oxford University Press, 1999.

Gentile, Domenic, with Gary D'Amato. *The Packer Tapes: My 32 Years with the Green Bay Packers.* Madison, WI: Prairie Oak Press, 1995.

George, Gary R. *Winning Is a Habit: Lombardi on Winning, Success, and the Pursuit of Excellence.* New York: HarperCollins, 1997.

Golenbock, Peter. *Cowboys Have Always Been My Heroes: The Definitive Oral History of America's Team.* New York: Warner Books, 1997.

Goodman, Murray, and Leonard Lewin. *My Greatest Day in Football.* New York: Barnes, 1948.

Goska, Eric. *Packer Legends in Facts: Your Most Accurate Source of Stats, Rosters, Team History and All Team Photos of the Green Bay Packers 1919–1995.* Germantown, WI: Tech/Data Publications, 1995.

Green, Jerry. *Super Bowl Chronicles: A Sportswriter Reflects on the First 25 Years of America's Game.* Grand Rapids, MI: Masters Press, 1991.

Gruver, Ed. *The Ice Bowl: The Cold Truth About Football's Most Unforgettable Game.* Ithaca, NY: McBooks Press, 1998.

———. *Nitschke: The Ray Nitschke Story.* Lanham, MD: Taylor Trade, 2002.

Harrington, Denis. *The Pro Football Hall of Fame: Players, Coaches, Team Owners and League Officials, 1963–1991.* Jefferson, NC: McFarland, 1991.

Harris, David. *The League: The Rise and Decline of the NFL.* New York: Bantam Books, 1986.

Heir to the Legacy: The Memorable Story of Mike Holmgren's Green Bay Packers. Louisville, KY: AdCraft, 1996.

Hersch, Hank. *The Greatest Football Games of All Time.* New York: Sports Illustrated [Time-Life], 1998.

Herskowitz, Mickey. *The Golden Age of Pro Football: NFL Football in the 1950s.* Dallas, TX: Taylor Publishing, 1990.

————. *The Quarterbacks: The Uncensored Truth About the Men in the Pocket.* New York: Morrow, 1990.

Hollander, Zander. *More Strange but True Football Stories.* New York: Random House, 1973.

Hornung, Paul, as told to Al Silverman. *Football and the Single Man.* Garden City, NY: Doubleday, 1965.

Hubbard, Mary Bell. *Strike Three! And You're Out: The Cal Hubbard Story.* MO: Walsworth, 1986.

Isaacson, Kevin, with Tom Kessenich. *Return to Glory: The Inside Story of the Green Bay Packers Return to Prominence.* Iola, WI: Krause Publications, 1996.

Izenberg, Jerry. *Championship: The Complete NFL Title Story.* New York: Four Winds Press, 1966.

Johnson, Chuck. *The Green Bay Packers: Pro Football's Pioneer Team.* New York: Thomas Nelson and Sons, 1963.

————. *The Greatest Packers of Them All.* New York: Putnam, 1968.

King, Peter. *Football: A History of the Professional Game.* New York: Bishop Books [Time. Inc. Home Entertainment], 1997.

————. *Greatest Quarterbacks.* New York: Bishop Books [Time. Inc. Home Entertainment], 1999.

Korth, Todd. *Greatest Moments in Green Bay Packers Football History.* Lenexa, KS: Addax Publishing Group, 1998.

Kramer, Jerry, ed. *Lombardi: Winning Is the Only Thing.* New York: World Publishing, 1970.

Kramer, Jerry, with Dick Schaap. *Distant Replay.* New York: G.P. Putnam, 1985.

Lahey, Lyle. *Packer Chronicles: Waiting for the Pack to Come Back.* Green Bay, WI: Green Bay News Chronicle, 1997.

Landry, Tom, with Gregg Lewis. *Tom Landry: An Autobiography.* Grand Rapids, MI: Zondervan Publishing, and New York: Harper Collins, 1990.

Lea, Bud. *The Magnificent Seven: The Championship Games That Built the Lombardi Dynasty.* Chicago: Triumph Books, 2002.

Leuthner, Stuart. *Iron Men: Bucko, Crazy Legs, and the Boys Recall the Golden Days of Professional Football.* New York: Doubleday, 1988.

Lombardi, Jr.,Vince. *What It Takes to Be Number One: Vince Lombardi on Leadership.* New York: McGraw-Hill, 2001.

Lombardi, Vince, with W.C. Heinz. *Run to Daylight.* Englewood Cliffs, NJ: Prentice-Hall, 1963.

Maraniss, David. *When Pride Still Mattered: A Life of Vince Lombardi.* New York: Simon and Schuster, 1999.

March, Harry. *Pro Football, Its "Ups" and "Downs:" A Lighthearted History of the Post Graduate Game.* Albany, NY: J.B. Lyon, 1934.

BIBLIOGRAPHY

Maule, Tex. *The Game: The Official Picture History of the NFL and AFL*. New York: Random House, 1967.

———. *The Players*. New York: New American Library, 1967.

McCallum, Jack, with Chuck Bednarik. *Bednarik: Last of the Sixty Minute Men*. Englewood Cliffs, NJ: Prentice-Hall, 1977.

McClellan, Keith. *The Sunday Game: At the Dawn of Professional Football*. Akron, OH: University of Akron Press, 1998.

McCullough, Bob. *My Greatest Day in Football: The Legends of Football Recount Their Greatest Moments*. New York: Thomas Dunne Books, 2001.

McGinn, Bob. *The Road to Glory: The Inside Story of the Packers Super Bowl XXXI Championship Season*. Louisville, KY: AdCraft Sports Marketing, 1997.

Merchant, Larry. *...And Every Day You Take Another Bite*. Garden City, New York: Doubleday, 1971.

Michael, Paul. *Professional Football's Greatest Games*. Englewood Cliffs, NJ: Prentice-Hall,1972.

Murphy, Austin. *The Super Bowl: Sport's Greatest Championship*. New York: Sports Illustrated [Time-Life], 1998

Names, Larry. *The History of the Green Bay Packers: Book I: The Lambeau Years Part One*. Wautoma, WI: Angel Press of WI, 1987.

———. *The History of the Green Bay Packers: Book II: The Lambeau Years Part Two*. Wautoma, WI: Angel Press of WI, 1989.

———. *The History of the Green Bay Packers: Book III: The Lambeau Years Part Three*. Wautoma, WI: Angel Press of WI, 1990.

———. *The History of the Green Bay Packers: Book IV: The Shameful Years*. Wautoma, WI: Angel Press of WI, 1995.

———. *The World Champion Green Bay Packers Facts and Trivia*. 5th ed. South Bend, IN: E.B. Houchin Company, 1997.

Neft, David S. Richard M. Cohen, and Richard Korch. *The Football Encyclopedia: The Complete History of Professional Football from 1892 to the Present*. New York: St. Martin's, 1994.

Nitschke, Ray, as told to Robert W. Wells. *Mean on Sunday: The Autobiography of Ray Nitschke*. 2nd ed. Madison, WI: Prairie Oak Press, 1999.

O'Brien, Michael. *Vince: A Personal Biography*. New York: William Morrow, 1987.

Olderman, Murray. *The Pro Quarterback*. Englewood Cliffs, NJ: Prentice-Hall, 1966.

———. *The Running Backs*. Englewood Cliffs, NJ: Prentice-Hall, 1969.

Packers of the Past: A Series of Articles Reprinted from the Milwaukee Journal Sept. 28–Dec. 9, 1965. Milwaukee, WI: Milwaukee Journal, 1965.

Peary, Danny. *Super Bowl: The Game of Their Lives*. New York: Macmillan, 1997.

Peterson, Robert. *Pigskin: The Early Years of Pro Football*. New York: Oxford University Press, 1997.

Phillips, Donald T. *Run to Win: Vince Lombardi on Coaching and Leadership.* New York: St. Martin's Press, 2001.

Plimpton, George. *One More July: A Football Dialogue with Bill Curry.* New York: Harper and Row, 1977.

————. *Paper Lion.* New York: Harper and Row, 1966.

Poling, Jerry. *Downfield! Untold Stories of the Green Bay Packers.* Madison, WI: Prairie Oak Press, 1996.

Porter, David L., ed. *Biographical Dictionary of American Sports: Football.* New York: Greenwood Press, 1987.

————. *Biographical Dictionary of American Sports: 1989–1992 Supplement for Baseball, Football, Basketball, and Other Sports.* New York: Greenwood Press, 1992.

————. *Biographical Dictionary of American Sports: 1992–1995 Supplement for Baseball, Football, Basketball, and Other Sports.* New York: Greenwood Press, 1995.

Pruyne, Terry W. *Sports Nicknames: 20,000 Professionals Worldwide.* Jefferson, NC: McFarland, 2002.

Rathet, Mike, and Don R. Smith. *Their Deeds and Dogged Faith.* New York: Rutledge Books, 1984.

Riffenburgh, Beau. *Great Ones: NFL Quarterbacks from Baugh to Montana.* New York: Viking, 1989.

Riger, Robert. *Best Plays of the Year 1962: A Documentary of Pro Football in the National Football League.* Englewood Cliffs, NJ: Prentice-Hall, 1963.

————. *Best Plays of the Year 1963: A Documentary of Pro Football in the National Football League.* Englewood Cliffs, NJ: Prentice-Hall, 1964.

Robinson, Eugene, with Kevin Isaacson and Rocky Landsverk. *Diary of a Super Bowl Season.* Iola, WI: Krause Publications, 1998.

Ross, Charles K. *Outside the Lines: African Americans and the Integration of the National Football League.* New York: New York University Press, 1999.

Rubin, Bob. *Green Bay's Packers: Return to Glory.* Englewood Cliffs, NJ: Prentice-Hall, 1974.

Sahadi, Lou. *Super Sundays I–XVI.* Chicago: Contemporary Books, 1982.

Schaap, Dick. *Paul Hornung: Pro Football Golden Boy.* New York: Macfadden-Bartell, 1962 (No. 13 in the Sport Magazine Library).

————. *Green Bay Replay: The Packers Return to Glory.* New York: Avon Books, 1997.

Schaap, Dick, ed. *Instant Replay: The Green Bay Diary of Jerry Kramer.* New York: World Publishing, 1968.

————. *Jerry Kramer's Farewell to Football.* New York: World Publishing, 1969.

————. *Quarterbacks Have All the Fun: The Good Life and Hard Times of Bart, Johnny, Joe, Francis, and Other Great Quarterbacks.* Chicago: Playboy Press, 1974.

Schachter, Norm. *Close Calls: The Confessions of a NFL Referee.* New York: Morrow, 1981.

Schoor, Gene. *Football's Greatest Coach: Vince Lombardi.* Garden City, NY: Doubleday, 1974.

———. *Bart Starr: A Biography.* Garden City, NY: Doubleday, 1977.

75 Seasons: The Complete Story of the National Football League 1920–1995. Atlanta, GA: Turner Publishing Inc., 1994.

Shropshire, Mike. *The Ice Bowl: The Green Bay Packers and Dallas Cowboys Season of 1967.* New York: Donald I. Fine Books, 1997.

Smith, Myron J. *Pro Football: The Official Pro Football Hall of Fame Bibliography.* Westport, CT: Greenwood Press, 1993.

———. *The Pro Football Bio-Bibliography.* West Cornwall, CT: Locust Hill Press, 1989.

Smith, Robert. *Illustrated History of Pro Football.* New York: Grossett and Dunlap, 1977.

Smith, Ron. *The Sporting News Selects Football's 100 Greatest Players: A Celebration of the 20th Century's Best.* St. Louis, MO: Sporting News, 1999.

Sports Illustrated Presents The Champions: 1996 Green Bay Packers. [United States]: Time Inc., 1997.

Starr, Bart, and John Wiebusch. *A Perspective on Victory.* Chicago: Follett Publishing, 1972.

Starr, Bart, with Murray Olderman. *Starr: My Life in Football.* New York: William Morrow, 1987.

Strother, Shelby. *NFL Top 40: The Greatest Football Games of All Time.* New York: Viking, 1988.

Sugar, Bert Randolph. *I Hate the Dallas Cowboys: And Who Elected Them America's Team Anyway.* New York: St. Martin's Griffin, 1997.

The Super Bowl: Celebrating a Quarter Century of America's Greatest Game. New York: Simon and Schuster, 1990.

Swain, Glenn. *Packers vs. Bears.* Los Angeles: Charles Publishing, 1996.

Thorn, John. *Pro Football's Ten Greatest Games.* New York: Four Winds Press, 1981.

———. *The Armchair Quarterback.* New York: Scribners, 1982.

Titletown: The Green Bay Packers Improbable Journey to Super Bowl XXXI. [Green Bay Press-Gazette] Louisville, KY: AdCraft Sports Marketing, 1997.

Torinus, John. *The Packer Legend: An Inside Look.* Revised ed. Neshkoro, WI: Laranmark Press, 1982.

Towle, Mike. *I Remember Vince Lombardi.* Nashville, TN: Cumberland House, 2001.

Wagner, Len. *Launching the Glory Years: The 1959 Packers—What They Didn't Tell Us.* Green Bay, WI: Coach's Books LLC [Jay Bengtson], 2001.

Ward, Arch. *The Green Bay Packers.* New York: Putnam, 1946.

Wells, Robert W. *Vince Lombardi: His Life and Times.* 2nd ed. Madison, WI: Prairie Oak Press, 1997.

White, Reggie, with Jim Denney. *In the Trenches: The Autobiography.* Nashville, TN: T. Nelson, 1996.

White, Reggie, with Steve Hubbard. *God's Playbook: The Bible's Game Plan for Life.* Nashville, TN: T. Nelson, 1998.

White, Reggie, with Terry Hill. *Reggie White: Minister of Defense.* Brentwood, TN: Wolgemuth and Hyatt, 1991

Whittingham, Richard. *What a Game They Played.* New York: Harper and Row, 1974.

Wiebusch, John, ed. *Lombardi.* Chicago: Follett Publishing, 1971.

———. *More than a Game.* Englewood Cliffs, NJ: Prentice-Hall, 1974.

Wolf, Ron, and Paul Attner. *The Packer Way: Nine Stepping Stones to Building a Winning Organization.* New York: St. Martin's Press, 1998.

Wright, Steve, with William Gildeau and Kenneth Turin. *I'd Rather Be Wright.* Englewood Cliffs, NJ: Prentice-Hall, 1974.

Zimmerman, David. *In Search of a Hero: Life and Times of Tony Canadeo Packers' Grey Ghost.* Hales Corner, WI: Eagle Books, 2001.

Zimmerman, Paul. *The New Thinking Man's Guide to Pro Football.* New York: Simon and Schuster, 1984.

———. *The Linebackers: The Tough Ones of Pro Football.* New York: Scholastic Books, 1973.

AUTHOR AWARDS

IF I WERE GIVING OUT AWARDS, THESE ARE THE BLUE RIBBON WINNERS BY CATEGORY IN MY OPINION:

REFERENCE—Eric Goska's *Packer Legends in Facts: Your Most Accurate Source of Stats, Rosters, Team History and All Team Photos of the Green Bay Packers 1919–1995* provides exactly what the subtitle says. For a self-published work of this sort, the amount of errors and typos is amazingly small. Honorable mention to *Total Packers: The Official Encyclopedia of the Green Bay Packers* edited by Bob Carroll, Michael Gershman, David Neft, and John Thorn. It contains just the Packer material derived from the authoritative football encyclopedia, *Total Football.* Both volumes are out of date.

PHOTOGRAPHIC WORKS—Almost 50 years worth of Vernon J. Biever's glorious photos are displayed in *The Glory of Titletown: The Classic Green Bay Packers Photography of Vernon Biever.*

TEAM HISTORY WORKS—Larry Names' four volume set *The History of the Green Bay Packers* covers the team from its founding till the coming of Lombardi. Names went back to the original source material of contemporary newspaper accounts and fashioned a familiar story retold with surprising new developments.

BIOGRAPHICAL WORKS—Brett Favre's autobiography *Favre: For the Record* is as entertaining as the quarterback himself. The old Ray Nitschke autobiography *Mean on Sunday* is also especially good reading.

SEASONAL DIARY—Jerry Kramer's diary edited by Dick Schaap, *Instant Replay: The Green Bay Diary of Jerry Kramer,* is still the best of its genre for football. Entertaining and insightful, it's still fun to read even if Kramer left out the juiciest stuff—women, drugs and so on. Honorable mention goes to Steve Wright's *I'd Rather Be Wright,* a memoir of his ordinary career. Wright was observant and perceptive and displayed these qualities in one of the funnier books about NFL football.

THE ICE BOWL—Two books were written just on this pivotal game. Both bore the same simple title and were published in the same year, but Ed Gruver's version, *The Ice Bowl: The Cold Truth About Football's Most Unforgettable Game,* is better researched and a more thoughtful book than Mike Shropshire's.

CATCHING UP ON THE PAST —Jerry Kramer and Dick Schaap returned to a familiar subject in *Distant Replay, Lombardi's Packers.* The appeal is similar to another book from the same era, *What Really Happened to the Class of 1965?* by Michael Medved and David Wallechinsky. These books show how different people answered the question that we all face upon completion of a major goal—What's Next? Honorable mention goes to Jerry Poling's *Downfield* and the obscure compilation of newspaper articles *Packers of the Past: A Series of Articles Reprinted from the Milwaukee Journal Sept. 28–Dec. 9, 1965.*

RIVALRIES —Gary D'Amato and Cliff Christl told the story of Bears and Packers rivalry with great wit and style in *Mudbaths and Bloodbaths: The Inside Story of the Bears-Packers Rivalry.* There is another book on the same subject, *Packers vs Bears* by Glenn Swain; it is more comprehensive but much drier reading.

SUPER BOWL XXXI—Dick Schaap melded the stories of the 1967 and 1996 Packers to create *Green Bay Replay: The Packers Return to Glory* in 1997. He made many fresh connections and wrote with great verve.

LOMBARDI—Wisconsin-native and Bill Clinton biographer David Maraniss wrote the definitive biography of Lombardi 29 years after the coach's death. *When Pride Still Mattered: A Life of Vince Lombardi* is a wonderful and weighty tome. Honorable mention goes to John Weibusch's compilation of quotes and photographs called simply *Lombardi* and the coach's own book *Run to Daylight,* which sounds a little stilted but is still worth reading.

ALL TIME ROSTER
WITH UNIFORM NUMBERS

Numbers within angle brackets <> are numbers assigned to players in game programs but not worn on the uniform. Players and numbers within parentheses refer to players who never actually played in a game although they were listed in a game program. NA is used for players who played before game programs and uniform numbers were instituted (1921–24). Numbers accompanied by an R were worn by 1987 strike replacement players.

Aberson, Cliff	B	1946	78
Abrams, Nate	E	1921	NA
Abramson, George	G/T	<1925>	<12>
Acks, Ron	LB	1974–76	57
Adams, Chet	T	1943	27
Adderley, Herb	DB	1961–69	26
Adkins, Bob	B	1940–41, 45	55, 79
Affholter, Erik	WR	1991	82
Afflis, Dick	G	1951–54	15, 62, 72, 75
Agajanian, Ben	K	1961	3
Aguiar, Louie	P	1999	10
Akins, Chris	S	2000–01	31
Albrecht, Art	T	1942	19
Aldridge, Ben	B	1953	40
Aldridge, Lionel	DE	1963–71	62, 82
Allerman, Kurt	LB	1980–81	60
Amsler, Marty	DE	1970	87
Amundsen, Norm	G	1957	62
Anderson, Aric	LB	1987	53
Anderson, Bill	TE	1965–66	88
(Anderson, Curtis)	DE	(1987)	(63 R)
Anderson, Donny	RB	1966–71	44
Anderson, John	LB	1978–89	59, 60
Anderson, Marques	DB	2002	20
Anderson, Vickey Ray	FB	1980	44
Andruzzi, Joe	G	1998–99	70
Ane, Charlie	C	1981	61
Apsit, Marger	B	1932	44
Archambeau, Lester	DE	1990–92	74
Ard, Billy	G/T	1989–91	67
Ariey, Mike	T	1989	76
Arnold, Jahine	WR	1999	88
Arthur, Mike	C	1995–96	50
Artmore, Rodney	S	1999	46
Ashmore, Roger	T	1928–29	35, 46
Askson, Bert	TE	1975–77	88
Atkins, Steve	RB	1979–81	32

Auer, Todd	LB	1987	72 R, 98 R
Austin, Hise	DB	1973	27
Avery, Steve	FB	1991	32
Aydelette, Buddy	G	1980	62
Bailey, Byron	HB	1953	20
Bailey, Karston	WR	2002	85
Bain, Bill	T	1975	69
Baker, Frank	E	1931	12
Baker, Roy	B	1928–29	5, 12, 17, 21
Balazs, Frank	B	1939–41	35
Baldwin, Al	E	1950	19
Banet, Herb	B	1937	21
Barber, Bob	DE	1976–79	70
Barker, Roy	DE	1999	94
Barnes, Emery	DE	1956	85
Barnes, Gary	E	1962	80
Barnett, Solon	T	1945–46	72
Barragar, Nate	C	1931–32, 34–35	30, 31, 56, 64
Barrett, Jan	E	1963	82
Barrie, Sebastian	DE	1992	67
Barry, Al	G	1954, 57	63, 66
Barry, Kevin	T	2002	71
Barry, Norm	B	1921	NA
Barton, Don	B	1953	43
Bartrum, Mike	TE	1995	48
Barzilauskas, Carl	DT	1978–79	75
Basing, Myrt	B	1923–27	<15>, 27
Basinger, Mike	DE	1974	71
Baxter, Lloyd	C	1948	33
Beach, Sanjay	WR	1992	82
Beasey, Jack	B	1924	NA
Beck, Ken	DT	1959–60	73
Becker, Wayland	E	1936–38	32
Beebe, Don	WR	1996–97	82
Beekley, Bruce	LB	1980	58
Bell, Albert	WR	1988	88
Bell, Ed	G/T	1947–49	82
Bell, Tyrone	CB	1999	47
Bennett, Earl	G	1946	15, 36
Bennett, Edgar	RB	1992–96	34
Bennett, Tony	LB	1990–93	90
Berezney, Paul	T	1942–44	47
Berrang, Ed	E	1952	81
Berry, Connie	E	1940	37
Berry, Ed	DB	1986	20
Berry, Gary	S	2000	21
Bettencourt, Larry	C	1933	29, 30, 39
Bettis, Tom	LB	1955–61	58, 65
Beverly, David	P	1975–80	11

Bidwell, Josh	P	2000–01	9
Bieberstein, Adolph	G	1926	?
Bilda, Dick	B	1944	22
Billups, Lewis	CB	1992	22
Biolo, John	G	1939	16, 32
Birney, Tom	K	1979–80	16, 19
Blackmon, Roosevelt	CB	1998	23
Blackshear, Jeff	G	2002	69
Blaine, Ed	G	1962	60
Blair, Michael	RB	1998	27
Bland, Carl	WR	1989–90	83
Bloodgood, Elbert	B	1930	11
Boedeker, Bill	B	1950	31
Boerio, Chuck	LB	1952	65
Bolden, Juran	CB	1998	46
Bolton, Scott	WR	1988	82
Bone, Warren	DE	1987	72 R
Bono, Steve	QB	1997	13
Booker, Vaughn	DE/DT	1998–99	96
Bookout, Billy	DB	1955–56	20
Boone, J.R.	B	1953	22, 43
Borak, Fritz	E	1938	9
Borden, Nate	DE	1955–59	87
Borgognone, Dirk	K	1995	9
Bowdoin, Jim	G	1928–31	19, 32, 34
Bowen, Matt	S	2001-02	28
Bowens, David	DE	2000	96
Bowman, Ken	C	1964–73	57
Boyarsky, Jerry	NT	1986–89	61
Boyd, Elmo	WR	1978	85
Boyd, Greg	DE	1983	72
Bracken, Don	P	1985–90	17
Brackins, Charlie	QB	1955	15
Bradford, Corey	WR	1998–2001	85
Bradley, Dave	G	1969–71	61
Brady, Jeff	LB	1992	51
Braggs, Byron	DE	1981–83	73
Branstetter, Kent	T	1973	71
Bratkowski, Zeke	QB	1963–68, 71	12
Bray, Ray	G	1952	63
Breen, Gene	LB	1964	61
Brennan, Jack	G	1939	37
Brock, Charley	C/LB	1939–47	29
Brock, Lou	B	1940–45	15, 16
Brock, Matt	DE/DT	1989–94	62, 94
Brockington, John	RB	1971–77	42
(Brooks, Aaron)	QB	(1999)	(2)
Brooks, Barrett	T	2002	77
Brooks, Bucky	CB	1996–97	22

Brooks, Robert	WR	1992–98	87
Bross, Mal	B	1927	6
Broussard, Steve	P	1975	11
Brown, Aaron	DE	1973–74	74
Brown, Allen	TE	1966–67	83
Brown, Bob	DT	1966–73	78
Brown, Buddy	G	1953–56	62
Brown, Carlos	QB	1975–76	19
Brown, Dave	CB	1987–89	32
Brown, Gary	T	1994–96	68, 71
Brown, Gilbert	DT	1994–99, 2001-02	71, 93
Brown, Jonathan	DE	1998	91
Brown, Ken	C	1980	74
Brown, Robert	LB/DE	1982–92	93
Brown, Tim	HB	1959	25
Brown, Tom	DB	1964–68	40
Browner, Ross	DE/NT	1987	79
Bruder, Hank	B	1931–39	5, 13, 18, 27, 47, 55
Brunell, Mark	QB	1993–94	8
Bucchianeri, Mike	G	1941, 44–45	17, 19, 33
Buchanon, Willie	CB	1972–78	28
Buck, Cub	T	<1921–25>	<10>
Buckley, Terrell	CB	1992–94	27
Buhler, Larry	B	1939–41	52
Buland, Walt	T	1924	NA
Bullough, Hank	G	1955, 58	61, 67
Bultman, Art	C	1932–34	17, 32, 33, 38, 45, 52
Burgess, Ronnie	DB	1985	39
Burnette, Reggie	LB	1991	55
(Burris, Henry)	QB	(2001)	(10)
Burris, Paul	G	1949–51	33
Burrow, Curtis	K	1988	5
Burrow, Jim	DB	1976	41
Bush, Blair	C	1989–91	51
Butler, Bill	B	1959	22, 25
Butler, Frank	C/T	1934–36, 38	26, 35, 48, 59, 60
Butler, LeRoy	CB/S	1990–2001	36
Butler, Mike	DE	1977–82, 85	77
Cabral, Brian	LB	1980	65
Cade, Mossy	DB	1985–86	24
Caffey, Lee Roy	LB	1964–69	60
Cahoon, Ivan	T	1926–29	<10>, 30, 40
Caldwell, David	NT	1987	73 R
Campbell, Rich	QB	1981–84	19
Campen, James	C	1989–93	63
Canadeo, Tony	B	1941–44, 46–52	3
Cannava, Al	B	1950	42
Cannon, Mark	C	1984–89	58
Capp, Dick	TE/LB	1967	88

PACKERS BY THE NUMBERS

Capuzzi, Jim	B	1955–56	23, 26
Carey, Joe	G	1921	NA
Carlson, Wes	G	<1926>	<11>
Carmichael, Al	HB	1953–58	42, 48
Carpenter, Lew	B	1959–63	33
Carr, Fred	LB	1968–77	53
Carreker, Alphonso	DE	1984–88	76
Carroll, Leo	DE	1968	67
Carruth, Paul Ott	RB	1986–88	30
Carter, Carl	CB	1992	21
Carter, Jim	LB	1970–75, 77–78	50
Carter, Joe	E	1942	58
Carter, Mike	WR	1970	36
Carter, Tony	FB	2002	39
Casper, Charley	B	1934	20, 44
Cassidy, Ron	WR	1979–81, 83–84	88
Cecil, Chuck	S	1988–92	26
Chandler, Don	K	1965–67	34
Cheek, Louis	T	1991	78
Cherry, Bill	C	1986–87	69
Chesley, Francis	LB	1978	53
Cheyunski, Jim	LB	1977	55
Childs, Henry	TE	1984	89
Chmura, Mark	TE	1993–99	89
Choate, Putt	LB	1987	57 R
Christman, Paul	QB	1950	28
Cifelli, Gus	T	1953	73
Cifers, Bob	B	1949	16
Clancy, Jack	WR	1970	80
Clanton, Chuck	DB	1985	23
Claridge, Dennis	QB	1965	10
Clark, Allan	RB	1982	34
Clark, Greg	LB	1991	55
Clark, Jessie	FB	1983–87	33
Clark, Vinnie	CB	1991–92	25
Clavelle, Shannon	DE	1995–97	91
Clayton, Mark	WR	1993	83
Clemens, Bob	FB	1955	33, 35
Clemens, Cal	B	1936	33
Clemons, Ray	G	1947	46
Clifton, Chad	T	2000–02	76
Cloud, Jack	FB	1950–51	82
Cobb, Reggie	RB	1994	32
Cody, Ed	B	1947–48	17
Coffey, Junior	RB	1965	41
Coffman, Paul	TE	1978–85	82
Coleman, Keo	LB	1993	54
Collier, Steve	T	1987	64, 70 R, 74 R, 92 R
Collins, Albin	HB	1951	65, 88

Collins, Bobby	TE	2001	87
Collins, Brett	LB	1992–93	55
Collins, Mark	CB	1997	26
Collins, Patrick	RB	1988	25
Collins, Shawn	WR	1993	81
Comp, Irv	B	1943–49	51
Compton, Chuck	DB	1987	41 R
Comstock, Rudy	G	1931–33	32
Concannon, Jack	QB	1974	10
Cone, Fred	FB/K	1951–57	31, 66
Conway, Dave	K	1971	35
Cook, James	G	1921	NA
Cook, Kelly	RB	1987	20
Cook, Ted	E/DB	1948–50	48
Cooke, Bill	DE	1975	78
Cooks, Kerry	S	1998	20, 45
Cooney, Mark	LB	1974	58
Copeland, Russell	WR	1998	16
Corker, John	LB	1988	53
Coughlin, Frank	T	1921	NA
Coutre, Larry	HB	1950, 53	27
Cox, Ron	LB	1996	54
Craig, Larry	E/B	1939–49	54
Crawford, Keith	CB/WR	1995, 99	45
Cremer, Ted	E	1948	18
Crenshaw, Leon	DT	1968	70
Crimmins, Bernie	G/B	1945	76
Croft, Milburn	T	1942–47	75
Cronin, Tommy	HB	1922	NA
Croston, Dave	T	1988	60
Crouse, Ray	RB	1984	21
Crowley, Jim	HB	1925	?
Crutcher, Tommy	LB	1964–67, 71–72	37, 56
Cuff, Ward	B	1947	21
Culbreath, Jim	FB	1977–79	31
Culver, Al	T	1932	54
Cumby, George	LB	1980–85	52
Curcio, Mike	LB	1983	57
Currie, Dan	LB	1958–64	58
Curry, Bill	C	1965–66	50
Curry, Scott	T	1999	61
Cvercko, Andy	G	1960	62, 67
Cyre, Hector	T	<1926>	<3>
Dahms, Tom	T	1955	78
Dale, Carroll	WR	1965–72	84
Danelo, Joe	K	1975	18
Daniell, Averell	T	1937	23
Danjean, Ernie	LB	1957	64
Darkins, Chris	RB	1996–97	44

Darling, Bernard	C	1927–31	17, 29
Davenport, Bill	HB	1931	16
Davenport, Najeh	RB	2002	44
Davey, Don	DE/DT	1991–94	99
Davidson, Ben	DE	1961	72
Davis, Anthony	LB	1999	50
Davis, Dave	WR	1971–72	47
Davis, Harper	B	1951	25
Davis, Kenneth	RB	1986–88	36
Davis, Paul	G	1922	NA
Davis, Ralph	G	1947–48	66
Davis, Rob	LS	1997–2002	60
Davis, Tyrone	TE	1997–2002	81
Davis, Willie	DE	1960–69	87
Dawson, Dale	K	1988	4
Dawson, Gib	HB	1953	26
Dean, Walter	FB	1991	42
Deeks, Don	T	1948	85
Dees, Bob	T	1952	76
Degrate, Tony	DE	1985	95
Del Gaizo, Jim	QB	1973	12
Del Greco, Al	K	1984–87	10
DeLisle, Jim	DT	1971	79
Dellenbach, Jeff	C/G	1996–98	67
DeLuca, Tony	NT	1984	98
Dennard, Preston	WR	1985	88
Dent, Burnell	LB	1986–92	56
Deschaine, Dick	P	1955–57	80
Detmer, Ty	QB	1992–95	11
Dickey, Lynn	QB	1976–77, 79–85	10, 12
Didier, Clint	TE	1988–89	80
Diggs, Na'il	LB	2000–02	59
Dillon, Bobby	DB	1952–59	44
Dilweg, Anthony	QB	1989–90	8
Dilweg, Lavvie	E	1927–34	22, 61
Dimler, Rich	DT	1980	92
Dingle, Antonio	DT	1999	74
DiPierro, Ray	G	1950–51	21
Disend, Leo	T	1940	18
Dittrich, John	G	1959	68
Don Carlos, Waldo	C	1931	24
D'Onofrio, Mark	LB	1992	58
Donohoe, Mike	TE	1973–74	86
Dorsett, Matthew	CB	1995	23
Dorsey, Dean	K	1988	9
Dorsey, John	LB	1984–88	99
Dotson, Earl	T	1993–2001	72
Dotson, Santana	DT	1996–2001	71
Douglas, George	C	1921	NA

Douglass, Bobby	QB	1978	19
Douglass, Mike	LB	1978–85	53, 65
Dowden, Corey	CB	1996	42
Dowden, Steve	T	1952	70
Dowler, Boyd	WR	1959–69	86
Dowling, Brian	QB	1977	12
Drechsler, Dave	G	1983–84	61
Dreyer, Wally	B	1950	16, 42
Driver, Donald	WR	1999–2002	80
Drost, Jeff	DT	1987	71 R
Drulis, Chuck	G	1950	18
Duckett, Forey	CB	1994	21
Duford, Wilfred	B	1924	NA
Duhart, Paul	B	1944	42
Dukes, Jamie	C	1994	63
DuMoe, Bill	E	1921	NA
Dunaway, Dave	WR	1968	29
Duncan, Ken	P	1971	18
Dunn, Red	B	1927–31	7, 11, 15, 16, 17, 32
Dunningan, Pat	E	1922	NA
Earhart, Ralph	B	1948–49	41
Earp, Jug	C	1922–32	<7>, 9, 29, 38, 39
Eason, Roger	G	1949	40
Ecker, Ed	T	1950–51	55
Edwards, Antuan	CB/S	1999–2001	24
Edwards, Earl	DT	1979	73
Ellerson, Gary	FB	1985–86	42
Elliott, Burton	B	1921	NA
Elliott, Carlton	E	1951–54	40, 80
Elliott, Tony	DB	1987–88	27 R
Ellis, Gerry	FB	1980–86	31
Ellis, Ken	CB	1970–75	48
Enderle, Dick	G	1976	67
Engebretsen, Paul	G	1934–41	34, 52, 69
Engelmann, Wuert	B	1930–33	25, 33
Enright, Rex	FB	1926–27	15, <20>
Epps, Phillip	WR	1982–88	85
Estep, Mike	G	1987	79 R
(Estes, Roy)	B	1928	(5)
Ethridge, Joe	T	1949	85
Evans, Dick	E	1940, 43	22, 53
Evans, Doug	CB	1993–97	33
Evans, Jack	B	1929	21
Evans, Lon	G	1933–37	17, 25, 39, 46, 51, 65
Falkenstein, Tony	FB	1943	18
Fanucci, Mike	DE	1974	71
Faverty, Hal	C/LB	1952	51
Favre, Brett	QB	1992–2002	4
Faye, Allen	E	1922	NA

PACKERS BY THE NUMBERS

Feasel, Greg	T	1986	77
Feathers, Beattie	B	1940	3
Ferguson, Howie	FB	1953–58	37
Ferguson, Robert	WR	2001–02	89
Ferragamo, Vince	QB	1985–86	5
Ferrario, Bill	G	2002	63
Ferry, Lou	T	1949	18
Fields, Angelo	T	1982	79
Finnin, Tom	T	1957	?
Fisher, Tony	RB	2002	40
Fitzgerald, Kevin	TE	1987	89 R
Fitzgibbon, Paul	B	1930–32	14, 18, 49
Flaherty, Dick	E	<1926>	<6>
Flanagan, Mike	C	1998–2002	58
Flanigan, Jim	LB	1967–70	55
Flanigan, Jim	DT	2001	75
Fleming, Marv	TE	1963–69	81
Flowers, Bob	C/LB	1942–49	35
Floyd, Bobby Jack	FB	1952	33
Flynn, Tom	S	1984–86	41
Folkins, Lee	DE	1961	81
Fontenot, Herman	RB	1989–90	27
Ford, Len	DE	1958	83
Forester, Bill	LB	1953–63	69, 71
Forte, Aldo	G	1947	40
Forte, Bob	B	1946–53	8, 26
Francis, Joe	B	1958–59	20
Frankowski, Ray	G	1945	15
Franks, Bubba	TE	2000–02	88
Franta, Herb	T	1930	55
Franz, Nolan	WR	1986	84
Franz, Todd	DB	2002	49
Frase, Paul	DE	1997	97
Freeman, Antonio	WR	1995–2001	86
Freeman, Bob	DB	1959	41
Fries, Sherwood	G/LB	1943	46
Fritsch, Ted	B	1942–50	64
Frutig, Ed	E	1941, 45	51, 80
Fuller, Joe	CB	1991	21
Fullwood, Brent	RB	1987–90	21
Fusina, Chuck	QB	1986	4
Gabbard, Steve	T	1991	72
Galbraith, Scott	TE	1998	47
Galbreath, Harry	G	1993–95	76
Gantenbein, Milt	E	1931–40	21, 22, 30, 46, 47
Garcia, Eddie	K	1983–84	11
Gardella, Gus	FB	1922	NA
Gardner, Milton	G	1922–26	<14>
Garrett, Bob	QB	1954	15

Garrett, Len	TE	1971–73	88
Gassert, Ron	DT	1962	73
Gatewood, Lester	C	1946–47	33, 77
Gavin, Buck	B	1921, 23	NA
Gaydos, Kent	WR	1975	86
Gbaja-Biamila, Kabeer	DE	2000–02	94
Getty, Charlie	T	1983	77
Gibson, Paul	WR	1972	41
Gillette, Jim	B	1947	16
Gillingham, Gale	G	1966–74, 76	68
Gillus, Willie	QB	1987	5 R
Girard, Jug	B	1948–51	36
Gizzi, Chris	LB	2000–01	57
Glass, Leland	WR	1972–73	46
Glenn, Terry	WR	2002	83
Glick, Eddie	B	1921–22	NA
Gofourth, Derrel	G/C	1977–82	57
Goldenberg, Charles	G/B	1933–45	21, 43, 44, 51
Goodman, Herbert	RB	2000–01	29
Goodman, Les	RB	1973–74	25
Goodnight, Clyde	E	1945–49	23
Gordon, Darrien	DB	2002	23
Gordon, Dick	WR	1973	7, 85
Gordon, Lou	T	1936–37	47, 53
Gorgal, Ken	DB	1956	26
Grabowski, Jim	RB	1966–70	33
Graham, Jay	FB	2002	35
Grant, David	DE	1993	70
Gray, Cecil	T	1992	71
Gray, Jack	E	1923	NA
Gray, Johnnie	S	1975–83	24
Green, Ahman	RB	2000–02	30
Green, Jessie	WR	1976	86
Greene, Tiger	S	1986–90	23
Greeney, Norm	G	1933	20
Greenfield, Tom	C/LB	1939–41	56
Greenwood, David	S	1986	49
Gregg, Forrest	T	1956, 58–70	75
Gremminger, Hank	DB	1956–65	46
Griffen, Harold	C	1928	25
Grimes, Billy	HB	1950–52	22
Grimm, Dan	G	1963–65	67
Gros, Earl	FB	1962–63	40
Grove, Roger	B	1931–35	10, 11
Gruber, Bob	T	1987	69 R
Gueno, Jim	LB	1976–80	51
Hackbart, Dale	DB	1960–61	40
Hackett, Joey	TE	1987–88	89
Haddix, Michael	FB	1989–90	35

PACKERS BY THE NUMBERS

Hadl, John	QB	1974–75	12, 21
Haley, Darryl	T	1988	74
Hall, Charlie	CB	1971–76	21
Hall, Lamont	TE	1999	49, 88
Hall, Mark	DE	1989–90	72
Hallstrom, Ron	G	1982–92	65
Hamilton, Ruffin	LB	1994	58
Hampton, Dave	RB	1969–71	25
Hanner, Dave	DT	1952–64	77, 79
Hanny, Frank	T	1930	19
Hansen, Don	LB	1976–77	58
Hanson, Chris	P	1999	7
Hanson, Hal	FB/E	1923	NA
Harden, Derrick	WR	1987	82 R
Harden, Leon	S	1970	28
Harding, Roger	C	1949	31
Hardy, Kevin	DT	1970	73
Hargrove, James	RB	1987	20 R
Harrell, Willard	RB	1975–77	40
Harris, Bernardo	LB	1995–2001	54, 55
Harris, Corey	WR/CB/KR	1992–94	30, 81
Harris, Jack	B	<1925–26>	<16>
Harris, Jackie	TE	1990–93	80
Harris, Leotis	G	1978–83	69
Harris, Raymont	RB	1998	29
Harris, Tim	LB	1986–90	97
Harris, William	TE	1990	89
Harrison, Anthony	DB	1987	46 R
Hart, Doug	DB	1964–71	43
Hartnett, Perry	G	1987	63 R
Hartwig, Keith	WR	1977	82
Harvey, Maurice	S	1981–83	23
Hasselbeck, Matt	QB	1999–2000	11
Hathcock, Dave	DB	1966	45
Hauck, Tim	S	1991–94	24
Havig, Dennis	G	1977	62
Haycraft, Ken	E	1930	21
Hayden, Aaron	RB	1997	24
Hayes, Chris	S	1996	40
Hayes, Dave	E	1921–22	NA
Hayes, Gary	DB	1984–86	27
Hayes, Norb	E	1923	NA
Hayhoe, Bill	T	1969–73	51, 77
Hays, George	DE	1953	88
Hearden, Les	HB	1924	NA
Hearden, Tom	B	1927–28	12
Heath, Stan	QB	1949	39
Hefner, Larry	LB	1972–75	51
Heimburger, Craig	G	1999	75

Held, Paul	QB	1955	15
Helluin, Jerry	DT	1954–57	72
Henderson, William	FB	1995–2001	30, 33
Hendrian, Dutch	B	1924	NA
Hendricks, Ted	LB	1974	56
Henry, Urban	DT	1963	83
Hentrich, Craig	P	1994–97	17
Herber, Arnie	B	1930–40	12, 16, 19, 26, 38, 41, 45, 68
Hickman, Larry	FB	1960	37
Highsmith, Don	RB	1973	32
Hill, Don	B	1929	14, 16
Hill, Jim	DB	1972–74	39
Hill, Nate	DE	1988	90
Hilton, John	TE	1970	86
Himes, Dick	T	1968–77	72
Hinkle, Clarke	FB	1932–41	27, 30, 33, 39, 41, 45, 48
Hinte, Hal	E	1942	15
Hobbins, Jim	G	1987	78R
Hoffman, Gary	T	1984	78
Holland, Darius	DT/DE	1995–97	90
Holland, Johnny	LB	1987–93	50
Holler, Ed	LB	1963	65
Holliday, Vonnie	DE	1998–2002	90
Hollinquest, Lamont	LB	1996–98	56
Holmberg, Rob	LB	2001	56
Holmes, Darick	RB	1998	22
Holmes, Jerry	CB	1990–91	44
Hood, Estus	DB	1978–84	38
Hope, Charles	G	1994	70
Horn, Don	QB	1967–70	13
Hornung, Paul	B	1957–62, 64–66	5
Houston, Bobby	LB	1990	60
Howard, Desmond	WR/KR	1996, 99	81, 82
Howard, Lynn	B	1921–22	NA
Howell, John	B	1938	49
Howton, Billy	E	1952–58	86
Hubbard, Cal	T	1929–33, 35	27, 38, 39, 40, 51
Huckleby, Harlan	RB	1980–85	25
Hudson, Bob	RB	1972	23
Huffman, Tim	G/T	1981–85	74
Hull, Tom	LB	1975	55
Humphrey, Donnie	DE	1984–86	79
Hunt, Cletidus	DE/DT	1999–2002	97
Hunt, Ervin	DB	1970	45
Hunt, Kevin	T	1972	64
Hunt, Mike	LB	1978–80	55
Hunter, Art	C	1954	70
Hunter, Scott	QB	1971–73	16
Hunter, Tony	RB	1987	31 R

Hutchins, Paul	T	1993–94	67
Hutson, Don	E/DB	1935–45	14
Hyland, Bob	C	1967–69, 76	50, 55
Ilkin, Tunch	T	1993	79
Iman, Ken	C	1960–63	53
Ingalls, Bob	C/LB	1942	53
Ingram, Darryl	TE	1992–93	88
Ingram, Mark	WR	1995	82
Isbell, Cecil	B	1938–42	17
Ivery, Eddie Lee	RB	1979–86	40
Jacke, Chris	K	1989–96	13
Jackson, Alcender	G	2002	64
Jackson, Chris	WR	2002	86
Jackson, Johnnie	S	1992	40
Jackson, Keith	TE	1995–96	88
Jackson, Mel	G	1976–80	71
Jacobs, Allen	HB	1965	35
Jacobs, Jack	B	1947–49	27
Jacunski, Harry	E	1939–44	48
Jakes, Van	CB	1989	24
James, Claudis	WR	1967–68	16, 27
Janet, Ernie	G	1975	63
Jankowski, Ed	B	1937–41	7, 25
Jansante, Val	E	1951	23
(Jarrell, Baxter)	T	(1947)	(28)
Jay, Craig	TE	1987	26 R, 81 R
Jefferson, John	WR	1981–84	83
Jefferson, Norman	DB	1987–88	38
Jenison, Ray	T	1931	31
Jenke, Noel	LB	1973–74	55
Jenkins, Billy	S	2001	23
Jennings, Jim	E	1955	85
Jensen, Greg	G	1987	54 R, 60 R
Jensen, Jim	RB	1981–82	33
Jervey, Travis	RB	1995–98	32
Jeter, Bob	DB	1963–70	21
Johnson, Bill	DE	1941	50
Johnson, Charles	DT	1979–80, 83	99
Johnson, Danny	LB	1978	58
Johnson, Ezra	DE	1977–87	78, 90
Johnson, Glenn	T	1949	35
Johnson, Howard	G/LB	1940–41	64
Johnson, Joe	HB	1954–58	40
Johnson, Joe	DE	2002	91
Johnson, Kenneth	DB	1987	39, 41
Johnson, KeShon	CB	1994	37
Johnson, LeShon	RB	1994–95	42
Johnson, Marvin	DB	1952–53	41
Johnson, Randy	QB	1976	16

Johnson, Reggie	TE	1994, 97	82, 88
Johnson, Sammy	RB	1979	39
Johnson, Tom	DT	1952	72
Johnston, Chester	B	1931, 34–38	15, 37, 54
Jolly, Mike	S	1980, 82–83	21
Jones, Bob	G	1934	55
Jones, Boyd	T	1984	71
Jones, Bruce	G	1927–28	24
Jones, Calvin	RB	1996	27
Jones, Daryll	DB	1984–85	43
Jones, Ron	TE	1969	88
Jones, Scott	T	1991	71
Jones, Sean	DE	1994–96	96
Jones, Terry	NT	1978–84	63
Jones, Tom	G	1938	37
Jordan, Charles	WR	1994–95, 99	80, 82
Jordan, Henry	DT	1959–69	74
Jordan, Kenneth	LB	1987	55 R
Jorgenson, Carl	T	1934	54
Joyner, Seth	LB	1997	54
Jue, Bhawoh	CB	2001-02	21
Jurkovic, John	NT	1991–95	64, 92
Kahler, Bob	B	1942–44	8
Kahler, Royal	T	1942	72
Kampman, Aaron	DE	2002	74
Katalinas, Leo	T	1938	11
Kauahi, Kani	C	1988	62
Keane, Jim	E	1952	81
Keefe, Emmett	T	1921	NA
Kekeris, Jim	T	1948	72
Kell, Paul	T	1939–40	41
Kelley, Bill	E	1949	26
Kelly, Joe	LB	1995	57
Kemp, Perry	WR	1988–91	81
Kercher, Bob	DE	1944	18, 23
Kern, Bill	T	1929–30	33
Keuper, Ken	B	1945–47	18
Kiel, Blair	QB	1988–91	10
Kiesling, Walt	G	1935–36	49, 60
Kilbourne, Warren	T	1939	58
Kimball, Bobby	WR	1979–80	85
Kimmel, J.D.	DT	1958	72
Kinard, Billy	B	1957–58	25
Kinder, Randy	CB	1997	43
King, David	DB	1987	40 R
King, Don	DT	1956	70
King, Don	DB	1987	17 R, 32 R
(Kinkade, Tom)	B	(1945)	(42)
Kirby, Jack	B	1949	43

PACKERS BY THE NUMBERS

Kitson, Syd	G	1980–81, 83–84	64
Kitts, Jim	FB	1998	48
Klaus, Fee	C	1921	NA
Kliebhan, Adolph	B	1921	NA
Knafelc, Gary	E	1954–62	84
Knapp, Lindsay	G	1996	65
Knutson, Gene	DE	1954, 56	81
Knutson, Steve	T	1976–77	60
Koart, Matt	DE	1986	92
Koch, Greg	T	1977–85	68
Koncar, Mark	T	1976–77, 79–81	79
Konopasek, Ed	T	1987	68 R
Koonce, George	LB	1992–99	53
Kopay, Dave	RB	1972	40
Kostelnik, Ron	T	1961–68	77
Kotal, Eddie	B	1925–29	10, <13>
Kovatch, John	E	1947	76
Kowalkowski, Bob	G	1977	67
Kramer, Jerry	G	1958–68	64
Kramer, Ron	TE	1957, 59–64	88
Kranz, Keneth	B	1949	42
Krause, Larry	RB	1970–71, 73–74	30
(Kresky, Joe)	G	(1930)	(25)
Kroll, Bob	S	1972–73	44
Kuberski, Bob	DT	1995–98	94
Kuechenberg, Rudy	LB	1970	59
Kurth, Joe	T	1933–34	28, 31, 58
Kuusisto, Bill	G	1941–46	45, 52
(Laabs, Kermit)	B	(1929)	(19)
LaBounty, Matt	DE	1995	97
Ladrow, Wally	HB	1921	NA
Lally, Bob	LB	1976	58
Lambeau, Earl "Curly"	B	1921–29	<1>, 14, 20, 42
Lammons, Pete	TE	1972	86
Lande, Cliff	E	1921	NA
Landers, Walt	FB	1978–79	42
Landeta, Sean	P	1998	7
Lane, MacArthur	RB	1972–74	36
Lankas, Jim	FB	1943	23
Larson, Bill	TE	1980	87
Larson, Fred	C	<1925>	<17>
Larson, Kurt	LB	1991	59
Laslavic, Jim	LB	1982	60
Lathrop, Kit	DT	1979–80	72
Lauer, Dutch	E	1922	NA
Lauer, Larry	C	1956–57	58
Laughlin, Jim	LB	1983	62
Lawrence, Jim	B	1939	51, 59
Laws, Joe	B	1934–45	24, 29, 38

Leaper, Wes	E	1921, 23	NA
Lee, Bill	T	1937–42, 46	40
Lee, Charles	WR	2000–01	82
Lee, Mark	CB	1980–90	22
Leigh, Charlie	RB	1974	23
Leiker, Tony	DE	1987	96 R
LeJeune, Walt	G	<1925–26>	<8>
Lenon, Paris	LB	2002	53
Leopold, Bobby	LB	1986	53
Lester, Darrell	C	1937–38	29
Letlow, Russ	G	1936–42, 46	46, 62
Levens, Dorsey	RB	1994–2001	25, 48
Lewellen, Verne	B	1924–32	<4>, 21, 31, 45, 46
Lewis, Cliff	LB	1981–84	56
Lewis, Gary	TE	1981–84	81
Lewis, Mark	TE	1985–87	89
Lewis, Mike	NT	1980	66
Lewis, Ron	WR	1992–94	85
Lewis, Tim	CB	1983–86	26
Lidberg, Carl	FB	1926, 29–30	<17>, 34, 38
Lipscomb, Paul	T	1945–49	47
Livingston, Dale	K	1970	37
Lofton, James	WR	1978–86	80
Logan, David	NT	1987	94
Logan, Dick	G	1952–53	67
Lollar, Slick	FB	1928	14
London, Antonio	LB	1998	57
Long, Bob	WR	1964–67	80
Longwell, Ryan	K	1997–2002	8
Loomis, Ace	B	1951–53	7, 43, 48
Losch, Jack	HB	1956	25
Lucky, Bill	DT	1955	71
Lueck, Bill	G	1968–74	62
Luhn, Nolan	E	1945–49	38
Luke, Steve	DB	1975–80	46
Lusteg, Booth	K	1969	32
Lyle, Dewey	E	1922–23	NA
Lyman, Del	T	1941	15
Lyon, Billy	DT/DE	1998–2002	98
Maas, Bill	NT	1993	77
Mack, Red	WR	1966	27
MacLeod, Tom	LB	1973	56
Maddox, George	T	1935	28
Majkowski, Don	QB	1987–92	5, 7
Malancon, Rydell	LB	1987	54 R, 60 R
Malone, Grover	B	1921	NA
Mandarich, Tony	T	1989–91	77
Mandeville, Chris	DB	1987–88	44
Manley, Leon	G	1950–51	90

Mann, Bob	E	1950–54	31, 87
Mann, Erroll	K	1968, 76	39
Manning, Brian	WR	1998	82
Mansfield, Von	DB	1987	44 R
Marcol, Chester	K	1972–80	13
Marks, Larry	B	1928	44
Marshall, Rich	DT	1965	70
Marshall, Torrance	LB	2001-02	41, 51
Martell, Herman	E	1921	NA
Martin, Charles	DE	1984–87	94
Martin, David	TE	2001-02	83
Martinkovic, John	DE	1951–56	39, 47, 83
Maryland, Russell	DT	2000	67
Mason, Dave	DB	1974	43
Mason, Joel	E	1942–45	7
Mason, Larry	RB	1988	34
Massey, Carlton	DE	1957–58	81
Masters, Norm	T	1957–64	78
Mataele, Stan	NT	1987	94 R
Mathys, Charlie	B	<1922–26>	<2>
Matson, Pat	G	1975	62
Matthews, Al	DB	1970–75	29
Matthews, Aubrey	WR	1988–89	88
Mattos, Harry	B	1936	23
Matuszak, Marv	LB	1958	63
Mayer, Frank	G	1927	19
Mayes, Derrick	WR	1996–98	80
Mayes, Kivuusama	LB	1999	56
McAuliffe, Jack	HB	<1926>	<19>
McBride, Ron	RB	1973	24
McBride, Tod	CB/S	1999–2002	27
McCaffrey, Bob	C	1975	58
McCarren, Larry	C	1973–84	54
McCaslin, Eugene	LB	2000	56
McCloughan, Dave	CB	1992	23
McConkey, Phil	WR	1986	88
McCoy, Mike C.	DB	1976–83	29
McCoy, Mike P.	DT	1970–76	76
McCrary, Herdis	B	1929–33	19, 28, 29, 38, 43, 53
McDonald, Dustin	G	1935	42
McDougal, Bob	B	1947	19
McDowell, John	G	1964	73
McElmurry, Blaine	S	1997	38
McGarrahan, Scott	S	1998–2000	43
McGarry, John	G	1987	61 R
McGaw, Walter	G	<1926>	<11>
McGeary, Clarence	DT	1950	44
McGee, Buford	FB	1992	31
McGee, Max	E	1954, 57–67	85

McGeorge, Rich	TE	1970–78	81
McGill, Lenny	CB	1994–95	22
McGrew, Sylvester	DE	1987	77 R
McGruder, Michael	CB	1989	20
McGuire, Gene	C	1996	60
McHan, Lamar	QB	1959–60	16, 17
McIlhenny, Don	HB	1957–59	42
McIntyre, Guy	G	1994	62
McJulien, Paul	P	1991–92	16
McKay, Roy	B	1944–47	3, 22
McKenzie, Keith	DE/LB	1996–99, 2002	95
McKenzie, Mike	CB	1999–2002	34
McKenzie, Raleigh	G	1999–2000	63
McLaughlin, Joe	LB	1979	62
McLaughlin, Lee	G	1941	37
McLean, Ray	B	1921	NA
McLeod, Mike	DB	1984–85	28
McMahon, Jim	QB	1995–96	9
McMath, Herb	DT	1977	61
McMichael, Steve	DT	1994	90
McMillan, Ernie	T	1975	70
McNabb, Dexter	FB	1992–93	44, 45
McNally, Johnny	B	1929–33, 35–36	14, 20, 24, 26, 55
McPherson, Forrest	T	1943–45	72
Meade, Mike	FB	1982–83	39
Mealey, Rondell	RB	2001-02	32
Meilinger, Steve	E	1958, 60	80
Melka, James	LB	1987	52 R
Mendoza, Ruben	G	1986	62
Mercein, Chuck	RB	1967–69	30
Mercer, Mike	K	1968–69	38
Merrill, Casey	DE	1979–83	78
Merrill, Mark	LB	1982	62
Merriweather, Mike	LB	1993	97
Mestnik, Frank	FB	1963	35
Metcalf, Eric	PR	2002	22
Meyer, Jim	T	1987	62 R
Michaels, Lou	K	1971	75
Michaels, Walt	G	1951	35
Michalske, Mike	G	1929–35, 37	19, 24, 28, 30, 31, 33, 36, 40, 63
Michels, John	T	1996–97	77
Mickens, Terry	WR	1994–97	85, 88
Middleton, Terdell	RB	1977–81	34
Midler, Lou	G	1941	27
Mihajlovich, Lou	DE	1954	41
Milan, Don	QB	1975	12
Millard, Keith	DE	1992	77
Miller, Don	B	1941–42	27
Miller, Don	B	1954	20

PACKERS BY THE NUMBERS

Miller, John	T	1960	72
Miller, John	LB	1987	97 R
Miller, Ookie	C	1938	48
Miller, Paul	B	1936–38	3
Miller, Tom	E	1946	76
Mills, Stan	B	1922–23	NA
Minick, Paul	G	1928–29	15, 23, 25
Mirer, Rick	QB	(1998)	(12)
Mitchell, Basil	RB	1999–2000	28
Mitchell, Charles	B	1946	16
Mitchell, Roland	CB/S	1991–94	47
Moffitt, Mike	WR	1986	82
Moje, Dick	E	1951	79
Molenda, Bo	B	1928–32	27, 30
Monaco, Ron	LB	1987	51 R
Monnett, Bob	B	1933–38	3, 5, 12, 18, 50, 66
Monroe, Henry	DB	1979	43
Moore, Allen	E	1939	55
Moore, Blake	C/G	1984–85	60
Moore, Brent	DE	1987	97
Moore, Jason	S	2000	40
Moore, Rich	DT	1969–70	70
Moore, Tom	HB	1960–65	25
Moran, Rich	G	1985–93	57
Moresco, Tim	DB	1977	37
Morgan, Anthony	WR	1993–96	81, 84
Morris, Jim Bob	DB	1987	30 R, 47R
Morris, Larry	RB	1987	43 R
Morris, Lee	WR	1987	48 R, 81 R, 85 R
Morrissey, Jim	LB	1993	51
Morton, Mike	LB	2000	53
Moselle, Dom	B	1951–52	47, 93
Moses, J.J.	PR	2002	86
Mosley, Russ	B	1945–46	8
Moss, Perry	QB	1948	10
Mott, Joe	LB	1993	55
Mott, Norm	B	1933	19
Mullen, Roderick	CB/S	1995–97	28
Mulleneaux, Carl	E	1938–41, 45–46	19
Mulleneaux, Lee	C	1938	28
Murphy, Mark	S	1980–85, 87–91	37
Murray, Jab	T	1921–24	NA
Nadolney, Romanus	G	1922	NA
(Nall, Craig)	QB	(2002)	(12)
Nash, Tom	E	1928–32	19, 21, 26, 35, 37
Neal, Ed	DT/T	1945–51	58
Neal, Frankie	WR	1987	80
Neill, Bill	NT	1984	77
Nelson, Bob	NT	1988–90	79

Nelson, Jim	LB	1998–99	57
Neville, Tom	T/G	1986–88, 92	61, 72
Newsome, Craig	CB	1995–98	21
Nichols, Hamilton	G	1951	46
Nickerson, Hardy	LB	2002	56
Niemann, Walter	C	1922–24	NA
Nitschke, Ray	LB	1958–72	33, 66
Nix, Doyle	DB	1955	41
Nixon, Fred	WR	1980–81	84
Noble, Brian	LB	1985–93	91
Noonan, Danny	NT	1992	97
Norgard, Al	E	1934	19, 62
Norseth, Mike	QB	1990	4
Norton, Jerry	DB	1963–64	23
Norton, Marty	B	<1925>	<13>
Norton, Rick	QB	1970	11
Nussbaumer, Bob	B	1946, 51	23, 48
Nuzum, Rick	C	1978	56
Nystrom, Lee	T	1974	70
Oakes, Bill	T	1921	NA
Oates, Brad	T	1981	72
Oats, Carleton	DT	1973	73
O'Boyle, Harry	B	1928, 32	41, 42
O'Connor, Bob	T	1935	24
Odom, Steve	WR	1974–79	84
O'Donahue, Pat	DE	1955	81
O'Donnell, Dick	E	1924–30	<5>, 20, 30
Odson, Urban	T	1946–49	63
Oglesby, Alfred	NT	1992	97
Ohlgren, Earl	E	1942	23
Okoniewski, Steve	DT	1974–75	73
Oliver, Muhammad	CB	1993	25
Olsen, Ralph	E	1949	19
Olsonoski, Larry	G	1948–49	46, 74
O'Malley, Tom	QB	1950	76
O'Neal, Andre	LB	2001	53
O'Neil, Ed	LB	1980	56
Orlich, Dan	E	1949–51	19, 49
Osborn, Dave	RB	1976	41
O'Steen, Dwayne	CB	1983–84	44
Owens, Rip	G	1922	NA
Palumbo, Sam	LB/C	1957	53
Pannell, Ernie	T	1941–42, 45	22
Pape, Orrin	B	1930	56
Papit, Johnny	HB	1953	22
Parilli, Babe	QB	1952–53, 57–58	10, 15, 16
Parker, De'Mond	RB	1999–2000	22
Parker, Freddie	RB	1987	39 R
Parlavecchio, Chet	LB	1983	57

Paskett, Keith	WR	1987	82
Paskvan, George	B	1941	68
Patrick, Frank	QB	1970–72	10
Patterson, Shawn	DE	1988–91, 93	96
Patton, Ricky	RB	1979	30
Paulekas, Tony	C	1936	39
Paup, Bryce	LB	1990–94	95
Payne, Ken	WR	1974–77	85
Pearson, Lindell	HB	1952	26
Peay, Francis	T	1968–72	71
Pederson, Doug	QB	1996–98, 2001-02	18
Pelfrey, Ray	E	1951–52	8, 26
Perkins, Don	FB	1944–45	23, 48, 53, 58
Perko, Tom	LB	1976	56
Perry, Claude	T	1927–35	24, 26, 27, 32, 37, 50
Pesonen, Dick	DB	1960	48
Peterson, Les	E	1932, 34	29, 43
Peterson, Ray	B	1937	33
Petitbon, John	DB	1957	20
Petway, David	S	1981	47
Pickens, Bruce	CB	1993	38
(Piotrowski, Ray)	C	(1947)	(35)
Pisarkiewicz, Steve	QB	1980	19
Pitts, Elijah	RB	1961–69, 71	22
Pitts, Ron	CB	1988–90	28
Ploeger, Kurt	DE	1986	71
Pointer, John	LB	1987	56 R
Pope, Bucky	WR	1968	80
Powers, Sammy	G	1921	NA
Prather, Guy	LB	1981–85	51
Pregulman, Merv	G	1946	17
Prescott, Harold	E	1946	31
Preston, Roell	WR/KR	1997–98	88
Prior, Mike	S	1993–98	39, 45
Pritko, Steve	E	1949–50	23
Prokop, Joe	P	1985	11
Provo, Fred	B	1948	80
Psaltis, Jim	G	1954	48
Purdy, Pid	B	1926–27	5, 7, <18>
Pureifory, Dave	DL	1972–77	75
Purnell, Frank	FB	1957	33
Quatse, Jess	T	1933	23, 36
Query, Jeff	WR	1989–91	85
Quinlan, Bill	DE	1959–62	83
Radick, Ken	E	1930–31	33, 35
Rafferty, Vince	C	1987	50 R
Randolph, Al	DB	1971	27
Randolph, Terry	DB	1977	23
Ranspot, Keith	E	1942	27

Rash, Lou	DB	1987	34 R
Ray, Baby	T	1938–48	44, 58
Redick, Cornelius	WR	1987	87 R
Regnier, Pete	B	1922	NA
Reichardt, Bill	FB	1952	37
Reid, Floyd	HB	1950–56	24, 80
Renner, Bill	P	1986–87	13 R
Reynolds, Jamal	DE	2001-02	99
Rhodemyre, Jay	C/LB	1949, 51–52	22, 50, 85
Rice, Allen	RB	1991	31
Richard, Gary	DB	1988	46
Riddick, Ray	E	1940–42, 46	5, 19, 22
Ringo, Jim	C	1953–63	51
Risher, Alan	QB	1987	11 R
Rison, Andre	WR	1996	84
Rivera, Marco	G	1997–2002	62
Roach, John	QB	1961–63	10, 18
Robbins, Austin	DT	2000	99
Robbins, Tootie	T	1992–93	73
Roberts, Bill	HB	1956	22
Robinson, Bill	HB	1952	41
Robinson, Charley	G	1951	18
Robinson, Dave	LB	1963–72	89
Robinson, Eugene	S	1996–97	41
Robinson, Michael	CB	1996	46
Robison, Tommy	G	1987	77
Roche, Alden	DE	1971–76	87
Rodgers, Del	RB	1982, 84	35
Rohrig, Herman	B	1941, 46–47	8, 80
Roller, Dave	DT	1975–78	74
Romine, Al	HB	1955, 58	23, 85
Rosatti, Rudy	T	1924, 26–27	<12>, 25
Rose, Al	E	1932–36	34, 37, 47, 49, 52
Rose, Bob	C	<1926>	<18>
Rosenow, Gus	B	1921	NA
Roskie, Ken	B	1948	34, 50
Ross, Dan	TE	1986	81
Rossum, Allen	CB/KR	2000–01	20
Rote, Tobin	QB	1950–56	18, 38
Rowser, John	DB	1967–69	28, 45
Rubens, Larry	C	1982–83	58
Rubley, T.J.	QB	1995	12
Rudzinski, Paul	LB	1978–80	58, 66, 70
Ruettgers, Ken	T	1985–96	75
Ruetz, Howard	DT	1951–53	75
Rule, Gordon	DB	1968–69	47
Rush, Clive	E	1953	81
Ruzich, Steve	G	1952–54	61
Salem, Harvey	T	1992	72

Salsbury, Jim	G	1957–58	67
Sample, Chuck	B	1942, 45	38
Sampson, Howard	DB	1978–79	36
Sams, Ron	G	1983	70
Sandifer, Dan	B	1952–53	20, 23
Sandusky, John	T	1956	77
Sarafiny, Al	C	1933	24
Satterfield, Brian	FB	1996	38
Sauer, George	B	1935–37	17, 25
Saunders, Russ	FB	1931	18
Scales, Hurles	DB	1975	38
Schammel, Francis	G	1937	37
Scherer, Bernie	E	1936–38	11, 16, 36, 40
Schlinkman, Walt	FB	1946–49	7
Schmaehl, Art	FB	1921	NA
Schmidt, George	C	1952	54
Schmitt, John	C	1974	52
Schneidman, Herm	B	1935–39	4, 51
Schoemann, Roy	C	1938	42
Schroeder, Bill	WR	1994, 97–2001	19, 84
Schroll, Charles	G	1951	86
Schuette, Carl	C/DB	1950–51	17
Schuh, Jeff	LB	1986	54
Schuh, Harry	T	1974	79
Schultz, Charles	T	1939–41	60
Schwammel, Ade	T	1934–36, 43–44	40, 50, 53, 57, 58
Scott, Patrick	WR	1987–88	83 R
Scott, Randy	LB	1981–86	55
Scribner, Bucky	P	1983–84	13
Secord, Joe	C	1922	NA
Seeman, George	E	1940	68
Seibold, Champ	T	1934–38, 40	37, 41, 57, 58
Self, Clarence	B	1952, 54–55	28
Serini, Wash	G	1952	73
Shanley, Jim	HB	1958	22
Sharpe, Sterling	WR	1988–94	84
Sharper, Darren	CB/S	1997–2002	42
Shelley, Dexter	B	1932	15
Shield, Joe	QB	1986	18
Shirey, Fred	T	1940	18
Shumate, Mark	NT	1985	71
Sikahema, Vai	RB/KR	1991	45
Simmons, Davie	LB	1979	61
Simmons, John	DB	1986	32
Simmons, Wayne	LB	1993–97	59
Simpkins, Ron	LB	1988	51
Simpson, Nate	RB	1977–79	48
Simpson, Travis	C	1987	67 R
Sims, Joe	T/G	1992–95	68

Singletary, Reggie	T	1991	68
Skaugstad, Daryle	NT	1983	91
Skeate, Gil	FB	1927	16
Skibinski, Joe	G	1955–56	63
Skinner, Gerald	T	1978	73
Skoglund, Bob	DE	1947	52
Skoronski, Bob	T	1956, 59–68	76
Sleight, Elmer	T	1930–31	34, 37
Smith, Barry	WR	1973–75	80
Smith, Barty	RB	1974–80	33
Smith, Ben	E	1933	23
Smith, Blane	G	1977	56
Smith, Bruce	LB	1945–48	42
Smith, Donnell	DE	1971	74
Smith, Earl	E	1922	NA
Smith, Ed	B	1937	28
Smith, Ed	HB	1948–49	21
Smith, Ernie	T	1935–37, 39	45, 61
Smith, Jermaine	DT	1997, 99	99
Smith, Jerry	G	1956	61
Smith, Kevin	FB	1996	49
Smith, Moe	RB	2002	43
Smith, Ollie	WR	1976–77	21, 89
Smith, Perry	DB	1973–76	45
Smith, Red	G	1927, 29	7, 15, 19, 28
Smith, Rex	E	1922	NA
Smith, Rod	CB	1998	31
Smith, Warren	G	1921	NA
Smith, Wes	WR	1987	84
Snelling, Ken	B	1945	42
Snider, Malcolm	T/G	1972–74	67
Snider, Matt	FB	1999–2000	38, 44
Sorenson, Glen	G	1943–45	33
Spagnola, John	TE	1989	89
Sparlis, Al	G	1946	21
Spears, Ron	DE	1983	79
Spencer, Joe	T	1950–51	34, 79
Spencer, Ollie	T	1957–58	77
Spilis, John	WR	1969–71	85
Spinks, Jack	G	1955–56	61
Sproul, Dennis	QB	1978	16
Stachowicz, Ray	P	1981–82	16
Staggers, Jon	WR	1972–74	22
Stahlman, Dick	T	1931–32	34, 36
Stanley, Walter	WR	1985–88	87
Stansauk, Don	T	1950–51	63, 66
Starch, Ken	RB	1976	32
Staroba, Paul	WR	1973	85
Starr, Bart	QB	1956–71	15, 16

PACKERS BY THE NUMBERS

Starret, Ben	B	1942–45	63
Steen, Frank	E	1939	36
Steiner, Rebel	DB	1950–51	74
Stenerud, Jan	K	1980–83	10
Stephen, Scott	LB	1987–91	54
Stephens, John	RB	1993	32
Stephenson, Dave	G/C	1951–55	44, 53, 69
Sterling, John	RB	1987	33 R
Stevens, Bill	QB	1968–69	10
Stewart, Steve	LB	1979	58
Stills, Ken	S	1985–89	29
Stokes, Barry	G/T	2000–01	79
Stokes, Tim	T	1978–82	76
Stonebraker, John	E	1942	51
Strickland, Fred	LB	1994–95	55
Sturgeon, Lyle	T	1937	26
Sullivan, Carl	DE	1987	95 R
Sullivan, John	DB	1986	38
Sullivan, Walter	G	1921	NA
Summerhays, Bob	B	1949–51	77
Summers, Don	TE	1987	86 R
Sutton, Mickey	CB	1989	49
Svendsen, Earl	C	1937, 39	7, 53, 66
Svendsen, George	C/LB	1935–37, 40–41	43, 66
Swanke, Karl	T/C	1980–86	67
Swiney, Erwin	DB	2002	26
Switzer, Veryl	B	1954–55	27
Sydney, Harry	FB	1992	42
Symank, John	DB	1957–62	27
Szafaryn, Len	T	1950, 53–56	47, 51, 68
Tagge, Jerry	QB	1972–74	17
Tassos, Damon	G	1947–49	15
Taugher, Claude	FB	1922	NA
Tauscher, Mark	T	2000–02	65
Taylor, Aaron	G	1995–97	73
Taylor, Cliff	RB	1976	27
Taylor, Jim	FB	1958–66	31
Taylor, Kitrick	WR	1992	85
Taylor, Lenny	WR	1984	84
Taylor, Willie	WR	1978	89
Teague, George	S	1993–95	31
Temp, Jim	DE	1957–60	82
Tenner, Bob	E	1935	36
Terrell, Pat	S	1998	40
Teteak, Deral	LB/G	1952–56	66
Thibodeaux, Keith	CB	2001	22
Thierry, John	DE	2000–01	91
Thomas, Ben	DE	1986	92
Thomas, Ike	DB	1972–73	37

Thomas, Lavale	RB	1987–88	45 R
Thomason, Bobby	QB	1951	28
Thomason, Jeff	TE	1995–99	83
Thompson, Arland	G	1981	71
Thompson, Aundra	WR	1977–81	43, 89
Thompson, Clarence	B	1939	50
Thompson, Darrell	RB	1990–94	26, 39
Thompson, John	TE	1979–82	83, 87
Thurston, Fuzzy	G	1959–67	63
Timberlake, George	LB/G	1955	53
Timmerman, Adam	G	1995–98	63
Tinker, Gerald	WR	1975	82
Tinsley, Pete	G/LB	1938–39, 41–45	21
Toburen, Nelson	LB	1961–62	61, 69
Tollefson, Chuck	G	1944–46	27, 46, (77)
Tomczak, Mike	QB	1991	18
Tomich, Jared	DE	2002	75
Toner, Tom	LB	1973, 75–77	59
Tonnemaker, Clayton	LB/C	1950, 53–54	35, 58
Torkelson, Eric	RB	1974–79, 81	26
Traylor, Keith	LB	1993	97
Troup, Bill	QB	1980	10
Tualo, Esera	NT/DE	1991–92	98
Tullis, Walter	WR	1978–79	20, 87
Tunnell, Emlen	S	1959–61	45
Turner, Maurice	RB	1985	20
Turner, Rich	NT	1981–83	75
Turner, Wylie	DB	1979–80	20
Turpin, Miles	LB	1986	53
Tuttle, George	E	1927	18
Twedell, Francis	G	1939	62
Uecker, Keith	G/T	1984–85, 87–88	70
Uram, Andy	B	1938–43	8, 42
Urban, Alex	E	1941, 44–45	18, 23, 79
Usher, Eddie	B	1922, 24	NA
Vairo, Dominic	E	1935	35
Vandersea, Phil	LB/DE	1966, 68–69	37, 83
Van Dyke, Bruce	G	1974–76	61
Van Every, Hal	B	1940–41	36
Vanoy, Vernon	DT	1972	73
Van Sickle, Clyde	C	1932–33	25, 31, 57
Vant Hull, Fred	G	1942	18
Van Valkenburg, Pete	RB	1974	40
Vataha, Randy	WR	1977	18
Veingrad, Alan	T	1986–87, 89–90	73
Verba, Ross	T/G	1997–2000	78
Vereen, Carl	T	1957	74
Vergara, George	E	<1925>	<6>
Viaene, David	T	1992	76

Villanucci, Vince	NT	1987	64 R
Vinson, Fred	CB	1999	31
Vogds, Evan	G	1948–49	79
Voss, Lloyd	T	1964–65	71
Voss, Walter	E	1924	NA
Waddy, Jude	LB	1998–99	54
Wade, Charley	WR	1975	89
Wafer, Carl	DT	1974	78
Wagner, Bryan	P	1992–93	9
Wagner, Buff	B	1921	NA
Wagner, Steve	DB	1976–79	21
Wahle, Mike	T/G	1998–2002	68
Walker, Cleo	C/LB	1970	52
Walker, Javon	WR	2002	84
Walker, Malcolm	C	1970	54
Walker, Randy	P	1974	18
Walker, Rod	DT	2001-02	95
Walker, Sammy	CB	1993	23
Walker, Val Joe	DB	1953–56	47
Wallace, Calvin	DE	1987	93 R
Walsh, Ward	RB	1972	26
Warren, Steve	DT	2000, 2002	95
Washington, Chuck	DB	1987	18 R, 38 R
Watts, Elbert	DB	1986	28
Wayne, Nate	LB	2000–02	54
Weathers, Clarence	WR	1990–91	87
Weatherwax, Jim	DT	1966–67, 69	73
Weaver, Gary	LB	1975–79	52
Webb, Chuck	RB	1991	30
Webber, Dutch	E	1928	43
Webster, Tim	K	1971	38
Weddington, Mike	LB	1986–90	52
Wehba, Ray	E	1944	17, 57
Weigel, Lee	RB	1987	25 R
Weisgerber, Dick	B	1938–40, 42	33
Weishuhn, Clayton	LB	1987	51
Wellman, Mike	C	1979–80	65
Wells, Don	E	1946–49	43, 84
Wells, Terry	RB	1975	37
West, Ed	TE	1984–94	49, 86
West, Pat	B	1948	25
Westbrook, Bryant	DB	2002	32
Wetnight, Ryan	TE	2000	83
Wheeler, Lyle	E	1921–23	NA
Whitaker, Bill	DB	1981–82	30
White, Adrian	S	1992	38
White, Gene	DB	1954	88
White, Reggie	DE	1993–98	92
Whitehurst, David	QB	1977–83	17

Whittenton, Jesse	DB	1958–64	47
Wicks, Bob	WR	1974	49
Widby, Ron	P	1972–73	20
Widell, Doug	G	1993	74
Wildung, Dick	T	1946–51, 53	45, 70
Wilkens, Elmer	E	<1925>	<18>
Wilkins, Marcus	LB	2002	55
Wilkerson, Bruce	T	1996–97	64
Wilkins, Gabe	DE/DT	1994–97	98
Willhite, Kevin	RB	1987	35 R
Williams, A.D.	E	1959	81
Williams, Brian	LB	1995–2000	51
Williams, Clarence	DE	1970–77	83
Williams, Delvin	RB	1981	20
Williams, Gerald	DE	1997	96
Williams, Howard	DB	1962–63	29
Williams, K.D.	LB	2000–01	50
Williams, Kevin	RB	1993	20
Williams, Mark	LB	1994	51
Williams, Perry	RB	1969–73	31
Williams, Travis	RB/KR	1967–70	17, 23
Williams, Tyrone	CB	1996–2002	37
Willig, Matt	T	1998	76
Willis, James	LB	1993–94	56
Wilner, Jeff	TE	1994–95	49, 83
Wilson, Ben	FB	1967	36
Wilson, Charles	WR	1990–91	88
Wilson, Faye	B	1930–31	17
Wilson, Gene	E/DB	1947–48	65
Wilson, Marcus	RB	1992–95	29
Wilson, Milt	G	1921	NA
Wilson, Ray	S	1994	35
Wimberly, Abner	E	1950–52	16, 85
Wingle, Blake	G	1985	61
Wingo, Rich	LB	1979, 81–84	50
Winkler, Francis	DE	1968–69	58
Winkler, Randy	G	1971	63
Winslow, Paul	HB	1960	23
Winter, Blaise	DE/NT	1988–90	68
Winters, Chet	RB	1983	20
Winters, Frank	C/G	1992–2002	52
Winther, Wimpy	C	1971	52, 54
Wisne, Jerry	T	2002	77
Withrow, Cal	C	1971–73	58, 74
Witte, Earl	B	1934	23
Wizbicki, Alex	B	1950	25
Wood, Bobby	T	1940	29
Wood, Willie	S	1960–71	24
Woodin, Whitey	G	1922–31	<9>, 23, 25

PACKERS BY THE NUMBERS

Woods, Jerry	S	1990	29
Woodside, Keith	RB	1988–91	33
Workman, Vince	RB	1989–92	46
Wortman, Keith	G	1972–75	65
Wright, Randy	QB	1984–88	16
Wright, Steve	T	1964–67	72
Wuerffel, Danny	QB	2000	7
Wunsch, Harry	G	1934	56
Young, Billy	G	1929	18
Young, Glenn	DB	1956	23
Young, Paul	C	1933	15
Zarnas, Gust	G	1939–40	63
Zatkoff, Roger	LB	1953–56	74
Zeller, Joe	G	1932	16
Zendejas, Max	K	1987–88	8
Zeno, Lance	C	1993	60
Zimmerman, Don	WR	1976	80
Zoll, Carl	G	1921–22	NA
Zoll, Dick	G	1939	52
Zoll, Martin	G	1921	NA
Zorn, Jim	QB	1985	18
Zuidmulder, Dave	B	1929–31	10, 12, 41
Zupek, Al	E	1946	25
Zuver, Merle	C	1930	14

CHRONOLOGICAL
PATH OF PLAYERS

1	Curly Lambeau (1921)
10	Cub Buck (1921)
2	Charlie Mathys (1922)
39	Jug Earp (1922)
46	Verne Lewellen (1924)
11	Red Dunn (1927)
22	Lavvie Dilweg (1927)
33	Mike Michalske (1929)
38	Cal Hubbard (1929)
55	Johnny Blood McNally(1929)
16	Arnie Herber (1930)
27	Hank Bruder (1931)
30	Clarke Hinkle (1932)
43	Buckets Goldenberg (1933)
52	Tiny Engebretsen (1934)
14	Don Hutson (1935)
45	Ernie Smith (1935)
49	Walt Kiesling (1935)
62	Russ Letlow (1936)
17	Cecil Isbell (1938)
29	Charley Brock (1939)
3	Tony Canadeo (1941)
58	Ed Neal (1945)
70	Dick Wildung (1946)
18	Tobin Rote (1950)
35	Clayton Tonnemaker (1950)
87	Bob Mann (1950)
72	Dick Afflis (1951)
83	John Martinkovic (1951)
44	Bobby Dillon (1952)
79	Hawg Hanner (1952)
86	Bill Howton (1952)
51	Jim Ringo (1953)
69	Bill Forester (1953)
85	Max McGee (1954)
65	Tom Bettis (1955)
15	Bart Starr (1956)
75	Forrest Gregg (1956)
76	Bob Skoronski (1956)
5	Paul Hornung (1957)
88	Ron Kramer (1957)
31	Jim Taylor (1958)
47	Jess Whittenton (1958)
64	Jerry Kramer (1958)

PACKERS BY THE NUMBERS

66	Ray Nitschke (1958)
6	Vince Lombardi (1959)
63	Fuzzy Thurston (1959)
74	Henry Jordan (1974)
24	Willie Wood (1960)
26	Herb Adderley (1961)
21	Bob Jeter (1963)
82	Lionel Aldridge (1963)
89	Dave Robinson (1963)
57	Ken Bowman (1964)
60	Lee Roy Caffey (1964)
34	Don Chandler (1965)
68	Gale Gillingham (1966)
78	Bob Brown (1966)
23	Travis Williams (1967)
53	Fred Carr (1968)
48	Ken Ellis (1970)
50	Jim Carter (1970)
42	John Brockington (1971)
13	Chester Marcol (1972)
28	Willie Buchanon (1972)
54	Larry McCarren (1973)
56	Ted Hendricks (1974)
61	Bruce Van Dyke (1974)
19	Carlos Brown (1975)
12	Lynn Dickey (1976)
90	Ezra Johnson (1977)
59	John Anderson (1978)
80	James Lofton (1978)
40	Eddie Lee Ivery (1979)
37	Mark Murphy (1980)
94	Charles Martin (1984)
91	Brian Noble (1985)
97	Tim Harris (1986)
7	Don Majkowski (1987)
84	Sterling Sharpe (1988)
77	Tony Mandarich (1989)
36	Leroy Butler (1990)
95	Bryce Paup (1990)
99	Don Davey (1991)
4	Brett Favre (1992)
92	Reggie White (1993)
93	Gilbert Brown (1993)
25	Dorsey Levens (1994)
96	Sean Jones (1994)
98	Gabe Wilkins (1994)
9	Jim McMahon (1995)
32	Travis Jervey (1995)

73	Aaron Taylor (1995)	
41	Eugene Robinson (1996)	
71	Santana Dotson (1996)	
81	Desmond Howard (1996)	
8	Ryan Longwell (1997)	
20	Allen Rossum (2000)	
67	Russell Maryland (2000)	

CHRONOLOGICAL PATH OF EVENTS

1	Curly Lambeau	Beginnings
2	Charles Mathys	1920s in a Box
10	Cub Buck	Of Runts, Grunts, and Punts
11	Red Dunn	Threepeat I
27	Hank Bruder	1930s in a Box
30	Clarke Hinkle	Head to Head with Nagurski
16	Arnie Herber	1936 Champs
52	Tiny Engebretsen	1938 Championship Game
17	Cecil Isbell	1939 Champs
29	Charley Brock	1940s in a Box
14	Don Hutson	The Greatest Packer and the 1941 Playoff
43	Buckets Goldenberg	1944 Wartime Champs
44	Bobby Dillon	1950s in a Box
86	Bill Howton	King of Siberia
6	Vince Lombardi	Winning
63	Fuzzy Thurston	The Sweep
74	Henry Jordan	1960s in a Box
69	Bill Forester	Bengtson of the Defense
65	Tom Bettis	1960 Championship Game
66	Ray Nitschke	Transformation
5	Paul Hornung	1961 Championship
31	Jim Taylor	1962 Championship
15	Bart Starr	Starr Quarterbacks
51	Jim Ringo	Oral Mystery
34	Don Chandler	1965 Champs
85	Max McGee	Super Bowl I
76	Bob Skoronski	Frozen Tundra
64	Jerry Kramer	Replay Man
26	Herb Adderley	Super Bowl II
89	Dave Robinson	Threepeat II
53	Fred Carr	End of the Dynasty
50	Jim Carter	Replacing the Legends
28	Willie Buchanon	1970s in a Box
42	John Brockington	1972 Playoff Return
61	Bruce Van Dyke	Dynasty After Dynasty
82	Lionel Aldridge	Tragic Adversity
59	John Anderson	1980s in a Box
80	James Lofton	1982 Playoffs
25	Dorsey Levens	The Nineties and Beyond in a Box
71	Santana Dotson	The Wolf Era

PACKERS BY THE NUMBERS

37	Mark Murphy	New Broom Sweeps Clean
84	Sterling Sharpe	Mid-West Coast Offense
95	Bryce Paup	1993 & 1994 Playoffs
92	Reggie White	1995 Playoffs
36	Leroy Butler	The Lambeau Leap
81	Desmond Howard	Super Bowl XXXI
98	Gabe Wilkins	Super Bowl XXXII
4	Brett Favre	Holmgren's Choice and Recent Playoffs

GENERAL TOPICS

GAME ON THE FIELD

8	Ryan Longwell	Specialists
12	Lynn Dickey	The Passing Game
13	Chester Marcol	The Kicking Game
18	Tobin Rote	Running Quarterbacks
23	Travis Williams	No Return
46	Verne Lewellen	Triple Threat
78	Bob Brown	Bench Strength

OFF THE FIELD

19	Carlos Brown	Going Hollywood
40	Eddie Lee Ivery	Troubles Troubles
41	Eugene Robinson	Lock Up Your Daughters
45	Ernie Smith	Work Ethic
70	Dick Wildung	Military Service
91	Brian Noble	Trading Cards and Memorabilia

RIVALRIES

9	Jim McMahon	Da Bears
47	Jesse Whittenton	Giant Rival
67	Russell Maryland	Cowboys
88	Ron Kramer	The Lions
93	Gilbert Brown	Vikings Rivalry
94	Charles Martin	Bears Rivalry II: Unnecessary Roughness

MEASURING AND ASSESSING

7	Don Majkowski	Majikal Comebacks
35	Clayton Tonnemaker	Pro Bowl and All Pro Honors
38	Cal Hubbard	All Time Teams and Hall of Fame
62	Russ Letlow	The Draft
48	Ken Ellis	The Packer Hall of Fame
49	Walt Kiesling	The Undeserving
68	Gale Gillingham	The Unheralded
75	Forrest Gregg	Coaching Legacies
77	Tony Mandarich	Draft Busts
97	Tim Harris	Leaders

FACTUAL TOPICS

3	Tony Canadeo	Long Time Service and Retired Numbers
20	Allen Rossum	Little Guys
21	Bob Jeter	Rival Leagues
22	Lavvie Dilweg	Family Ties
24	Willie Wood	Undrafted Free Agents

INDEX

PACKERS BY THE NUMBERS

PACKERS BY THE NUMBERS

PACKERS BY THE NUMBERS

PACKERS BY THE NUMBERS